H

and
The Art of Being

An introduction to
the philosophy and practice of
the spiritual teachings of
Bhagavan Sri Ramana

(Second Edition)

Michael James

ISBN: 1475111576
ISBN-13: 978-1475111576

First PDF edition: December 2006
Second PDF edition: March 2007
Third PDF edition: August 2007
First print edition (Canada): August 2007
First print edition (India): August 2007
Second print edition (US): March 2012
Second print edition (India): March 2012
Fourth PDF edition: March 2012
First Kindle edition: March 2012

Author's website and blog:
www.happinessofbeing.com
www.happinessofbeing.blogspot.com

DEDICATION

To

Bhagavan Sri Ramana,
who taught me all that I know,
and gave whatever inspiration created this book,

and to his closest disciples,
especially

Sri Sivaprakasam Pillai,
who first elicited and recorded his basic teachings,
which he later formed into his precious treatise
Nāṉ Yār? (Who am I?),

Sri Muruganar,
who not only elicited his finest philosophical poems and verses,
but also recorded his oral teachings
most comprehensively, profoundly and poetically in
Guru Vācaka Kōvai,

and

Sri Sadhu Om,
who helped me to understand his teachings
more clearly and deeply.

Contents

Introduction

Happiness lies deep within us, in the very core of our being. Happiness does not exist in any external object, but only in us, who are the consciousness that experiences happiness. Though we seem to derive happiness from external objects or experiences, the happiness that we thus enjoy in fact arises from within us.

Whatever turmoil our mind may be in, in the centre of our being there always exists a state of perfect peace and joy, like the calm in the eye of a storm. Desire and fear agitate our mind, and obscure from its view the happiness that always exists within it. When a desire is satisfied, or the cause of a fear is removed, the surface agitation of our mind subsides, and in that temporary calm our mind enjoys a taste of its own innate happiness.

Happiness is thus a state of being – a state in which our mind's habitual agitation is calmed. The activity of our mind disturbs it from its calm state of just being, and causes it to lose sight of its own innermost happiness. To enjoy happiness, therefore, all our mind need do is to cease all activity, returning calmly to its natural state of inactive being, as it does daily in deep sleep.

Therefore to master the art of being happy, we must master the art and science of just being. We must discover what the innermost core of our being is, and we must learn to abide consciously and constantly in that state of pure being, which underlies and supports (but nevertheless remains unaffected by) all the superficial activities of our mind: thinking, feeling and perceiving, remembering and forgetting, and so on.

The art of just being, remaining fully conscious but without any activity of the mind, is not only an art – a practical skill that can be cultivated and applied to produce an experience of inexpressible beauty and joy – but also a science – an attempt to acquire true knowledge by keen observation and rigorous experiment. And this art and science of being is not only the art and science of happiness, but also the art and science of consciousness, and the art and science of self-knowledge.

The science of being is incredibly simple and clear. To the human mind, however, it may appear to be complex and abstruse, not because it is in any way complex in itself, but because the mind which tries to comprehend it is such a complex bundle of thoughts and emotions – desires, fears, anxieties, attachments, long-cherished beliefs and preconceived ideas – that it tends to cloud the pure simplicity and clarity of being, making what is obvious appear to be obscure.

Like any other science, the science of being begins with observation and analysis of something that we already know but do not fully understand, and proceeds by reasoning to formulate a plausible hypothesis that can explain what is observed, and then rigorously tests that hypothesis by precise and critical experiment. However, unlike all other sciences, this science does not study any object of knowledge, but instead studies the very power of knowing itself – the power of consciousness that underlies the mind, the power by which all objects are known.

Hence the truth discovered by means of this science is not something that can be demonstrated or proved objectively by one person to another. It can, however, be directly experienced as a clear knowledge in the innermost core of each person who scrupulously pursues the necessary process of experiment till the true nature of being – which is the true nature of consciousness, and of happiness – is revealed in the full clarity of pure unadulterated self-consciousness.

Just as the science of being is fundamentally unlike all other sciences, so as an art it is fundamentally unlike all other arts, because it is not an art that involves doing anything. It is an art not of doing but of non-doing – an art of just being.

The state of just being is one in which our mind does not rise to do, think or know anything, yet it is a state of full consciousness – consciousness not of anything else but only of being. The skill that is to be learnt in this art is not simply the skill to be – because we always are and therefore require no special skill or effort to be –, nor is it merely the skill to be without doing or thinking anything – because we are able to be so each day in deep dreamless sleep. The skill to be cultivated is the skill to remain calmly and peacefully without doing or thinking anything, but nevertheless retaining a perfectly clear consciousness of being – that is, consciousness of our own being or essential 'am'-ness. Only in this pristine state of clear non-dual self-conscious being, unclouded by the distracting agitation of thought and action, will the true nature of being become perfectly clear, obvious, self-evident and free from even the least scope for doubt or confusion.

Our first and most direct experience of being is that of our own being or existence. First we know that we exist, and then only can we know of the existence of other things. But whereas our own existence is self-conscious, the existence of each other thing depends on us to be known.

We know our own being because we are consciousness. In other words, our being is itself the consciousness that knows itself. It knows itself because it is essentially self-conscious. Thus it is reasonable to hypothesise that consciousness is the primal and essential form of being. Without consciousness, being would be unknown, and without being, consciousness would not exist.

Our being and our consciousness of being are inseparable – in fact they are identical – and both are expressed by the single phrase 'I am'. This being-consciousness, 'I am', is our most fundamental experience, and the most fundamental experience of every sentient being. 'I am' is the one basic consciousness – the essential non-dual self-consciousness – without which nothing would be known. 'I am' is therefore the source and foundation of all knowledge.

What then is the use of knowing anything else if we do not know the truth of our own being-consciousness, our self-consciousness, 'I am', on the basis of which all else is known? All that we know about the world and all that we know about God – all our sciences and all our religions – are of no real value to us if we do not know the truth about ourself, who desire to know the truth about the world and God.

We are the being-consciousness 'I am', yet our knowledge about this 'I am' is confused. We all believe 'I am this body', 'I am a person', 'I am called so-and-so, and was born on such-and-such a date at such-and-such a place'. Thus we identify our consciousness 'I am' with a particular body. This identification is the result of a confused and unclear knowledge of the true nature of consciousness.

Our consciousness 'I am' is not something material, whereas our body is merely a bundle of physical matter, which is not inherently conscious. Yet somehow we are deluded into mistaking this material body to be our consciousness 'I'. As a result of our unclear knowledge of consciousness, we mistake matter to be conscious, and consciousness to be something material.

That which thus mistakes this body to be 'I' is our mind. Our mind comes into existence only by imagining itself to be a body. In deep sleep we are unaware of either our mind or our body. As soon as we wake up, our mind rises feeling 'I am this body, I am so-and-so', and only after thus identifying itself as a particular body does it perceive the external world through the five senses of that body.

Exactly the same thing happens in dream – our mind identifies itself as a particular body and through the five senses of that body it perceives a seemingly real and external world. When we wake up from a dream, we understand that the body we mistook to be 'I' and the world we mistook to be real and external were both in fact only figments of our imagination.

Thus from our experience in dream we all know that our mind has a wonderful power of imagination by which it is able to create a body, to mistake that imaginary body to be 'I', and through that body to project a world which, at the time we perceive it, appears to be every bit as real and external to us as the world that we now perceive in this waking state.

Knowing that our mind possesses this wonderful power of creation and self-deception, is it not reasonable for us to suspect that the body we take to be 'I' and the world we take to be real in our present waking state may in fact be nothing more than a mere imagination or mental projection, just like the body and world that we experience in dream? What evidence do we have that the body and world we experience in this waking state are anything other than a creation of our own mind? We may be able to point out certain differences between waking and dream, but on analysis we will discover that those differences are superficial, being concerned with quality or quantity rather than with substance.

If we compare the world drama we see in waking or dream to a drama we see on a cinema screen, we may say that the drama seen in waking is a better quality and more impressive production than that seen in dream, but both are productions none the less – productions not of some external agency but of our mind which sees them.

In substance, there is no essential difference between our experience in waking and that in dream. In both states our mind rises, attaching itself to a body by taking it to be 'I', and through the senses of that body it sees a world bound within the limits of time and space, and filled with numerous people and other objects, both sentient and insentient, all of which it is convinced are real. How can we prove to ourself that what we experience in the waking state exists at all outside our own imagination, any more than a dream exists outside our imagination?

When we carefully analyse our experience in our three states of waking, dream and deep sleep, it is clear that we are able to confuse our consciousness 'I' to be different things at different times. In waking we mistake our present body to be 'I', in dream we mistake some other imaginary body to be 'I', and in sleep we mistake unconsciousness to be 'I' – or at least on waking from sleep what we remember is that 'I was unconscious'.

What we were in fact unconscious of in sleep was our mind, our body and the world, but not our own existence or being. Our experience in sleep was not that we ceased to exist, but only that we ceased to be aware of all the thoughts and perceptions that we are accustomed to experiencing in the waking and dream states. When we say, 'I slept peacefully, I had no dreams, I was unaware of anything', we are confidently affirming that 'I' was in sleep – that is, that we existed and knew that we existed at that time.

Because we associate consciousness with being conscious of all the thoughts and perceptions that make up our life in waking and in dream, we consider sleep to be a state of unconsciousness. But we should examine the so-called unconsciousness of sleep more carefully. The consciousness that knows thoughts and perceptions is our mind, which rises and is active in waking and dream, but which subsides in sleep. But this rising and subsiding consciousness is not our real consciousness. We are conscious not only of the two states of waking and dream, in which our mind rises to experience thoughts and perceptions, but also of a third state, sleep, in which our mind has subsided in a state devoid of thoughts and perceptions.

This fact that we are conscious of sleep as a state distinct from waking and dream clearly indicates that we are the consciousness that underlies the rising and subsiding of the transient consciousness that we call 'mind'. The consciousness that enables us to affirm confidently, 'I did exist in sleep, but I was unconscious of anything', is not our 'rising consciousness' but our 'being consciousness'.

This 'being consciousness', which exists in all our three states, is our real consciousness, and is what is truly denoted when we say 'I am'. Our mind, the 'rising consciousness' that appears in waking and dream and disappears in sleep, is only a spurious form of consciousness, which on rising mistakes itself to be both our basic consciousness 'I am' and this material body.

Thus, by analysing our experience in our three states of waking, dream and deep sleep, we can understand that though we now mistake ourself to be a body limited by time and space, we are in fact the consciousness that underlies the appearance of these three states, in only two of which the sense of being a body and the consequent limitations of time and space are experienced.

However, a mere theoretical understanding of the truth that we are only consciousness will be of little use to us if we do not apply it in practice by endeavouring to gain real experiential knowledge of that truth. By itself, a theoretical understanding will not and cannot give us true and lasting happiness, because it cannot destroy our deep-rooted sense of identification with the body, which is the root of all ignorance, and the cause of all misery.

That which understands this truth theoretically is only our mind or intellect, and our mind cannot function without first identifying itself with a body. Since our mind or intellect is thus a confused knowledge whose existence is rooted in ignorance about who or what we really are, no intellectual understanding can ever by itself give us true self-knowledge. Self-knowledge can only be gained by direct experience of the pure unlimited consciousness which is our real self, because only such experience can root out the ignorance that we are anything other than that consciousness.

Therefore a theoretical understanding of the truth can be of real benefit to us only if it prompts us to investigate our essential consciousness of being – our simple self-consciousness, 'I am' – and thereby attain through direct experience a clear knowledge of our own true nature. Only by attaining such a clear knowledge of the consciousness that is truly 'I', can we destroy our primal ignorance, the confused and mistaken knowledge that we are the mind, the limited form of consciousness that identifies a body as 'I'.

If we truly understand that we are not a body, nor the mind which imagines itself to be a body, and that every form of unhappiness that we experience is caused only by our mistaken identification with a body, we will endeavour to destroy that false identification by undertaking practical research to discover who or what we really are. To know what we really are, we must cease attending to any other things, and must attend instead to ourself, the consciousness that knows those other things.

When we attend to things other than 'I', our attention is a 'thought' or activity of the mind. But when we attend to our essential consciousness 'I', our attention ceases to be an activity or 'thought', and instead becomes mere being. We know other things by an act of knowing, but we know ourself not by an act of knowing but by merely being ourself. Therefore, when we attend to the innermost core of our being – that is, to our essential and real self, which is simple thought-free non-dual self-conscious being – we cease to rise as the incessantly active mind and instead remain merely as our naturally actionless consciousness of being. Therefore self-attention is self-abidance, the state of merely being what we really are.

So long as we attend to things other than ourself, our mind is active, and its activity clouds and obscures our natural clarity of self-consciousness. But when we try to attend to ourself, the activity of our mind begins to subside, and thus the veil that obscures our natural self-consciousness begins to dissolve. The more keenly and intensely we focus our attention upon our basic consciousness 'I', the more our mind will subside, until finally it disappears in the clear light of true self-knowledge.

In this book, therefore, I will attempt to explain both the theory and the practice of the art of knowing and being our real self. The theory of this science and art of self-knowledge is necessary and helpful to us insofar as it enables us to understand not only the imperative need for us to know the reality, but also the practical means by which we can achieve such knowledge.

All the unhappiness, discontent and misery that we experience in our life is caused only by our ignorance or confused knowledge of who or what we really are. So long as we limit ourself by identifying a body as 'I', we will feel desire for whatever we think is necessary for our survival in that body, and for whatever we think will make our life in that body more comfortable and pleasant. Likewise we will feel fear and dislike of whatever we think threatens our survival in that body, and of whatever we think will make our life in it less comfortable or pleasant. When we do not get whatever we desire or like, and when we cannot avoid whatever we fear or dislike, we feel unhappy, discontented or miserable.

Thus unhappiness or suffering is the inevitable result of desire and fear, or likes and dislikes. Desire and fear, and likes and dislikes, are the inevitable result of identifying a body as 'I'. And identifying a body as 'I' results from our lack of clear knowledge of our real nature – our essential self-conscious being. Therefore if we want to be free of all forms of misery and unhappiness, we must free ourself from our ignorance or confused knowledge of what we really are.

In order to free ourself from this confused knowledge, which makes us feel that we are a body, we must attain a clear knowledge of our real self. The only means by which we can attain such clear self-knowledge is to turn our attention away from our body, our mind and all other things, and to focus it keenly upon our own essential self-consciousness – our fundamental consciousness of our own being, 'I am'.

Thus the theory that underlies the science and art of self-knowledge enables us to understand that all we need do in order to experience perfect and unlimited happiness is to attain true self-knowledge, and that the only means to attain true self-knowledge is to practise keen scrutinising self-attention. Unless we know ourself as we really are, we can never experience true and perfect happiness, untainted by even the least unhappiness or dissatisfaction, and unless we keenly attend to our essential consciousness of our own mere being – our simple non-dual self-consciousness, 'I am' – we can never know ourself as we really are.

For the majority of spiritual aspirants, the process of attaining self-knowledge, like the process of learning any other art or science, is said to be a threefold process of repeated *śravaṇa*, *manana* and *nididhyāsana*, or learning, assimilation and practice. The Sanskrit word *śravaṇa* literally means 'hearing', but in this context it means learning the truth by hearing, reading or studying. The word *manana* means thinking, pondering, musing, reflection or meditation, that is, dwelling frequently upon the truth that we have learnt through *śravaṇa* in order to imbibe it and understand it more and more clearly, and to impress it upon our mind more and more firmly. And the word *nididhyāsana* means keen observation, scrutiny, attentiveness or profound contemplation, that is, in our context, putting what we have learnt and understood by *śravaṇa* and *manana* into practice by keenly scrutinising, attending to or contemplating upon our essential self-conscious being, 'I am'.

In the life of a serious spiritual aspirant, this threefold process of *śravaṇa*, *manana* and *nididhyāsana* should continue repeatedly until the experience of true self-knowledge is attained. In our day-to-day lives our mind encounters innumerable different impressions through our five senses, and thinks innumerable thoughts about those impressions, so the impression made by one thing is quickly replaced by the impression made by other things. Therefore even though we have once learnt about the spiritual truth – the truth that we are not the limited body but are only the unlimited spirit or consciousness – the impression made by that truth will quickly fade if we do not repeatedly study books that remind us of it, and frequently reflect upon it in our mind.

However mere reading and thinking about the truth will be of little benefit to us if we do not also repeatedly attempt to put it into practice by turning our attention back to our mere consciousness of being, I am', whenever we notice that it has slipped away to think of other things. To stress the paramount importance of such practice, Sri Adi Sankara declared in verse 364 of *Vivēkacūḍāmaṇi* that the benefit of *manana* is a hundred times greater than that of *śravaṇa*, and the benefit of *nididhyāsana* is a hundred thousand times greater than that of *manana*.

For some very rare souls, repeated *śravaṇa*, *manana* and *nididhyāsana* is not necessary, because as soon as they first hear the truth, they at once grasp its meaning and importance, turn their attention selfwards, and thereby immediately experience true self-knowledge. But the majority of us do not have the spiritual maturity to be able to experience the truth as soon as we hear it, because we are too strongly attached to our existence as an individual person, and to all that is associated with our life as a person.

By repeated *nididhyāsana* or self-contemplation, supported by the aid of repeated *śravaṇa* and *manana*, our consciousness of our own essential being and our corresponding understanding of the truth will become increasingly clear, and by that increasing clarity we will steadily gain more love to know ourself as we really are, and more detachment from our individuality and all that is associated with it. Therefore, until we gain such true spiritual maturity – the willingness and love to lose our individual self in the experience of true non-dual self-knowledge – we have to continue the process of repeated *śravaṇa*, *manana* and *nididhyāsana*.

Even more rare than those highly mature souls who are able to experience the truth as soon as they hear it, there are some people who without ever hearing the truth experience it spontaneously. But such people are very rare indeed.

All that I write in this book is what I have learnt and understood from the teachings of the sage known as Bhagavan Sri Ramana Maharshi, who was one such extremely rare being who experienced the truth spontaneously without ever having heard or read anything about it. He spontaneously attained the experience of true self-knowledge one day in July 1896, when he was just a sixteen-year-old schoolboy. That day he was sitting alone in a room in his uncle's house in the south Indian town of Madurai, when suddenly and with no apparent cause an intense fear of death arose within him. Instead of trying to put this fear out of his mind, as most of us would do, he decided to investigate and discover for himself the truth about death.

'All right, death has come! What is death? What is it that dies? This body is going to die – let it die.' Deciding thus, he lay down like a corpse, rigid and without breathing, and turned his mind inwards to discover what death would actually do to him. He later described the truth that dawned upon him at that moment as follows:

'This body is dead. It will now be taken to the cremation ground, burnt, and reduced to ashes. But with the destruction of this body, am I also destroyed? Is this body really "I"? Although this body is lying lifeless as a corpse, I know that I am. Unaffected in the least by this death, my being is shining clearly. Therefore I am not this body which dies. I am the "I" which is indestructible. Of all things, I alone am the reality. This body is subject to death, but I, who transcend the body, am that which lives eternally. The death that came to this body cannot affect me.'

Although he described his experience of death in so many words, he explained that this truth actually dawned upon him in an instant, not as reasoning or verbalised thoughts, but as a direct experience, without the least action of mind. So intense was his fear and consequent urge to know the truth of death, that without actually thinking anything he turned his attention away from his rigid and lifeless body and towards the innermost core of his being – his essential, unadulterated and non-dual self-consciousness 'I am'. Because his attention was so keenly focused on his consciousness of being, the true nature of that being-consciousness revealed itself as a flash of direct and certain knowledge – knowledge that was so direct and certain that it could never be doubted.

Thus Sri Ramana discovered himself to be the pure transpersonal consciousness 'I am', which is the one, unlimited, undivided and non-dual whole, the only existing reality, the source and substance of all things, and the true self of every living being. This knowledge of his real nature destroyed in him for ever the sense of identification with the physical body – the feeling of being an individual person, a separate conscious entity confined within the limits of a particular time and place.

Along with this dawn of non-dual self-knowledge, the truth of everything else became clear to him. By knowing himself to be the infinite spirit, the fundamental consciousness 'I am', in which and through which all other things are known, he knew as an immediate experience how those other things appear and disappear in this essential consciousness. Thus he knew without the least doubt that everything that appears and disappears depends for its seeming existence upon this fundamental consciousness, which he knew to be his real self.

When reading some of the recorded accounts of his death experience, people often get the impression that when he lay down like a corpse, Sri Ramana merely simulated the signs of physical death. But he explained on several occasions that he did not merely simulate it, but actually underwent the experience of physical death at that time. Because he fixed his whole attention so firmly and intensely upon his non-dual consciousness of being, not only did his breathing cease, but his heart stopped beating, and all the other biological functions that indicate life also came to a standstill. Thus his body literally lay lifeless for about twenty minutes, until suddenly life surged through it once again, and his heartbeat and breath started to function as normal.

However, though life returned to his physical body, the person who had previously identified that body as 'I' was dead, having been destroyed forever by the clear light of true self-knowledge. But though he had died as an individual person, he had thereby been born again as the infinite spirit – the fundamental and unlimited consciousness of being, the non-dual self-consciousness 'I am'.

Though outwardly he appeared to behave as an individual person, his personality was in fact just an appearance that existed only in the view of other people, like the charred form of a rope that remains after the rope itself has been burnt. Inwardly he knew himself to be the all-inclusive consciousness that transcends all limitations, and not merely a separate individual consciousness confined within the limits of a particular body. Therefore, the conscious being that other people saw acting through his body was not really an individual person at all, but was only the supreme spirit – the infinite and absolute reality that we usually refer to as 'God'.

Soon after this true self-knowledge dawned upon him, Sri Ramana left his childhood home and travelled a few hundred miles north to Tiruvannamalai, a temple town nestled at the foot of the holy mountain Arunachala, where he lived as a *sādhu* or religious mendicant for the remaining fifty-four years of his bodily life. Since he had ceased to identify himself with the body that other people mistook to be him, he also ceased to identify with the name that had previously been given to that body. Therefore, from the time he left home, he stopped using his childhood name Venkataraman, and he signed his parting note with just a line.

Thus when he first came to Tiruvannamalai, no one there knew his name, so they referred to him by various names of their choosing. More than ten years later, however, one of his devotees, who was a Sanskrit poet and Vedic scholar, announced that he should be called 'Bhagavan Sri Ramana Maharshi', and somehow this became the name by which he was generally known thereafter.

However, till the end of his bodily life, Sri Ramana never claimed this or any other name as his own, and he always declined to sign any signature, even when asked to do so. When he was once asked why he never signed his name, he replied, 'By what name am I to be known? I myself do not know. At various times various people have called me by various different names'. Because he did not experience himself as an individual person, but knew himself to be the one reality, which is the source and substance of all names and forms, but which has no name or form of its own, he responded to whatever name people called him, without ever identifying any of those names as his own.

Of the four words of the name 'Bhagavan Sri Ramana Maharshi', only the word 'Ramana' is a personal name, and the other three words are titles of various sorts. 'Ramana' is a shortened form of 'Venkataramana', a variant of his childhood name 'Venkataraman', and is a word that is commonly used as a term of affection. Whereas in the name 'Venkataraman', the letter 'a' in the syllable 'ra' is a long form of the vowel and is therefore pronounced with a stress, in the name 'Ramana' all the three 'a's are short forms of the vowel, and therefore none of the three syllables are pronounced with any stress. Etymologically, the word *ramaṇa* comes from the verbal root *ram*, which means to stop, to set at rest, to make steady or calm, to delight or to make happy, and is a noun that means 'joy' or that which gives joy, that which is pleasing, charming or delightful, and by extension is used as an affectionate term meaning a beloved person, a lover, husband or wife, or the lord or mistress of one's heart.

The word *bhagavān* is an honorific and affectionate title meaning the glorious, adorable and divine Lord, and is used generally as a term meaning 'God', and more particularly as a title of veneration given to a person who is considered to be an incarnation of God or a human embodiment of the supreme reality, such as the Buddha, Sri Adi Sankara, or most commonly Sri Krishna, whose teachings are given in the *Bhagavad Gītā* and in parts of the *Śrīmad Bhāgavatam*. The word *śrī* is a sacred monosyllable meaning light, lustre, radiance or splendour, and is customarily used as an honorific prefix appended to the names of holy people, places, texts or other objects of veneration. As a reverential prefix, it means 'sacred', 'holy' or 'venerable', but it is also commonly used as a simple title of respect which may be appended to the name of any person in place of the English title 'Mister'. The word *maharṣi* (which is commonly transcribed as 'maharshi') means a great *ṛṣi* (commonly transcribed as 'rishi') or 'seer'.

To the world at large, particularly outside India, Sri Ramana is generally known as 'Ramana Maharshi' (probably because to a western mind the title 'Maharshi' placed after his personal name appears to be a surname, which it is not), and since he is so frequently referred to as such, some people even refer to him simply as 'the Maharshi'. However those who are close to him seldom use the title 'Maharshi' when referring to him. In Indian history and mythology, the term *ṛṣi* originally denoted one of the inspired poets or 'seers' who 'saw' and wrote down the hymns of the Vēdas, or any person who was adept in the performance of Vedic rituals and had thereby attained psychic or supernatural powers, but in later times it was used more generally to denote an ascetic or saint who was considered to have achieved some degree of spiritual attainment. The term *ṛṣi* has therefore never specifically meant a person who has 'seen' or attained true self-knowledge, and nor has the term *maharṣi* (*maha-ṛṣi*). The few *ṛṣis*, such as Vasishtha, and later Viswamitra, who did attain true knowledge of *brahman*, the absolute reality or God, were called not merely *maha-ṛṣis* but *brahma-ṛṣis*, a term that denotes a *ṛṣi* of the highest order. Hence many people feel that it is not particularly appropriate to apply the title 'Maharshi' to Sri Ramana, who had attained true knowledge of *brahman*, and who therefore can be accurately described as being nothing less than a *brahma-ṛṣi*.

Besides being not particularly appropriate, the title 'Maharshi' sounds rather cold and distant when applied to Sri Ramana, so rather than referring to him as 'the Maharshi', his disciples and devotees usually prefer to refer to him by the more affectionate and respectful title 'Bhagavan'. Therefore, if I were writing this book for people who are already his followers, in accordance with the usual custom I would refer to him as 'Bhagavan' or 'Sri Bhagavan'. However, since I am writing it for a wider audience, and particularly for people who have no previous acquaintance with his teachings, I will refer to him by his personal name as 'Sri Ramana' or 'Bhagavan Ramana'.

However, by whatever name I or anyone else may refer to him, to all those who have followed his teachings and thereby attained the blissful state of true self-knowledge, he is 'Ramana', the beloved giver of joy, and 'Bhagavan', a gracious embodiment of God, the supreme reality, which he discovered to be his own true self, and which he prompted and guided each one of us to discover likewise as our own true self. Sri Ramana is not merely an individual person who lived sometime in the past, nor does he belong to any particular religion or culture. He is the eternal and unlimited spirit, the ultimate and absolute reality, our own true self, and as such he always lives within each one of us as our pure and essential consciousness of being, which we each experience as 'I am'.

Bhagavan Sri Ramana never sought of his own accord to teach anyone the truth that he had come to know, because in his experience that truth – the consciousness 'I am' – alone exists, and hence there is no person either to give or to receive any teaching. However, though he inwardly knew that consciousness is the only reality, he was nevertheless outwardly a personification of love, compassion and kindness, because, knowing both himself and all other things to be nothing but the consciousness 'I am', he saw himself in everything, and hence he quite literally loved all living beings as his own self. Therefore, when people asked him questions about the reality and the means of attaining it, he patiently answered their questions, and thus without any volition on his part he gradually revealed a wealth of spiritual teachings.

Many of the answers that he thus gave were recorded in writing, more or less accurately, by his devotees and disciples, but the most accurate and authentic record of his teachings lies in the poetry that he himself wrote, mostly in Tamil, and also in Sanskrit, Telugu and Malayalam. Most of the poetry he wrote was in response to requests made by his disciples, but some of it was composed by him spontaneously. His poetry falls into two general categories – poems that directly convey spiritual teachings, and devotional hymns that convey spiritual teachings indirectly in the allegorical language of mystical love.

Since he was asked questions on a wide range of subjects by people whose interests and level of understanding varied greatly, the answers that he gave were in each case tailored to the needs of the person he was talking to, and hence they did not always reflect the essence of his teachings. Therefore when we read the various records of the conversations that he had with people, they may appear to contain inconsistencies, and to convey no single, clear or coherent set of teachings. However, a very clear, coherent and consistent account of his central teachings can be found in his poetry and other writings, and if we read all the records of his conversations in the light of those central teachings, we can clearly understand that he had a very definite message for all who were ready to hear it.

Before he attained the experience of true self-knowledge, Sri Ramana had not read or heard anything that described that experience, or prepared him in any way for it. Having been brought up in a normal family of south Indian brahmins, he was familiar with the outward forms of the Hindu religion and with a few devotional texts, and having been educated in a Christian missionary school, he was familiar with the outward forms of Christianity and with the Bible. Moreover, having had some childhood friends who were from Muslim families, he also had some familiarity with the outward forms of Islam. But though he had a general idea that all these religions were just different ways of worshipping the same one God, he had had no opportunity to learn anything about the real inner essence that lies behind the outward forms of all religions.

The teachings that he gave in later years were therefore derived entirely from his own inward experience, and did not originate from any outward learning. However, whenever anyone asked him to explain any sacred or spiritual text, he would read it and would often recognise that in one way or another it was expressing the truth that was his own experience. Thus he was able to interpret such texts with authority and to explain their inner meaning in clear and simple words. Since the cultural and religious milieu in which he lived was predominantly Hindu, and since most of the people who sought his spiritual guidance were either born Hindus or were familiar with traditional Hindu philosophy, the texts he was most often asked to explain were those of the Hindu philosophical tradition known as *advaita vēdānta*. Thus Sri Ramana's teachings are often identified with *advaita vēdānta* and are taken to be a modern expression or interpretation of that ancient philosophy.

The word *vēdānta* literally means the 'conclusion' or 'end' (*anta*) of 'knowledge' (*vēda*), and denotes the philosophical conclusions of the Vēdas. These philosophical conclusions are contained in Vedic texts known as the *Upaniṣads*, and were later expressed more clearly and in greater detail in two other ancient texts known as the *Brahma Sūtra* and the *Bhagavad Gītā*. These three bodies of literature, which are known as the 'triple source' (*prasthāna-traya*) of *vēdānta*, have been interpreted in very different ways, giving rise to three distinct systems of *vēdāntic* philosophy, the pure monistic system known as *advaita*, the dualistic system known as *dvaita*, and the qualified monistic system known as *viśiṣṭādvaita*. Of these three systems of philosophy, *advaita* is not only the most radical but also the least convoluted interpretation of the ancient *prasthāna-traya* of *vēdānta*, and hence it is widely recognised as being *vēdānta* in its purest and truest form.

However, *advaita* is more than just a scholarly interpretation of some ancient texts. Like the literature of any other system of religious or spiritual philosophy, the literature of *advaita* includes a huge amount of elaborate and abstruse material written by and for scholars, but such material is not the essence or basis of the *advaita* philosophy. The life and heart of *advaita vēdānta* lies in a number of crucial texts that contain the sayings and writings of sages like Sri Ramana who had attained true self-knowledge, and whose words therefore reflect their own direct experience of the reality. Thus *advaita vēdānta* is a system of spiritual philosophy that is based not upon mere reasoning or intellectual speculation, but upon the experience of sages who have attained direct knowledge of the non-dual reality that underlies the appearance of all multiplicity.

The word *advaita* literally means 'no-twoness' or 'non-duality', and denotes the truth experienced by sages – the truth that the reality is only one, a single undivided whole that is completely devoid of any duality or multiplicity. According to sages who have attained true self-knowledge, all multiplicity is a mere appearance, a distorted view of the one reality, like the illusory appearance of a snake seen in a dim light. Just as the reality underlying the illusory appearance of the snake is just a rope lying on the ground, so the reality underlying the illusory appearance of multiplicity is only the non-dual consciousness of being that we each experience as 'I am'.

Sri Ramana's teachings are therefore identified with *advaita vēdānta* for three main reasons: firstly because he experienced and taught the same non-dual reality that was experienced by the sages whose sayings and writings formed the foundation of the *advaita vēdānta* philosophy; secondly because he was often asked to explain and elucidate various texts from the classical literature of *advaita vēdānta*; and thirdly because in his teachings he made free but nevertheless selective use of the terminology, concepts and analogies used in that classical literature. The reason he thus used the terminology and concepts of *advaita vēdānta* more than those of any other spiritual tradition, such as Buddhism, Taoism, Jewish or Christian mysticism, or Sufism, is that most of the people who sought his spiritual guidance were more familiar with *advaita vēdānta* than with those other spiritual traditions, and hence it was easier for them to understand such terminology and concepts. However, whenever anyone asked him to elucidate any text or passage from the literature of those other spiritual traditions, he did so with the same ease, clarity and authority that he elucidated the texts of *advaita vēdānta*.

Though in his teachings Sri Ramana borrowed some of the terminology, concepts and analogies commonly used in the classical literature of *advaita vēdānta*, his teachings are not merely a repetition of the old and familiar teachings contained in that literature. Because he was teaching the truth that he had known from his own direct experience, and not merely learnt from books, he was able to set aside all the dense mass of non-essential, complex and ponderous arguments and concepts found in that literature, and to throw a fresh and clear light upon the inner essence of *advaita vēdānta*.

In his teachings he has revealed the true spirit of *advaita vēdānta* in a clear and simple manner that can easily be understood even by people who have no previous acquaintance with such philosophy. Moreover, the simplicity, clarity and directness of his teachings have helped to clear the confusion created in the minds of many people who have studied the classical literature of *advaita vēdānta*, but have been misled by the many well-established misinterpretations of it made by scholars who had no direct experience of the truth. In particular, his teachings have cleared up many misunderstandings that had long existed about the practice of *advaita vēdānta*, and have clearly revealed the means by which we can attain the experience of true self-knowledge.

Since the means to attain self-knowledge is for some reason seldom stated in clear and unambiguous terms in the classical literature of *advaita vēdānta*, many misconceptions exist about the spiritual practice advocated by *advaita vēdānta*. Therefore perhaps the most significant contribution made by Sri Ramana to the literature of *advaita vēdānta* lies in the fact that in his teachings he has revealed in very clear, precise and unambiguous terms the practical means by which self-knowledge can be attained.

Not only has he explained this practical means very clearly, he has also explained exactly how it will lead us infallibly to the state of self-knowledge, and why it is the only means that can do so. Unlike many of the older texts of *advaita vēdānta*, the teachings of Sri Ramana are centred entirely around the practical means by which we can attain self-knowledge, and all that he taught regarding any aspect of life was aimed solely at directing our minds towards this practice.

Though this practical means is essentially very simple, for many people it appears difficult to comprehend, because it is not an action or state of 'doing', nor does it involve any form of objective attention. Since the practice is thus a state beyond all mental activity – a state of non-doing and non-objective attention – no words can express it perfectly. Therefore, to enable us to understand and practise it, Sri Ramana has expressed and described it in various different ways, each of which serves as a valuable clue that helps us to know and to be the pure consciousness that is our own true self.

Sri Ramana spoke and wrote mostly in Tamil, his mother tongue, but he was also conversant in Sanskrit, Telugu, Malayalam and English. Tamil is the oldest surviving member of the Dravidian family of languages, and has a rich and ancient classical literature. Though in its origins it belongs to a family of languages that is entirely independent of the Indo-European family, for the past two thousand years or so Tamil literature has made rich and abundant use of words borrowed from Sanskrit, the oldest surviving member of the Indo-European family. Therefore, most of the terms Sri Ramana used to describe the practical means by which we can attain self-knowledge are either Tamil words or words of Sanskrit origin that are commonly used in Tamil spiritual literature.

The words he thus used in Tamil have been translated in English by a variety of different words, some of which convey the import and spirit of his original words more clearly and accurately than others. Perhaps two of the clearest and most simple terms used in English to convey the sense of the words that he used in Tamil to describe the practical means to attain self-knowledge are 'self-attention' and 'self-abidance'. The term 'self-attention' denotes the knowing aspect of the practice, while the term 'self-abidance' denotes its being aspect.

Since our real self, which is non-dual self-consciousness, knows itself not by an act of knowing but merely by being itself, the state of knowing our real self is just the state of being our real self. Thus attending to our self-consciousness and abiding as our self-consciousness are one and the same thing. All the other words that Sri Ramana used to describe the practice are intended to be clues that help to clarify what this state of 'self-attention' or 'self-abidance' really is.

A few of the terms which he used to describe the practice of 'self-attention' or 'self-abidance' are in fact terms already used in some of the classical texts of *advaita vēdānta*. However though such texts have used some of the same terms that Sri Ramana used to express the practice, they have seldom explained the true import of those terms in a clear and unambiguous manner. Thus, even after thoroughly studying the classical literature of *advaita vēdānta*, many people are left with only a vague understanding of what they can do to attain self-knowledge. As a result, many misconceptions about the practice of *advaita vēdānta* arose, and some of these misconceptions have been prevalent among students and scholars of *advaita vēdānta* since time immemorial.

One of the terms that occurs in the classical literature of *advaita vēdānta* and that Sri Ramana frequently used to denote the practice of self-attention is *vicāra* (which is commonly transcribed as *vichara*, since the 'c' in *vicāra* represents the same sound as 'ch' in chutney), but the significance of this term was not clearly understood by most of the traditional scholars of *advaita vēdānta*. According to the Sanskrit-English dictionary of Monier-Williams, the term *vicāra* has various meanings, including 'pondering, deliberation, consideration, reflection, examination, investigation', and it is in these senses that this same word is used in Tamil, as is clear from the Tamil Lexicon, which defines it both as 'deliberation' or 'consideration', and as 'unbiased examination with a view to arriving at the truth' or 'investigation'. Therefore the term *ātma-vicāra*, which Sri Ramana frequently used to describe the practice by which we can attain self-knowledge, means 'self-investigation' or 'self-examination', and denotes the practice of examining, inspecting or scrutinising our fundamental and essential consciousness 'I am' with a keen and concentrated power of attention.

Though the term *ātma-vicāra* can best be translated in English as 'self-investigation', 'self-examination', 'self-inspection', 'self-scrutiny', 'self-contemplation', or simply 'self-attention', in most English translations of Sri Ramana's teachings it has been translated as 'self-enquiry'. This choice of the English word 'enquiry' to translate *vicāra* has had unfortunate consequences, because it has created an impression in the minds of some people that *ātma-vicāra*, or the *vicāra* 'who am I?' as Sri Ramana often called it, is merely a process of questioning or asking ourself 'who am I?'. This is clearly a misinterpretation, because in Sanskrit the word *vicāra* means 'enquiry' in the sense of 'investigation' rather than in the sense of 'questioning'. When Sri Ramana spoke of the *vicāra* 'who am I?' he did not intend it to imply that we can attain the non-dual experience of true self-knowledge simply by asking ourself the question 'who am I?'. The *vicāra* 'who am I?' is an investigation, examination or scrutiny of our fundamental consciousness 'I am', because only by keenly scrutinising or inspecting our consciousness 'I' can we discover who we really are – what this consciousness 'I' actually is.

Besides describing the means to attain self-knowledge by the use of terms that mean 'self-attention' or 'self-abidance', Sri Ramana also described it by terms that mean 'self-surrender' or 'self-denial'. By using the latter terms, he affirmed that the ultimate aim of all forms of dualistic devotion – devotion to a God who is conceived as other than the devotee – is in fact the non-dual state of true self-knowledge. In order to know our true self, we must give up our identification with the false individual self that we now mistake to be 'I'. Therefore, surrendering or denying our personal self – our mind, which is our confused and distorted consciousness 'I am this body, a person called so-and-so' – is essential if we are to know our true unadulterated consciousness 'I am', which is our real self.

Our individual self, which is the limited and distorted consciousness that we call our 'mind' or 'ego', and that in theological terminology is called our 'soul', nourishes its seeming existence by attending to things other than itself. When we cease attending to other things, as in sleep, our mind or individual self subsides, but as soon as we begin to think of other things, it again rises and flourishes. Without thinking of things other than 'I', our mind cannot stand. Therefore, when we attempt to turn our attention away from all objects and towards our fundamental consciousness 'I', we are surrendering or denying our individual self, our mind or ego. Self-attention or self-abidance is thus the perfect means to attain the state of 'self-surrender' or 'self-denial'.

This is why in verse 31 of *Vivēkacūḍāmaṇi* Sri Adi Sankara defines *bhakti* or 'devotion' as *sva-svarūpa-anusandhāna* or 'self-attention', the investigation or close inspection of our own true form or essential nature, which is our fundamental self-consciousness – our non-dual consciousness of our own being, 'I am'. Sri Ramana expresses the same truth in verse 15 of *Upadēśa Taṉippākkaḷ*, but at the same time explains why it is so:

> Since God exists as *ātmā* [our essential 'spirit' or real self], *ātma-anusandhāna* [self-investigation, self-inspection or self-attention] is *parama-īśa-bhakti* [supreme devotion to God].

He also expresses a similar idea in the thirteenth paragraph of his brief treatise *Nāṉ Yār?* (Who am I?):

> Being completely absorbed in *ātma-niṣṭha* [self-abidance, the state of just being as we really are], giving not even the slightest room to the rising of any thought other than *ātma-cintana* [the thought of our own real self], is giving ourself to God. […]

People who practise dualistic devotion believe that the highest form of devotion to God – the purest form of love – is to surrender ourself wholly to him. In order to surrender themselves to him, they try to deny themselves by giving up their attachment to all that they consider as 'mine', and in particular by renouncing their own individual will. Thus the ultimate prayer of every true devotee is, 'Thy will be done – not my will, but only thine'.

However, so long as the mind exists, it will inevitably have a will of its own. Desire and attachment are inherent in the mind, the very fabric of which it is made. Therefore, so long as we feel ourself to be an individual 'I', we will also have an individual will, and will feel a sense of attachment to 'mine'. The only way we can surrender our own will and give up all our attachments is to surrender the mind that has an individual will and feels attachment to the body and other possessions.

Trying to surrender our individual will and sense of 'mine' – our desires and attachments – without actually surrendering our individuality, our ego or sense of being a separate 'I', is like cutting the leaves and branches off a tree without cutting its root. Until and unless we cut the root, the branches and leaves will continue sprouting again and again. Similarly, until and unless we surrender our ego, the root of all our desires and attachments, all our efforts to give up our desires and attachments will fail, because they will continue to sprout again and again in one subtle form or another. Therefore self-surrender can be complete and final only when our individual self, the limited consciousness that we call our 'mind' or 'ego', is surrendered wholly.

So long as we feel that we exist as an individual who is separate from God, we have not surrendered ourself wholly to him. Though we are in truth only the pure, unlimited and non-personal consciousness 'I am', which is the spirit or true form of God, we feel that we are separate from him because we mistake ourself to be a limited individual consciousness that has identified itself with a particular body.

This individual consciousness – our feeling 'I am a person, a separate individual, a mind or soul confined within the limits of a body' – is merely an imagination, a false and distorted form of our pure consciousness 'I am', but it is nevertheless the root cause of all desire and all misery. Unless we give up this individual consciousness, this false notion that we are separate from God, we can never be free of desire, nor of misery, which is the inevitable consequence of desire.

True self-surrender is therefore nothing but giving up the false notion that we are separate from God. In order to give up this false notion, we must know who we really are. And in order to know who we really are, we must attend to the consciousness that we feel to be 'I'.

Though the consciousness that we now feel to be 'I' is only a false consciousness, a limited and distorted form of the real consciousness that is God, by attending to it keenly we can know the real consciousness that underlies it. That is, attending keenly to this false form of consciousness is similar to looking closely at a snake that we imagine we see lying on the ground in the dim light of dusk. When we look closely at the snake, we discover that it is in fact nothing but a rope. Similarly, if we keenly attend to the limited and distorted individual consciousness that we now feel to be 'I', we will discover that it is in fact nothing but the real and unlimited consciousness 'I am', which is God. Just as the illusory appearance of the snake dissolves and disappears as soon as we see the rope, so the illusory feeling that we are a separate individual consciousness confined within the limits of a body will dissolve and disappear as soon as we experience the pure non-dual consciousness, which is the reality both of ourself and of God.

We can thus achieve complete and perfect self-surrender only by knowing ourself to be the real consciousness that is devoid of all duality and separateness. Without knowing our true self, we cannot surrender our false self, and without surrendering our false self, we cannot know our true self. Self-surrender and self-knowledge are thus inseparable, like the two sides of one sheet of paper. In fact, the terms 'self-surrender' and 'self-knowledge' are just two ways of describing one and the same state – the pure non-dual state of consciousness devoid of individuality.

Since true self-knowledge is therefore the state in which our individual consciousness, our mind or ego, is known to be a false appearance that never existed except in its own imagination, Sri Ramana often described it as the state of 'egolessness', 'loss of individuality' or 'destruction of the mind'. Another term that is commonly used, both in Buddhism and in *advaita vēdānta*, to describe this state of annihilation or extinction of our personal identity is *nirvāṇa*, a word that literally means 'blown out' or 'extinguished'. This is the same state that most religions refer to as 'liberation' or 'salvation', because only in this state of true self-knowledge are we free or saved from the bondage of mistaking ourself to be a separate individual, a consciousness that is confined within the limits of a physical body.

The sole reality that exists and is known in this state of egolessness, *nirvāṇa* or salvation is our fundamental and essential consciousness 'I am'. Since it does not identify itself with any delimiting adjunct, our essential and pure consciousness 'I am' is a single, undivided and unlimited whole, separate from which nothing can exist. All the diversity and multiplicity that appears to exist so long as we identify ourself with a physical body, is known only by our mind, which is merely a distorted and limited form of our original consciousness 'I am'. If this consciousness 'I am' did not exist, nothing else could appear to exist. Therefore, our fundamental consciousness 'I am' is the source and origin of all knowledge – the one basis of all that appears to exist.

Our essential consciousness 'I am' is thus the ultimate reality, the original source from which everything arises, and the final destination towards which all religions and spiritual traditions seek to lead us. Most religions call this fundamental reality 'God' or the 'Supreme Being', or else they refer to it in a more abstract manner as the true state of being. But by whatever name they may call it – and whether they describe it as a being or a state of being – the truth is that the supreme and absolute reality is not anything other than our own being, the consciousness which we experience as 'I am'.

In his true form, his essential nature, God is not something or some person who exists outside us or separate from us, but is the spirit or consciousness that exists within us as our own essential nature. God is the pure consciousness 'I am', the true form of consciousness that is not limited by identifying itself with a physical body or any other adjunct. But when we, who are that same pure consciousness 'I am', identify ourself with a physical body, feeling 'I am this body, I am a person, an individual confined within the limits of time and space', we become the mind, a false and illusory form of consciousness. Because we identify ourself with adjuncts in this manner, we seemingly separate ourself from the adjunctless pure consciousness 'I am', which is God. By thus imagining ourself to be an individual separate from God, we violate his unlimited wholeness and undivided oneness.

The inner aim of all religions and spiritual traditions is to free us from this illusory state in which we imagine that we are separate from God, the one unlimited and undivided reality. For example, in Christianity this state in which we violate the oneness and wholeness of God by imagining ourself to be an individual separate from him is called the 'original sin', which is the root cause of all misery and unhappiness. Because we can become free from this 'original sin' only by knowing the truth, Christ said, '[…] ye shall know the truth, and the truth shall make you free' (*John* 8.32). The truth that we must know in order to be made free is the truth that we are nothing but the adjunctless pure consciousness 'I am' – that 'I am' which is the true form of God, as disclosed by him when he revealed his identity to Moses saying, 'I AM THAT I AM' ('*ehyeh asher ehyeh*' – *Exodus* 3.14).

To 'know the truth' does not mean to know it theoretically, but to know it as a direct and immediate experience. In order to destroy the illusion that we are a limited individual consciousness, a person separate from the perfect whole which is called God, we must experience ourself as the unlimited and undivided pure consciousness 'I am'. Therefore, to know the truth and thereby be made free from the illusion called 'original sin', we must die and be born again – we must die to the flesh and be born again as the spirit. That is why Christ said, 'Except a man be born again, he cannot see the kingdom of God. […] Except a man be born of […] the Spirit, he cannot enter into the kingdom of God. That which is born of the flesh is flesh; and that which is born of the Spirit is spirit' (*John* 3.3 & 3.5-6).

That is, to experience and enter into the true state of God, we must cease to exist as a separate individual, a consciousness that identifies itself with the flesh and all the limitations of the flesh, and must rediscover ourself to be the unlimited and undivided spirit, the pure, unadulterated and infinite consciousness 'I am', which is the absolute reality that we call 'God'. When we identify ourself with a body made of flesh, we become that flesh, but when we cease to identify ourself with that flesh and know ourself to be mere spirit, we are born again as our original nature, the pure spirit or consciousness 'I am'.

The need for us to sacrifice our individuality in order to be born anew as the spirit is a recurring theme in the teachings of Jesus Christ. 'Except a corn of wheat fall into the ground and die, it abideth alone: but if it die, it bringeth forth much fruit. He that loveth his life shall lose it; and he that hateth his life in this world shall keep it unto life eternal' (*John* 12.24-25). 'Whosoever shall seek to save his life shall lose it; and whosoever shall lose his life shall preserve it' (*Luke* 17.33). 'And he that taketh not his cross, and followeth after me, is not worthy of me. He that findeth his life shall lose it: and he that loseth his life for my sake shall find it' (*Matthew* 10.38-39). 'If any [man] will come after me, let him deny himself, and take up his cross, and follow me. For whosoever will save his life shall lose it: and whosoever will lose his life for my sake shall find it. For what is a man profited, if he shall gain the whole world, and lose his own soul? or what shall a man give in exchange for his soul?' (*Matthew* 16.24-26, and also *Mark* 8.34-37 and *Luke* 9.23-25).

That is, in order to rediscover our true and eternal life as the spirit, we must lose our false and transient life as an individual. If we seek to preserve our false individuality, we shall in effect be losing our real spirit. This is the price we have to pay to live as an individual in this world. Therefore, whatever we may gain or achieve in this world, we do so at the cost of losing our real self, the state of perfection and wholeness (which in this context is what Christ means by the term our 'own soul'). In exchange for regaining our original and perfect state of wholeness, we have only to give up our individuality and all that goes with it. Which is truly profitable, to lose the whole and gain merely a part, or to give up a mere part in exchange for the whole?

In order to give up or lose our individuality, as Christ had done, he says that we must follow him by denying ourself and taking up our cross. To deny ourself means to refrain from rising as an individual separate from God, who is the whole – the 'fullness of being' or totality of all that is. To take up our cross means to embrace the death or destruction of our own individuality, because in the time of Christ the cross was a powerful symbol of death, being the usual instrument of execution. Thus, though he used somewhat oblique language to express it, Christ repeatedly emphasised the truth that in order to rediscover our real life as the spirit we must sacrifice our false life as an individual.

This sacrifice of our individuality or identification with the flesh, and our consequent resurrection or rebirth as the spirit, was symbolised by Christ through his own crucifixion and subsequent resurrection. By dying on the cross and rising again from the dead, Christ gave us a powerful symbolic representation of the truth that in order to become free from the 'original sin' of identification with the flesh and thereby to enter the 'kingdom of God', we must die or cease to exist as a separate individual, and thereby rise again as the pure spirit, the infinite consciousness 'I am'.

The 'kingdom of God' which we can see and enter only by being born again as the spirit is not a place – something that we can find externally in the material world of time and space, or even in some celestial world called heaven. When Christ was asked when the kingdom of God would come, he answered, 'The kingdom of God cometh not with observation: neither shall they say, Lo here! or, lo there! for, behold, the kingdom of God is within you' (*Luke* 17.20-21).

The kingdom of God cannot be found by observation, that is, by any form of objective attention – by looking externally here or there. It cannot be found in any place outside us, either here in this world or there in heaven, nor indeed is it something that will come in the future. It exists within us even now. To see and enter into it, we must turn our attention inwards, away from the external world of time and space that we observe by means of the limited flesh-bound consciousness that we call our 'mind', and towards our true consciousness 'I am', which is the underlying base and reality of the observing consciousness 'I am so-and-so'.

The exhortation 'behold' that Christ used in the above passage is very important. He did not merely tell us the fact that the kingdom of God is within ourself, but exhorted us to look and see that it is within ourself. That is, he did not merely tell us the truth that he saw, but told us that we should each see it for ourself. In more modern English, we would express the passage '[…] neither shall they say, Lo here! or, lo there! for, behold, the kingdom of God is within you' as '[…] and they should not say, 'Look here or look there', because, see, the kingdom of God is within you'. This exhortation that Christ makes to us not to look here or there but to see that the kingdom of God is within ourself, is the essence of the spiritual practice taught by Sri Ramana and all other true sages. We should give up attending to anything outside ourself, and should instead turn our attention inwards to see the reality that exists within us.

The kingdom of God is not a place but a state – our natural state of pure self-conscious being. When we see it within ourself by turning our attention towards the innermost core of our being, we enter into it and become one with it. This is the state of being born again as the spirit – the state of mystical union with God that all Christian contemplatives seek to attain. In this state called the 'kingdom of God', the pure consciousness 'I am', which is the spirit or true form of God, exists and shines alone in all the splendour and glory of its undivided oneness and unlimited wholeness.

The teachings of Sri Ramana thus throw a fresh light upon the spiritual teachings contained in the Bible. In the same manner, they also throw fresh light upon the spiritual teachings of all other religions. Though his teachings are easily recognised as a fresh and clear expression of the ancient teachings of *advaita vēdānta*, they in fact clarify the inner essence not only of *advaita vēdānta* but also of all other spiritual traditions. The truth that he taught is not a relative truth that is limited to any particular religion or human culture, but is the absolute truth which underlies all human experience, and which is the source and foundation of the spiritual teachings of all religions. For certain cultural or other reasons, in some religions this truth is expressed less openly and clearly than in others, but it is nevertheless the truth that lies at the heart of every religion.

Though this truth is not recognised by most of the followers of the various religions, particularly by the followers of those religions in which it is hidden more obscurely, it is nevertheless expressed in some form or other in the scriptures and the philosophical and mystical writings of every religion, and it can be discerned and recognised by all who have the eyes to see it. The teachings of Sri Ramana, if understood clearly and correctly, give us the eyes or insight required to discern and recognise it wherever it is expressed, no matter how seemingly obscure may be the words that are used to express it.

All words are open to interpretation – and misinterpretation. This is particularly true of words that speak about the spirit – the reality that lies beyond the limitations of physical matter, and that therefore cannot be perceived by the five senses, or known as an object of consciousness. All interpretations of such words fall into two distinct categories – interpretations that are strictly non-dualistic, admitting no division of the one and only reality, and interpretations that are either completely dualistic, or that at least concede that within the one reality there are divisions and distinctions that are real. Ultimately the interpretation that we each choose to accept depends not upon the truth itself – because the nature of the truth cannot be proved objectively – but upon our own personal preferences.

Most people – whether they hold religious beliefs or cherish a more materialistic outlook on life – prefer to take a dualistic view of reality, because such a view assures them of the reality of their own individuality, and of the world they perceive through their senses, and (if they choose to believe in God) of God as a separately existing entity. Therefore the only basis for a dualistic view of reality is the attachment that people have to their own individuality, to the world that they think gives them happiness, and to their idea of a God who they believe will give them the things that will make them happy.

There is no way that a dualistic view of reality can be proved to be correct and valid. All our knowledge of duality is obtained by our mind and exists only within our mind. If our mind is real, then duality may be real. But the reality of our mind is open to question and doubt.

If we are not overly attached to our existence as a separate individual, we can begin to question and doubt the reality of our mind. If we do so, we will be led unavoidably to a non-dualistic view of reality. Of all the knowledge we know, the one knowledge whose reality we cannot reasonably doubt is our own essential consciousness 'I am'. Knowledge can exist only if there is a consciousness to know it. Since all knowledge depends for its seeming existence upon consciousness, consciousness is the one fundamental, irreducible and indubitable truth of our experience. Because we know, our consciousness is undoubtedly real.

The one essential quality of consciousness is that it is always self-conscious – it always knows its own existence or being – and that consciousness of its own existence is what we experience as 'I am'. However, in addition to knowing its own existence, our consciousness sometimes seems to know other things also. When our consciousness thus appears to know things other than itself, we call it our 'mind'.

What exactly is this 'mind', this consciousness that knows otherness and duality? Is it the true form of our consciousness, or merely a false superimposition upon our real self-consciousness 'I am'? Is it real, or is it merely a false appearance?

Whenever our mind rises, it rises in conjunction with a body, with which it identifies itself, feeling 'I am this body'. Without identifying itself with a body, our mind cannot rise. Once it has risen, identifying itself with a particular body, through the five senses of that body it perceives the world. Thus our mind's identification with a body is fundamental to its ability to know the world.

But how does this identification with a body arise? Our mind is a form of consciousness, whereas this body is a physical form composed of inconscient matter. By identifying itself with this body, our mind is confusing two different things as one. It is confusing consciousness, which is not physical matter, with the physical form of this body, which is not consciousness. Therefore our mind is a confused and spurious form of consciousness, a phantom which is neither our real consciousness 'I am', nor the physical form of this body, but which mixes these two different things together, feeling 'I am this body'.

Though our mind usurps the properties of both our consciousness 'I am' and this physical body, it is in fact neither of these two things. Since it appears and disappears, and constantly undergoes change, it is not our real consciousness 'I am', which neither appears nor disappears, but exists and knows its own existence at all times and in all states without ever undergoing any change. And since our mind is conscious, it is not this body, which is inconscient matter.

Moreover, our mind does not always identify the same body as 'I'. In waking it takes one body to be 'I', but in each dream it takes some other body to be 'I'. Since it can identify itself with different bodies at different times, it cannot really be any of those bodies.

By identifying itself with a body, our mind deludes itself into experiencing our consciousness 'I am' as being something confined within the limits of a body, and a body composed of inconscient matter as being something that is endowed with consciousness. If our mind did not delude itself in this manner, it would not exist as a separate entity called 'mind', but would remain as pure consciousness, undefiled by any form of limitation. Because the very nature of our mind is to delude itself into experiencing that it is what it is not, Sri Ramana said that our mind itself is *māyā*, the primordial power of delusion, illusion or self-deception – the power that makes what is real appear to be unreal, and what is unreal appear to be real.

In dream our mind projects an imaginary body, which it identifies as 'I', and through the five senses of that body it perceives an imaginary world. So long as our mind continues to be in that state of dream, it takes the body and world that it experiences in dream to be real. However absurd some of the things which it experiences may appear to be, still our mind deludes itself into believing that those things are real. So long as our mind experiences itself as a body, it cannot but experience all that it perceives through the senses of that body as real. But when we wake up from a dream, we cease to experience the dream body as 'I', and we simultaneously cease to experience the dream world as real.

Thus from our experience in dream, and our contrasting experience on waking from dream, we can clearly understand that by the power of its imagination our mind has the ability to create a world of duality and simultaneously convince itself that that world is real. When we know that our mind has this power of simultaneous creation and self-deception, we have to doubt whether all the duality that it now experiences in the waking state is anything other than a product of its own self-deceiving power of imagination.

The only thing whose reality we cannot doubt is our consciousness of our own existence – our non-dual self-consciousness, 'I am'. Other than this non-dual and fundamental consciousness 'I am', everything that we experience is open to doubt. Hence we cannot reasonably avoid doubting the reality of all duality, and suspecting that in fact the only reality is our non-dual consciousness of our own being, 'I am'.

By what standard can we determine whether or not something is real? A thing can be truly said to be real only if it is absolutely, unconditionally and independently real, and not if its reality is in any way relative, conditional or dependent upon something else. Therefore, according to Sri Ramana, something can be called real only if it satisfies three essential criteria: it must be eternal, unchanging and self-shining.

If something is not eternal, though it may appear to be real for a certain period of time, it was not real before it came into existence, and it will not be real after it ceases to exist, so in fact it is unreal even while it appears to be real. Because it is confined within the limits of time, its seeming reality is relative and conditional. That which is absolutely and unconditionally real must be real at all times, and cannot be limited in relation to anything else.

Moreover, if something undergoes change during the course of time, it is one thing at one time, but becomes another thing at another time, and hence it does not exist eternally as any one thing. Being impermanent, that which changes is not real.

However, the most important criteria by which we can determine something as real is that it must be self-shining. By the term 'self-shining', Sri Ramana means 'self-knowing' or 'self-conscious', that is, knowing itself by its own light of consciousness. That which is absolutely and unconditionally real need not depend upon any consciousness other than itself to be known. If something depends upon something else in order to be known as existing or real, then its reality depends upon the reality of the consciousness that knows it. Since it does not know itself to be real, it is not real at all, but merely appears to be real so long as it is known by the consciousness that knows it.

Measured by this standard, the only existing reality is our fundamental consciousness 'I am', because among all the things that we experience or know, it is the only thing that is permanent, the only thing that never undergoes any change, and the only thing that knows its own existence without the aid of any other thing.

Unlike this consciousness 'I am', our mind is impermanent, because it appears in the states of waking and dream, and disappears in deep sleep. Even while it does appear to exist, our mind is constantly undergoing change, thinking of one thing at one moment and another thing at another moment. And though our mind appears to know itself by its own power of consciousness, in fact the consciousness by which it knows itself and all other things is only our basic consciousness 'I am', which it seemingly usurps as its own, but which is nevertheless independent of it.

Our mind is distinct from our essential consciousness 'I am', by the light of which it seemingly knows the existence of itself and other things, because our consciousness 'I am' can exist in the absence of our mind, as in sleep. Whereas our consciousness 'I am' is permanent, our mind is impermanent. Whereas our consciousness 'I am' is ever unchanging being, which always remains as it is, our mind is a constantly changing flow of thoughts. And whereas our consciousness 'I am' is always conscious of its own being, our mind is sometimes conscious of itself and other things, and sometimes conscious neither of itself nor of any other thing. Therefore our consciousness 'I am' is real, whereas our mind is merely an unreal appearance.

If the essential nature of something is consciousness, it must always be conscious, because nothing can ever be separated from its essential nature. Because consciousness is the essential nature of our consciousness 'I am', it is conscious at all times and in all states. Similarly, because the essential nature of our consciousness 'I am' is also being or existence, it exists at all times and in all states.

In contrast, since our mind is conscious only during the waking and dream states, and ceases to be conscious in sleep, its essential nature cannot be consciousness. Similarly, since it exists only in waking and dream, but ceases to exist in sleep, its essential nature cannot be being or existence.

In fact, there is nothing that can be pointed out as being the essential nature of our mind, because it is not constantly any one thing. The body cannot be its essential nature, because though it identifies itself with a particular body in the waking state, in dream it identifies itself with some other body, and in sleep it identifies itself with no body at all. Similarly, its essential nature cannot be any thought or even the act of thinking, because throughout the waking and dream states the thoughts it thinks are constantly changing, and in sleep it ceases to think any thought. Though our mind in fact has no essential nature of its own, in the waking and dream states its essential nature appears to be consciousness. However, since it ceases to be conscious in sleep, the consciousness that appears to be its essential nature in waking and dream is in fact borrowed by it from our real consciousness 'I am'.

Since our mind therefore has no essential nature of its own, we can definitely conclude that it has no reality of its own, but borrows its seeming reality only from our essential consciousness 'I am'. Our mind is therefore an unreal phantom, something that is in fact neither one thing nor another. It is a false appearance, an illusion or hallucination, a self-deceiving imagination that appears and disappears in our one real consciousness 'I am'.

However, though our mind deceives itself by appearing in and as our real consciousness 'I am', it does not deceive our consciousness 'I am', which always remains as it is, knowing only its own existence, and being affected by nothing else whatsoever. Because our real consciousness 'I am' always remains as pure consciousness, undefiled by the knowledge of anything other than itself, nothing that appears or disappears can ever affect it even in the least. That is, whatever else may appear or disappear, we always know 'I am'.

The essential nature of our real consciousness 'I am' is only self-consciousness – consciousness of our own existence or being – and not consciousness of anything other than ourself. Because our consciousness of other things appears and disappears, it cannot be the essential nature of our real underlying consciousness 'I am'. In its real and essential nature, our consciousness 'I am' is ever unchanging, and ever unaffected by any change that may appear to occur. Therefore, whatever other knowledge may appear or disappear, it cannot affect our fundamental consciousness of our own being, 'I am', which exists and knows its own existence in all states and at all times.

Our mind is therefore a false form of consciousness, an imaginary, confused and self-deceiving form of knowledge, a spurious entity that has no real existence of its own. Since all duality or multiplicity is known only by this mind, it depends for its seeming existence upon this mind – this imaginary, confused, self-deceiving and unreal form of consciousness. Hence our mind is the root cause of the appearance of duality. Without our mind to know it, no duality could exist. Therefore duality can only be as real as our mind, which knows it. Since our mind is an unreal appearance that rises and subsides in our real consciousness 'I am', all duality is likewise an unreal appearance.

Therefore we can reasonably conclude that our pure consciousness 'I am' is the only existing reality, and that our mind and all the duality or multiplicity which is known by it is only an unreal appearance – an appearance that is unreal because it is impermanent, constantly changing, and dependent for its seeming existence upon the one real consciousness 'I am'.

Thus, if we have the courage and intellectual honesty to seriously doubt and question the reality of our mind, and to analyse its nature impartially, we will be led unavoidably to a non-dualistic view of reality – to the conclusion that the only existing reality is our fundamental consciousness of our own essential being, our pure non-dual self-consciousness 'I am', and that all else is only an illusion or false appearance, an imagination created and known only by our imaginary mind.

This non-dual reality is the one truth about which all religions speak. Though they do not always describe the non-dual nature of this truth in explicit terms, all religions do so implicitly in one way or another.

No religion has a monopoly on the truth. What is true in one religion is true in every religion. The truth can never be in any way exclusive, because if it were, it would only be a partial truth and not the whole truth – a relative truth and not the absolute truth. To be wholly and absolutely true, the truth must be all-inclusive – it must be the one whole that includes everything within itself.

The one whole truth that does include everything within itself is the infinite spirit, the single consciousness that we all know as 'I am'. Everything that appears to exist does so only within this consciousness. Though the manifold forms in which things appear are unreal as such, the one real substance of all things is the consciousness in which they appear. Therefore the one truth about which all religions speak is the single, all-inclusive and non-dual whole, the spirit or consciousness in which all things appear and disappear.

However, because they interpret the spiritual teachings of their religion in a dualistic manner, most of the followers of the various religions tend to believe that their own religion somehow has a monopoly or exclusive claim upon the truth, and is therefore the only means to salvation. For example, throughout the history of Christianity, most ordinary Christians have believed that true salvation can be attained only through the person of Jesus Christ, and that atheists, agnostics and the followers of other religions can be saved only by converting to Christianity. They have justified this unreasonable and arrogant belief by their dualistic interpretation of Christ's saying, 'I am the way, the truth, and the life: no man cometh unto the Father, but by me' (*John* 14.6). Because of their dualistic understanding of his spiritual teachings, they interpret the words 'I am' and 'me' that he used in this passage to denote only the individual person Jesus Christ, who was born at a certain time in a certain place called Bethlehem.

However, Christ did not mistake himself to be merely an individual person whose life was limited within a certain range of time and place. He knew himself to be the real and eternal spirit 'I am', which is unlimited by time and place. That is why he said, 'Before Abraham was born, I am' (*John* 8.58). The person who was Jesus Christ was born long after the time of Abraham, but the spirit which is Jesus Christ exists always and everywhere, transcending the limits of time and place. Because that spirit is timeless, he did not say, 'Before Abraham was born, I was', but, 'Before Abraham was born, I am'.

That timeless spirit 'I am', which Christ thus knew to be his own real self, is the same 'I am' that God revealed to be his real self when he said to Moses, 'I AM THAT I AM' (*Exodus* 3.14). Therefore, though Christ appears to us to be a separate individual person, he and his Father God are in fact one and the same reality, the spirit that exists within each one of us as our fundamental consciousness 'I am'. That is why he said, 'I and the Father are one' (*John* 10.30).

Therefore, when Christ said, 'I am the way, the truth, and the life: no man cometh unto the Father, but by me' (*John* 14.6), by the words 'I am' and 'me' he was referring not merely to the time-bound individual called Jesus, but to the eternal spirit 'I am', which he knew to be his own real self. The inner meaning of his words can therefore be expressed by rephrasing them thus, 'The spirit "I am" is the way, the truth, and the life: no man cometh unto the spirit "I am", which is the Father or source of all things, but by this same spirit'.

The spirit 'I am' is not only the truth or reality of all things, the source from which they all originate, and the life or consciousness that animates every sentient being, but is also the only way by which we can return to our original source, which we call by various names such as 'God' or the 'Father'. Except by turning our attention within towards the spirit, the consciousness that we each experience as 'I am', there is no way by which we return to and become one with our source. Therefore true salvation can only be attained not merely through the person who was Jesus Christ, but through the spirit which is Jesus Christ – the eternal spirit 'I am' that exists within each one of us.

Not only did Christ affirm his oneness with God, his Father, he also wanted us to become one with him. Before his arrest and crucifixion, Christ prayed for us, 'Holy Father, [...] that they may be one, as we [are]. [...] that they all may be one; as thou, Father, [art] in me, and I in thee, that they also may be one in us [...] that they may be one, even as we are one: I in them, and thou in me, that they may be made perfect in one' (*John* 17.11 & 21-23). That is, the aim of Christ was that we should cease to mistake ourself to be an individual separate from God and should know ourself to be the one indivisible spirit, the pure fundamental consciousness 'I am', which is the reality of God. Thus oneness or non-duality is the central aim of the spiritual teachings of Jesus Christ.

Every religion consists of a vital central core of non-dualistic truth, expressed either explicitly or implicitly, and a thick outer shell of dualistic beliefs, practices, doctrines and dogmas. The differences that we see between one religion and another – the differences that throughout the ages have given rise to so much conflict, intolerance and cruel persecution, and even to bloody wars and terrorism – lie only in the superficial forms of those religions, their outer shells of dualistic beliefs and practices.

All the disharmony, conflict and strife that exist between one religion and another arise only because most of the followers of those religions are too attached to a dualistic view of reality, which limits their vision and prevents them from seeing what all religions have in common, namely the one underlying truth of non-duality. Therefore true peace and harmony would prevail among the adherents of the various religions only if they were all willing to look beyond the external forms of those religions and see the one simple and common truth of non-duality that lies at the heart of all of them.

If we accept and truly understand the truth of non-duality, we will have no cause to quarrel or fight with anyone. We will be happy instead to let each person believe what they want to believe, because if a person is so attached to their individuality that they are unwilling to doubt its reality, no amount of reasoning or argument will convince them of the truth of non-duality. Therefore no one who truly understands this truth would ever try to convince the unwilling. If anyone does try to force the truth of non-duality upon someone who is unwilling to accept it, they are only displaying their own lack of correct understanding of that truth.

Non-duality is not a religion that needs evangelists to propagate it, or converts to join its ranks. It is the truth, and will remain the truth whether or not anyone chooses to accept and understand it. Therefore we can and should do no more than make this truth available to whomsoever is ready to understand it and apply it in practice.

Many religious people believe that it is blasphemy or sacrilege to say that we are one with God, because they mistake such a statement to mean that an individual is claiming himself to be God. But when we say that we are God, what we mean is not that we as a separate individual are God, which would be absurd, but that we are not an individual separate from God. By thus denying that we have any existence or reality separate from God, we are affirming that the reality we call God is one, whole and undivided.

If instead we were to claim that we are in reality separate from God, as most religious people believe us to be, that would be blasphemy or sacrilege, because it would imply that God is not the one and only reality. If we were to have any reality of our own separate from God, then he would not be the whole truth, but only a part or division of some larger truth.

If we believe that the reality that we call God is truly the infinite 'fullness of being', the one undivided whole, then we must accept that nothing can exist as other than or separate from him. He alone truly exists, and all else that seems to exist as separate from him is in fact nothing but an illusion or false appearance whose sole underlying reality is God. Only in the state of perfect non-duality is the true glory, wholeness and fullness of God revealed. So long as we experience a state of seeming duality by mistaking ourself to be an individual separate from God, we are degrading and demeaning him, denying his indivisible oneness, wholeness and infinity, and making him into something less than the only existing reality that he truly is.

Though the inner aim of all religions is to teach us the truth of non-duality, in their scriptures this truth is often expressed only in an oblique manner, and can be discerned only by people who are able to read between the lines with true insight and understanding. The reason why the truth is not expressed more openly, clearly and unambiguously in many of the scriptures of the various religions is that at any given point in time the majority of people have not yet reached a state of sufficient spiritual maturity to be able to digest and assimilate it if it is told as it is. That is why Christ said, 'I have yet many things to say unto you, but ye cannot bear them now' (*John*

16.12). However, though most of us may be unable to bear and accept the raw and naked truth of non-duality now, with the passing of time we will each eventually gain the spiritual maturity required to understand and accept the truth as it is, and not merely as we would now like it to be.

Our life in this world is a dream that is occurring in our long sleep of self-forgetfulness – forgetfulness or ignorance of our true state of pure non-dual self-consciousness. Until we wake from this sleep of self-forgetfulness by regaining our true and natural state of self-knowledge, dreams such as our present life will continue recurring one after another. When our present body 'dies', that is, when we cease to identify ourself with this body, which by our wonderful power of imagination we have now projected as 'I' and through which we see the present world, we will subside temporarily in the sleep of self-forgetfulness, but will sooner or later rise again to project another dream body as ourself and see through it another dream world. This process of passing from one dream to another in the long sleep of self-forgetfulness is what is called 'rebirth'.

As we thus pass through one dream life after another, we undergo many experiences that gradually enkindle within us a clarity of spiritual discrimination, by means of which we come to understand that our life as a separate individual is a constantly fluctuating flow of pleasurable and painful experiences, and that we can therefore experience true and perfect happiness only by knowing our real self and thereby destroying the delusion that makes us feel ourself to be a separate individual. Thus the truth of non-duality is the ultimate truth that each and every one of us will eventually come to understand and accept.

However, a mere theoretical understanding and acceptance of the truth of non-duality is of no real value to us in itself, because it will not remove the basic self-forgetfulness or self-ignorance that underlies our delusion of individuality. Acceptance of the truth of non-duality is only of use to us if it prompts us to turn our attention within towards our real self – our fundamental consciousness of our own being, which we each experience as 'I am'.

We can never experience the truth of non-duality merely by studying scriptures or other spiritual books, no matter how correctly we may understand and interpret their inner meaning. The truth itself can be discovered and experienced only within us, in the very core of our own being, and not in books or in words, no matter how sacred they may be. Books or words can be helpful to us only if they enable us to understand that we can experience true knowledge only by turning our attention away from the world of objects and ideas and towards the consciousness by which all things are known.

In every religion and authentic spiritual tradition throughout the ages there have been people who have attained the same non-dual experience that Sri Ramana attained – the experience of true self-knowledge. In this book I shall refer to such people as 'sages', a term which I will use not just in the usual general sense of a 'person of great wisdom' but in the more specific sense of a 'person of self-knowledge'. Thus whenever I use the term 'sage', I use it as an English equivalent of the Sanskrit term *jñāni*, which means a 'person of *jñāna* or [true] knowledge', or more specifically *ātma-jñāni*, a 'person of *ātma-jñāna* or self-knowledge'.

Just because a person is said to be a saint, prophet, seer, *ṛṣi*, mystic or some such revered being, he or she may not necessarily be a true sage, because such appellations do not specifically denote a person who has attained true self-knowledge. True sages are however the cream of the saints, prophets, seers, *ṛṣis* and mystics of all religions and all times, and a sample of such sages may be found in every religion and spiritual tradition.

Many such sages have remained unknown to the world, because though they experienced the ultimate truth, they never attempted to express it in words, or even if they did so, their words were never recorded. However, in every culture and every religion some sages have expressed the truth either in writing or in speech, and hence between them they have left the world a large legacy of spiritual literature, all of which testifies to the non-dual experience they attained.

Though all such sages have experienced the same truth, the words they have each used to express it often differ greatly, and sometimes they may even seem to contradict one another. The reason for this is that no words can adequately express the truth of non-duality, because it lies beyond the range of the dualistic consciousness we call 'mind'. Words are an instrument used by the mind to convey its feelings, ideas, perceptions and so on, all of which arise from its experience of duality. Since the mind is a form of consciousness that feels itself to be distinct from whatever it knows, it can know only duality, and can never know the non-dual reality that underlies itself.

The words that sages use to express the truth are therefore only pointers, drawing our attention to that which is beyond our mind, yet which lies deep within us, and which contains within itself all things. The true import of their words cannot be understood by the normal worldly intelligence that we use to understand other things, but it can be understood by the inner clarity that shines naturally in our mind when its surface agitation caused by the storm of desire and attachment is calmed at least partially. If we attempt to experience the truth that is indicated by their words by scrutinising our fundamental consciousness 'I am' and thereby cultivating skill in the art of just being, we will gain increasingly the inner clarity that is required to perceive the true import of their words.

Because no words can adequately express the truth, all sages have declared it to be ineffable, and many of them have therefore chosen to use the language of allegory to express the inexpressible. The allegorical language that sages have used most commonly to express the journey that we must take in order to merge in the source from which we originated is the language of mystical love. In this language, the individual soul seeking union with God is described as a young girl seeking union with her beloved. Much of the finest spiritual literature in the world is the poetry composed by sages in this language of mystical love, and samples of such poetry can be found in many diverse cultures. When we read such poetry with an understanding of the truth of non-duality, we can clearly see in it an unmistakable expression of that truth.

In the language of allegory the truth is implied rather than stated explicitly, and can therefore remain hidden from readers who have no prior understanding of it. Therefore some sages, when questioned by people who earnestly seek to know the truth, have set aside the language of allegory and have instead attempted to use the language of philosophy to express the truth more explicitly and clearly. However, even the language of philosophy cannot express the truth perfectly, but can only indirectly indicate the nature of it and the means of attaining it.

The philosophical terminology that sages in different cultures and different ages have used to express the truth differs greatly, and if understood only superficially may often appear to be conflicting. For example, many sages have used terms such as 'God' to refer to the absolute reality, while others like Buddha and Mahavira have avoided using such a term. This has led some people to claim that such sages have denied the existence of God. But such a claim is misleading, and arises from an overly simplistic understanding both of the reality and of the term 'God'.

The sole aim of the teachings of Buddha and Mahavira, like that of all other sages, was to lead us to the one absolute reality. The terminology they each used when talking about that reality may vary, but the reality about which they all talked is the same. That reality can be known only by direct non-dual experience, and can never be conceived by the mind, nor expressed by words. Being infinite, it transcends all the conceptual qualities that our finite minds attribute to it, so it cannot be correctly described as being either this or that. It is everything, and at the same time it is nothing. Therefore it is equally correct, and also equally incorrect, either to refer to it as 'God' or not to refer to it as 'God'.

The term 'God' has no fixed meaning. In certain contexts it means one thing, and in other contexts it means another thing, because it is a name given to a wide range of notions that people hold about the supreme or ultimate reality. Some of our notions about God are decidedly anthropomorphic, whereas others are more abstract, but none of them are either entirely correct or entirely incorrect.

In *vēdānta*, therefore, a distinction is made between two basic forms of God. One form is called *saguṇa brahman*, which means '*brahman* with *guṇas*', and the other form is called *nirguṇa brahman*, which means '*brahman* without *guṇas*'. The word *brahman* means the absolute reality, the supreme being or God, and the word *guṇa* means quality or attribute. Thus *saguṇa brahman* is the relative form of God, God with qualities and attributes as conceived by the human mind, while *nirguṇa brahman* is the absolute and real form of God, God without any conceivable quality or attribute. The God of human conception, whatever that conception may be, is *saguṇa brahman*, whereas the reality of God, which transcends all human conception, is *nirguṇa brahman*. Thus *nirguṇa brahman* is the substance or absolute reality that underlies *saguṇa brahman*, the God of our limited conception.

Though God as *saguṇa brahman* is not the ultimate or absolute reality, he and all the divine qualities we attribute to him are as real as our own individuality. Therefore so long as we take ourself to be a separate individual, God and all his divine qualities are for all practical purposes real. But when we attain the experience of true self-knowledge and thereby destroy the false notion that we are an individual consciousness that is separate from God, God will remain as our own real self or essential being, the absolute reality or *nirguṇa brahman*, which transcends all human conception.

Because the aim of the Buddha and Mahavira was to teach us the means by which we can attain the absolute reality, which is beyond all *guṇas*, qualities or attributes, they did not consider it necessary to talk about 'God', a term that is generally understood to mean *saguṇa brahman*, the supreme being endowed with divine qualities. Other sages, however, have used the term 'God' either as a word referring to *nirguṇa brahman*, the absolute reality that transcends all qualities, or because they understood that the people to whom they were speaking had need of a concept of a personal God who would aid them in their efforts to attain the transpersonal reality. There is thus no fundamental difference between the teachings of sages who have used the term 'God' and those who have not used this term. Both are speaking about the same absolute reality, but have simply chosen to express it in different terms.

The fact that the Buddha clearly acknowledged the existence of the absolute reality or *nirguṇa brahman* is evident from one of his important and well-known teachings, which is recorded in the *Tipiṭaka* 2.5.3.8.3 (*Udāna* 8.3):

> There is, mendicants, that which is not born, that which has not come into being, that which is not made, that which is not fabricated. If there were not, mendicants, that which is not born, that which has not come into being, that which is not made, that which is not fabricated,

> here [in this world or in this lifetime] escape from that which is born, from that which has come into being, from that which is made, from that which is fabricated, would therefore not have been [a state that could be] clearly known [or experienced]. But because, mendicants, there is indeed that which is not born, that which has not come into being, that which is not made, that which is not fabricated, therefore escape from that which is born, from that which has come into being, from that which is made, from that which is fabricated, is [a state that can be] clearly known [or experienced].

Though there is a wealth of profound meaning in these words of the Buddha, this is not a suitable place to examine them in depth, so we will study them in more detail in a sequel to this book that I have already begun to write.

Another superficial difference between the teachings of the Buddha and those of *advaita vēdānta* is that the Buddha taught the truth of *anattā*, a Pali term that is a modified form of the Sanskrit word *anātmā*, which means 'no self', whereas sages of the *advaita vēdānta* tradition teach that *ātmā* or 'self' is the sole existing reality. Some people claim that this is a fundamental contradiction between their respective teachings, whereas in fact this is merely a superficial difference in terminology.

When Buddha taught that there is no 'self' or *ātmā*, he was referring only to our finite individual self or *jīvātmā*, which all sages of the *advaita vēdānta* tradition also say is unreal. And when those sages teach that 'self' or *ātmā* is the sole existing reality, they are referring not to our false individual self but only to our real self – our true being or essential 'am'-ness, our pure, unlimited, undivided, unqualified and absolutely non-dual consciousness of our own being, which alone remains in the state of *nirvāṇa*, in which the false appearance of our individual object-knowing consciousness is completely extinguished. Thus there is no contradiction at all between the truth of 'no self' or *anattā* taught by the Buddha and the truth that 'self' or *ātmā* is the sole existing reality taught by *advaita vēdānta*.

The teachings of different sages appear to differ from one another, or even to contradict one another, for three main reasons. Firstly, it is because of the different terminology that they have used to teach the truth, which words can never express perfectly, but can only indicate. Secondly, it is because they had to adapt their teachings to suit the receptivity of the people they were teaching. And thirdly, it is because their original teachings have often become mixed with the ideas of their followers, many of whom had no direct experience of the truth they taught, nor even a clear and correct understanding of it.

The records that have survived of the teachings of many sages were not written by those sages themselves, but were recorded by their followers, often long after their lifetime. Therefore such records often do not reflect the teachings of those sages perfectly, but only reflect the understanding that some of their literate followers had of their teachings.

In almost all religions and spiritual traditions, the original teachings of sages have become mixed up with elaborate systems of theology, cosmology, philosophy and psychology, which bear very little relation to the actual experience of those sages. Such theologies and cosmologies originate from the minds of people who were unable to understand the simplicity and immediacy of the truth taught by the sages, and who therefore created such elaborate and complex systems of belief in an attempt to explain what they themselves could not understand. Because they originated in this manner, all the complex theologies and cosmologies that exist in every religion only serve to confuse people and obscure from their minds the simple truth of non-duality taught by sages.

However, in spite of all the confusing complexity found in the spiritual literature of the world, running throughout that literature there is a common thread of simple truth, which we can easily discern if we are able to understand the original teachings of the real sages. Because the same fundamental truth of non-duality has been expressed in the recorded words of sages from so many diverse cultures throughout the ages, modern students of philosophy often call it the 'perennial philosophy', a term that corresponds to the ancient Sanskrit term *sanātana dharma*, which literally means 'that which always upholds' or 'that which is ever established', and which therefore by implication means the 'eternal truth', the 'eternal law', the 'eternal principle', the 'eternal support', the 'eternal foundation', the 'eternal nature', the 'eternal essence', the 'eternal way' or the 'eternal religion'.

Fortunately for us, Sri Ramana's teachings were not only recorded in his lifetime by many of his followers, some of whom understood them very clearly, but were also written by him in various poems and other works. Since he composed poetry not only in the language of allegory and mystical love, but also in the language of philosophy, and since in his poetry he described the reality and the means of attaining it in very clear and unambiguous terms, he has made it extremely easy for us to understand the simple truth that underlies the teachings of all sages.

Having read and understood his teachings, if we read the teachings of any other real sage, we can easily recognise that the same truth is expressed in all of them. Moreover, his teachings also serve as a key that enables us to unravel and extract the true teachings of the sages from the dense mass of extraneous theologies, cosmologies and philosophies with which they have become mixed in every religion and spiritual tradition.

Therefore readers who are already familiar with the *sanātana dharma*, the timeless and universal truth or 'perennial philosophy' taught by all sages, will find that the teachings of Sri Ramana also express that same basic philosophy. However, they will also find that his teachings throw a clear and fresh light upon that philosophy, elucidating many subtle and profound truths that have seldom been expressed so explicitly by other sages, particularly with regard to the practical means by which we can attain the true experience of non-dual self-knowledge.

Because the teachings of Sri Ramana are a simple yet very profound revelation of the fundamental and absolute reality that underlies the appearance of all multiplicity and diversity, they express the ultimate truth that is the inner essence of all religions and spiritual traditions. Hence people of many diverse religious and cultural backgrounds have recognised that his teachings are a profoundly insightful and authentic exposition of the true import of their own religion or spiritual tradition, and have understood that after studying his teachings they need not study any other spiritual texts.

Though the same simple truth of non-duality can be found expressed in all the spiritual literature of the world if we search for it hard enough, it is not necessary or advisable for us to waste our time searching for it in the vast jungle of scriptures and sacred writings, where it is usually hidden among a dense mass of extraneous ideas. That is why in verse 60 of *Vivēkacūḍāmaṇi* Sri Adi Sankara warned all serious spiritual aspirants to avoid excessive study of the scriptures or *śāstras*, which he described as a 'great forest of delusive snares of noisy words' (*śabda jālaṁ mahāraṇyaṁ*) and a 'cause of unsteadiness, bewilderment and confusion of mind' (*citta-bhramaṇa kāraṇam*), and advised us that with the guidance of a sage who knows the truth we should instead try to investigate and know the truth of our self through direct experience.

For us to attain such direct non-dual experience of our own real self, all the guidance required can be found expressed in an extremely clear and simple manner in the teachings of Sri Ramana. If we read and understand his teachings, there will be no need for us to study any other scriptures or sacred writings, because from his teachings we will learn that the truth does not lie outside us in any books, but only within us, in the innermost core of our being, and that the only means to experience it is therefore to turn our attention selfwards to know the reality of the consciousness by which we know all other things.

Though Sri Ramana wrote and spoke comparatively little, and that too mostly only in response to questions put to him or requests made to him by other people, through those relatively few words that he wrote and spoke he has given us a complete set of spiritual teachings – a set of spiritual teachings which are so clear, simple, profound and all-embracing that they contain the seed or foundation of an entire philosophy and science of ourself and of every essential aspect of our whole life as an individual existing in this world of duality and multiplicity.

In this book I attempt to develop this seed and build upon this foundation by presenting in the clear light of his spiritual teachings a detailed analysis of our entire experience of ourself in our three normal states of consciousness, waking, dream and deep sleep, of our experience of the world that we perceive around us, and of the notions and beliefs that we hold not only about ourself and the world, but also about God and many other crucial aspects of our life as an individual in this world of baffling diversity and complexity. However, though I initially intended to explore his teachings in this book from a broad and comprehensive range of different angles, when I actually attempted to cover all the many different aspects of his teachings in sufficient detail and depth, I found that what I had written and what I still had to write was far more than could be comfortably contained within a single volume. Therefore I decided to limit myself in this present book to an in-depth exploration of only the most essential aspects of his teachings, and to cover more peripheral aspects in some subsequent books.

The detailed analysis that I present in this book consists of ideas that I have learnt from three principal sources. In part it consists of ideas that I have learnt directly from the writings and recorded sayings of Sri Ramana, in particular from the most comprehensive and profound record of his sayings that his pre-eminent disciple Sri Muruganar preserved in the form of Tamil verses in *Guru Vācaka Kōvai*. In part it consists of ideas that I learnt personally from Sri Sadhu Om, who was one of the closest disciples of Sri Ramana (by which term I mean not those who merely lived close to him physically, but those who followed his teachings most closely and truly), who was a lucid and extremely profound exponent of his teachings, in whose close company I had the good fortune to live for more than eight years, and under whose guidance I studied *Guru Vācaka Kōvai* and all the original writings of Sri Ramana in minute detail and great depth. However, for the most part it consists of my own understanding of Sri Ramana's teachings, an understanding that I have gained by studying his teachings deeply and in the original Tamil in which he wrote and spoke them, by reflecting upon them for many years, and by attempting to practise the empirical technique of self-investigation that he taught as the only means by which we can experience true self-knowledge.

However, though the ideas that I express in this book are a mixture of ideas that I have learnt directly from the writings or recorded sayings of Sri Ramana, of ideas that I have learnt through the channel of the profound explanations of his teachings that I heard from Sri Sadhu Om, and of ideas that I have formed from my own reflections upon and understanding of his teachings, I believe that the actual source of all these ideas is only Sri Ramana, without whose inspiration and inner guidance I would not have been able to understand his teachings with any degree of clarity, or thereby to write this book.

Whereas what I write is based merely upon my repeated *śravaṇa* and *manana* and my limited experience of *nididhyāsana* – that is, upon what I have read, upon my own personal reflections, and upon the limited experience that I have gained by attempting to practise contemplation, the empirical method of self-investigation taught by Sri Ramana – I believe that his words are derived from his direct, perfect and complete experience of the non-dual true knowledge about which he speaks. Similarly, I believe that the words of his foremost disciples, such as Sri Muruganar and Sri Sadhu Om, are based upon the experience of true self-knowledge that they attained by his grace and inner guidance, which drew their attention inwards and thereby dissolved their separate individuality in the non-dual consciousness of being, 'I am', which is the true form of Sri Ramana, and the real and essential nature of each and every one of us.

Therefore I believe that the ideas that I express in this book, which are based largely on what I have learnt and understood from the words of Sri Ramana and these two disciples of his, are not merely speculative hypotheses, but are facts that have been verified by their transcendent experience, and by the transcendent experience of many other sages. However, as Sri Ramana himself emphasised, mere belief in certain ideas is not true knowledge, so we must all hold our beliefs tentatively, and must endeavour to verify them for ourself by seeking to attain true experiential knowledge of the fundamental and absolute reality through empirical research, that is, through practical self-investigation. Therefore, the sole aim of all the theory discussed in this book is to guide us and encourage us in our practical quest for the direct, immediate, non-dual and absolute experience of true self-knowledge.

When I first started to write the material that is contained in this book, I had no idea that I would later decide to form the ideas that I was writing into a book. I have for long been in the habit of writing my private reflections about the teachings of Sri Ramana, but I always did so for my own benefit, because I find that writing helps me to clarify my thinking and to enkindle in my mind fresh ideas and new angles or ways of understanding his teachings. In my experience, musing on his teachings, and expressing my musings in writing, is a great aid and encouragement in my attempt to practise his teachings in the midst of my day-to-day life.

However, the greatest obstacle that for many years has prevented me from devoting enough of my time to this valuable exercise of writing my musings has been the necessity to work long hours and to expend a great deal of mental energy in a 'nine-to-five' job for which I felt no affinity. I felt that for the sake of earning a living I was wasting too much of my life engaged in activities that were draining my energy and diverting my attention away from the real purpose of life, which for each of us is to turn our attention inwards to know who we really are.

Since I believe that I had been singularly blessed to have had the opportunity to study the teachings of Sri Ramana in great depth under the close and clear guidance of Sri Sadhu Om, whose unique clarity of understanding arose both from his wholehearted and single-minded devotion to Sri Ramana and his teachings, and from his own profound spiritual experience, which resulted from such devotion, I recently began to feel that if I were to share my writings with others by forming them into a book, some people might be interested to read them and a few might perhaps be benefited by them. In particular I felt that my writings might help people who were entirely unacquainted with the teachings of Sri Ramana and with the philosophical, spiritual, religious and cultural background against which they were set, because not only have I studied them in the original Tamil in which he wrote them, but I am also able to rethink them in English, which is my own native language, as a result of which I am able to understand them from the perspectives of both a Hindu and a non-Hindu mindset.

With these thoughts in mind, I began tentatively to edit all that I had written into the form of a book, thinking that at least I could see what shape it would take and thereby test whether or not it might prove useful to any sincerely interested readers. While doing this, I found that I needed to write many more ideas in order to form a coherent and comprehensive exposition of his teachings, and I became pleasantly surprised to find a wealth of fresh ideas arising in my mind and finding expression in my writings.

Nevertheless, I continued to feel diffident about the idea of publishing my private musings upon the teachings of Sri Ramana, and I felt so for two main reasons. Firstly and most importantly, I do not wish to fall victim to the subtle and powerful delusion of pride and egoism that might result if my writings were to be appreciated by many people. And secondly, since the spiritual teachings of Sri Ramana are the love of my life, and since I revere them as the most worthy object of meditation, adoration and inward worship, I am not entirely comfortable about the idea of utilising my love of them as a means to earn a livelihood.

However I have gradually overcome these two reservations. I have overcome the first one by deciding that pride and egoism are challenges that we all have to face if we are to follow the spiritual path, and that we can conquer them not merely by avoiding external circumstances that could strengthen them, but only by facing them with an honest recognition of our own weaknesses and imperfections, and a consequent sense of complete dependence upon the protecting power of divine grace. And I have overcome the second one by reconciling my mind to the fact that, since I have to earn a livelihood in some manner, I may as well try to do so writing about the subject I love, since this will help me to keep my mind immersed in the teachings of Sri Ramana, rather than allowing it to become immersed in any more worldly occupation. Therefore, after much hesitation, I have finally decided to take the plunge and have this first volume published.

When I began to form my writings as a book, I planned to divide it into two parts in one volume. According to the initial outline I had in mind, the first part was going to be called 'The Essentials' and would be largely concerning ourself, both our true self and our false self, whereas the second part was going to be called 'The Peripherals' and would be largely concerning things that we imagine to be other than ourself, such as the world and God. As this idea developed, my proposed outline came to consist of this introduction, ten chapters in the first part, eighteen chapters in the second part, and an appendix.

However, by the time I had written almost two hundred thousand words, but had still not completed writing even half of what I expected to write, I understood that it would be far too much to fit into a single volume. Therefore I decided to form this introduction and the proposed first part into this present book, *Happiness and the Art of Being*, to form the proposed second part into a separate book, which I have tentatively entitled *The Truth of Otherness*, and to form the proposed appendix into a third book entitled *Yōga and the Art of Being*.

When I decided to split the then partially written book into these three volumes, I had already written many portions of each of these volumes, but none of them were complete. Though the material that I had written for this present book came to nearly one hundred thousand words, most of the chapters were still incomplete and some had not even been started. Therefore, since this book was logically the first volume in the series of then partially developed books, and since it would form the foundation of the subsequent volumes, I decided that I should try to complete it first. In order to complete the next two volumes, I still have much to write, and by the time I have finished, it may be necessary for me to split them further into more volumes.

Because this book has been formed from a collection of material written at different times, some chapters contain a certain amount of material that is not directly pertinent to the title of that chapter, but is nevertheless connected to the other material within that chapter. For the same reason, within certain chapters the overall flow of ideas is not entirely sequential, and may sometimes appear to have taken a few steps backwards. Though I have taken trouble to edit the material in an easy flowing and logically coherent fashion, in many places I decided not to sacrifice certain valuable ideas just for the sake of a perfectly polished flow. I am aware, therefore, that some of the ideas in this book are presented in a slightly rambling fashion, but I believe that the overall value of such ideas will justify their inclusion.

Moreover, certain ideas in this book are repeated in several different contexts. I have allowed such repetition to occur because each time a particular idea is repeated, it is examined from a fresh angle, and therefore its repetition will help us to understand it more deeply and in a broader perspective. Furthermore, by reiterating a particular idea in a new context, we are not only able to examine it from a fresh angle, but are also able to use it to clarify whatever subject is then under discussion.

In a book such as this, repetition of certain central ideas is in fact unavoidable. Though the material in this book and in the subsequent volumes covers a wide range of subjects, all these subjects are in one way or other related to the central subject, which is our search for true and absolute happiness, a happiness that can be experienced only in the state of actionless, thought-free and therefore perfectly peaceful being, which is the state of true self-knowledge, the state in which we remain only as our own real self, knowing nothing other than our own essential being. Because we examine all these subjects from the perspective of our search for true self-knowledge, certain central themes necessarily recur throughout this book, and will also recur in the subsequent volumes.

Of all the central themes that recur throughout this book, the centremost is our fundamental, essential and non-dual consciousness of our own being, our simple self-consciousness 'I am', which is not only our true self, but is also the one and only absolute reality, the source and substance of all things, and the abode of perfect, eternal and infinite happiness. This self-consciousness 'I am' is the only thing that we experience permanently, and it is the centre and foundation of all our knowledge and experience. As such, it has to be the primary concern of any serious philosophical or scientific investigation. Unless we know the true nature of this fundamental consciousness, without which we would know nothing else, the truth of any knowledge that we may have about anything else is dubious and open to question.

All the other recurring themes in this book are closely related to this one centremost theme, our fundamental self-consciousness 'I am', and the more frequently they recur, the more important they are to our search for true self-knowledge. Their recurrence serves an important purpose, because it enables us to explore the foundations of this philosophy and science of self-knowledge from various different perspectives, and thereby to develop a deeper and more comprehensive understanding of it.

The deeper and more comprehensive our understanding grows, the firmer will become our conviction that we can experience infinite happiness only if we know the true nature of our own self, and that the most important and essential thing in our life is therefore to seek and attain true self-knowledge.

The firmer this conviction becomes, the more strongly we will be motivated to withdraw our attention from all other things, and to fix it wholly and exclusively in the core of our being – in our essential self-consciousness, 'I am'.

Though the philosophy presented in this book is based largely upon the testimony of Sri Ramana and other sages, we cannot attain true knowledge merely by understanding this philosophy intellectually. The reason why sages have expressed their experience of the absolute reality in words is only to prompt us and guide us to attain that same experience. Therefore the philosophy presented here is not an end in itself, but is only a means to a much greater end, the experience of true self-knowledge. This philosophy is not only a theoretical philosophy but also a practical science, and hence the sole purpose of all its theory is to motivate us and guide us in its practice, the empirical method of self-investigation and consequent self-surrender.

When we begin to study any science, whether it be one of the many sciences concerned with knowing some aspect of the objective world, or this science of self-knowledge, which is concerned not with knowing any object but only with knowing the consciousness by which all objects are known, it is necessary for us to have tentative trust in the experience and testimony of those who have already acquired practical knowledge of that science. When we study physics, for example, we initially have to accept many of its advanced discoveries, such as the theory of relativity, on trust. Only later, when we become personally involved in experimental physics, will we be in a position to test the truth of such theories for ourself. If from the outset we were to refuse to believe any of the truths discovered by physicists until we ourself had tested and verified each one of them, we would unnecessarily impede our speed of learning, and we would never have time to acquire the knowledge required to engage in advanced experimental physics.

All learning requires a keen, inquisitive and questioning mind, but just as honest doubt plays an important part in the learning process, so too does tentative trust. Knowledge is acquired most efficiently and effectively by an intelligent use of both doubt and trust. A discriminating student knows what is to be doubted, and what is to be tentatively trusted.

More than in any other science, in this science of self-knowledge doubt is essential, because to know the truth that underlies all appearances, we must doubt the reality of everything – not just the reality of the objects known by our mind, but the reality of our knowing mind itself. However, though doubt plays such a vital role in the process of acquiring self-knowledge, tentative trust in the testimony of sages, who have already attained the experience of true self-knowledge, is nevertheless extremely helpful.

Since the testimony of sages challenges us to question and doubt all the beliefs that we have cherished for so long about what we are and about the reality of our life in this world, we may initially find it difficult to trust their words. That is why, rather than asking us to believe anything that we do not already know, Sri Ramana based his teachings upon an analysis of our own everyday experience. When we critically analyse our experience of the three states of consciousness that we undergo each day, we cannot reasonably avoid doubting most of what we normally take for granted about who we are and about the reality of all that we experience in these states.

In order to acquire knowledge that we cannot reasonably doubt, we must first disentangle ourself from all the confused and uncertain knowledge we now have about ourself. Such disentanglement can be achieved only by turning our attention away from all objects of knowledge and towards ourself, the consciousness by which everything is known. This process of disentanglement is the journey of self-discovery that all sages urge us to undertake.

As explained above, this book presents a philosophical analysis of our everyday experience of ourself, and the purpose of this analysis is only to enable us to obtain a clear theoretical understanding of who we really are, and thereby to ascertain the practical means by which we can attain direct experience of our own real nature. Though in this journey of self-discovery we will be guided by the revelations of Sri Ramana and other sages, we will nevertheless be relying primarily upon our own personal experience of our being or consciousness, and thus we will as far as possible avoid the need to rely upon belief in what we ourself do not actually know. If we take this journey depending always upon our own experience of ourself as our guide, we will be able to verify for ourself the truth of all that has been revealed through the words of sages, who have taken this journey before us.

However, while we are proceeding on this journey of self-discovery, and before we complete it, we are likely to discover that our rational analysis of our already existing experience of our own being and consciousness, together with our experience of practising the art of self-conscious being, will inspire in our mind a steadily increasing trust in the words of sages. Such trust should not be mistaken to be mere 'blind belief', because it is a trust born not of intellectual blindness but of a deep inner clarity of mind gained by dwelling repeatedly upon the true light of self-consciousness, which ever shines in the core of our being, as the core of our being, but which till now we have always habitually ignored due to our infatuation with the external world of sense perceptions.

Though it is possible for us to turn our attention away from the external world and towards our own essential consciousness 'I am' in order to discover our true nature even without our placing our trust in the words of anyone, in practice while pursuing the journey of self-discovery, and while confronting all the obstacles that inevitably arise on the way, we can derive much benefit by trusting and learning from the testimony of those who have taken and completed this journey before us. Therefore in the forthcoming sequel to this book, while investigating certain peripheral subjects which, though not essential, are nevertheless closely related to the journey of self-discovery, we will come across certain explanations which have been given by Sri Ramana and other sages who have completed that journey, but which we cannot verify from our own experience until we complete the journey and discover for ourself the truth that they have experienced. Each one of us is free to decide for ourself whether or not we wish to trust such explanations.

However, though we may not be able to verify the truth of such explanations until we attain the experience of true self-knowledge, we can at least understand that they are all logical implications, or at least reasonably possible implications, of the conclusions and truths that we arrive at by analysis and deduction in this present book. Therefore if we have been convinced by the conclusions that we deduce in this book from our critical analysis of our everyday experience of our three states of consciousness, waking, dream and deep sleep, it should not be too difficult for us to trust at least tentatively most of the explanations that are given in the sequel to this book.

If we do trust them, or at least accept them as tentative hypotheses to be tested by means of self-investigation, we will find them to be helpful to us in our attempts to turn our attention away from the external world and towards our essential self-consciousness 'I am' in order to remain merely as this fundamental consciousness of our own being. However, even if we are unwilling to trust anything that we do not already know for certain, we can still pursue this journey of self-discovery by taking all our doubts to their logical conclusion – by doubting the reality of our doubting mind, and therefore turning our attention towards the consciousness that underlies it in order to know the ultimate source from which it has arisen along with all its doubts.

The aim of this book or any subsequent books is not to persuade anyone to believe anything, but is only to prompt all of us who have a truly enquiring mind to question critically our habitual view of ourself, the world and God, and to encourage us to embark upon the journey of self-discovery by investigating our consciousness 'I am', which is the centre and fundamental basis of all our experience and knowledge.

Let us now embark upon this journey of self-discovery, and verify for ourself the truth revealed in the words of Sri Ramana and other sages.

CHAPTER 1

What is Happiness?

What is the one thing that all sentient beings desire? Is it not happiness? In the final analysis, are not all our desires just various forms of our one fundamental desire to be happy? Is not our fundamental desire for happiness the essence of every form of desire that we may ever have?

Our desire for happiness is the driving force behind all the countless forms of effort that we are always making. We do not do anything – whether through mind, speech or body – that is not driven by our fundamental desire to be happy. Each and every one of our actions is motivated by our desire to be perfectly happy.

For whom do we desire happiness? Do we not each desire happiness for ourself? First and foremost, we each want ourself to be happy. Though we may also want other people to be happy, we want them to be happy because seeing their happiness makes us feel happy. All our actions of mind, speech and body are impelled by our desire for our own happiness.

However unselfish we may think our actions to be, they are still all motivated by our desire for our own happiness. Even if we sacrifice our time, our money, our comforts and conveniences, or anything else that is precious to us, in order to do some altruistic action, whether to help some other person or to support some noble cause, the ultimate driving force behind such sacrifice is our desire to be happy. We do altruistic actions only because doing so makes us feel happy.

Because we feel unhappy when we see other people suffering, we are ready to do anything to alleviate their suffering, even if by doing so we seem to cause some suffering to ourself. We feel happier suffering to help other people than we would feel if we did nothing to help them. In fact we may derive positive happiness from our suffering, because we know we are undergoing it for the sake of others.

Taking this to an extreme, some people actually choose to suffer for the sake of suffering, because they cannot feel happy unless they feel that they are suffering. They derive pleasure by undergoing what appears to be suffering, because for them that seeming suffering is not really suffering but is only a form of pleasure. Whatever extreme form our desire may take, whether some truly noble altruistic form or some deeply perverse masochistic form, in essence it is still only a desire for our own happiness.

Why is our desire for our own happiness the fundamental and ultimate cause of our desire for the happiness of other people? Why do we desire their happiness primarily because it contributes to our own happiness? Why, in other words, do we ultimately desire our own happiness more than we desire the happiness of others?

We are primarily concerned with our own happiness because we love ourself more than we love any other person or thing. We love other people and things because we believe that they can contribute to our own happiness. We love each of them only to the extent to which we believe that they are able to make us happy, and if we thought that they did not or could not in some way or other contribute to our happiness, we would feel no particular love for them.

Our greatest love is only for ourself, and it is for our own sake that we love other people and things. We love our family, our friends and our possessions because we feel that they are *ours*, and because loving them makes *us* feel happy. Our love for our own happiness is inseparable from our love for our own self.

Because we love our own self above all other things, we desire our own happiness above all other things. We love and desire whatever makes us happy, and we dislike and fear whatever makes us unhappy. All our likes and dislikes, all our desires and fears, are rooted in our love for our own happiness, which in turn is rooted in our love for our own self.

Why do we love our own self more than we love any other person or thing? The reason we love certain other people and certain other things is because we feel that they make us happy, or at least can make us happy. That is, we love whatever we believe can give us happiness. If we know that something does not make us happy, and cannot make us happy, we do not feel any particular love for it. Is not happiness, therefore, the fundamental cause of all forms of love? Is not all the love that we feel for various people and things in essence only our love for our own happiness? Do we not love only those things that are potential sources of happiness for us? Therefore, since we love our own self above all other things, is it not clear that we ourself are foremost among all the potential sources of our happiness?

In fact, we are the only true source of all our happiness, because whatever happiness we seem to derive from other people or things arises only from within us. Since all our happiness ultimately comes only from within us, is it not clear that happiness is something inherent in us? In fact, happiness is our own true and essential nature. Therefore, the reason why we love our own self more than any other person or thing is simply that we ourself are happiness – the fullness of perfect happiness, and the one ultimate source of all the various forms of happiness that we seemingly derive from other people and things.

Our love for our own self and for our own happiness is not wrong. It is perfectly natural, and therefore unavoidable. It becomes wrong only when, due to our lack of correct understanding about where true happiness lies, it impels us to do actions that cause harm to other people. Therefore, in order to avoid doing any harm to anyone – to avoid making anyone else unhappy – it is essential that we understand what true happiness is and where our true happiness lies.

In order to understand this, we must first understand more about ourself. Since love and happiness are subjective feelings that are experienced by us, we cannot understand the true nature of either of them without first understanding the true nature of ourself. Only if we understand our own true nature will we be able to understand how the desire for happiness arises within us, and why we love our own self and our own happiness above all other things.

The converse side of our desire to be happy is our desire to be free from pain, suffering, misery or any other form of unhappiness. What we all desire is to be perfectly happy, free from even the least form of unhappiness. In fact, what we call happiness is just the state in which we are free from unhappiness.

Our natural state is to be happy. Our desire for happiness is our desire for our natural state. Consciously or unconsciously, we are all seeking what is natural for us. For example, when we have a headache, why do we wish to be free of it? Because a headache is not natural to us, when we experience one, we desire to be free of it. The same is the case with all other things that are not natural to us. We cannot feel entirely comfortable or happy with anything that is not truly natural to us. That is why we never feel perfectly happy, in spite of all the material, mental and emotional pleasures that we may be enjoying. All such pleasures come and go, and hence they are not natural to us.

Whatever is truly natural to us – whatever is inherent in our essential nature – must be with us always. Since the physical body that we now take to be ourself is experienced by us only in our present waking state, and not in dream or in deep sleep, it is not our essential nature. Likewise, since our mind is experienced by us only in the states of waking and dream, and not in the state of deep sleep, even it is not our essential nature. Because in deep sleep we remain peacefully and happily without either our mind or our body, neither of them is natural to us.

Though this contention that we exist in the absence of our mind and body in deep sleep may initially seem strange to us, and may therefore on superficial observation appear to be questionable, if we consider it carefully, we will clearly understand that it is not merely a dubious supposition, but is in fact the obvious truth that each one of us actually experiences in deep sleep, as we shall see more clearly when we examine our three states of consciousness in greater detail in the next chapter. Therefore, since our mind and body are not natural to us, we can never feel completely at ease or happy with either of them, or with any of the material, sensual, mental, intellectual or emotional pleasures that we may enjoy through them.

Why should we think that happiness is our natural state, and that unhappiness is something unnatural to us? If our true nature is really happiness, why do we not feel perfectly happy at all times? How does unhappiness arise?

We can understand this by critically analysing our experience of our three states of consciousness, waking, dream and deep sleep. In our waking and dream states we experience a mixture of pleasure and pain, or happiness and unhappiness. But what do we experience in deep sleep, when this mixture of pleasure and pain is removed? In the absence of this mixture, do we experience happiness or unhappiness? In the state of deep sleep, do we not feel perfectly happy, and free from all misery or unhappiness? Is it not clear therefore that neither unhappiness, nor a mixture of happiness and unhappiness, is natural to us? Since we can exist in the absence of unhappiness, it cannot be our real nature. Unhappiness is merely a negation of happiness, which is natural to us.

If unhappiness cannot be our real nature because we can exist in its absence, can we not say the same about happiness? When we are unhappy, are we not existing in the absence of happiness? No, happiness is something that is never entirely absent.

Unhappiness is a relative state, one which exists relative only to happiness. Without the underlying existence of happiness, there would be no such thing as unhappiness. We feel unhappy only because we desire to be happy. If happiness were ever to become absolutely non-existent, we would not feel any desire for it, and hence we would not feel unhappy. Even in a state of the most intense unhappiness, happiness still exists as something for which we feel desire. There is therefore no such thing as absolute unhappiness.

If unhappiness is something that is merely relative, can we not say the same about happiness? Is not happiness also a relative state, one which exists relative only to unhappiness? The happiness that we experience in waking and dream is certainly relative, and is therefore always incomplete or imperfect. But can we say the same about the happiness that we experience in deep sleep? Does the happiness of deep sleep exist relative only to unhappiness?

No, in deep sleep unhappiness is totally absent. When we are asleep, unhappiness does not exist even as a thought, or as something that we fear or desire to avoid. Therefore, since unhappiness cannot exist without a desire for happiness, but happiness can exist without even the slightest notion of unhappiness, unhappiness is entirely relative, whereas happiness may be either relative or absolute.

The relative happiness and unhappiness that we experience in our waking and dream states are a distorted reflection of the absolute happiness that is our true nature, and that underlies all our three states of waking, dream and deep sleep. We experience relative happiness and unhappiness in the waking and dream states because at that time our real nature of absolute happiness is somehow clouded over and obscured.

What is it in the waking and dream states that obscures our natural state of absolute happiness? Why in deep sleep do we experience perfect happiness, untainted by even the least trace of unhappiness, whereas in the waking and dream states we experience only a mixture of relative happiness and unhappiness? What is the difference between deep sleep and our other two states that allows us to experience absolute happiness in the former, but only relative happiness and unhappiness in the latter?

In deep sleep our mind is absent, and along with it all forms of thought are absent, whereas in the waking and dream states our mind has risen and is active, thinking thoughts of innumerable different things. When our mind and all its thoughts are absent, as in deep sleep, we experience perfect happiness, whereas when our mind is active, thinking one thought after another, as in waking and dream, we experience only a mixture of partial happiness and partial unhappiness. Is it not clear, therefore, that the rising of our mind and its thoughts is what obscures our natural state of absolute happiness?

Even now, in this waking state, our true and essential nature is absolute happiness, but that absolute happiness is clouded over and obscured by the persistent activity of our mind. Therefore, since our mental activity is the cloud or veil that obscures from our experience our own inherent and natural happiness, all we need do to experience that happiness in full is to put an end to all our mental activity – to cease rising as a mind to think anything. Since we experience perfect happiness in sleep due to the cessation of mental activity, we can experience the same happiness even now in the waking state, provided we refrain from all thought or mental activity.

Since our natural and absolute happiness is thus obscured by our mind's constant flow of thoughts, which rise one after another in rapid succession, how in the midst of that flow do we experience varying degrees of relative happiness and unhappiness? Since our activity of thinking is the cloud that obscures our natural happiness, the more intense that activity grows, the more densely it obscures our inherent happiness.

When our mind is extremely agitated, that is, when its activity of thinking becomes very intense, we are unable to experience more than a glimmer of our inherent happiness, and therefore we feel restless and unhappy. But when our mind becomes relatively calm, that is, when its activity of thinking decreases, we are able to experience our inherent happiness more fully, and therefore we feel comparatively peaceful and happy.

Thus calmness and peace of mind makes us feel relatively happy, while restlessness and agitation of mind makes us feel relatively unhappy. Is this not the experience of all of us? Do we not all feel peaceful and happy when our mind is calm and at rest? And do we not all feel restless and unhappy when our mind is agitated and disturbed?

The reason why we experience perfect happiness in deep sleep is that our mind has then become perfectly calm and peaceful, having subsided by withdrawing from all its activity. Since no thoughts rise in deep sleep to disturb our natural state of peaceful being, in that state we experience our inherent happiness without the least obstruction.

Is it not clear, therefore, that happiness is a state of being, and unhappiness is a state of doing? So long as our mind is active or doing something, thinking one thought or another, we experience only a mixture of happiness and unhappiness, and whatever happiness we do experience in the midst of that mixture is imperfect, limited and relative. We experience perfect, unlimited and absolute happiness only when our mind becomes perfectly still.

Our own essential being is therefore happiness. When we remain merely as being, without rising to think or do anything, as in deep sleep, we experience perfect happiness, untainted by even the least sorrow, unhappiness or discontent. But as soon as we rise as this thinking mind, we experience restlessness, discontent and unhappiness.

Since we thus experience perfect happiness in the absence of all mental activity, as in our deep sleep, is it not clear that such happiness is something that is inherent within us, and that our mental activity is the only obstacle that prevents us from experiencing it in full in our waking and dream states? Therefore whatever limited happiness we may experience in the waking and dream states when our mind becomes comparatively calm and peaceful, is only a fraction of the happiness that is already inherent within us.

Happiness is something that arises from within ourself, and not something that comes from outside us. Why then do we think that we derive pleasure or happiness from material objects and external circumstances? Does happiness actually lie in any material object or any external circumstance? No, happiness is obviously not something that exists in any object or circumstance outside us.

How then do we seem to obtain happiness from certain objects and circumstances? Whatever relative happiness we may seem to obtain from them is actually a state of our own mind. Happiness is something that is latent within us, and it sometimes becomes manifest when we experience certain material objects or external circumstances. How does this happen?

Whenever we obtain something that we like, and whenever we avoid or get rid of something that we dislike, we feel happy. Conversely, whenever we lose or are unable to obtain something that we like, and whenever we cannot avoid or get rid of something that we dislike, we feel unhappy. In other words, we feel happy when our desires are fulfilled, and unhappy when they are not fulfilled.

Thus the real cause of the happiness that we seem to obtain from external objects and circumstances is not those objects or circumstances themselves, but is only the fulfilment of our desire for them. Whenever we experience a desire, whether in the form of a like or a dislike for a certain thing, our mind is agitated by it. So long as that desire persists in our mind, the agitation caused by it persists, and that agitation makes us feel unhappy. But when our desire is fulfilled, that agitation subsides, and in the temporary calm that results from its subsidence, we feel happy.

The happiness that we thus experience when one of our desires is fulfilled is a fraction of the happiness that always exists within us. When a desire arises and agitates our mind, our inherent happiness is obscured, and hence we feel restless and unhappy until that desire is fulfilled. As soon as it is fulfilled, the agitation of our mind subsides for a short while, and because our inherent happiness is thus less densely obscured, we feel relatively happy.

Therefore, though happiness is our own true nature, and though in reality there is no happiness at all in anything outside us, we nevertheless feel happy whenever our desire for anything is fulfilled, and hence we wrongly believe that we derive happiness from the objects of our desire. We feel love or desire for other people and for external objects and circumstances only because we believe that we can derive happiness from them. And we believe this only because we experience happiness whenever any of our desires for those external things are satisfied.

Our delusion that happiness comes from the things that we desire, and that therefore by desiring and acquiring more things we will become more happy, is thus a vicious circle. Because we desire something, we feel happy when we obtain it, and because we feel happy when we obtain it, we desire more of it. In this way our desires are always continuously increasing and multiplying.

The raging fire of our desires can never be quenched by the objects of our desire. The more we acquire those objects, the more intensely our desire for them and for other such objects will rage. Trying to quench the fire of our desires by fulfilling them is like trying to quench a fire by pouring petrol upon it.

The objects of our desire are the fuel that keeps the fire of our desires burning. The only way we can extinguish this fire of our desires is by knowing the truth that all the happiness that we seem to derive from the objects of our desire does not actually come from those objects but only from within ourself.

However, we should not think that understanding this truth by means of our intellect or power of reasoning is the same as actually knowing it. We cannot actually know this truth without experiencing ourself as happiness. So long as we feel ourself to be a limited individual consciousness that experiences relative degrees of happiness and unhappiness, we clearly do not experience the truth that we ourself are absolute happiness.

No amount of intellectual understanding can give us the true experiential knowledge that happiness is our own true nature, and is not something that we obtain from the objects of our desire. We can understand something intellectually, but nevertheless actually experience something that is quite contrary to what we understand. For example, if we see water in a desert, we may understand that it is only a mirage, but we nevertheless continue to see it as something that looks quite real, and the mere sight of it continues to make us feel thirsty. Similarly, though we may understand intellectually that happiness is our true nature and that we do not actually obtain happiness from anything outside ourself, we nevertheless continue to feel ourself to be somehow lacking in happiness, and therefore continue to experience desire for things outside ourself, as if happiness could really be obtained from them.

Intellectual knowledge is only a superficial and shallow form of knowledge, because our intellect is only a function of our mind, which is itself just a superficial and shallow form of consciousness. Our delusion that makes us feel that happiness comes from things outside ourself and not from within us is, on the other hand, deeply rooted in our mistaken identification of ourself with a physical body, which is in turn rooted in our lack of clear self-knowledge.

In fact, the delusion that makes us feel that happiness comes from things outside ourself is the same delusion that makes us feel that we are something that we are not. This fundamental delusion of ours arises only because we do not clearly know what we really are, and hence it can be destroyed only by a clear and correct knowledge of our own real nature. No intellectual knowledge, therefore, can destroy this deep-rooted delusion of ours. The only knowledge that can destroy it is true experiential knowledge of what we really are.

When by true experiential self-knowledge we thus destroy the delusion that we are anything other than the fullness of absolute happiness, the fire of our desires will automatically be extinguished.

Though no amount of intellectual understanding can destroy our deeply rooted delusion, a clear intellectual understanding of the truth is nevertheless necessary, because without such an understanding we would not know how to discover what true happiness is. A clear and correct understanding of the true nature of happiness will enable us to know not only where we should seek happiness, but also how we should actually endeavour to seek it. Let us therefore analyse more deeply how our delusion that we obtain happiness from external objects and circumstances arises.

Let us suppose that we like chocolate. In our mind we associate the bittersweet taste of chocolate with the feeling of pleasure that we are accustomed to experience whenever we taste it. But does the taste of chocolate necessarily create a feeling of pleasure? No, it creates such a feeling in us because we like it so much, but it will create no such feeling in a person who is indifferent to it, and it will create a feeling of disgust in a person who positively dislikes it. Moreover, if we eat too much chocolate and thereby make ourself sick, we will begin to feel an aversion for it, at least temporarily, so if we eat more of it at that time, it will not create any feeling of pleasure but only a feeling of disgust. Therefore it is clear that the happiness we think we derive from eating chocolate is determined not by the actual taste of chocolate, but only by our liking for that taste.

The same is the case with any of the pleasures that we experience through our five senses. Our senses can only tell us the impressions created by a thing, for example the taste, aroma, texture and colour of chocolate, and the crinkling sound of the silver foil in which it is wrapped, but it is our mind which determines whether or not we like those impressions. If we like them, we do not even have to taste chocolate to feel pleasure from it. Even the sight or smell of chocolate, or the sound of its silver foil being opened, will give us pleasure.

In fact we often seem to derive more pleasure from the anticipation of enjoying something, than we do when we actually experience it. Therefore even the thought of some object of our desire can give us pleasure, though that pleasure will always be mixed with a restlessness to experience it actually. Only when we actually experience it, will our desire for it be fully satisfied. However, since that satisfaction is usually experienced only momentarily, we may sometimes appear to enjoy more pleasure from the cumulative build-up of our anticipation for it than we actually enjoy when we experience it.

Moreover, if our mind is distracted by other thoughts, we may not feel any particular pleasure when we eat chocolate, even though we have so much liking for it. Only when our mind is relatively free of other thoughts can we really enjoy the taste of chocolate, or the pleasure of satisfying any of our other desires.

A clear illustration of this is something that most of us have probably experienced. If we are watching a good film or an entertaining programme on television while eating a meal, no matter how tasty and to our liking that meal may be, we will hardly notice its taste and we will experience no particular pleasure in eating it. After the programme and meal are both finished, we may notice that we failed to enjoy that tasty meal at all, and we may wish we had eaten it when we were not distracted by watching the television. Because we were more interested in the programme or film we were watching than in the meal we were eating, we failed to enjoy the meal. And the reason why we took greater interest in enjoying the film than in enjoying our meal was that at that time our desire for the enjoyment of the film was greater than our desire for the enjoyment of the meal.

However, if we had been really hungry before sitting down to eat that meal and watch that film, we would probably have enjoyed the meal with great relish and would therefore have hardly noticed the film we were watching. Even if the meal were not particularly tasty, if we had been really hungry we would have enjoyed it nonetheless. When we are really hungry, that is, when our desire for food is very intense, we can relish and enjoy even the most tasteless meal.

Our hunger or real desire for nourishment is the best of all condiments. The spice of real hunger will give the pleasantest taste even to the most tasteless food, and even to food that would normally taste positively unpleasant. Conversely, if the spice of real hunger is missing, we can eat even the most tasty food without particularly relishing it.

Is it not clear, therefore, that the relative degrees of happiness that we derive from enjoying the objects of our desires are not only entirely subjective and dependent upon our relative degree of liking for those objects, but are primarily determined by the fluctuations of our mind and of the successive waves of excitement of our desires, our anticipations and our ultimate satisfactions?

In the midst of all this excited activity of our mind, how do the fragments of happiness that we experience appear? These successive waves of our mental excitement have their peaks and their troughs. They rise to their peaks when our mind is most agitated by its desires, and they subside to their troughs when our mind experiences the satisfaction of anticipating or actually enjoying the objects of its desires. During the brief troughs between the successive peaks of our desires, our mind is momentarily calm, and in that calmness the happiness that is always inherent in us is less densely obscured and therefore manifests itself more clearly.

So long as our mind is active, it is constantly fluctuating between the peaks of its desire or dissatisfaction and the troughs of its contentment or satisfaction. Our desires and our fears, our likes and our dislikes, our cravings and our aversions, all agitate and impel the activity of our mind to the peaks of its intensity, and such intense peaks of activity obscure our inherent happiness and thereby make us feel dissatisfied, discontented and unhappy.

The more intense and agitated the activity of our mind becomes, the more rapidly it rises from one peak to another, and hence the briefer and shallower the troughs between those peaks become. However, if we are able to restrain our desires, fears, likes, dislikes, cravings, aversions and other such passions, the activity of our mind will become less intense, that is, its peaks will be less frequent and will rise less high, and the troughs between those peaks will be wider and deeper. Thus, when the agitated and passionate activity of our mind becomes less intense, we feel calmer and more contented, and hence we are able to experience more clearly the happiness that is always within us.

The happiness that we derive from eating a piece of chocolate comes not from that piece of chocolate itself, but only from the satisfaction we feel as a result of the gratification of our desire for it. When such a desire is gratified, from where does the resulting feeling of satisfaction or happiness actually come? It clearly does not come from the object of our desire, or from anything else outside us, but only from within ourself. If we carefully observe the feeling of happiness that we experience when we eat a piece of chocolate, or when we enjoy any other object of our desire, we will clearly see that it arises from within ourself, and as a result of the temporary subsidence of our mental agitation caused by that desire.

Our satisfaction and the happiness that seems to result from it are both subjective feelings that arise from our innermost being, and that we accordingly experience only within ourself. Since all happiness thus comes only from our own innermost self, is it not clear that happiness already exists within us, at least in a latent form? Why then should we waste our time and energy trying to experience that happiness in a roundabout manner by gratifying our desires for external objects and circumstances? Why should we not try instead to experience it in a direct manner by turning our attention within to discover the source from which all happiness arises?

Desire arises within us in various forms – as likes or dislikes, as cravings or aversions, as hopes or fears – but in whatever form it rises, it disturbs the natural peace of our mind, and thereby obscures the happiness that is always within us. All the misery or unhappiness that we experience is caused only by our desires. Therefore, if we wish to experience perfect happiness, untainted by even the least misery, we must free ourself from all our desires.

But how can we actually do this? Our desires are deeply engrained within us and cannot easily be changed. Though we may be able to modify them to a certain extent, our ability to do so is nevertheless limited. Our present desires, or likes and dislikes, have been formed by our previous experiences, not only in the lifetime of the physical body that we now identify as ourself, but also in the lifetimes of all the physical bodies that we formerly identified as ourself, whether in our dreams or in some other states of consciousness similar to our present so-called waking state.

One of our strongest desires is our desire for sexual pleasure. Though the intensity of this desire may vary with age and circumstances, it always exists within us, at least in the form of a dormant seed. As anyone who has tried to 'conquer' lust knows only too well, we can never entirely overcome it.

Like all our other desires, our lust or desire for carnal pleasure is rooted in our wrong identification of ourself with a physical body. Because we mistake a physical body to be ourself, we mistake the natural biological urges of that body to be our natural urges. All our desires will therefore remain at least in seed form so long as we continue to have the habit of identifying ourself with a physical body, whether our present physical body in this waking state, or some other physical body in dream.

Therefore the only way to put an end to all our desires is to put an end to their root, which is our mind, our limited consciousness that feels 'I am this body'. Unless and until we know what we really are, we cannot be free from our desires, which arise only due to our mistaking ourself to be what we are not.

By fighting our desires we can never get rid of them, because we who try to fight them are in fact the cause, source and root of them. That which seeks to fight our desires is our mind, which is itself the root from which all our desires spring. The very nature of our mind is to have desires. Without desires to impel it, our mind would subside and merge in the source from which it originally arose. Therefore the only way to conquer our desires is to bypass our mind by seeking the source from which it has arisen. That source is our own real self, the innermost core of our being, our fundamental and essential consciousness 'I am'.

Our mind is a limited form of consciousness that arises within us, and that mistakes a particular body to be itself, and all the other objects that it knows to be other than itself. In fact all that our mind knows, including the body that it mistakes to be 'I', are only its own thoughts, products of its own power of imagination. Therefore nothing that is known by our mind is actually other than itself. However, because it mistakes the objects of its imagination to be other than itself, it feels desire for those objects that it thinks will contribute to its happiness, and aversion for those objects that it thinks will detract from its happiness.

So long as we experience otherness or duality, we cannot but feel desire for some of the things that we see as other than ourself, and aversion for some of the other things. Because we mistake a particular body to be ourself, certain things are necessary for our survival and our comfort in that body, and certain things are a threat to our survival and our comfort in it. As a general rule, therefore, we feel desire for those things that contribute to our bodily survival and comfort, and aversion for those things that threaten our survival or detract from our comfort.

However, even after we have secured all the things that we require for our bodily survival and comfort, we still do not feel satisfied. Because we fear for our future, we strive to acquire more than we actually require at present. Because of our restlessness caused by our concern for our future happiness and wellbeing, we seldom enjoy the present moment to the fullest, but instead think constantly about what we may or may not enjoy in future.

Most of our thoughts are not concerned with the present moment, but only with what is already past, or what may or may not happen in future. We live much of our life in varying degrees of anxiety, mostly about what may happen to us in future, but also sometimes about what we did or what happened to us in the past. We wish the past were other than it was, and we hope the future will be better than it probably will be.

Because our mind is filled with thoughts about the past, and with aspirations for or anxiety about the future, we seldom feel completely satisfied with the present moment, and with all that we now enjoy and possess. All our lack of satisfaction or contentment with the present moment is caused only by our desires, and by their inevitable consequences, our fears.

Desire and fear are in fact not two different things, but just two aspects of the same one thing. So long as we desire whatever things appear to contribute to our happiness, we will inevitably fear whatever things appear to detract from our happiness. Fear is therefore simply the converse side of desire. Every fear is in fact a form of desire, because our fear of a particular thing is simply our desire to avoid or be free of that thing. However, whatever form our desire may take – whether it manifests as a hope or a fear, a like or a dislike, a craving or an aversion – it always deprives us of our natural peace or contentment. Therefore so long as we have any form of desire, we can never be perfectly satisfied.

However favourable and pleasant our present circumstances may be – however much material wealth we may have, however many possessions we may have accumulated, however much security we may have surrounded ourself with, however many friends and admirers we may have, however affectionate and kind our relatives and associates may be – we still do not feel perfectly satisfied, and we restlessly search for something more. Even if we do not attach much importance to wealth and material possessions, we still seek satisfaction and happiness outside ourself, in some form of external pursuit or entertainment such as a social activity, an involvement in politics, an intellectual pastime, a religion, a philosophy, a science, an art, a profession, a sport or a hobby. Through all our mental and physical activities, of whatever kind they may be, we are seeking to obtain happiness and to avoid misery, and our activities will not cease permanently until we experience happiness in full, untainted by even the least misery, sorrow or unhappiness.

All our efforts to attain happiness will continue until our all-consuming desire for perfect happiness is permanently satisfied. We know from experience that this fundamental desire of ours is never completely satisfied in spite of all our efforts to obtain happiness from external objects and circumstances. Nothing and no person in this material world can ever make us perfectly happy. However happy we may sometimes feel ourself to be, our happiness is nevertheless imperfect and short-lived, and hence we continue to search restlessly for more happiness.

Every effort that we make through our mind, speech and body – every thought, word and deed of ours – is impelled only by our desire for happiness and our fear of unhappiness. Because of our mistaken conviction that happiness and unhappiness both come from external objects and circumstances – a conviction that is so strong and deep-rooted that it persists in spite of all our intellectual understanding that happiness actually comes only from within us, and that unhappiness is caused only by the agitated activity of our mind – we unceasingly direct our attention and efforts towards those external objects and circumstances.

Whenever we experience something that we desire, the agitation of our mind caused by that desire subsides temporarily, allowing us to experience for a short while the happiness that always exists within us. However, because we fail to recognise that the happiness that we thus experience already exists within us, we always wrongly associate it with the objects of our desire, and thus we have developed a strong and deeply rooted conviction that we obtain happiness from people, objects and circumstances outside ourself. Because of this strong conviction, we continue to desire those things that we believe to be potential sources of happiness for us. Our desires can therefore never be satisfied fully, because whenever we experience a little happiness from the satisfaction of one of our desires, our fundamental desire for complete and perfect happiness impels us to seek greater happiness by attempting to satisfy more of our desires.

Therefore, the happiness that we experience when one of our desires is fulfilled is very short-lived, because some other desire immediately arises in our mind. That is, we experience such happiness only in the temporary period of calm that results from the satisfaction of one of our desires, and such a period of calm creates an opportunity for some other desire to arise. Innumerable desires exist in our mind in a dormant or latent form, and each one of them is awaiting a suitable opportunity to rise to the surface of our mind.

At any single moment our mind can attend to only one thought. Therefore each of our thoughts can rise only when our previous thought has subsided. However, since our thoughts rise and subside in rapid succession, we feel that we are thinking of several things simultaneously. That is, just as the speed at which the frames of a movie film are projected on a cinema screen is so rapid that we are unable to perceive the gap between two consecutive frames, and hence we see a continuous moving picture, so the speed at which our thoughts rise and subside is so rapid that we are unable to perceive the extremely brief gap between two consecutive thoughts, and hence we experience a continuous and unbroken flow of thoughts.

However, though our thoughts rise and subside so rapidly, there is nevertheless a limit to the number of thoughts that can rise in our mind during each fraction of a second, because at any precise moment only one thought can be active. Hence, in order to rise to the surface of our mind, each of our many latent thoughts or dormant desires must await a suitable gap between the subsiding and rising of our other thoughts or desires. Therefore, as soon as a relative quiescence occurs in our mental activity due to the satisfaction of one of our desires, many of our other desires will clamour to rise in its place.

This process of some thought or other rising as soon as a relative quiescence occurs in our mental activity can be clearly perceived by us if we deliberately try to quieten the activity of our mind by some form of meditation. Whenever we try to avoid thinking of one thing, the thought of some other thing will rise in our mind. The more we try to quieten our mental activity, the more vigorously other thoughts will arise to take the place of the thoughts we are trying to avoid. All such thoughts that arise in our relatively quiescent mind are impelled by our desire to obtain happiness from things other than our own essential self.

So long as we mistake ourself to be this limited form of consciousness that we call our 'mind', we will experience desire to obtain those things other than ourself that we believe will make us happy, and to avoid those things that we believe will make us unhappy, and so long as such desire persists, our mind will continue to think one thought after another. Whenever our mind becomes tired of this restless activity of thinking innumerable thoughts, it subsides temporarily in deep sleep. But from such sleep it will soon be roused once again by its dormant desires, and will thereby experience either a dream or a state such as our present one, which we take to be a state of waking. Therefore, until we put an end to our mistaken identification of ourself with our mind, which is the root of all our desires, we can never put an end to all our desires, and hence we can never remain without either thinking of things other than our essential self, or instead falling temporarily into the state of deep sleep.

Throughout our waking and dream states, our mind experiences an unceasing turmoil of desires. One desire or another is always raging in our mind. All our mental activity is driven only by desire. Every thought that rises in our mind is impelled by some desire, and every desire is a form of thought. Desire and thought are therefore inseparable. In the absence of desire, as in deep sleep, there is no thought or mental activity, and in the absence of mental activity, there is no desire. The more intensely we experience a desire, the more active and agitated our mind becomes.

Whenever our mind is active, that activity obscures to a greater or lesser extent the happiness that always exists within us. The more intense our mental activity becomes, the more densely our natural happiness is obscured. Therefore, since all our mental activity is caused only by our desires, is it not clear that desire is the sole cause of all our unhappiness? Whatever form of unhappiness we may experience, we can always trace its origin back to some desire that exists in our mind.

The raging of countless petty desires in our mind is usually so intense that we fail to notice how they obscure our natural sense of peaceful happiness, and how the fragments of happiness that we experience in the midst of all our restless mental activity result only from certain moments of temporary slackness in the intensity of that activity. Often so many desires are active in our mind that we are not fully aware of most of them. That is, because our mind is usually so busy thinking so many different thoughts in such rapid succession, it often fails to notice all the desires that are niggling away inside it. Only when a certain unnoticed desire is fulfilled and we experience the resulting feeling of relief or pleasure, do we actually become aware how strong that desire was and how much it was irritating our mind.

For example, when our mind is busy with some activity that engages its entire attention, we may not notice that we have a strong urge to go to the toilet. Only when we go to the toilet and experience the resulting relief, do we actually become aware how strong our urge to do so was. The satisfaction of our unnoticed desire to relieve ourself may be so intense that for a while we consciously feel a positive pleasure arising from our sense of great relief. In this way, we sometimes become aware of one of our desires, and discover how strong it is and how much uneasiness or agitation it causes in our mind, only when we experience the happiness that results from the perhaps quite accidental satisfaction of it.

When a desire rises, our mind becomes agitated, and that agitation obscures the happiness which is our true nature. When no desire rises, as in deep sleep, our mind remains perfectly inactive, and hence we experience not even the least unhappiness. Therefore, if we were perfectly contented – free of all desires and fears – our mind would remain perfectly calm, and hence we would experience in full the absolute happiness that always exists in the very core of our being.

In reality, in the innermost core or depth of our being we are always perfectly calm and happy, no matter how much our surface mind may be agitated. All our agitation and unhappiness is experienced only by our mind, and not by our real self – our fundamental and essential self-consciousness, which is conscious only of our own unqualified being, 'I am'.

Our essential being always remains calm and peaceful, just like the eye of a storm. No agitation of our mind can ever disturb it even in the least, because it is perfectly non-dual self-consciousness, and hence it knows nothing other than 'I am'. No matter what our mind may be doing, we are – that is, we exist, and we remain essentially as our own self-conscious being, 'I am'. No amount of doing can ever prevent us from being.

Being is what underlies all forms of doing, just as consciousness underlies all forms of knowing, and happiness underlies all forms of love or desire. Our essential being is consciousness, and our essential consciousness of our being is happiness. Thus our essential being, our essential consciousness and our essential happiness are all one and the same reality – the one absolute reality, which is our true and essential self.

Relative existence and non-existence, relative consciousness and unconsciousness, and relative happiness and unhappiness, are all only a distorted reflection of our own absolute being, absolute consciousness and absolute happiness. Because we are distracted by all the superficial activity of our mind, we overlook our own essential being, consciousness and happiness, which are our own true self or fundamental nature. And because we overlook this essential and fundamental nature of our own true self, we mistake ourself to be the limited consciousness that we call our 'mind', through which we experience our absolute being, consciousness and happiness only in their relative forms as the pairs of opposites: existence and non-existence, consciousness and unconsciousness, and happiness and unhappiness.

Therefore, if we wish to experience complete and perfect happiness, free from even the least taint of unhappiness, all we need to do is to know our own true self as it really is. So long as we experience ourself as anything other than absolute being, consciousness and happiness, we cannot experience true and perfect happiness. So long as we continue to seek happiness outside our own essential self, we will continue to experience only relative happiness and unhappiness.

Since the activity of our mind is what seemingly obscures our essential nature as absolute being, consciousness and happiness, in order to experience our essential nature we must put an end to all our mental activity – to all the thoughts that are constantly rising and raging in our mind. All forms of thought or mental activity are nothing but the attention that we pay to objects – to things that are seemingly other than ourself. Throughout our waking and dream states, we are constantly thinking only about things other than our own essential being or fundamental consciousness.

So long as we attend to anything other than our mere consciousness of being, 'I am', our mind is active. However, if we try to turn our attention back on ourself to know our own essential self-conscious being, the activity of our mind will begin to subside. If we are able to focus our attention wholly and exclusively upon our consciousness of being, 'I am', then all our thoughts or mental activity will subside completely, and we will clearly know the true nature of our own real self, which is perfect and absolute being, consciousness and happiness.

Did we not see earlier that happiness is a state of being, and unhappiness is a state of doing? In deep sleep we remain as mere being, without rising to do anything, and hence we experience perfect happiness. In waking and dream, on the other hand, we forsake our essential and natural state of mere being by rising as our mind, whose nature is to be constantly doing, and hence we experience happiness mixed with unhappiness. Whereas deep sleep is a state of mere being, and therefore a state of perfect happiness, waking and dream are states in which our essential being is mixed with and obscured by all our doing, and are therefore states in which our essential happiness is mixed with and obscured by varying degrees of unhappiness.

Since our being is permanent and our doing is impermanent, our being is natural and all our doing is unnatural. Hence our happiness is natural, because it is our essential being, and all our unhappiness is unnatural, because it is a result of our doing or thinking.

The root of all our doing, and hence the root of all our unhappiness, is only the rising of our mind. Whenever our mind rises, it is active, thinking thoughts of innumerable different kinds. Our mind cannot remain for a moment without activity – without thinking of something other than our own essential being. As soon as our mind ceases to think of anything other than our own being, it subsides and merges motionlessly in our natural state of mere being, which is the source from which it rose. Thus, whenever our mind becomes inactive, it ceases to be the thinking entity that we call 'mind', and remains instead as our essential self-conscious being, which is its own true nature.

Though in deep sleep our mind subsides and remains merely as our essential being, the perfect happiness that we experience in that state appears to be short-lived, because our mind driven by its dormant desires eventually rises again to experience a state of waking or dream. Therefore in sleep our mind and its inherent desires are not destroyed completely, but have merely subsided in a state of abeyance, dormancy or temporary quiescence.

If we wish to experience our natural and perfect happiness permanently, therefore, we must not merely make our mind subside temporarily in a state of abeyance like sleep, but must destroy it completely. Since the rising of our mind is the rising of all our unhappiness, the temporary quiescence of our mind is the temporary quiescence of all our unhappiness, and the destruction of our mind is the destruction of all our unhappiness.

Why is our mind, which is the root of all our desires and therefore the cause of all our unhappiness, not destroyed in deep sleep? Why does it rise again from that state? To answer this, we must understand why it rose in the first place.

As we saw earlier, this individual entity that we call our 'mind' is a limited form of consciousness that always identifies a physical body as itself. In our present waking state, our mind mistakes this particular body to be itself, whereas in each dream it mistakes some other body to be itself. Because it takes one body to be itself in the waking state, and another body to be itself in dream, our mind clearly does not know what its real self is.

Therefore, so long as we mistake ourself to be our mind, and the particular body that our mind at any given time mistakes to be itself, we do not know who or what we really are. In sleep we do not mistake ourself to be our mind or any particular body, whereas in waking we mistake ourself to be our mind and this particular body, and in dream we mistake ourself to be our mind and some other particular body.

In sleep, when we do not take ourself to be our mind or any body, what do we take ourself to be? As we shall see when we address this question in more detail in later chapters, all we know of ourself in sleep is 'I am'. However, though in sleep we know *that we are*, we do not clearly know *what we are*.

For some inexplicable reason, our knowledge of ourself in sleep is somehow obscured and vague. In sleep we definitely know that we are, because if we did not, we would not be able to remember so clearly in the waking state 'I slept happily and peacefully, and did not know anything at that time'. What we did not know in sleep is anything other than ourself – our own essential self-consciousness, our fundamental consciousness of our own being, 'I am'. However, just as in waking and dream we appear to identify our fundamental and essential consciousness 'I am' with our mind and some particular body, in sleep we appear to identify it with a seeming lack of clarity of self-knowledge.

Because we do not clearly know our real self in waking, dream or deep sleep, we are able to mistake ourself to be our mind and some particular body in waking and dream. Thus our lack of clear self-knowledge is the root cause for the rising of our mind, and the consequent rising of all our desires, thoughts and unhappiness. If we clearly knew what we really are, we could not mistake ourself to be anything other than that. Therefore the only way to put an end permanently to all our desires, thoughts and consequent unhappiness is to know what we really are.

Since our mind is a form of false or wrong knowledge, a knowledge or consciousness that wrongly knows itself as 'I am this body' and that wrongly knows all its other thoughts as being objects other than itself, it can be destroyed only by our experiencing a true or correct knowledge of our own essential being, 'I am'. Until and unless we know the true nature of our own real self, we cannot free ourself from the self-delusive grip of our mind, and we therefore cannot permanently experience the natural and absolute happiness which is our own real nature.

All that we have examined and discovered in this chapter about the nature of happiness is expressed succinctly by Sri Ramana in the opening sentence of his introduction to his Tamil translation of Sri Adi Sankara's great philosophical poem, *Vivēkacūḍāmaṇi*:

> Since all living beings in the world desire that they should always be happy [and] devoid of misery, just as [they desire] that they should be happy as always [by] getting rid of those [experiences] such as illness which are not their own nature, since all [living beings] have love completely only for their own self, since love does not arise except for happiness, and since in sleep [all living beings have] the experience of being happy without anything, when what is called happiness is [therefore] only [their own real] self, only due to [their] ignorance of not knowing [their real] self do they rise and engage in *pravṛtti* [extroverted activity], whirling in boundless *saṁsāra* [the state of restless and incessant wandering of the mind], forsaking the path [of self-discovery] which bestows [true] happiness, [believing] as if attaining the pleasures of this world and the next were alone the path to happiness.

Sri Ramana expresses the same truth even more tersely in the opening paragraph of *Nāṉ Yār?* (Who am I?), a brief twenty-paragraph treatise that he wrote about the need for us to attain true self-knowledge, and the means by which we can do so:

> Since all living beings desire to be always happy [and] devoid of misery, since all [of them] have greatest love only for their own self, and since happiness alone is the cause of love, [in order] to attain that happiness, which is their own [true] nature that they experience daily in [dreamless] sleep, which is devoid of the mind, knowing [their own real] self is necessary. For that, ***jñāna-vicāra*** [scrutinising our consciousness to know] **'who am I?' alone is the principal means.**

The crucial practical conclusion with which Sri Ramana ends this paragraph, '*jñāna-vicāra* "who am I?" alone is the principal means', was highlighted by him in bold type in the original Tamil. The term *jñāna-vicāra* literally means 'knowledge-investigation', and is the process (or rather the state) of investigating our essential self-consciousness 'I am', which is our primary knowledge and the base of all our other knowledge, in order to attain true knowledge of our own real self.

What Sri Ramana means here by the term 'knowledge-investigation "who am I?"' is therefore not a mere intellectual analysis of our knowledge 'I am', but is an actual examination or deep scrutiny of our fundamental knowledge or consciousness 'I am' in order to know through direct experience what it really is. Such an investigation or scrutiny cannot be done by thinking, but only by turning our attention back on ourself to know our own essential consciousness of being. When our attention or power of knowing is turned outwards to know things other than ourself, it becomes our thinking mind, but when it turns back inwards to know our essential self, it remains in its natural state as our essential self – that is, as our true non-dual self-conscious being.

Further on, in the fourteenth paragraph of the same treatise, Sri Ramana explains more about the true nature of happiness:

> What is called happiness is only *svarūpa* [the 'own form' or essential nature] of *ātmā* [self]; happiness and *ātma-svarūpa* [our own essential self] are not different. *Ātma-sukha* [the happiness of self] alone exists; that alone is real. Happiness is not obtained from any of the objects of the world. We think that happiness is obtained from them because of our lack of discrimination. When [our] mind comes out, it experiences unhappiness. In truth, whenever our thoughts [or wishes] are fulfilled, it [our mind] turns back to its proper place [the core of our being, our real self, which is the source from which it arose] and experiences only the happiness of [our real] self. In the same way, at times of sleep, *samādhi* [a state of intense contemplation or absorption of mind] and fainting, and when a desired thing is obtained, and when termination occurs to a disliked thing [that is, when our mind avoids or is relieved from some experience that it dislikes], [our] mind becomes introverted and experiences only the happiness of self. In this way [our] mind wavers about without rest, going outwards leaving [our essential] self, and [then] turning [back] inwards. At the foot of a tree the shade is delightful. Outside the heat of the sun is severe. A person who is wandering outside is cooled by going into the shade. Emerging outside after a short while, he is unable to bear the heat, so he again comes to the foot of the tree. In this way he continues, going from the shade into the sunshine, and going [back] from the sunshine into the shade. A person who acts in this manner is someone lacking in discrimination. But a person of discrimination will not leave the shade. Similarly, the mind of a *jñāni* [a person of true self-knowledge] does not leave *brahman* [the fundamental and absolute reality, which is our own essential being or self]. But the mind of an *ajñāni* [a person lacking true self-knowledge] continues to undergo misery by roaming about in the world, and to obtain happiness by returning to *brahman* for a short while. What is called the world is only thought [because all that we know as the world is nothing but a series of mental images or thoughts that we have formed in our mind by our power of imagination]. When the world

disappears, that is, when thought ceases, [our] mind experiences happiness; when the world appears, it experiences unhappiness.

What Sri Ramana here describes as the restless wavering or oscillation of our mind, fluctuating repeatedly between going outwards and turning back inwards, is the same process that we described earlier as the rising and subsiding of our thoughts. Each moment of our waking and dream lives innumerable thoughts rise and subside in our mind in rapid succession. With the rising of each thought our mind or power of attention goes outwards, leaving our real self or essential being and thereby forgetting the happiness that is always within us, while with the subsiding of each thought our mind turns back towards ourself to experience momentarily the happiness of just being.

However, because this rising of our mind or thoughts is impelled by innumerable strong desires, no sooner does one thought subside than another one rises in its place, and hence the gap between the subsiding and rising of two consecutive thoughts is so extremely brief that we are hardly aware of the peaceful being or happiness that we experience in that gap. This is the reason why in our waking and dream states our attention is so absorbed in thinking of other things that we barely notice our own peacefully self-conscious being, and the happiness that is inherent in it. Generally, the only occasion on which we are clearly aware of the peaceful happiness of being that we experience between two consecutive thoughts is during sleep, because sleep is a comparatively long gap between two consecutive thoughts, brought about by the sheer exhaustion of our mind.

Nevertheless, though we may hardly notice it, even during waking and dream, in the extremely brief moment between the subsiding of each thought and the rising of the next, we do in fact experience our own essential self-conscious being or *brahman* in its true and perfectly pure form, uncontaminated by thinking or doing. Moreover, whenever one of our desires – whether a desire to experience something that we like or a desire to avoid experiencing something that we dislike – is fulfilled, the momentum with which thoughts rise in our mind slows down temporarily, so not only does each thought rise with less vigour, but also the momentary gap between two consecutive thoughts becomes slightly longer. Thus for a short while we are able to experience the peaceful happiness of our own being more clearly, until some other desire takes hold of our mind, thereby reanimating the momentum and vigour with which our thoughts rise, and thus once again obscuring our happiness of being more densely.

The true, motionless, unadulterated and thought-free form of our own essential being or *brahman*, which we experience momentarily between each two consecutive thoughts, is both our fundamental consciousness of being, 'I am', and the perfect happiness of our thus being conscious only of our being. Therefore, if we wish to experience our own natural and perfect happiness constantly, our attention must penetrate beneath the wavering or oscillation of thoughts on the surface of our mind in order to experience in its pure unadulterated form our essential and fundamental consciousness of our own being, 'I am', which always underlies our wavering mind.

Thus we can permanently experience perfect and absolute happiness only in the state of true self-knowledge – the state in which we always remain merely as our own essential being, our fundamental self-consciousness 'I am', without rising to think or do anything. Therefore, let us now examine the knowledge that we have about ourself at present in order to understand not only how it is a wrong knowledge, but also what the correct knowledge of ourself really is, and how we can attain immediate experience of that correct knowledge.

CHAPTER 2

Who am I?

In order for us to determine the means by which we can discover who or what we really are, it is necessary for us first to gain a clear theoretical understanding of what we are and what we are not. We can gain such an understanding only by carefully and critically analysing our experience of ourself. For such an analysis to be complete and thorough, we must consider our experience of ourself not only in our present waking state, but also in each of our other two states of consciousness, dream and sleep.

This approach is similar to the well-established method of research adopted in all the objective sciences. In those sciences, researchers first carefully consider all the already known facts about the subject under investigation in order to formulate a reasonable hypothesis that can explain those facts, and then they proceed to test that hypothesis by rigorously conducted experiments.

The hypothesis formulated by spiritual scientists, or sages as they are more commonly called, is that we are not the body composed of inconscient matter, nor are we the mind consisting of thoughts, feelings and perceptions, but that we are the essential underlying consciousness by which the body and mind are both known. This hypothesis has been independently tested and verified by many sages before us, but unlike the findings of the objective sciences, the findings of this spiritual science cannot be demonstrated objectively. Therefore, to be truly benefited by this science of self-knowledge, we each have to test and verify this hypothesis for ourself.

In order to do so, we must each experiment to see whether or not the consciousness that we experience as 'I' can stand alone without our body or mind. If we are able to remain as consciousness in the absence of any kind of body or mind, we will prove to ourself that we are neither of those two objects known by us.

In order to remain as our mere consciousness 'I am' without any awareness of our body or mind, it is necessary for us to know our consciousness in its pure form, devoid of any contents – devoid of any objects of knowledge. We are so accustomed to identifying our consciousness 'I am' with our body and mind that it may initially appear difficult for us to distinguish our essential consciousness from these objects known by it. Because of this identification of our consciousness with its objects or contents, our knowledge of it appears to be clouded and unclear. Therefore, in order to distinguish between our consciousness and its objects, we must gain a clear knowledge of it as it really is.

Whether we are a scientist or just any ordinary person, when we seek to obtain knowledge about something, the primary and essential instrument we use is our power of attention. Without paying attention to something, we cannot know it.

In their experiments, scientists often use mechanical aids to observe things that they cannot perceive directly through their five senses, but it is nevertheless only through their five senses that they are able to read and interpret the information provided by those mechanical aids. It is only by means of one or more of our five senses that we can obtain knowledge about anything in the external world.

However, though our five senses provide us with information about the external world, we can only know that information by attending to it. If we do not pay attention to the information provided by our senses, we can fail to see something that happens right in front of our eyes, or to hear a conversation between two people sitting just beside us. Therefore all knowledge is ultimately obtained by us only by means of our power of attention.

Since our consciousness is not an object, it cannot be observed by means of any mechanical aid, nor can it be observed by means of any of our five senses. The one and only instrument by which we can observe and know our consciousness is our own power of attention, unaided by anything else. Since we are consciousness, and since our consciousness knows itself without any sort of aid, all we need to do to obtain a clear knowledge of our consciousness as it really is, is to withdraw our attention from all the objects known by our consciousness and to concentrate it only upon our consciousness itself.

Since our power of attention is our power of knowing or consciousness, which we are free to direct towards whatever we wish to know, concentrating our attention upon our own consciousness means concentrating our attention upon itself, or concentrating our consciousness upon itself. Since we experience our consciousness or power of knowing as 'I', as our own essential self, attending to it is not any form of objective attention, but is a purely subjective attention – a perfectly non-dual self-attention, an attention to our own essential self or 'I'.

Only by thus attending to our own essential consciousness, which we experience as 'I', will we be able to distinguish between this consciousness and all the objects known by it, including the body and mind that we now mistake to be 'I'. By thus attending to our consciousness and thereby distinguishing it from its contents, we can experiment and know for certain whether or not we can remain as mere consciousness, entirely separate from our body, our mind and all its thoughts, feelings and perceptions. If we are able to do so, we will prove to ourself that in essence we are only consciousness, and that we are neither the body nor the mind that we now mistake to be 'I'.

Let us therefore now analyse our experience of ourself thoroughly, examining how exactly we experience ourself in each one of our three states of consciousness, waking, dream and sleep, in order to obtain a clear theoretical understanding of what we are and what we are not. By doing so, we will be able to verify for ourself whether or not we can reasonably arrive at the hypothesis mentioned above.

When we analyse our experience of ourself in our present waking state, we can see that our knowledge of who or what we are is confused and unclear. If we are asked, 'Who are you?', we reply, 'I am Michael James', 'I am Mary Smith', or I am whatever else our name may be. This name is the name given to our body, and we identify ourself with this name because we take our body to be 'I'. We feel 'I am sitting here, reading this book' because we identify ourself with our body.

This sense of identification, 'I am this body', is so strong that it remains with us throughout our waking state. In fact it is the basis of all that we experience in this waking state. Without first feeling this body to be 'I', and thereby limiting ourself within its confines, we would not know or experience any of the things that we experience in this waking state.

Not only is the external world known by us only through the five senses of this body, but even the thoughts and feelings that we experience within our mind are felt by us to be occurring only within this body. All our perceptual, emotional, mental and intellectual life in the waking state is centred in this body. All that we take ourself to be, and all that we take to be ours, is centred in and around this body. For us this body is not only the centre of our life, it is the centre of the whole world that we perceive around us.

However, we identify ourself not only with our body, but also with our mind, and though our body and our mind are obviously very closely connected, we speak of them as two different things. Since we simultaneously identify ourself with two things that we take to be different, is it not clear that in our present waking state our knowledge of who or what we actually are is confused and uncertain?

Moreover, though our sense of identification with this body is the foundation of all that we experience in our present waking state, we cease to identify this body as 'I' as soon as we fall asleep, or go into a coma or any other such state. In sleep, we either remain in the state of deep dreamless sleep, in which we are not aware of any body or any other thing, or we dream some imaginary experiences. In dream, as in waking, we identify ourself with a body, and through the five senses of that body we perceive a seemingly external world consisting both of inanimate objects and of people and other sentient beings like ourself.

While we are in a dream state, we identify a dream body as 'I' in exactly the same manner that we identify our present body as 'I' in this waking state, and we take the dream world that we see to be real in exactly the same manner that we take the world that we see in this waking state to be real. But as soon as we wake up from a dream, we understand without the least doubt that all that we experienced in that dream was only a product of our own imagination, and was therefore unreal. Thus the dream state clearly demonstrates to us that by the power of its imagination our mind has the ability not only to create a body and world, but also simultaneously to delude itself that that imaginary body is 'I' and that that imaginary world is real.

Knowing that our mind possesses this wonderful power of creation and self-deception, can we reasonably avoid doubting whether the body we take to be 'I' and the world we take to be real in our present waking state are in fact any more real than the body and world we experience in a dream? Do we not have good reason to suspect that our body and this world that we experience in our present waking state are merely imaginary creations of our own mind, just as the body and world that we experienced in dream were? What evidence do we have that our body in this waking state and the world we perceive through the senses of this body are anything other than a creation of our mind?

In this waking state we understand that the bodies and worlds we experience in our dreams are merely products of our imagination, and exist only within our own mind, yet we generally assume without question that the body and world we now experience are not mere products of our imagination, but exist independently, outside our mind. We believe that this body and world exist even when we are unaware of them, as in dream and deep sleep, but how can we prove to ourself that this is so?

'Other people who were awake when we were asleep can testify that our body and this world continued to exist even when we were unaware of them' is the answer that immediately comes to our mind. However, those other people and their testimony are themselves part of the world whose existence in sleep we want to prove. Relying on their testimony to prove that the world exists when we do not perceive it is like relying on the testimony of a confidence trickster to prove that he did not swindle our money.

The people we meet in a dream may testify to us that the world we perceive then existed even before we perceived it, but when we wake up we realise that their testimony proves nothing, because they were just a part of the world that our mind had temporarily created and deluded itself into believing to be real. There is no way we can prove to ourself that the world exists independent of our perception of it, because any proof we may wish to rely upon can come only from the world whose reality we are doubting.

'But the body and world that we experience in dream are fleeting and insubstantial. They appear one minute, and disappear the next. Even within one dream, we flit from one scene to another – one moment we are in a certain place, and the next moment it has become another place; one moment we are talking with a certain person, and the next moment that person has become someone else. In contrast, the world we experience in waking is consistent. Each time we wake up from sleep or from a dream, we find ourself to be in the same world that we were in before sleeping. Though the world we see in the waking state is constantly changing, those changes are all happening in a reasonable and comprehensible manner. If we are in one place now, we do not suddenly find ourself to be in another place the next moment. If we are talking to a certain person, that person does not suddenly become some other person. Therefore what we experience in waking is definitely more real than what we experienced in dream.' In this way we reason with ourself and convince ourself that it is reasonable for us to believe that the body and world that we experience in waking are not merely a product of our imagination, like the body and world that we experience in dream, but really exist independent of our imagination.

However, none of these superficial differences that we can point out between our experience in waking and our experience in dream can actually prove that what we experience in waking is any more real than what we experienced in dream. These superficial differences are not differences in substance, but only differences in quality. Just because the world we perceive in waking appears to be more lasting and internally consistent than the world we perceive in dream, we cannot reasonably conclude thereby that it is not merely a product of our wonderful power of imagination and self-deception.

The differences that we can point out between our experience in waking and our experience in dream can be reasonably accounted for in another way. The reason why the world we perceive in waking appears to be more lasting and internally consistent than the world we perceive in dream is that we are more strongly attached to our waking body than we normally are to any body that we identify as ourself in a dream.

If we experience any severe shock, pain, fear or excitement in a dream, we usually wake up immediately from that dream, because we do not feel strongly attached to the body that we then identify as 'I'. In contrast, we can usually bear a much greater degree of shock, pain, fear or excitement in the waking state without swooning, because we feel very strongly attached to this body that we now identify as 'I'. Thus, because our attachment to the body that we identify as 'I' in a dream is usually quite tenuous, our experience of the world that we see in that dream is fleeting, fluid and often inconsistent. In contrast, because our attachment to this body that we now identify as 'I' in this waking state is very strong, our experience of the world that we now perceive around us generally appears to be more lasting, substantial and consistent.

However, even in our waking state there are times when this world appears to be dream-like and unreal, for example after we have been deeply absorbed in a reverie or daydream, or in reading a book or watching a film, or after we have experienced an intense shock, joy or bereavement. The reality that we attribute to our body and this world is therefore subjective and relative. All that we know of this world is what we experience in our own mind, and is therefore coloured by our mind.

In this waking state our mind tells us that the world we are now experiencing is real and that the world we experienced in dream is unreal, but in dream our same mind told us that the world we were then experiencing was real. The differences that we now imagine to exist between that state and our present state did not appear to exist then. In fact, while dreaming, we generally think we are in the waking state. If we were to discuss the reality of waking and dream with someone in a dream, we would probably agree with each other that this 'waking state' – as we would then take our dream to be – is more real than a dream.

Our experience of our body and this world is entirely subjective, because it exists only in our own mind. Likewise, the reality that we attribute to our experience of them is entirely subjective. What we know of our body and this world is only our sense perceptions. Without our five senses, we would know neither our body nor this world. Every sense perception is an image or thought that we have formed within our own mind by our power of imagination, yet we imagine that each one of them corresponds to something that actually exists outside our mind. Since we cannot know anything about our body or this world except the images or thoughts that our mind forms about them within itself, we have no way of knowing for certain that either of them actually exists outside our mind.

Therefore, since we know from our experience in dream that our mind not only has the power to create a seemingly real body for itself, and to perceive a seemingly real world through the five senses of that body, but also has the power to delude itself into mistaking its imaginary creations to be real, and since we have no way of knowing for certain that our body and this world that we now experience in this waking state are not just imaginary creations of our own mind, like the body and world that we experienced in dream, we have good reason to suspect neither our body nor the world actually exists outside our own mind. If they do not exist outside our mind, then they do not exist when we do not know them, as in dream and deep sleep.

Since we can be sure that our body exists only when we know it, and since we know our present body in only one of our three states of consciousness, our notion that this body is ourself is open to serious doubt. Since we know that we exist in dream, when we do not know the existence of this present body, is it not reasonable for us to infer that we are the consciousness that knows this body, rather than this body itself?

If we are consciousness, that is, if consciousness is our real and essential nature, we must be consciousness in all the states in which we exist. Since our consciousness cannot know anything else without first knowing itself – without knowing 'I am', 'I know' – the essential nature of our consciousness is self-consciousness, the consciousness of its own being or existence. Whatever else it knows, our consciousness always knows 'I am', 'I exist', 'I know'.

Since it always knows itself as 'I am', our consciousness cannot be something that it knows at one time and does not know at another time. Therefore, if we are consciousness, we must be something that we know in all the states in which we exist, something that we know whenever we exist.

Since we now feel ourself to be not only this body, but also the consciousness that knows this body, and since we feel ourself to be the same consciousness in dream, even though at that time we also feel ourself to be some other body, is it not clear that this consciousness that knows these bodies is more real than either of them? Since we are the same consciousness in both waking and dream, and since we are conscious of one body as ourself in waking, and of some other body as ourself in dream, is it not clear that our identification with either of these bodies is an illusion – a mere imagination?

Can we then say that we are the consciousness that knows our body and this world in the waking state, and that knows some other body and world in dream? No, we cannot, because the consciousness that knows these bodies and worlds is a transient form of consciousness, which appears to exist only in waking and in dream, and which disappears in dreamless sleep. If we exist in deep dreamless sleep, we cannot be this form of consciousness that knows a body and world, because this object-knowing form of consciousness does not exist as such in deep sleep.

Do we exist in deep sleep? Yes, obviously we do, because when we wake up we know clearly and without any doubt 'I slept'. If we did not exist in sleep, we could not now know that we slept. Since sleep is a state that we actually experience, it is not only a state in which we exist, but is also a state in which we are conscious of our existence. If we were not conscious in sleep, we could not know our experience in sleep – we could not know with such certainty that we slept and did not know anything at that time. What we are unconscious of in sleep is anything other than our own being or existence, 'I am', but we are not unconscious of our own being.

Let us imagine a conversation that might occur between two people, whom we shall call A and B, just after B has woken up from a deep dreamless sleep.

A: Did someone come into your room ten minutes ago?
B: I do not know, I was asleep.
A: Are you sure you were asleep?
B: Yes, of course, I know very well that I was asleep.
A: How do you know that you were asleep?
B: Because I did not know anything.

If someone were to question us as A questioned B, would we not normally answer in words similar to those used by B? What can we infer from such answers?

When we say that we did not know anything in sleep, what we mean is that we did not know any external object or event at that time. But what about our own being – did we know that we existed in sleep? If someone were to ask us if we are sure we were asleep, we would answer like B, 'I know very well that I was asleep'. That is, we have no doubt that we existed, even though we were in a state that we call 'sleep'.

When we say, 'I know I was asleep', what exactly do we mean? These words express a certainty that we all feel when we wake up from sleep. From this certainty that we each of us feel, it is clear not only that we did exist in sleep, but also that we knew we existed in sleep, even though we did not know anything else at that time. Moreover, just as we feel with certainty, 'I know I was asleep', so we feel with equal certainty, 'I know I knew nothing in sleep'. Since we know this with such certainty, it is clear that we did exist in sleep as the consciousness that knew that state of nothingness.

After we wake up from a deep sleep, we do not need anyone else to tell us that we have been asleep, because sleep was a state that we ourself consciously experienced. What we experienced in sleep was a state in which we were not conscious of anything else. But though we were not conscious of anything else in that state, we were nevertheless conscious that we were in that state in which we knew nothing. The so-called 'unconsciousness' of sleep was a conscious experience for us at that time.

In other words, though we are not conscious of anything else in sleep, we are nevertheless conscious of being in that seemingly unconscious state. Therefore, since the so-called 'unconsciousness' of sleep is a state clearly known by us, sleep is in fact a conscious state of being. Hence, rather than describing sleep in negative terms as a state of 'unconsciousness' – a state of being unconscious of anything – it would be more accurate to describe it in positive terms as a state of 'consciousness' – a state of being conscious of nothing other than our own being.

How do we come to be so sure that we know nothing in sleep? How exactly does this knowledge of not knowing anything in sleep arise? In waking this knowledge takes the form of a thought, 'I did not know anything in sleep', but in sleep no such thought exists. The absence of knowledge in sleep is known by us only because at that time we know that we exist. That is, because we know that we exist, we are able to know that we exist without knowing any other thing. In waking we are able to say that we knew nothing when we were asleep because in sleep we not only existed in the absence of all other knowledge, but also knew that we existed thus.

However, it is important to remember that though in our present waking state we say, 'I knew nothing in sleep', the knowledge that we actually experience while asleep is not 'I know nothing', but is only 'I am'. In sleep what we actually know is 'I am', and nothing but 'I am'. Since this knowledge or consciousness 'I am' exists in all our three states of consciousness, and since nothing else exists in all three of them, is it not clear that we are in reality only this essential consciousness 'I am' – or to be more precise, this essential self-consciousness 'I am'?

Thus by critically analysing our experience of ourself in each of our three states of consciousness, we come to understand that we are in essence only self-consciousness – our fundamental consciousness of our own being, 'I am'. Unless we analyse our experience of our three states of consciousness in this manner, we cannot arrive at a clear, certain and correct understanding of who or what we really are. This critical analysis is thus the essential foundation upon which the entire philosophy and science of true self-knowledge is built.

Therefore, since this analysis is so essential to our correct understanding of ourself, let us delve into it more deeply, examining our experience of our three states of consciousness from several alternative angles. Though certain ideas may appear to repeat themselves when we do so, it is nevertheless useful to explore the same ground again from various different perspectives, because unless we gain not only a clear understanding but also a firm conviction about our real nature from our critical analysis of our three states of consciousness, we will lack the motivation required to pursue the rigorous and extremely demanding empirical research or investigation into our own essential self-conscious being, 'I am', without which we cannot attain direct and immediate experience of true self-knowledge.

Do we not all feel ourself to be a particular human body? When we say, 'I was born at such-and-such a time in such-and-such a place. I am the son or daughter of so-and-so. I have travelled to so many different places. Now I am sitting here, reading this book', and suchlike, is it not clear that we identify ourself with our body so strongly that we habitually refer to it as 'I'? But do we not at the same time also feel ourself to be the consciousness within this body, and do we not therefore refer to this body not only subjectively as 'I', but also objectively as 'my body'?

Are we then two different things, this physical body that we call 'I', and the consciousness that feels itself to be within this body, but at the same time regards this body as an object that it calls 'my body'? No, we obviously cannot be two different things, because we all know very clearly 'I am one'. That is, we each feel that we have only one self or 'I', and not two or more different 'I's. When we say 'I', we refer to a sense of selfhood that is intrinsically single, whole and indivisible.

Does that then mean that this physical body and the consciousness within it that feels it to be 'my body' are not two different things, but are one and the same? No, they are very clearly two quite different things, because we all know that our body is not inherently conscious. Though we cannot know our own body when our consciousness is separated from it, we do know that when the body of some other person dies, it remains just as a lump of insentient matter, devoid of any consciousness. Since a physical body can thus remain without being conscious, the consciousness that appears to be united with it when it is alive and awake is clearly something that is different from it.

Moreover, and more importantly, just as we know that a body can remain without any consciousness of its own, we also know from our experience in dream that our own consciousness can remain without this body that we now mistake to be 'I'. In dream we are conscious, both of ourself as a body and of a world around us, but we are not conscious of this body, which at that time is supposedly lying asleep on a bed, unconscious of the world around it. Is it not clear, therefore, that our consciousness and our body are two different things?

Since we thus know from our own experience that our consciousness and this body are two separate and distinct things, and since in the waking state we feel ourself to be both our consciousness and this body, can we say that we are not just one or other of these two separate things, but are a compound formed by the union of the two of them? If we are indeed just a compound of these two separate things, we must cease to exist when they are parted. Our consciousness is united with this body only in the waking state, and parted from it in both dream and deep sleep. Since we continue to exist in both dream and deep sleep, we must be something more than just a compound of our consciousness and this body.

When our consciousness and this body are separated, which of these two things are we? Since we are conscious of our existence not only in the waking state, but also in dream and in deep sleep, is it not evident that we cannot be either this body or a compound of our consciousness and this body, but must be some form of consciousness that can separate itself from this body, and that persists through all these three passing and contrasting states?

Is it not clear, therefore, that the knowledge we have at present about who or what we are is confused and uncertain? Are we this body, which is composed of inconscient matter, or are we our consciousness, which knows this body as an object distinct from itself? Since we feel ourself to be both, and refer to both as 'I', it is evident that we have no clear knowledge of what our 'I' actually is.

When we say, 'I know I am sitting here', we are equating and thereby confusing the knowing 'I', which is our consciousness, with the sitting 'I', which is this body. In this way, throughout our waking and dream states, we persistently confuse our consciousness with whatever body it currently appears to be confined within.

Our confusion about our true identity, which is obvious enough from our experience in waking, is made still more clear by our experience in dream. In that state, this body that we now identify as 'I' is supposedly lying unconscious either of itself or of the world around it, but we are nevertheless conscious of another body, which we mistake to be 'I', and another world, which we mistake to be real. Does not this experience that we have in every dream clearly demonstrate to us that we have the ability to delude ourself into believing that we are a body which is in reality nothing but a figment of our own imagination?

How are we able to delude ourself in this manner? If we clearly knew exactly what we are, we could not mistake ourself to be something that we are not. Is it not clear, therefore, that all our confused and mistaken notions about what we are arise only from our lack of true and clear self-knowledge? Until and unless we gain a clear and correct knowledge about what we really are, we will continue to be confused and to delude ourself into believing that we are a body, a mind, a person, or some other thing that we are not.

So long as our knowledge of our own real self thus remains unclear, uncertain and confused, can we really be sure about anything else that we may know? All the so-called knowledge about other things that we think we now possess rests solely upon the unsteady foundation of our confused and uncertain knowledge about ourself. How can we rely upon or feel confident about any such knowledge?

Which is actually real, the body and world that we experience in the waking state, or the body and world that we experience in dream? Or are neither of them real? As far as we know when we are dreaming, the body and world of this waking state are non-existent. Even now, when we are in the waking state, the idea that they existed when we were unconscious of them, as in the states of dream and deep sleep, is merely an assumption for which we have no concrete evidence.

Like all our other assumptions, this assumption is based upon our first and most fundamental assumption – our wrong assumption that we are somehow a mixture of both a physical body and the consciousness that knows that body not only subjectively as 'I' but also objectively as 'my body'. Before we seek to acquire any knowledge about other things, all of which we merely assume to be real, but which are quite possibly nothing more than figments of our own imagination, is it not necessary for us first to question this fundamental assumption about who or what we are?

Since in dream and in deep sleep we are consciously separated from this body that we now in the waking state identify as 'I', is it not clear that this body cannot actually be our real self? In dream we identify another body as 'I', and through the five senses of that body we see a world of objects and people around us, just as in waking we identify this body as 'I', and through the five senses of this body we see a world of objects and people around us. Does not dream therefore clearly demonstrate to us that our mind has a power of imagination that is so strong and self-deceptive that it can not only create for us a body and a whole world, but can also deceive us into believing that that body is 'I' and that world is real?

Does this not give us a very compelling reason to doubt the reality of this body and world in the waking state? Is it not quite possible that this body and the world full of objects and people that it sees around it are just another creation of the same self-deceptive power of imagination that created a very similar body and world in dream – a body and world that at that time seemed just as real as this body and world now seem to be?

In both waking and in dream we appear to be a confused mixture of both consciousness and a physical body. This confused mixture or compound that is formed by our identification of our consciousness with a physical body is what we call our 'mind'. Since this mind is a confused and transitory form of consciousness that appears to exist only when it identifies itself with a body in either waking or dream, and ceases to exist when it relinquishes its identification with any body in sleep, can it be anything more than a mere illusion – an unreal appearance, a phantom product of our self-deceptive power of imagination?

Since all things other than our fundamental consciousness 'I am' are known by us only through the unreliable medium of this confused, self-deceiving and transitory form of consciousness called 'mind', can we confidently say that any of them are real? Is it not reasonable for us instead to suspect that they are all nothing more than an illusory and unreal apparition, just like all the things that we see in a dream?

Since the body that we mistake to be 'I' in the waking state, and the body that we mistake to be 'I' in a dream, are both transitory appearances, appearing as they each do in one state and not in another, is it not clear that we cannot be either of these two bodies? If we are neither of them, then what in fact are we?

We must be something that exists in both waking and dream. Though the body and world that we now know in the waking state and the body and world that we knew in dream may be very similar to each other, they are clearly not the same body and world. Is there anything that exists and remains the same in both of these two states, and if so what is it? On superficial observation, the only thing that is common to these two states is our mind, the consciousness that knows them. Are we then this consciousness that knows both waking and dream, and that identifies one body as 'I' in waking and another body as 'I' in dream?

We cannot answer this question without first asking another. Are we this same consciousness not only in waking and dream, but also in sleep? No, this consciousness that knows a body and world in the waking and dream states ceases to exist in deep sleep. But do we also cease to exist in deep sleep? No, though we cease to be conscious of any body or world in the state of deep sleep, we nevertheless do exist in that state, and we also know our own existence at that time.

When we wake up from deep sleep, we are able to say with certainty, 'I slept peacefully and happily. I knew nothing at that time, and was not disturbed by any dream'. Does not this certain knowledge that we have about our experience in sleep clearly indicate not only that we did exist at that time, but also that we knew we existed?

Generally we think of deep sleep as a state of 'unconsciousness'. But what we were unconscious of in sleep was only things other than 'I', such as any body or world. We were not, however, unconscious of our own existence. We need other people to tell us that our body and the world existed while we were asleep, but we need no one to tell us that we existed at that time. Without the help or testimony of any other person or thing, we know clearly and without any doubt 'I slept'.

In sleep we may not have known exactly what we were, but we did know very clearly that we were. The clear knowledge that we possess about our experience in sleep, and that we express when we say 'I slept peacefully, and knew nothing at that time', would not be possible if in sleep we had not been conscious of that experience – or to be more precise, if we had not been conscious of ourself as the consciousness that was unconscious of anything other than our own peaceful and happy being.

If we did not know 'I am' while we were asleep, now after we have woken from sleep we could not know so clearly 'I slept'. That is, we could not now know so clearly that we were then in the state that we now call 'sleep' – in other words, that we did indeed exist in that state. We know that we existed in sleep because in that state we did actually experience our own existence – our essential self-conscious being, 'I am'.

Since in the waking state we know clearly not only that we slept, but also that in sleep we did not know anything, is it not clear that sleep was a state that we actually experienced? The seeming 'unconsciousness' of sleep – the absence at that time of any knowledge about anything other than 'I am' –

was our own experience, something that we ourself experienced and knew at that time.

We can employ another parallel line of reasoning to demonstrate the fact that we were conscious of our existence in sleep. After we wake up from sleep, do we not have a clear memory of having slept, and of having known nothing while we slept? Since we can have no memory of something unless we have actually experienced it, our memory of having slept and having known nothing while asleep is a clear proof of the fact that we did experience ourself sleeping and knowing nothing at that time.

If we did not truly remember our experience in sleep, we could not know with such certainty that we were unconscious of anything at that time. What we would know about sleep is not the positive knowledge that we slept and knew nothing at that time, but merely a negative knowledge that we do not remember any such state at all.

Instead of remembering a clear gap between one period of waking and the next – a thought-free gap in which we were clearly unconscious of anything other than our own being – we would remember no break at all between two such consecutive periods of waking. The end of one period of waking would in our experience simply merge without any perceptible break into the beginning of the next period of waking, and all our many consecutive periods of waking would appear to us to be one single continuous and unbroken period of waking, just as the many frames of a movie film when projected in rapid succession upon a screen appear to be one single continuous and unbroken moving picture. If there were no continuity of our consciousness during sleep, the gap that exists between one period of waking and the next would be imperceptible to us, just as the gap between each frame of the movie film is imperceptible to us.

Deep sleep is thus a state of which we do have a direct and first-hand experience. Since there can be no experience without consciousness, the fact that we experience sleep clearly proves that we certainly do have some level of consciousness even in that state. That level of consciousness that we experience in sleep is our deepest and most fundamental level of consciousness – our simple non-dual consciousness of our own essential being, which is our true self-consciousness 'I am'.

We are so accustomed to associating consciousness only with our mind, the consciousness that knows things other than itself, that with regard to sleep we overlook the obvious. We overlook the fact that the 'unconsciousness' of sleep is something that we ourself have experienced, and that in order to have experienced that so-called 'unconsciousness' in sleep we ourself must have been conscious.

Therefore, as far as we can ever possibly know, there is no such thing as a state of absolute unconsciousness. Such a state of absolute unconsciousness would be a state that could never be known or experienced. The only type of unconsciousness that we can experience and know is not a state of absolute unconsciousness, but merely a state of relative unconsciousness – a state in which the consciousness of duality with which we are familiar in the waking and dream states has subsided, a state in which we are not conscious of anything other than our mere being, our fundamental non-dual self-consciousness 'I am'.

If we were really unconscious in sleep, or at any other time, we could not be consciousness, because consciousness can never be unconscious. However, since we are conscious of sleep and other such states of relative unconsciousness, we are the absolute consciousness that underlies and supports yet transcends all states of relative consciousness and unconsciousness.

Does not the fact that we experience waking, dream and deep sleep as three distinct states clearly prove that we exist and are conscious of our existence in all these three states? There is thus a continuity of our existence and our consciousness through all our three states of waking, dream and deep sleep.

However the consciousness of our existence or mere being that continues unbroken in all these three states is distinct from the consciousness that knows a body and world in just two of them, namely waking and dream. Our simple and fundamental consciousness of our own mere being that continues throughout our three states is our pure uncontaminated consciousness 'I am', whereas the consciousness that identifies itself with a particular body and that knows a world through the five senses of that body is the mixed and contaminated consciousness 'I am this body'.

This mixed consciousness that identifies itself with a body is a limited and distorted form of our original and fundamental consciousness 'I am'. Since this distorted consciousness, which we call our 'mind', appears only in the states of waking and dream, and disappears in deep sleep, it cannot be our real nature, our true and essential self. Our real nature is only our pure, uncontaminated and unlimited consciousness 'I am', which underlies and supports the passing appearance of our three states.

Thus from our critical analysis of our experience in our three ordinary states of consciousness, we can conclude that we are the underlying consciousness that knows both the conscious states of waking and dream and the seemingly unconscious state of sleep. Or to be more precise, we are that fundamental consciousness which always knows 'I am', and which in sleep knows nothing but 'I am', but which in waking and dream appears to know other things in addition to 'I am'.

Neither the consciousness of things other than 'I' that we experience in waking and dream, nor the unconsciousness of other things that we experience in sleep, are ever able to conceal completely our fundamental consciousness 'I am'. Nevertheless they do appear to cloud over and obscure this consciousness 'I am', making us feel in waking and dream 'I am this body' and in sleep 'I am unconscious', and thereby they deprive us of our clear knowledge of our true state of mere self-conscious being. Therefore, to know clearly the true nature of our being, we must use our power of knowing to attend to our fundamental and essential consciousness 'I am', thereby penetrating beyond the transitory appearances of both the objective consciousness of waking and dream, and the seeming unconsciousness of sleep.

We normally think of sleep as a state of unconsciousness because we are accustomed to associating consciousness with the state of knowing things other than ourself in waking and dream. When the knowing of other things subsides in sleep, we experience a state of seeming darkness or emptiness that we mistake to be unconsciousness. So accustomed have we become to associating consciousness with knowing things other than our own being, that we overlook the fact that in sleep we are clearly conscious of our being. The reason why we thus overlook our clear consciousness of our own being in sleep is because we have habituated ourself to overlooking it in waking and in dream.

In both waking and dream we usually spend all our time paying attention only to the thoughts and feelings in our mind, and to the objects and events in the seemingly external world, and we seldom if ever pay any attention to our mere being, our self-consciousness 'I am'. Because we habitually ignore our consciousness of our own being, we mistakenly believe that our dualistic consciousness – our consciousness that knows things that are seemingly other than ourself – is the only consciousness there is. Since this dualistic consciousness subsides in sleep, that state appears to us to be a state of unconsciousness.

The consciousness that knows other things is a transitory phenomenon that exists only in waking and dream, but it is not the only form of consciousness that exists. Even in waking and dream, a more subtle form of consciousness exists, underlying and supporting the transitory appearance of our dualistic consciousness. This more subtle form of consciousness is our non-dual consciousness of our own being, the consciousness by which we each know 'I am'. Thus our consciousness in waking and dream has two distinct forms: our fundamental 'being consciousness', by which we know 'I am', and our superficial 'knowing consciousness', by which we know everything else.

Though we can thus distinguish two forms of our consciousness, these are not two different consciousnesses, but just two forms of one and the same consciousness – the one and only consciousness that exists. The relationship between these two forms of consciousness is similar to the relationship between the illusory appearance of a snake and the rope that underlies and supports that illusory appearance. When walking in a dim light, we may mistake a rope lying on the ground to be a snake. Because we see the rope as a snake, we fail to see the rope as it is, and hence we mistakenly think that what is lying on the ground is only a snake. Similarly, because we experience our 'being consciousness' as a 'knowing consciousness', we fail to know our 'being consciousness' as it is, and hence we mistakenly think that the only form of consciousness that exists is our 'knowing consciousness'.

Just as the rope underlies and supports the illusory appearance of the snake, so our 'being consciousness' underlies and supports the transitory appearance of our 'knowing consciousness'. Whereas our 'knowing consciousness' is a transitory and illusory appearance, like the snake, our 'being consciousness' is not a transitory and unreal appearance, but is our true self, our essential being, which exists and is known by us at all times, in all places, and in all states.

Since our 'knowing consciousness', which is what is commonly called our 'mind', appears in waking and dream but disappears in sleep, it is impermanent, and hence it cannot be our real self – our true and natural form of being and consciousness. Since our 'being consciousness', on the other hand, exists in all our three states of consciousness, waking, dream and deep sleep, it is permanent, and hence it is our real self, the very core and essence of our being – our true and natural form of consciousness.

Since both the 'being' form and the 'knowing' form of our consciousness are experienced by us in the waking state, we have a choice of attending either to the thoughts, feelings, objects and events that are known by the knowing form of our consciousness, or to the 'I am' that is known by the being form of our consciousness. When we attend to things other than our being, we seemingly become our false form of 'knowing consciousness', which is our mind, whereas when we attend only to our own being, 'I am', we remain as our essential form of non-dual 'being consciousness', which is our real self.

The nature of our essential 'being consciousness' is just to be, and not to know anything other than itself. Since it is consciousness, it knows itself merely by being itself. Its knowledge of itself is therefore not an action, a 'doing' of any sort, but is just being.

In order to know our real self, therefore, all we need do is just be. What seemingly prevents us from knowing our real self, our mere 'being consciousness', is our 'doing', our rising to know things that we imagine to be other than ourself. Whereas knowing ourself is not a 'doing' but just 'being', knowing other things is a 'doing' or action. The very nature of our 'knowing consciousness' or mind is therefore to be constantly doing.

Our ‘knowing consciousness’ comes into existence only by an act of imagination – by imagining itself to be a body, which it creates by its power of imagination. Thus it is nothing but a form of imagination. Since it is itself an imagination, all that it knows is likewise an imagination. Since imagining is a doing or action, the very formation of our ‘knowing consciousness’ in our imagination is a doing, and of all doings it is the first.

Since the rising of our ‘knowing consciousness’ from sleep is a doing or act of imagination, all that it gives rise to – all our dualistic knowledge, which rises in the form of our thoughts, some of which appear to exist externally as our body and the other objects of this world – is just a product of doing, a result of our repeated acts of imagination. Thus from the moment it rises from sleep till the moment it subsides once again in sleep, our mind or ‘knowing consciousness’ is in a state of constant activity or doing. Without doing, without thinking or knowing something other than itself, our mind cannot stand. As soon as it ceases doing, it subsides in sleep, which is a state of mere being.

However, though in sleep we remain as our mere ‘being consciousness’, we somehow appear to lack a perfect clarity of self-knowledge in that state. If we clearly knew our true nature in sleep, we could not again mistake ourself to be a body or anything else that we are not, and hence we would never rise again as our ‘knowing consciousness’ or mind.

Throughout all our normal three states of consciousness, we experience our ‘being consciousness’ as ‘I am’, yet we somehow imagine that it is obscured by a lack of clarity of self-knowledge. This lack of clarity of true self-knowledge is only imaginary, but because in our imagination it appears to be real, it enables us to imagine that we are a ‘knowing consciousness’ in waking and dream, and that we do not clearly know ourself even in sleep, when that ‘knowing consciousness’ has temporarily subsided.

How exactly we are able to sustain this imaginary lack of clarity of self-knowledge even in sleep cannot be understood by our mind or ‘knowing consciousness’. However, if we are able now in our present waking state to scrutinise our ‘being consciousness’ sufficiently keenly, we will discover that this imaginary lack of clarity of self-knowledge never really existed.

That is, if we turn the attention of our ‘knowing consciousness’ away from all forms of duality and focus it keenly upon our non-dual ‘being consciousness’, which we always experience as ‘I am’, we will begin to experience our ‘being consciousness’ more clearly. The more clearly we experience it, the more keenly we will be able to focus our attention upon it. By constantly practising self-attention, therefore, we will eventually be able to focus our attention so keenly upon our ‘being consciousness’ that we will experience it with full and perfect clarity. When we thus come to experience our ‘being consciousness’ with perfect clarity, we will discover that we never really experienced any lack of clarity of self-knowledge.

Our 'being consciousness' always knows itself perfectly clearly, and never experiences any lack of clarity of self-knowledge. Our seeming lack of clarity of self-knowledge is merely an illusion, an unreal product of our self-deceptive power of imagination, and is experienced only by our mind or 'knowing consciousness'. Therefore, as soon as we experience our 'being consciousness' with perfect clarity, we will discover that in reality our imaginary lack of clarity of self-knowledge is ever non-existent, and thus the illusion of it will be destroyed forever.

Since our entire experience of duality or multiplicity arises only in our mind, and since our mind is built upon the flimsy foundation of our imaginary lack of clarity of self-knowledge, when this mist-like imaginary lack of clarity is dissolved in the clear light of unadulterated self-consciousness, our mind and all the duality that it now experiences will disappear for ever, just as a dream disappears as soon as we wake up from sleep. Therefore in verse 1 of *Ēkātma Pañcakam* Sri Ramana says:

> Having forgotten ourself [our real self, our pure unadulterated consciousness 'I am'], having thought '[this] body indeed is myself', [and] having [thereby] taken innumerable births, finally knowing ourself [and] being ourself is just [like] waking from a dream of wandering about the world. See [thus].

Our present waking state is in fact just a dream that is occurring in our long sleep of self-forgetfulness or lack of clarity of true self-knowledge. So long as this sleep persists, we will continue dreaming one dream after another. Between our dreams we may rest for a while in dreamless sleep, but such rest can never be permanent.

Our sleep of self-forgetfulness is imaginary, but from the perspective of our mind, which is a product of it, it appears to be quite real. That is, so long as we feel ourself to be this mind, we cannot deny the fact that we do appear to lack clear knowledge of our real self, as a result of which the knowledge of ourself that we now appear to experience is confused and uncertain.

This lack of clarity of true self-knowledge is what Sri Ramana describes as 'self-forgetfulness'. He also describes it as a 'sleep', because sleep is a state in which we forget our normal waking self. Just as in our everyday sleep we forget our present waking self, so in our primal sleep of imaginary self-forgetfulness we seem to have forgotten our real self, which is our ever-wakeful consciousness of our own essential and infinite being.

So long as we experience this state of imaginary self-forgetfulness, we do not experience ourself as we really are – that is, as infinite and absolute being, infinite and absolute consciousness, and infinite and absolute happiness. Instead we experience ourself as a finite and relative being – a person who seems to exist now but apparently did not exist before his or her birth, and apparently will not exist after his or her death, a person who sometimes rises as this finite and relative consciousness that we call our mind, and sometimes subsides in the state of relative unconsciousness that we call sleep, a person who experiences only finite and relative happiness, mixed with equally finite and relative unhappiness.

In the state of relative unconsciousness that we call sleep, we do not experience ourself as a person, but simply as our own happy self-conscious being. Though in sleep we do not actually experience any form of relativity or finitude, from the perspective of our present waking mind we have to say that sleep is only a relative and therefore finite state, because it is a state which we seem to enter and from which we seem to rise repeatedly. Therefore, though sleep is not finite in itself, relative to our other two states, waking and dream, it does appear to be finite.

Since sleep is a state in which our mind has subsided, it transcends our mind, and hence it cannot be defined categorically as being either finite or infinite, or as being either relative or absolute. From the perspective of our mind, sleep is a finite and relative state, but from the perspective of our true non-dual self-consciousness, 'I am', it is our real and natural state of infinite and absolute being, infinite and absolute consciousness, and infinite and absolute happiness.

What we actually experience in sleep is only our non-dual consciousness of our own essential being, 'I am', so as such sleep is a state devoid of any form of relativity or finitude. What makes sleep appear to be a relative and therefore finite state is the rising of our mind in the two truly relative and finite states of waking and dream.

As Sri Sadhu Om used to say, if we raise two walls in a vast open space, that one open space will appear to be divided into three confined spaces. Similarly, when our mind imagines the existence of two different types of body – the body that it imagines to be itself in its current state, which it considers to be waking, and the body that it imagined to be itself in another state that it now considers to be dream – the infinite space of our true and absolute self-conscious being appears to be divided into three separate and therefore finite states, which we call waking, dream and sleep.

In reality, the state that we now call 'sleep' is our true, natural, infinite and absolute state of unadulterated self-consciousness. However, so long as we feel ourself to be this relative and finite consciousness that we call our mind, we cannot know sleep as it really is. That is, since we do not experience our essential self-consciousness 'I am' in its true unadulterated form in our present waking state, from the perspective of this waking state we cannot recognise the fact that we did experience our self-consciousness 'I am' in its true unadulterated form in sleep. Therefore, in order to discover what we really experienced in sleep, we must experience our fundamental self-consciousness 'I am' in its true unadulterated form in our present waking state.

In the perspective of our real self, which is the non-dual consciousness that knows nothing other than itself, the state that we call sleep is a state of infinite, absolute and unadulterated self-consciousness. However, in the perspective of our real self, our other two states, which we call waking and dream, are equally states of infinite, absolute and unadulterated self-consciousness. That is, in the infinite perspective of our real self, there is only one state, and that state is our single, non-dual, true and natural state of absolute consciousness of our own essential being, 'I am'.

However, in the limited and distorted perspective of our mind, our one true state of non-dual self-consciousness appears to be three distinct states, which we call waking, dream and sleep. Since in the perspective of our waking and dreaming mind sleep appears to be a separate state, which exists relative to waking and dream, it seems to us now to be a limited state of relative unconsciousness – a state that results from a temporary forgetfulness of our waking and dreaming self, which is the object-knowing consciousness that we call our mind.

Most forms of philosophy and science are concerned only or at least principally with what we experience in our present waking state. Even when they study our other two states, dream and sleep, they do so only from the perspective of our waking mind. Therefore, since all such forms of philosophy and science are centred around the experience of our waking mind, they tend to consider our experience in our other two states as being of only secondary importance.

However, in our search for the absolute reality, dream and sleep are both crucially important states of consciousness, since they each give us essential clues concerning the true nature of our real self. Dream is important to us because it clearly demonstrates the fact that our mind has a wonderful power of imagination by which it is not only able to create a body and a whole world, but is also able to delude itself into mistaking its own imaginary creation to be real. Sleep is important to us because it clearly demonstrates the fact that we can exist and be conscious of our own existence even in the absence of our mind.

In our search for the absolute reality, which transcends all the limitations created by our mind, sleep is in fact the most important of our three states of consciousness, because it is the only state in which we experience our fundamental knowledge – our essential self-consciousness, 'I am' – devoid of any other knowledge. Not only does sleep provide us with incontrovertible evidence of the fact that our essential nature is only our non-dual self-consciousness – our unadulterated consciousness of our own being, 'I am' – but it also provides us with the vital clue that we require in order to practise self-investigation effectively.

That is, self-investigation or self-scrutiny, which is the practical research that we must perform in order to experience true self-knowledge, is a state of non-dual self-consciousness – a state in which we knowingly abide as nothing other than our own essential self-conscious being. If we did not already have a taste of this non-dual self-consciousness in sleep, it would be difficult for our mind (which is always accustomed to experiencing only duality or otherness throughout its two states of activity, waking and dream) to comprehend what this state of non-dual self-consciousness actually is, and hence when we attempt to practise self-investigation, which Sri Ramana revealed to us is the only means by which we can experience true self-knowledge, it would not be so easy for us to abide knowingly as our own essential self-conscious being, 'I am'.

Sri Ramana sometimes described sleep as a sample of our true state of non-dual self-consciousness, and at other times he described it as an imaginary state of self-forgetfulness. Why did he refer to sleep in these two different ways, which are seemingly contradictory?

Sleep appears to be a state of self-forgetfulness only from the perspective of our mind, which is itself an imaginary product of our seeming self-forgetfulness. If we had not seemingly forgotten our real self, we could not now imagine ourself to be this mind, which appears to be something other than our real self – our true non-dual consciousness of our own essential being or 'am'-ness. Therefore, though our self-forgetfulness is truly imaginary, from the perspective of our mind it is a fact that is undeniably real.

Our imaginary self-forgetfulness is like a sleep. Just as sleep is the seeming darkness or lack of clarity without which no dream could appear, so our self-forgetfulness is the seeming darkness or lack of clarity without which we could not imagine ourself to be experiencing the states of dualistic knowledge that we call waking and dream.

Though our mind disappears in sleep every day, it reappears from sleep as soon as it has thereby recuperated sufficient energy to engage in another period of activity. It appears, therefore, that in sleep our mind somehow continues to exist in a seed form – a dormant and unmanifest form, which will again become manifest as soon as the conditions become favourable, the favourable conditions in this case being a sufficient internal store of energy to become active once again.

Since our mind reappears after a period of rest in sleep, from the perspective of this mind our idea that in sleep we continue to be unaware or forgetful of our real self – our true non-dual consciousness of our own essential being, 'I am' – appears to be quite true. Therefore, when talking from the perspective of our mind, Sri Ramana used to describe sleep as an imaginary state of self-forgetfulness.

However, when we analyse our experience in sleep more deeply, as we have done in this chapter, it becomes clear to us that though we now imagine that we did not experience any consciousness in sleep, we did in fact experience our fundamental consciousness of our own essential being, 'I am'. Therefore, though sleep does appear to our waking mind to be a state of self-forgetfulness, on more careful consideration we cannot deny the fact that we did indeed experience our natural and eternal self-consciousness even in sleep. Hence, when talking from the perspective of the absolute reality, which is our own infinite self-consciousness, 'I am', Sri Ramana used to describe sleep as our true state of non-dual self-consciousness.

The truth is that we do indeed know that we are even in sleep. However, though in sleep we know *that we are*, we appear not to know *what we are*. Nevertheless, though we appear not to know what we are in sleep, we should remember that this seeming ignorance or forgetfulness of our real self in sleep is imaginary and therefore unreal, just as our present ignorance or forgetfulness of our real self is imaginary and unreal.

We have never truly forgotten our real self, or been ignorant of it. We merely imagine that we do not know ourself as we really are. However, as Sri Ramana repeatedly pointed out to us, this imaginary self-ignorance or self-forgetfulness is experienced only by our mind, and not by our real self, which always experiences itself as infinite and eternally happy consciousness of just being.

Since in sleep we do not experience our mind, which alone imagines the existence of self-forgetfulness, sleep cannot really be a state of self-forgetfulness. Indeed, in sleep no individual consciousness exists to experience self-forgetfulness. All that exists in sleep is our unadulterated consciousness of our own real self or essential being, 'I am'. Therefore, though the relative truth about sleep is that it is a state of self-forgetfulness, the absolute truth about sleep is that it is a state of perfect self-consciousness or self-knowledge.

However, though the absolute truth is that sleep is a state of infinite non-dual self-consciousness, which is the only existing reality, so long as we imagine ourself to be this mind, for all practical purposes we have to concede that sleep does indeed appear to be a relative state of self-forgetfulness. Only if we recognise the fact that the sole cause of the appearance of our mind is our imaginary self-forgetfulness or self-ignorance, will we be able to understand that the only means by which we can transcend the limitations that are seemingly imposed upon us by our mind is to destroy this illusion of self-forgetfulness.

In order to destroy this illusion, we must know ourself as we really are, and in order to know ourself as we really are, we must attend to ourself – to our fundamental consciousness of our own essential being, 'I am'.

Therefore, though Sri Ramana experienced the absolute truth – the truth that we have never really forgotten ourself, because we are the perfectly non-dual self-consciousness, which never knows anything other than itself – in his teachings he accepted the relative reality of our present imaginary self-forgetfulness or self-ignorance. This is the reason why he began the above verse of *Ēkātma Pañcakam* with the words, 'Having forgotten ourself'.

After saying, 'Having forgotten ourself', Sri Ramana says, 'having thought "[this] body indeed is myself"', because our present imagination that we are this body arises as a result of our self-forgetfulness. If we clearly knew what we really are, we could not imagine ourself to be anything that we are not. Therefore we could not imagine ourself to be this body if we did not first imagine our seeming self-forgetfulness or lack of clarity of self-consciousness.

Whenever our mind becomes active, whether in waking or in dream, it first imagines itself to be a body, and then through the five senses of that imaginary body it perceives an imaginary world. Our mind cannot function without first limiting itself within the confines of an imaginary body, which it mistakes to be 'I'. Hence our mind is an intrinsically limited and therefore distorted form of consciousness.

Without imagining itself to be something finite, our mind could not imagine anything that is other than itself. All otherness or duality is an imagination that can come into existence only when we imagine ourself to be a separate and therefore finite consciousness. Though we are in reality the infinite consciousness of just being – the essential non-dual self-consciousness 'I am' – we imagine ourself to be this finite object-knowing consciousness that we call our mind.

All that we know as other than ourself – all our thoughts, feelings and perceptions – are merely products of our own imagination, and they appear to exist only because we imagine ourself to be something separate from them. In sleep we experience our non-dual self-consciousness 'I am', but we do not experience any otherness, separation or duality. Even in waking and dream we experience this same non-dual self-consciousness 'I am', but along with it we also experience the illusion of otherness, separation or duality.

Nothing that we experience is actually other than our own essential consciousness. Our consciousness is the fundamental substance that appears as all other things. Other things are all products of our imagination. What we call our imagination is a power or faculty that our consciousness possesses to modify itself seemingly into the form of our thoughts, feelings and perceptions.

When we imagine our experience of thoughts, feelings and perceptions, we create a seeming separation between ourself and these objects of our consciousness. Therefore if we did not first imagine ourself to be something separate – something limited or finite – we could not experience anything as being other than ourself. Hence, in order to imagine the existence of things other than ourself, we must begin by imagining ourself to be one among the many finite things that we thus imagine.

Thus in order to experience a world, whether this world that we perceive in our present waking state or the world that we perceive in any of our other dreams, we must simultaneously imagine ourself to be a particular body in that world. We can clearly recognise this fact when we consider our experience in dream.

We do not experience a dream in the same manner that we experience a cinema show. When we watch a cinema show or television programme, we experience ourself as a spectator who exists outside the moving picture that we are watching, but when we experience a dream, we experience ourself as a person – a body and mind – who is a part of the dream world that we are experiencing. Similarly, when we experience our present waking state, we experience ourself as a person – a body and mind – who is a part of this waking world that we are now experiencing.

The consciousness that experiences both waking and dream is our mind, and our mind always experiences itself as being a particular body, which is a part of the world that it is currently experiencing. If we did not limit ourself as a body and as a body-bound mind, we could not experience anything as being other than ourself, because in reality we are the unlimited consciousness in which this entire dream of duality appears.

Since we are the infinite consciousness in which all things appear and disappear, we alone really exist, and nothing that appears to exist can really be other than ourself. Therefore our real consciousness can never know anything other than itself – our own real self or essential being, 'I am'. All otherness is experienced only by our mind, which is a limited and distorted form of our real consciousness.

A dream actually appears within our own mind, but our mind experiences itself as being a body that exists within that dream. Such is the self-delusive power of our imagination. Therefore in verse 3 of *Ēkātma Pañcakam* Sri Ramana says:

> When [our] body exists within ourself [who are the basic consciousness in which all things appear], a person who thinks himself [or herself] to be existing within that inconscient [material] body is like someone who thinks that the screen, [which is] the *ādhāra* [the underlying support or base] of a [cinema] picture, exists within that picture.

In the *kaliveṇbā* version of *Ēkātma Pañcakam* Sri Ramana added the compound word *sat-cit-ānanda*, which means 'being-consciousness-bliss', before the initial word of this verse, *taṉṉuḷ* or 'within [our] self', thereby reminding us that what we are in essence is only the perfectly peaceful consciousness of being, 'I am'. Other than our basic consciousness of our own being, everything that we know appears within the distorted object-knowing form of our consciousness that we call our mind, which arises within us during waking and dream, and subsides back into ourself during sleep. Our true consciousness of being – our essential self-consciousness 'I am' – is therefore like the screen on which a cinema picture is projected, because it is the one fundamental *ādhāra* or underlying base that supports the appearance and disappearance of our mind and everything that is known by it.

Just as a dream appears within our own mind, so everything that we experience in this waking state appears within our own mind. However, though the world that we now perceive is experienced by us within our own mind, we imagine ourself to be a particular body, which is one among the many objects that exists in this world.

Therefore if we wish to know the truth about ourself and this world, should we not determine which of these two conflicting experiences is real and which is an illusion? Does this world really exist only in our own mind, or is our mind really something that exists only within a particular body in this world? Is this entire universe, which seems to be so vast, extending with no known limit in time or space, merely a series of thoughts in our mind, or are we merely an insignificant person who lives for a few brief years in a small corner of this universe? In other words, is this whole world really in us, or are we really in it?

If this body and world actually exist only in our own mind, as the body and world that we experience in a dream do, our experience that we are confined within the limits of this body cannot be real, and must therefore be an illusion. We could know that it is real, and not an illusion, only if we could prove to ourself that this body and world really do exist outside of and independent of our own mind.

Can we ever prove to ourself that anything that we know exists independent of our own mind? No, except our own essential self-consciousness, 'I am', which we experience in sleep in the absence of our mind, we cannot prove to ourself that anything is more than a mere imagination that is created and experienced only in and by our own mind. All we know of our body and this world is only the thoughts or mental images of them which we have formed in our mind by our power of imagination. Except our fundamental consciousness of our own being, 'I am', everything that we know can be known by us only within our own mind.

Our belief that our body and this world really exist outside our mind is just wishful thinking. It is a blind belief, because it is not based upon any adequate evidence, and is therefore without any real foundation. When we know in this waking state that the world we perceived and the body we mistook to be ourself in a dream were in fact just figments of our imagination, and therefore existed only in our own mind, what reasonable grounds do we have for believing that our present body and the world that we now perceive are anything more than mere figments of our imagination?

In the eighteenth paragraph of *Nāṉ Yār?* Sri Ramana says:

> Except that waking is *dīrgha* [long lasting] and dream is *kṣaṇika* [momentary or lasting for only a short while], there is no other difference [between these two imaginary states of mental activity]. To the extent to which all the *vyavahāras* [doings, activities, affairs or occurrences] that happen in waking appear [at this present moment] to be real, to that [same] extent even the *vyavahāras* that happen in dream appear at that time to be real. In dream [our] mind takes another body [to be itself]. In both waking and dream thoughts and names-and-forms [the objects of the seemingly external world] occur in one time [that is, simultaneously].

Though in the first sentence of this paragraph Sri Ramana says that the only difference between waking and dream is that in their relative duration waking is long and dream is short, in verse 560 of *Guru Vācaka Kōvai* he points out that even this difference is merely an illusion:

> The answer which stated that dream appears and disappears momentarily, [whereas] waking endures for a long time, was given as a consoling reply to the question asked [that is, it was a concession made in accordance with the then level of understanding of the questioner]. [In truth, however, time is merely a product of our mind's imagination, and hence the illusion that waking endures for a long time whereas dream is momentary is] a deceptive trick that occurs due to the adherence of mind-*māyā* [our power of *māyā* or self-delusion, which manifests in the form of our own mind].

Since time is a figment of our imagination, we cannot measure the duration of one state by the standard of the time that we experience in another state. We may experience a dream which appears to last a long time, but when we wake up we may find that according to the time experienced in this waking state we have slept for only a few minutes.

Though it may now appear to us that our present waking state endures for many hours each day, and resumes every day for many years, and that in contrast each of our dreams lasts for only a short period of time, this seeming distinction appears to be real only in the perspective of our mind in this waking state. In dream our same mind experiences that dream as if it were a waking state, and imagines that it is a state that endures for many hours each day, and resumes every day for many years.

Time is an imagination that we do not experience in sleep, but is a part of each of the worlds that we experience in waking and dream. Since the world that we experienced in a dream is not the same world that we experience now in this present waking state, the time that we experienced as part of that dream world is not the same time that we are experiencing now. Therefore if we try to judge the duration of dream by the standard of time that we experience now, our judgement will inevitably be distorted and therefore invalid.

The relative reality of all that we experience in waking and dream cannot be correctly judged from either of these two states. When we are dreaming, we mistake everything that we experience in that dream to be real, but when we are in our present waking state, we understand that everything that we experienced in that dream is actually a figment of our imagination. Just as we can correctly judge the reality of all that we experienced in dream only when we step outside that dream into our present waking state, so we will be able to judge correctly the reality of all that we experience now in this so-called waking state only when we step outside it into some other state that transcends it.

From the perspective of the all-transcending state of true self-knowledge, which is the state of non-dual and therefore absolute self-consciousness, Sri Ramana and other sages have been able to judge correctly the relative reality of all that we experience in waking and dream, and they have testified the fact that these two states are equally unreal, because they are both mere figments of our imagination.

In the second sentence of the eighteenth paragraph of *Nāṉ Yār?* Sri Ramana says, 'To the extent to which all the occurrences that happen in waking appear to be real, to that extent even the occurrences that happen in dream appear at that time to be real'. This is a fact that we all know from our own experience, but what inference should we draw from it? Since we now know that whatever we experienced in a dream was just our own thoughts, even though at that time it appeared to be as real as whatever we experience in this waking state now appears to be, is it not reasonable for us to infer that whatever we experience in this waking state is most probably likewise just our own thoughts?

Though this is a logical inference for us to draw, we can verify it for certain only when we ascertain the truth about ourself. Unless we know by our own experience what we really are, we cannot be sure of the reality of anything else that we know.

In order to know ourself, we must keenly scrutinise ourself – that is, we must focus our attention wholly and exclusively upon our essential consciousness of our own being, 'I am'. So long as we have any desire, attachment, fear or aversion for anything other than our own essential self-consciousness, whenever we try to focus our attention upon ourself, we will be distracted by our thoughts of whatever other things we desire, fear or feel averse to. And so long as we believe that those other things exist outside our own imagination and are therefore real in their own right, we will not be able to free ourself from our desire, attachment, fear or aversion for them.

Therefore to help us to free ourself from all our desires, attachments, fears and aversions, Sri Ramana and other sages teach us the truth that everything other than our own self-consciousness, 'I am', is unreal, being a mere figment of our own imagination. This is why in verse 559 of *Guru Vācaka Kōvai* he confirmed the inference that we can draw from the fact that whatever we experienced in a dream appeared then to be as real as what we experience in this waking state appears now to be, stating explicitly:

> If dream, which appeared [and was experienced by us as if it were real], is a mere whirling of [our own] thoughts, waking, which has [now] occurred [and is being experienced by us as if it were real], is also of that [same] nature [that is, it is likewise a mere whirling of our own thoughts]. As real as the happenings in waking, which has [now] occurred, [appear to be at this present moment], so real indeed [the happenings in] dream [appeared to be] at that time.

Sri Ramana affirms emphatically that waking and dream are both a 'mere whirling of thoughts'. That is, they are each a series of mental images that we form in our own mind by our power of imagination. In other words, except our fundamental self-consciousness 'I am', everything that we experience in either waking or dream is just a figment of our own imagination.

The state that we now experience as waking is in fact just another dream. Just as we now mistake our present state to be waking, in a dream we likewise mistake our then current state to be waking. We always mistake whatever state we are currently experiencing to be our waking state, and we consider all our other states to be dreams.

What distinguishes one state of dream from another is that in each such state or each series of such states we mistake a different body to be ourself. Since we remember a series of consecutive states in which we mistook ourself to be the same body that we now mistake ourself to be, we consider each of those states to be a resumption of this same waking state. However, we also remember other states in which we mistook ourself to be various other bodies, so we consider those other states to be dreams.

Since the fact that we take various different bodies to be ourself is what makes us imagine that there is a basic distinction between our present so-called waking state and our other states of dream, in the third sentence of the eighteenth paragraph of *Nāṉ Yār?* Sri Ramana says, 'In dream [our] mind takes another body'. In our present state of dream, we consider certain other states of dream to be real, because in them we took this same body to be ourself, but we consider yet other states of dream to be unreal, because in them we mistook other bodies to be ourself.

How exactly do we 'take another body' in each of our dreams? In a dream we imagine the existence of some other body, and we simultaneously imagine that body to be ourself. Similarly, in our present so-called waking state we imagine the existence of this body and simultaneously imagine it to be ourself. Just as the body that we mistook to be ourself in a dream was merely a product of our own imagination, so this body that we now mistake to be ourself is merely a product of our own imagination.

The relationship between ourself and our body is similar to the relationship between gold and a gold ornament. Just as gold is the one substance of which the ornament is made, so we are the one substance of which our body and all the other objects of this world are made. Therefore in verse 4 of *Ēkātma Pañcakam* Sri Ramana says:

> Is [an] ornament other than [the] gold [of which it is made]? Having separated [freed or disentangled] ourself, what [or how] is [our] body? One who thinks himself [or herself] to be [merely a finite] body is an *ajñāni* [a person who is ignorant of our one real, infinite and non-dual self], [whereas] one who takes [himself or herself] to be [nothing other than our one real] self is a *jñāni*, [a sage] who has known [this one real] self. Know [yourself thus as this one infinite self].

In the *kaliveṇbā* version of *Ēkātma Pañcakam* Sri Ramana added the word *vattuvām*, which means 'which is the substance', before the initial word of this verse, *poṉ* or 'gold'. The word *vattu* is a Tamil form of the Sanskrit word *vastu*, which means 'substance', 'essence' or 'reality', and which is a word that is often used in philosophy to denote the absolute reality, our own self-conscious being, which is the one essential substance of which all things are formed. Since Sri Ramana is here using gold as an analogy for our real self, by describing gold as the *vastu* or 'substance' he implies that we ourself are the one real substance of which our body and all other things are merely imaginary forms.

The rhetorical question 'Having separated ourself, what is [our] body?' expresses two closely related truths. Firstly, it expresses the truth that our present body does not exist when we separate ourself from it, as we do in both sleep and dream. Secondly, and in this context more importantly, this question is an idiomatic way of expressing the truth that just as an ornament cannot be other than the gold of which it is made, so our body cannot be other than our real self, which is the one substance of which all things are made.

That is, we are consciousness, and everything that we know is merely a form or image that appears in our consciousness – that is, in us – like waves that appear on the surface of the ocean. Just as the water of the ocean is the one substance of which all waves are formed, so our consciousness is the one substance of which all our thoughts – that is, all the objects known by us, including our body – are formed.

Our body and everything else that we know are just a series of thoughts or mental images, which we form in our own mind by our power of imagination. Since everything other than our own consciousness is just a figment of our imagination, our consciousness alone is real, and hence it is the one true substance of which all other things are formed.

In the final sentence of the eighteenth paragraph of *Nāṉ Yār?* Sri Ramana says, 'In both waking and dream thoughts and names-and-forms occur simultaneously'. In this context the plural form of the compound word *nāma-rūpa*, which literally means 'name-forms' and which I have translated as 'names-and-forms', denotes all the objects of the world, which we imagine exist outside ourself. In each of our states of mental activity, whether we imagine that state to be waking or dream, we experience the fact that the objects that we recognise as being merely thoughts that we have formed in our own mind, and the objects that seem to exist outside ourself, both appear simultaneously.

Therefore in verse 555 of *Guru Vācaka Kōvai* Sri Ramana says:

> Sages say that those [two seemingly different states] that are called waking and dream are [both] creations of our confused [agitated and deluded] mind, [because] in both [states] called waking and dream thoughts and names-and-forms come into existence simultaneously [and] in conjunction. Know for certain that [this is so].

As Sri Ramana often pointed out, all the objects of the seemingly external world are in fact experienced by us only as images that we form in our own mind by our power of imagination, and hence they are only our own thoughts. This is the reason why in the absence of all thoughts, as in sleep, no knowledge of any object is experienced, whereas as soon as our mind becomes active, as in waking and dream, our knowledge of external objects appears together with our other thoughts.

Even now in our present waking state, if we turn our attention away from all thoughts towards our own essential self-consciousness, 'I am', all our knowledge of external objects will disappear. Is it not clear, therefore, that all our objective knowledge depends upon our thoughts about the objects that we know? We appear to know an object only when we form an image of it in our mind. Since mental images are what we otherwise call thoughts, all that we know of external objects is only the thoughts of them that we form in our own mind by our power of imagination.

Except our essential self-consciousness, 'I am', everything that we know or experience is only a thought – one among the many mental images that we form in our own mind. Just as we understand that everything that we experience in a dream is merely our own imagination, by impartial and thorough analysis we can understand that everything that we experience in our present waking state is likewise merely our own imagination.

Our belief that our knowledge of this seemingly external world corresponds to something that actually exists outside ourself is merely an imagination – one among the many thoughts that we form in our mind. There is absolutely no evidence – and there never can be any evidence – that the world we now experience actually exists outside ourself, any more than there is any evidence that the world we experienced in a dream actually exists outside ourself.

In verse 1 of *Ēkātma Pañcakam*, after the first two clauses, 'Having forgotten ourself' and 'having thought "[this] body indeed is myself"', Sri Ramana adds a third clause, 'having [thereby] taken innumerable births'. What exactly does he mean by this? How actually do we 'take innumerable births'?

As we have discussed earlier, our present waking life is actually just a dream that is occurring in our imaginary sleep of self-forgetfulness or self-ignorance. When we imaginarily ignore or forget our real self, which is infinite being, consciousness and happiness, we seemingly separate ourself from the perfect happiness that is our own self. Therefore until we reunite with our own reality, which is absolute happiness, we cannot rest, except during the brief but necessary interludes that we experience in sleep, death and other such states, in which our mind subsides in a state of temporary abeyance or inactivity.

Because we have imaginarily separated ourself from our own infinite happiness, we feel perpetually dissatisfied, and hence our innate love for happiness impels us to search restlessly for the happiness that we have lost. Thus our natural love for happiness, which is our own true being, is seemingly distorted, manifesting in the form of desire, which impels us to be active, thereby driving ourself further away from our true state of being. Whereas true love is our natural state of just being, desire gives rise to 'doing' or activity, which distracts us from our essential being.

How does our love for happiness become distorted as desire? Having imaginarily separated ourself from our infinite real self, we now feel happiness to be something other than ourself, and therefore we seek it outside ourself in objects and experiences that we imagine to be other than ourself. In our natural state of true self-knowledge, we experience happiness as our own self, and hence our love for happiness impels us just to be ourself. In our imaginary state of self-ignorance, on the other hand, we experience happiness as if it were something other than ourself, and hence our simple love for happiness is distorted as innumerable desires for things other than ourself – for objects and experiences that we imagine will give us the happiness for which we crave.

Because our self-ignorance clouds our natural clarity of discrimination, it deludes us, making us imagine that in order to be happy we must obtain things other than ourself – whether material objects, sensual experiences or intellectual knowledge. We imagine that certain experiences will make us happy, and certain other experiences will make us unhappy, and hence we desire those experiences that we imagine will make us happy, and we fear or feel averse to those experiences that we imagine will make us unhappy.

Thus our self-ignorance inevitably gives rise to our desires and fears, which impel us to be constantly active, striving by mind, speech and body to experience the happiness for which we yearn so intensely. Until we attain the non-dual experience of true self-knowledge, thereby dissolving the illusion of self-ignorance and all its progeny, we will not be able to free ourself from the gripping vice of desire and fear.

Even when our mind subsides temporarily in a state of abeyance such as sleep or death, our deeply rooted desires and fears are not dissolved, because our basic self-ignorance persists in a dormant form. Therefore as soon as we are sufficiently rested, our dormant desires and fears rouse us from sleep, giving rise either to the experience of this waking state or to the experience of a dream.

All our dreams are caused by our latent desires and fears, and our present waking state is just one of our dreams. Just as all that we experience in a dream is our own thoughts, which are formed by our latent desires and fears, so all that we experience in our present waking state is our own thoughts, which are likewise formed by our latent desires and fears.

Since our present waking life is actually just a dream in our imaginary sleep of self-forgetfulness or self-ignorance, the state that we call death is merely the final termination of this particular dream. The entire life of our present body is one continuous dream, which is interrupted each day by a brief period of rest in sleep, but which resumes as soon as we have recuperated sufficient energy to engage in another period of mental activity. One feature of this dream is that the imaginary body that we now mistake to be ourself appears to grow gradually older and more worn out, until eventually we forsake it permanently. The state in which we thus permanently cease to imagine our present body to be ourself is what we generally call death.

Since death is just the ending of an extended dream, it is merely a state of abeyance or temporary subsidence of our mind, like the sleep that we experience every day. After we have rested for a while in sleep, our latent desires and fears impel our mind to rise and become active once again in another state of dream. Similarly, after we have rested for a while in death, our latent desires and fears impel our mind to rise once again in another state of activity, in which we imagine some other body to be ourself.

Therefore when Sri Ramana said, 'having taken innumerable births', he was referring to this repeated process of forsaking one dream body and imagining another dream body to be ourself. Rebirth or reincarnation is therefore not real, but is just a dream – an imaginary event that occurs repeatedly in our seemingly long sleep of imaginary self-ignorance.

Though rebirth is merely a figment of our imagination – a dream created by our own desires and fears – it is as real as our present life in this world, which is itself just as real as our mind, the limited and distorted form of consciousness that experiences this and so many other dreams. Until we know what we really are, thereby putting an end to our imaginary sleep of self-forgetfulness or self-ignorance, we will continue to experience one dream after another, and in each of those dreams we will mistake ourself to be a body that we have created by our own imagination.

Since the fundamental cause of all the suffering and lack of perfect happiness that we experience in this dream-life and so many other dream-lives is our imaginary self-forgetfulness or self-ignorance, we can end all our suffering and attain perfect happiness only by experiencing the absolute clarity of true self-knowledge. Since the illusion of duality is caused by our self-forgetfulness – our forgetfulness of our fundamental non-dual consciousness of our own infinite and absolute being – it will be dissolved only when we experience perfectly clear non-dual self-knowledge or self-consciousness.

By seemingly forgetting our real self, we enable ourself to imagine that we have become a body. Therefore though we have never really ceased to be our infinite real self, we do appear to have become something else. Hence in this first verse of *Ēkātma Pañcakam* Sri Ramana says that having forgotten our real self, having repeatedly imagined ourself to be a body, and having thereby seemingly taken birth in innumerable different bodies, when we finally know ourself we become ourself once again.

Though he says, '[…] finally knowing ourself [and thereby] becoming ourself […]', he does not mean to imply that the attainment of true self-knowledge is really a process of becoming. Relative to our present state of self-forgetfulness, in which we seem to have become a body and mind, the state of self-knowledge may appear to be a state in which we will once again become our real self, but in reality it is just our natural state of being, in which we remain as we always have been – that is, as our immutable real self.

The word that Sri Ramana actually uses in this verse is *ādal*, which is a gerund that primarily means 'becoming' but can also mean 'being'. Therefore, though the words '*iṟudi taṉṉai-y-uṇarndu tāṉ-ādal*', which form the subject of this verse, could be translated as 'finally knowing ourself [and thereby] becoming ourself', they can be translated more accurately as 'finally knowing ourself [and thereby just] being ourself'.

The state of true self-knowledge is our natural, eternal, immutable and non-dual state of self-conscious being. Since it is the absolute reality, which underlies the appearance of all relativity, it can never undergo any form of change or becoming. It never has become anything, and it never will become anything. It just is.

When we imagine that we know anything other than ourself, we seem to become something limited. However, such becoming is only imaginary. In reality, we always remain as we really are – that is, as infinite and absolute being, consciousness and happiness. Hence when we know ourself as we really are, we do not become anything, but simply remain as the infinite and absolute reality that we always have been and always will be. Therefore in verse 26 of *Upadēśa Undiyār* Sri Ramana says:

> Being [our real] self is indeed knowing [our real] self, because [our real] self is that which is devoid of two. [...]

Since we are the absolute reality, we are in truth devoid of any form of duality, and hence we can know ourself only by being ourself, which is what we always are. Therefore the state that we call self-knowledge is not a state in which we know anything new, but is only the state in which we shed all knowledge of everything other than ourself.

When we wake up from a dream, we do not become anything new or know anything new. We merely shed the imaginary experience of our dream, and remain as we previously were. Similarly, when we wake up from our imaginary sleep of self-forgetfulness, in which we have experienced innumerable dreams, we will not become anything new or know anything new. We will merely shed the imaginary experience of our self-forgetfulness and all our resulting dreams, and remain as the infinite and absolutely non-dual self-consciousness that we always have been.

Therefore Sri Ramana concludes this first verse of *Ēkātma Pañcakam* by saying:

> [...] finally knowing ourself [and] being ourself is just [like] waking from a dream of wandering about the world. See [thus].

When we wake up from a dream, we know that everything that we experienced in that dream was merely our own imagination, and was therefore entirely unreal. Similarly, when we attain the non-dual experience of true self-knowledge, we will know that everything that we experienced in this state of self-forgetfulness (including our self-forgetfulness itself) is merely our own imagination, and is therefore entirely unreal.

In our present experience, the only thing that is real is our own self-consciousness, 'I am'. If we did not exist, we could not know our own existence, nor could we imagine the existence of anything else.

The one real basis of all our knowledge and all our experience is our own consciousness. When we say 'I know' or 'I experience', we imply 'I am conscious'. However, though we sometimes appear to be conscious of things other than ourself, our consciousness of those other things appears and disappears. Being impermanent, it is only relatively real.

The only thing of which we are permanently conscious is ourself – our own being, 'I am'. Even when we are conscious of nothing else, as in sleep, we continue to be conscious of our own being, because our being is inherently self-conscious. In other words, we are self-consciousness, and hence we always experience ourself as 'I am'.

Since our consciousness of other things appears only when our mind is active, it is merely an imagination. But since we are the consciousness that experiences both that imagination and the absence of it in sleep, we are the real consciousness that underlies the imaginary consciousness of otherness.

Since the only form of consciousness that we experience permanently is our own self-consciousness, we can definitely conclude that it is the true and essential form of consciousness. In other words, since we are the fundamental self-consciousness that underlies the appearance of all other forms of consciousness, we alone are the true and essential form of consciousness.

We can also conclude that we are the absolute reality, because we are the fundamental non-dual self-consciousness 'I am', which is essentially unqualified and unconditioned, being free from all limits and any form of dependence upon any other thing. Whatever else may appear or disappear, and whatever change or other action may seem to happen, our essential self-consciousness always remains unchanged and unaffected. Therefore, whereas all other things are relative, our true self-consciousness is absolute.

We are absolute being, absolute consciousness and absolute happiness. Therefore if we wish to free ourself from all unhappiness and all forms of limitation, we must know ourself as we really are. That is, we must actually experience ourself as the absolute non-dual self-consciousness that we really are, and that we now understand ourself to be.

In order to know ourself thus, we must concentrate our entire attention upon our essential self-consciousness 'I am'. This concentration of our attention upon ourself is the practice of *ātma-vicāra* – self-investigation, self-examination, self-scrutiny or self-enquiry – which Sri Ramana taught as the only means by which we can experience true non-dual self-knowledge.

Before concluding this chapter, in which we have attempted to find a satisfactory theoretical answer to the crucial question 'who am I?', it is worth narrating an important event in the early life of Sri Ramana. The first person who asked him truly pertinent and useful questions was a humble and self-effacing devotee called Sri Sivaprakasam Pillai, who first came to him in 1901, when he was just twenty-one years old. The first question Sri Sivaprakasam Pillai asked him was 'Who am I?', to which he replied simply, 'Knowledge [or consciousness] alone is I'.

The actual Tamil words spoken by Sri Sivaprakasam Pillai were '*nāṉ yār?*', which literally mean 'I [am] who?', and the words that Sri Ramana, who seldom spoke in those early times, wrote in reply with his finger on the sandy ground were '*aṟivē nāṉ*'. The Tamil word *aṟivu* means 'knowledge' in the broadest sense, and is therefore used to denote many different forms of knowledge, including consciousness, wisdom, intelligence, learning, sense perception, anything that is known, and even *ātmā*, our real self, which is our fundamental knowledge 'I am'. In this context, however, it means only our fundamental knowledge 'I am' – our essential consciousness of our own being. The letter *ē* that he appended to *aṟivu* is a suffix that is commonly used in Tamil to add emphasis to a word, conveying the sense 'itself', 'alone' or 'indeed', and the word *nāṉ* means 'I'.

In these two simple words, *aṟivē nāṉ*, Sri Ramana summarised the essence of his experience of true self-knowledge, which is the basis of the entire philosophy and science that he taught. What he meant by these simple words is that our true and essential nature is only our fundamental knowledge or consciousness 'I am', which is the conclusion that we have to arrive at if we critically analyse our experience of ourself in our three ordinary states of consciousness, as we have done in this chapter.

The next question that Sri Sivaprakasam Pillai asked him was 'What is the nature of [such] knowledge?', to which he replied either 'The nature of knowledge is *sat-cit-ānanda*' or more probably just '*sat-cit-ānanda*'. The compound word *sat-cit-ānanda* (which is actually fused into one word, *saccidānanda*), is a well-known philosophical term, which is of Sanskrit origin, but which is widely understood and frequently used in Tamil and all other Indian languages. It is a term used to describe the nature of the absolute reality, and though it is composed of three words, it is not intended to imply that the absolute reality is composed of three distinct elements, but only that the single non-dual nature of the one absolute reality can be described in three different ways.

The word *sat* basically means 'being' or 'existing', but by extension also means 'that which really is', 'reality', 'truth', 'existence', 'essence', 'real', 'true', 'good', 'right', or 'that which is real, true, good or right'. The word *cit* means 'consciousness' or 'awareness', from a verbal root meaning 'to know', 'to be conscious of', 'to perceive', 'to observe', 'to attend to' or 'to be attentive'. And the word *ānanda* means 'happiness', 'joy' or 'bliss'. Thus *saccidānanda*, or as it is more commonly spelt in roman script, *sat-cit-ānanda*, means 'being-consciousness-bliss', that is, being which is both consciousness and bliss, or consciousness which is both being and bliss, or bliss which is both being and consciousness.

True being and true consciousness are not two different things. If consciousness were not the essential nature of being, being would have to depend upon some consciousness other than itself in order to be known, and hence it would not be absolute being, but only relative being – being that existed only in the view of some other existing consciousness.

If we postulate that there is an absolute being that is not conscious of its own existence, and that exists even though it is not known either by itself or by any consciousness other than itself, such a being would be a mere supposition or imagination – a being that exists only in our own mind – and hence it would not be real being. We have no valid reason to suppose that any such unknown being exists. The term 'being' or 'existence' has a valid meaning only if it is applied to something that is known to exist, and not if it is applied to something whose existence is merely imaginary. Therefore true and absolute being must always be conscious of its own being, and hence consciousness must be its very nature.

Similarly, the very nature of consciousness must be being, because if being were not the essential nature of consciousness, consciousness would not be – it would not exist. A non-existent consciousness, a consciousness that is not, would have absolutely no reality. It would be nothing, and hence it would not be conscious. To be conscious means to be, just as to be truly means to be conscious – to know that 'I am'.

True and absolute being, being that exists unconditionally and independent of any other thing, must be self-conscious being, being that knows 'I am'. Though it does not know any other thing, because there is nothing other than it for it to know, it must always know itself. Therefore the consciousness that knows its own being as 'I am' is the only true, independent, unconditional and absolute being. Any other being, any being that does not know itself as 'I am', is merely a figment of our imagination.

Since in its essential nature being or consciousness has no form, it is devoid of limits, and includes everything within itself. Since a thing can be said to be a thing only if it is, nothing exists separate from or other than being. Everything that exists is therefore in its essential nature just being.

Though a thing can be said to be only if it is known to be, most things do not actually know their own being. A thing that does not know that it is, and that is known only by some consciousness that is seemingly other than itself, does not exist independently or absolutely. Its seeming existence as a 'thing' is only relative. Therefore it is not real as the 'thing' that it appears to be, but is real only as the mere 'being' that is its essence.

The only 'thing' that is real as such is consciousness, because only consciousness knows its own being. Therefore, since being is the essential nature of everything, and since being is always conscious of its own being, anything that does not know 'I am' is a mere imagination – an illusion, an apparition that, though unreal as the thing that it appears to be, is nevertheless real in its essential nature as mere being.

Though being has no form of its own, it is the indefinable essence of all forms. Being essentially formless, being is devoid of all forms of limitation, and hence it is infinite. Since the infinite includes all things within itself, it is essentially single and non-dual. There cannot be more than one infinite reality, because if there were, none of those 'infinite realities' would actually be infinite. Being is therefore the non-dual infinite whole – the totality of all that is.

However, though being is infinite and non-dual in itself, it nevertheless includes within itself all that is finite and dual. Though duality appears to exist in being, it is not the essential nature of being, but is a mere illusion. It is an illusory form of being, an imagination that appears and disappears in being, yet does not affect the essential, formless, infinite and non-dual nature of being even in the least. However, though it is an illusory imagination, duality could not even appear to exist without the underlying support of the essential, infinite and non-dual being.

Just as being is non-dual, so the consciousness of being is non-dual, because it knows only its own being and nothing else. The consciousness that appears to know things that it imagines to be other than itself is not the infinite, absolute and therefore real consciousness, but is only a finite, relative and therefore unreal form of consciousness.

Just as any finite, relative or dual form of being is not the true and essential nature of being, so any finite, relative or dual form of consciousness is not the true and essential nature of consciousness. Therefore the compound word *sat-cit* denotes only the real and essential being-consciousness, which is completely unconditional, independent, non-dual, infinite and absolute.

Just as the essential, absolute and infinite reality is both being and the consciousness of being, so it is also perfect happiness or bliss. Unhappiness is not a natural condition, any more than either non-existence or unconsciousness is natural. Non-existence, unconsciousness and unhappiness are not in any way absolute, but are merely relative conditions that appear to arise only when we mistake ourself to be the finite form of a physical body.

In sleep, when we do not mistake ourself to be a body or any other finite thing, we exist happily knowing only our own being. Our being, our consciousness of being, and the happiness that we enjoy when we are conscious only of our being, are therefore our essential nature. When everything else is taken away from us, what remains is only our essential nature, and that is our perfectly peaceful and happy consciousness of our own being, 'I am'. Unhappiness is an unnatural and therefore unreal condition that appears to arise only when by our power of imagination we superimpose some other knowledge upon our fundamental and essential knowledge 'I am'.

Therefore, as Sri Ramana stated in answer to the second question of Sri Sivaprakasam Pillai, the nature of our fundamental knowledge 'I am' is *sat-cit-ānanda* or 'being-consciousness-bliss'. This does not mean that our true nature, which we always experience as 'I am', is any relative or finite form of being, consciousness or happiness, but only that it is absolute, infinite, eternal, immutable, undivided and non-dual being-consciousness-bliss, as Sri Ramana states explicitly in verse 28 of *Upadēśa Undiyār* and verse 18 of *Upadēśa Taṉippākkaḷ*:

> If we know what our [real] nature is, then [we will discover it to be] beginningless, endless [and] unbroken *sat-cit-ānanda* [being-consciousness-bliss].
>
> If we know our real form in [our] heart [in the innermost core or depth of our being], [we will discover it to be] being-consciousness-bliss, which is fullness [infinite wholeness, completeness or perfection] without beginning [or] end.

Though these two verses express the actual truth experienced by Sri Ramana and all other real sages, the idea that we ourself are the infinite and absolute reality may appear to many of us to be fanciful and far-fetched. Though by critically analysing our experience of ourself in our three ordinary states of consciousness, as we did earlier in this chapter, we may have been convinced that in essence we are nothing other than our fundamental consciousness of being, 'I am', we may still find it hard to comprehend the fact that our fundamental consciousness or knowledge 'I am', which is our real self, is in truth the infinite and absolute reality. Let us therefore examine this idea more closely in order to ascertain whether or not we have any reasonable grounds for believing it to be the truth.

Because sages experience this truth as their own real nature, they do not need any philosophical analysis or theoretical arguments to convince them that it is the truth, but for those of us who mistake ourself to be a finite individual, a clear understanding of the rationality of this idea is necessary to convince us that it is the truth, and that it is the one and only experience that is truly worthy for us to make effort to attain. Let us therefore see what reasonable grounds we may have, if any, to conclude that we are in truth the infinite and absolute reality.

Assuming that we have all been convinced by our earlier analysis that our essential nature is only our basic self-consciousness – our fundamental consciousness of our own being, 'I am' – let us take that conclusion as our starting point. Unlike our mind, our superficial 'knowing consciousness', which always mistakes itself to be a particular body, our real self, our fundamental 'being consciousness', does not mistake itself to be any particular thing, and hence it has no particular form or dimension. Therefore, whereas our mind has limited itself within the dimensions of time and space by identifying itself with a finite body, our real consciousness of being is not limited in any way.

In sleep, when we cease to mistake ourself to be a finite body, we do not feel that we exist in any particular time or place, but feel only 'I am'. The limits of time and space are ideas that arise only when we imagine ourself to be a particular body in either waking or dream.

Even now in this waking state, if we try for a moment to ignore our body and mind and to be conscious only of our own being, 'I am', we will be able to recognise that our consciousness 'I am' is not something that is limited within the bounds of our physical body. It just is, and is not something that can be located at any particular point in time or space.

Even when we identify ourself with a body and therefore feel ourself to be located at a particular point in time and space, we always know 'I am'. Our consciousness or knowledge 'I am' is therefore unaffected by any changes in time and space. It exists unconditionally, and since it exists in all our three states of consciousness, it exists independent of any body, and therefore independent of time and space.

Just as the time and space that we perceive in a dream are both ideas that exist only in our own mind, so the time and space that we perceive in our present waking state are likewise both ideas that exist only in our own mind. When our mind subsides, as in sleep, time and space both cease to exist, or at least they disappear and are no longer known by us. Therefore, since we have no reason to suppose that they exist in any way independent of or separate from the idea or mental image that we have of them, we can reasonably hypothesise that they are both mere thoughts, a fact that is confirmed by Sri Ramana and other sages. Since time and space as we know them arise only in our mind, and since our mind rises only in our fundamental being-consciousness 'I am', is it not reasonable for us to infer that our being-consciousness transcends both time and space?

Just as it transcends time and space, it transcends every other imaginable dimension. Only that which has a particular definable form, and which therefore occupies a distinct and definable extent in one or more dimensions, can be said to be limited or finite. But since our fundamental and essential being-consciousness 'I am' has no definable form or extent, it is not limited in any way, and is therefore infinite. Since everything that we know arises in our mind, and since our mind arises in our being-consciousness, all finite things are contained in our infinite being-consciousness, 'I am'.

So long as we do not imagine ourself to be a body or any other object that seems to appear in our consciousness, we are infinite. Our being and our consciousness of being are both infinite, or to be more precise, they are both the one infinite and non-dual reality. Since our being is infinite, nothing can be separate from it, and hence it alone truly exists.

However, when we imagine ourself to be a body, innumerable other objects seem to arise in our consciousness, and we imagine that each of them truly exists. Thus by our power of imagination we give a seeming being or reality to many things, and thereby we delude ourself into believing that each thing has its own independent and finite being.

In reality, however, nothing has an independent or separate being. Being is not a finite thing that can be divided into parts, but is the one infinite and therefore indivisible whole, other than which nothing can be. Since it is infinite, it includes everything within itself, and hence it is the one essential being of each and every thing. No particular thing is real as the particular thing that it appears to be – as its particular form, or as the particular name, description or definition that we give to its form – but is real only as the being that it essentially is. Other than being, nothing is.

Since we always know ourself as 'I am', our essential being is itself our consciousness of our being. Our consciousness of our being, our knowledge 'I am', is the one fundamental basis of all our other knowledge. If we did not know 'I am', we could not know any other thing. Whatever we may know, we know it only because we first know our own being as 'I am'. Therefore our fundamental knowledge 'I am' – our real and essential self-consciousness or being-consciousness – is the true foundation that underlies and supports the seeming existence of all other things.

Without depending upon the support of our being, nothing else could appear to be. All other things appear to be only because we are. We are therefore the one fundamental and absolute being, other than which nothing is. Since nothing is other than us, we are infinite, and include all things within ourself – that is, within our own self-conscious being. We are therefore the one non-dual and infinite being.

Because the one non-dual and infinite being is our own essential self, which we always experience as 'I am', we refer to it as 'our own' being. However, though we have no real being other than the one infinite reality, is it correct for us to consider it to be just 'our' being? Since it is the only being that really is, is it not the essential being of all things – of everything that appears to exist?

Yes, to the extent that 'things' exist, they do all share in the one common being of the infinite reality. However, there is a fundamental difference between the being that we imagine we see in other things and the being that we experience in ourself.

All the things that we know as other than ourself are only thoughts or mental images that exist in our own mind, and therefore they are known not by themselves but only by our mind. But whereas other things are not conscious of their own being, we are conscious of our own being. Therefore, though in other things we know only being, in ourself we know both being and consciousness.

The consciousness that we imagine we see in other people and in other creatures is not actually experienced by us, but is only inferred by us, just as we infer that each person and creature that we see in a dream has consciousness. The only consciousness that we know directly and not by mere inference is our own consciousness. Since we know that our consciousness is, and since we do not exist apart from our consciousness, our consciousness is itself our being, and hence we experience it as 'I am'.

Just as the consciousness that we see in all other people and creatures is only inferred by us, so the being that we see in all other things is only inferred by us. The only being we know directly is our own being. The being or existence of all other things is known by us not directly but only through the imperfect channel of our mind, our limited and distorted consciousness that feels 'I am this body'. The seemingly separate being or existence of other things deludes us and reinforces in our mind the illusion that being or reality is divided, mutable and relative.

The seemingly separate being of other things depends upon the seemingly separate being of our mind, because it is known only by our mind, and not by our essential non-dual consciousness of being, which knows only itself and no separateness or otherness. The seemingly separate being of our mind depends upon the real being of our essential consciousness 'I am', because without identifying that real consciousness as itself our mind would not appear to know either its own being or the being of any other thing.

However, since it appears and disappears, the separate being or existence of our mind is not real being, but is only a semblance of real being. A thing that appears to be at one time, and ceases to be at some other time, is not real being, but is only a seeming form of being – a being which depends upon time and is therefore conditional. If a thing really is, it must be at all times and under all conditions.

The only being that is at all times and under all conditions is our own essential being, which we always know as 'I am'. Not only does it exist at all times and under all conditions, but it also exists immutably, without ever undergoing any change. In contrast, the being of all other things appears and disappears, and constantly undergoes change. Moreover, unlike all other things, our own essential being always knows itself, and does not depend upon any other thing to be known. Therefore it is the only being that really is.

Since the being of all other things is not real but is only an illusion or apparition, and since the only real being is our own essential being, 'I am', real being is in fact never divided, even though it appears to be divided as many separate 'beings' – as the separate being of each of the many different things that appear to be. Our own real and essential being is always single, non-dual and indivisible, and since nothing exists apart from it, it is infinite and includes all things within itself.

Therefore what Sri Ramana and other sages tell us about their experience of true self-knowledge, namely that they know themself to be the one and only truly existing reality, whose nature is beginningless, endless, eternal, undivided, non-dual and infinite being, consciousness and bliss, is not as fanciful and far-fetched as it may initially appear to be.

What they experience as the truth of their own real self or being is also the truth of our own real self or being, because our being is no different from their being. We appear to be separate from them only because we mistake ourself to be a finite body, but even when we mistake ourself to be such, we still know our essential being as 'I am'. In reality, therefore, what each and every one of us experiences as 'I am' is the one eternal, undivided, non-dual and infinite being.

The fundamental difference between the experience of sages such as Sri Ramana, who know themself to be the one infinite and undivided self-conscious being, and the experience of those of us who imagine ourself to be anything other than this one infinite and undivided self-conscious being, which is our true and essential self, lies only in the limitations that we imaginarily superimpose upon our truly infinite being. This fundamental difference is expressed by Sri Ramana in verses 17 and 18 of *Uḷḷadu Nāṟpadu*:

> [Both] to those who do not know themself [and] to those who have known themself, the body [is] indeed 'I'. [However] to those who do not know themself 'I' [is limited to] only the extent of the body, [whereas] to those who have known themself within the body 'I' itself shines devoid of limit [boundary or extent]. Understand that this indeed is the difference between them.
>
> [Both] to those who do not have knowledge [that is, true self-knowledge] [and] to those who do have [true self-knowledge], the world is the reality. [However] to those who do not know [themself] the reality is [limited to] the extent of the world, [whereas] to those who have known [themself] the reality abides [or pervades] devoid of form as the *ādhāra* [support, substratum, foundation or base] to [the imaginary appearance of] the world. Understand [that] this is the difference between them.

That which limits a finite thing is only its form, because its form defines its extent in time and space, and thereby separates it from all other forms. If we are a definite form, we are limited within the confines or extent of that form, but if we have no definite form, we are unlimited or infinite.

Because we imagine ourself to be the form of this body, we have seemingly limited ourself within a certain extent of time and space, and hence we feel ourself to be separate from everything that exists outside this limited extent of time or space. Moreover, because we imagine the form of this body to be 'I', we mistake it to be real, and hence we mistake all the other forms that we perceive outside this body to be real.

Since Sri Ramana and other sages teach us that we are not the body that we imagine ourself to be, and that the world is not real as we imagine it to be, it is reasonable for us to infer that such sages do not experience their body as 'I' or this world as real. Why then does Sri Ramana say in these two verses that to sages, who are those who have known themself as they really are, their body is 'I' and the world is real?

To understand why he says this, we have to understand the exact meaning of what he says in the second half of each of these two verses. In verse 17 he says that for sages 'I' shines devoid of any limit, boundary or extent, thereby implying that in their experience 'I' is the infinite reality that is the essence or true substance of everything, including this body. Similarly, in verse 18 he says that for sages the reality is the formless substratum, foundation or base that supports the world, thereby implying once again that in their experience the reality is the one essence or true substance that underlies everything, including all the manifold forms of this world.

That is, since our true self or real 'I' is the infinite reality, nothing can be separate from or other than it. Therefore it alone truly exists, and whatever else appears to exist is not anything other than it, but is just an imaginary form that it appears to be. Since neither our body nor this world can have any reality other than our own consciousness, in which they appear as thoughts or mental images, they are in essence nothing but our own consciousness.

Since sages experience only the absolute reality, which is infinite, indivisible and therefore perfectly non-dual self-conscious being, they do not experience any forms or any limitations. They know only the formless and limitless reality, which is their own true self.

Since they know that the one real 'I' alone is, they know that there is nothing that is not 'I' or not real. Hence from their absolute non-dual perspective, they say that everything is 'I' and is therefore real. That is, since they do not experience this body or world as limited forms but only as their own formless and therefore unlimited reality, they say that this body is 'I' and this world is real.

Therefore, when Sri Ramana says that for sages this body is 'I' and this world is real, he does not mean that our body as such is 'I' or this world as such is real, but only that as our own formless and limitless real self, which is their true essence and sole reality, they are both 'I' and real.

Therefore what Sri Ramana is affirming in these two verses is not the reality of the limited forms of this body and world, but is only the reality of our own essential formless and therefore infinite being, which always experiences itself and nothing other than itself.

Though we are infinite and absolute being, we do not know ourself as such because we ignore our essential being and imagine ourself to be a finite body. So habituated have we become to ignoring our own being that even in sleep, when we cease imagining ourself to be a body, and therefore cease knowing any other thing, we appear to be ignorant of the real nature of our essential being, 'I am'.

However, though we appear to be ignorant of our real nature in all our three states of consciousness, in truth our essential being always knows itself clearly as the infinite, absolute and non-dual consciousness 'I am'. Our essential being never ignores or is ignorant of our real nature. That which is ignorant of our real nature is only our mind, and therefore we appear to be ignorant of our real nature only because we imagine ourself to be our mind.

Since our self-ignorance is therefore not real but only imaginary, in order to put an end to it all we need do is cultivate the habit of remembering or being attentive to our own essential being, 'I am'. As Sri Ramana says in the eleventh paragraph of *Nāṉ Yār?*:

> […] If one clings firmly to uninterrupted *svarūpa-smaraṇa* [remembrance of one's own essential nature or real self, 'I am'] until one attains *svarūpa* [that is, until one attains true knowledge of one's own essential nature], that alone [will be] sufficient. […]

In this one sentence, Sri Ramana encapsulates the empirical method of *ātma-vicāra* or self-investigation, which is the only means by which we can attain true self-knowledge – true experiential knowledge of our own real nature. Since we appear not to know the true nature of our essential being, our own real self, only because of our long-established habit of ignoring it, we can know it only by cultivating the opposite habit of constantly remembering or being attentive to it.

In practice we may initially be unable to remember our being-consciousness 'I am' uninterruptedly, but by remembering it repeatedly and frequently, we can gradually cultivate the habit of remembering it even while we are engaged in other activities. Whatever we may be doing or thinking, we *are*, and therefore we can remember our 'being' even while we seem to be 'doing'. As we become more accustomed to remembering our being, we will find that we remember it more frequently and easily, in spite of any amount of distracting external influences.

As our self-remembrance thus becomes more firmly established, our clarity of self-consciousness will gradually increase, until finally we are able to experience and know our essential being with full and perfect clarity. When we once experience ourself as we really are, our delusion of self-ignorance will be destroyed, and thus we will discover that we are nothing but our own real and essential being, which always knows itself with perfect and ever-unfading clarity.

Since we have examined in so much detail Sri Ramana's replies to the first two questions that Sri Sivaprakasam Pillai asked him, it is appropriate to mention here another fact that is related to them. Following on from his first two questions, Sri Sivaprakasam Pillai asked Sri Ramana many other questions, and Sri Ramana answered most of them by writing either on the sandy ground, or on a slate or slips of paper that Sri Sivaprakasam Pillai gave him. Sri Sivaprakasam Pillai copied many of these questions and answers in a notebook, and more than twenty years later he was requested by other devotees to publish them as a small booklet. The first edition of this booklet was published in 1923 under the title *Nāṉ Yār?*, which means 'Who am I?', or more precisely 'I [am] Who?'.

Before its publication, a draft of this booklet was shown to Sri Ramana for his approval, and when he read it he noticed that Sri Sivaprakasam Pillai had expanded his original answer to the first question, adding a detailed list of things that we mistake ourself to be, but that in fact we are not. On seeing this, he remarked that he had not answered in such a detailed manner, but then explained that, because Sri Sivaprakasam Pillai was familiar with *nēti nēti*, he had added such detail thinking that it would help him to understand his answer more clearly.

By the term *nēti nēti*, Sri Ramana meant the rational process of self-analysis described in the ancient texts of *vēdānta*, a process that involves the analytical elimination or denial of everything that is not 'I'. The word *nēti* is a compound of two words, *na*, which means 'not', and *iti*, which means 'thus', and hence *nēti nēti* literally means 'not thus, not thus'. The ancient texts of *vēdānta* use these words *nēti nēti* when explaining the rational basis for the theory that our body, our senses, our life-force, our mind and even the ignorance that we seemingly experience in sleep are all not 'I'.

During the ten years or so that followed the first publication of *Nāṉ Yār?* various versions of it were published, and various other versions of it exist in manuscript form in the notebooks of Sri Sivaprakasam Pillai. Each of these versions has a different number of questions and answers, with slight variation in their actual wording, and with a varying amount of content in some particular answers. The standard and most authentic version, however, is the essay version that Sri Ramana himself wrote a few years after the first version was published.

Sri Ramana formed this essay version, which consists of twenty paragraphs, by rewriting the first published question and answer version, and possibly by drawing on some of the other versions, and while doing so he made several improvements, removing all but the first question, rearranging the order in which the ideas in his answers were presented, and making some changes to the actual wordings.

Of all the changes he made, the most significant was to add an entirely new paragraph at the beginning of the essay. This opening paragraph, a translation of which is given in the previous chapter of this book, serves as a suitable introduction to the subject 'Who am I?', because it explains that the reason why we need to know who we are is that happiness is our real nature, and that we can therefore experience true and perfect happiness only by knowing ourself as we really are.

However, though he made such changes, out of respect for Sri Sivaprakasam Pillai he did not remove the detailed *nēti nēti* portion that he had inserted, but instead simply instructed that the first question and the actual words of his first two answers should be printed in bold type in order to distinguish them from the inserted portion. The first question, the inserted portion and Sri Ramana's first two answers together constitute the second paragraph, the meaning of which is as follows:

> **Who am I?** The *sthūla dēha* [the 'gross' or physical body], which is [composed] of the *sapta dhātus* [the seven constituents, namely chyle, blood, flesh, fat, marrow, bone and semen], is not 'I'. The five *jñānēndriyas* [sense organs], namely the ears, skin, eyes, tongue and nose, which individually [and respectively] know the five *viṣayas* [sense 'domains' or types of sense perception], namely sound, touch [texture and other qualities perceived by touch], form [shape, colour and other qualities perceived by sight], taste and smell, are also not 'I'. The five *karmēndriyas* [organs of action], namely the vocal cords, feet [or legs], hands [or arms], anus and genitals, which [respectively] do the five actions, namely speaking, walking, holding [or giving], defecation and [sexual] enjoyment, are also not 'I'. The *pañca vāyus* [the five 'winds', 'vital airs' or metabolic forces], beginning with *prāṇa* [breath], which perform the five [metabolic] functions, beginning with respiration, are also not 'I'. The mind, which thinks, is also not 'I'. The ignorance [the absence of all dualistic knowledge] that is combined with only *viṣaya-vāsanās* [latent inclinations, impulsions, desires, liking or taste for sense perceptions or sense enjoyments] when all sense perceptions and all actions have been severed [as in sleep], is also not 'I'. Having done *nēti* [negation, elimination or denial of whatever is not ourself by thinking] that all the abovesaid things are not 'I', not 'I', the **knowledge** that [then] stands detached **alone is 'I'. The nature of** [this] **knowledge** ['I am'] **is *sat-cit-ānanda*** [being-consciousness-bliss].

The qualification of the word 'knowledge' by the addition of the defining clause 'that stands detached [separated or alone] having done *nēti* [by thinking] that all the abovesaid things are not I, not I' is potentially misleading, because it could create the impression that simply by thinking *nēti nēti*, 'not thus, not thus' or 'this is not I, this is not I', we can detach our essential consciousness or knowledge 'I am' from everything with which we now confuse it. In fact, many scholars who attempt to explain the ancient texts of *vēdānta*, which often describe this process of *nēti nēti* or negation of all that is not our real self, interpret it to be the actual means by which we can attain self-knowledge. However, the sages who first taught the rational process of self-analysis called *nēti nēti* did not intend it to be understood as the actual technique of practical or empirical research, but only as the theoretical basis upon which the empirical technique of *ātma-vicāra* or self-investigation should be based.

The rational and analytical process which is described in the ancient texts of *vēdānta* as *nēti nēti* or 'not thus, not thus' is essentially the same as the logical analysis of our experience of ourself that we described earlier in this chapter. If we did not first critically analyse our experience of ourself in this manner, we would not be able to understand either the reason why we should seek true self-knowledge, or what exactly we should scrutinise in order to know our real self.

So long as we imagine that we are really our physical body, our thinking mind or any other object, we will imagine that we can know ourself by attending to such things, and hence we will not be able to understand what is really meant by the terms *ātma-vicāra*, self-investigation, self-examination, self-scrutiny, self-enquiry, self-attention, self-attentiveness or self-remembrance. Only when we understand the essential theory that we are nothing other than our fundamental non-dual self-consciousness – our adjunct-free consciousness of our own mere being, which we experience just as 'I am' and not as 'I am this' – will we be able to understand what actually is the 'self' or 'I' that we should scrutinise or attend to.

Once we have understood that we are truly not our physical body, our thinking mind or any other object known by us, we should not continue thinking, 'this body is not I', 'this mind is not I', and so on, but should withdraw our attention from all such things, and focus it wholly and exclusively upon our real and essential being. We cannot know our real self by thinking of anything that is not 'I', but only by investigating, scrutinising or attending keenly to that which is really 'I' – to that which we really are, to our essential being. Unless we withdraw our attention entirely from all other things, we will not be able to focus it wholly and exclusively upon our essential being, which we always experience as 'I am', and unless we focus it thus upon our essential being, we will not be able to attain the non-dual experience of true self-knowledge.

For those of us who happen to be familiar with all the concepts and terminology of ancient Indian philosophy and science, the portion added by

Sri Sivaprakasam Pillai may appear to be of some use as an aid to understanding Sri Ramana's simple answer, 'Knowledge alone is I'. However, the presentation and wording of this added portion does not truly reflect Sri Ramana's natural style of teaching, or his usual choice of words.

His natural style was always to answer questions briefly, simply and to the point. Unless he was talking to someone whose mind was already steeped in the complex and often obscure concepts and terminology of traditional *vēdānta*, he generally avoided using such concepts and terminology, and instead used only simple Tamil words, or words borrowed from Sanskrit whose meaning was clear and straightforward. Since many people who came to him were not well versed in traditional *vēdāntic* or *yōgic* concepts, he avoided as far as possible cluttering and burdening their minds with such concepts, except for a few that were really useful and pertinent.

In particular, he avoided all the detailed descriptions and classifications of the 'non-self' – whatever is not our real self –, which are given in many traditional texts. As he writes in the seventeenth paragraph of *Nāṉ Yār?*:

> Just as no benefit [is to be gained] by a person, who should sweep up and throw away rubbish, scrutinising it, so no benefit [is to be gained] by a person, who should know [his or her real] self, calculating that the *tattvas*, which are concealing [our real] self, are this many, and scrutinising their qualities, instead of gathering up and rejecting all of them. It is necessary [for us] to consider the world [which is composed of these *tattvas*] like a dream.

That is, in plainer English, just as we would derive no benefit by scrutinising a mass of rubbish, instead of just sweeping it up and throwing it away, so we will derive no benefit by enumerating and investigating the nature of the *tattvas*, which constitute all that is 'non-self' and which therefore obscure our knowledge of our real self, instead of rejecting all of them and thereby knowing our real self, which is the one true being or essential substance that underlies their imaginary appearance.

The word *tattva*, whose etymological meaning is 'it-ness' or 'that-ness', basically means that which is real, true and essential, the 'reality', 'truth' or 'essence', but it is commonly used to mean any basic element or constituent quality that is considered to be real. In this context, therefore, the plural term *tattvas* denotes all the ontological principles – the basic elements, essential components or abstract qualities of which all things are supposed to be made. The various schools of Indian philosophy each give their own classification of these so-called *tattvas*, and each reckon that there are a different number of them, a number that usually does not exceed thirty-six.

However, though some of them may use a different word to describe it, most of these schools agree that the original and fundamental *tattva* is *paramātman*, the 'supreme self' or 'transcendent spirit', which is also called *puruṣa*, the primal 'person' or 'spirit'. This *puruṣa* or *paramātman* is in fact our own real self, our own spirit or essential self-conscious being, which we always experience as 'I am'. Since this primal spirit 'I am' is the only *tattva* that exists permanently, without either appearing or disappearing, it is the only real *tattva*.

That is why in verse 43 of *Śrī Aruṇācala Akṣaramaṇamālai* Sri Ramana prays to Arunachala, who is our real self in its function as *guru*, the power of grace that bestows true self-knowledge:

> *tāṉē tāṉē tattuvam idaṉai-t*
> *tāṉē kaṭṭuvāy aruṇācalā*

The Tamil word *tāṉ* is a singular reflexive pronoun meaning 'oneself', 'myself', 'itself', 'yourself' and so on, and the letter *ē* that is appended to it is an emphatic suffix that conveys the sense 'itself', 'alone' or 'indeed'. Thus the meaning of this quintessential prayer is:

> Myself itself alone is *tattva* [the reality]. Show this [to me] yourself, Arunachala.

Our real self is the only truly existing *tattva*, the one non-dual, infinite and absolute reality, and we can know this only when it shows itself to us, which it does by drawing our mind or power of attention inwards, towards itself, thereby dissolving us and absorbing us as one with itself, our own essential being. So long as we pay even the least attention to anything other than our essential being, we cannot know ourself as we really are.

Since all the other so-called *tattvas* – which include our intellect, our ego, our mind, our five sense-organs, our five organs of action, the five *tanmātras*, which are the subtle essences of each of the five forms of sense perception, namely sound, touch, form, taste and smell, and the five elements, namely space, air, water, fire and earth – appear and disappear, they are merely ephemeral apparitions or illusions, and hence they are not real *tattvas*. Since the world is composed of these ephemeral and illusory *tattvas*, it is itself a mere illusion, and therefore Sri Ramana concludes the seventeenth paragraph of *Nāṉ Yār?* by saying that we should consider it to be a mere dream. Hence, since our body is a part of this illusory and dream-like world, we should consider it likewise to be merely an unreal illusion, a product of our own power of imagination.

Since none of these other *tattvas* are real, neither they nor anything composed of them can be our true self, and therefore we should not waste our time and energy thinking about them, enumerating them, classifying them or examining their properties, but should ignore them entirely and instead attend only to our real 'I' – our fundamental and essential consciousness of our own true being. The only need we have to consider our body, our mind and all our other adjuncts is to understand the fact that they are unreal, and are therefore not 'I'.

Hence in verse 22 of *Upadēśa Undiyār* Sri Ramana briefly states the essential conclusion that we should arrive at by means of the rational process of self-analysis, which in the ancient texts of *advaita vēdānta* is called *nēti nēti* or 'not thus, not thus':

> Since [our] body, mind, intellect, life and darkness [the seeming absence of knowledge that we experience in sleep] are all *jaḍa* [inconscient] and *asat* [unreal or non-existent], [they are] not 'I', which is [*cit* or consciousness and] *sat* [being or reality].

The five objects that Sri Ramana declares in this verse to be not 'I', namely our body, mind, intellect, life and darkness, are generally known in *vēdānta* as the *pañca-kōśas* or 'five sheaths', because they are the five adjuncts that seemingly cover and obscure our consciousness of our real self. These five adjuncts or 'sheaths' are the *annamaya kōśa* or 'sheath composed of food', which is our physical body, the *prāṇamaya kōśa* or 'sheath composed of *prāṇa*, life, vitality or breath', which is the life-force that animates our physical body, the *manōmaya kōśa* or 'sheath composed of mind', which is our mind or faculty of mentation and cognition, the *vijñānamaya kōśa* or 'sheath composed of discriminative knowledge', which is our intellect or faculty of discernment or judgement, and the *ānandamaya kōśa* or 'sheath composed of happiness', which is the happy but seemingly unconscious form in which we experience ourself in sleep.

However, instead of using these technical Sanskrit terms to denote these five adjuncts, Sri Ramana used five simple Tamil words, which literally mean body, mind, intellect, life and darkness. The word *uḍal* or 'body' here denotes our physical body or *annamaya kōśa*, the word *poṟi*, which usually means 'sense organ', here denotes our mind or *manōmaya kōśa*, the word *uḷḷam*, which usually means 'heart' or 'mind', here denotes our intellect or *vijñānamaya kōśa*, the word *uyir* or 'life' denotes our life-force or *prāṇamaya kōśa*, and the word *iruḷ* or 'darkness' denotes our *ānandamaya kōśa*, the blissful absence of objective knowledge that we experience in sleep.

However, what is important in this verse is not the terms that are used to denote these adjuncts that we imagine to be ourself, but is the conclusion that they are not actually our real self. Our real self is *sat* and *cit*, being and consciousness, whereas our body, our life-force, our mind, our intellect and the seeming darkness of sleep are all *asat* and *jaḍa*, that is, they have no real being or consciousness of their own. They appear to exist only when we know them, and we do not know any of them in all our three normal states of consciousness.

Of these five adjuncts, we experience our mind and intellect, which are actually just two functions of the one individual consciousness that we generally call our mind or ego, in both waking and dream, but not in sleep. We experience our present physical body and the life-force within it only in this waking state, and in each of our other states of dream we experience some other physical body and its corresponding life-force. And we experience the fifth adjunct, the seeming darkness of sleep, only in sleep.

Therefore, since we experience none of these five adjuncts in all our three states of consciousness, they cannot be our real self. They are not our real being, or our real consciousness. They are merely impostors – phantoms that we imagine to be ourself for a short period of time, but from which we are able to separate ourself at other times. Independent of our real self-conscious being, 'I am', they do not exist, nor do they know their own existence.

Though our mind may appear to be conscious of itself now, it is not conscious of itself at all times and in all states. Its seeming self-consciousness is therefore not inherent in it, and hence is not real. It borrows its seeming self-consciousness from our real self-consciousness, which alone is conscious of itself at all times and in all states.

The being and the consciousness of our body, our mind and our other adjuncts are not real, but are mere apparitions – illusions created by our power of imagination. Their being and their consciousness appear to be real only when we mistake them to be ourself. By our power of imagination we superimpose these adjuncts upon our own real being and consciousness, and hence they appear to exist and to be conscious.

Because these adjuncts have no inherent and permanent being or consciousness of their own, Sri Ramana concludes that they are all *asat* – unreal or devoid of true being or existence – and *jaḍa* – inconscient or devoid of true consciousness. Therefore they cannot be 'I', our real self, which is absolute being or *sat* and absolute consciousness or *cit*.

Once we have thus understood that our body, our mind and all our other adjuncts are not our real self, we should ignore them. Instead of wasting our time and energy examining or thinking about them or anything else that is not our real self, we should direct all our energy and effort into scrutinising only ourself – our own essential self-conscious being, which we always experience as 'I am' – because we can know who or what we really are only by keenly scrutinising or attending to our own real and essential self.

As we have seen in this chapter, by analysing our experience of ourself in our three states of consciousness, we are able to gain a clear theoretical understanding of what we really are. However, this theoretical understanding is not an end in itself, but is merely the means to discover how we can gain true experiential knowledge of our real nature. Since we have learnt by our critical analysis that our true nature, our real self, is only our non-dual 'being consciousness', which we always experience as 'I am', all we need do in order to gain true experiential self-knowledge is to scrutinise our 'being consciousness' with a keenly focused power of attention.

Our real consciousness is only our 'being consciousness' – our essential self-consciousness 'I am'. Our mind or 'knowing consciousness' is merely an unreal form of consciousness, which exists only in its own imagination, and which is therefore experienced only by itself, and not by our real 'being consciousness'. Since the imaginary rising of this unreal 'knowing consciousness' is the cloud that seemingly obscures our real 'being consciousness', preventing us from experiencing it as it really is, let us now proceed to examine the nature of this unreal 'knowing consciousness' – our own self-deceptive mind.

Though our ultimate aim, as we discussed above, is to ignore our mind and to attend only to our own true self, which is the reality that underlies it, we will nevertheless derive great benefit from examining the nature of our mind more deeply and thereby understanding it more clearly. There are two main reasons for this:

The first and most important reason is that it is essential that we should understand and be firmly convinced of the fact that our mind is unreal and is therefore not our true self or 'I' – our essential and real form of consciousness. Since our mind is an impostor who deludes us into mistaking it to be ourself, we must be able to see through its self-deceptive nature in order to recognise our real self, which underlies its false appearance, just as a rope underlies the false appearance of an imaginary snake.

The second reason is that when we try to scrutinise our real self, the only obstacle that will actually stand in our way will be our own mind. Since our mind is the primary enemy that will oppose and obstruct all our efforts to know our real self, we should understand this enemy correctly in order to use it to our advantage and to avoid falling a prey to all its subtle and self-delusive tricks. In particular, we should understand the unreality and insubstantiality of our mind, because only then will we be truly convinced of the fact that the only means to overcome it and all its self-delusive tricks is to ignore it by attending only to our real underlying consciousness – our essential non-dual self-consciousness 'I am'.

Therefore, before investigating the nature of our real consciousness in chapter four, let us first investigate the nature of this unreal consciousness that we call our 'mind'.

CHAPTER 3

The Nature of Our Mind

In the previous chapter we saw that what we call our 'mind' is just a limited and distorted form of our original and fundamental consciousness 'I am' – a spurious form of consciousness that identifies itself with a particular body, and that appears to exist only in the states of waking and dream, and disappears in deep sleep. Since this mind is the primary obstacle that stands in the way of our knowing ourself as we really are, let us now examine it more closely. What is the nature of this limited and distorted form of consciousness that we call our 'mind'?

Our mind as we now know it is just a bundle of thoughts – thoughts, that is, in the very broadest sense of the term, namely anything that our mind forms and experiences within itself, such as any perception, conception, idea, belief, feeling, emotion, desire, fear or suchlike. All thoughts are just images that our mind forms within itself by its power of imagination. Except our fundamental consciousness 'I am', each and everything that our mind knows or experiences is only a thought that it forms within itself.

Even our perceptions are only thoughts or mental images that our mind forms within itself by its wonderful power of imagination. Whether perceptions in the waking state are formed only by our mind's power of imagination without any external stimuli, as in dream, or whether they are formed by our mind's power of imagination in response to actual external stimuli, is something we can know for certain only when we discover the ultimate truth about our mind.

Because the fact that all our perceptions are only thoughts is so important, let us examine it a little more closely, using the example of sight. According to the 'scientific' explanation of the process of seeing, light from the outside world enters our eyeballs and stimulates electrochemical reactions in the light-sensitive cells at the back of them. These cells then stimulate a chain of further electrochemical reactions along our optic nerves, and these in turn reach our brain and cause more electrochemical activity to take place there. Thus far the process is very clear-cut and simple to understand. But then something mysterious happens. Our mind, which is a form of consciousness that interfaces with our brain, then somehow interprets all this electrochemical activity by forming images within itself that we believe to correspond to the shape, colour and size of external objects, and to their relative distance from our body. But all we actually know when we see something is the image that our mind has formed within itself.

Our belief that such images correspond to actual external objects, and all our scientific explanations of the supposed process by which light from those objects stimulates our mind to form such images, are also only images or thoughts that our mind has formed within itself. The same applies to all the images of sound, smell, taste and touch that our mind forms within itself, supposedly in response to external stimuli.

Therefore all that we know of the external world is actually only the images or thoughts that our mind is constantly forming within itself. Do we not have to accept, therefore, that the world that we think we perceive outside ourself may in fact be nothing other than thoughts that our mind has formed within itself, just as the worlds that we see in our dreams are? Even if we are not ready to accept the fact that the world may actually be nothing but our own thoughts, must we not at least accept the fact that the world as we know it, and as we ever can know it, is indeed nothing but thoughts?

Of all the thoughts that are formed in our mind, the first is the thought 'I'. Our mind first forms itself as the thought 'I', and only then does it form other thoughts. Without an 'I' to think or know them, no other thoughts could be formed.

All the other thoughts that are formed in our mind are constantly coming and going, rising and then subsiding, but the thought 'I' persists so long as our mind itself persists. Thus the thought 'I' is the root of all other thoughts, and is the one essential thought without which there would be no such thing as 'mind' and no such action as 'thinking'.

Therefore our mind consists of two distinct aspects, namely the knowing subject, which is our root thought 'I', and the known objects, which are all the other thoughts that are formed and experienced by this 'I'. However, though it consists of these two distinct aspects or elements, the one fundamental and essential element of our mind is only our causal thought 'I'.

Hence, though we use the term 'mind' as a collective term for both the thinker and its thoughts, our mind is in essence just the thinker, the basic thought 'I' that thinks all other thoughts. This simple but important truth is expressed succinctly by Sri Ramana in verse 18 of *Upadēśa Undiyār*:

> [Our] mind is only [a multitude of] thoughts. Of all [the countless thoughts that are formed in our mind], the thought 'I' alone is the root [base, foundation or origin]. [Therefore] what is called 'mind' is [in essence just this root thought] 'I'.

Just as on analysis our mind can thus be resolved into being in essence only this fundamental thought 'I', so on further analysis this fundamental thought 'I' can in turn be resolved into being in essence only consciousness. Because it knows other thoughts, this thought 'I' is a form of consciousness, but because it rises or is formed only by feeling 'I am such-and-such a person', and because it subsides and loses its separate form in sleep, when it ceases to feel thus, it is not our permanent and real form of consciousness, our pure consciousness 'I am'. Because it can rise only by identifying a physical body as 'I', as it does in both waking and dream, it is a mixed and contaminated form of consciousness, a consciousness that confuses itself with a body, feeling mistakenly 'I am this body, an individual person called so-and-so'.

What we mean when we say 'I am such-and-such a person' is that we are an individual consciousness that identifies itself with an adjunct – a particular body. This identification of our consciousness with a particular body is what defines us as a person or individual. Our individuality or separate and distinct existence is thus nothing other than this adjunct-bound consciousness that feels 'I am this body'.

By mistaking itself to be a particular body, this consciousness confines itself within the limits of that body, and feels itself to be separate from all the objects and people it perceives outside that body. This seemingly separate individual consciousness 'I am this body' is what we call by various names such as the mind, the ego, the psyche or the soul, and it is the first thought that gives rise to and experiences all other thoughts.

In religious terminology, our limited individual consciousness 'I am this body' is what is called our 'soul', whereas our unlimited fundamental consciousness 'I am' is what is called our 'spirit', our 'heart' or the 'core of our soul'. The popular belief that our whole self is a compound of these three elements, our body, our soul and our spirit, is rooted in our wrong identification of ourself with a particular body. Though we know ourself to be one, because of our mistaken identification of ourself with a body, we wrongly imagine ourself to be all these three different things. This notion of ours is logically absurd, because since we are one, how can three quite different things be ourself?

Every day in sleep both our body and our soul (our mind or individual consciousness) disappear, yet we continue to exist, and to know that we exist. Therefore, since we remain in sleep without either our body or our soul, neither of these two elements can be our real self. In truth, therefore, these three elements constitute only our false individual self, which is a mere illusion, and not our real self. Our real self, our whole and complete self, does not consist of three elements, but of only one element, the fundamental and essential element that we call our 'spirit', which is our single non-dual consciousness of our own being – our true self-consciousness 'I am'.

Because this non-dual spirit is entirely distinct from our body and our individual soul, it is not limited in any way, nor is it divided. Therefore the spirit that exists as the heart or core of each individual soul is essentially the same single, undivided, non-dual and infinite consciousness of being. What each one of us experiences as our own essential consciousness of being, 'I am', is the same non-dual real consciousness that exists in every other living being.

Because our mind or soul is a form of consciousness that has limited itself within the confines of a particular body, and because it sees many other bodies, each of which seems to have a consciousness of its own, in the outlook of our mind there appear to be many other minds or souls. However, because the fundamental consciousness 'I am', which is experienced by each one of us as the essential core of our own being, always exists as it is, without limiting itself in any way by identifying itself with an adjunct, there is in reality only one consciousness 'I am', even though due to our distorted individualised consciousness we think that the 'I am' in each person is different to that in every other person.

The mind or separate individual 'I' that we see in each person is just a different reflection of the one original 'I' that exists in the innermost depth of each one of us, just as the bright light that we see in each fragment of a broken mirror lying on the ground is just a different reflection of the one sun shining brightly in the sky. Therefore though it is formed only by imagining itself to be a particular body, the mind of each one of us nevertheless contains within itself the light of our original non-dual consciousness 'I am'. Just as each reflected sun lying on the ground could not be formed without borrowing both the light of the sun and the limited form of a fragment of mirror, so without borrowing the light of consciousness from its original source, 'I am', and without at the same time borrowing all the limitations of a physical body, our mind – our root thought 'I' – could not be formed or rise into existence.

Thus our mind is a mixture composed of two contrary and discordant elements, the essential element of consciousness and the superimposed element of physical limitations. As Sri Ramana says in verses 24 and 25 of *Uḷḷadu Nāṟpadu*:

> The inconscient body does not say 'I'; *sat-cit* [being-consciousness, that is, our fundamental consciousness of our own being, 'I am'] does not rise [that is, it does not newly appear or come into being]. [However] between [these two], [some spurious consciousness that feels itself to be] 'I' rises [imagining itself to be limited] as the extent [dimension, size or nature] of [a] body. Know that this [the spurious consciousness that knows itself as 'I am this body'] is *cit-jaḍa-granthi* [the 'knot between consciousness and inconscient matter'], bondage, the soul, the subtle body [the subtle seed-form of all the gross physical bodies that the mind creates for itself in waking and in dreams], the ego, this *saṁsāra* [the mundane state of persistent activity], and the mind.

> Grasping form [a body] it comes into existence. Grasping form [that body] it persists. Grasping and feeding on form [thoughts or objects] it flourishes abundantly. Leaving form [one body] it grasps form [another body]. If [we] examine [it], [this] formless phantom ego takes flight. Know [that is, know this truth, or experience this disappearance of the ego by examining it].

That is, our mind or ego is a spurious entity, an impostor that poses both as consciousness and as a body composed of inconscient matter. It seems to come into existence and to endure only by grasping an imaginary body as itself, and it feeds itself and flourishes by constantly attending to thoughts or imaginary objects. If we scrutinise it closely, however, it disappears, having no form or real existence of its own.

As Sri Ramana says in verses 17 and 20 of *Upadēśa Undiyār*:

> When [we] scrutinise the form of [our] mind without forgetfulness [interruption caused either by sleep or by thinking other thoughts], [we will discover that] there is no such thing as 'mind' [separate from or other than our fundamental consciousness 'I am']. For everyone, this is the direct path [the direct means to experience true self-knowledge].

> In the place [the state of clear self-knowledge] where 'I' [our mind or spurious individual consciousness] merges [by thus scrutinising its own form], the one [real being-consciousness] appears spontaneously as 'I [am] I'. That itself is the whole [the unlimited and undivided reality].

That is, when our mind or root thought 'I' – this mixed and limited consciousness that feels 'I am this body' – turns its attention inwards to scrutinise itself, it loses its grasp on its imaginary body and all its other thoughts, and since it has no separate form of its own, it subsides and disappears. What then remains and is known in the absence of this spurious and limited consciousness 'I am this body' is our one, non-dual, real and unlimited consciousness 'I am', which experiences itself not as 'I am this' or 'I am that', but only as 'I am I'.

Whereas our adjunct-bound consciousness that feels 'I am this' or 'I am that' is a dual form of consciousness, our adjunct-free consciousness that feels only 'I am I' is the non-dual, undivided and infinite whole. Since it is infinite, nothing can truly be separate from or other than it. Anything that appears to be separate is merely a false appearance – an apparition or illusion, a figment of our own imagination. Hence our true adjunct-free and therefore non-dual consciousness 'I am I' is the sole truly existing reality – the one and only absolute reality.

Sri Ramana also expresses this same truth in verse 2 of *Āṉma-Viddai*:

> Since the thought 'this body composed of flesh is I' is the one string on which [all our] various thoughts are attached, if [we] go within [ourself scrutinising] 'who am I? what is the place [the source from which this fundamental thought 'I am this body' rises]?', [all] thoughts will disappear, and within the cave [the core of our being] self-knowledge will shine spontaneously as 'I [am] I'. This alone is silence [the silent or motionless state of mere being], the one [non-dual] space [of infinite consciousness], the sole abode of [true unlimited] happiness.

The words '*nāṉ ār iḍam edu*' used here by Sri Ramana can be taken to mean either one question, 'what is the place where I abide?', or two questions, 'who am I? what is the place?', depending upon whether the word *ār* is taken to be an interrogative pronoun meaning 'who' or a verbal adjective meaning 'where [I] abide'.

As in many other instances in his teachings, Sri Ramana here uses the word *iḍam*, which literally means 'place' or 'space', in a figurative sense to denote our real being or self, because our real self is the source or 'birthplace' from which our individual sense of 'I' arises, and because it is also the infinite space of consciousness in which our mind resides. Since all other things are only thoughts that we form in our mind by our power of imagination, the infinite space of our non-dual consciousness of being, 'I am', is the original source and only abode not only of our own mind, but also of all other things.

When Sri Ramana says, 'The thought "this body composed of flesh is I" is the one string on which [all our] various thoughts are attached', what exactly does he mean by the word 'thought'? In this context the word 'thought' does not mean merely a verbalised or conceptualised thought. It means anything that we form in our mind by our power of imagination. Everything that we form and experience within our mind is a thought or imagination – whether we call it a thought, a feeling, an emotion, a desire, a fear, a belief, a memory, an idea, a conception or a perception. In other words, any other form of objective knowledge or dualistic experience is a thought – an idea or image that we have formed in our mind.

Of all our many thoughts, Sri Ramana says that the one basic thought that supports all our other thoughts is our thought or imagination that a particular body is ourself. Each of our other thoughts is linked directly to this basic thought 'I am this body', and they are all held together by it, just as the pearls in a necklace are all held together by a string. That is, since the 'I' that thinks all other thoughts is our mind, which creates and sustains itself by imagining itself to be a body, this fundamental feeling that we are a body underlies and supports every thought that we think.

Whenever our mind is active, whether in waking or in dream, we always feel ourself to be a body. Even when we daydream, whatever we imagine is centred around our basic imagination that we are a body. Even if we imagine ourself being in some state of existence that is beyond this present material world, such as either heaven or hell, we imagine ourself being some form of subtle or ethereal body in that other world.

Though we now consider that the body that we experienced ourself to be in a dream, or the body that we will experience ourself to be in some other state such as heaven or hell, is not a material body but is a more subtle body – a mind-created or ethereal body –, when we actually experience such a body, as in dream, we do not feel it to be a subtle body but a solid material body – a body of flesh and blood. That is why Sri Ramana says, 'The thought "this body composed of flesh is I" is the one string on which [all our] various thoughts are attached'.

The feeling or imagination that a particular body is ourself is the foundation upon which our mind and all its activity is based. In both waking and dream we always feel ourself to be a body. Our mind first forms itself by imagining itself to be a physical body, and then only can it think of any other thing.

Like all our thoughts, this feeling that a body is ourself is an imagination. It is our first and fundamental imagination – our original and most basic thought, which Sri Ramana otherwise refers to as our root thought 'I'. Whenever our mind rises, whether in waking or in dream, it always does so by imagining itself to be a body. Without this first imagination, we cannot imagine any other thought. Therefore every other thought that we think depends entirely upon this first thought 'I am this body'.

In fact, the basic and essential form of our mind is only this root thought 'I' – our deeply rooted imagination that we are a material body. So why and how does this imagination arise? It arises only due to our imaginary self-ignorance. Because we first imagine that we do not know what we really are, we are then able to imagine that we are something that we are not.

Since our mind – our finite individual consciousness, which arises by imagining itself to be a body – is an illusion that comes into existence due to our imaginary self-ignorance, it will be destroyed only when we experience true self-knowledge – that is, only when we experience ourself as we really are. In order to experience ourself thus, we must cease attending to any of our thoughts, and must instead attend keenly to our essential self-consciousness 'I am'.

When we do so, the clarity of our vigilant self-consciousness will dissolve the illusion of our self-ignorance, and hence we will cease to imagine ourself to be a body or anything else that we are not. Since our basic imagination that we are a body will thereby be dissolved, along with it all our other thoughts will also be destroyed. That is why Sri Ramana says in this verse, '[…] if [we] go within [ourself scrutinising] "who am I? what is the place [the source from which this fundamental thought 'I am this body' rises]?”, [all] thoughts will disappear, and within the cave [the core of our being] self-knowledge will shine spontaneously as “I [am] I” […]’.

Since all our other thoughts depend for their seeming existence upon our first and fundamental thought ‘I am this body’, and since everything that we know as other than ourself is just one of our thoughts – an image that we have formed in our mind by our power of imagination – when we discover that we are not this body but are only the adjunct-free and therefore infinite non-dual self-consciousness ‘I am’, everything that appears to be other than this fundamental and essential self-consciousness will disappear, just as an imaginary snake will disappear when we discover that what we mistook to be that snake is in fact only a rope.

Therefore, since our body and this whole world are only a series of thoughts or images that we have formed in our mind by our power of imagination, they will all disappear along with our mind when we attain the non-dual experience of true self-knowledge. This truth is clearly implied by Sri Ramana in verse 1 of *Āṉma-Viddai*:

> Though [our] self uninterruptedly [and] undoubtedly [or imperishably] exists as real [that is, though it is the one constant, indivisible, imperishable and undoubtable reality], [this] body and world, which are unreal, sprout and arise as [if] real. When thought [our mind], which is [composed of] the unreal darkness [of self-ignorance], is dissolved [or destroyed] without reviving even an iota [that is, in such a manner that it can never revive even to the slightest extent], in the heart-space [the innermost core of our being], which is [the one infinite] reality, [our real] self, [which is] the sun [of true knowledge or consciousness], will indeed shine spontaneously [that is, by and of itself]. The darkness [of self-ignorance, which is the basis for the appearance of our mind, being the background darkness in which the cinema-show of our shadow-like thoughts is projected] will [thereby] disappear, suffering [which we experience in this darkness of self-ignorance due to the intense activity of our thoughts] will cease, [and] happiness [which is always our true and essential nature] will surge forth.

In this verse Sri Ramana emphatically states that our body and the world that we seem to perceive through it are both unreal, and he implies that they arise as mere thoughts in our mind. Since our mind, which is the sole cause for the seeming existence of both our body and this world, is composed only of thoughts, in this context he uses the word *niṉaivu* or ‘thought’ to denote it, and he describes it as *poy mai-y-ār*, which means ‘which is [composed of] unreal darkness’, because it is formed from the darkness of self-ignorance, which is itself unreal, being nothing but an imagination.

Our body and this world are both mere thoughts that we form in our mind by our power of imagination, and like all our thoughts, including our fundamental thought 'I am this body', we imagine them due to the darkness of our self-ignorance. Therefore when we destroy this darkness of self-ignorance by experiencing the absolute clarity of true non-dual self-knowledge, our body, this world and all our other thoughts will be destroyed in such a manner that they will never reappear even to the slightest extent.

This state of absolute annihilation of our mind and all its progeny – all our thoughts, including our body, this entire universe and every other world that we imagine – is the state that Sri Ramana describes when he says, '*poy mai-y-ār niṉaivu aṇuvum uyyādu oḍukkiḍavē*', which means, 'when thought, which is [composed of] unreal darkness, is dissolved [or destroyed] without reviving even an iota'. Just as when the sun rises the darkness of night is dissolved by its bright light, so when the sun of true self-knowledge dawns our mind, which is formed from the unreal darkness of self-ignorance, will be dissolved by the true light of our absolutely clear self-consciousness.

Though Sri Ramana says in this verse, 'when thought is destroyed', he does not explicitly specify how exactly we can bring about this destruction of our mind. This is why in the next verse of *Āṉma-Viddai*, which we discussed above, he first explains that all our thoughts depend upon our basic thought or imagination that a body is 'I', and he then says that if we penetrate within ourself by keenly scrutinising ourself in order to know 'who am I?' or 'what is the source from which this thought that a body is myself originates?' all our thoughts will disappear.

That is, since the cause and foundation of all our thoughts is our basic imagination that a body is ourself, we can destroy all our thoughts only by destroying this basic imagination, and since this basic imagination is an illusion – a mistaken knowledge about what we are – we can destroy it only by keenly scrutinising it in order to discover the reality that underlies it. We cannot kill an imaginary snake by beating it with a stick, but only by scrutinising it carefully in order to discover the reality that underlies it. Likewise, we cannot destroy our imaginary feeling that we are a body by any means other than keen self-scrutiny or self-attention.

When we look carefully at a snake that we imagine we see lying on the ground in the dim light of night, we will discover that it is not really a snake but is only a rope. Similarly, when we carefully scrutinise our basic consciousness 'I am', which we now experience as our mind, our limited consciousness that imagines itself to be a body, we will discover that we are not really this finite mind or body, but are only the infinite non-dual consciousness of our own being.

When we thus experience ourself as being nothing other than our own absolutely non-dual self-consciousness 'I am', our primal imagination that a body is ourself will be destroyed, and along with it all our other thoughts will be destroyed, since they are merely shadows that can be formed only in the obscured and therefore limited light of self-ignorance. That is, though we allow our unlimited natural clarity of non-dual self-consciousness to be obscured by an imaginary self-ignorance, we never entirely cease to be conscious of ourself, and hence in the dim light of our distorted self-consciousness, which we experience as our mind, the shadow-play of our thoughts appears to take place. However, since this shadow-play is unreal, it can occur only in the dim light of our imaginary self-ignorance, and hence it will disappear in the clear light of true self-knowledge, in which we experience ourself as the infinite consciousness of being that we always really are.

Thus in this second verse of *Āṉma-Viddai* Sri Ramana teaches us the truth that when we turn our attention within, towards the core of our being, in order to know the true nature of our real 'I', which is the source from which our spurious individual sense of 'I' arises, we will discover that we are not this body composed of flesh, but are only the infinite space of non-dual being-consciousness, which is the silent and peaceful abode of perfect happiness. Since all our thoughts depend for their seeming existence upon our mind, which is nothing but the spurious consciousness that imagines 'I am this body composed of flesh', they will all disappear for ever when we thus discover that we are not this body but are only the non-dual infinite spirit – the one real self or *ātman*, which is the sole absolute reality.

This non-dual infinite spirit is our adjunct-free and therefore unadulterated consciousness of our own true being, which in truth we experience eternally as 'I am', 'I am I', 'I am nothing but I', 'I am only what I am', or to quote the words of God in *Exodus* 3.14, 'I AM THAT I AM'.

The same truth that Sri Ramana expresses in the second verse of *Āṉma-Viddai* is expressed by him in more mystical language in verse 7 of *Śrī Aruṇācala Aṣṭakam*:

> If the thought 'I' does not exist, no other thing will exist. Until then, if [any] other thought rises, if, [responding to each such thought by investigating] 'To whom [does this thought occur]? To me [this fundamental thought 'I']. What is the place from which [this fundamental thought] "I" rises and [in which it] merges?', we sink within [ourself] and reach [our] heart-seat [the innermost core of our being, which is the source from which all our thoughts rise], [we will merge and become one with] the Lord under the shade of the unique umbrella [the non-dual infinite spirit, which outwardly manifests as God, the supreme Lord of all that is]. [In that state of non-dual being] the dream of [duality with all its imaginary pairs of opposites such as] inside and outside, the two *karmas* [the two kinds of action, good and bad], death and birth, happiness and misery, and light and darkness, will not exist, O boundless ocean of light of grace called Aruna Hill,

who dance motionlessly within the court of [our] heart.

The 'boundless ocean of light of grace called Aruna Hill', whom Sri Ramana addresses in this verse, is the non-dual infinite spirit, which outwardly manifests as God, who is worshipped in the form of the holy hill Arunachala. This is not the place to answer the question why the non-dual spirit should be worshipped dualistically as an external form, but this question will be answered in the sequel to this present book. Suffice it to say here that Sri Ramana wrote this verse as part of a hymn written in the allegorical and poetic language of mystical love.

The 'boundless ocean of light of grace called Aruna Hill' is therefore an allegorical description of God, and he is said to 'dance motionlessly within the court of our heart' because he is our unlimited consciousness of being, which shines motionlessly yet vividly as 'I am' in the innermost core of our being. The 'Lord under the shade of the unique umbrella' is likewise an allegorical description of God, the supreme Lord of all that is, whose reality is nothing but our infinite non-dual consciousness of being, 'I am'. Therefore, though Sri Ramana describes it allegorically in the language of dualistic devotion, what he is actually describing in the later part of this verse is only the state of perfect non-duality, which we can experience only when we put an end to our dream of duality.

Our dream of duality is known only by our mind, our fundamental thought 'I', which is the limited consciousness that feels 'I am this body'. If we do not rise as this limited consciousness, we cannot know any duality. Since all duality is only an imagination, it does not exist when we do not know it. Therefore Sri Ramana begins this verse by stating the fundamental and all-important truth, 'If the thought "I" does not exist, no other thing will exist'.

That is, all things depend for their seeming existence upon the seeming existence of our fundamental thought 'I', which is a limited and distorted form of our fundamental consciousness of being, 'I am'. Therefore, in order to put an end to the illusory appearance of duality, we must put an end to the illusory appearance of our first and fundamental thought 'I'.

In this verse Sri Ramana explains in a few very simple words how we can put an end to the illusory appearance of this primal thought 'I'. Since every thought that rises in our mind is formed and known only by our first thought 'I', and since our first thought 'I' rises from and always depends upon our essential consciousness of being, 'I am', whatever thought may rise, we can know it only because we first know 'I am'. Thus every thought can serve as a reminder to us of our own being. In order to show us how we can make the rising of any thought an opportunity for us to remember our being, Sri Ramana gives us the simple formula, 'To whom? To me. What is the place from which I rise?'.

By giving us this formula, Sri Ramana does not mean that we should constantly question ourself, 'To whom has this thought occurred? Only to me. What is the place from which this "me" has risen?'. What he means is that we should use any thought that rises to remind ourself of our thinking mind, which we now feel to be 'I', because remembering this 'I' that thinks and knows each thought will in turn remind us of our essential consciousness of our own being, 'I am', which underlies the feeling that we are thinking and knowing thoughts, and which is thus the 'place' or source from which our thinking mind arises. That is, whatever thought rises, we should remember, 'I know this thought because I am', and thereby we should turn our attention away from the thought towards our own essential consciousness of being – our real self-consciousness 'I am'.

When we thus turn our attention towards our consciousness of being, 'I am', our mind, which had risen to think thoughts, will begin to subside in our true self-conscious being, which is the source from which it has risen. If we are able to focus our attention wholly and exclusively upon our consciousness of being, our mind will subside completely into the innermost core of our being, and thus we will experience our own true being with absolutely unadulterated clarity of non-dual self-consciousness.

When we once experience our true being with such perfect clarity, we will discover that we are the non-dual infinite spirit, and thus we will destroy for ever the illusion that we are a body, a mind or anything other than that spirit. When this illusion is thus destroyed, the dream of duality, which depends upon it, will also come to an end.

This technique of using the rising of each thought to remind ourself of our own essential being, which Sri Ramana explains very concisely in this verse, is explained by him in more detail in the sixth paragraph of *Nāṉ Yār?*:

> Only by [means of] the investigation 'who am I?' will [our] mind subside [shrink, settle down, become still, disappear or cease to be]; the thought 'who am I?' [that is, the effort we make to attend to our essential being], having destroyed all other thoughts, will itself in the end be destroyed like a corpse-burning stick [that is, a stick that is used to stir a funeral pyre to ensure that the corpse is burnt entirely]. If other thoughts rise, without trying to complete them [we] must investigate to whom they have occurred. However many thoughts rise, what [does it matter]? As soon as each thought appears, if [we] vigilantly investigate to whom it has occurred, 'to me' will be clear [that is, we will be clearly reminded of ourself, to whom each thought occurs]. If [we thus] investigate 'who am I?' [that is, if we turn our attention back towards ourself and keep it fixed firmly, keenly and vigilantly upon our own essential self-conscious being in order to discover what this 'me' really is], [our] mind will return to its birthplace [the innermost core of our being, which is the source from

> which it arose]; [and since we thereby refrain from attending to it] the thought which had risen will also subside. When [we] practise and practise in this manner, to [our] mind the power to stand firmly established in its birthplace will increase [that is, by repeatedly practising turning our attention towards our mere being, which is the birthplace of our mind, our mind's ability to remain as mere being will increase]. When [our] subtle mind goes out through the portal of [our] brain and sense organs, gross names and forms [the thoughts or mental images that constitute our mind, and the objects that constitute this world] appear; when it remains in [our] heart [the core of our being], names and forms disappear. Only to [this state of] retaining [our] mind in [our] heart without letting [it] go outwards [is] the name '*ahamukham*' ['I-facing' or self-attention] or '*antarmukham*' ['inward-facing' or introversion] [truly applicable]. Only to [the state of] letting [it] go outwards [is] the name '*bahirmukham*' ['outward-facing' or extroversion] [truly applicable]. Only when [our] mind remains firmly established in [our] heart in this manner, will [our primal thought] 'I', which is the root [base, foundation or origin] of all thoughts, go [leave, disappear or cease to be], and will [our] ever-existing [real] **self** alone shine. The place [that is, the state or reality] devoid of even a little [trace] of [our primal] thought 'I' is *svarūpa* [our 'own form' or essential self]. That alone is called '*mauna*' [silence]. Only to [this state of] just being [is] the name '*jñāna-dṛṣṭi*' ['knowledge-seeing', that is, the experience of true knowledge] [truly applicable]. That [state] which is just being is only [the state of] making [our] mind to subside [settle down, melt, dissolve, disappear, be absorbed or perish] in *ātma-svarūpa* [our own essential self]. Besides [this state of non-dual being], these [states of dualistic knowledge] which are knowing the thoughts of others, knowing the three times [what happened in the past, what is happening now, and what will happen in future], and knowing what is happening in a distant place cannot be *jñāna-dṛṣṭi* [the experience of true knowledge].

Since our mind rises only by attending to thoughts, which it imagines to be other than itself, it subsides only by withdrawing its attention from all thoughts. Though our mind subsides in this way every day in deep sleep, and occasionally in other states such as swooning, general anaesthesia, coma, bodily death, or in a similar state of subsidence brought about artificially by certain forms of meditation or by the *yōgic* practice of breath-control, in all such states it subsides without clear consciousness of its being.

Therefore in all such states, though we know 'I am', our consciousness of our being is not perfectly clear, so though we know *that we are*, we do not know exactly *what we are*. Because we do not experience a perfect clarity of true self-knowledge or self-consciousness in such states of subsidence, our mind sooner or later rises again from such states, attending once again to its own thoughts, which it imagines to be other than itself.

The reason why our consciousness of our being is not perfectly clear in such states is that our mind subsides in them merely by withdrawing its attention from its thoughts, but without focusing its attention clearly on itself. Only if we focus our attention wholly and exclusively upon our own consciousness of being, 'I am', will our mind subside with perfect clarity of self-consciousness. If we are able to make our mind subside in this manner, we will not only know *that we are*, but also know exactly *what we are*.

Since we thus experience a perfect clarity of true self-knowledge in that state, we will never again be able to mistake ourself to be anything that we are not, and hence our mind will never rise again. Thus the subsidence of our mind that we can achieve by attending to our consciousness of being will be permanent.

The subsidence of our mind which Sri Ramana discusses in the above paragraph of *Nāṉ Yār?* is not the usual dull and temporary form of subsidence that we experience in states like sleep, which we bring about by merely withdrawing our attention voluntarily or involuntarily from all thoughts, but is the clear and permanent form of subsidence that we can experience only in the state of true self-knowledge, which we can bring about only by focusing our attention intentionally upon our consciousness of our own being, 'I am'. Therefore, when he says, 'Only by the investigation "who am I?" will the mind subside', he means that we can make our mind subside permanently and with full clarity of self-consciousness only by investigating, examining, inspecting or scrutinising our own consciousness of being, 'I am'.

Even though our essential being is eternally self-conscious – that is, even though we are always conscious of ourself as 'I am' – so long as our mind is active, we will feel we have to make an effort to scrutinise or attend to our essential self-consciousness, our consciousness of our own being. Therefore, since self-attention involves an effort made by our mind, Sri Ramana refers to that effort as 'the thought "who am I?"' and says that, after destroying all other thoughts, it will also be destroyed.

Every thought that we form in our mind is a form of effort, because we can form and know any thought only by making an effort to do so. Because we think with great desire and enthusiasm, and because we are thoroughly habituated to doing so, it appears to us that we think effortlessly. However, thinking does in fact require effort, and therefore as a result of thinking we become tired.

Because thinking is tiring, our mind needs to rest and recuperate its energy every day, which it does by subsiding and remaining for a while in sleep. In sleep our mind remains subsided temporarily in our own real self – our true state of self-conscious being – and because our real self is the source of all power, our mind is able to recharge its energy by remaining for a while in sleep.

The energy or power that impels our mind to think is our desire to do so. Desire is the driving force behind all thought and all activity. Unless impelled by some desire, we do not think or do anything. When we make effort to attend to our consciousness of being, we do so because of our desire or love for true self-knowledge.

When we repeatedly practise such self-attention, the clarity of our consciousness of our own mere being increases, and because of the happiness we find in such clarity, our love to attend to our being increases. Since this love to attend to our being is the power that enables us to do so, Sri Ramana says, 'When [we] practise and practise in this manner, to [our] mind the power to stand firmly established in its birthplace will increase'.

The more we experience the joy of just being, the less we will feel desire to think or do anything, and thus by the practice of self-attention our tendency to think will be gradually weakened and will finally be destroyed. When we have no desire to think anything, we will remain effortlessly established in our own essential being, and thus even our effort to attend to our being will subside. This is what Sri Ramana means by saying that the thought or effort to know 'who am I?' will destroy all other thoughts and will itself finally be destroyed.

Sri Ramana says, 'If other thoughts rise, without trying to complete them [we] must investigate to whom they have occurred'. What he means by saying that we should not try or make effort to complete a thought is that we should not continue attending to it.

Our thoughts rise only because we attend to them, and the more we attend to them the more they flourish. If, instead of thus allowing our effort or attention to flow outwards to think thoughts, we direct it inwards to know the consciousness to whom those thoughts are known, the vigour with which we form our thoughts will begin to wane.

Therefore Sri Ramana says, 'As soon as each thought appears, if [we] vigilantly investigate to whom it has occurred, "to me" will be clear'. The verb he uses to mean 'will be clear' is *tōṉḏṟum*, which also means 'will be visible', 'will appear', 'will spring up', 'will rise into existence', 'will come to mind' or 'will be known', so by the words 'to me will be clear' he means that we will be clearly reminded of ourself, the 'me' to whom each thought occurs. In other words, our attention will turn back on itself, away from the thought that it had begun to think.

Though the 'me' who knows thoughts is not our real self, our 'being consciousness', but is only our mind, our spurious 'knowing consciousness' or 'rising consciousness', when we turn our attention towards it, it will automatically subside in and become one with our 'being consciousness'. This is what Sri Ramana means when he then says, 'If [we thus] investigate "who am I?", [our] mind will return to its birthplace'.

Because he first says, 'if [we] vigilantly investigate to whom this [thought] has occurred', and then in the next sentence says, 'if [we] investigate who am I', some people wrongly mistake him to mean that we should first ask ourself to whom each thought has occurred, and that after remembering that it has occurred to me, we should then ask ourself who this 'me' is, or 'who am I?'. In fact, however, since by the mere remembrance of 'me' our attention turns back towards ourself, we do not then need to do anything further except to keep our attention fixed on ourself.

Since we can investigate 'who am I?' only by scrutinising or attending to our consciousness of our own being, which we always experience as 'I am', the mere remembrance of the 'me' to whom each thought occurs is itself the beginning of the process of investigating 'who am I?'. Thus all we need do after remembering that 'this thought has occurred to me' is to keep our attention fixed on that 'me'.

Therefore we can best understand the connection between these two sentences by interpolating the words 'thus' or 'continue thus to': 'if [we thus] investigate who am I', or, 'if [we continue thus to] investigate who am I'. Even if we choose to interpolate the word 'then' instead the word 'thus', we should still understand this 'then' in the sense of 'then continue to': 'if [we then continue to] investigate who am I'. That is, we should not understand this clause to mean, 'if we then initiate a fresh process of investigation by newly thinking "who am I?"', but should understand it to mean, 'if we then continue this state of investigation (which we initiated when we remembered 'me') by keeping our attention firmly and keenly fixed on our self-conscious being, "I am"'.

When Sri Ramana says, 'If [we thus] investigate "who am I?", [our] mind will return to its birthplace', what exactly does he mean by saying that our 'mind will return to its birthplace'? In this context the term 'birthplace' denotes the source from which our mind has risen, which is our fundamental consciousness of our own being, 'I am'. Since our mind seemingly rises or leaves its birthplace only by attending to thoughts – which it forms by its power of imagination, but which it imagines to be other than itself – it returns to its birthplace only by withdrawing its attention from all its thoughts.

However, if we are not only to return to our birthplace, but also to be fully conscious of that 'place' or natural state of being to which we are thus returning, we must not only withdraw our attention from all our thoughts, but must also turn it back towards ourself, focusing it keenly upon our essential consciousness of our own being. Thus when Sri Ramana says that our 'mind will return to its birthplace', he means that our attention will turn back towards our natural self-consciousness, and thus our mind will subside in that perfectly clear consciousness of our own being.

Our mind is in fact nothing but our power of attention. When we direct our power of attention towards thoughts and objects, which we imagine to be other than ourself, we rise as our mind, leaving our natural state of mere being. But when instead we direct our power of attention back towards ourself, we return to our natural state of mere being, and so long as we keep our attention fixed on ourself, without allowing it to stray out towards anything else, we remain as our mere being – that is, as our own essential self. In other words, our outward facing attention is our mind, whereas our inward or 'I'-ward facing attention is our real self – our own simple and essential self-conscious being.

Our power of attention, which is our power of consciousness or knowing, is not anything separate from us. It is ourself – our own true and essential being. In other words, we ourself are the power of attention or consciousness by which all is known.

When we misuse our power of consciousness by imagining that we are knowing things other than ourself, we seemingly become the separate and therefore finite individual consciousness that we call 'mind'. But when we do not misuse our power of consciousness in this manner, we remain as we always really are – as the true infinite non-dual consciousness of mere being, 'I am'.

When we thus remain as our true consciousness of our own mere being, we experience ourself as 'I just am', but when we imagine ourself to be a separate individual consciousness or 'mind', we experience ourself as 'I am this' or 'I am that' – 'I am this body', 'I am a person', 'I am so-and-so', 'I am such-and-such', 'I am knowing', 'I am doing' and so on and so forth. Our mind and all that it knows or experiences is therefore just an imaginarily distorted and limited form of our own natural non-dual consciousness of being, 'I am', which is our true self.

What we call 'attention' is the power that we as consciousness have to direct or focus ourself. When we focus our consciousness upon itself, that is, when we focus ourself upon ourself – upon our mere self-conscious being – we experience the true knowledge 'I just am'. But when we focus ourself or our consciousness upon anything other than our own essential self, we experience the false knowledge 'I am knowing this thing other than myself'.

This focusing of our consciousness upon anything other than ourself is what we call 'imagination', because everything other than our own essential self-conscious being, 'I am', is merely a thought or image that we have formed in our mind by our power of imagination. Since this 'imagination', which is another name for our mind, causes us to delude ourself into experiencing things that do not truly exist, it is also called *māyā*, a word that means 'delusion' or 'self-deception'. Thus our mind or object-knowing attention is merely a product of our own self-deceiving power of imagination, which is the distorted use that we make of our power of consciousness when we use it to imagine that we are experiencing anything other than ourself.

Because our attention is the focusing of our entire being upon something, it has tremendous power. In fact it is the only power that truly exists, and it is the source from which all other forms of power arise. From our experience in dream we know that by misusing our power of attention to imagine and know things other than ourself, we can create an entire world and delude ourself into mistaking that world to be real. Since we know that we can create a seemingly real world by our mere power of imagination in dream, we have no valid reason to suppose that the world we experience now in this so-called waking state is anything other than a creation of our same power of imagination.

Thus our attention has the power to create a world that does not truly exist, and in the process of doing so, it deludes us into mistaking that world to be real. All the power that we see in the world that we imagine to be outside ourself appears to exist only because of our power of attention. All that we experience appears to be real only because we attend to it. Since our attention is so powerful, it is a dangerous weapon that we should use carefully and wisely.

The wise way to use our power of attention is to know ourself. Until we know the truth of ourself, who know all other things, we cannot know the truth of anything else. To know ourself we must attend to ourself – to our own essential self-conscious being, 'I am'.

Other things appear to come into existence only when we attend to them, and they disappear when we cease attending to them. This is why Sri Ramana says, 'When [our] subtle mind goes out through the portal of [our] brain and sense organs, gross names and forms appear; when it remains in [our] heart, names and forms disappear'.

What exactly does he mean when he says this? When we attend to or know anything that is seemingly other than our consciousness of being, we feel that our mind or attention is going outwards, away from ourself. When our attention thus goes outwards, it does so either through just the portal or gateway of our brain, or through the portals of both our brain and one or more of our five sense organs. When our attention goes out only through the portal of our brain, we experience thoughts that we recognise as existing only within our own mind, but when our attention goes out still further, not only through our brain but also through our sense organs, we experience objects that we imagine to exist outside and independent of our mind.

Sri Ramana describes both the thoughts that we recognise as existing only within our own mind and the objects that we imagine to exist outside our mind as 'names and forms', because every thought is just a mental form or image, and every external object is likewise just a form or image that we experience in our own mind, and because we give or can give a name to every form that we know. Thus in this context the word 'names' denotes our verbalised thoughts, whereas the word 'forms' denotes our pre-verbalised thoughts. However, since our verbalised and pre-verbalised thoughts are intimately associated and interwoven, the distinction between them is blurred, and hence in Indian philosophy they are regarded as an indistinguishable whole, which is expressed by the compound word *nāma-rūpa*, which means 'name-form'.

Because all the thoughts that we think and all the objects that we know are nothing but 'names and forms', this compound word *nāma-rūpa* or 'name-form' is frequently used in *advaita vēdānta* to denote collectively all thoughts and all external objects. One important reason why this term *nāma-rūpa* is thus used so frequently to denote all thoughts and external objects is that it clearly distinguishes them from our essential consciousness of being, 'I am', which is nameless and formless, because it has no definable form and is therefore beyond all mental conception.

Since our mind is in essence mere consciousness, and since it therefore has no form of its own, Sri Ramana describes it as 'subtle', whereas he describes all thoughts and external objects as 'gross', because they are all mere forms – images that we form in our mind by our power of imagination.

We form all such mental images only by allowing our mind or attention to go outwards, away from ourself. Therefore, when we retain our attention within ourself, not allowing our mind to rise to know anything other than 'I am', all such mental images disappear. This is what Sri Ramana means when he says, 'when it remains in [our] heart, names and forms disappear'. By the word 'heart' he means only the core of our being, which is our own fundamental and essential self-consciousness 'I am', and which is the source or 'birthplace' of our imaginary mind.

Sri Ramana describes this state of retaining our attention in our 'heart' or the core of our being as 'introversion', but while doing so he significantly uses not just one but two Sanskrit terms to denote 'introversion'. The second of these two terms is *antarmukham*, which is the term most commonly used in both Sanskrit and Tamil philosophical literature to denote introversion, and which is a compound of two words, *antar* and *mukham*. The word *antar* means 'within', 'inside', 'internal', 'interior' or 'inward', while the word *mukham* means 'face', 'direction', 'facing', 'turning towards', 'turned towards' or 'looking at'. Thus the compound word *antarmukham* means 'facing inward', 'looking inward', 'turned inward' or 'directing attention inward'.

The first of the two terms that he uses to describe the state of introversion is *ahamukham*, which is a more rarely used term, but which is actually more meaningful than *antarmukham*. Like *antarmukham*, *ahamukham* is a compound of two words, *aham* and *mukham*. In Sanskrit the word *aham* means only 'I', but in Tamil it not only means 'I' or 'self', but also from another root it means 'inside', 'mind', 'heart', 'abode', 'home', 'house', 'place' or 'space'. Thus the compound word *ahamukham* means not only 'introversion', but also more specifically 'facing I-ward', 'facing selfward', 'looking selfward', 'turned selfward' or 'directing attention towards I'.

Sri Ramana then goes on to say that when our mind or attention thus remains firmly established in our heart or *hṛdaya*, the innermost core of our being, our first and fundamental thought 'I' will vanish, and only our ever-existing real **self** will shine or be known. That is, when we are able to keep our attention firmly fixed in our consciousness of being, the clarity of self-consciousness that we experience in that state – the clarity of self-consciousness that always exists in our heart, but which we experience only when we keep our attention firmly fixed upon it – will destroy forever our tendency to rise as the thought 'I', the spurious individual consciousness that imagines itself to be a body, and thus our real and essential **self** will remain alone, shining clearly as 'I am' or 'I am I'.

In order to emphasise the fact that the non-dual reality which alone remains after our individual consciousness 'I' has ceased to exist is not anything alien to us but is only we ourself, in the original Tamil text, in the final and main clause of this sentence, '[...] [our] ever-existing **self** alone will shine', Sri Ramana highlighted in bold type the pronoun *tāṉ*, which means 'self' or 'ourself'. Though we always experience this ever-existing **self** as 'I am', it will destroy our mind or individual consciousness only if we fix our attention firmly upon it.

Sri Ramana then describes our essential self or *svarūpa* as being the 'place' in which not even the slightest trace of the thought 'I' exists. That 'place' is our 'heart', the innermost core of our being. He refers to it figuratively as a 'place' for two reasons, firstly because it is the source or birthplace of our mind (and of all the progeny of our mind, namely its thoughts and the objects that constitute this world), and secondly because we experience it as the core of our being – the central point in the space of our mind, the point from which we conceive all thoughts and perceive all external objects. Besides being described as a 'place', it can also be described as a 'state', because it is the state of perfect egolessness, the state in which we experience only our pure, uncontaminated and adjunctless consciousness of mere being, 'I am'.

Sri Ramana also describes this 'place' or state of egolessness as being *mauna* or 'silence', because it is the state of perfectly silent or motionless being. Since our real self is thus the state of perfect silence, we can know it only by remaining silent, that is, by just being, without rising to think anything. That is, since the restless activity or chattering of our mind is the noise that prevents us from knowing the silence of pure being, we can experience that silence only by silencing all our mental activity. Therefore silence in this context does not mean mere silence of speech, but complete silence of mind.

Sri Ramana further describes this state of silence or egoless being as the state of 'just being'. The Tamil words that he uses to mean 'just being' are *summā iruppadu*. The word *summā* is an adverb meaning 'just', 'merely', 'silently', 'quietly', 'peacefully', 'restfully', 'leisurely', 'without doing anything', 'motionlessly', 'freely' or 'continuously', while *iruppadu* is a gerund or verbal noun meaning 'being', from the root *iru*, which is an imperative that means 'be'.

This term *summā iruppadu* is a key concept in Tamil philosophical literature, and its imperative form, *summā iru*, which means 'just be', is considered to be the ultimate and most perfect form of spiritual instruction. The reason for the pre-eminence given to this term is that it expresses as perfectly as any words can express the state of true self-knowledge, which is the state of perfect silence. Sri Ramana defines it simply as 'making [our] mind to subside [settle down, melt, dissolve, disappear, be absorbed or perish] in *ātma-svarūpa* [our own essential self]'.

The Sanskrit word *ātman*, which is used in Tamil in various modified forms such as *ātmā*, *āttumā* and *āṉmā*, means 'self', 'spirit', 'life', 'soul', 'mind', 'supreme spirit', 'essence' or 'nature', and is also used as the singular reflexive pronoun for all three persons and all three genders, 'oneself', 'myself', 'yourself', 'himself', 'herself' or 'itself', or as the genitive form of the reflexive pronoun, in the sense 'one's own', 'my own' and so on. In a spiritual context, *ātman* means our real self, our spirit or essential being, which is also called *brahman*, the supreme spirit or absolute reality, the essence or sole substance of all things.

The Sanskrit word *svarūpa*, which in Tamil is usually modified as *sorūpam*, is a composite noun formed of two parts, *sva*, which means 'own', 'one's own', 'my own', 'your own', 'his own', 'her own', 'its own', 'our own' or 'their own', and *rūpa*, which means 'form', 'appearance', 'image' or 'nature'. Thus the compound word *ātma-svarūpa* literally means 'oneself's own true nature', that is, the true nature of our own real self, which is our mere consciousness of being – our essential self-consciousness 'I am'.

Since our mind is our false self, a spurious form of consciousness that we mistake to be ourself, we can effect its dissolution only by fixing our attention firmly in our real self, the innermost core of our being, which we always experience as our fundamental and essential consciousness 'I am'. When we dissolve our mind thus in our real own self, the true nature of our real self will reveal itself as mere being – being which is silent, peaceful and devoid of any movement or activity. This state in which we thus dissolve our mind in our real self is therefore described as *summā iruppadu*, the state of 'just being' – that is, the state in which we merely are as we truly ever are, devoid of even the least activity or 'doing'.

Sri Ramana says that only this state of 'just being' can be called *jñāna-dṛṣṭi* or the 'experience of true knowledge'. The Sanskrit word *jñāna*, which is derived from the verbal root *jñā* meaning 'to know', 'to cognise' or 'to experience', means 'knowing' or 'knowledge', and in a spiritual context it means true knowledge – that is, knowledge of our own real self. The Sanskrit word *dṛṣṭi* means the act of 'seeing', 'beholding' or 'looking at', or the faculty of 'sight', the 'eye', a 'look', a 'glance' or a 'view'. Thus the compound word *jñāna-dṛṣṭi* means the 'seeing' or experience of true knowledge. Therefore, since the experience of true knowledge is nothing other than the experience of knowing our own real self, and since we can know our real self only by being nothing other than our real self, the state of just being what we always really are is the experience of true knowledge or *jñāna-dṛṣṭi*.

In the popular imagination, however, the term *jñāna-dṛṣṭi* is wrongly believed to mean the power or ability to know certain things that could not normally be known by the human mind, such as what other people are thinking, what will happen in the future, or what is happening in some faraway place. But such miraculous or supernatural powers do not in fact have anything to do with true knowledge. On the contrary, they are merely additional forms of ignorance, delusion or self-deception – forms of delusion that only add to the density of our already existing and deeply rooted delusion about who or what we really are.

Since our mind has created this entire universe by the power of its imagination, there would be nothing that it could not do if only it could master complete control over its imagination. However, since our power of imagination is a power of delusion and self-deception, we can never master it perfectly. If we try to control it in one way, it will deceive us in some other way.

Nevertheless, since our mind is so powerful, it is possible for us to manipulate our power of imagination by certain techniques (such as certain forms of meditation, concentrated repetition of certain *mantras* or sounds that are supposedly endowed with some mystical power, certain *yōgic* practices, occult rites and rituals, carefully controlled use of certain entheogenic or so-called mind-expanding herbs, fungi or other drugs, certain other forms of magic that supposedly enable a person to invoke the aid of spirits, *jinn*, demons, angels, petty deities or *dēvas*, or some other such artificial means) in such a way as to delude ourself and others into believing that we possess certain miraculous powers, just as in dream we are able to manipulate our power of imagination in such a way as to delude ourself into believing that we are actually flying.

However, since the world we see in this waking state is no more real than the world we saw in a dream, any miraculous powers that we may be able to display in this waking state are no more real than our ability to fly in a dream. Therefore, in verse 35 of *Uḷḷadu Nāṟpadu* Sri Ramana says:

> Knowing and being the [absolute] reality [our own essential being], which is [eternally] *siddha* [attained], is [the only true] *siddhi* [attainment]. All other *siddhis* [attainments such as miraculous powers] are merely [like] *siddhis* that [we] experience in dream. If [we] consider [such *siddhis* after we have woken up] leaving sleep, will they [still appear to us to] be real? Consider [likewise], will those who have left [or ended] unreality [by experiencing and] abiding in the real state [of true self-knowledge] be deluded [by the deceptive illusion of miraculous powers]?

Whatever we experience in a dream appears to us to be real only so long as we are experiencing that dream. When we wake up and consider what we had experienced, we understand clearly and without any doubt that it was all unreal, being merely a figment of our imagination.

Likewise, all that we experience in this so-called waking state appears to us to be real only so long as we are experiencing this state. When we wake up into our real waking state, which is the non-dual state of perfectly clear self-consciousness or self-knowledge, we will discover that all the duality that we are now experiencing in our present state of self-ignorance is as unreal as all the duality that we experienced in our dream, being nothing but a mere figment of our own imagination.

When we clearly know ourself as we really are – that is, as our non-dual consciousness of our own essential being, 'I am', which is the one and only absolute reality – we will discover that we alone are real, and that everything that formerly appeared to be other than ourself is therefore entirely unreal. Experiencing and abiding firmly in this state of absolute clarity is therefore the only attainment or *siddhi* that is truly worth achieving.

By achieving this self-attainment or *ātma-siddhi*, we will free ourself from the delusion that we are this mind, the false finite form of consciousness that imagines itself to be experiencing duality or otherness, and thereby we will transcend all our present imaginary knowledge of otherness. Having thus discarded the entire fabrication of duality, will we be deluded by any appearance such as the display of miraculous powers?

If we understand that this whole world is a mere dream, we will find no wonder and take no delight in miracles or any such display of supernatural power. Miracles happen according to people's faith in them, and such faith is nothing but an act of imagination.

We are only able to fly in a dream because at that time we believe that we can fly. If we did not believe that we could fly, we would not even attempt to do so. Similarly, we would not look for miracles in this world if we did not believe that miracles were possible. If we see a miracle, we must have already believed, either consciously or unconsciously, that such a miracle was possible. We may attribute such miracles to some form of divine agency, but in fact they are nothing but a product of our own imagination, just as this whole world is a product of our own imagination.

Therefore, if we have understood at least theoretically that all knowledge of duality or otherness is merely a figment of our own imagination, like all the knowledge we have of things other than ourself in a dream, we will feel no desire to acquire any form of supernatural power or to perform any miracle. If we were able to perform miracles, we may be able to delude other people, but by doing so the first person we would delude is ourself. Therefore, in verse 8 of *Upadēśa Taṉippākkaḷ* Sri Ramana says:

> A conjuror will delude the people of this world without himself being deluded, [my] son, but a *siddha* [a person who has acquired *siddhis* or miraculous powers] deludes the people of this world and is himself [also] deluded [believing his own powers and miracles to be real]. What a wonder this is!

Whatever supernatural power of knowing we may have, whether the power to know what other people are thinking, the power to know what will happen in the future, or the power to know what is happening in faraway places, such power is only a power to know something other than ourself, and it cannot help us to know ourself. All such powers are therefore only a means of self-deception, and cannot be a means to true self-discovery.

No knowledge of anything other than ourself can be true knowledge, because all such knowledge is acquired by us through the delusive and self-deceiving consciousness that we call our 'mind'. The only knowledge that is true or real is the correct and uncontaminated knowledge of our own real self – our essential non-dual consciousness of our own being, 'I am'.

The knowledge of anything other than 'I am' is merely a form of imagination, and is therefore not really knowledge but only ignorance. Therefore if we wish to attain true knowledge, without which we cannot experience true and perfect happiness, we should not waste our time and energy practising meditation, *yōga* or any other occult technique with an aim to acquire any form of supernatural power.

Since we know from our own experience in dream that our mind has the power to create an entire world within itself, and since we therefore have to suspect that even this world that we experience in our present waking state is likewise a mere creation of our mind, we know that our mind is already endowed with immeasurable power. However, all the wonderful power of our mind – all its present power and all its potential power – is nothing but the power of our own imagination.

Moreover, all such power is only a power of extroversion, a power that is directed outwards, away from ourself, and therefore it only serves to delude us and to obscure from our experience the clarity of true self-consciousness or self-knowledge, which always exists in the core of our being. That is, since the outward-going power of our mind, the power of our mind to know anything other than ourself, is the power of *māyā*, the power of delusion or self-deception, it is the obstacle that stands in the way of our knowing our real self.

Hence, if we attempt to increase the outward-going power of our mind in any way, we will merely succeed in increasing the density of our ignorance – the density of the cloud of false knowledge that obscures our ever-existing inner clarity of true self-knowledge. Therefore, in verse 16 of *Uḷḷadu Nāṟpadu Anubandham* Sri Ramana asks:

> Since [absolute] peace [or calmness] of mind alone is *mukti* [liberation from the bonds of self-ignorance or delusion], which is [in truth always] attained, tell [me], how can those whose minds are bound to [the desire for] *siddhis* [supernatural powers of mind], which cannot be attained without activity of mind, immerse in the bliss of *mukti*, which is [completely] devoid of movement [oscillation, wavering or activity] of mind?

The opening words of this verse, *cittattiṉ śānti*, which literally mean 'peace of mind', denote the state in which our mind has subsided and dissolved in the absolute peace of mere being, which is completely devoid of any kind of movement or activity. Only in that state of absolute peace and calmness can we experience full and perfect clarity of true self-knowledge.

This peaceful state of true self-knowledge is often described as being the state of *mukti*, which means 'liberation' or 'emancipation', because only true self-knowledge can free us from our bondage to finite existence, which is caused by our self-ignorance – our imaginary delusion that we are something other than the infinite and absolute reality, which is what we really are. Sri Ramana describes this state of *mukti* as being *siddha*, which means 'attained', because it is in truth our ever-existing or eternally attained natural state of being.

Sri Ramana expresses the central idea in this verse in the form of a rhetorical question, a question whose answer is clearly implied in its wording. Since we can experience infinite and absolute happiness only in the perfectly peaceful state of liberation or true self-knowledge, the state in which all mental activity has ceased, it is obvious that we cannot experience such happiness if we allow our mind to be bound by the desire for any form of *siddhi*, supernatural or miraculous power of mind, because all such mental powers can be attained only by mental activity.

So long as our mind is active we cannot know our real self, which is perfectly peaceful and inactive being, because our mind becomes active only when we imagine ourself to be the limited form of a particular body. When we do not imagine ourself to be any body, as in sleep, all the restless activity of our mind subsides, and we remain peacefully and happily in the state of mere being.

As soon as our mind rises, either in the state of waking or in a state of dream, we imagine ourself to be a body, and through the five senses of that body we see a world, which we imagine to be separate from ourself. Therefore, since all forms of dualistic knowledge, and all forms of activity, come into existence only when our mind rises, the rising of our mind obscures our natural state of peaceful, blissful and inactive being, in which we experience only the non-dual knowledge of our own real self, 'I am'.

Since the appearance of this world in the waking state, or of any other world in a dream, is caused only by the rising of our mind, we cannot experience the peaceful non-dual state of true self-knowledge so long as we perceive this world. Therefore in the third paragraph of *Nāṉ Yār?* Sri Ramana says:

> If [our] mind, which is the cause of all [dualistic, relative or objective] knowledge and of all activity, subsides [becomes still, disappears or ceases to exist], [our] perception of the world will cease. Just as knowledge of the rope, which is the base [that underlies and supports the appearance of the snake], will not arise unless knowledge of the imaginary snake ceases, *svarūpa-darśana* [true experiential knowledge of our own essential nature or real self], which is the base [that underlies and supports the appearance of the world], will not arise unless [our] perception of the world, which is an imagination [or fabrication], ceases.

The world and everything else that we know – except our own real self, our non-dual consciousness of our own essential being, 'I am' – is merely a figment of our imagination, a fabrication or illusion created by our own mind, which is the power of *māyā*, our delusive and self-deceiving power of imagination. Therefore in the seventh paragraph of *Nāṉ Yār?* Sri Ramana says:

> That which actually exists is only *ātma-svarūpa* [our essential self]. The world, soul and God [which are the three basic elements of finite existence] are imaginations [or fabrications] in it [our essential self], like [the imaginary] silver [that we see] in a shell. These three [basic elements of relativity or duality] appear at the same time [such as

> when we rise up from sleep] and disappear at the same time [such as when we subside in sleep]. [Our] *svarūpa* [our 'own form' or essential self] alone is the world; [our] *svarūpa* alone is 'I' [the consciousness that appears as our individual self, our mind or soul]; [our] *svarūpa* alone is God; everything is *śiva-svarūpa* [our essential self, which is *śiva*, the absolute and only truly existing reality].

Since our individual self or soul, and the world and God (that is, God as a separate entity) that appear along with it, are all mere imaginations superimposed upon the one fundamental reality, which is our own real self, their appearance prevents us from experiencing that reality as it actually is, that is, as our own absolutely inactive, non-dual, self-conscious being. Therefore we cannot experience the true nature of our own real self unless we cease imagining the existence of any such form of duality or relativity.

Any world that we may perceive is nothing but a series of mental images or thoughts that we form in our mind by our power of imagination. Since the world is therefore nothing but our own thoughts, and since the root of all our thoughts is our primary thought 'I am this body', the appearance of the world, which includes the appearance of the body that we mistake to be ourself, obscures our true knowledge of ourself – our non-dual consciousness of our own essential being, 'I am'. This process of obscuration is explained clearly by Sri Ramana in the fourth paragraph of *Nāṉ Yār?*:

> That which is called 'mind' is an *atiśaya śakti* [an extraordinary or wonderful power] that exists in *ātma-svarūpa* [our essential self]. It projects all thoughts [or causes all thoughts to appear]. When [we] see [what remains] having removed [relinquished, discarded, dispelled, erased or destroyed] all [our] thoughts, [we will discover that] solitarily [separate from or independent of thoughts] there is no such thing as 'mind'; therefore thought alone is the *svarūpa* [the 'own form' or basic nature] of [our] mind. Having removed [all our] thoughts, [we will discover that] there is no such thing as 'world' [existing separately or independently] as other [than our thoughts]. In sleep there are no thoughts, [and consequently] there is also no world; in waking and dream there are thoughts, [and consequently] there is also a world. Just as a spider spins out [a] thread from within itself and again draws [it back] into itself, so [our] mind projects [this or some other] world from within itself and again dissolves [it back] into itself. When [our] mind comes out from *ātma-svarūpa* [our essential self], the world appears. Therefore when the world appears, *svarūpa* [our 'own form' or essential self] does not appear [as it really is, that is, as the absolute and infinite non-dual consciousness of just being]; when *svarūpa* appears (shines) [as it really is], the world does not

> appear. If [we] go on investigating the nature of [our] mind, '*tāṉ*' alone will finally appear as [the one underlying reality that we now mistake to be our] mind. That which is [here] called '*tāṉ*' [a Tamil reflexive pronoun meaning 'oneself' or 'ourself'] is only *ātma-svarūpa* [our own essential self]. [Our] mind stands only by always following [conforming or attaching itself to] a gross object [a physical body]; solitarily it does not stand. [Our] mind alone is spoken of as *sūkṣma śarīra* [our 'subtle body', that is, the subtle form or seed of all the imaginary physical bodies that our mind creates and mistakes to be itself] and as *jīva* [our 'soul' or individual self].

The world that we imagine we perceive outside ourself is in fact nothing but our own thoughts, a series of mental images that our mind projects from within itself, and experiences within itself. It is therefore a creation and projection of our own mind, just like the world that we experience in a dream.

Since our thoughts are the veil that obscures our true nature, which is perfect peace and happiness, our experience of thoughts and the world created by our thoughts is the real cause of all our unhappiness. As Sri Ramana says at the end of the fourteenth paragraph of *Nāṉ Yār?* (a complete translation of which is given in the final pages of the first chapter):

> […] What is called the world is only thought. When the world disappears, that is, when thought ceases, [our] mind experiences happiness; when the world appears, it experiences unhappiness.

The happiness that we experience when the world disappears along with all our other thoughts is our own real self, our essential being. Though Sri Ramana says that our mind experiences happiness when our thoughts cease, that which actually experiences happiness at that time is not our mind as such, but is only our true self, which is the sole reality underlying the false appearance of our mind. Our mind as such is only thoughts. In the absence of thoughts, what remains is not our mind but only our own essential being – our pure self-consciousness, 'I am', which is ever uncontaminated by any thought.

So long as we attend to thoughts, our mind appears to exist, but when we turn our attention away from all thoughts to scrutinise the essential consciousness aspect of our mind, we will discover that our mind is truly not a separate entity but is only our own real self, the nature of which is non-dual consciousness of being, 'I am'. This is what Sri Ramana means in the fourth paragraph of *Nāṉ Yār?* when he says cryptically, 'If [we] go on investigating the nature of [our] mind, "self" alone will finally appear as [our] mind'.

The Tamil verb *muḍiyum*, which I have here translated as 'will finally appear', literally means 'will end', but also has many other meanings such as 'will be accomplished', 'will be complete' or 'will appear'. When he says, '[...] "self" alone will end as mind', he means that when we persistently scrutinise the essential nature of our mind we will finally discover that what now appears to be our mind is in fact nothing other than our real self, our fundamental consciousness of our own being, 'I am'. He expresses this same truth in verse 17 of *Upadēśa Undiyār*:

> When [we] scrutinise the form of [our] mind without forgetfulness, [we will discover that] there is no such thing as 'mind' [separate from or other than our real self]. For everyone, this is the direct path [the direct means to experience true self-knowledge].

We are nothing but pure and absolute consciousness – not consciousness of anything other than ourself, but just consciousness of our own essential being, which we always experience as 'I am'. When we imagine that we are conscious of anything other than 'I am', we appear to be our mind, a separate object-knowing consciousness. But when we examine this consciousness that appears to know things other than itself, it will dissolve and disappear, and what will remain is only our true non-dual consciousness of being, because there is truly no such thing as 'mind' other than our fundamental and essential self-consciousness 'I am'.

When our mind appears, the world appears along with it. The appearance of the world depends upon the appearance of our mind. But our mind cannot stand alone without a world. Whenever our mind appears, it does so by attaching itself to a physical body, which it mistakes to be itself. The body which we mistake to be ourself is a part of the world, but due to our identification of that one particular body as 'I', we create an artificial distinction between what we imagine to be ourself and what we imagine to be other than ourself.

This false distinction is created by our mind, but without it our mind cannot stand. Though the world is its own imaginary creation, our mind cannot imagine a world without simultaneously imagining itself to be a particular body in that world.

This is why in the fourth paragraph of *Nāṉ Yār?* Sri Ramana says, '[Our] mind stands only by always following [conforming or attaching itself to] a gross object [a physical body]; solitarily it does not stand'. This is our experience in both waking and dream. We never experience our mind without feeling ourself to be a particular body in a seemingly objective world. Therefore Sri Ramana often described our mind as the consciousness 'I am this body', for which he sometimes used the traditional Sanskrit term *dēhātma buddhi*, which literally means 'body-self sense', that is, the sense, feeling, thought or imagination that our body is ourself. He also says that our mind is what is called the *sūkṣma śarīra* or 'subtle body', because it is the seed or subtle form of all the imaginary physical bodies that it creates by its power of imagination and mistakes to be itself.

Our imagining a particular body to be 'I' is prerequisite to our perception of the world, because it is through the five senses of the body that we imagine to be ourself that we perceive the world. As Sri Ramana says, this world is projected by our mind, and in the process of this projection, the five senses of our body function like the lens in a cinema projector. Though we feel that we perceive the world through our five senses, we in fact not only perceive it but also project it through our senses.

Just as thinking is a two-fold process of forming and experiencing thoughts in our mind, so perception is a two-fold process of projecting and experiencing the world. Forming a thought and experiencing it are not two separate actions, but are just two inseparable aspects of the single process of thinking. Similarly, projecting external objects and experiencing them are not two separate actions, but are just two inseparable aspects of the single process of perception.

Thinking and perception are both processes of imagination. The only difference between them is that we recognise that the thoughts we think exist only in our own mind, whereas we imagine that the world we perceive exists outside our mind. However, this distinction is not real, but exists only in our own imagination.

In a dream we imagine that the world we perceive at that time exists outside our mind, but when we wake up we recognise that it actually existed only within our mind. The world that we perceive now in this so-called waking state is experienced by us in exactly the same manner that we experience that world in our dream, so we have no valid or adequate reason to suppose that it is not merely a figment of our imagination, just as that other world was.

In both waking and dream we first experience a body, which we mistake to be ourself, and then through the five senses of that body we experience a world that seems to exist outside ourself. Whenever we experience a body as ourself and a world as existing outside ourself, whether in waking or in dream, that experience appears to us to be real. Only after waking up from a dream are we able to recognise without the least doubt that it was only a figment of our imagination, a projection of our own mind.

In a dream the body that we mistake to be ourself is a projection of our own mind. When we begin to dream, the first thing we do is simultaneously to imagine a body and to delude ourself into experiencing that body as ourself. Without this self-induced delusion that an imaginary body is ourself, we could not experience the imaginary world that we perceive at that time. Whenever we perceive a world, we always do so from within the confines of a particular body, which we feel to be ourself.

Hence our perception of any world is dependent upon our imagining ourself to be a body in that world, which in turn is dependent upon our mind, the finite consciousness that imagines itself to be that body. Therefore in verses 5, 6 and 7 of *Uḷḷadu Nāṟpadu* Sri Ramana says:

> [Our] body [is] a form [composed] of five sheaths [the *pañca kōśas* or five adjuncts that seemingly cover and obscure our consciousness of our real self when we imagine any of them to be ourself]. Therefore all five [of these 'sheaths' or adjuncts] are included in the term 'body'. Without [some kind of] body, is there [any such thing as a] world? Say, having left [all kinds of] body, is there [any] person who has seen [this or any other] world?
>
> The world [is] nothing other than a form [composed] of five [kinds of] sense perception [sight, sound, smell, taste and touch]. Those five [kinds of] sense perception are objects [known] to [our] five sense organs. Since [our] mind alone cognises the world through [these] five sense organs, say, without [our] mind is there [any such thing as a] world?
>
> Though the world and [our] mind rise and subside as one [that is, together and simultaneously], the world shines [or is known only] by [our] mind. Only that [our own real self] which shines without [ever] appearing or disappearing as the space [or base] for the appearing and disappearing of the world and [our] mind [is] *poruḷ* [the true substance, essence or absolute reality], which is the whole [the infinite totality of all that is].

Sri Ramana begins verse 5 by saying that our body is a form composed of five sheaths, and that all these five sheaths are therefore included in the term 'body'. As we saw when we discussed the meaning of verse 22 of *Upadēśa Undiyār* in the final pages of the previous chapter, the *pañca-kōśas* or 'five sheaths' are our physical body, the life-force in our body, our mind, our intellect and the darkness of relative ignorance that we experience in sleep.

These five 'sheaths' or adjuncts appear to obscure our natural consciousness of our real self because we imagine ourself to be one or more of them in each of our three usual states of consciousness, waking, dream and sleep. In waking and dream we experience ourself as a combination of four of our five sheaths – a physical body, the life in that body, our mind and our intellect – and hence through the five senses of our physical body we experience a world of material objects.

In sleep, on the other hand, we cease to experience ourself as any of those outer four sheaths. Instead we identify ourself with our innermost sheath, which is a seeming darkness or ignorance, because we imagine ourself to be unconscious of anything, and hence at that time we do not know any world other than that darkness.

We perceive a physical world only when we imagine ourself to be a physical body in that world. Therefore in verse 5 of *Uḷḷadu Nāṟpadu* Sri

Ramana asks, '[…] Without [some kind of] body, is there [any such thing as a] world? Say, having left [all kinds of] body, is there [any] person who has seen [this or any other] world?'.

In verse 6 he points out the obvious truth that everything that we call the 'world' is just a combination of the five types of sense perception – sights, sounds, smells, tastes and tactile sensations – which we experience through the medium of our five sense organs. However, that which actually experiences these five types of sense perception is only our mind. Therefore Sri Ramana asks, '[…] Since [our] mind alone cognises the world through [these] five sense organs, say, without [our] mind is there [any such thing as a] world?'.

That is, the appearance of any world depends not only upon our body, through the five senses of which we perceive it, but also upon our mind, which is the consciousness that actually knows it. This dependence of the appearance of any world upon our mind is further emphasised by Sri Ramana in verse 7, in which he says, 'Though the world and [our] mind rise and subside together, the world shines by [our] mind'.

What exactly does he mean by saying that the world shines by our mind? Here the word *oḷirum* or 'shines' means 'appears', 'becomes perceptible' or 'is known'. That is, the world appears or is known only due to our mind, which is the consciousness that cognises it.

Any world appears or is known only when our mind attends to it. In our present waking state this world appears because our mind attends to it, whereas in dream some other world appears because at that time our mind is attending to it. Therefore our mind does not depend upon the appearance of any particular world, whereas the appearance of any particular world does depend upon our mind.

Though the world and our mind both appear and disappear, underlying their appearance and disappearance is a reality that neither appears nor disappears. That reality is our own real self – our essential non-dual consciousness of our own being, which we always experience as 'I am'. In both waking and dream our mind appears along with a world, whereas in sleep our mind and all worlds disappear. However in all these three states we continue to experience ourself as 'I am'.

Since our essential self-consciousness – our knowledge that we are – persists even in the absence of our mind, it is clearly more real than our mind. Since it transcends all the limitations that are experienced by our mind, it is not limited in any way, and hence it is both infinite and absolute. It is the one enduring reality, and hence it is the true substance that appears as our mind, our body, this world and every other thing.

Therefore, referring to our basic self-consciousness 'I am', which we experience continuously, Sri Ramana concludes verse 7 by expressing his own transcendent experience of true self-knowledge:

> [...] Only that which shines without [ever] appearing or disappearing as the space [or base] for the appearing and disappearing of the world and [our] mind [is] *poruḷ* [the true substance, essence or absolute reality], which is the whole [the infinite totality of all that is].

Just as a rope appears to be a snake without ever ceasing to be a rope, so our non-dual self-consciousness 'I am', which is the one absolute reality, appears as our mind and all the duality experienced by our mind without ever ceasing to be what it really is.

Sri Ramana summarises the truth that he expresses in the above three verses of *Uḷḷadu Nāṟpadu* in verse 99 of *Guru Vācaka Kōvai*:

> [This or any other] world does not exist without [a corresponding] body [that we imagine to be ourself], [any such] body does not exist at any time without [our] mind, [our] mind does not exist at any time without [our essential] consciousness, and [our essential] consciousness does not exist at any time without [our true] being [our own reality or 'am'-ness].

The existence of any world is dependent upon the body through which we perceive it. The existence of any such body is dependent upon our mind, which experiences it as 'I'. The existence of our mind is dependent upon our essential consciousness, without which it could not know either its own existence or the existence of any other thing.

How exactly does this sequence of dependence take place? Our real consciousness – that is, our basic self-consciousness 'I am' – does not depend upon any other thing, because it always exists and knows its own existence. Our mind, on the other hand, does not always exist, or at least it does not always know its own existence. It knows its own existence only in waking and dream, but not in sleep. It appears to know its own existence only when it superimposes an imaginary body upon our real self-consciousness 'I am', thereby experiencing that body as 'I', and only after it has thus imagined itself to be a body is it able to experience a world through the five senses of that body. Therefore the appearance of the world depends upon our body, the appearance of our body depends upon our mind, and the appearance of our mind depends upon our essential self-consciousness 'I am'.

After expressing this sequence of dependence, Sri Ramana concludes by saying, '[...] consciousness does not exist at any time in the absence of being'. By saying this, he does not mean to imply that consciousness is some separate thing that is dependent upon being, but only that consciousness itself is being.

If consciousness were other than being, it would not be – that is, it would not exist – and hence it could not know either itself or any other thing. Similarly, if being were other than consciousness, it could not know itself, and hence it would have to depend upon some consciousness other than itself in order to be known. Hence in order to be independently and therefore absolutely real, being must be conscious of itself, and consciousness must be.

The real being is only our own being, because our being is self-conscious, whereas the seeming being or existence of every other thing is known only by us, and is therefore dependent upon us. Since our being is self-conscious, it is a perfectly non-dual consciousness, and hence it is not dependent upon any other thing either to be or to be known to be. Being completely independent, it is free from all forms of limitation, all conditions and all relativity. It is therefore the one infinite and absolute reality.

In this verse of *Guru Vācaka Kōvai* the word that I have translated as 'being' is *uṇmai*, which usually means 'truth' or 'reality', but which etymologically means 'is'-ness or 'am'-ness. Since real being or 'am'-ness is self-conscious, it is not an objective form of being, but is the one infinite reality that underlies and supports the appearance of all objectivity or duality. It is the fundamental consciousness that makes the appearance of all other things possible.

Since our mind, our body, this world and every other conceivable thing depend upon our non-dual self-conscious being, and since they all appear and disappear, they are all mere imaginary appearances, and the sole reality that underlies and supports their appearance is only our own being or consciousness. In other words, the one substance that appears as everything is only our own essential being-consciousness, 'I am'.

Whereas every other thing is only relatively real, being a mere imagination, our own consciousness is the one and only absolute reality. In essence, therefore, everything is only our own consciousness. Hence our consciousness alone is real. Other than it, nothing truly exists. This is the final conclusion to which Sri Ramana leads us.

However, understanding theoretically that everything is only our own consciousness is not an end in itself. Sri Ramana leads us to this conclusion in order to convince us that the only means by which we can experience the absolute reality is to experience ourself as the infinite non-dual consciousness of being that we really are. In order to experience ourself thus, we must divert our attention away from all other things, and focus it wholly and exclusively upon ourself – that is, upon our own self-conscious being, which we always experience as 'I am'.

Our present knowledge of duality or otherness is what obstructs us from experiencing our own consciousness as the adjunct-free and absolutely non-dual self-consciousness that it truly ever is. Since our knowledge of duality arises only when we imagine ourself to be a body, we cannot experience ourself as the infinite, undivided, non-dual and absolute reality so long as we experience the seeming existence of any other thing.

In order to remove our imaginary knowledge of duality, we must cease to imagine ourself to be this or any other body, and in order to cease imagining ourself thus, we must know ourself as we really are. Our mind rises, imagining itself to be a body and thereby experiencing things that appear to be other than itself, only because of our self-ignorance, and hence it will be destroyed only by true self-knowledge.

Our primal imagination that we are a physical body is the foundation upon which our mind is built. Whenever our mind rises, whether in a dream or in a so-called waking state, it always imagines itself to be a body. Without this fundamental imagination 'I am this body', it could not rise and imagine any other thing.

When our mind is active, perceiving the world or thinking thoughts (all of which pertain to the world in one way or another), we always feel, 'I am a person called so-and-so, I am distinct from this world around me, and from all the other people and creatures that I see in this world', and these feelings are all rooted in our fundamental imagination that a particular body is ourself. Whatever else we may be experiencing, this fundamental imagination 'I am this body' is always there in the background, underlying all our experiences.

In our essential nature, we are just formless consciousness, and as such we do not think any thoughts or experience anything other than 'I am'. We experience this natural state of formless consciousness in deep sleep, which is a state in which we know nothing other than our essential being, 'I am'. The fact that we can be and can know our being in the formless state of deep sleep clearly indicates that in our essential nature we are not any form, but are just formless consciousness of being.

Though we are formless consciousness, in the waking and dream states we imagine ourself to be the form of a particular body. The form-bound consciousness that seemingly comes into existence when we thus attach ourself to a body is what we call our 'mind'. Our mind, which in reality is just formless consciousness, forms itself as a form-bound consciousness by imagining itself to be the form of a particular body.

The basic form that our mind takes upon itself is its fundamental imagination 'I am this body'. This fundamental imagination is itself our mind. Other than this imagination 'I am this body', our mind does not exist as a separate entity. Our mind arises only when it forms itself as this fundamental imagination, and only after forming itself thus does it begin to form all its other imaginations. Therefore the root of all imagination is our primal imagination 'I am this body'.

In the fifth paragraph of *Nāṉ Yār?* Sri Ramana describes more about this primal imagination 'I am this body', which he refers to as the thought 'I' that rises in this body:

> What rises in this body as 'I', that alone is [our] mind. If [we] investigate in what place the thought 'I' rises first in [our] body, [we] will come to know that [it rises first] in [our] heart [the innermost core of our being]. That alone is the birthplace of [our] mind. Even if [we] remain thinking 'I, I', it will take [us] and leave [us] in that place. Of all the thoughts that appear [or arise] in [our] mind, **the thought 'I' alone is the first thought**. Only after this rises do other thoughts rise. Only after the first person appears do the second and third persons appear; without the first person the second and third persons do not exist.

Though our body is an imagination, an image that our mind has formed within itself, our mind cannot rise without imagining this mental image to be itself. Such is the enigmatic nature of *māyā*, our self-deceptive power of imagination.

Being a mental image, our body actually exists only in our mind, but we delude ourself into imagining that our mind exists only within our body. As a result of this delusion, when our mind rises we feel that it rises within the confines of our body.

The limited feeling 'I' that rises within this body, mistaking it to be itself, is our mind. Though this feeling 'I', which is a thought or mental image, seems to arise or originate within this body, if we scrutinise it keenly in order to ascertain from where in this body it originates, we will discover that it does not actually originate from any place within this body, but only from the innermost core of our being.

In spiritual literature this innermost core of our being, which is our fundamental and essential consciousness 'I am', is what is called our 'heart' or *hṛdaya*. As Sri Ramana often explained, the word 'heart' in this context does not denote any organ within our body, but is synonymous with our real self, the formless and infinite spirit, which is the absolute reality and which we always experience as our fundamental consciousness of mere being, 'I am'.

Our fundamental consciousness 'I am' is referred to as our 'heart' or the core of our being because we experience it as the centre from which we experience all other things. In every experience and every knowledge our fundamental consciousness 'I am' is present as both the centre and the base.

All our knowledge is based upon and centred in our first and fundamental knowledge 'I am'. All our other forms of knowledge appear and disappear, but this knowledge or consciousness 'I am' remains as our only constant and unchanging knowledge. It is therefore the 'heart' or core of all that we consider to be ourself, and of all that we as an individual know, experience and do.

Because it is the source from which our mind and everything known by our mind arises, Sri Ramana says that our 'heart' or real self is the 'birthplace' of our mind. Though he uses the word 'place' to denote the core or 'heart' of our being, he does not use it in the literal sense of a place existing within the limited dimensions of time and space, but only in a figurative sense. That is, though the core of our being is not confined within the limits of time and space, he refers to it figuratively as a 'place' because we always experience it as the central point in time and space, as the 'now' and 'here', the single point from which we perceive and conceive all other points in time and space.

Some people appear to have difficulty in understanding the simple fact that our true being is formless and infinite consciousness, presumably because they are either unable or unwilling to conceive of any consciousness beyond their present finite consciousness of themself as a physical body. Because they cannot conceive that they are anything more than their limited mind-body complex, and because some of them are therefore enamoured by the idea of *cakras* or mystic centres located at certain points within the physical body, such people often used to ask Sri Ramana at which point in the physical body the *hṛdaya* or spiritual 'heart' is located. Knowing that such people were unable or unwilling to comprehend the simple truth that the word 'heart' truly denotes the infinite reality, the formless spirit or consciousness, Sri Ramana used to appease their curiosity by saying that the spiritual 'heart' is located two digits to the right from the centre of our chest.

The reason why he specified this particular point as being the location of the 'heart' in our physical body is that this is the point in our body at which our sense of 'I' appears to originate and from which it spreads throughout our body. However this location of our 'heart' is not absolutely true, but is true only relative to our body. This location is only as real as our body, and our body is no more real than our mind, of which it is a creation. Since our body is a mere imagination, like the whole world of which it is a part, how can any point in it be our true 'heart', the core of our being, which is the infinite and absolute reality?

Therefore, to all people who were able to understand the simple truth of his teaching, namely that our essential self is the sole reality, and that our mind and everything known by it except 'I am' is a mere figment of our self-deceiving imagination, Sri Ramana often emphasised the truth that the spiritual 'heart' is not any place in our body but is only our own real self, our fundamental and essential consciousness of being, 'I am'.

Not only is the location of our spiritual 'heart' in this physical body merely a relative truth, it is also a truth which is of no practical value. When someone once asked him whether we should meditate on the right side of our chest in order to meditate upon our spiritual heart, he replied, 'The "heart" is not physical. Meditation should not be on the right or on the left. Meditation should be on our self. We all know "I am". What is this "I"? It is neither inside nor outside, nor is it on the right or on the left. "I am" – that is all'. For practical purposes, all we need know about the spiritual 'heart' is that it is our basic consciousness 'I am', which is the core of our being, and the centre of all that we experience.

In this fifth paragraph of *Nāṉ Yār?* Sri Ramana teaches that the means by which we can experience a clear knowledge of this 'heart', which is the source or 'birthplace' of our mind, is to keenly scrutinise our primal thought 'I' in order to ascertain from 'which place' or from what it has originated. Though he expresses this process of self-investigation or *vicāra* by saying, 'If [we] investigate in what place the thought "I" rises first in [our] body, [we] will come to know that [it rises first] in [our] heart. That alone is the birthplace of [our] mind', this is essentially the same process that he expresses more directly in the sixth paragraph (which we cited in full earlier in this chapter) by saying, 'If [we] investigate "who am I?", [our] mind will return to its birthplace'.

Our mind or attention returns to its source or 'birthplace', the innermost core of our being, whenever we cease thinking of anything other than our own essential self-conscious being, which we always experience as 'I am'. Our mind rises from its source only by thinking, that is, by imagining and attending to anything other than itself, so it naturally subsides and merges in its source whenever it stops thinking. This subsidence and merging of our mind in our essential being happens every day when we fall asleep. However in sleep we do not experience a clear unclouded knowledge of our true being, because we subside in sleep only by withdrawing our attention from other things, but without focusing it keenly upon our own consciousness of being – our essential self-consciousness 'I am'.

Our mind rises due to the cloud of self-forgetfulness or self-ignorance with which we have seemingly obscured our natural clarity of pure self-consciousness. We mistake ourself to be this finite body-bound consciousness called 'mind' only because we have chosen seemingly to ignore our true being, the infinite and uncontaminated consciousness 'I am'. This voluntary self-ignorance or self-forgetfulness persists until we choose to remember what our true being really is. We can remember what we really are only by focusing our attention wholly and exclusively upon our essential being, our consciousness 'I am', because the true nature of our essential being is pure non-dual self-consciousness.

Since we subside and merge in the state of sleep without focusing our attention wholly and exclusively upon our essential consciousness of being, 'I am', the cloud of our self-ignorance or self-forgetfulness continues to exist in sleep. The ordinary sleep that we experience every day is just a state in which our mind rests from its ceaseless activity and recuperates its energy to engage in more activity. By temporarily merging and becoming one with its original source, which is the true source of all power, our mind is able to recharge its energy, which it then expends on another bout of activity in either waking or dream. Having expended its limited supply of energy, our mind must again merge in sleep to renew that supply.

No machine can gain energy merely by ceasing to be active. We cannot recharge a battery simply by ceasing to use it for a while. In order to recharge it, we have to connect it to some source of power, such as the mains electricity or a generator. Likewise, our mind does not renew its energy in sleep merely because it is inactive. It does so because in sleep it is connected to a source of power, which is our own essential being. The power that our mind derives by remaining for a while in sleep does not come from anywhere outside ourself. It comes only from a source within ourself, and that source is our own real self or spirit, the essential nature of which is our mere consciousness of being – our self-consciousness 'I am'.

In sleep all that we experience is 'I am'. But by merely experiencing this consciousness 'I am' for a while, our mind is able to recharge its energy. However, though we do experience the knowledge 'I am' in sleep, we do not experience it with perfect clarity. Though our mind has subsided in sleep together with all its knowledge of other things, the clouding influence of our basic self-forgetfulness persists. Therefore though in sleep we know *that we are*, we do not clearly know *what we are*.

The reason why we do not clearly know what we are in sleep is that we subside in that state merely by withdrawing our attention from other things, but without focusing it upon ourself. In order to know what we are, we must focus our attention keenly upon our own essential being. This focusing of our attention wholly and exclusively upon ourself, our consciousness of being, 'I am', is what Sri Ramana calls 'self-investigation' or *ātma-vicāra*.

Sri Ramana describes this simple process of 'self-investigation' in various different ways, each of which is suited to a particular context. In the sixth paragraph of *Nāṉ Yār?*, in the context of how we should deal with other thoughts, which tend to distract us whenever we try to attend to our mere being, he describes it as a process of investigating, 'To whom do these thoughts occur? To me. Who am I?'. In the fifth paragraph, in the context of how our mind always rises as a limited sense of 'I' that is seemingly confined within a body, he describes it as a process of investigating in what place the thought 'I' rises first in our body.

Because our mind always rises in a body by imagining that body to be 'I', Sri Ramana says that we should investigate in what place it rises in our body. However he explains that when we do so we will discover that it does not actually rise from any place within our physical body but only from our 'heart', the non-physical core of our being.

In order to ascertain from where our mind rises as 'I', we must focus our attention keenly upon the essential consciousness that we experience as 'I'. When we do so, our attention will automatically be withdrawn from our body and from everything else, and will be centred entirely in our basic sense of being – our own fundamental self-consciousness, 'I am'. Therefore, by suggesting that we investigate from where in this body our mind rises as 'I', Sri Ramana is providing us with a trick to divert our attention away from our body towards the essential consciousness that, when seemingly contaminated with our cognition of this body and the world that we perceive through it, enables us to feel that this body is 'I'.

In whatever way he may describe this process of self-investigation or self-scrutiny, the sole aim of Sri Ramana is to provide us with clues that will help us to divert our attention away from our thoughts, our body and all other things, and to focus it wholly and exclusively upon our fundamental and essential consciousness of being, which we always experience as 'I am'. In his writings and sayings there are many examples of how he does this. In this fifth paragraph of *Nāṉ Yār?*, for instance, after first suggesting that we should investigate in what place the thought 'I' rises in our body, he goes on to give us a still simpler means by which we can consciously return to the source from which we have risen, saying, 'Even if [we] remain thinking "I, I", it will take [us] and leave [us] in that place'.

He expresses this same truth in slightly different words in verse 716 of *Guru Vācaka Kōvai*:

> Even if [we] incessantly contemplate that [divine] name 'I, I' [or 'I am I'], with [our] attention [thereby fixed firmly] in [our] heart [that is, in our real 'I', which is the core of our being], it will save [us], taking one [that is, ourself] into the source from which [our] mind [or thought] rises [in such a manner as] to destroy [our] ego, [which is] the body-bound embryo [germ, cause or foundation from which all other things arise].

In this verse the words 'that name' refer to the name 'I', 'am', 'I am' or 'I [am] I', which he declared in the preceding verses 712 to 715 to be the original and most appropriate name of God. When we contemplate this name 'I', our attention will be drawn to our basic self-consciousness, which we always experience as 'I am', and thereby our mind will be drawn back to its own source.

When our mind or ego thereby sinks back into our real self, which is the source from which it had risen, it will be destroyed, being consumed in the infinite clarity of unadulterated self-consciousness. Since our mind deludes us, causing us to imagine ourself to be bound within the limitations of a physical body, the destruction of our mind in the clear light of true self-knowledge is the only real salvation, and hence Sri Ramana says that we will be saved by contemplating upon the original name of God, which is 'I', 'I am' or 'I am I'.

Sri Ramana describes our mind as *ūṉ ār karu ahandai*, which means the 'ego, [which is] the body-bound embryo', because it comes into existence only by imagining itself to be a body, and because it thereby gives rise to the appearance of all other things. The Tamil word *karu*, which I have translated as 'embryo', also means 'germ', 'efficient cause', 'substance' or 'foundation', and it derives from the Sanskrit word *garbha*, which means 'womb' or 'the interior'. In this context, therefore, it implies that our ego or mind is the embryo or seed from which all duality or otherness is born, the substance of which it is formed, the active cause or creator that brings it all into being, the foundation that supports its appearance, and the womb inside which it is all contained.

Since our body and all other things are imaginary appendages that distract our attention away from our essential self-consciousness 'I am', we can free ourself from them only by keeping our attention fixed firmly upon our self-consciousness. A simple and easy means by which we can draw our attention back towards our self-consciousness, and which will help us to a certain extent to keep it fixed there, is to remember the name 'I' or 'I am' incessantly.

This is a very practical clue given to us by Sri Ramana, and it is particularly useful for those people who initially have difficulty in understanding what exactly is meant by the term 'self-attention'. Such people are so accustomed to objective attention that they cannot understand how we can attend to our non-objective and formless consciousness 'I am', and hence they complain that they cannot find any such thing as 'I' to attend to. Because they imagine that they must look for an 'I' as if it were some kind of subtle object, they complain that it is too elusive for them to be able to attend to it.

The real cause of their imagined difficulty, however, is that our consciousness 'I' is not an object of any kind, but is the subject that knows all objects. We cannot objectify our first person consciousness 'I', and if we try to do so we will be diverting our attention away from the real 'I' that we should be attending to. Though our consciousness 'I am' is not an object, it is nevertheless something that we always know. None of us doubt the obvious truth 'I am', even though we do not have a perfectly clear knowledge of what exactly this 'I am' is.

Since many people experience such difficulty in grasping exactly what Sri Ramana means when he says that we should attend to our mere consciousness 'I am', he sometimes suggested that they should continuously think 'I, I, I' or 'I am, I am, I am'. If we think thus, our attention will naturally be drawn back to the consciousness that is denoted by the words 'I' and 'I am'.

Whenever we think of the name of a person or an object, a remembrance of that person or object naturally comes to our mind. The thought of any name will bring to our mind the form or thing denoted by that name. Likewise, the thought of the name 'I' or 'I am' will draw our attention to the subject, the non-objective consciousness denoted by that name. Therefore thinking 'I, I, I' is a useful aid to the practice of self-attention, at least until such time as we become familiar with the experience of attending to our mere consciousness of being.

However, since even the verbalised thought 'I' or 'I am' is an object known by us, the practice of thinking 'I, I, I' or 'I am, I am, I am' can become a distraction, preventing our attention from penetrating deep into the consciousness that is actually denoted by the words 'I' or 'I am'. This practice of thinking continuously 'I, I' is therefore beneficial only to a certain extent, but it will drop off naturally when it has become unnecessary, that is, when we have become sufficiently accustomed to the experience of true self-attention. However, even when we have become accustomed to attending to our mere being, we may sometimes find that thinking 'I, I' or 'I am, I am' a few times can be an aid to divert our attention away from other thoughts and to centre it exclusively upon our own essential self-conscious being.

In this extremely valuable small treatise *Nāṉ Yār?* Sri Ramana has given us many other clues that can help us to practise self-attention. For example in the eleventh paragraph, when describing how we must overcome all our *viṣaya-vāsanās*, our deeply rooted mental impulsions or desires to attend to things other than our own real self, he says:

> [...] If one clings firmly to uninterrupted *svarūpa-smaraṇa* [remembrance of one's own essential nature or real self, 'I am'] until one attains *svarūpa* [that is, until one attains true knowledge of one's own essential nature], that alone [will be] sufficient. [...]

In plain English the Sanskrit term *svarūpa-smaraṇa* can best be translated as 'self-remembrance', which is just another way of describing the state of self-attention. However, every word has its own particular flavour, and by using the word *smaraṇa* or 'remembrance' in this context Sri Ramana is able to convey a shade of meaning that would not have been conveyed if he had instead used the word 'attention'. The word 'remembrance' suggests something that we already know but have forgotten or overlooked.

We always know 'I am', but we somehow overlook or ignore it because we are too enthralled by the delusive attraction of other things. If we wish to free ourself of the bondage of attachment to anything other than our own real self, all we need do is to remember uninterruptedly our essential consciousness of being, 'I am'. Since our self-forgetfulness is the root cause of all our unhappiness and all our other problems, self-remembrance is the only antidote that will cure all our problems.

Moreover, whereas terms such as 'self-investigation', 'self-examination', 'self-enquiry', 'self-scrutiny' and 'self-attention' tend to suggest an active process of investigating, examining, enquiring into, scrutinising or attending to ourself, the term 'self-remembrance' tends to suggest a more passive state of simply remembering ourself. All these words do of course denote the same 'process' or state, which is not actually a process of doing anything, but is only a state of just being. However, though they all denote the same state of just being, each of them depicts that state in a subtly different manner, so Sri Ramana used whichever such term was most appropriate to the context in which he was speaking.

Another two terms that he often used to denote this same state of just being were *ātma-niṣṭha*, which means 'self-abidance', and *ātma-cintana*, which literally means 'self-thought' or the 'thought of ourself'. The first of these two terms, 'self-abidance', is particularly significant, because it implies the truth that attending to and knowing ourself is not an action, but is just the state of consciously abiding as our real self, or in other words, simply being what we really are, which is perfectly thought-free self-conscious being. However, the other term, 'self-thought', could easily be mistaken to imply that self-attention is an act of 'thinking' of ourself.

Though these two terms seem to imply conflicting meanings, Sri Ramana uses both of them in the first sentence of the thirteenth paragraph of *Nāṉ Yār?* in the context of describing the state of complete self-surrender:

> Being completely absorbed in *ātma-niṣṭha* [self-abidance], giving not even the slightest room to the rising of any thought except *ātma-cintana* [the thought of our own real self], is giving ourself to God. […]

The reason why he uses the term *ātma-cintana* or 'self-thought' in this context is to emphasise the fact that in order to abide in the state of perfect self-surrender we should not attend to or 'think of' anything other than our own essential being, 'I am'. If we think of anything else, we rise as this separate object-knowing consciousness that we call our 'mind'. Thinking is therefore what separates us from God. Hence, if we truly wish to surrender our individual self or mind entirely to God, we must refrain from thinking anything.

Why then does Sri Ramana say 'except *ātma-cintana*' in this sentence? He makes this exception because *ātma-cintana* or 'self-thought' is not actually a thought like any other thought that we think. Thinking of anything other than our true self is an action, and as such it requires the rising of our mind or individual self to perform that action, whereas 'thinking of' our true self is not an action. When we try to 'think of' our true self, our attention turns inwards, towards our essential self-conscious being, and thus our mind subsides in the source from which it originated. This subsidence of our mind in the innermost core of our being, 'I am', which is the true form of God, is the state of true and perfect self-surrender.

Therefore, though *ātma-cintana* literally means 'self-thought' or the 'thought of ourself', it is truly not a state of thinking but is simply the state of just being. Whenever Sri Ramana talks about 'thought of ourself', 'thinking of ourself' or 'thinking of I', he is not using the words 'thought' or 'thinking' in a precise sense, but is using them loosely to mean 'attention' or 'attending'.

A thought or the act of thinking is actually just the act of paying attention to something. When we attend to anything other than our essential being, our attention takes the form of an action, which we call 'thinking', but when we attend only to our essential being, our attention remains as being. Therefore if we try to 'think' of ourself – of our true being or 'I am' – our mind will become motionless, all our thinking will cease, and we will remain in the state of just being.

In its strict sense, thinking is the act of forming and experiencing a thought in our mind. Our forming a thought and our experiencing that thought are not two separate actions, because we form a thought by our very act of experiencing or knowing it. As such, thinking is a process of imagination, a process by which we conjure up the experience of images, thoughts or feelings in our mind.

This process of thinking is what gives our mind a seeming identity or separate existence. When we think, we rise as the separate consciousness we call our 'mind', and when we do not think, this mind of ours subsides and dissolves in its source, which is our essential being or true self.

Our mind is the separate and finite consciousness in which we form and experience all our thoughts or imaginations. However, it is not only that in which all our thoughts are formed and experienced, but also that by which they are formed and experienced. Moreover, since our mind forms itself by its act of thinking, it is itself a thought, a product of its own imagination. Therefore, since our mind always experiences itself as the 'I' which thinks all other thoughts, Sri Ramana often refers to it as the thought 'I'.

In the fifth paragraph of *Nāṉ Yār?*, after explaining that this thought 'I', which seems to rise in our body, actually rises from our 'heart', the innermost core of our being, and that by attending to this thought 'I' we can return to that source, Sri Ramana goes on to say:

> […] Of all the thoughts that appear in [our] mind, **the thought 'I' alone is the first thought**. Only after this rises do other thoughts rise. Only after the first person appears do the second and third persons appear; without the first person the second and third persons do not exist.

In the clause 'the thought "I" alone is the first thought', which is highlighted in bold type in the original Tamil text, the word that I have translated as 'first' is *mudal*, which has various related meanings such as first, foremost, primary, root, base, basis, origin and cause, all of which are appropriate in this context. Not only is this basic thought 'I' the first thought to rise and the last thought to subside, it is also the origin and cause of all other thoughts. Without it no other thought can rise, because this primal thought 'I' is the thinker that thinks all those other thoughts.

Being not only a thought but also the thinker, it is fundamentally different to all our other thoughts, because it is the knowing subject, whereas they are all just known objects. That is, it is the only thought that is endowed with an element of consciousness. It is conscious both of all other thoughts, and of itself as 'I'. However, because it appears to be limited within the confines of a physical body, it is not a pure uncontaminated form of consciousness, but is a mixture of consciousness and all the limitations of this body that it imagines to be 'I'.

When Sri Ramana says, 'Of all the thoughts that appear in [our] mind [...]', he means every type of thought, including all our verbalised thoughts, our concepts, our beliefs, our memories, our dreams, our feelings and our perceptions. Except our essential consciousness 'I am', everything that we know is a thought, an impression or image that appears in our mind.

When describing the dependence of all our other thoughts upon our primal thought 'I', Sri Ramana refers to the latter as the 'first person', and the former as the 'second and third persons'. Which of our other thoughts does he refer to as 'second persons', and which does he refer to as 'third persons'? Our 'second person' thoughts are all those thoughts that we recognise as existing only in our own mind, and which we therefore feel are most close and intimate to us, whereas our 'third person' thoughts are all those thoughts that we imagine to be external objects that we perceive through one or more of our five senses.

All our other thoughts – that is, both our 'second person' thoughts and our 'third person' thoughts – arise in our mind only after our 'first person' thought 'I' has arisen. In the absence of our first person thought 'I', neither our second person thoughts nor our third person thoughts can exist. Except our essential consciousness 'I am', everything that we know depends for its seeming existence upon our mind, our first person thought 'I', which is the consciousness that knows them.

Our mind, our compound consciousness 'I am this body', is merely an imagination superimposed upon our real consciousness 'I am', just like an imaginary snake that is superimposed upon a rope. In the dim light of dusk, when we see a rope lying on the ground, we may imagine it to be a snake. But if we look closely at that imaginary snake, we will see that it is in fact nothing but a rope. Similarly, if we look at the compound consciousness 'I am this body' sufficiently closely and keenly, we will discover that it is in reality nothing but the pure and simple consciousness 'I am', and that the adjunct 'this body' is merely an illusion superimposed upon it by our power of imagination.

This illusory body, and all the other objects or thoughts known by our mind, will continue to appear real so long as we attend to them, just as a dream continues to appear real so long as we experience it. Our power of attention is what gives a seeming reality to the things that we know. The delusion 'I am this body' will therefore be sustained so long as we continue to attend to this body or to any of the objects that we know through the media of its five senses. To disperse this delusion, we must cease attending to any object known by our mind, and must instead turn our attention back on ourself in order to know our underlying consciousness 'I am'.

Therefore in order to experience our real consciousness 'I am' as it is, unlimited and undefiled by identification with any form, we must turn our attention away from all forms – all objective thoughts, feelings or mental images such as our body and this world – towards the one essential element of our mind – our basic consciousness 'I am'. So long as we continue to cling or attend to any form of objective thought, we can never experience our consciousness 'I am' as it really is. Instead, we will continue to delude ourself into believing that our mind and everything known by it are real.

Can anything known by our mind actually be real? Or rather, can anything that *we* know through the deceptive medium that we call our 'mind' be real? Except our essential self-consciousness 'I am', each and everything that we know is only a thought of some form or another. All thoughts are a form of knowledge, and conversely, all knowledge other than our basic consciousness 'I am' is a form of thought.

All thoughts are known by us only through the medium of our mind, which is our first thought 'I', but our essential consciousness 'I am' is known by us directly, not through our mind or any other medium. All the knowledge that we have of everything other than 'I am' depends for its seeming reality upon the reality of the mind through which we know it. If our mind is unreal, all things known by it must also be unreal, since they are only thoughts that it has formed within itself.

The only thing that appears to be known by our mind yet is nevertheless not dependent upon our mind for its reality is our fundamental consciousness 'I am', because it is not merely a thought that our mind has formed within itself. Even in the absence of our mind, in thought-free states such as sleep, we experience this basic consciousness 'I am'. Moreover, what our mind actually knows is not our consciousness 'I am' as it really is, but is only our consciousness 'I am' obscured by our imagination 'I am this body'. On waking from sleep, the first thing our mind knows is 'I am', but as soon as it knows 'I am' it superimposes upon it this false identification 'I am this body'.

Thus from its very outset our mind is a lie, a false mixture of our fundamental consciousness 'I am' with a physical body composed of inconscient matter. When its most basic knowledge, the knowledge it has of itself, is thus a lie or falsehood, how can we trust any other knowledge that our mind may acquire? All that our mind knows is based upon its first knowledge, its wrong knowledge 'I am this body'. Because it always superimposes this false identification 'I am this body' upon our pure, original and fundamental consciousness 'I am', our mind can never know our pure uncontaminated consciousness as it really is.

The one essential quality of consciousness is that it is always self-conscious – it always knows its own existence or being – and that consciousness of its own existence is what we call 'I am'. However, in addition to knowing its own existence, consciousness sometimes also seems to know other things. When our consciousness thus knows other things, we call it our 'mind'.

The nature of our mind is to know otherness or duality. Our mind is thus a mixed consciousness, a consciousness in which our fundamental knowledge 'I am' is mixed with the knowledge of other things. However, whereas the knowledge of other things is something that appears and disappears, and while appearing constantly undergoes change, our basic knowledge 'I am' does not appear or disappear, but exists permanently and without undergoing any change. Moreover, whereas the knowledge of otherness depends upon our consciousness in order to be known, our basic knowledge 'I am' does not depend upon anything else in order to be known, because it is itself the consciousness by which all things are known.

Thus in the mixed consciousness that we call our 'mind', what is real is only our fundamental consciousness 'I am'. This fundamental and uncontaminated consciousness 'I am' seems to become the mixed consciousness called 'mind' only when we superimpose upon it the knowledge of other things. But whereas our basic consciousness 'I am' is permanent and therefore real, all our knowledge of other things is merely a temporary appearance, and is therefore unreal. Our consciousness 'I am' alone is real because it alone satisfies all three conditions by which we can judge something to be real. That is, it is permanent, unchanging, and not dependent upon any other thing, either to exist or to be known to exist.

Our mind is a temporary form of consciousness that appears and disappears, and that constantly undergoes change during the time of its appearance. Though it appears to know its own existence as 'I am', it actually borrows this knowledge of its own existence from our real consciousness, which underlies it and gives it a seeming existence of its own.

Our knowledge 'I am' is experienced by us even in sleep, when our mind has disappeared, but when our mind appears in waking or in dream, it usurps from us this basic knowledge 'I am', and masquerades as if this knowledge were its own. Our knowledge or consciousness 'I am' is our real self, and hence it is the one thing that we experience always, but our mind is not our real self, because we only experience it temporarily.

There is therefore a clear distinction between our knowledge 'I am' and our mind, which merely assumes this knowledge in waking and dream, as if it were its own, but is separated from it in sleep. Thus the seeming union of our mind with our knowledge 'I am' is not a real oneness, but is only a transitory appearance. Therefore our mind is not independently conscious of its own existence. To know its own existence as 'I am', it depends entirely upon our real consciousness, without whose support it could not appear to exist.

Being impermanent, constantly subject to change, and entirely dependent upon our real consciousness, both for its seeming existence and for its seeming knowledge of its own existence, our mind is not real. Whatever reality it appears to have is only relative, and not absolute. That which is only relatively real is not truly real at all, but merely appears to be real. Only that which is absolutely and unconditionally real can be called 'real' in the truest sense of this word.

In the previous chapter we described our mind as our 'knowing consciousness', because its nature is to be always knowing things that it imagines to be other than itself. Since it rises and subsides, or appears and disappears, we can also describe it as our 'rising consciousness', in contrast to our real consciousness, which is our 'being consciousness', the consciousness that just is, and that never rises to know anything other than itself.

Our mind or 'rising consciousness' cannot rise or come into existence without imagining itself to be a distinct and separate entity, and without simultaneously imagining something other than itself to know. It imagines itself to be a separate entity by imagining a physical body and by simultaneously imagining that imaginary physical body to be itself. Thus our mind or 'rising consciousness' rises by imagining 'I am this body', and it simultaneously imagines that it knows things other than itself. Without simultaneously imagining both of these things, our mind cannot rise.

As soon as we wake up from sleep, we feel as if we have woken up or risen in a particular body, which we feel to be ourself, and we simultaneously feel as if we have become aware of a world around us, which we feel to be other than ourself. This feeling of rising as a body and of knowing other things is all an imagination, but so long as we identify ourself with our 'rising consciousness' it appears to us to be quite real.

We are able to know things other than ourself only through the medium of our mind, our limited 'rising consciousness'. Generally we divide all the objects that we know into two broad categories, our thoughts and the external objects perceived by us. In this context the term 'our thoughts' includes all the 'second person' objects known by us, that is, all our thoughts, feelings and emotions, and everything else that we recognise as existing only in our own mind. The term 'external objects', on the other hand, includes all the 'third person' objects known by us, that is, everything that we perceive through any of our five senses, and that we therefore imagine exists outside of and independent of our mind.

If we are asked whether we think that our thoughts exist apart from our knowledge of them, most of us would readily admit that they can exist only if we know them. We may think that we are only vaguely aware of some of the thoughts in the background of our mind, but any thought exists only to the extent to which we know it. A thought is essentially just an image in our mind, an object that exists only in our own consciousness, and as such it exists only because we know it.

However, though we recognise that for their seeming existence our thoughts depend upon our knowledge of them, we imagine that the external objects that we perceive through our five senses somehow exist independent of our knowledge of them. But this distinction that we make between our 'thoughts' and 'external objects' is false.

Whatever we know, we know only in our own mind. Even the 'external objects' that we think we perceive outside ourself are actually experienced by us only as images in our own mind, and therefore they are also thoughts that we form and know by our power of imagination. Except our basic consciousness of our own being, 'I am', everything that we know is just a thought that we have formed in our mind.

Knowing anything other than ourself is therefore synonymous with thinking. It is a process of imagination, and can happen only when we imaginarily limit our consciousness as something other than the thoughts and objects that we know. Limiting ourself as a mind, a separate individual form of consciousness, is therefore the fundamental and essential factor in the process of thinking or knowing things other than ourself.

Though we usually imagine that our mind rises as soon as we wake up from sleep, and does not subside until we again fall into sleep, our mind actually rises and subsides countless times each second. With the rising of each thought, our mind rises to think and know it, and with the subsidence of each thought our mind momentarily subsides, before rising almost instantaneously to think and know some other thought.

Thinking is essentially a process of forming and simultaneously knowing thoughts. As we discussed earlier, our forming a thought and our knowing that thought are not actually two separate actions, because we form thoughts only by imagining them, and imagination necessarily involves knowing what we imagine.

Since our mind forms its thoughts only by imagining them, and since imagining something essentially involves attending to and knowing a mental image or thought, all thoughts are ultimately formed only by our attention or power of knowing. In other words, our power of imagination, which forms all our thoughts, is just a faculty of our power of knowing or consciousness.

Since at any single moment our mind can attend to and know only one thought, it cannot imagine or form more than one thought at the same time. Therefore, as we discussed in the first chapter, our thoughts rise and subside in our consciousness one at a time. Each consecutive thought can rise or be formed only after the previous thought has subsided or dissolved.

However, because each individual thought rises and subsides in an infinitely small period of time, during each second a countless number of consecutive thoughts can rise and subside in rapid succession. Therefore, because of the rapidity with which thoughts thus rise and subside, our surface mind is unable to discern the rising and subsiding of each individual thought, and therefore cognises only the collective impression formed by a series of such individual thoughts.

This is similar to our eye being unable to discern each individual spot of light on a television screen, as a result of which it cognises only the collective impression formed by a series of such spots covering the entire screen in rapid succession. The picture that we see on the screen of a cathode-ray tube television is formed by many horizontal lines of light, each of which is formed by many individual spots of light of varying colours and intensity. These individual spots of light, which are known as pixels (the syllable 'pix' standing for pictures, and 'el' standing for element), are formed on the screen one at a time by a ray of electrons discharged from the cathode at the back of the tube. Controlled by the steady sequence of oscillations of the magnetic or electrostatic field through which the ray of electrons is sprayed, in a fraction of a second the entire television screen is covered with a series of pixels of varying colours and intensity, thereby collectively forming a complete picture.

Because each individual pixel is formed only momentarily, and dissolves almost immediately, within a fraction of a second the oscillating ray of electrons is able to form another pixel of different colour and intensity upon the same spot on the screen, and thus in each successive fraction of a second it forms a slightly different picture upon the screen. Because the cognitive power of our eyes is not sufficiently subtle and refined for us to be able to perceive distinctly the rapid formation and dissolution of each individual pixel, or even the slightly less rapid formation and dissolution of each entire picture that is formed on the screen by a single sweep of the ray of electrons, what we cognise is not many rapidly changing individual spots of light but only a complete and continuously changing picture.

Each individual thought that momentarily rises and subsides in our mind is similar to a pixel that is momentarily formed and dissolved on a television screen. Because each individual thought rises or is formed only momentarily, and subsides or dissolves almost immediately, within an infinitely small fraction of a second our mind can form another thought in its place. Because the cognitive power of our mind is usually not sufficiently subtle and refined for us to be able to discern distinctly the extremely rapid formation and dissolution of each individual thought, what we usually cognise is not many rapidly rising and subsiding individual thoughts but only a single but continuously changing flow of thoughts.

However, if we practise being attentive to our infinitely subtle consciousness of being, 'I am', our power of attention or cognition will gradually become more subtle and refined, and eventually we will be able to cognise each individual thought as it rises. When by the practice of self-attentiveness our power of attention is thus refined and made sufficiently subtle to be able to detect distinctly the rising or formation of each individual thought, it will also be able to cognise clearly our pure and essential being, which always underlies and supports the formation of our thoughts, and which momentarily remains alone in the gap between the dissolution of one thought and the formation of our next thought.

When our power of attention or cognition thus becomes sufficiently refined to enable us to experience clearly our essential consciousness of our own being, 'I am', in the clarity of that pure self-consciousness or self-knowledge our mind will be dissolved, being a mere apparition that had risen only due to our lack of clear self-knowledge. That is, since our mind is merely a limited form of consciousness that feels 'I am this body', it cannot arise or be formed in the bright light of true self-knowledge, which shines only as our adjunct-free and therefore unadulterated self-consciousness 'I am'. And since this illusory feeling 'I am this body' is our first and fundamental thought, which is the root or base of all our other thoughts, when this feeling is dissolved by true self-knowledge no other thought will be able to rise or be formed in our consciousness.

As we saw earlier in this chapter, our mind first forms itself as our root thought 'I', and then only does it form each other thought. Our root thought 'I' is the thinker, the agent who thinks all other thoughts. Therefore underlying the formation of each individual thought is the formation of our root thought 'I'.

No thought can be formed without our thought 'I' being formed first. That is, we cannot form any other thought without first forming ourself as the thought 'I', which is the agent that thinks that thought. However, the obvious corollary of this truth is that we cannot form ourself as the thinker or first thought 'I' without simultaneously thinking or forming some other thought.

Without forming some other thought to cling to, we cannot rise as the thinking thought 'I'. The nature of our first thought 'I' is to think other thoughts, and without thinking other thoughts it cannot appear to be formed as a separate individual consciousness. That is, our essential consciousness of being, 'I am', seemingly forms itself into our first thought 'I am this body' only by thinking some other thought.

Therefore, along with the formation and dissolution of each of our other thoughts, our thought 'I' is formed and dissolved. In other words, the repeated formation and dissolution of our fundamental thought 'I' is part and parcel of the formation and dissolution of each of our other thoughts. Hence in the brief gap between the dissolution and formation of each two consecutive thoughts, our mind or root thought 'I' is itself dissolved and re-formed.

Thus this gap between each two thoughts is a miniature sample of sleep, and the rising and subsiding of each thought is a miniature sample of waking or dream. Therefore our states of waking and dream are a macrocosm of which the formation and dissolution of each one of our individual thoughts is the microcosm.

Therefore if we gradually refine our power of attention or cognition by our persistent practice of self-attentiveness, we will eventually be able to cognise the underlying reality that remains between each successive subsidence and subsequent rising of our mind or root thought 'I'. That underlying reality is our essential self-consciousness, which we always experience as 'I am'.

Though we always experience our true self-consciousness 'I am', at present we do not experience it as it really is, because we are experiencing it mixed with the distorting limitation of our mind. Therefore if we are able to experience it clearly in the momentary mind-free gap that exists between the subsidence of one thought and the rising of the next thought, we will be able to know it as it really is, unadulterated by even the slightest form of duality or otherness.

Hence when we practise self-attentiveness, our aim is to experience our own natural self-consciousness unadulterated by even the slightest appearance of our mind or any object known by our mind. Instead of experiencing ourself as a body or any other adjunct, we should attempt to experience ourself clearly as our true adjunct-free self-consciousness 'I am'.

The immediate substratum, background or screen upon which our states of waking and dream, and all our individual thoughts within those states, are formed and dissolved is the state of sleep, in which we experience only our own essential consciousness of being, but in a manner that is somehow not perfectly clear or distinct. However, the ultimate substratum or space in which not only waking and dream but also sleep are formed and dissolved is our true state of self-conscious being, 'I am', in which we experience our fundamental and essential consciousness of being in its full, natural and absolute clarity.

Therefore, since the entire universe and the physical space in which it is contained are nothing but thoughts that we have formed in our mind by our own power of imagination, in *advaita vēdānta* it is said that the physical space or *bhūtākāśa* is contained within the space of our mind or *cittākāśa*, and that the space of our mind is contained within the space of our true consciousness or *cidākāśa*.

If we can cognise how within our own consciousness we form and dissolve our thoughts, we will have understood the secret of how the entire universe is created and destroyed. To attain first-hand and immediate knowledge of this secret, we need not tax our mind pondering over any of the various religious or scientific theories of the origin of the universe, but need only scrutinise our own consciousness, which is the source from which and the space in which all our thoughts and this entire universe arise, momentarily stand, and then again subside. Both 'Genesis' and the 'Big Bang', which are each believed by certain groups of people to account for the appearance of this universe, occur in our mind every moment, with the formation of each one of our thoughts.

CHAPTER 4

The Nature of Reality

What is reality? What do we mean when we use the nouns 'reality' and 'truth', and their corresponding adjectives 'real' and 'true'? We consider many things to be real or true, but are any of those things absolutely real, or is their reality merely relative? If the reality of something is only relative, can it actually be called real in the strictest sense of the term?

If something is relatively real, it is also relatively unreal. It may appear to be real at certain times or under certain conditions, but it ceases to be real at other times and under other conditions, so its reality is impermanent. Because its reality is dependent upon certain conditions, it is not independently real. Its so-called reality is limited by and relative to the reality of whatever conditions it depends upon, and is therefore imperfect. Being relative, conditional and dependent, it is not real in its own right, but merely appears to be real under certain conditions.

That which appears at one time will inevitably disappear at some other time. Since it is not real either before it appears or after it disappears, it is in truth not real even when it appears to be real. Its seeming reality is only a transitory appearance or apparition, and is therefore not absolutely true. That which appears at one time and disappears at another time merely appears to exist, but does not really exist. That which really exists, that which really is, must be at all times. Hence all temporal forms of existence are mere appearances, and are therefore not real.

Only that which is absolutely, unconditionally, independently and permanently real is real in the strictest sense of the term. That which is perfectly real must be real at all times, in all circumstances and under all conditions. Its reality must not be in any way dependent upon, limited by or relative to any other thing. Moreover, it must not change, or cease to be as it once was.

That which changes exists in one form at one time, and in some other form at some other time, so it has no permanent form of its own. Being impermanent, none of its forms are absolutely real. Moreover, since change occurs within time, that which changes is time-bound, and hence its reality is dependent upon, limited by and thus relative to time. Only that which is unchanging and immutable, therefore, is real in an absolute sense.

Thus a thing can be considered to be absolutely real only if it is permanent, immutable, unaffected by the passing of time and the changing of conditions, independent of any other thing, unlimited by any other thing, and in no way relative to any other thing.

If we are satisfied with things that are impermanent, imperfect, changeable, relative, conditional and dependent, we may take such things to be real. But are any of us really satisfied with such things? Do we not all consciously or unconsciously seek happiness that is permanent, perfect, immutable, absolute, unconditional and independent?

We cannot attain such happiness from anything that is impermanent, imperfect, changeable, relative, conditional and dependent, and therefore we can never be truly satisfied with any such thing. Something that is relatively real can give only relative happiness, and only that which is absolutely real can give absolute happiness.

Therefore, if we are serious in our desire for absolute happiness, we should accept only an absolute definition of reality. If instead we choose to accept a relative definition of reality, we clearly have not understood that what we really desire is only absolute happiness. Because we wrongly think that we can obtain the happiness that we desire from objects and circumstances in this relative and temporal world, we delude ourself into thinking that such relative and transient objects and circumstances are real. However, so long as we continue to believe that such transient and relative things are real, we can never experience the absolute happiness that we all desire, and that can be found only in that which is absolutely real.

We are all free to choose either to accept the relative as real, or to accept only the absolute as real. Therefore the definition we give to reality is dependent upon what we truly want. If we think we can be satisfied with things that are relative, we will accept a relative definition of reality. But if we understand that we can never be satisfied with any form of relative reality, we will not accept any definition of reality that is not absolute.

Since this book is concerned only with the attainment of absolute happiness and absolutely true knowledge, the definition of reality upon which the reasoning in this book is based is an absolute one. Therefore, unless the context clearly indicates otherwise, wherever the nouns 'reality' or 'truth', or the adjectives 'real' or 'true', are used in this book, they should be understood to mean only that which is absolutely, unconditionally, independently, permanently and immutably real.

When we say that our mind, our body and this world, and the God who is believed to have created all these things, are all unreal, we do not mean to deny the fact that they are real in a relative sense. What we mean to say is that they are not absolutely real – permanently, immutably, unconditionally and independently real. They are all transitory appearances that are conceived or perceived by our own mind, and hence their apparent reality depends upon our mind, which is itself impermanent and ever changing.

Though our mind, and all that is known by our mind as other than itself, is unreal, it could not appear to be real if there were not some reality underlying it. The reality that underlies all relativity is absolute. What is the nature of that absolute reality?

Since every form of duality is relative, the absolute reality cannot be more than one. It is therefore single and non-dual. There cannot be more than one absolute reality, because if there were, each such reality would be limited, and would be relative to each other one, and hence none of them would be the unrestricted whole.

To be absolute is to be free of all conditions, restrictions, limitations and modifying influences – to be infinite, whole, complete, uncontaminated, perfect and independent. Therefore the absolute reality is by definition only one perfectly non-dual whole, apart from which nothing else can exist.

Everything else that appears to exist is not actually other than the one non-dual absolute reality. The absolute reality is like the rope, and everything else is like the snake that that rope is mistaken to be. Just as only the rope really exists, and the snake is merely an imaginary appearance that is superimposed upon it, so the absolute reality alone truly exists, and all the duality and relativity that appears in it is merely an imagination that is superimposed upon it. The absolute reality is not only the substratum underlying the appearance of all duality and relativity, it is their sole substance, because other than it nothing exists.

So long as we see the illusory snake, we cannot see the real rope as it is. Similarly, so long as we experience duality, we cannot know the non-dual absolute reality as it is. Therefore, if we wish to attain true experiential knowledge of the absolute reality, we must stop attributing reality to any form of duality and relativity.

So long as we believe that duality and relativity are real, our mind will continue to attend to them, believing that it can attain real happiness thereby. Only if we are firmly convinced that all forms of duality and relativity are illusory and unreal appearances – mere figments of our own imagination – will we be willing to turn our mind away from them to seek the absolute reality that underlies them.

Does such an absolute reality actually exist, and if so can we attain true experiential knowledge of it? Before deciding whether it actually exists, we must first decide exactly what its nature must be. We have already seen that the absolute reality must be permanent, unchanging, unconditional and independent, but there is one other necessary quality of the reality that we have not yet examined.

According to Sri Ramana, the definition of reality is that it is that which is eternal, unchanging and self-shining. To be eternal is to be permanent, so we have already examined the first two elements of Sri Ramana's definition, eternal and unchanging. But what does he mean by self-shining, and why should self-shining be a defining quality of the absolute reality?

Self-shining means the quality of knowing oneself by the light of one's own consciousness. If something is known only by some consciousness other than itself, or if it cannot know itself without the aid of some 'light' that is other than itself, it cannot be real, because it must depend on that other thing in order to be known. Since it cannot be known without the aid of that other thing, its seeming reality is dependent upon the reality of that other thing, and hence it is not absolutely real.

If the absolute reality were not consciousness, it could not know itself, and hence it would have to depend upon some consciousness other than itself in order to be known. However, if it had to depend upon anything other than itself for any reason whatsoever, it would not be absolute.

Therefore, a necessary quality of the reality is that it should not only exist permanently and without ever undergoing any form of change, but that it should also know its own existence or being. The absolute reality is, and it knows that it is. That is, it is not only being, but is also the consciousness of being. Since it is non-dual, the absolute reality is both being and consciousness. Its being and its consciousness are not two different things, but are one and the same essence.

But does any such reality actually exist, or is it merely a hypothetical concept? Do we know anything that exists always, that never undergoes any change, and that always knows itself by its own self-shining light of consciousness?

All the objects that we know, and our mind through which we know them, are impermanent and subject to change. Though our mind seems to know itself, it cannot be the absolute reality, because it is impermanent and constantly changing. Our mind seems to exist and to know itself in waking and dream, but in sleep it ceases to know itself, and ceases to exist as the thinking and object-knowing consciousness that we call 'mind'.

However, as we have seen earlier, underlying our mind we have a deeper level of consciousness that continues to know itself in all our three states of consciousness, waking, dream and sleep. This deeper level of consciousness is our fundamental consciousness of our own being – our true and essential self-consciousness 'I am'.

This fundamental and essential consciousness of our own being exists permanently, not only throughout our three normal states of consciousness, but beyond the limits of the life of the physical body that we now imagine to be ourself. Since this physical body is merely an imaginary product of our own mind, just as any body that we mistake to be ourself in a dream is, our mind will retain its power to create imaginary bodies to identify as 'I' even after the life of this body – the dream that we call our present waking life – has come to an end. The existence of our mind is not limited to the lifetime of this present body, because this lifetime is merely one of the many dreams that our mind imagines and experiences in its long sleep of self-forgetfulness. So long as our mind remains in this slumber of self-forgetfulness or lack of clarity of self-knowledge, it will continue to imagine such dreams, and thus it will continue to reappear after each occasion that it disappears temporarily either in sleep or in death. Since the essential foundation that underlies and supports the appearance and disappearance of our mind is our fundamental consciousness of being, 'I am', it endures throughout our sleep of self-forgetfulness, in which so many dreams or so-called lives appear and disappear.

Like our mind, which appears in it, our sleep of self-forgetfulness is just a temporary apparition. Though we seem to lack a clear knowledge of what we really are, this lack of clarity affects only our mind, our superficial object-knowing consciousness. Our real consciousness, which is our fundamental consciousness of our own essential being, always knows itself clearly as 'I am'. It is therefore unaffected by the illusory appearance and disappearance of our seeming self-forgetfulness.

Our self-forgetfulness or lack of clarity of self-knowledge exists only in the view of our mind, and not in the view of our real consciousness 'I am'. Therefore our real non-dual consciousness of being exists and knows its own existence eternally, whether or not our sleep of self-forgetfulness appears to occur.

Not only does our fundamental and essential consciousness of being exist eternally, but it also remains without ever undergoing any change. All change is an appearance that is experienced only by our mind, which is a limited and distorted form of our original consciousness of being, 'I am', and not by the true form of this consciousness. That is, our original consciousness of being knows nothing but itself, 'I am', which alone truly exists. Therefore it never knows the illusory appearance of our changeful mind, or any of the ever-changing knowledge of duality that our mind experiences.

Our fundamental consciousness 'I am' therefore remains unaffected by any changes that may appear to occur within it. Whatever we may be doing or thinking, or whatever experiences we may be undergoing, we always know our being, 'I am', even if we do not pay any particular attention to it. Thus from our own experience we clearly know that our essential consciousness of being remains ever unchanged.

Moreover, our fundamental and essential consciousness of our own being is self-shining, because we continue to know ourself as 'I am' both when our mind appears and when it disappears. We require the aid of our mind to know all the imaginary duality that it creates by its power of imagination, but we do not require the aid of anything to know 'I am'. Even in sleep, when our mind and everything else has disappeared, we continue to know 'I am'. In sleep nothing else exists, yet in that absence of all other things our essential consciousness continues to know itself as 'I am'. Since it knows itself without any external aid, our consciousness of our own being is eternally and immutably self-shining.

Thus our consciousness of being is the only thing we experience that has all the essential qualifications required to be the absolute reality. It is eternal, unchanging and self-shining, it is non-dual, it is not affected in the least by the passing of time and the changing of conditions, and it is independent of any other thing, unlimited by any other thing, and in no way relative to any other thing. Therefore, is it not clear that the one and only absolute reality is our essential consciousness of our own being – our fundamental non-dual self-consciousness, 'I am'?

When we clearly know that our own self-consciousness is absolutely real, how can we accept that any transitory and relative phenomenon like our mind or any of the things known by it are real? Though they may appear to be real from a relative standpoint, from an absolute standpoint they are all unreal. The only thing that is real in an absolute sense is our non-dual consciousness of our own being, 'I am'.

As we have seen, our being is itself our consciousness of our being. Our essential being and our essential consciousness are one and the same reality. Since our being is consciousness, it knows itself just by being itself. And as we saw in the first chapter, perfect happiness is only the state in which we remain merely as our essential consciousness of being. That is, being conscious of ourself as mere being is the state of supreme happiness.

Why do we experience perfect happiness when we thus remain as our mere consciousness of being? It is because happiness is our essential nature. Our being is not only consciousness but is also happiness. Our essential being, our essential consciousness and our essential happiness are not three separate things, but are all one and the same reality.

Being, consciousness and happiness appear to be three separate things only in the view of our mind. That is, they appear to be separate only from a relative standpoint. In the limited and distorted view of our mind, we exist throughout the lifetime of our physical body. But though we recognise that we exist whether our mind is in the state of waking, dream or deep sleep, it appears to us that we are conscious only in waking and dream, and that we become unconscious in sleep. And it appears to us that our happiness is even more fleeting than our consciousness. Our experience of happiness appears to be so transient and relative that it even seems to have different degrees of intensity, and to be constantly fluctuating from one degree to another.

From the relative perspective of our mind, not only do being, consciousness and happiness appear to be three separate things, but they each also appear to have an opposite, and their opposites appear to be as real as them. We imagine that we exist for a certain period of time, and are non-existent at all other times – that we came into existence when our body was born, and that we may or may not continue to exist after our body dies. We also imagine that we are conscious in some states and unconscious in other states, and that we are happy sometimes and unhappy at other times. Likewise, we imagine that all other things come into existence at one time, and become non-existent at other times, that they are either conscious or unconscious, and that if they are conscious they may be happy or unhappy.

In the view of our mind, existence and non-existence, consciousness and unconsciousness, and happiness and unhappiness are all equally real. However, the reality of each of these opposites is only relative. Their reality is time-bound and dependent upon circumstances, and the knowledge of their reality is dependent upon our mind. Therefore none of these opposites is absolutely real.

Since everything that is known by our mind is only relatively real, is there no such thing as absolute existence or non-existence, absolute consciousness or unconsciousness, or absolute happiness or unhappiness? Let us first consider the negative qualities. A negative quality such as non-existence, unconsciousness or unhappiness can never be absolute, because a negative quality can only 'exist' relative to its corresponding positive quality. In fact a negative quality does not really 'exist', but is only the absence or non-existence of a corresponding positive quality.

Non-existence or non-being can never really exist, because it is just an absence or negation of existence or being. There is truly no such thing as non-existence or non-being, because if there were, it would be an 'existent non-existence', which is a contradiction in terms. Non-existence or non-being is therefore real only as a mental concept, and it does not exist except as an idea or thought in our mind. As such, non-existence is an essentially relative quality, and can therefore never be absolute.

Similarly, there can be no such thing as absolute unconsciousness. What we call 'unconsciousness' is just an absence of consciousness, but in a complete absence of consciousness no 'unconsciousness' could be known or experienced. Like non-existence, unconsciousness is therefore real only as a mental concept. The consciousness or unconsciousness of other people, creatures and things can never be known by us directly, but is only inferred by our mind, and as such it is real only as an idea or thought in our own mind. Moreover, though we do know our own consciousness, we can never know our own unconsciousness. Unconsciousness is therefore something that we can never actually know, either in ourself or in anything else, and hence it is merely a hypothetical condition, and not a condition that is ever really experienced.

When we wake up from sleep, we think that we were unconscious in sleep, but we did not actually know or experience complete unconsciousness in that state. What we actually experienced in sleep was merely the absence of any knowledge or consciousness of anything other than ourself. When we say, 'I know that I was unconscious in sleep', we are describing our actual experience in sleep, but we are doing so in very loose terms, because we have not reflected deeply about what we actually experienced at that time, or what exactly we mean by the term 'unconscious'. In order to know that we were unconscious in sleep, we must have been conscious of that seeming 'unconsciousness'. That is, we were able to experience the relative 'unconsciousness' of sleep only because we were actually conscious at that time.

When we say, 'I was unconscious', we do not mean that we were absolutely unconscious, but only that we were unconscious of our body, the world and all the other things that we are accustomed to knowing in our waking and dream states. Our 'unconsciousness' or lack of objective knowledge in sleep is relative only to our objective knowledge in waking and dream. The absence of all objective knowledge in sleep, which is what we mean to describe when we say, 'I was unconscious', is not merely inferred by our mind, but was actually experienced by us in sleep.

When we say, 'I did not know anything in sleep', we do so with a strong sense of certainty, because we remember what we actually experienced at that time, which was a relative absence of knowledge. The fact that we now remember having experienced at that time an absence of all objective knowledge clearly proves that we were conscious in sleep. Though we call that experience of no objective knowledge as a state of 'unconsciousness', it is only a relative unconsciousness, because we were present as consciousness to know that condition of seeming unconsciousness.

We can therefore definitely say that non-existence and unconsciousness are real only as mental concepts, and can never exist or be known as absolute qualities, but can we say the same about unhappiness? Is not unhappiness something that we actually experience? If we reword our description of unhappiness as 'suffering', 'pain' or 'misery', does it not become a positive quality?

Firstly, we cannot equate the word 'pain' with unhappiness. Pain is a word that is usually used to describe a physical sensation, and a physical sensation of pain makes us feel unhappy only because we strongly dislike it and are unwilling to tolerate it. As we all know, a person can be in great physical pain yet feel quite happy and cheerful. To the extent to which we are willing to tolerate pain, we are able to feel happy in spite of it.

However if we use the word 'pain' in the sense of mental anguish, it does then describe a state of actual unhappiness. We can mentally detach ourself from physical pain, and thereby remain unaffected by it, but we cannot so easily detach ourself from mental pain, and if we are able to do so, then it will cease to be mental pain.

Though we may use positive terms such as 'suffering', 'misery', 'pain' or 'anguish' to describe it, unhappiness is still just a relative state, and is experienced by us as a lack or absence of something that we desire and feel is rightfully ours. We desire happiness because we feel it is natural to us, and we are uncomfortable with suffering or misery because it feels unnatural and alien to us.

If we did not have any desire or liking to be happy, or any aversion for feeling unhappy, happiness would not make us feel happy, and suffering would not make us feel miserable. What we suggest in this sentence is of course a self-contradictory absurdity. But more than being just absurd, it is in fact an impossibility, because our experience of happiness is inseparable from our love for happiness, and our experience of unhappiness is inseparable from our aversion for unhappiness. Happiness makes us feel happy because we love it, and we love it because it makes us feel happy. Likewise, unhappiness makes us feel unhappy because we are averse to it, and we are averse to it because it makes us feel unhappy.

Though we speak of them as if they were two different things, our love for happiness and our aversion for unhappiness are actually one and the same thing. These two terms, 'love for happiness' and 'aversion for unhappiness', are just two ways of describing the same single feeling, a feeling that is inherent in our very being. The words 'aversion for unhappiness' are just a negative description of our positive feeling of love for happiness. Because we love happiness, and because unhappiness is a state in which we are deprived of the happiness that we love, when we are confronted with unhappiness we experience our love for happiness as an aversion for that unhappiness.

Even if we use seemingly positive words such as 'suffering' or 'misery' to describe it, unhappiness is essentially just a deprivation of happiness. Whatever way we look at it, we cannot avoid the conclusion that unhappiness, suffering or misery is basically just a negation, an absence of the happiness that we all desire. Therefore, since unhappiness exists only in contrast to happiness, it is an essentially relative quality, and hence there can be no such thing as absolute unhappiness.

If non-existence, unconsciousness and unhappiness are each necessarily just relative qualities, qualities that can never have any absolute reality, can we not say the same of their opposites? Are not existence, consciousness and happiness likewise just relative qualities?

Yes, when we speak of each of these qualities as one of a pair of opposites, they are certainly relative, and cannot be absolute. For example, when we speak of existence and non-existence, the existence we are speaking of is relative to its opposite, non-existence. When we consider existence to be a quality in contrast to its opposite, it is only a relative quality.

However, just because in the limited and distorted view of our mind existence, consciousness and happiness all appear to be just relative qualities, does this mean that there can be no such thing as absolute existence, absolute consciousness and absolute happiness? To answer this question, we must again consider what we mean by the word 'absolute'.

Etymologically, absolute means 'loosed from' or 'freed from', and hence to be absolute is to be free from all conditions, restrictions and limitations, free from all forms of confinement, free from all dimensions such as time and space, free from all boundaries or limits, free from all divisions and parts, free from all relationships and modifying influences, free from all dependence, free from all forms of imperfection or incompleteness, free from all finiteness, relativity and duality. Or to express it in more positive terms, absolute means complete, whole, infinite and perfect. Therefore our question is whether or not there is any such thing as an existence, consciousness or happiness that is infinite, undivided, independent and free of all conditions and relativity.

Infinitude does not allow for the existence of any other. To be infinite, a thing must be the one single whole, apart from which nothing else can exist. If anything were to exist apart from, outside of or independent of the infinite, that would set a limit upon the infinite, and hence it would cease to be infinite.

Not only can there be nothing other than the infinite, there can also be no divisions within the infinite, because a division is an internal form of restriction or limitation, and the infinite is by definition devoid of all limits, both internal and external. Therefore, if there is any such thing as an infinite or absolute reality, it must be the only reality, the whole reality, and a reality that is essentially single, undivided and non-dual.

There cannot be more than one absolute reality. Hence, if there is indeed an absolute existence or being, an absolute consciousness and an absolute happiness, they cannot be three separate things, but must be one and the same reality. Is there such a reality, and if so is it existence, consciousness and happiness?

To answer this, we must first consider consciousness, because consciousness is the starting-point and foundation of everything, the basis of all that we know or ever can know. If the absolute reality were not consciousness, it could not know its own existence or being, and since there can be nothing other than the absolute to know it, it could never be known and would therefore be merely a hypothetical concept or supposition.

All talk of being or existence presupposes consciousness, because without consciousness to know it, who could say that it is? The very word 'exist' etymologically means to 'stand out', because a thing can be said to be or to exist only if it 'stands out' in consciousness. An unknown being or existence is a mere imagination, an unfounded supposition, and as such it cannot be real.

Is there therefore any such thing as an absolute consciousness, a consciousness that is free of all conditions and limitations, free of all external boundaries and internal divisions, free of all modifying influences, free of all dependence, and free from all relativity and duality? Since we cannot know any consciousness other than our own consciousness, we can answer this question only by applying it to our own consciousness.

Faced with this question, most of us would conclude superficially that our mind is the only consciousness that we know, and that our mind meets none of the criteria required to be called absolute. It is of course true that our mind is not absolute, but is our mind the only consciousness that we know? Since we are conscious of our own being in sleep, when our mind is absent, we are clearly a consciousness that transcends our mind and all its limitations. Our real consciousness is therefore not our mind, but is some other more basic consciousness that underlies our mind. That basic underlying consciousness is our essential self-consciousness, our non-dual consciousness of our own being, which we always experience as 'I am'.

Applying the above question to our own fundamental self-consciousness, 'I am', we will find that it meets all the criteria that distinguish the absolute reality. It is free from all conditions, restrictions and limitations. It is free from all forms of confinement. It is free from all dimensions such as time and space. It is free from all boundaries or limits. It is free from all divisions and parts. It is free from all relationships and modifying influences. It is free from all dependence. It is free from all forms of imperfection or incompleteness. It is free from all finiteness, relativity and duality. It is therefore complete, whole, infinite and perfect.

This fundamental self-consciousness is non-dual and devoid of all relativity because it is not a consciousness of any other thing, but only of itself – of its own essential being, which it experiences as 'I am'. Since it is, and is conscious of its 'is'-ness, or rather of its 'am'-ness, it is not only consciousness but is also being.

However, though it is being, it is not any form of objective being or existence, because objective being requires some consciousness other than itself in order to be known. Whereas the existence of any other thing depends upon consciousness to be known, the existence of consciousness cannot be known by anything other than itself.

Consciousness is not an object, and hence its existence or being can never be known objectively. Though there may be objective signs or indications of the existence of the finite consciousness we call 'mind', the actual existence of that consciousness can never be known by anything other than itself. When even that finite consciousness, which interacts with the objects known by it, cannot be known objectively or by anything other than itself, how can the real infinite consciousness be known as an object?

The being or existence of our fundamental consciousness 'I am' is perfectly self-conscious being, and therefore it is non-dual, undivided and entirely independent of all other things. All other things depend for their seeming existence upon this fundamental consciousness, but this fundamental consciousness depends upon nothing. It is, and it knows its 'is'-ness or being without the help of any other thing. Its being and its consciousness of its being are therefore one and the same thing – the one non-dual, undivided, unlimited and absolute reality.

Because it is not confined within any limits or boundaries, our essential self-conscious being, 'I am', is the infinite fullness of being. It is truly the only being that is. The being of any other thing is only a limited and distorted reflection of this one real being, which experiences itself eternally as 'I am'. True being is not any being that is experienced either as 'is'-ness or as 'are'-ness, because 'is' and 'are' both denote an objectified experience of being. True being is only that being which is experienced as 'am'-ness, because the first person singular verb 'am' alone denotes the self-conscious and non-dual experience of being as it really is.

Thus we have established the fact that our fundamental and essential consciousness 'I am' is the absolute reality, and that it is also the infinite fullness of being. However, it is not only absolute consciousness and absolute being, but is also absolute happiness.

We experience unhappiness only in the states of waking and dream, in which our mind has risen and is active, but in the state of deep sleep we experience no such thing. In sleep we only experience happiness, and while we experience that happiness it is not relative to any other thing. Though it appears to come to an end when we wake up, the happiness that we experience in sleep does not actually cease to exist but is merely obscured when our mind rises.

In sleep we experience no duality, so whatever we experience at that time must be one with our essential being and our consciousness of our being. Therefore, since we experience happiness in sleep, which is a perfectly non-dual state of pure self-conscious being, happiness must be the very nature of our essential being. Hence, since our essential being is the infinite and absolute reality, and since it is also perfect happiness, the absolute reality must not only be the fullness of consciousness and being, but must also be the fullness of perfect happiness.

Therefore, though there can be no such thing as absolute non-existence, absolute unconsciousness or absolute unhappiness, there is a single reality that is absolute being or existence, absolute consciousness and absolute happiness. However we should not confuse this absolute existence, consciousness and happiness with relative existence, consciousness and happiness, which each possess a corresponding opposite quality.

Like all other forms of duality, these pairs of opposites, existence and non-existence, consciousness and unconsciousness, and happiness and unhappiness, are all relative and therefore mutually dependent. Absolute existence, consciousness and happiness, on the other hand, are one single reality, which is entirely independent and completely free of all forms of duality and relativity.

The non-dual and absolute reality, which is infinite being, consciousness and happiness, transcends these relative pairs of opposites, existence and non-existence, consciousness and unconsciousness, and happiness and unhappiness, and is entirely unaffected either by their appearance or by their disappearance. However, though the absolute reality is in no way related to these pairs of opposites, they are intimately and unavoidably related to it. It is their substratum and support, and without it they could not even appear to be real.

The absolute reality is not related to any form of duality or relativity, because in truth it alone exists. In its view, therefore, there is no such thing as duality or relativity, or anything other than itself. Hence it transcends and is unaffected by any relationship that other things may appear to have with it.

In the view of our mind, however, all other things that appear to be are known by the consciousness that knows itself as 'I am', and are therefore unavoidably related to it. The truth is, therefore, that all things are related to our mind, because it is the consciousness that knows them, and our mind is related to the absolute reality, because the absolute reality is the fundamental consciousness 'I am' that our mind mistakes to be its own.

Our mind exists only in its own view, and not in the view of our true, non-dual and absolute consciousness of being, which knows nothing other than itself. Therefore the relationship between our mind and our absolute consciousness 'I am' appears to be real only from the standpoint of our mind, whose view of our real consciousness is distorted.

In the limited and distorted view of our mind, our being, our consciousness and our happiness, which are the one non-dual and absolute reality, are mistaken to be three separate things, each of which is experienced as one member of a pair of opposites. What our mind sees as relative existence and non-existence is merely a limited and distorted reflection of our true and absolute being. Similarly, what it sees as relative consciousness and unconsciousness is merely a limited and distorted reflection of our true and absolute consciousness, and what it sees as relative happiness and unhappiness is merely a limited and distorted reflection of our true and absolute happiness.

What is it that imparts a seeming reality to duality and relativity? It is only our mind. But how is our mind able to impart such reality to things that exist only in its own imagination?

Because our mind is a confused mixture of our real consciousness 'I am' and a set of unreal limitations, it mistakes itself together with all its limitations to be real. And because it mistakes this mixture of itself and all the limitations it has imposed upon itself to be real, it also mistakes everything known by it to be real.

In a dream we see and experience many things, all of which appear to be real, but when we wake up, we find that all those things that we experienced were in fact unreal, being mere figments of our imagination. After waking up, we feel that the only thing that was real in our dream was ourself, that is, our own mind, the consciousness that experienced that dream. However, the truth is that our mind is as unreal as the dream that it experienced.

Our mind was confused about the reality of the dream it experienced because it was and is confused about its own reality. And just as it was confused about the reality of everything that it experienced in a dream, it is also confused about the reality of everything that it is now experiencing in this so-called waking state.

In dream we felt, 'I am walking, I am talking, I am seeing all these things and hearing all these sounds', but in fact we were not walking or talking, nor were we seeing or hearing anything. We were only imagining all these things. We felt that we were walking and so on because we mistook ourself to be a particular body, but that body was in fact just a figment of our imagination. We mistook ourself to be that imaginary body because we are confused about what we really are.

As our essential consciousness 'I am' we are real, but as our mind we confuse this real consciousness 'I am' with various limitations, all of which are unreal. Because we are real as 'I am', and because we confuse this real 'I am' with an imaginary body and its imaginary actions such as walking, talking, seeing and hearing, we mistake that imaginary body and its imaginary actions to be real.

Since that imaginary body is part of an imaginary world, and since we perceive that imaginary world by means of our imaginary actions such as seeing and hearing, everything that we perceive or experience, whether in a dream or in this so-called waking state, appears to us to be as real as the imaginary body and imaginary actions that we have confused with 'I am'.

Our confused knowledge of 'I am' is therefore the root cause that imparts reality to all the duality and relativity that we experience. So long as we imagine any experience such as 'I am this body, I am this person, I am walking, I am talking, I am seeing, I am hearing, I am thinking' and so on, we cannot but mistake all these experiences to be real, because they are all superimposed upon and identified as 'I am', which is the only thing that is actually real.

Therefore, if we wish to free ourself from all confusion, and to know what is truly real, we must first endeavour to know the reality of our fundamental consciousness 'I am'. Until we gain a clear and unconfused knowledge of our own consciousness 'I am', all our knowledge about other things will remain confused, and we will be unable to distinguish clearly between reality and our own imagination.

So long as we mistake duality and relativity to be real, we cannot experience the absolute reality as it truly is. Conversely, and more importantly, until we experience the absolute reality as it truly is, we cannot avoid mistaking duality and relativity to be real. Therefore, in order to transcend and free ourself from all duality and relativity, and all the confusion that results therefrom, we must gain true experiential knowledge of the absolute reality.

If there were no absolute reality, or if the absolute reality were something that we could not know, we would be doomed to remain for ever in confusion, both about our own reality and about the reality of all other things. So long as we experience only relative reality, our knowledge of reality will always be confused, because relative reality is a knowledge that we experience only through the medium of our mind, which is itself an inherently confused knowledge or consciousness. Since we are the consciousness that knows all other things, we cannot know the reality of any of those other things unless we know the reality of ourself.

What is the reality of ourself? Are we merely a finite and relative reality, or are we the infinite and absolute reality? If there is indeed an infinite and absolute reality, we cannot be separate from or other than it, and conversely, it cannot be separate from or other than us. The absolute reality must therefore be our own essential being.

Hence we cannot know the absolute reality as an object, as something separate from ourself, but can only know it as our own true and essential self. Therefore in order to experience the absolute reality, and thereby to transcend all relative knowledge, we must know our own real self – that is, we must attain the non-dual experience of true and perfectly clear self-knowledge.

Many people feel confused and frightened when they are first told that their mind is not real, and that the world perceived by their mind and the God in whom their mind believes are both as unreal as their mind. Though this truth may at first appear to be very daunting and unpalatable, and for many people therefore quite unacceptable, it is not actually as terrible or as unpalatable as it may appear to be.

'If this world is unreal, like a dream, why should I not behave in any way I wish? In an unreal world, what need is there for ethics or morality? If all other people are just figments of my imagination, like the people I saw in a dream, why should I care for their feelings, and why should I feel compassion when I see them suffering? If this world is just a dream, why should I not just enjoy it to my heart's content, unmindful of any suffering that I may thereby appear to cause to other people? Even if I cannot bring myself to behave in such a heartless and uncaring manner, if everyone is told that this world is just a dream, will not many of them begin to behave in such a manner?'.

Questions such as these arise in the minds of some people when they first come to know that sages such as Sri Ramana have taught that our life in this world is just a dream, and some people even remark that this is potentially a very dangerous philosophy, because it could induce people to act irresponsibly. However these questions are all based upon a basic misunderstanding of the truth taught by Sri Ramana and other sages. When they say that this world and everything else that we know, except our basic self-consciousness 'I am', is unreal, they mean only that none of these things are absolutely real, and they do not mean to deny the relative reality of anything.

The world we perceive, and the God we believe in, are both as real as our mind. So long as we feel ourself to be real as an individual, the world and God are also equally real, as are all our actions and their consequences. The other people and creatures that we see in this world are as real as our mind, which sees them, and hence their feelings – their happiness and their sufferings – are all as real as our own feelings.

If our actions cause harm to any other sentient being, we will have to suffer the consequences of those actions, because the consequences we experience are as real as the actions that we do. The laws of *karma* – which include the fact that we must sooner or later experience the consequences of each of our actions, whether good or bad, and the fact that the appropriate time, place and manner in which we must experience those consequences are all ordained by God in such a way that we gradually develop spiritual maturity – are all real so long as we mistake ourself to be real as an agent or 'doer' of action, and as the one who experiences the 'fruit' or consequences of action.

As Sri Ramana says in verse 38 of *Uḷḷadu Nāṟpadu*:

> If we are the doer of action, we will experience the resulting fruit [the consequences of our actions]. When [we] know ourself [by] having investigated 'who is the doer of action?', *kartṛtva* [our sense of doership, our feeling 'I am doing action'] will depart and the three *karmas* will slip off [vanish or cease to exist]. [This state devoid of all actions or *karmas* is] the state of liberation, which is eternal.

The compound word *vinai-mudal*, which I have translated as 'the doer of action', literally means the origin or cause of an action, but is used idiomatically, particularly in grammar, to mean the subject or agent who performs an action. In the context of *karma* or action, the word 'fruit' is used idiomatically in both Tamil and Sanskrit to mean the moral consequences that result from any of our actions, whether good or bad, in the form of correspondingly pleasant or unpleasant experiences that we must sooner or later undergo.

Each action that we do by mind, speech or body is like a seed, as indicated by the words *vittu-p-pōṉḏṟa*, which Sri Ramana added before the first line of this verse when, in order to make it easy for people to memorise and chant *Uḷḷadu Nāṟpadu*, he appended an additional one and half metrical feet between each of its consecutive verses, thereby transforming it from two plus forty verses in *veṇbā* metre to one single verse in *kaliveṇbā* metre. These words, *vittu-p-pōṉḏṟa*, which mean 'seed-like', are appended to the opening sentence of this verse, which in combination with them mean, 'If we are the doer of actions, which are like seeds, we will experience the resulting fruit'.

Just as a fruit contains two elements, its edible portion and its seed, so the consequence of each of our actions is twofold. One element of the consequence of each action is the pleasure or pain that we must sooner or later experience as a result of it. This element is like the edible portion of a fruit. The other element, which is like the seed contained within that fruit, is the resulting *karma-vāsanā*, the tendency or inclination to do that same action again.

That is, our *karmas* or actions are habit forming. The more we indulge in any particular type of action, the more we will generate and nourish a corresponding *vāsanā*, an inclination or liking that will impel us to do the same type of action again. Therefore in verse 2 of *Upadēśa Undiyār* Sri Ramana says:

> The fruit [produce, result or consequence] of [any] action having perished [passed away or ceased, as it does as soon as it has been appropriately experienced by us in the form of a pleasure or pain], will as [a] seed make [us] fall into the ocean of action. [Therefore action and its results, its fruits and its seeds] will not give liberation.

The truly harmful consequence of any action that we do is not just the pleasant or unpleasant experience that will sooner or later result from it, but is the seed or latent impulse that it generates or nourishes within our mind. Just as the edible part of a fruit passes away when we eat it, so the potential experience that results as the moral consequence of an action will pass away when we undergo it. But though that experience passes away, a harmful residue of our action will still remain in our mind in the form of a *vāsanā*, an inclination or liking to repeat such an action. That is, just as the seed survives the consumption of a fruit, waiting for a suitable opportunity to germinate and produce more such fruit, so the tendency or impulse to do such an action again will remain within us in a dormant form, waiting to assert itself either when some seemingly external experience prompts it or when no other stronger impulse has a hold on our mind.

These *karma-vāsanās* or mental impulses are the seeds of our desires, which are the forces that impel us to do actions by mind, speech and body. Whether any particular action can be classified from a relative perspective as being a good action or a bad action, the impulse or latent desire to do such an action again is yet another knot that helps to bind us to the perpetually revolving wheel of *karma* or action.

If bad actions are like iron chains that bind us and immerse us in the restless ocean of action, good actions are like golden chains that bind us and immerse us in that same ocean. The only difference between the seeds left by good actions and the seeds left by bad actions is that the former will impel us to do more good actions, which will yield relatively pleasant fruit or resulting experiences, whereas the latter will impel us to do more bad actions, which will yield relatively unpleasant fruit or resulting experiences.

Therefore Sri Ramana says in verse 2 of *Upadēśa Undiyār* that any action that we may do will only immerse us further in the ocean of action, and will therefore not liberate us from the bondage of compulsively doing more action. Since this bondage results from our illusion that we are this body-bound mind, which is the doer of actions and the experiencer of the resulting pleasant and unpleasant fruits, it cannot be removed by any action that this mind may do, but can only be removed by the absolutely clear experience of true self-knowledge.

So long as we do any action, we will perpetuate the illusion that we are this mind and body, which are the instruments that actually do such actions. Since we are in reality not this ever-active mind or body, but only the underlying self-conscious being, 'I am', in which they appear and disappear, in order to experience ourself as we really are we must separate ourself from these instruments of action by remaining unswervingly as our ever-inactive self-conscious being.

Therefore we cannot attain liberation by 'doing' anything but only by just 'being'. That is, liberation from the bondage of our present illusion that we are a finite individual, who does actions by mind, speech and body, cannot be achieved by our doing action of any sort whatsoever, but only by our being just the absolutely non-dual self-conscious being that we always really are. Since the goal that we seek to achieve is just action-free self-conscious being, the only path or means by which we can achieve it is likewise just action-free self-conscious being.

This oneness of the path and the goal is expressed by Sri Ramana clearly and emphatically in verse 579 of *Guru Vācaka Kōvai*:

> Because of the non-dual nature [or greatness] of [our eternally] enduring *svarūpa* [our own essential self], [and] because of the

> [consequent] fact that excluding [this non-dual] self there is no other *gati* [refuge, remedy or way to attain it], the *upēya* [the goal] which is to be reached is only self and the *upāya* [the means to reach it] is only self. [Therefore] see that they [our goal and our path] are *abhēda* [not different].

In this verse Sri Ramana emphasises three times the truth that our goal and the path to reach it are essentially the same. Firstly he says that because our ever-existing self is non-dual there is no way by which we can experience it other than this self itself. Hence our essential self is our only refuge if we wish to be saved from the bondage of *karma* or action, that is, from the illusion that we are a finite person who is ensnared in duality and who consequently does actions and experiences their results. Secondly he says, '*upēyamum tāṉē upāyamum tāṉē*', which means 'the aim is only self, and the means is only self'. And finally he concludes emphatically that our goal and our path are therefore *abhēda* or 'not different'.

That is, since our essential self is eternally and absolutely non-dual self-conscious being, it is devoid of all otherness and therefore of all action or 'doing', and hence there can be no means to attain it or experience it other than just to be as it is – that is, to remain simply as the thought-free non-dual self-conscious being that we always truly are.

The 'three *karmas*' that Sri Ramana mentions in verse 38 of *Uḷḷadu Nāṟpadu* are (1) our present actions, which we perform by our free will under the influence of our *vāsanās* or the latent 'seeds' of our desires, and which therefore generate not only more such 'seeds' but also 'fruits' to be experienced by us later, (2) the store of the 'fruits' of our past actions that are yet to be experienced by us, and (3) our present destiny or fate, which is the set of those 'fruits' of our past actions that God has selected and ordained for us to experience now. These 'three *karmas*' will all appear to be real so long as we mistake ourself to be a doer and an experiencer, that is, an individual who does actions and experiences pleasure and pain, which are the 'fruits' or consequences of actions that we have done in the past.

If we investigate 'who am I, who now feel that I am doing actions?' – that is, if we keenly scrutinise our own essential consciousness 'I am', which we now confuse with the mind, speech and body that do actions – we will discover that we are actually not a finite individual who does actions by mind, speech and body, but are only the infinite consciousness that just is. When we thus come to know ourself as we really are, we will cease to mistake ourself to be either the doer of any action or the experiencer of the fruit of any action.

In the absence of any such sense of doership or experiencership, all our 'three *karmas*' will slip off us like the skin that slips off a snake. Sri Ramana describes the state in which we will then remain as the state of *mukti* –

liberation, emancipation or salvation – which he says is *nitya*, a word that is usually translated as 'eternal' or 'perpetual', but that also means 'internal', 'innate', 'natural' or 'one's own'.

What is the significance of his using this word *nitya* or 'eternal' to describe the state of true self-knowledge, in which we are liberated from our sense of doership and from all the 'three *karmas*', which result from that sense? This state is eternal because it is the only state that really exists. There is truly never a time when we do not clearly know ourself as we really are.

Our sense of doership, 'I am doing this or that', and all our other confused knowledge about ourself is experienced only by our mind, and not by our real self, which is the infinite and eternal non-dual consciousness that knows only 'I am'. Our mind is a mere apparition or imagination, and it exists only in its own distorted view of the reality. When we know what we really are, we will discover that we have always known only our own real self, and that our mind is a phantom that never really existed.

However, though the absolute truth is that our mind has never really existed, so long as we imagine ourself to be this mind, its existence will appear to be real, but only in its own distorted view. And so long as our mind thus experiences itself as real, it will also experience everything that is known by it as equally real.

That is, all that our mind experiences appears to it to be as real as it itself appears to be. However, except our basic knowledge 'I am', neither our mind nor anything that is known by it is absolutely real. But though none of our knowledge of anything other than 'I am' is absolutely real, it is all relatively real. That is, in relation to our mind, which experiences it, all our knowledge of otherness or duality is real.

Moreover, because our entire experience of duality is real in relation to our mind, each individual element in our experience of duality is also real in relation to certain other individual elements. However, though a particular element may be real in relation to certain other elements, it may appear to be unreal in relation to various other elements. The reality or unreality of anything that we experience within the realm of duality is therefore relative.

For example, in a dream we may feel hungry, and if we eat some food in that dream our hunger will be appeased. Though neither our hunger nor the food that we ate was absolutely real, they were both real in relation to each other, and also in relation to our mind, which experienced them both in the same state of dream. Because the dream food was as real as our dream hunger, it was able to appease it, or rather to give rise to a sense of appeasement, which was as real as our former sense of hunger.

However, shortly before experiencing that dream, we may actually have eaten a full meal in the waking state. In relation to the full belly we experienced before falling asleep, the hunger we experienced in dream was unreal. But our mind had forgotten the full meal it had just enjoyed in the waking state, so the hunger it felt in dream appeared to it to be real.

Though the reality of what we experience in one state may negate the reality of what we experienced in another state, we cannot say that either state is more real than the other. Just because we really felt hungry in dream, we cannot conclude that we did not really have a full belly in the waking state. The reason why the two sets of reality that we appear to experience in these two states seem to contradict each other is that the body we imagine to be ourself in one state is different from the body we imagine to be ourself in the other state. Relative to our waking body, our feeling of fullness is real, but relative to our dream body, our feeling of hunger is equally real.

What we experience in each one of these states is just as real as what we experience in the other one, but neither of them is the absolute reality. Our same mind, which takes one set of experiences to be real in one state, takes another set of experiences to be real in another state.

Because the reality that we experience in waking and the reality that we experience in dream are both only relative forms of reality, neither of them can permanently and conclusively establish the unreality of the other. In waking we may think that we know our experiences in dream to be unreal, but before long we will again mistake our experiences in another dream to be real. However clever we may think we are, our mind will always delude us and make us mistake our present imaginations to be real.

Not only does the reality that we experience in waking fail to convince us permanently that the reality that we experience in dream is unreal, and vice versa, but in fact both these sets of reality have a quite opposite effect. That is, they both serve only to reconfirm the reality of our mind, and in doing so they each reinforce the basic delusion that makes us feel that whatever state our mind currently happens to be experiencing is real.

So long as we experience our mind as real, we cannot but experience whatever we are currently knowing through the medium of our mind as equally real. Only in contrast to some other experience that our mind may later experience will it then be able to conclude that what it is now experiencing was unreal.

Our mind will always feel that what it is now experiencing is more real than what it experienced in the past or will experience in the future. The present moment in time is always experienced by our mind as being relatively the most real moment, and every other moment is felt by it to be relatively less real. Therefore since we always feel that our present set of experiences is real, when we are awake we always feel that our present waking experiences are real, whereas when we are dreaming we always feel that our then present dream experiences are real.

Since our mind is the root cause that makes all our relative experiences appear real, and since our experiences in both waking and dream reinforce the seeming reality of our mind, nothing that we experience in either of these two states, except of course our basic and permanent consciousness 'I am', can enable us to discover with absolute clarity and certainty the unreality of all relative experience. Only in the real, absolute and non-dual state of true self-knowledge will all relative knowledge be dissolved permanently. That is, we can know for certain that our mind and all that it experiences in both waking and dream are entirely unreal only when we actually experience the absolute reality of our own essential consciousness of being, 'I am'.

Until we experience the absolute reality of our own essential self, we will continue to experience our mind and its knowledge of duality and otherness as real. However, though we experience them as if they were real, neither our mind nor anything known by it, except 'I am', is absolutely real. Therefore the reality of our mind and of all the duality and otherness that it experiences is only relative.

Relative to our mind or individual consciousness, this world is real. Since it is real, everything that exists in it is equally real, including all the people and the innumerable other sentient creatures, and all their various actions and experiences. However, though they are real, none of these things are absolutely real, but are only relatively real. They are in fact all just figments of our imagination, but that does not make them any less real than our mind, which simultaneously imagines and experiences them, because our mind is also just a figment of our imagination.

In a dream we imagine not only the dream world, but also the person who experiences that dream world. Unlike a cinema show, in which the spectators are not actually participants in the drama they are watching, but are quite separate from it, in a dream we are not only the spectator but also a participant who is intimately involved in the drama we are experiencing. We do not experience a dream as an outsider looking in, but as an insider who is actually a part of the dream world. In a dream we cease to be the person we were in the waking state, who is then supposedly lying asleep in a bed, and we become another person – another body – who is engaged in various activities and experiences in some other imaginary world.

The imaginary world that is experienced in a dream is as real as the imaginary person who experiences it. So long as we are dreaming, we mistake that person to be ourself, but when we wake up we understand that he or she was only a product of our imagination. Similarly in our present waking state, we have not only imagined this world, but have also imagined this person who experiences this world. This world is therefore as real as this person, whom we mistake to be ourself so long as we remain in this waking state. In dream we cease to mistake this imaginary person to be ourself, but instead mistake some other imaginary person to be ourself, and in sleep we cease to mistake ourself to be any imaginary person whatsoever.

Though the imaginary person we mistake to be ourself in waking and the imaginary person we mistake ourself to be in a dream are essentially the same person, in that it is our same mind that as each of them experiences a corresponding world, we speak of them as if they were two different persons for two closely related reasons. Firstly and most obviously, the body that we mistake to be ourself in a dream is not the same body that we mistake to be ourself in this waking state. Secondly, in a dream we not only identify ourself with another imaginary body, but we also consequently identify ourself with the experiences we undergo in that body, whereas when we wake up we cease to identify ourself either with that body or with those experiences.

For example, in dream we may have felt, 'I am hungry', but in waking we think, 'I was not really hungry'. In dream we may have felt that we had injured ourself, but in waking we think, 'I was not really injured'. Thus in each state we dissociate ourself both from the body and from the experiences of the person we mistook ourself to be in another state, and in doing so we in effect deny the reality of that person who experienced that other state.

In these two states, waking and dream, we experience two distinct and independent sets of relative reality, and each of those sets of relative reality include a distinct and independent person whom we mistake to be ourself. When we wake up from a dream, we allow the relative reality of this waking state to supplant and supersede the relative reality of that dream. Likewise, when we begin to dream, we allow the relative reality of that dream to supplant and supersede the relative reality of this waking state. Therefore when we wake up from a dream in which the person we mistook ourself to be was hungry or injured, and when we find the person we now mistake ourself to be is neither hungry nor injured, we allow the relative reality of this waking person to supplant and supersede the relative reality of that dream person, and hence we think 'I was not really hungry' or 'I was not really injured'.

The non-hungry and uninjured person of our present waking state is in fact no more real than the hungry or injured person of our dream state, but because we now mistake this waking person to be ourself, he or she appears to us to be more real than the person we mistook to be ourself in dream. Exactly the same thing happens when we begin to dream. The hungry person we mistake ourself to be in our dream is no more real than the person we mistook ourself to be in the waking state, who had just gone to bed with a full belly. However, because in our dream we mistake that hungry person to be ourself, at that time he or she appears to us to be more real than the person we mistook to be ourself in the waking state, and hence the reality of his or her hunger supersedes the reality of the full belly of the waking person.

The person we now mistake ourself to be and the person we mistook ourself to be in our dream are both figments of our imagination, and are therefore both equally unreal. However, at the time that we actually experience each one of these persons to be ourself, that person and his or her experiences appear to be quite real, whereas the other person and his or her experiences appear to be quite unreal. Therefore the judgement that we now make in this waking state about the reality of our present experience and the unreality of our dream experience is one-sided and therefore unfair.

However, we continue to maintain this biased and prejudiced judgement in favour of the reality of our present experience in this waking state only so long as we mistake this waking person to be ourself. As soon as we begin to mistake some other person to be ourself in dream, we make another equally biased and unfair judgement in favour of the reality of our experience in that state.

For example, in a dream we may meet a friend who had died many years before in our waking state, and though we may be surprised to see that friend alive, we nevertheless feel happy to be able to talk to him and tell him all that has happened in our life since we last met him. Though we remember that he was supposed to have died long ago, now that we actually see him we are unable to doubt his present reality, and so we feel convinced that our memory of his having died is somehow not quite correct. In this way, our judgement of reality will always favour whatever state we are currently experiencing.

The reason why we always feel our present state to be real is that at this particular moment we mistake this particular person, who is not only experiencing but also participating in this present state, to be ourself. We cannot but feel that what we mistake to be ourself is real. In a dream, because we mistake that dream person to be ourself, we cannot but mistake him or her to be real, and therefore we mistake all of his or her experiences to be real. Exactly the same happens in this waking state. Because we now mistake this waking person to be ourself, we cannot but mistake him or her to be real, and therefore we mistake all of his or her experiences to be real.

Therefore, if we analyse our experiences in waking and dream carefully and without partiality, we will have to conclude that our waking experiences have no greater claim to reality than our dream experiences. Both are relatively real while we experience them, even though they each appear to be unreal while we are experiencing the other state. Each is real relative only to the person who experiences them, whom at that time we mistake to be our real self. However, though they each appear to be real from the standpoint of the person who experiences them, they are both actually mere products of our imagination.

What gives all our imaginary experiences a seeming reality is only the actual reality of ourself. Our experiences all appear to be real while we experience them because they are experienced by us. But what is the actual reality of ourself, who experience them? We experience them as a person, and that person is a part of our imaginary experience. What reality does that imaginary person have? There is only one element of actual reality in that imaginary person, and that is our essential consciousness of being, 'I am'. Because we feel 'I am experiencing this', whatever we experience appears to be real.

However, though our simple consciousness 'I am' is absolutely real, our compound consciousness 'I am experiencing' is unreal. That is, it is unreal in the sense that it is not absolutely real. It is a mere imagination, a transient apparition, which appears at one time and disappears at another time.

Moreover, not only is its appearance transient, but it appears only in its own view, and not in the view of our simple adjunct-free consciousness 'I am'. In the view of this simple self-consciousness 'I am', only 'I am' exists. Other than this simple and basic consciousness 'I am', everything is an imagination, and is experienced only by the imaginary consciousness that imagines 'I am experiencing'.

This imaginary consciousness 'I am experiencing' is our mind, which is what becomes one person in one state and another person in another state. This imaginary consciousness cannot remain without becoming a person, because it needs to limit itself as an imaginary form in order to be able to imagine and experience things other than itself. The basic form in which it always limits itself is a physical body, which it imagines to be itself, and through the five senses of that imaginary body it experiences an imaginary world. The compound consciousness that arises when we imagine 'I am this body' is what constitutes the person we become.

In each state of dualistic experience – that is, in each of the many dreams that we experience, of which our present waking state is just one – we become a person, who is an intimate part of that dualistic state, and who is therefore entirely caught up in the seeming reality of everything that he or she experiences in that state. Since everything that we experience in any state of duality is a product of our own imagination, the imaginary person that we mistake ourself to be whenever we experience such a state is no more real than any of the other imaginary people and things that we experience in that state.

The only thing about this imaginary person that distinguishes him or her from all the other imaginary people in that state is that our experience of this imaginary person is mixed and confused with our consciousness 'I am', and therefore we feel 'I am this person who is experiencing all this'. Because we thus imagine ourself to be this experiencing person, who is a part of the world that we are experiencing in that state, we become entangled and ensnared in the seeming reality of all that we are then experiencing.

That is, because we confuse our essential consciousness 'I am' with this imaginary person, who seems to be experiencing the current state, we mistake him or her to be real. And because we thus attribute reality to this experiencing person, we thereby attribute the same degree of reality to all that he or she is experiencing. Therefore, though everything that we experience is just as real as this experiencing person, whom we imagine to be ourself, everything that we experience actually derives its seeming reality only from this experiencing person, who in turn derives his or her seeming reality only from our own essential self-consciousness 'I am'.

In a dream we may sometimes think that we are just dreaming, but even then we are unable to change what we are experiencing in that dream. Since the dream is our own imagination, why can we not imagine it in any way we wish?

The reason is that we who wish to change that imaginary experience are ourself a part of it. Because we have imagined ourself to be a person who is not only experiencing an imaginary world, but is also a part of that imaginary world, we have in effect become a figment of our own imagination. Being a part of the dream we have imagined, we are powerless to change it. Our power of imagination is so intense and vivid that whenever we imagine something, we become ensnared in our own imagination.

Since we who experience our imagination are unable to control it, who or what does control it? Is it running haphazardly, or is it being regulated in some way? Though there does often appear to be an element of disorderliness and haphazardness in the events we experience in a dream, at least in our waking world there does appear to be a high degree of order and regularity. What then is the power or controlling force that regulates all the events that we experience in this imaginary world that we are now experiencing? Clearly it is not us as an individual, because as a part of this imaginary world we are subject to the order by which it is running. We cannot change this world at will, just as we cannot change our dream world at will.

Though the world we experience is a product of our own imagination, as an individual in this world we are unable to regulate the order by which it is running. Therefore the power that is regulating this imaginary world is separate from this individual that we now imagine ourself to be. What then is that power? Is it our real self?

No, it cannot be, because our real self is just being, and knows nothing other than mere being. Our real self is just our essential consciousness of being, 'I am', and since it knows only its own being, in its view there is no imagination or any product of imagination. Since it is infinite, undivided and non-dual, it alone truly exists, and there is nothing other than it for it to know. That is, our real self is the absolute reality, and as such it has no function, but is just the substratum, support and only true substance of this world of relativity and duality.

Since it is not us as our individual mind, nor us as our real self, the power that regulates all that we imagine appears to us to be something separate from us. That seemingly separate power is what we commonly refer to as 'God'.

Though God appears to be separate from us, his separateness exists only in the limited and distorted view of our mind. In the unlimited view of God, neither we nor this world are separate from him, but are just distorted forms of his own essential being.

In reality, God is not other than our own real self, but what seemingly distinguishes him from our real self is his function. The only 'function' of our real self is to be, whereas the function of God is to regulate this entire world of our imagination. Because he has this function of regulating or governing this entire world, God is in effect an entity or being that is separate both from the world and from us as individuals.

In reality neither this world, which we imagine we experience through our five senses, nor God, who regulates exactly what we experience in this world, are separate from us, that is, from our real self. However, because we have separated ourself as a finite mind or individual consciousness, the world and God both appear to be separate from us. Therefore the root cause of the seeming separation or division that we experience between ourself, the world and God is our basic imagination that we are a separate individual consciousness.

In a state devoid of form, there can be no separation, so we are able to separate ourself only by imagining ourself to be a form. Because we imagine ourself to be a distinct form, other forms that are separate from us also appear to exist. The basic form that we imagine to be ourself is our physical body, but by imagining ourself to be this body, we also give rise to a more subtle form, namely our mind, which is the individual consciousness that feels 'I am this body', and we thereby feel ourself to be this more subtle form also. Thus the form that distinguishes us as an individual is a compound form consisting of the physical form of this body and the subtle form of this mind.

By imagining this compound form to be ourself, we seemingly divide or separate ourself from our own absolute reality – our formless, infinite and indivisible real self – and having separated ourself thus, we experience our own self as two other basic entities, namely the world and God. Because we imagine the world and God to be separate from us, we imagine them to be forms like us. Therefore in verse 4 of *Uḷḷadu Nāṟpadu* Sri Ramana says:

> If we are a form, the world and God will be likewise. If we are not a form, who could see their forms, [and] how? Can the sight [whatever

> is seen] be otherwise than the eye [the consciousness that sees it]? We, that eye [the formless consciousness 'I am'], are the limitless eye [the infinite consciousness].

The form in which this world exists in our imagination is a physical form, like our physical body, and the form in which God exists in our imagination is a more subtle form, like our mind. Just as we cannot see our mind as a physical entity, we cannot see God as a physical entity, but that does not mean that he does not have a form. Though we cannot see his form in the same manner that we see the physical form of this world, he is not for that reason any less real than this world.

Just as our mind is the soul that animates the physical form of our body, so God is the soul that animates the physical form of this entire world. We cannot see the mind in the physical body of another person, but from the behaviour of that physical body we are able to infer that a mind is present within it. Likewise we are able to infer the presence of God in this world even though we cannot see him.

Just as our mind is a subtle and intangible form, a form that we experience as our first thought 'I', so God is also a subtle and intangible form, a form that we can experience only as a thought, a concept, a belief or a mental image. However, just because the form of God as we know him is only a thought or mental image, this does not mean that he is unreal. As a form or separate being, God is as real as this world and as our individual self.

Even the physical forms of our body and of this entire world are actually only thoughts or mental images, but that does not mean that they are unreal. Our individual self, the world and God are all thoughts, and as such they are real, but only relatively real. As separate entities, none of them is the absolute reality, but they are each a relative reality. The world and God are both as real as our mind, our individual consciousness, which experiences them both as mental images.

As distinct mental images, not only the world and God but even our own individual self or mind exists only in our imagination. As soon as we imagine ourself to be a separate individual, the world and God also come into existence as separate entities. The reality of each one of these three basic entities is inseparable from the reality of the other two. Though all three of them are imaginary, so long as we experience the existence of ourself as an individual, we will also experience the existence of the world and God.

As Sri Ramana says in the seventh paragraph of *Nāṉ Yār?*, which we discussed in the previous chapter:

> That which actually exists is only *ātma-svarūpa* [our own essential self]. The world, soul and God are *kaṟpaṉaigaḷ* [imaginations, mental

> creations or fabrications] in it [our essential self], like [the imaginary] silver [that we see] in a shell. These three [basic elements of relativity or duality] appear at the same time and disappear at the same time. [Our] *svarūpa* [our 'own form' or essential self] alone is the world; [our] *svarūpa* alone is 'I' [our mind or individual self]; [our] *svarūpa* alone is God; everything is *śiva-svarūpa* [our essential self, which is *śiva*, the absolute and only truly existing reality].

Therefore, though God as a separate entity is only a figment of our own imagination, he is nevertheless as real as this world, and also as real as our mind, which imagines him to be separate from itself. So long as we experience our mind as if it were real, we cannot deny the relative reality of God. Since he is the infinitely subtle power that regulates everything that we experience in this or any other world, he is as real as anything else that we experience.

As we saw above, the function of God is to regulate or govern this world and all the individuals in it. His overall function of governing everything in this universe includes many aspects or sub-functions, including various material functions such as ensuring that all the physical objects in this universe obey the various 'laws of nature' – the laws of mathematics, physics, chemistry, biology and so on. However, his most important and significant function is his most subtle one, which is to bestow his 'grace' or 'blessing' upon all us individual souls in such a manner as to guide us towards and along the path that leads to 'salvation' or true self-knowledge.

This function of bestowing grace includes ordaining the time, the place and the manner in which each of the 'fruits' or consequences of all our past actions should be experienced by us. We generate these 'fruits' by thought, word and deed, that is, by using our free will to perform *karmas* or actions through our mind, speech and body. All these actions that we thus perform by our free will are driven by the force of our desires.

When our desires are strong and we do not keep them in check, they rage wildly as thoughts in our mind and impel us to speak and act rashly, selfishly and without concern for the effects that our words and actions will have upon others. Such selfishly motivated thoughts, speech and actions are 'bad *karmas*' or 'sins', and by such sins we generate bad 'fruits', which we will later have to experience as some form of suffering or pain.

When we keep a check on our desires, and shape them with due concern for other people and creatures, we will think, speak and act more carefully and with greater compassion, not wishing to cause any harm to any other living being. Such actions of mind, speech and body that we perform with due care and true compassion are 'good *karmas*', by which we generate good 'fruits', which we will later have to experience as some form of pleasure.

Good desires lead to good actions, which in turn yield good 'fruit', while bad desires lead to bad actions, which in turn yield bad 'fruit'. The rate at which we generate 'fruit' is determined by the strength of our desires. Whether they are good desires or bad desires, or as is usually the case, a mixture of both, if our desires are strong we will generate 'fruit' rapidly. We can avoid generating fresh 'fruit' only by surrendering our will to God, that is, by giving up all our desires, both good and bad.

However, because our desires are generally very strong, we usually generate fresh 'fruit' at a much greater rate than we are able to experience them. Thus in each single lifetime we generate far more 'fruit' than we could possibly experience in a single lifetime, so during the course of many lifetimes we have each accumulated a vast store of 'fruits' that we are yet to experience. Even if our desires are now greatly reduced due to our efforts to surrender our own will and to yield ourself to the will of God, we will still have a vast stock of 'fruits' that we have accumulated as a result of our past desires.

From the vast store of the 'fruits' of our past actions that we have not yet experienced, God is able to select carefully those 'fruits' that will be most beneficial for us to experience now, and he therefore ordains that those 'fruits' should be experienced by us as our destiny or fate in this present lifetime. The 'fruits' that he destines us to experience now are those that will be most conducive to the development of our spiritual maturity, that is, to enkindling in our mind the clarity of discrimination that will enable us to free ourself from our desires, fears and attachments, and to develop the true love just to be. Since everything that we experience is our destiny, and since our destiny is those 'fruits' of our past actions that for our own greatest good God has carefully selected and ordained for us to experience now, whatever we happen to experience is truly the 'will of God'.

All the divine qualities of God that are described by our various religions are true. Most importantly, he is all-loving, all-knowing and all-powerful. Because he is omniscient or all-knowing, nothing can happen in this world that he does not know. Because he is omnipotent or all-powerful, nothing can happen in this world without his consent. And because he is all-loving, or rather because he is love itself, nothing can happen in this world that is not for the ultimate good of all concerned.

All this is true, but only as true as our existence as a separate individual consciousness. If we are real as a separate individual, then the God and all his divine qualities are also real. In other words, until we attain true self-knowledge and thereby merge in our own real self, losing our separate individuality, God will exist as a separate all-loving, all-knowing and all-powerful being, and he will always be guiding and assisting us in our efforts to know ourself. However, when we do finally know our real self and thereby become free from the delusion that we are a separate individual, God will also cease to exist as a separate being, and will instead be experienced by us as our own real self.

As a separate being, God is real, but only relatively real. So long as we imagine him to be separate from us, he cannot as such be the absolute reality, which is infinite and therefore separate from nothing. However, his separation from us is real only in the limited and distorted view of our mind. In his real nature or essential being, God is always one with our own essential being, so when we experience our essential being as it really is, we will discover that God is our own real self, and that as such he is the absolute reality.

So long as we feel ourself to be a person, a distinct and finite individual, we have a tendency to consider God to be some sort of a person – not a limited person like ourself, but somehow a person nonetheless. We believe God to be infinite, yet we nevertheless consider him to be a person. How can we reconcile this obvious contradiction, and what is the actual basis of this almost universally held concept of God?

How can God be both the infinite fullness of being and any sort of person, even if we consider that person to be the 'Supreme Person'? If he is truly infinite, he cannot be a person of any sort whatsoever, because a person is by definition a finite individual, a distinct and separate being. What then are we to infer from the fact that we have this confused notion of an infinite yet personal God? Does this not indicate that none of our concepts of God are actually an adequate depiction of his true nature, because in reality he transcends all human conception?

It is true that God is infinite, but as such he cannot be separate either from ourself or from any other thing. Since he is the infinite fullness of being, he is the whole that includes all things within itself, and as such he is the essence of everything. However, so long as we do not experience his infinite being as our own real self – our own true essence – we mistake ourself to be a finite individual, and this mistaken view of ourself distorts our conception of the infinite reality that we call God, making us feel that he is somehow separate from us.

Given the fact that we mistake ourself to be somehow separate from the infinite reality that we call God, relative to this mistaken view both of ourself and of God do we have any valid reason to consider God to be a person? Is our concept of a personal God even a remote approximation to the truth of his nature? Surprising though it may seem, our conception of God as a person does in fact have a reasonable and valid basis in reality. What is that basis?

The ultimate reality of God is that he is our own real self, our essential being. As we have seen earlier, an intrinsic characteristic of ourself is that we love ourself and we love happiness, because happiness is our own true nature. When we remain as we really are, that is, as our pure self-conscious being, devoid of all 'doing' and dualistic 'knowing', we experience perfect happiness, because our essential being, which is our adjunct-free non-dual consciousness of being, is itself the infinite fullness of happiness. However, when we imagine ourself to be a finite individual, we seemingly separate ourself from the infinite happiness which is our own true being, and hence we become restless, hankering to experience once again that infinite happiness.

Our love to be happy is inherent not only in us as an individual, but also in us as the infinite and non-dual consciousness of being. Love is in fact our true nature – our own essential being. We can never for a moment remain without love for happiness, because we are that love. Our true self-conscious and perfectly happy being is infinite love, because happiness and love are inseparable. We love whatever makes us happy, and we are made happy by experiencing whatever we love. The ultimate happiness lies in experiencing that which we love most, which is ourself – our own true self-conscious being.

When we imagine ourself to be a finite individual, we seemingly separate ourself from God, who is in reality nothing other than our own true being, which is perfect peace and absolute happiness. Whether we know it or not, our love for happiness is love for God, because 'God' is a name that we give to the infinite happiness that we all seek.

Since God is in truth our own real self, he loves us as himself, and his only 'will' or 'desire' is that we should be perfectly happy. Because he loves each and every living being as himself, and because he therefore loves us all to be infinitely happy as he is, all religions teach the fundamental truth that God is love.

Because we each feel ourself to be a human being, we cannot avoid thinking of the love of God in anthropomorphic terms. Due to our deluded experience of ourself as an individual person, we mistake love to be something personal, and we are unable to conceive of a love that is impersonal, or rather, transpersonal. Hence, though in reality the love of God transcends all forms of limitation, including the limitation that is inherent in the love of one person for another person, we are not entirely mistaken in considering God to be a person whose love is all-embracing. That is, from the limited standpoint of our human mind, the love that God has for each one of us does function in a manner that is very similar to the love between one person and another.

The love that is the true nature of God, and that manifests in our view as a seemingly personal love for each one of us, is the basis of our belief in a personal God. Though in reality he is not a person, but is the essential substance and infinite totality of all that is, from the finite standpoint of our human mind, he does in effect appear to act as a person who has unbounded love for each and every one of us.

Therefore, though our belief in the seemingly personal nature of God may appear to be incompatible with the ultimate truth of his nature, namely that he is the infinite, indivisible, non-dual and absolute reality, which is our own true self or essential being, this superficial incompatibility is reconciled by the fact that God is not only infinite being and consciousness, but is also infinite love.

Because he is infinite being, and because there is therefore nothing that is separate from or other than him, he is indeed all-powerful or omnipotent. Because he is infinite consciousness or knowledge, being the ultimate foundation and essential substance of all forms of knowledge, he is indeed all-knowing or omniscient. And because he is infinite love, having unbounded love for everything as his own self, he is indeed all-loving.

So long as we imagine ourself to be a particular person, the almighty, all-knowing and all-loving infinite reality that we call 'God' does appear to function as a person, and therefore we are able to experience an intensely personal love for him, even though we may understand the truth that he is the impersonal absolute reality. By cultivating such love for him in our heart, we can learn to surrender our self-deluded individual will to his divine 'will' – which is the simple love just to be – and thereby we can attune ourself to his true nature of non-dual self-conscious being.

The personal love that we feel for God is by no means a love that is one-sided on our part. In fact, if it is in any way one-sided, it is on his part and not ours, because his love for us is infinitely greater than our love for him. Therefore, when we cultivate sincere love for him, he responds in far greater measure, helping us to surrender ourself entirely to him by drawing our mind inwards, thereby establishing it firmly in our fundamental consciousness of our own being, 'I am', which is his real nature.

In truth, however, God does much more than just respond to the love that we feel for him, because he is actually responsible for enkindling such love in our heart. That is, since he is the ultimate source of all love, whatever love we feel for him originates only from him.

Though we speak of our personal relationship with God in this apparently dualistic manner, the duality that seems to exist in the love between him and us actually exists only in the inherently dualistic outlook of our own mind, and not in the inherently non-dualistic outlook of his real being. Since he knows us and loves us as his own essential self, his love is in truth always perfectly non-dual, and therefore completely non-personal. Nevertheless, though the absolute truth is that his love for us is non-dual and non-personal, from the relative standpoint of our mind the seemingly dualistic and personal nature of his love is quite real.

That is, his personal love for us is every bit as real as our seeming existence as a separate individual person. So long as we mistake ourself to be a person, the non-dual love that God has for us will appear to us to be a personal love, albeit a love that is infinite. Only when we respond to his infinite love by surrendering our mind or separate individuality entirely to him – sacrificing it in the clarity of our own self-conscious being, which is his true essence – will we be able to experience the real non-dual and transpersonal nature of his love.

Though in the limited and distorted view of our mind God appears to perform certain functions, in reality he is just being, and hence he does not do anything. All the functions that he appears to perform happen due to his mere presence, without him actually doing anything. This fact is explained graphically by Sri Ramana in the fifteenth paragraph of *Nāṉ Yār?*:

> Just as in the mere presence of the sun, which rose without *icchā* [wish, desire or liking], *saṁkalpa* [volition or intention], [or] *yatna* [effort or exertion], a crystal stone [or magnifying lens] will emit fire, a lotus will blossom, water will evaporate, and people of the world will engage in [or begin] their respective activities, do [those activities] and subside [or cease being active], and [just as] in front of a magnet a needle will move, [so] *jīvas* [living beings], who are caught in [the finite state governed by] *muttoḻil* [the threefold function of God, namely the creation, sustenance and dissolution of the world] or *pañcakṛtyas* [the five functions of God, namely creation, sustenance, dissolution, concealment and grace], which happen due to nothing but the special nature of the presence of God, move [busy themselves, perform activities, make effort or strive] and subside [cease being active, become still or sleep] in accordance with their respective *karmas* [that is, in accordance not only with their *prārabdha karma* or destiny, which impels them to do whatever actions are necessary in order for them to experience all the pleasant and unpleasant things that they are destined to experience, but also with their *karma vāsanās*, their inclinations or impulsions to desire, think and act in particular ways, which impel them to make effort to experience certain pleasant things that they are not destined to experience, and to avoid certain unpleasant things that they are destined to experience]. Nevertheless, he [God] is not *saṁkalpa sahitar* [a person connected with or possessing volition or intention]. Even one *karma* does not adhere to him [that is, he is not bound or affected by any *karma* or action whatsoever]. That is like world-actions [the actions happening here on earth] not adhering to [or affecting] the sun, and [like] the qualities and defects of the other four elements [earth, water, air and fire] not adhering to the all-pervading space.

Like the sun, whose mere presence causes so many things to happen on this earth, God has no *icchā* or *saṁkalpa*, desire or intention, and hence he never makes any *yatna* or effort to do anything, yet his mere presence causes all living beings to act, each according to his or her own destiny and personal inclinations. Though all that happens happens due to his mere presence, he remains completely unaffected by anything that happens – either by any action or by its effects. He does not do anything, and he is not affected by anything that appears to be done, because he is pure being.

Being is the single, non-dual, undivided and infinite 'is'-ness or essence of all that is, and as such it just is, and never does anything. Whatever we or anything else may appear to do, our essential 'is'-ness or being remains as it is. All *karma*, all action or 'doing', is finite and therefore relative and superficial. That which is infinite, absolute and essential is only being. All 'doing' depends upon 'being', and it can happen only in the presence of 'being'. Unless we are, we cannot do, but whatever we do does not in any way affect, change or modify the fact that we are. Being therefore transcends all forms of doing.

God is the infinitude or fullness of being. He is the 'is-ness' or essence of all that is. Because he is the essence of everything, he is present everywhere, in all places and at all times. His all-pervading presence is therefore just his being, which is the essential being or 'is'-ness of everything. Because he is the one infinite whole or fullness of being, nothing can exist apart from him, and hence he is present in everything as everything.

Because he is everything, he is also said to be *mahākartā*, the 'great doer', or *sarvakartā*, the 'all doer', the one who does everything, including the five fundamental actions or *pañcakṛtyas*, namely *sṛṣṭi*, the creation or projection of this entire appearance of duality, which we call the 'world' or 'universe', *sthiti*, the sustenance or maintenance of this appearance, *saṁhāra*, the dissolution or withdrawal of this appearance, *tirōdhāna* or *tirōbhāva*, the concealment or veiling of the reality, which not only enables *sṛṣṭi*, *sthiti* and *saṁhāra* to take place, but also more specifically enables living beings to continue to do *karmas* and to experience their consequences so long as they have desire to do so, and *anugraha* or grace, the revealing of the reality, which enables us to experience true self-knowledge and thereby to transcend the unreal state of duality in which all these *pañcakṛtyas* appear to happen.

However, though in our limited outlook it appears that God does all these 'five actions' or *pañcakṛtyas*, he does not in fact do anything. He just is, and due to the mere presence of his 'is'-ness or being all these *pañcakṛtyas* happen automatically and spontaneously.

Therefore, if we wish to say that God does everything, that is true only in the sense that he does it all by just being. This is why Sri Ramana says that these *pañcakṛtyas* all happen due to *īśaṉ sannidhāna viśēṣa mātra*, which means 'nothing but the special nature of the presence of God'.

The fact that God is just the infinite fullness of being and therefore does not do anything is the ultimate and absolute truth. However, from the limited standpoint of our finite mind, the fact that he is separate from us and has certain functions to perform is relatively real. That is, so long as we feel ourself to be a doer of action, it will appear to us that the functions of God are actions that he is actually doing.

So long as any action is done, there has to be something or someone who is doing that action, so from our relative standpoint we are correct in believing that God is the ultimate doer of everything. The fact that he is just being, and that due to his mere being or presence all actions appear to be done, can be fully comprehended by us only when we experience ourself as just being, and thereby discover that we have never done anything, and that all action or 'doing' was a mere imagination that existed only in the distorted view of our unreal mind.

All 'doing' is merely a distortion of being. Though being is truly the only reality, and though it just is, in the limited and distorted view of our mind it is experienced as doing. Though all doing is an unreal appearance, being a mere figment of our imagination, it could not even appear to be real if it were not supported by the underlying reality of being. Before we can imagine that we are doing anything, we must first know that we are. The imagination that we are doing appears and disappears, but the knowledge that we are endures. Since our being alone endures, it is the only permanent and absolute reality, and therefore the appearance of doing is an illusion that can occur only due to being, or rather, due to our mind's distorted view of being.

Just as we are real in two very distinct senses, so God is real in the same two distinct senses. As a finite individual consciousness that imagines 'I am this body', 'I am doing this or that', we are relatively real, but as the infinite consciousness 'I am', we are absolutely real. Likewise, as a separate all-doing, all-loving, all-knowing and all-powerful being, God is relatively real, but as our own infinite consciousness 'I am', which is the limitless fullness of being, love, knowledge and power, he is absolutely real.

So long as God and ourself appear to be two separate beings, the world will also appear to exist. Relative to our individual self or mind, God and the world are both perfectly real. None of these three separate entities is any less real than the other two. We cannot experience either the world that we perceive or the God who governs it as unreal so long as we experience our experiencing mind as real.

Understanding theoretically that our mind, the world and God are all unreal is necessary, but it is of practical value to us only to the extent that it enables us to develop true inward detachment from our mind and our entire life in this world, and true love to know and to be our own real self. If we believe that we have understood the world to be unreal, but we still have desire to enjoy any of the seeming pleasures of this world, we are only deluding ourself. The sole purpose and benefit of our understanding the theory of spiritual philosophy is to enable ourself to develop the true love to experience only our own essential self, which is the one and only absolute reality, and the true freedom from any desire to experience anything else.

If we really understand that this world, our mind and everything other than our essential consciousness of being is unreal, we should turn our attention inwards to discover what is real. However, until we actually experience the absolute and infinite reality as our own self, we will continue to experience our finite mind as ourself, and hence we will inevitably experience our mind and everything known by it as real. So long as we experience ourself to be this mind-body complex, we will continue to experience the world as real.

Though for our true inward purpose of discovering the absolute reality we must develop the understanding and conviction that this world is unreal, for all outward purposes we must behave as if this world were real, because it is unreal only from the standpoint of the absolute reality, and not from the standpoint of our equally unreal mind.

Relative to our mind, this world is real, so we must interact with it accordingly. For example, the fact that fire burns may not be the absolute reality, but it is definitely a relative reality. Though we may imagine that we have understood fire to be unreal, if we touch it we will still feel pain. The fire, our pain and our mind, which experiences that pain, are all equally real.

Therefore in the non-dualistic philosophy of *advaita vēdānta*, an important distinction is always made between absolute reality and relative reality, which in Sanskrit are called respectively *pāramārthika satya* and *vyāvahārika satya*. The word *satya* means 'truth' or 'reality', and the word *pāramārthika* is an adjectival form of *paramārtha*, which in this context means the 'ultimate substance' or essence. Thus the term *pāramārthika satya*, which is usually translated as the 'supreme reality' or 'absolute reality', literally means the reality that is the ultimate substance or essence of all things. The word *vyāvahārika* is an adjectival form of *vyavahāra*, which means doing, action, practice, conduct, behaviour, occupation, activity or any worldly interaction such as business, trade, commerce or litigation, and thus *vyāvahārika satya* means mundane, practical, interactive reality. Hence in *advaita vēdānta* the term *vyāvahārika satya* is used to denote the relative reality of our mind and all that it experiences, while the term *pāramārthika satya* is used to denote the absolute reality of our essential being.

In addition to these two quite distinct forms of reality, some scholars like to distinguish a third form of reality called *prātibhāsika satya*. The word *prātibhāsika* is an adjectival form of *pratibhāsa*, which means an appearance, a semblance or an illusion, and thus *prātibhāsika satya* means 'seeming reality' or 'illusory reality'. In certain philosophical texts of *vēdānta* the world that we experience in the waking state is described as *vyāvahārika satya* or 'practical reality', whereas the world that we experience in dream is described as *prātibhāsika satya* or 'seeming reality'. However the same texts also say that certain things that we experience in the waking state, such as a mirage or the illusion of a snake in a rope, are not *vyāvahārika satya* but only *prātibhāsika satya.* Thus the distinction that is supposed to exist between *vyāvahārika satya* and *prātibhāsika satya* is that the former is a reality experienced 'objectively' by many people, whereas the latter is a reality experienced 'subjectively' by just one person.

However, this distinction is false, and it appears to be true only in relation to our present experience in this waking world. Just as we now imagine that this waking world is experienced objectively by many people, so in dream we imagined that that dream world was experienced objectively by many people. In both states, however, the 'many people' exist only as images in our own mind. All forms of relative reality or *vyāvahārika satya* are in fact only an illusion, a seeming reality or *prātibhāsika satya*, and conversely, all forms of seeming reality are real relative to the mind that experiences them. Therefore, though the distinction between *vyāvahārika satya* and *prātibhāsika satya* may appear to be true from a mundane standpoint, from a strictly philosophical standpoint both these terms denote the same form of reality, the relative but illusory reality experienced by our mind.

Basically there are just two forms of reality, absolute reality and relative reality. Everything that we experience is either absolutely real or only relatively real. Since there can truly be only one absolute reality, everything else is only a form of relative reality. Though we may be able to distinguish different forms of relative reality, such distinctions are of no use to us if our aim is to experience the absolute reality.

We distinguish relative reality from absolute reality only because, in order to experience the absolute reality, we must learn to ignore everything that is not absolutely real, and to focus our attention only on that which is absolutely real. However, when we do actually experience the absolute reality as it is, we will discover that it alone exists, and that there is nothing other than it. In that state all relative reality will have merged and disappeared, being found to be nothing other than the one infinite, undivided and non-dual absolute reality.

Some scholastic philosophers describe absolute reality and relative reality as being different 'levels' or 'planes' of reality. However, absolute reality and relative reality cannot be compared in this manner. The absolute reality is absolutely real, so it is relative to nothing, and therefore cannot be compared in any way to anything else.

However, from the limited and distorted perspective of relative reality, we have to say that the absolute reality is the ultimate foundation, substratum or support of all this relative reality. Therefore, though the absolute reality is not related in any way to relative reality, relative reality is intimately, intrinsically and unavoidably related to the absolute reality, because it is entirely dependent upon it. That is, all relativity depends for its own seeming reality upon the true reality of the one absolute essence, which is our own self-conscious being or 'am'-ness, whereas this absolute essence does not depend upon anything else.

The concept of such a one-way relationship would be meaningless and self-contradictory if it were formed with respect to anything other than this 'relationship' between the absolute reality and relative reality. However, we cannot explain this particular 'relationship' as being anything other than a one-way relationship, because of the two partners in this relationship, only the former is truly real, while the latter is a mere apparition – an illusion that exists only in the outlook of our mind, which is itself part of the illusion that it experiences.

The concept of 'levels' or 'planes' of reality can therefore be applied only to the various different forms of relative reality. So long as relative reality appears to exist, there may appear to be any number of different 'levels' or 'planes' of such reality. However, since our aim is to transcend all relative reality and to experience only the non-dual absolute reality, we need not concern ourself with any analysis of or discussions about any different 'levels' or 'planes' of reality, because in truth there is only one reality, and we are that.

To our minds, which are long accustomed to the idea that the problems of life are complex and difficult to comprehend fully, and that the solutions to those problems are equally complex and obscure, the account of reality given here may appear to be excessively simple and free of obscurity, and as such to be overly simplistic. However, the absolute reality is indeed perfectly simple and free of all obscurity.

Complexity and obscurity belongs only to the realm of relativity, and not to the realm of the absolute. That which is absolute is by its very definition perfectly simple and clear. To be absolute it must be perfectly non-dual, because all duality is by its very nature relative. So long as we imagine any form of duality in the reality, that reality is not absolute but only relative.

If we consider the countless relative problems of life, they are indeed extremely complex and impossible to comprehend fully or adequately, and the aim of our discussion here is not to pretend otherwise. What we are considering here is not any relative problems, but is only the absolute reality that underlies all relativity, and since it is absolute that reality must be perfectly simple and free of all obscurity.

Since the absolute reality cannot be limited in any way, it must be infinite and undivided, and as such it must be single, non-dual and free of all complexity. Since it is infinite, nothing can be other than it, so it must be the true and essential being of everything, including ourself. Therefore the absolute reality is nothing other than our own essential being, which we always experience as our perfectly simple, self-knowing and therefore ever clearly self-evident consciousness 'I am'. The absolute reality is as simple and as obvious as that.

The root of all the relative problems that we experience in our life is our mind. Our mind by its power of imagination creates all duality and relativity, and duality and relativity inevitably give rise to conflict and complexity. The problems of the relative world will persist in one form or other so long as we seek to solve them only by relative means.

No relative solution can solve a relative problem perfectly or absolutely. As soon as one relative problem is solved, or appears to be solved, another relative problem pops up. In a relative world, therefore, a problem-free life is inconceivable. Utopia can never be experienced in a world of duality and relativity, but only in a state beyond all duality and relativity – in a state of absolute non-duality.

Since all duality and relativity are experienced only within our own mind, if we wish to find a perfect solution to all the relative problems of life, we must look beyond our mind to the absolute reality that underlies its appearance. Our mind is a relative form of consciousness, and as such it is extremely complex and fraught with problems. In fact our mind thrives on complexity and problems, and it instinctively shies away from a perfectly simple and problem-free state of non-dual self-consciousness. Why? Because in a state of perfectly clear non-dual consciousness, a state of simple and true self-knowledge, our mind cannot survive.

Being an illusory phantom, our mind can appear to exist only in the confusion and darkness of the complex duality of its own self-created state of relative consciousness. In the state of perfectly clear non-dual self-consciousness, all that is known is our simple consciousness of our own being, 'I am'. In the clarity of such absolute non-dual self-consciousness, therefore, the illusory appearance of the relative object-knowing consciousness called 'mind' – the consciousness that feels not merely 'I am' but 'I am knowing this' or 'I am knowing that' – will dissolve and disappear.

CHAPTER 5

What is True Knowledge?

What is 'true knowledge'? Can any knowledge that we now have be called true knowledge, or is all our knowledge just a semblance of true knowledge? Is there indeed any such thing as true knowledge, and if so how can we know what it is? Is it something that we can attain, or is it beyond the power of the human mind to grasp? If it is beyond the power of our mind to grasp, do we have any deeper level of consciousness by which we can experience it? How can we experience true knowledge?

Let us first decide what knowledge can be considered as true. To qualify as being true knowledge in the strictest sense of the term, the knowledge in question must be absolutely true – perfectly, permanently, unconditionally and independently true. That is, it must be a knowledge that is true in its own right, a knowledge that is true at all times, in all states and under all conditions, a knowledge whose truth is not in any way dependent upon, limited by or relative to any other thing, a knowledge whose truth is ever unchanging and immutable, being unaffected by anything else that may appear or disappear, or by any changes that may occur around it. It must also be self-evident, perfectly clear and absolutely reliable – devoid of even the least ambiguity or uncertainty – and must be known directly – not through any intervening media upon whose truth and reliability its own truth and reliability would then depend. Only such knowledge can be considered to be true knowledge in an absolute sense.

Knowledge that is not true from such an absolute standpoint but only from a relative standpoint is not perfectly true. It may be true under some conditions, but it is not true under all conditions. It may be true at one time or in one state, but it is not true at all times or in all states. It is true only relative to certain other things, and hence its truth is dependent upon and limited by the truth of those other things, and is affected by their appearance and disappearance, and by changes that may take place within them. Such relative knowledge is uncertain and unreliable, particularly since it is invariably obtained by us not directly but only through the intervening media of our mind and our five senses, whose truth and reliability are (as we shall see later) open to serious doubt. Knowledge which is thus true only relatively and not absolutely does not warrant the name 'true knowledge' in a strict analysis of what knowledge can be considered as true or real.

Therefore whenever the term 'true knowledge' is used in this book, it means only knowledge that is absolutely true, and not just relatively true.

The aim of this book is not to deny the relative truth or validity of any of the many forms of relative knowledge that we experience, but is to investigate our experience deeply in order to discover whether or not any knowledge within our experience is absolutely true.

If we can discover some knowledge that is absolute, from the perspective of that absolute knowledge we will be able to appreciate better the relativity of all the relative forms of knowledge that we now experience. Because we think that we do not now experience anything that is absolute, we attribute undue reality and give undue credence to the seeming truth of all our relative knowledge. This book, therefore, is primarily concerned not with determining the relative truth of any knowledge, but only with investigating whether there is any absolutely true knowledge that we can experience.

Most of the knowledge that we now take to be true is only relatively true. For example, we generally accept that, with the exception of optical illusions such as a mirage, and other such sensory misperceptions, the knowledge that we acquire by means of our five senses is true. However, all such knowledge is relative, because it is dependent upon the questionable reliability of our five senses, and because it is limited to their range of perception. Since our physical senses are strictly limited and not entirely reliable, they are an imperfect media for acquiring true knowledge. Though they may provide us with knowledge that is relatively true and that meets many of our relative needs, including our biological survival, they cannot provide us with any knowledge that is absolutely true.

Not only is all the knowledge that we acquire by means of our five senses merely relative, but so also is all the knowledge that we acquire by means of our mind. Like our five physical senses, our mind is an imperfect medium for acquiring true knowledge, because it is a limited and unreliable instrument.

We all recognise the fact that much of the knowledge that our mind takes to be true at certain times is not actually true. For example, our mind may mistake an illusion to be true while it is experiencing it, but it later recognises that it was at that time mistaken in its judgement of what is true or real. Likewise, our mind mistakes its experiences in a dream to be true while it is actually experiencing that dream, but it later recognises that all those experiences were imaginary and therefore not true. Since we know that our mind is easily deceived into believing that whatever it is currently experiencing is true, how can we rely upon our mind as a dependable instrument through which we can acquire true knowledge?

Our mind is not just deluded temporarily into mistaking its own imaginations to be true, but is also deluded repeatedly into making this same mistake. Having once understood that in dream it was deluded into mistaking the unreal to be real, it does not thereby become immune from being again deluded in the same manner. The same delusion repeats itself again and again whenever our mind experiences a dream.

Since it is unable to learn from its repeated mistakes, our mind is a very unreliable judge of what knowledge is true and what knowledge is false. When it is so frequently incapable of recognising its own imaginations as false, how can we be sure that anything that it experiences is not merely an illusion, an unreal product of its own imagination?

Our mind has access to only two basic sources of objective knowledge, namely its five physical senses, which it believes provide it with knowledge obtained from outside itself, and its own internally generated knowledge such as its thoughts, feelings, emotions, beliefs, concepts and so on. Neither of these two sources can provide it with consistently reliable information. Its physical senses often provide it with misperceptions, and its internally generated knowledge often provides it with dreams, and when it actually experiences such misperceptions or dreams, it is usually unable to distinguish them from all its other knowledge, which it assumes to be true.

Moreover, our mind is unable to distinguish between the knowledge that it is supposed to have obtained from each of these two sources. In a dream our mind believes that the world it is experiencing is perceived by it through its physical senses, and that that world therefore exists outside itself. However, when it wakes from that dream, our mind recognises that the world in its dream was not actually perceived by it through any physical senses, but was only an internally generated imagination.

Even now in our present waking state, our mind has no means of knowing for certain that the knowledge that it seems to obtain from outside itself through its physical senses is not actually just an internally generated imagination. All the knowledge that our mind experiences is experienced by it within itself, so it has no reliable means of knowing for certain that any of its knowledge is actually derived from outside itself.

Whether we imagine it to be derived from some external source or to be internally generated, or a combination of both, any knowledge we have of anything other than ourself is objective knowledge. All objective knowledge is dualistic and therefore relative, because it involves a distinction between the knowing subject and the known objects. Any knowledge that involves any form of duality must necessarily be relative.

Since the knowledge we have of everything else is objective, dualistic and therefore relative, the only knowledge we have that can possibly qualify as absolute is our subjective and therefore non-dual knowledge of ourself. Our knowledge of ourself, that is, of our own essential being, is the only knowledge that is devoid of all duality and relativity.

To know ourself, that is, to experience our own essential being as 'I am', we do not need the aid of our five senses or even of our mind. We know our own being, 'I am', even in sleep, when we are completely unaware either of our body and its five senses, or of our mind. Therefore our basic knowledge 'I am' is not dependent upon any other thing. In the complete absence of all otherness, such as in sleep, we know 'I am'.

Whatever else we may know, and even when we know nothing else, we always know 'I am'. Therefore our basic knowledge 'I am' is not only completely independent of all other knowledge, it is also permanent and unchanging. Other forms of knowledge may come and go, and they may even appear to be superimposed temporarily upon our basic knowledge 'I am', thereby seemingly obscuring it (though never actually hiding it), but this knowledge 'I am' itself remains permanently, without ever coming or going, appearing or disappearing, or beginning or ending, and without ever undergoing any change. Therefore this basic knowledge of our own being, 'I am', is the only absolute knowledge we experience.

The reason why we always know ourself as 'I am' is that we are consciousness, and consciousness is necessarily and essentially self-conscious. As consciousness, we always know our own being, not because our being is an object known by us, but because it is ourself, our own essential consciousness. We are therefore both being and consciousness. Our being and our consciousness are a single non-dual whole. Our consciousness is being, because it is, and our being is consciousness, because it knows itself.

However, when we say this, we are expressing the oneness of our being and our consciousness crudely and imperfectly, because we are speaking about them in the third person, as if they were objects. Our being-consciousness does not know itself objectively as a third person, but only subjectively as the first person. Therefore, rather than saying that our consciousness is being because it is, we can express the truth more accurately by saying that we are being because we are. Likewise, rather than saying that our being is consciousness because it knows itself, we can express the truth more accurately by saying that we are consciousness because we know ourself.

Still more accurately, we can express the truth by saying that I am being because I am, and I am consciousness because I know myself, because not only does our being-consciousness know itself only subjectively as the first person, but it also knows itself not as the first person plural, but only as the perfectly non-dual first person singular.

In his teachings, whether he happened to be referring to our real self or to our individual self, Sri Ramana often used the first person plural pronoun 'we' rather than the first person singular pronoun 'I', but he did not mean to imply thereby that there is any sense of plurality or duality in our real self. He referred to our real self as 'we' in order to include whomever he was speaking to or writing for, and to indicate that we are all one reality.

In many cases, if he had used 'I' instead of 'we', it would have created the impression that our real self is exclusive, whereas in truth it is all-inclusive. Therefore, wherever he has used the term 'we' in reference to our real self, we should understand that he used it as the first person *inclusive* pronoun rather than as the first person *plural* pronoun.

All our objective knowledge is known by us indirectly through the imperfect media of our mind and five senses, whereas consciousness is known by us directly as our own self. No form of indirect or mediate knowledge can be absolute, because such knowledge is inherently partitioned and dualistic, since it involves a distinction between the subject that is knowing, the object that is known, and the medium through which the subject knows the object. Since absolute knowledge must be free of all limitations, both internal and external, it must be devoid of any divisions, parts or duality. It must therefore be direct and immediate knowledge, knowledge that knows itself, in itself and by itself, without the aid of any internal or external medium.

Absolute knowledge must therefore be self-conscious – perfectly and singly self-conscious. It must be known by itself, and only by itself. It cannot be known by anything other than itself, because if it were it would not be absolute. The existence of anything other than it that could know it would set a limitation upon the wholeness of its being, and would therefore mean that it was not absolute in the fullest sense of the word.

Absolute knowledge cannot exist in relation to anything else, but only in itself and by itself. In order to be absolute, a knowledge must be the only truly existing knowledge. All knowledge that appears to be other than it must be false. Conversely, to be true – absolutely and perfectly true – a knowledge must be absolute.

Since true knowledge must therefore by definition be absolute, it must be a single, infinite, whole, undivided, non-dual, immediate and self-conscious knowledge. The only knowledge that knows itself is our essential consciousness of our own being, 'I am'. Even our mind is not truly self-conscious, because it does not know itself as it really is, and because its seeming self-consciousness is limited to the two imaginary states of waking and dream. The only knowledge that is truly self-conscious, therefore, is our fundamental consciousness 'I am', because it knows itself always, undisturbed and unaffected by the passing of the three transient states of waking, dream and sleep.

Our essential consciousness 'I am' is not only immediately and eternally self-conscious, it is also single, undivided and non-dual. Is it, however, infinite? Is it the unlimited whole, other than which nothing can exist? Yes, it is, because it has no form of its own, and hence it is free of all boundaries and limits. Therefore, since it is not limited in any way, nothing can truly be other than it.

Everything else that appears to exist depends for its seeming existence upon our basic consciousness 'I am'. No other knowledge could exist if our first and original knowledge 'I am' did not exist. Since all other knowledge appears and disappears in our mind, and since our mind appears and disappears in our underlying consciousness 'I am', no knowledge is truly separate from or other than this fundamental consciousness 'I am'.

The 'otherness' of all other knowledge – our feeling that what we know is separate from or other than ourself – is caused by the limitations that we seemingly impose upon ourself when we imagine ourself to be a finite creature, a consciousness that experiences itself as 'I am this body'. However, even when we experience this illusion of separation or 'otherness', all our 'other' knowledge is known in us and by us, so it is truly not separate from or other than ourself. It is in fact all just a product of our imagination, and our imagination is just a distorted function of our consciousness.

The apparent 'being' of every 'other' thing that we know is just a projection of our own true being, which is consciousness. Though other things appear to exist outside ourself, the outside in which they occur is actually just a part of our imagination. The process by which they are projected from within ourself into a seeming outside is in fact just an internal distortion of our consciousness – a distortion that nevertheless occurs not really but only seemingly.

None of the things that we know have any being or existence apart from our knowledge of them, and hence in the final analysis all 'things' are only knowledge, and knowledge is only consciousness. In a dream we experience knowledge of things that appear to be separate from and other than ourself, but when we wake up we recognise that all such knowledge was created by our imagination, and therefore had no independent existence outside our consciousness.

Like any other form of imagination, a dream is just an internal distortion of our natural consciousness. All the knowledge that we experience in our dream is formed in our own consciousness, and of our own consciousness. That is, the substance of which all our imaginations are formed is our own consciousness.

Other than our consciousness, there is no substance from which all our imaginations – our thoughts, feelings, perceptions and every form of dualistic knowledge – could be formed. The only substance we truly know is our own consciousness or being. Everything else that we seem to know is generated by our consciousness within itself and from its own substance.

However, there is an important distinction between our consciousness that seems to imagine and experience other forms of knowledge, and our real consciousness, which experiences only our own being, 'I am'. Our consciousness that imagines that it is experiencing 'otherness' – knowledge of things other than itself – is what we call our 'mind'. Though this mind is in essence just our real and infinite consciousness of being, 'I am', it experiences itself as a finite consciousness because it imagines the appearance of things other than itself. Its separation or distinction from our real consciousness is therefore just an imagination.

Nevertheless, when we are critically analysing our various forms of knowledge or consciousness and testing their reality, this distinction between our object-knowing consciousness and our self-knowing consciousness is one that we have to make in order to be able to experience the latter as it really is. Because this distinction is the root cause of all duality, it is in effect very real and significant so long as we experience even the slightest trace of any duality or 'otherness'.

Since our aim is to experience our true and essential knowledge or consciousness as it really is, a need inevitably arises for us to distinguish it from all the unreal forms of knowledge that we have seemingly superimposed upon it by our power of imagination. Since all other forms of knowledge are experienced in and by our mind, in order to distinguish our true knowledge 'I am' from every other knowledge we need only distinguish it from our mind.

Our mind is just a distorted form of our true consciousness of being, 'I am', and it has become distorted only by imagining things other than itself. Since knowing itself just as 'I am' is the very nature of consciousness, the natural 'target' or resting-place of its attention is itself. That is, in its true and natural state, the focus or attention of our consciousness rests automatically and effortlessly upon itself, and not upon any other thing. Our attention becomes diverted away from ourself towards 'other things' only when we imagine them or form them in our consciousness.

So long as the focus of our consciousness or attention rests naturally upon ourself, we remain as the infinite real consciousness or true knowledge that we always are, but when the focus of our consciousness seems to be diverted towards imaginary objects or thoughts, we seem to become the finite consciousness that we call our 'mind'. Therefore, if our mind wishes to experience the true knowledge that is its own real self, all it need do is withdraw its attention from all other things and to focus it keenly upon its own essential consciousness, 'I am'. This state in which our mind thus rests its attention in itself, knowing only its own being or consciousness, is described by Sri Ramana in verse 16 of *Upadēśa Undiyār* as the state of true knowledge:

> [Our] mind knowing its own form of light, having given up [knowing] external objects, alone is true knowledge.

When our mind knows 'external objects' or things other than itself, it does so by mistaking itself to be a physical body, which is one among those other things that it knows. But when it withdraws its attention back towards itself, it will cease to know any other thing, and thereby it will cease to mistake itself to be a physical body or any other product of its imagination.

By thus attending only to its own essential consciousness or 'form of light', and thereby giving up attending to any form of imagination, our mind will experience itself as its own natural consciousness of being, 'I am'. In other words, by attending to and knowing only its own true consciousness of being, our mind will merge and become one with that consciousness. This non-dual experience of true self-consciousness is the state of true and absolute knowledge.

What exactly does Sri Ramana mean when he speaks of our 'mind knowing its own form of light, having relinquished external objects'? What is our mind's 'own form of light'?

Our mind, as we saw in chapter three, is our compound consciousness 'I am this body', which is composed of two elements, our essential and fundamental consciousness 'I am', and the superimposed adjunct 'this body'. Since the adjunct 'this body' appears at one time and disappears at another time, and since it changes its form, appearing as one body in waking and another body in dream, it is merely a superficial appearance, a spurious and unreal apparition. Therefore the only real element of our mind is our fundamental consciousness 'I am', our essential consciousness of our own existence, because this fundamental and essential consciousness is permanent – not something that appears at one time and disappears at another time – and never changes its form. Since this fundamental consciousness of our own being is thus the true and essential form of our mind, and since it is the 'light' that enables our mind to know not only itself but also all other things, in this verse Sri Ramana refers to it as our mind's 'own form of light'.

When our mind turns its power of attention back on itself, away from all other things, focusing its attention keenly and exclusively upon its fundamental and essential consciousness of its own being, 'I am', it will subside and disappear, merging in and becoming one with that fundamental consciousness. That is, when we, who now mistake ourself to be this limited individual consciousness that we call 'mind', focus our attention exclusively upon our fundamental adjunct-free consciousness 'I am', we will discover this adjunct-free consciousness to be our own real self, and thus we will no longer mistake ourself to be this mind, the adjunct-bound consciousness 'I am this body'.

However, so long as we attend to things other than ourself, we will perpetuate the illusion that we are this mind. In order to know ourself as we really are, therefore, we must stop attending to other things and must attend only to our own essential being – our adjunct-free consciousness 'I am'.

Therefore, when our mind gives up its habit of attending to external objects, and instead knows only its own true form of light – our clear self-luminous consciousness 'I am' – it will no longer appear to be a separate entity called 'mind', but will instead shine only as its own true and essential being, which is our eternally self-knowing consciousness 'I am'. Hence, that which knows our adjunct-free consciousness 'I am' is not actually our mind, but is only our adjunct-free consciousness itself. Since it knows only itself, and is known only by itself, our adjunct-free consciousness 'I am' is essentially non-dual.

Therefore, our 'mind knowing its own form of light, having relinquished external objects' is the non-dual state in which, by knowing its own true and essential nature, our mind has ceased to be the imaginary adjunct-bound, object-knowing consciousness called 'mind', and instead remains only as our essential adjunct-free self-consciousness – our true consciousness, which always knows only its own being, 'I am'.

As Sri Ramana says, this non-dual state of clear self-consciousness or self-knowledge is alone the state of true knowledge. Why is this so? The only thing we know with absolute certainty is 'I am'. If we ourself did not exist, we could not know any other thing. Therefore, because we are conscious, we do exist.

We may not know exactly *what we are*, but we cannot reasonably have any doubt about the fact *that we are*. Our consciousness 'I am' is therefore the only knowledge that we can be absolutely sure is a true knowledge.

Unlike all our other knowledge, which is only relatively or conditionally true, our consciousness 'I am' is absolutely and unconditionally true, because it is permanent, unchanging and perfectly self-evident. Since it is known directly by itself, and not by anything else or through any other medium, its truth or reality does not depend upon any other thing. Because it is true at all times, in all states and under all conditions, and because it is ever unchanging and immutable, being unaffected by anything else that may appear or disappear, or by any changes that may occur around it, it is true in its own right – absolutely, unconditionally and independently true.

Since it is the only thing we experience at all times, in all states and under all conditions, and since it always remains as it is without ever undergoing any change, this fundamental consciousness 'I am' must be our real self, our true and most essential nature. However, though we already know this consciousness 'I am', we do not clearly know it as it is, because it seems to be clouded by the superimposition of our mind – the spurious consciousness that always knows itself mixed with adjuncts, and that can never know itself free of adjuncts as the mere consciousness 'I am'. Therefore, rather than being the means to true knowledge, our mind is in fact the primary obstacle to true knowledge.

Why can no knowledge other than self-knowledge – the non-dual state in which we clearly know and firmly abide as the consciousness that knows only its own being, 'I am' – be considered to be true knowledge? All knowledge other than our real adjunct-free non-dual consciousness 'I am' is known only by our mind – our false adjunct-bound consciousness 'I am this body'. Whereas our unadulterated consciousness 'I am' is essentially non-dual, because it knows only its own being, our mind is an intrinsically dual form of consciousness, because it appears as a separate individual consciousness only by seemingly knowing things other than itself.

All dual knowledge, that is, all knowledge in which what is known is separate from or other than that which knows it, is relative knowledge. That which is known as an object distinct from the knowing subject exists relative to that subject which knows it, and is therefore dependent for its seeming reality upon that subject. Unless the knowing subject is itself real, none of its knowledge of objects can be real.

All the knowledge that we have of objects is only thoughts that our mind has formed within itself by its power of imagination. We cannot know any objects – anything other than our own being, 'I am' – except through the medium of our mind. Hence we cannot know whether any object really exists independent of the thought of it that we have formed in our mind. Therefore all our knowledge about everything other than 'I am' is nothing but thoughts, which are only as real as our mind that has formed them.

As we have seen earlier, our mind, together with all its knowledge of duality, is merely an imagination superimposed upon the one real knowledge, which is our non-dual consciousness 'I am'. Our consciousness 'I am' is non-dual because it knows only itself – its own essential being – and not any other thing. That which knows things that are seemingly other than itself is only our mind.

All objective knowledge – all knowledge of duality, all knowledge other than 'I am' – is known only by our mind, and therefore exists only relative to our mind. Hence all knowledge other than 'I am' is dualistic and relative knowledge, and as such it depends for its seeming reality upon our mind that knows it.

Our mind is an unreal form of consciousness, because it comes into existence as a separate object-knowing consciousness only by falsely identifying itself – its essential consciousness 'I am' – with an adjunct, 'this body', which is merely one of its own thoughts – an image that it has formed within itself by its power of imagination. Since our mind is thus formed only by our power of imagination, all that is known by it is also only a product of our imagination.

How can any such imaginary, relative, dualistic and objective knowledge be considered to be true knowledge? Is it not clear, therefore, that the only true knowledge that we can attain is the clear knowledge of ourself as we really are, devoid of any superimposed adjuncts – that is, knowledge of ourself as our unadulterated and essential self-consciousness, 'I am', which is the absolute non-dual consciousness that knows only itself?

All objective knowledge involves a basic distinction between the subject, who is knowing, and the object, which is known. It also involves a third factor, the subject's act of knowing the object.

Because our knowledge of ourself involves only the inherently self-conscious subject, and no object, we know ourself just by being ourself, and we do so without the aid of any other thing. Because we are naturally self-conscious, we do not need to do anything in order to know ourself. Therefore unlike all our objective knowledge, our knowledge of ourself involves neither an object nor any act of knowing, and hence it is a perfectly non-dual knowledge.

Objective knowledge involves an act of knowing because of the seeming separation that exists between the knowing subject and the known object. That is, because the object is something that seems to be other than the subject, in order to know the object the attention of the subject must move away from itself towards the object. This movement of our attention away from ourself towards something that seems to be other than ourself is an action or 'doing'.

Whereas we know ourself by just being ourself, we can know other things only by actively attending to them – that is, only by directing our mind towards them. When we know ourself, our attention, which is our power of knowing or consciousness, rests in itself, without moving anywhere. But when we know any other thing, our attention must be diverted from ourself towards that other thing.

This act of directing our attention towards something that appears to be other than ourself is what we call thinking. Every thought involves a movement of our attention away from ourself towards some image in our mind. Our mind forms all its thoughts or mental images only by seemingly moving its attention away from itself.

Since all our objective knowledge is just thoughts or mental images that our mind has formed within itself by seemingly moving its attention away from itself, it appears to exist only because of this action, which we call by various names such as thinking, knowing, cognising, experiencing, seeing, hearing, remembering and so on. Likewise, all the objects that we know come into existence only because of our act of knowing them. That is, since all objects are thoughts or images that arise in our mind, they are formed by our action of thinking or imagining them – an action that can occur only when we allow our attention to move seemingly away from ourself.

Thus all objective knowledge involves three basic elements, the knowing subject, its act of knowing and the objects known by it – or in other words, the knower, the knowing and the known. These three basic elements or factors of objective knowledge are known in Sanskrit as *triputi* and in Tamil as *muppuḍi*, two terms which both literally mean 'that which is threefold' but which can be translated more comfortably by the word 'triad'.

Of these three factors of objective knowledge, the first and foremost is the knower, which is our own mind or object-knowing consciousness. Without this first factor, the other two factors could not appear to exist. Therefore our knowing mind is the root or original cause of the appearance of these three factors of objective knowledge. In other words, what these three factors depend upon for their appearance or seeming existence is the appearance of our mind. Hence they will appear to exist only so long as our mind appears to exist.

This truth is clearly stated by Sri Ramana in verse 9 of *Uḷḷadu Nāṟpadu*:

> The pairs and the triads exist [only by] clinging always to one [that is, to our mind or object-knowing consciousness]. If [we] look within [our] mind 'what is that one?', they will slip off [because we will discover that their cause and supporting base, our mind, is itself non-existent]. Only those who have [thus] seen [the non-existence of our mind and the sole existence of our real self] are those who have seen the reality [the absolute reality or true 'am'-ness]. They will not be deluded [confused or agitated by again imagining the existence of such pairs and triads]. See [this absolute reality, which is our own true self – our essential non-dual consciousness of our own being, 'I am'].

In this verse the word *iraṭṭaigaḷ* or 'pairs' means the pairs of opposites such as life and death, existence and non-existence, consciousness and unconsciousness, happiness and unhappiness, real and unreal, knowledge and ignorance, light and darkness, good and bad, and so on. The word *muppuḍigaḷ* or 'triads' means the various forms that the 'triad' or set of three factors of objective knowledge assumes, such as the knower, the knowing and the known, the thinker, the thinking and the thought, the perceiver, the perceiving and the perceived, the experiencer, the experiencing and the experienced, and so on.

The unreality both of these 'triads', which form the totality of our objective knowledge, and of these 'pairs', which are an inherent part of our objective knowledge, being objective phenomena experienced by our knowing mind, is emphasised by the word *viṇmai*, which Sri Ramana added between the previous verse and this verse in the *kaliveṇbā* version of *Uḷḷadu Nāṟpadu*. Being placed immediately before the opening words of this verse, *iraṭṭaigaḷ muppuḍigaḷ*, this word *viṇmai*, which literally means 'sky-ness' – that is, the abstract quality or condition of the sky, which in this context implies its blueness – defines the nature of these 'pairs' and 'triads'. That is, these basic constituents of all our objective or dualistic knowledge are unreal appearances, like the blueness of the sky.

Just as the sky is actually just empty space, which is devoid of colour, so we are actually just the empty space of unadulterated self-consciousness, which is devoid of duality or otherness. But just as the seeming blueness of the sky is formed because the light of the sun is refracted when it enters the earth's atmosphere, so the appearance of duality is formed in the undivided space of our consciousness because the clear light of our non-dual self-consciousness is seemingly divided into many thoughts or mental images when the phantom of our mind arises within us.

This is why Sri Ramana says that these pairs of opposites and triads exist only by 'clinging always to one'. The 'one' to which they always cling is our mind or object-knowing consciousness, and they are said to cling to it because for their seeming existence they all depend upon its seeming existence. When our mind seems to exist, as it does in waking and dream, the pairs of opposites and the triads also seem to exist, and when it does not seem to exist, as in sleep, they also do not seem to exist.

Therefore Sri Ramana says that if we look within our mind to see what that 'one' is, the pairs of opposites and the triads will slip off. That is, if we keenly scrutinise ourself in order to know what this object-knowing consciousness really is, we will discover that it is actually just our essential non-dual self-consciousness, which knows nothing other than itself, and hence all the otherness and duality that it now appears to know will vanish.

Our mind or object-knowing consciousness appears to exist only when we ignore our true non-dual self-consciousness, and hence it will cease to exist when we attend only to ourself – that is, to our fundamental and essential self-consciousness. When we look closely at an imaginary snake, it will disappear, and in its place only the real rope will remain. Similarly, when we look closely at this imaginary object-knowing consciousness that we call our 'mind', it will disappear, and in its place only our real non-dual self-consciousness will remain.

Just as the snake disappears because it is imaginary and therefore never really existed, so our mind will disappear because it is imaginary and has therefore never really existed. And just as the sole reality underlying the imaginary appearance of the snake is the rope, so the sole reality underlying the imaginary appearance of our mind is our fundamental non-dual self-consciousness, 'I am'.

When we look closely at the object-knowing consciousness that we call our 'mind', we will discover that it is non-existent as such, being nothing other than our real consciousness – our non-dual self-consciousness 'I am', which never knows anything other than itself. When we thus discover that our object-knowing mind is non-existent as such, we will also discover that all the duality that appeared to be known by it was likewise non-existent.

This is why Sri Ramana says that if we look within our mind to see what this object-knowing consciousness really is, the pairs of opposites and the triads will 'slip off' – that is, they will disappear along with their root cause, our mind.

After saying that the pairs of opposites and the triads will slip off if we see what the one object-knowing consciousness really is, Sri Ramana says, 'Only those who have seen [thus] are those who have seen the reality'. Here the word *kaṇḍavarē*, which I have translated as 'only those who have seen', means only those who have thus 'seen' or experienced the non-existence of our mind and the sole existence of our real self. The word *uṇmai*, which I have translated as 'the reality', but which etymologically means 'is'-ness or 'am'-ness, here denotes the absolute reality, which is our true 'am'-ness – our own essential non-dual self-conscious being.

Sri Ramana then declares, '*kalaṅgārē*', which means, 'They will certainly not be deluded, confused or agitated'. That is, since all delusion, confusion and agitation arise only due to our knowledge of duality or otherness, which in turn arises only due to the imaginary appearance of our mind, and since our mind will disappear for ever when we experience the absolute and only truly existing reality, which is our own perfectly non-dual self-conscious being, after we have experienced this reality we will never again be deluded or confused by the imaginary appearance of duality.

Thus in this verse Sri Ramana emphasises the fact that our mind is the one foundation upon which this entire imaginary appearance of duality is built, and that we can therefore experience the absolute reality that underlies this appearance only by scrutinising its foundation, our mind. Until we thereby free ourself from our self-delusive imagination that this mind is our real self, we will continue to experience the unreal knowledge of duality, and we will therefore be unable to experience the non-dual true knowledge that is our own real self.

The knowledge that our mind has about the world is twofold, taking the form of knowledge about some things and ignorance about other things. Such relative knowledge and ignorance (which is one of the pairs of opposites to which Sri Ramana refers in verse 9 of *Uḷḷadu Nāṟpadu*) is possible only about things other than ourself.

About ourself we can never really be ignorant, because we always know ourself as 'I am'. However, until we know ourself without the obscuring veil of superimposed adjuncts, we do not know ourself as we really are, but know ourself wrongly as 'I am such-and-such a person'.

Though this wrong knowledge that we seem to have about our true nature is sometimes called 'self-ignorance', 'ignorance of our real self' or 'spiritual ignorance', it is not in fact real, but is merely an appearance that seems to exist only in the outlook of our mind. That is, it is just a seeming ignorance that is experienced only by our mind, and not by our real consciousness, which always knows itself merely as 'I am'. In the experience of our real consciousness 'I am', there is no such duality as knowledge and ignorance, because it is the sole reality underlying all appearances, and hence nothing exists apart from or other than it for it either to know or not to know.

Like all the other knowledge and ignorance that is experienced by our mind, our seeming ignorance of our true and essential nature is only relative. Moreover, even the state of self-knowledge that we now seek to attain exists only relative to our present state of self-ignorance. However, it is relative only from the standpoint of our mind, which seeks to attain it as if it were some knowledge that we do not now possess, and that we can therefore newly experience at some time in future.

This concept that our mind has about self-knowledge is a false image of what the true experience of self-knowledge really is. When we actually experience the state of true self-knowledge, we will discover that it is not something that we have newly attained at a particular point in time, but is the one and only real state, which we have always experienced and will always experience, because it exists eternally, beyond the relative dimensions of time – past, present and future. That is, in that state we will clearly know that we have always been only the pure consciousness of being, 'I am', and that ignorance – the wrong knowledge 'I am this body' – never really existed, just as when we finally see the rope as it really is, we will understand that we were always seeing only that rope, and that the snake we imagined we saw never really existed.

Even when we imagine that we do not know our real self and therefore try to attend to ourself in order to know what we really are, we are in fact nothing other than our real self, which always knows itself as it really is. Our seeming ignorance of the true non-dual nature of our real self is only an imagination, and the sole purpose of our effort to know ourself is only to remove this imagination. This truth is stated emphatically by Sri Ramana in verse 37 of *Uḷḷadu Nāṟpadu*:

> Even the argument that says, 'Duality [is real] in [the state of] spiritual practice, [whereas] non-duality [is real] in [the state of] attainment [of self-knowledge]', is not true. Both when we are lovingly [earnestly or desperately] searching [for ourself], and when [we] have attained ourself, who indeed are we other than the tenth man?

The word *daśamaṉ* or 'the tenth man' refers to an analogy that is often used in *advaita vēdānta*. According to the traditional story on which this analogy is based, ten dull-witted men once forded a fast-flowing river. After crossing the river, they decided to count how many they were in order to make sure that they had all crossed safely. Each one of them counted the other nine men, but forgot to count himself, so they all imagined that they had lost one of their companions, and instead of trying to know who that missing 'tenth man' was, they all began to lament his loss.

Seeing them weeping over the loss of their supposedly missing companion, a passer-by understood that each of them had forgotten to count himself, so to convince them that none of them was really missing, he suggested that he would tap each of them one by one, and that starting from 'one' each man should count the next number in sequence as he was tapped. When the last man was tapped he counted 'ten', whereupon they all understood that none of them was ever really missing.

Who then was the 'tenth man' whom they had each imagined they had lost? Each man, who had counted the other nine men but forgotten to count himself, was himself the supposedly missing 'tenth man'. Just as the 'tenth man' appeared to be missing only because each one of them had ignored himself and counted only the others, so we appear not to know ourself only because we habitually ignore ourself and attend only to things that appear to be other than ourself.

Therefore when Sri Ramana asks, '[…] who indeed are we other than the tenth man?', what he means by the word *daśamaṉ* or 'the tenth man' is only our own real self, which we now imagine we do not know. Hence the meaning of the rhetorical question that Sri Ramana asks in the last sentence of this verse is that we are always truly nothing other than our own real self, both when we are searching for it, and when we have discovered ourself to be it.

Just as the loss of the 'tenth man' was merely an imagination, so our present state of self-ignorance is likewise a mere imagination. Therefore, since all the duality that we experience in this state is a result of our imaginary self-ignorance, it is also a mere imagination. Hence, even in our present state of seeming self-ignorance, the only reality is our own essential non-dual self-consciousness, 'I am'.

In order for any of the ten men to discover the missing 'tenth man', all that was required was for him to remove his imagination that one of them was missing, and that could be achieved only by drawing his attention to himself. Similarly, in order for us to discover our own real self, all that is required is for us to remove our imagination that we know anything other than our real self, and that can be achieved only by drawing our attention towards ourself. That is, since the cause of our imaginary experience of duality or otherness is our seeming self-ignorance, it can be removed only by the experience of clear non-dual self-knowledge, which we can achieve only by attending keenly and exclusively to ourself.

The necessity for spiritual practice – for our making effort to be keenly and exclusively attentive to our own self-conscious being – arises only because we imagine ourself to be anything other than our real self, which is our essential non-dual self-consciousness. This is the meaning implied by two words that Sri Ramana added before the opening words of this verse in the *kaliveṇbā* version of *Uḷḷadu Nāṟpadu*, namely *aṟiyādē muyalum*, which mean 'which [we] attempt [or make effort to do] only [due to] not knowing'.

Being placed before the initial word of this verse, *sādhakattil*, which means 'in [the state of] spiritual practice', these two words imply that we make effort to do any form of spiritual practice, including the ultimate practice of *ātma-vicāra* or self-investigation, only because we do not experience true self-knowledge – the true knowledge that we are just absolutely non-dual and therefore perfectly clear self-conscious being. Though this self-ignorance or lack of true self-knowledge is only imaginary, so long as we experience ourself as being anything other than absolutely unadulterated self-consciousness – consciousness that knows nothing other than itself, its own essential being or 'am'-ness – it is necessary for us to practise self-investigation, which is the real spiritual practice of abiding undistractedly as our own true self-conscious being.

However, since our present self-ignorance is truly imaginary, when as a result of our practice we do experience our real self – our absolutely non-dual self-conscious being – we will discover that we have never known anything other than it. Just as the 'tenth man' was never anyone other than the man who imagined him to be missing, so the real self that we are now seeking is never anything other than ourself, who now imagine it to be something that we do not clearly know. Therefore Sri Ramana says that it is not true to say that duality is real when we are seeking our real self. Even now we are truly nothing other than the non-dual real self that we seek.

Since we ourself are the real self that we now seek, and since the true nature of our real self is to know nothing other than itself, we have never really experienced any duality. Our present experience of duality is therefore just a dream – an imagination that exists only in our own mind. Since our mind is itself just an imagination, and since it will therefore disappear when we experience ourself as we really are, our dream of duality will be dissolved by our experience of true self-knowledge.

In the state of true self-knowledge we will discover that we are the one non-dual self-consciousness, 'I am', which never knows anything other than itself. Since this true non-dual self-consciousness is our real self, we are actually this at all times and in all states, even when we imagine ourself to be something else.

Therefore, since we are the one non-dual, undivided, infinite, eternal and immutable self-consciousness, we ourself are the only true knowledge. That is, we are the one absolute knowledge that transcends all relativity – all knowledge and ignorance, all distinctions such as that between the knowing subject, the act of knowing, and the objects known, all time and space, and all other forms of duality.

All forms of duality or relativity exist only in the imagination of our mind, which itself is no more than a figment of our imagination – something which in truth has never really existed. However, though true knowledge transcends not only all forms of duality or relativity, but also our mind, by which all forms of duality and relativity are known, it is nevertheless the ultimate substratum that underlies and supports the appearance of all of them.

True knowledge is therefore only the absolute knowledge that underlies yet transcends all relative knowledge and ignorance. It transcends them because, though it is their ultimate substratum or support, it nevertheless remains distinct from, independent of and unaffected by them, just as a cinema screen is the support that underlies the appearance of the pictures that flit across it, yet nevertheless remains distinct from, independent of and unaffected by them. Just as the screen is not burnt when a picture of a raging fire is projected upon it, nor does it become wet when a picture of a flood is projected upon it, so true knowledge – our real non-dual self-consciousness 'I am' – is not affected in the least by any relative knowledge or ignorance that may seem to arise within it.

Though our true, absolute and non-dual knowledge 'I am' is the ultimate support or substratum that underlies all forms of duality or relativity, it is not their immediate support or base. The immediate base upon which all duality depends, and without which it ceases to exist, is only our wrong knowledge 'I am this body', which is our individualised sense of selfhood, our ego or mind. Therefore in verse 23 of *Uḷḷadu Nāṟpadu* Sri Ramana says:

> This body does not say 'I' [that is, it does not know 'I am', because it is just inconscient matter]. No one says 'in sleep I do not exist' [even though in sleep this body does not exist]. After an 'I' has risen [imagining 'I am this body'], everything rises. [Therefore] by a subtle intellect scrutinise where this 'I' rises.

What exactly Sri Ramana means by saying in the first sentence of this verse, 'This body does not say "I"', was clarified by him in the *kaliveṇbā* version of *Uḷḷadu Nāṟpadu*, in which he added before it the words *mati-y-iladāl*, which mean 'since it is devoid of *mati*'. The word *mati* usually means mind, intellect or power of discernment and understanding, but in this context Sri Ramana uses it in a deeper sense to mean consciousness.

That is, since our body has no consciousness of its own, it cannot by itself say 'I am'. Here 'say' is not used objectively to mean 'make sound by mouth', but is used more subjectively to mean 'testify', 'bear witness', 'declare' or 'make known'. Our body does not experience or witness its own existence, any more than a corpse does, and hence it cannot testify 'I am'. That which now experiences its seeming existence is only we – the consciousness or mind within this body – and since we imagine it to be ourself, we feel 'I am this body'. Hence, when this body seems to say 'I', it is in fact we who speak through it referring to it as 'I'.

Our mind, ego or individual sense of 'I', which now feels this body to be itself, is actually neither this body nor our real consciousness 'I'. It is not this body because this body is just inconscient matter, which does not know its own existence as 'I am', and it is not our real 'I', because we know that we exist in sleep, even though we do not experience our mind in that state.

Because our mind does not exist in sleep, no duality exists in that state. Duality or multiplicity appears to exist only after our mind has risen, posing itself as our real 'I'. Therefore the cause of the appearance of duality in waking and dream is only the appearance of our mind or ego, which arises by imagining itself to be a body.

Since our mind or individual sense of 'I' is not real, but arises merely as an imagination, Sri Ramana concludes this verse by advising us to scrutinise the source from which it rises. That source is ourself – our real 'I' or essential self-consciousness, which we experienced even in sleep. If we scrutinise ourself with a 'subtle intellect', that is, with a clearly refined and therefore deeply penetrating power of discernment, cognition or attention, we will experience ourself as the true non-dual self-consciousness that we really are, and thus our mind or ego will vanish.

In the last line of this verse, the two words *nuṇ matiyāl*, which literally mean 'by a subtle intellect', are very significant, and in order to understand their meaning more clearly we should compare them with two similar words that Sri Ramana uses in verse 28, namely *kūrnda matiyāl*, which literally mean 'by a sharp intellect' or 'by a pointed intellect', that is, by a sharp, keen, intense, acute and penetrating power of discernment, cognition or attention. Since he says in verse 28 that by such a 'sharp intellect' or *kūrnda mati* we 'should know the place [or source] from which [our] rising ego rises', it is clear that the 'subtle intellect' that he refers to in verse 23 is the same as the 'sharp intellect' that he refers to in verse 28.

Our real self is infinitely subtle, because it is formless consciousness, whereas in comparison all our thoughts are gross, because they are forms or images that appear to be other than ourself. Therefore if we are habituated to attending only to thoughts or objects, our intellect or power of discernment will have become comparatively gross, blunt and dull, having lost its natural subtlety, sharpness and clarity, and hence it will not be able to discern clearly our true, subtle, adjunct-free self-consciousness.

Since by constantly attending to gross thoughts and objects we have lost our natural subtlety, sharpness and clarity of attention or discernment, in order to regain these qualities we must attempt to attend repeatedly to our infinitely subtle self-consciousness. The more we practise such self-attentiveness, the more subtle, sharp and clear our power of attention or discernment will become, and as its subtlety, sharpness and clarity thus increase we will be able to discern our true self-consciousness more clearly, precisely and correctly, until eventually we will experience it in its absolutely pristine purity. This pristine experience of our real non-dual self-consciousness is alone the state of absolute true knowledge.

The result that will be achieved when with a truly subtle power of attention we scrutinise our essential self-consciousness, 'I am', which is the source from which our mind or false finite sense of 'I' arises, is stated by Sri Ramana explicitly in the words that he added at the end of this verse in the *kaliveṇbā* version of *Uḷḷadu Nāṟpadu*. The final word of this verse is *eṇ*, which is an imperative that in this context means 'scrutinise', but in the *kaliveṇbā* version he modified it as *eṇṇa*, which is the infinitive form of the same verb that is used idiomatically to mean 'when [we] scrutinise', and he added a concluding verb *naṙuvum*, which literally means 'it slips off', 'it steals away' or 'it escapes', and which therefore implies that it will depart, disappear, vanish, evaporate, dissolve or become entirely non-existent. Thus the meaning of this final sentence in the *kaliveṇbā* version is: 'When [we] scrutinise by a subtle intellect where this "I" rises, it [this rising 'I'] will vanish'.

This rising 'I', our mind or ego, appears to exist only when we imagine ourself to be a body, and hence its seeming existence depends upon our turning our attention away from our own essential self-conscious being, 'I am', towards a body and other thoughts, all of which are objects that we have created by our own power of imagination. When we do not attend to any imaginary object, such as this body, the world or any of the other thoughts in our mind, our mind or finite sense of 'I' cannot stand, and hence it subsides and vanishes within us, being found to be entirely non-existent. Therefore when we scrutinise the source of our finite rising 'I' – that is, when we turn our attention away from all thoughts or mental images and focus it wholly and exclusively upon our own essential self-conscious being – this false 'I' will vanish in the absolute clarity of our perfectly adjunct-free non-dual self-consciousness.

In the second half of verse 23 of *Uḷḷadu Nāṟpadu* Sri Ramana points out the obvious truth that everything – that is, all duality or otherness – rises only after our mind or individual sense of 'I' has risen, and he advises us that we should therefore scrutinise with a 'subtle intellect' the source from which this 'I' arises. He also adds that when we scrutinise thus, this 'I' will slip away, vanish or become entirely non-existent. The inference that we should understand from his statement, 'After an "I" has risen, everything rises', from his subsequent advice, 'By a subtle intellect scrutinise where this "I" rises', and from his final statement that this 'I' will then vanish, is stated by him clearly in verse 26 of *Uḷḷadu Nāṟpadu*:

If [our] ego comes into existence [as in the waking and dream states],

> everything comes into existence. If [our] ego does not exist [as in sleep], everything does not exist. [Hence our] ego indeed is everything [this entire appearance of duality or relativity]. Therefore, know that examining 'what is this [ego]?' is indeed relinquishing everything.

In the *kaliveṇbā* version of *Uḷḷadu Nāṟpadu* Sri Ramana added the word *karu-v-ām*, which means 'which is the *karu*', before the first word of this verse, which is *ahandai* or 'ego'. As I explained in chapter three when discussing the meaning of verse 716 of *Guru Vācaka Kōvai*, the word *karu* means 'embryo', 'germ', 'efficient cause', 'substance', 'foundation' or 'womb', and Sri Ramana describes our ego or mind as being the *karu* because it is the embryo or seed from which everything – all duality or otherness – is born, the substance of which everything is formed, the active cause or creator that brings everything into being, the foundation that supports the appearance of everything, and the womb inside which everything is born and contained.

Except our essential self-consciousness 'I am', everything that we know or experience is just a thought or image that we have formed in our mind by our power of imagination. Therefore everything is just an expansion of our own mind, our ego or root thought 'I'. This is why Sri Ramana states emphatically that our 'ego indeed is everything'.

Why does he then proceed to say that examining or scrutinising our ego in order to know what it is, is renouncing or casting off everything? Examining our ego is similar to examining the seeming snake that we see lying on the ground in the half-light of dusk. When we look carefully at the snake, we will discover that what we were seeing was never really a snake, but was always only a rope. Similarly, when we scrutinise our ego or individual sense of selfhood with a keen and subtle power of attention, we will discover that what we have always been aware of as 'I' was never really a limited adjunct-bound consciousness, but was always only the unlimited adjunct-free consciousness 'I am'.

Just as the snake as such never really existed, so our ego as such has never really existed. And just as the sole reality underlying the illusory appearance of the snake was merely a rope, so the sole reality underlying the illusory appearance of our ego is only our own true self, our adjunct-free consciousness 'I am'. Therefore, when we carefully examine our ego and discover that it is non-existent as such, the entire appearance of duality, which depended for its seeming reality upon the seeming reality of the ego, will cease to exist – or rather, it will be found to be truly ever non-existent.

In reality, therefore, the true knowledge 'I am' alone exists, and all other forms of knowledge – all relative knowledge and ignorance – are ever non-existent. However, so long as we experience the illusion of relative knowledge and ignorance, it must, like every illusion, have some reality underlying it, and that reality can only be our true and absolute knowledge 'I am'.

Our true knowledge 'I am' is the support or base underlying our false knowledge 'I am this body', and our false knowledge 'I am this body' is in turn the support or base underlying our illusion of relative knowledge and ignorance. Therefore, to experience true knowledge as it is, we must not only remove the illusion of relative knowledge and ignorance, but must also remove its base, which is our false sense of individual selfhood, our knowledge 'I am this body'.

This truth is expressed by Sri Ramana in verses 10, 11 and 12 of *Uḷḷadu Nāṟpadu*:

> Without [relative] ignorance, [relative] knowledge does not exist. Without [relative] knowledge, that [relative] ignorance does not exist. The knowledge that knows [the non-existence of] that [individual] self which is the base [of all our relative knowledge and ignorance], [by investigating] thus 'that [relative] knowledge and ignorance [are known] to whom?' is indeed [true] knowledge.
>
> Knowing [any] other thing without knowing [the non-existence of our individual] self, which knows [such other things], is ignorance; instead [can it be] knowledge? When [we] know [the non-existence of our individual] self, [which is] the *ādhāra* [the support or container] of knowledge and [its] opposite, [both] knowledge and ignorance will cease to exist.
>
> That which is [completely] devoid of both knowledge and ignorance is indeed [true] knowledge. That which knows [that is, our mind or individual self, which alone knows things other than itself] is not true knowledge. Since it [our real self] shines [as the only existing reality] without [any] other [thing] to know or to make known [that is, either for it to know, or to make itself or anything else known], [our real] self is [true] knowledge. It is not a void. Know [this truth].

Though our real self, our essential adjunct-free consciousness 'I am', is completely devoid of knowledge and ignorance about anything other than itself, it is not merely an empty void, because it is the fullness of being – the fullness of perfectly clear self-conscious being, which is the fullness of true self-knowledge. Therefore the term *śūnya* or 'void', which is used to describe the absolute reality not only in Buddhism but also in some texts of *advaita vēdānta*, is in fact intended to be understood only as a relative description of it – a description of it relative to the multiplicity of relative knowledge that our mind now experiences.

Though the absolute reality, which is our essential self-conscious being, is devoid of all relative knowledge – all knowledge of duality or otherness – it is not an absolute void, because it is not devoid of true knowledge, which is the absolute clarity of perfectly non-dual self-consciousness. Therefore rather than describing the absolute reality as a state of *śūnya*, 'emptiness' or 'void', it is more accurate to describe it as the state of *pūrṇa*, 'fullness', 'wholeness' or 'completeness', because it is the absolute fullness of true knowledge.

The same truth that Sri Ramana expresses in verse 12 of *Uḷḷadu Nāṟpadu* is expressed by him even more succinctly in verse 27 of *Upadēśa Undiyār*:

> The knowledge which is devoid of both knowledge and ignorance [about objects], alone is [true] knowledge. This [true knowledge] is the [only existing] reality, [because in truth] there is nothing to know [other than ourself].

Why is there truly nothing for us to know other than our own self? All knowledge of otherness or duality is known only by our mind, which is merely a false form of knowledge – an apparition that appears only when by our power of imagination we superimpose some illusory adjuncts upon our true knowledge 'I am'. When we examine this illusory apparition, it disappears, being truly non-existent, like the illusory snake that we created by our power of imagination. When we thus discover that our mind is truly non-existent, we will also discover that all other things, which were known only by our mind, are equally non-existent.

However, though all our knowledge of duality is unreal as such, we are able to imagine that we experience such knowledge of duality only because we experience the true knowledge 'I am'. If we did not know our own existence, 'I am', we could not imagine that we know any other thing. Therefore our imaginary knowledge of duality is only an illusory form of our true knowledge 'I am', as explained by Sri Ramana in verse 13 of *Uḷḷadu Nāṟpadu*:

> [Our true] self [our essential being], which is knowledge [our essential knowledge or consciousness 'I am'], alone is real. Knowledge which is many [that is, knowledge of multiplicity] is ignorance. [However] even [that] ignorance, which is unreal, does not exist apart from [our true] self, which is [the only real] knowledge. The multiplicity of ornaments is unreal; say, does it exist apart from gold, which is real?

This verse is a terser but more content-rich version of an earlier verse that Sri Ramana composed, which is included in *Upadēśa Taṉippākkaḷ* as verse 12:

> Knowledge [the true knowledge 'I am'] alone is real. Ignorance, which is nothing other than the [false] knowledge [our mind] that sees [the one real knowledge 'I am'] as many, itself does not exist apart from [our true] self, which is [the only real] knowledge. The

> multiplicity of ornaments is unreal; say, does it exist apart from gold, which is real?

The diversity of gold ornaments is merely a diversity of transient forms, and as such it is unreal. What is real and enduring in all those diverse ornaments is only the substance of which they are made, namely gold. Similarly, though the knowledge of multiplicity is unreal, being merely a transitory appearance, its underlying reality or substance is only the true knowledge 'I am', without which it could not even appear to exist.

Therefore the only thing that is worth knowing is our own real self, our essential consciousness 'I am'. That is why Sri Ramana says in verse 3 of *Āṉma-Viddai*:

> What [worth does all our knowledge have] if [we] know whatever else without knowing [our real] self? If [we] know [our real] self, then what [else] is there to know? When [we] know in ourself that [real] self, which shines undivided [as the unlimited, adjunct-free consciousness 'I am'] in all the divided [or separate] living beings, within ourself the light of self [the clarity of true self-knowledge] will shine. [This is] indeed the shining forth of grace, the annihilation of 'I' [our ego, mind or separate individual self], [and] the blossoming of [true and eternal] happiness.

Just as in verse 16 of *Upadēśa Undiyār*, which we discussed earlier in this chapter, Sri Ramana used the term 'its own form of light' to denote our mind's essential consciousness 'I am', so in this verse he uses the term 'the light of self' to denote the clear consciousness or knowledge of our real self. Why does he use the word 'light' in this figurative manner to denote consciousness or knowledge? Since our consciousness 'I am' is that by which both ourself and all other things are made known, in the poetic language of mysticism it is often described as being the true 'light' that illumines everything, including the physical light that we see with our eyes.

This metaphorical use of the word 'light' to denote our true consciousness of being, 'I am', can be found in the sayings and writings of sages from all traditions and all cultures. Jesus Christ, for example, referred to our consciousness 'I am' as the 'light of the world'. Since it is the light that enables us to know the world, and since it shines as the essential being of each and every one of us – including even God, who declared himself to be that 'I am' when he said to Moses, 'I AM THAT I AM. […] Thus shalt thou say unto the children of Israel, I AM hath sent me unto you' (*Exodus* 3.14), and Christ, who indicated that he was that same timeless 'I am' when he said, 'Before Abraham was born, I am' (*John* 8.58) –, Christ not only said, 'I am the light of the world' (*John* 8.12 and 9.5), but also addressing people said, 'Ye are the light of the world' (*Matthew* 5.14).

Hence this consciousness 'I am' can rightly be said to be the 'spark of divinity' within each one of us. Indeed, this pure consciousness of our being, which we each know as 'I am', is itself the ultimate and absolute reality, which in English is called 'God' or the 'Supreme Being', and which in Sanskrit is called *brahman*. This truth is affirmed not only by the above-quoted statement of God in the Bible, 'I AM THAT I AM', but also by the four 'great sayings' or *mahāvākyas* of the Vēdas, which declare the oneness of ourself and that absolute reality.

Of these four *mahāvākyas*, one is contained in each of the four Vēdas, in the portions of them that are known as the *upaniṣads*, which are some of the earliest known expressions of *vēdānta*, the 'end' or philosophical conclusion and essence of the Vēdas. The *mahāvākya* of the Ṛg Vēda is '*prajñānaṁ brahma*', which means 'pure consciousness is *brahman*' (*Aitarēya Upaniṣad* 3.3), that of the Yajur Vēda is '*ahaṁ brahmāsmi*', which means 'I am *brahman*' (*Bṛhadāraṇyaka Upaniṣad* 1.4.10), that of the Sāma Vēda is '*tat tvam asi*', which means 'it [*brahman*] you are' (*Chāndōgya Upaniṣad* 6.8.7), and that of the Atharva Vēda is '*ayaṁ ātmā brahma*', which means 'this self is *brahman*' (*Māṇḍūkya Upaniṣad* 2).

Our oneness with the absolute reality called 'God' is explained by Sri Ramana more clearly in verse 24 of *Upadēśa Undiyār*:

> By [their] nature which is [that is, in their essential nature or being, 'I am', which merely is], God and souls are only one *poruḷ* [substance or reality]. Only the adjunct-sense is [what makes them appear to be] different.

We feel ourself to be a soul or individual being because we identify ourself with certain adjuncts, and these adjuncts distinguish us from God and from every other living being. Just as we identify ourself with a certain set of attributes or adjuncts, we identify God with another set of attributes or adjuncts. However, none of the attributes that we ascribe either to God or to ourself are actually inherent in or essential to the fundamental being which is the true nature of both himself and ourself, but are all merely adjuncts that are superimposed upon it.

Since all such attributes or adjuncts are mere thoughts or mental images created by our power of imagination, Sri Ramana refers to them collectively as *upādhi-uṇarvu*, the 'adjunct-sense' or 'adjunct-consciousness' – that is, the feeling, notion or experience of adjuncts. Though the exact meaning of *upādhi* is a 'substitute' or thing that is put in place of something else, it actually comes from the verbal root *upādhā* meaning to place upon, impose, seize, take up, add, connect or yoke, and therefore by extension it also means a disguise, a phantom, a deceptive appearance, an attribute, an adjunct, a qualification or a limitation. Thus in our present context it means any extraneous adjunct, anything that is superimposed upon some other thing, making itself appear to be that other thing. Therefore whatever is not actually ourself but we mistake to be ourself, such as our body or mind, is one of our *upādhis* or limiting adjuncts, and our mistaken notion or imagination that such adjuncts are ourself is our *upādhi-uṇarvu*.

Since we superimpose such *upādhis* or limiting adjuncts not only upon ourself but also upon God, we experience an *upādhi-uṇarvu* or feeling of adjuncts both with respect to ourself and with respect to God. However, since our experience of adjuncts that distinguish us from God is created only by our own power of imagination, and not by God, all these distinguishing adjuncts exist only in the outlook of our mind and not in the outlook of God, who is in reality only our own true self-conscious being – our being that knows only itself.

Therefore, in order to know God as he really is, all we need do is to eradicate our own illusory sense of adjuncts. When we thus cease to identify ourself with any adjuncts, we will no longer imagine God as having any adjuncts, but will discover him to be nothing other than our own true and essential self-conscious being. Therefore in verse 25 of *Upadēśa Undiyār* Sri Ramana says:

> Knowing [our real] self, having relinquished [all our own] adjuncts, itself is knowing God, because [he] shines as [our real] self.

The knowledge that remains when we relinquish all of our adjuncts is only our essential non-dual consciousness of our own being, which is the true nature of God. That which experiences this true self-knowledge is not our mind but is only our own real self, our essential being, which is ever conscious of itself as 'I am'. Our mind is our essential consciousness mixed with adjuncts, which are the various forms of wrong knowledge that we have about ourself, and it therefore cannot survive as such in the perfectly clear state of true self-knowledge.

Thus the state in which we know ourself as we really are, and in which we thereby know God as our own self, is the state in which our mind has been entirely consumed in the absolute clarity of true self-knowledge. Therefore in verse 21 of *Uḷḷadu Nāṟpadu* Sri Ramana says:

> If [it is] asked what is the truth of [the supreme state that is indicated in] many sacred texts which say '[our] self seeing [our] self' [and] 'seeing God', [we have to reply with the counter questions] since [our] self is one, how [is our] self seeing [our] self [possible]? If it is not possible [for us] to see [ourself], how [is] seeing God [possible]? Becoming food [to God] is seeing [him].

Our mind can only know things other than itself, because if it turns its attention selfwards to know itself, it will subside and drown in its own essential self-conscious being. When it truly knows itself, or rather, when we truly know ourself, we will cease to be the mind or object-knowing consciousness that we now imagine ourself to be, and will remain instead in our natural state as our own non-dual consciousness of being.

Knowing or seeing, when understood from the distorted perspective of our mind, means experiencing duality – a separation between the consciousness that knows and the object that is known. Therefore, since we are one, we cannot know or see ourself as an object. We can know or see ourself only by being ourself, and not by any act of knowing or seeing. Therefore Sri Ramana asks, 'Since [our] self is one, how [is our] self seeing [our] self [possible]?'.

Since it is not possible for us to see ourself as an object, how is it possible for us to see God as an object? That is, since God is the reality of ourself, we cannot see him as an object any more than we can see ourself as an object. Therefore Sri Ramana asks, 'If it is not possible [for us] to see [ourself], how [is] seeing God [possible]?'.

Since we cannot know either ourself or God by an act of objective knowing, in order to know both ourself and God we must give up all objective knowing. That is, we must cease to be this object-knowing mind, and must instead remain as our natural non-dual consciousness of our own being – our true and essential self-consciousness 'I am'. Therefore Sri Ramana concludes, '*ūṇ ādal kāṇ*', which means, 'Becoming food [is] seeing'. That is, we can see God only when we are wholly consumed by him, thereby becoming one with the infinite self-conscious being that is the absolute reality of both himself and ourself.

Until and unless we know and remain as our own real self, our simple non-dual consciousness of our own being, 'I am', we cannot know God. If we imagine that we are seeing God as an object other than ourself, we are seeing only a mental image. Therefore in verse 20 of *Uḷḷadu Nāṟpadu* Sri Ramana says:

> Leaving [ignoring or omitting to know our own] self [our individual self or mind], which sees [all otherness or duality], [our] self seeing God is [merely] seeing a mental vision [sight, image or appearance]. Only he who sees [his real] self, [which is] the base [or reality] of [his individual] self, is a person who has [truly] seen God, because [our real] self – [which alone remains after all our mental images or objective forms of knowledge have disappeared due to their causal] root, [our individual] self, having gone [perished or ceased to exist] – is not other than God.

The wording of this verse is very terse and therefore difficult to translate exactly into fluent English, but its sense is quite clear. The opening words, 'leaving self which sees', refer to our usual habit of ignoring and making no attempt to know the reality of our individual self or mind, which is the self-deceiving consciousness that imagines itself to be seeing or knowing things other than itself. The remainder of the first sentence, 'self seeing God is seeing a mental vision', means that, when we do not know the truth of ourself who is seeing, if we imagine that we are seeing God, what we are seeing is actually nothing but a mind-made or *manōmaya* vision – a vision that is made or formed by and of our own mind.

The words that Sri Ramana uses in the original are *manōmayam-ām kāṭci*, which literally mean a 'sight which is composed of mind'. Though the word *kāṭci* literally means 'sight', 'vision' or 'appearance', being derived from the verbal root *kāṇ*, which literally means 'to see', but which is often used in a broader sense to mean 'to perceive', 'to cognise' or 'to experience', like its verbal root it can imply any form of experience. In this context, therefore, it implies not only a vision of God in some visual form such as Siva, Sakti, Krishna, Rama, Buddha or Christ, but also any other experience of God in which he is felt to be other than ourself, such as hearing the 'voice' of God or feeling his presence. So long as the 'presence of God' that we feel is experienced by us as something other than our own simple self-conscious being, 'I am', it is only a *manōmayam-ām kāṭci*, a mental image, thought or conception. Any experience of God as other than ourself is known only by our mind, and is therefore a product of our own imagination.

The second sentence of this verse is still more terse. For poetic reasons it begins with its main clause, which in Tamil prose would normally conclude such a sentence. The meaning of this main clause, 'only he who sees self is a person who has seen God', is quite clear. That is, we can truly see God only by 'seeing' or knowing our own real self.

The next two words, *taṉ mudalai*, are linked in meaning to the word 'self' in the opening words of the main clause, 'only he who sees self'. The word *taṉ* is the possessive form of the reflexive pronoun *tāṉ*, and therefore means 'of self', 'one's own', 'our own' or 'his own'. The word *mudalai* is the accusative form of *mudal*, a word whose primary meaning is 'first' or 'beginning', and which in this context means the source, base, reality or essential substance. Thus these two words here mean 'the base [or reality] of [the individual] self', and they are a description applied to the real self referred to in the first clause, which with their addition means, 'only he who sees [his real] self, [which is] the base [or reality] of [his false individual] self, is a person who has seen God'.

In the next group of words, *tāṉ mudal pōy*, *tāṉ* refers to our individual 'self', *mudal* means 'root', and *pōy* means 'having gone', 'having perished' or 'having ceased to exist'. Thus three words together mean 'the root, [which is our individual] self, having gone [perished or ceased to exist]'. The reason why our individual self is thus described as the 'root' is that it is the root or primary cause of the appearance of all duality, otherness or objective knowledge. Whereas our essential being or real self is the ultimate *mudal* or base of our false individual self, our false individual self is the immediate *mudal* or base of every other thing.

The final words are 'because [or since] self is not other than God'. Here the word *tāṉ* or 'self' denotes our real self, and coming immediately after the previous three words, *tāṉ mudal poy*, it implies that our real self is that which remains after our false individual self, the base of all our objective knowledge, has ceased to exist.

Thus the meaning conveyed by this second sentence can be paraphrased as follows: Since our real infinite self, which remains alone after our false finite self, the base of all our objective knowledge, has ceased to exist, is not anything other than the absolute reality called God, when we 'see' or experience our own real self, the base of our false self, we will truly be seeing God.

Thus the combined conclusion of verses 20 and 21 of *Uḷḷadu Nāṟpadu* is that we can see or know God only by knowing our own real self, because our own real self is itself the absolute reality that we call God, and that we can know our own real self only by ceasing to exist as our false individual self, that is, by surrendering ourself entirely to God, the infinite fullness of being, thereby becoming a prey to him and being wholly consumed in his absolute, infinite, undivided, unqualified and perfectly non-dual self-conscious being.

The only means by which we can thus experience God as our own real self or essential being is then clearly explained by Sri Ramana in verse 22 of *Uḷḷadu Nāṟpadu*:

> Except [by] turning [folding or drawing our] mind back within [and thereby] keeping [it] immersed [sunk, settled, subsided, fixed or absorbed] in the Lord, who shines within that mind, giving light to [our] mind, how [can we succeed in] knowing the Lord by [our] mind? Know [the Lord by thus turning back within and immersing in him].

The 'Lord' or *pati* referred to in this verse is God, who is the infinitely luminous light of pure self-consciousness. As we saw earlier, in spiritual literature our own essential consciousness of being is figuratively described as the original light, the light by which all other lights are known, because just as physical light enables us to see physical objects, our consciousness of being is that which enables us to know all things.

However, whereas our basic consciousness of our own being is the true and original light, the consciousness that we call our mind, which is the light by which we know all other things, is merely an illusory reflected light, because it comes into existence only when our original light of self-consciousness is seemingly reflected in imaginary adjuncts or *upādhis* such as our body and our individual personality. Therefore, when Sri Ramana says that the Lord shines within our mind giving light to it, he means that he shines within our mind as our fundamental consciousness of our own being,

'I am', thereby giving it the consciousness by which it is able to know all other things.

Because everything other than our essential self-consciousness – that is, all otherness, duality or multiplicity – is known only by our mind, in the *kaliveṇbā* version of *Uḷḷadu Nāṟpadu* Sri Ramana added the words *evaiyum kāṇum*, which mean 'which sees everything', before the initial word of this verse, *mati* or mind. Since our mind is an object-knowing form of consciousness, its nature is to know everything other than its own real self, but in order to know all those other things it must borrow the light of consciousness from its real self – from its own essential self-conscious being, which is the absolute reality that we call 'God' or the 'Lord'.

Since God is the original light of consciousness – that is, the true light of non-dual self-consciousness – which shines within our mind, enabling it to know all other things, how can our mind know him except by turning itself back within itself, thereby drowning itself in his infinite light? So long as our attention is turned outwards, we can only know things that appear to be other than ourself, which are all merely products of our own imagination. Since God is the true light of consciousness, which enables us to know all other things, we can never know him as he really is so long as we are misusing his light to know any other thing. Only when we turn our mind or attention back to face him within ourself, will we be able to know him truly.

However, even when we turn back to attend to him within ourself, we will not know him as an object, because our object-knowing mind will drown and be dissolved in his infinite light of adjunct-free self-consciousness. Therefore when we turn back within ourself, we will know him by becoming one with his true self-conscious being.

If we use a mirror to reflect the light of the sun upon objects here on earth, that reflected ray of light will illumine those objects, enabling us to see them clearly. But if we turn that mirror towards the sun itself, its reflected ray of light will merge and dissolve in the brilliant light of the sun. Similarly, the reflected light of consciousness that we call our mind enables us to know the objects of our imagination so long as we turn it towards them. But when we turn it back within ourself to face our own essential self-conscious being, which is the source of its light, it will merge and dissolve in the infinitely luminescent and therefore all-consuming light of that source.

The state in which the limited light of our mind dissolves in the infinite light of God, thereby disappearing as a separate entity and becoming one with him, is the state that Sri Ramana described in the last sentence of the previous verse when he said, 'Becoming food [to God] is seeing [him]'. The fact that the only means by which we can truly see or experience God, the absolute reality, is to become one with his essential self-conscious being by carefully examining or scrutinising our own essential self-conscious being and thereby subsiding and dissolving in it, is also emphasised by Sri Ramana in verse 8 of *Uḷḷadu Nāṟpadu*:

> Whoever worships [the absolute reality or God] in whatever form giving [it] whatever name, that is a path [or means] to see that [nameless and formless] reality in [that] name and form. However, becoming one [with that reality], having carefully scrutinised [or known] one's own truth [essence or 'am'-ness] and having [thereby] subsided [or dissolved] in the truth [essence or 'am'-ness] of that true reality, is alone seeing [it] in truth. Know [thus].

The word *ēttiṉum*, which I have translated as 'worships', literally means 'even if or though [anyone] praises', but in this context it implies the act of worshipping in any manner, whether by body, speech or mind. However, as Sri Ramana explains in verse 4 of *Upadēśa Undiyār*:

> This is certain, *pūjā* [ritual worship], *japa* [vocal repetition of a *mantra* or name of God] and *dhyāna* [meditation] are [respectively] actions of body, speech and mind, [and hence each succeeding] one is superior to [the preceding] one.

That is, vocal worship such as the chanting of hymns or the repetition of a name of God is superior to any form of physical worship such as the performance of rituals, and mental worship such as silent meditation upon a name or form of God is superior to vocal worship, the word 'superior' or *uyarvu* meaning in this context more efficacious. Therefore as a means to see God in any chosen name and form, meditating with love upon that name and form is the most efficacious form of worship.

By saying, 'Whoever worships [the absolute reality or God] in whatever form giving [it] whatever name', Sri Ramana indicates that we are free to worship God in any name or form that attracts our love and devotion, because God himself has no particular name and form of his own. No matter in what name or form a devotee may worship God, if that worship is sincere and performed with true love for him, God will certainly respond to it favourably, because even though his devotee may not know it, he knows that the true object of his devotee's love and worship is his nameless and formless reality or true being.

Therefore any sectarian form of religion or theology that teaches that only one particular name or form of God is his true name or form, and that all other names and forms are merely false 'gods', has failed to understand the true, infinite and all-transcendent nature of God. No concept or mental image that we may have of God (including even the concept espoused by certain religions that he is formless and therefore should not be worshipped in the form of any idol, icon, symbol or 'graven image') can truly define God or adequately depict him as he really is, because he is the absolute and infinite reality that transcends all concepts and mental forms of knowledge.

In the words *pēr-uruvil*, which Sri Ramana placed in this verse before the words 'a path to see that reality', the terminating syllable *il* can either be the locative case ending meaning 'in', or a negative termination signifying non-existence or absence. Thus in this context they can mean both 'in name and form' and 'nameless and formless'. In the sense 'nameless and formless' they qualify 'that reality', indicating the fact that the absolute reality is completely devoid of all names and forms. In the sense 'in name and form' they qualify the manner in which we can see that reality by worshipping it in name and form. That is, though the absolute reality transcends all names and forms and therefore has no name or form of its own, it is possible for us to see or experience it in any name and form in which we choose to worship it.

However, seeing God thus in name and form is not seeing him as he really is, but is only seeing him as we imagine him to be. No matter how real such a vision of God in name and form may appear to be, it is in fact just a *manōmayam-ām kāṭci* or 'mind-made image', as Sri Ramana says in verse 20 of *Uḷḷadu Nāṟpadu*.

In both the first and the second sentence of verse 8, the word that I have translated as 'reality' is *poruḷ*, which literally means 'thing', 'entity', 'reality', 'substance' or 'essence', and which is used in Tamil philosophical literature to denote the absolute reality or God as the true substance or essence of all things. In the second sentence Sri Ramana further clarifies the sense in which he uses this word *poruḷ* by qualifying it with the word *mey*, which means 'true' or 'real', thereby forming the compound word *meypporuḷ*, which means 'true essence' or 'real substance', and which is another term commonly used in Tamil philosophical literature to denote God. Thus the nameless and formless reality which he is discussing in this verse is absolute self-conscious being, which is the true essence or real substance both of God and of ourself.

In order to see or know this absolute reality or essential being 'in truth', that is, as it really is, Sri Ramana says that we must become one with it by scrutinising and knowing our own truth and thereby subsiding and dissolving in the truth of that real essence. The word that I have translated as 'truth', which he uses three times in the second sentence of this verse, is *uṇmai*, which etymologically means *uḷ-mai*, 'am'-ness or 'is'-ness, and which is therefore a word that is commonly used to denote existence, reality, truth, veracity, or the intrinsic nature or essential being of anything.

Since *uḷ* is the base of a tenseless verb meaning 'to be', in its basic form *uḷ* it just means 'be', and hence *uḷ-mai* or *uṇmai* literally means 'be'-ness. Because it is a verbal base, *uḷ* does not denote specifically the first person, second person or third person, so from a purely grammatical perspective *uḷ-mai* can equally well be taken to mean 'am'-ness, 'are'-ness or 'is'-ness.

However, since true being is self-conscious, and since it is known by nothing other than itself, from a philosophical perspective *uḷ-mai* is more accurately described by the term 'am'-ness than by the terms 'are'-ness or 'is'-ness. That is, true being is only our own self-conscious being, which we always experience as 'I am', and not any other objective being that we experience either as 'you are' or as 'he is', 'she is' or 'it is'. Therefore, since Sri Ramana uses the word *uṇmai* here to denote true being, in this context its etymological meaning is best translated as 'am'-ness.

Since true, self-conscious and unqualified being is single, infinite, indivisible and hence absolutely non-dual, the 'am'-ness of God and of ourself is truly one. Hence, by scrutinising and knowing our own 'am'-ness, we will subside and dissolve in the infinite 'am'-ness that is God, thereby becoming one with it, as in truth we always are. Becoming one with God, having thus known our own 'am'-ness and having thereby dissolved in his true 'am'-ness, is alone seeing him as he really is. Such is the true non-dual experience of Sri Ramana, as expressed by him in this verse.

The true nature or essential being both of God and of ourself is only that which merely is, and not that which is either 'this' or 'that'. That which merely is, and is not contaminated by association with any adjuncts such as 'this' or 'that', is what is described in philosophy as 'pure being' or 'pure existence'. This pure adjunct-free being is the one true substance of which all things are formed – the sole reality underlying all appearances. In truth, therefore, pure being alone exists.

Hence, since nothing can exist as other than being or existence, there can be no consciousness other than being to know being. If consciousness were other than being, consciousness would not be. Since consciousness exists, it cannot be other than being or existence. Therefore that which knows that which is, is only that which is, and not some other thing which is not.

Since that which knows pure being is thus pure being itself, pure being is itself consciousness. Our being and our consciousness of our being are one. Both are expressed when we say 'I am', because the words 'I am' signify not only that we are, but also that we know that we are. Therefore in verse 23 of *Upadēśa Undiyār* Sri Ramana says:

> Because of the non-existence of [any] consciousness other [than 'that which is'] to know 'that which is', 'that which is' is consciousness. [That] consciousness itself exists as 'we' [our essential being or true self].

Since we are both being and consciousness, we need not know ourself in the same manner in which we know other things. We know other things by an act of knowing, and hence all our knowing of other things is an activity of our mind – an activity that we describe by various terms such as 'thinking', 'feeling', 'perceiving' and so on. But no such activity or act of knowing is required for us to know ourself. We know ourself merely by being ourself, because our being is self-conscious – that is, our being is itself our consciousness of our being. Therefore in verse 26 of *Upadēśa Undiyār* Sri Ramana says:

> Being [our real] self is indeed knowing [our real] self, because [our real] self is that which is devoid of two. This is *tanmaya-niṣṭha* [the state of being firmly established in and as *tat* or 'it', the absolute reality called *brahman*].

Because our real self is totally devoid of even the least duality or two-ness, the only way we can know it is by being it – by relinquishing all our adjuncts and thereby being entirely absorbed in and firmly established as the one absolute reality, which in the philosophical terminology of *vēdānta* is known as *tat* or 'it', and which is our own pure, adjunct-free, essential self-conscious being, 'I am'.

The state of true knowledge, therefore, is not a state of knowing anything, but is just a state of being – a state of being our own real self-conscious self. It is the state in which we simply abide as pure knowledge, which is our fundamental non-dual knowledge or consciousness of our own essential being, 'I am'.

Pure knowledge, which is our own real self or essential being, is absolute and non-dual. However, though we are always pure knowledge, and nothing other than that, we imagine ourself to be a finite individual consciousness that knows objects. Therefore the state which is described as 'being our real self' or 'abiding as pure knowledge' is the state in which we refrain from imagining ourself to be an object-knowing consciousness. Thus true knowledge is just our present knowledge of our own being, bereft of our imaginary activity of 'knowing' anything.

Our real self, 'I am', is not only pure being and pure consciousness, it is also pure happiness. All misery and unhappiness exist only in our mind, and when our mind subsides, as in deep sleep, we experience perfect peace and happiness. The peaceful happiness that we experience in deep sleep is the very nature of our true self. Because our mind always thinks in terms of duality and differences, we think of being, consciousness and happiness as being three different things, but in essence they are one and the same reality. Just as absolute being is itself absolute consciousness, so it is also itself absolute happiness.

There is no such thing as absolute non-existence, because non-existence does not exist. If at all something called 'non-existence' does exist, it is not absolute non-existence, but just a non-existence that only exists relative to some other equally relative existence. Likewise, there is no such thing as absolute unconsciousness, because unconsciousness can be said to exist only if some consciousness other than it exists to know it. Any unconsciousness that is known to exist, exists relative only to the equally relative consciousness that knows its existence. For example, the unconsciousness that we experience in deep sleep exists relative only to our mind, the relative consciousness that we experience in waking and dream, because the state of deep sleep is a state of unconsciousness only in the outlook of our mind.

Just as both non-existence and unconsciousness are merely relative, so unhappiness is also merely relative. Since unhappiness is merely an absence or negation of happiness, and since a negation can only be relative, requiring something other than itself to negate, there can be no such thing as absolute unhappiness. Only that which is positive, and not that which is negative, can be absolute, because that which is positive does not require anything other than itself either to negate or to relate to in any other way.

However, though our real self, which we may call either our essential being, our essential consciousness or our essential happiness, is in truth absolute, in the outlook of our mind these three essential and absolute qualities appear to be relative to their opposites, non-existence, unconsciousness and unhappiness. Since the vision of our mind is essentially dualistic, it can only experience relativity, and can never experience the absolute as it is.

However, since our mind could not appear to exist without the absolute reality that underlies its appearance, it always knows that absolute reality, but only in a distorted form. Just as it knows the absolute reality 'I am' in the distorted form of a relative entity that feels 'I am this body', so it knows absolute being, absolute consciousness and absolute happiness as three relative pairs of opposites, existence and non-existence, consciousness and unconsciousness, and happiness and unhappiness. These relative pairs of opposites are each merely a distorted reflection of the absolute quality to which they correspond.

Our mind experiences many relative pairs of opposites, but not all of those relative pairs of opposites correspond to a particular quality of the absolute reality. For example, long and short, or rich and poor, do not correspond to any particular quality of the absolute reality. Why then should we say that certain pairs of opposites, such as existence and non-existence, consciousness and unconsciousness, and happiness and unhappiness, do correspond to a particular quality of the absolute reality?

We know that each these three pairs of opposites do indeed correspond to a particular quality of the absolute reality because in deep sleep, when our mind has subsided along with all its knowledge of duality and relativity, we experience our natural being, our natural consciousness, and our natural happiness, devoid of any notion of their opposites. Therefore from our experience in deep sleep, we know that our natural being, consciousness and happiness do exist beyond our mind, and hence beyond all duality and relativity.

Therefore, though no words can adequately express the true nature of the absolute reality, which is beyond the range of thoughts or words, in *advaita vēdānta* – the philosophy of *advaita* or non-duality, the essence of which is declared in the Vēdas as their *anta* or ultimate conclusion – the absolute reality or *brahman* is often described as being-consciousness-happiness or *sat-cit-ānanda*.

Though in its true nature the absolute reality 'I am' is totally devoid of any form of duality or relativity, it is nevertheless the essential substance that underlies and gives a seeming reality to the appearance of all forms of duality or relativity, just as a rope is the essential substance that underlies and gives a seeming reality to the appearance of the imaginary snake. Therefore, since the absolute reality is the essential being that underlies and gives a seeming reality to the appearance of relative being and non-being, or existence and non-existence, we can aptly describe it as *sat*, true and absolute being or existence. Since it is the essential consciousness that underlies and gives a seeming reality to the appearance of relative consciousness and unconsciousness, or knowledge and ignorance, we can aptly describe it as *cit*, true and absolute consciousness or knowledge. And since it is the essential happiness that underlies and gives a seeming reality to the appearance of relative happiness and unhappiness, we can aptly describe it as *ānanda*, true and absolute happiness or bliss.

However, though these three separate words, being, consciousness and happiness, are used to describe the absolute reality, which is our true self, we should not think that this implies that the absolute reality is anything more than one single whole. The absolute reality is essentially non-dual, and hence these three different words are used to describe it only because they are in fact words that all denote the same single reality. Being is itself the consciousness of being, and is also the happiness of merely being as that consciousness of being. True being or existence, true consciousness or knowledge, and true happiness or love, are all only the one non-dual absolute reality that we always experience as 'I am'.

In most of the major religions of this world, the absolute reality or 'God' is described as being not only the fullness of being, the fullness of consciousness or knowledge, and the fullness of perfect happiness, but also the fullness of perfect love. Why is the absolute reality thus said to be infinite love?

We all love ourself, and such love of oneself is natural to all living beings. What do we all love above everything else? If we analyse deeply, it will be clear that we all love ourself more than we love any other thing. We love other things because we believe that in some way or other they are giving, will give or can give happiness to ourself.

We love whatever gives us happiness, and because absolute happiness is our true and essential nature, we love ourself above all other things. Happiness and love are inseparable, because they are in fact one and the same reality – our own essential non-dual nature, 'I am'. Happiness makes us love, and love gives us happiness. We love ourself because being ourself and knowing ourself is the supreme happiness. Therefore, a term that is sometimes used in *advaita vēdānta* in place of *sat-cit-ānanda* or being-consciousness-bliss is *asti-bhāti-priya*, which means being-luminescence-love.

The state of true self-knowledge is thus the state of pure and perfect being, consciousness, happiness and love. Therefore in verse 28 of *Upadēśa Undiyār* Sri Ramana says:

> If we know what our [real] nature is, then [what will remain and be known as the sole reality is] *anādi ananta akhaṇḍa sat-cit-ānanda* [beginningless, endless and unbroken being-consciousness-bliss].

The Sanskrit word *ananta*, which literally means 'endless' or 'limitless', also means 'eternal' and 'infinite'. In the original Tamil verse, the adjectives 'beginningless' and 'endless' are appended before the noun 'being', *anādi ananta sat*, and the adjective 'unbroken' is appended before the nouns 'consciousness-bliss', *akhaṇḍa cit-ānanda*, but these words are formed in this manner only to fit the poetic metre. Since being, consciousness and bliss are one single non-dual reality, the implied meaning of these words is that being-consciousness-bliss as a single whole is beginningless, endless and unbroken.

Why does Sri Ramana describe the one absolute reality, which exists and shines as being-consciousness-bliss, as beginningless, endless and unbroken? A beginning, an end or a break are each a limit or a boundary, and as such they can occur only in time, in space or in some other dimension. Anything that has a beginning, an end or a break is therefore finite and relative, and hence it cannot be the absolute reality. That which is absolute is by definition infinite, because it is free of all limits and boundaries, and hence it cannot have any beginning, any end or any break.

A being, a consciousness or a happiness that has a beginning, an end or a break is finite, and hence it cannot be absolutely real. True being, true consciousness and true happiness must therefore be absolute, and as such they can have no beginning, end or break. Being absolute and infinite, they have no limits or boundaries in time, in space or in any other conceivable dimension, and therefore they are all-transcending.

Being is the essence of each and every thing that is, and consciousness is the essence of our knowledge of each of those things. Though things appear to be many, they are divided and made manifold only due to the limitations inherent in their respective forms. However, in their essence, which is their 'is'-ness or being, they are undivided. Similarly, though knowledge appears to be manifold, it is divided and made manifold only by the limitations inherent in its various forms, which are thoughts or mental images. However, in its essence, which is consciousness, knowledge is undivided.

The being which is the essence of all things, and the consciousness which is the essence of all knowledge, are not two separate things, because no thing can be separated or distinguished from our knowledge of that thing. Indeed, the notion that being and consciousness could in essence be two separate things is a logical absurdity, because if they were, consciousness would not be, and therefore being would be unknown.

Being and consciousness are therefore one essence, and being the essence of everything and every knowledge, they have no limits or boundaries. Since true being and true consciousness are therefore one single reality, and since that one reality has no limits or boundaries, it is beginningless, endless and unbroken.

The beginning and the end of something are its external boundaries, boundaries that limit and define its extent in time, space or some other dimension. Since that which is absolutely real is infinite, it is free of all such external boundaries, and it transcends the limits of all dimensions. Therefore, since there is no limit to its extent either in time or in space, it is eternal and omnipresent.

Moreover, being infinite and absolute, it is not only free of all external boundaries or limits, but also of all internal boundaries. Whereas a beginning and an end are external boundaries, a break or division is an internal boundary, and hence the absolute reality is not only devoid of any beginning or end, but is also devoid of any break or division.

Because it is unlimited in its extent, nothing can be separate from or other than the absolute and essential being-consciousness, and therefore it exists alone, without anything outside itself. And because it is unbroken and undivided in itself, it consists of no parts. It is therefore perfectly non-dual. It is the single, infinite, eternal and omnipresent whole, other than which nothing exists.

Since no other thing exists to disturb the perfect peace of its being, the absolute being-consciousness is also absolutely peaceful and happy. Hence, since peace and happiness are inherent in being, the non-dual, infinite and absolute whole is not merely being-consciousness but is being-consciousness-happiness. Therefore, being devoid of all internal and external limits, it is indeed beginningless, endless and unbroken being-consciousness-happiness.

Since it is beginningless, endless and unbroken both in time and in space, it is eternal and omnipresent. There is no time and no place in which it does not exist. Since no break ever occurs in the continuity of its being or existence, it does not cease to exist at one moment and begin to exist again at another moment. Moreover, because it is unbroken, it is devoid of all forms of division and all distinctions. It is a single, partless and indivisible whole, and hence there is absolutely no distinction between its being, its consciousness and its happiness.

Being-consciousness-bliss is the eternally undivided infinite whole, other than which nothing exists. Though all appearances seem to arise and subside in it, it is not itself divided or affected in any way by such appearances, because in reality it merely exists as it is, devoid of the appearing or disappearing of anything. All that appears and disappears does so only in the view of our mind, which is itself a mere apparition that never truly exists, and not in the view of the absolute reality, which, being without any beginning, end or break, never undergoes any kind of change or modification.

However, though we speak of the beginningless, endless and unbroken being-consciousness-bliss as 'it', as if it were a third person, it is in fact the sole reality of the first person 'I', which is in turn the cause, foundation and support of all second and third persons. Therefore the unlimited, undivided, eternal, omnipresent, infinite and absolute being-consciousness-bliss is our own true and essential self, and hence we can experience it only by knowing what our real nature is.

The state in which we thus know what our real nature is and thereby experience ourself as infinite being-consciousness-bliss is the state of true knowledge. Because this state of true self-knowledge has no beginning, end or break, it is our eternal state. Thus when we cease to mistake ourself to be our time-bound mind, we will discover that true self-knowledge has always existed, and that we have therefore always known ourself as we really are. Hence we will not experience self-knowledge as something newly attained, but as that which always exists, without any beginning, break or end.

When we discover by keen self-examination that our mind is truly non-existent, we will also discover that time is likewise truly non-existent, being nothing more than a product of our mind's power of imagination. Beginning, break and end are all phenomena that can occur only within the limits of time and space, but time and space are themselves phenomena that are known only by our mind.

In the state of true self-knowledge, all that exists and is known is only being-consciousness-bliss – the infinite joy of being and knowing our own true self, 'I am'. In that perfect non-dual state of true knowledge, time, space and all other forms of duality or relativity are non-existent. Therefore the absolute reality, which is *sat-cit-ānanda* or the blissful state of being conscious of ourself as mere being, 'I am', is that which is without *ādi* or beginning, *khaṇḍa* or break, and *anta* or end.

Though the absolute reality is given many names and descriptions such as God, *allāh*, *brahman*, the absolute, the eternal, the infinite, the fullness of being, *pūrṇa* or the whole, pure knowledge, *sat-cit-ānanda* or being-consciousness-bliss, *tat* or 'it', *nirvāṇa*, the kingdom of God and so on, Sri Ramana often said that the words that express its real nature most perfectly and accurately are 'I' and 'am', or their combined form 'I am'.

This is so because what these words 'I' and 'am' express is not only being, but also the essential self-consciousness of being. Therefore, no matter in which language these words are expressed, the first person singular pronoun, 'I', and the equivalent first person singular form of the basic verb to be, 'am', both express the whole truth as accurately as any words possibly can express it.

This is why in most of the major religions of the world the name 'I am' is revered as the first, foremost and ultimate name of God. The supreme sanctity of this divine name 'I am' is expressed and enshrined in the Old Testament (upon which are based the three great religions of west Asian origin, Judaism, Christianity and Islam) in the words spoken by God to Moses, 'I AM THAT I AM' (*Exodus* 3.14), and also in the Vēdas (upon which are based the broad family of south Asian religions known as Hinduism) in the *mahāvākya* or great saying 'I am *brahman*' (*Bṛhadāraṇyaka Upaniṣad* 1.4.10).

The fact that 'I' and 'am' are the original and natural names of the absolute reality or God is stated emphatically by Sri Ramana in verses 712, 713, 714 and 715 of *Guru Vācaka Kōvai*:

> When *meypporuḷ* [the 'real substance', 'true essence' or absolute reality], which is called *uḷḷam* [the 'heart' or 'core'], itself [seemingly] comes out and spreads gradually from the heart as consciousness [that is, when it seems to manifest outwardly as innumerable names and forms, which are actually just imaginary distortions of the one true formless and undivided consciousness 'I am', which is that 'real substance' itself], among the thousands of [sacred] names that are [attributed] to [this] *uḷḷa-poruḷ* [the 'being-essence' or absolute reality], know that when [we] scrutinise [we will discover that] 'I' indeed is the first [the original and foremost].
>
> Since [together] with that 'I', which was previously [in the above verse] said to be the primary name [of the absolute reality or God], as its *meypporuḷ-viḷakkam* [the light which is its real essence] it ['am'] always exists as 'I am' [in the heart of each one of us], that name 'am' also is [the primary name of the absolute reality or God].
>
> Among the many names [attributed to God in all the different religions and languages of this world], which are thousandfold, no name has [such] real beauty [or] is [so] truly appropriate to *kaḍavuḷ* [God, who is *kaḍandu-uḷḷavaṉ*, 'he who exists transcending'], who abides in [our] heart devoid of thought, like this name ['I' or 'am']. [That is, 'I' or 'am' is the most beautiful and truly appropriate name of God, because he exists in our heart as our naturally thought-free self-conscious being, 'I am'.]

> Among all [the names of God] that are known, only the [original, natural and true] name of God, [which is experienced] as 'I [am] I', will thunder [its sole supremacy] to those whose attention is selfward-facing, shining forth as the *mauna-parā-vāk* [the supreme word, which is absolute silence], filling the space of [their] heart, in which [their] ego has been annihilated.

When we turn our attention selfwards and thereby experience ourself as we really are, our mind or ego will be annihilated, all duality will disappear, and in the thought-free space of our heart, which is the infinite space of being-consciousness-bliss, only our non-dual self-consciousness 'I am' will remain shining clearly in all its pristine purity. Since there is nothing to disturb the perfect peace of this experience of true self-knowledge, and since it reveals its own absolute reality more clearly than any spoken or written words could ever do, Sri Ramana describes it as the *mauna-parā-vāk*, the 'supreme word' or *parā-vāk*, which is absolute silence or *mauna*.

The power of the silent clarity of unadulterated self-consciousness to reveal itself as the absolute reality is expressed by Sri Ramana poetically in verse 5 of *Ēkātma Pañcakam*:

> That which always exists is only that *ēkātma vastu* [the one reality or substance, which is our own true self]. Since the *ādi-guru* at that time made that *vastu* to be known [only by] speaking without speaking, say, who can make it known [by] speaking?

The word *ēka* means 'one', *ātma* means 'self', and *vastu* is the Sanskrit equivalent of the Tamil word *poruḷ*, which means the absolute reality, substance or essence. Therefore the *ēkātma vastu*, which Sri Ramana declares to be *eppōdum uḷḷadu*, 'that which always is', is the one absolute reality or essential substance, which is our own true self.

In the *kaliveṇbā* version of *Ēkātma Pañcakam* Sri Ramana added two more words to qualify *uḷḷadu*, which means 'that which is', namely *taṉadu oḷiyāl*, which mean 'by its own light'. Thus he declared not only that the *ēkātma vastu* is the only thing that always exists, but also that it is 'that which always exists by its own light', that is, by its own light of non-dual self-consciousness, 'I am'.

The compound word *ādi-guru* means the 'original *guru*', and is a term that denotes Sri Dakshinamurti, a form of God that symbolises the revelation of the absolute reality through silence, which is the 'supreme word' or *parā-vāk*, and which Sri Ramana describes poetically as 'speaking without speaking', that is, communicating the truth without thought or spoken words. Since the *ēkātma vastu* is our own thought-free and therefore absolutely silent self-conscious being, it can only reveal itself by shining within us silently and clearly as 'I am I', without the obstruction of any thoughts or words.

Since this silent, thought-free, peaceful and absolutely clear experience of pure non-dual self-conscious being, 'I am', is the true and natural state of our real self, which is the one absolute reality or essential substance that we call 'God', Sri Ramana says that the original and most beautifully appropriate name of God is only 'I', 'am', 'I am' or 'I am I'.

Though 'I' and 'am' are two separate words, they both denote our single, non-dual and absolutely indivisible sense of self – our essential consciousness of our own being, our fundamental knowledge of our own existence. Each of these two words is therefore implied in the other.

The pronoun 'I' implies that we exist, and this existence of ourself is expressed by the verb 'am'. Conversely, the verb 'am' implies the existence of nothing other than ourself, which is expressed by the pronoun 'I'. In many languages, therefore, either of these two words can be used on its own, since its counterpart is implied in it and is therefore clearly understood. In such languages, the compound form 'I am' is an option that is used only for added emphasis.

In this respect, English is an exception. For example, if we wish to say that we are a human being, in English we have to use both the words 'I' and 'am' and say, 'I am a human being', whereas in many other languages it is sufficient in such a context to use either just 'I' or just 'am'. In Tamil, for example, we need not say the long-winded sentence '*nāṉ māṉiḍaṉāy irukkiṟēṉ*', which means 'I am [a] man', because we can convey exactly the same sense simply by saying either '*nāṉ māṉidaṉ*', which means 'I [am a] man', or '*māṉidaṉāy irukkiṟēṉ*', which means '[I] am [a] man'. Similar is the case with many other ancient and modern Asian and European languages, of which Sanskrit, Hebrew, Greek and Latin are a few examples.

In the *Gospel according to St John*, which was originally written in a form of ancient Greek, there are many well-known 'I am' sayings of Jesus, in several of which he is alluding more or less clearly to the Old Testament usage of the words 'I am' to denote the essential self-conscious being of God. This allusion is particularly clear in the seven verses (8.24, 8.28, 8.58, 13.19, 18.5, 18.6 and 18.8) in which he uses 'I am' without appending any predicate to it, and which Biblical scholars therefore describe as being instances of his 'absolute' use of 'I am'.

In each of these seven verses, the best known of which is, 'Before Abraham was born, I am' (8.58), his saying ends with the Greek words *ego eimi*, which mean 'I am'. By using these two words together, and by placing them at the end of each respective sentence, these verses succeed in placing great emphasis upon the meaning of 'I am' intended by Jesus, but in some cases this emphasis has unfortunately been lost in translation.

Besides these seven instances of his 'absolute' use of 'I am', there are more than thirty other sayings in which he uses 'I am' with a predicate, but whereas in some of these sayings the words *ego eimi* are used in the original Greek, in others the word *eimi*, which means 'am', is used on its own without the word *ego*, which means 'I'.

Such a valid use of the verb 'am' without its logical subject 'I' is common in those languages in which all verbs take a particular form in each of the three persons and each of the two or more tenses. One such language is Latin, and therefore in Latin the word *sum*, which means 'am', and also the first person singular forms of other verbs can be used without the word *ego* or 'I'. For example, when Descartes famously concluded, '*cogito ergo sum*', which means '[I] think, therefore [I] am', he did not need to use the word *ego* either before *cogito* or before *sum*, because it is clearly implied in the grammatical form of each of these verbs. As we shall see in the next chapter, this conclusion of Descartes is really putting the cart before the horse, but I cite it here only as an example of the verb 'am' conveying a complete sense without the explicit use of its corresponding pronoun 'I'.

In the original Hebrew in which *Exodus* was written, the words that are usually translated as 'I AM THAT I AM' are '*ehyeh asher ehyeh*'. The word *ehyeh* actually means just 'am', and the pronoun 'I' is simply implied in it, so a more literal translation would be 'AM THAT AM' or 'AM WHAT AM'.

In ancient Hebrew there were no tenses as such, but only two 'aspects' of a verb, the 'perfect' and the 'imperfect'. The 'perfect aspect' of a verb was used to denote an action that has been completed or ended, and was therefore equivalent in function to the past tense, whereas the 'imperfect aspect' was used to denote an action that was not yet completed or ended, and was therefore used in cases in which we would use either the present or the future tense.

Since *ehyeh* is the first person 'imperfect' form of the verb 'to be', it implies a continuous present tense, which we could translate as 'am being'. Thus '*ehyeh asher ehyeh*' could be translated as '[I] AM BEING WHAT [I] AM BEING', or more freely as '[I] ALWAYS AM WHAT [I] ALWAYS AM'.

Some Biblical scholars suggest that it should be translated as a future tense, '[I] SHALL BE WHAT [I] SHALL BE', but if it is translated thus, it should be understood in the sense '[I] SHALL ALWAYS BE WHAT [I] SHALL ALWAYS BE' or '[I] SHALL ALWAYS BE WHAT I ALWAYS AM', because it is not an exclusively future tense, but only a tense continuing into the future. However, since the essential being that is God is eternal and ever present, *ehyeh* is most appropriately translated in this context by a continuous present tense, 'am' or 'am being'.

Since being is in reality always present, it transcends the three divisions of time, past, present and future. This eternally continuous nature of being is aptly expressed by the word *ehyeh*, which as an 'imperfect aspect' of the verb 'to be' implies an unended and continuing state of being.

Being as such never begins or ends, nor does it ever undergo any change.

It always remains as it is, so in future it will always be what it always has been, and will never become anything new. Therefore the true nature or absolute reality of God is just eternal and unchanging being, and is not any form of 'becoming'. Becoming implies change, and change requires time, but the true being of God transcends the limits of time, and is therefore beyond all change and becoming.

Moreover, since true being is self-conscious, and since it can therefore never be an object of knowledge, a second or third person, but always experiences itself as the first person, the first person 'imperfect' form *ehyeh* is a perfect expression of the true nature of being.

However we may choose to translate this profound expression of the true nature of being, '*ehyeh asher ehyeh*', what is important is that we understand the truth that it expresses. On its own, the word *ehyeh* expresses the fact that being is self-conscious, non-objective and continuous – or in other words, that being is the eternally present self-conscious reality of the first person. This truth about being, which is expressed perfectly by the first person continuous verb *ehyeh* or 'am', is reiterated and emphasised by the whole sentence '*ehyeh asher ehyeh*'.

That is, by saying '[I] AM WHAT [I] AM', these words further emphasise the truth that the eternal self-conscious first person being 'am' is absolutely single and non-dual. They imply, 'I am only what I am', 'I am nothing but what I am', or more simply, 'I am just I, and nothing other than I'.

Because this Biblical saying, 'I AM THAT I AM', is such a perfect expression of the absolute, eternal, non-dual, non-objective, self-conscious, first person nature of being, Sri Ramana used to say that it is the greatest *mahāvākya*, even greater than the four *mahāvākyas* or 'great sayings' of the Vēdas. Though the import of each of the Vedic *mahāvākyas*, 'pure consciousness is *brahman*', 'I am *brahman*', 'it you are' and 'this self is *brahman*', is essentially the same as that of this Biblical saying, they are actually less perfect and accurate expressions of the reality because they each contain one or more words that are not first person in form.

That is, in 'I AM THAT I AM' the first person sense of being, 'am', is equated only with itself and not with anything else, whereas in each of the Vedic *mahāvākyas* it is equated either with a third person noun, *brahman*, which means the absolute reality or supreme spirit, or with the third person pronoun, 'it', which denotes the same absolute reality. Though 'I am' is truly the absolute reality or *brahman*, as soon as we think that it is so, our attention is diverted away from our natural first person consciousness of being towards an unnatural and alien mental conception of 'the absolute reality'. To help us fix our whole and undivided attention upon 'I am', it is better that we are told that 'I am' is just 'I am', rather than being told that 'I am' is God, *brahman* or the absolute reality.

Just as the absolute truth of being is expressed by God in *Exodus* by equating 'am' only with 'am', and with nothing besides 'am', whenever Sri Ramana expressed the eternal experience of our being that is revealed when the imaginary obscuration caused by our mind is removed, he expressed it by equating 'I' only with 'I', and with nothing besides 'I'.

When doing so, he used the minimum words, just '*nāṉ nāṉ*', which literally mean 'I I', but which, in accordance with the Tamil custom of omitting 'am' whenever its sense is made clear by the use of 'I', clearly imply 'I [am] I'. That is, just as '*nāṉ yār?*' means 'I [am] who?' and '*edu nāṉ?*' means 'what [am] I?', or just as '*nāṉ maṉidaṉ*' means 'I [am a] man' and '*nāṉ iṉṉāṉ*' means 'I [am] so-and-so', so '*nāṉ nāṉ*' clearly means 'I [am] I'.

Three important instances of his use of these words '*nāṉ nāṉ*' or 'I [am] I' to describe the state of true self-knowledge are verse 20 of *Upadēśa Undiyār*, verse 30 of *Uḷḷadu Nāṟpadu* and verse 2 of *Āṉma-Viddai*, in which he says:

> In the place [the core of our being] where 'I' [our mind or individual self] merges [or becomes one], the one [true knowledge] appears [or shines forth] spontaneously [or as ourself] as 'I [am] I'. That itself [or that, which is ourself] is the whole [the infinite totality or fullness of being, consciousness and happiness].

> When [our] mind reaches [our] heart [the core of our being] by inwardly scrutinising 'who am I?' [and] when he [our mind] who is 'I' [our ego or individual self] is [thereby] subdued [literally, 'when he suffers head-shame', that is, when he subsides, bowing his head in shame], the one [true knowledge] appears [or shines forth] spontaneously [or as ourself] as 'I [am] I'. Though it appears, it is not 'I' [our individual self]. It is the whole *poruḷ* [the infinite essence, substance or reality], the *poruḷ* which is [our own real] self.

> Since the thought 'this body composed of flesh is I' is the one string on which [all our] various thoughts are attached, if [we] go within [ourself scrutinising] 'who am I? what is the place [the source from which this fundamental thought 'I am this body' rises]?', [all] thoughts will disappear, and within the cave [the core of our being] self-knowledge will shine spontaneously [or as ourself] as 'I [am] I'. This alone is silence [the silent or motionless state of mere being], the one [non-dual] space [of infinite consciousness], the sole abode of [true unlimited] happiness.

Though Sri Ramana describes this experience of true self-knowledge as 'appearing' or 'shining forth' spontaneously as 'I [am] I', it does not actually appear anew, because it is the eternal and infinite whole, the fullness of being and consciousness, which we always experience as 'I am'.

However, because we imagine ourself to be our mind or individual consciousness, the natural clarity of our non-dual self-consciousness or true self-knowledge now appears to be obscured. Therefore, when we scrutinise our basic consciousness 'I am', which is the essence of what we now feel to be our mind, and when our mind thereby ceases to exist as a separate individual consciousness, being found to be nothing other than our essential consciousness 'I am', we will experience this natural mind-free consciousness 'I am' as if it were a new and fresh knowledge.

However, the newness and freshness of this self-knowledge will be experienced as such only at the precise moment that our mind vanishes. What will remain thereafter is the clear knowledge that we are and always have been nothing other than this simple consciousness of our being, 'I am', which is the one, only, eternal and infinite reality. Therefore, in verse 30 of *Uḷḷadu Nāṟpadu*, after saying that it will appear or shine forth spontaneously as 'I am I', Sri Ramana adds:

> […] Though it appears [or shines forth], it is not 'I' [our individual self, which appears and disappears]. It is the [eternally existing] whole essence [substance or reality], the essence which is [our real] self.

Because we now experience ourself as a limited individual consciousness that mistakes itself to be this body, our knowledge of ourself now appears in the form 'I am this'. When this false and illusory knowledge of ourself is destroyed by the clarity of true self-knowledge, we will cease to feel 'I am this' and will instead feel only 'I am I'.

However, as soon as this fresh experience 'I am I' appears, we will recognise it as our eternal and natural state of being, which we always experience as 'I am', and thus we will no longer feel it to be new or fresh in the sense that it was previously absent, but will instead experience it as the infinite whole, which transcends the imaginary dimension of time and is therefore eternally new and fresh.

To emphasise the fact that this 'whole' or infinite totality of being, which is the absolute clarity of true self-knowledge or self-consciousness that shines as 'I [am] I', is not something that ever appears or disappears, even though it momentarily appears to be newly experienced at the precise instant that our mind is dissolved in and entirely consumed by it, after saying in verse 20 of *Upadēśa Undiyār* that it appears spontaneously as 'I [am] I' when our mind or ego, our finite individual sense of 'I', merges and becomes one with it, in verse 21 Sri Ramana affirms that, since it is always experienced by us as our own essential being, it is eternal:

> That [one infinite whole that shines thus as 'I am I'] is at all times [in the past, present and future, and in all eternity] the [true] import of the word 'I', because of the absence of our non-existence even in sleep,

which is devoid of [any separate or finite sense of] 'I'.

The opening words of this verse are *nāṉ eṉum sol-poruḷ*, which I have translated as 'the import of the word I'. However, though I have translated the word *poruḷ* as 'import', there is actually no adequate word in English to convey its full meaning, particularly as it is used in this context. When it is combined with the word *sol*, which means 'word', to form the compound word *soṯporuḷ*, as it is here, it would normally mean just the true 'import', 'meaning' or 'significance' of whichever word it refers to. However, when used in philosophy, *poruḷ* has a much deeper significance, because it denotes the absolute reality, the true substance or essential being of all that is. Therefore in this context *nāṉ eṉum sol-poruḷ* means the absolute reality or essential being that is denoted by the word 'I'.

That is, though due to our confused knowledge of ourself we frequently use this word 'I' to denote our body or mind, what we actually feel when we say 'I' is our essential self-consciousness – our fundamental consciousness of our own being. Because we are conscious of our being, we feel 'I am', but because we confuse our being with this body and mind, we misapply this word 'I' by using it with reference to these extraneous adjuncts.

When we thus confuse our consciousness of our being with a body, the resulting mixed consciousness that feels 'I am this body' is the limited and distorted form of consciousness that we call our 'mind'. This mind or adjunct-bound consciousness is our finite 'I', our individual self or ego.

Though we experience this mind in waking and dream, it disappears in sleep. However, though this mind or individual 'I' is absent in sleep, we do not feel that we cease to exist at that time. Therefore in the second half of this verse Sri Ramana says, '[…] because of the absence of our non-existence even in sleep, which is devoid of "I"'.

Here the words 'because of the absence of our non-existence' are a poetic way of saying 'because we are not non-existent'. That is, even though our mind becomes non-existent in sleep, we continue to exist and to know our existence as 'I am', and hence our mind is not our real 'I' but only an impostor, an apparition or phantom which poses as 'I'. Our real 'I' can only be that which we are at all times and in all states.

Because we know 'I slept', we clearly recognise and acknowledge our continued existence or being in sleep, even though at that time we did not feel ourself to be this limited mind or adjunct-bound 'I' that we mistake to be ourself in waking and dream. Therefore, since we continue to exist even in the absence of this false 'I', it cannot be the true import of the word 'I'.

That is, since the word 'I' denotes ourself, its true import must be that which we are at all times, and not that which we appear to be only at certain times. Hence the true import of the word 'I' – the reality that is truly denoted by it – can only be our ever-present consciousness of our own essential being, which we always experience as 'I am', even in sleep.

Since our essential being remains eternally distinct from and untouched by any adjuncts or *upādhis* that may appear to be superimposed upon it, it never feels 'I am this' or 'I am that', but is always clearly conscious of itself only as 'I am' or 'I am I'. Since this 'I am' does not become non-existent even in sleep, when our false adjunct-bound 'I' ceases to exist, it is at all times and in all states our true being – the real import of the word 'I'.

Therefore, since it is not limited in any way by any finite adjuncts, or by any finite dimensions such as time or space, our essential consciousness of being, which we always experience as 'I am', is eternal and infinite. Since it is not limited as 'this' or 'that', it is not separate from anything. Since we always experience it as the base of all our knowledge of everything, it is in fact the true essence of all things. Since it alone endures through and beyond all time, while all other forms of knowledge appear and disappear within time, it is the only knowledge that is absolutely true.

All other forms of knowledge appear and disappear because they are known only by our mind, which itself appears and disappears. Since it appears only in waking and dream, and disappears in sleep, our mind cannot be our real self – the true import of the word 'I'. Therefore in verse 717 of *Guru Vācaka Kōvai* Sri Ramana says:

> Since the body-soul [the embodied soul, the finite consciousness that imagines itself to be a body] itself appears and disappears, [it cannot be the enduring reality denoted by the word 'I', and hence] *ātmā* [our real self], which is the abiding base of the body-soul, alone is the correct [direct or honest] *poruḷ* [import, significance or reality] of the word that [each embodied soul] says as 'I'. Know that when [we] scrutinise, [we will discover only our own *ātmā* or fundamental self-consciousness] to be the conclusive *poruḷ* [the ultimate reality denoted by the word 'I'].

The basic reality that underlies the imaginary appearance and disappearance of our body-bound mind is only our own essential self-conscious being, which we always experience as 'I am'. Though everything else appears and disappears, our basic self-consciousness neither appears nor disappears, because it endures in all states and at all times, and hence it alone is the reality that is truly denoted when we say the word 'I'.

Because Sri Ramana often used the terminology of *advaita vēdānta*, making free use of many of its standard terms such as *sat-cit-ānanda* or being-consciousness-bliss, his philosophy is generally considered to be a fresh expression of that ancient philosophy. However, he did not arrive at his philosophy by studying any of the philosophical texts of *advaita vēdānta*, but did so even before he had had any opportunity to become acquainted with those texts.

His philosophy was an expression of his own direct experience of true self-knowledge, which he attained at the age of sixteen when, prompted by a sudden and intense fear of death, he turned his attention inwards and focused it keenly and exclusively upon his consciousness of being, 'I am', in order to discover whether or not his 'I' would die when his body died. As a result of this keenly focused self-scrutiny, he discovered that he was not the perishable body, but only the imperishable reality, which is beginningless, endless and unbroken being-consciousness-bliss. Only much later, when people asked him questions to clear their doubts about what they had read in the texts of *advaita vēdānta*, did he have occasion to read such texts, and when he did so he recognised that they were describing his own experience.

Advaita vēdānta is an ancient Indian system of philosophy, and its name etymologically means the philosophy of 'non-duality' (*advaita*) or 'no two-ness' (*a-dvi-tā*), which is the 'end' (*anta*) of all 'knowledge' (*vēda*), or the ultimate conclusion of the Vēdas. Though most of the knowledge expressed in the four Vēdas concerns only duality, in their later portions each of the Vēdas finally give some expression of the knowledge of non-duality. Where all the knowledge of duality (*dvaita*) expressed in the Vēdas comes to an end (*anta*), there remains the knowledge of non-duality (*advaita*).

That is, the true non-dual knowledge 'I am' that alone remains when all dualistic knowledge – which is the central concern not only of the Vēdas but also of most other scriptures, philosophies and sciences – has finally come to an end, is the knowledge of non-duality or *advaita* expressed in *vēdānta*.

In truth, therefore, *advaita vēdānta* is not a philosophy that is exclusive to the Vedic tradition of India, but is the 'perennial philosophy' that underpins all true forms of mysticism, metaphysics and radically profound philosophy. That is to say, though in the context of the Vedic tradition the philosophy of non-duality is named *advaita vēdānta*, the essential philosophy of non-duality that is so named can be found expressed in other words in many other mystical and philosophical traditions throughout the world. However, while discussing the philosophy of non-dual true knowledge, it is often useful to refer specifically to *advaita vēdānta*, because in the post-Vedic tradition known as *vēdānta* this philosophy has been given a particularly clear expression.

Therefore, when it is said that the philosophy of Sri Ramana is a modern expression of the ancient philosophy of *advaita vēdānta*, this does not mean either that his philosophy is derived from *advaita vēdānta*, or that it is relevant only in the context of the Vedic religion and culture known as Hinduism. His philosophy expresses a truth that is beyond all religious and cultural differences, and that can be found expressed in some form or other in most of the major religions and cultures of this world.

All the philosophical verses and other writings of Sri Ramana that I quote in this book express the experience of a being who is in a state of consciousness that is quite different to the body-bound state of consciousness with which we are all familiar. Since he is talking about a state of absolute non-dual knowledge of which we personally have no experience (or rather, of which our experience has seemingly been obscured, and of which we therefore imagine that we have no experience), is there any reason why we should believe all that he says, or at least accept it tentatively?

Sri Ramana does not ask us to believe anything blindly. He begins his exposition of the philosophy of non-duality by asking us to analyse critically our own experience of ourself in our three states of consciousness, waking, dream and deep sleep, which we all experience every day. All the rest of his exposition of this philosophy follows on logically from the conclusions that we arrive at by means of this critical analysis.

Nothing that he says is unreasonable, nor is it based upon unsound premises. Therefore, though we may not at present be able to verify immediately from our own experience all that he says about the absolute reality, which is the state of true knowledge, we cannot reasonably refute it, and hence there is no reason why we should not accept it at least tentatively.

Moreover, when he spoke about the state of absolute true knowledge, he did not do so with the intention that we should merely believe his words. Believing something that we do not know for certain is of little use to us if it does not help us to attain certain knowledge of it. Therefore Sri Ramana not only told us the nature of the absolute reality, which is perfectly non-dual being-consciousness or true self-knowledge, but also told us the means by which we could attain direct experience of that reality.

The means that he taught fits logically into the whole philosophy of non-duality that he expounded. Since our critical analysis of our experience of ourself in our three states of consciousness leads us to understand that our essential self-consciousness 'I am' is the sole reality underlying the appearance of these three states, being the only thing which we experience continuously throughout all of them, it is reasonable for us to conclude that, before trying to know any other thing, we should first try to know the true nature of this fundamental consciousness 'I am'.

Since we cannot know something without attending to it, the only way we can know the true nature of this consciousness is to scrutinise it with a keenly focused attention. This simple yet profound method of self-investigation, self-scrutiny or self-attention is therefore quite logically the only means by which we can discover the true nature of the reality that underlies all the diverse forms of knowledge that we now experience.

Thus the philosophy of non-dual true knowledge expounded by Sri Ramana is not only a well-reasoned philosophy, but also a practical and precise science. Because it begins with a minute analysis of our own consciousness, which is the base of all our knowledge, and thereby builds for itself a foundation of carefully thought out and clearly reasoned theory, the quest for true knowledge or self-discovery that Sri Ramana urges us to undertake is a philosophy in the truest and most profound sense of that word. And because from that theory it naturally leads us on to the practice of the simple empirical technique of turning our power of attention – our power of knowing or consciousness – back on itself, towards our basic consciousness 'I am', in order to discover what this 'I' really is, this quest for true self-knowledge is also a true science. Thus it is a complete philosophy-science, one in which both theory and practice are necessary and inseparable parts of the whole.

The theory of this science of self-knowledge is necessary to start us, to guide us and to motivate us in its practice. But if we never commence the practice, or if we do not follow it through to its conclusion, all the theory is of little use to us. The theory by itself can never give us true knowledge, but only an intellectual understanding about it. Such intellectual understanding is merely a superficial and dualistic knowledge, a knowledge in which what is known is distinct from the person who knows it.

No intellectual understanding can ever be true knowledge, because our intellect is merely a function of our mind, our limited adjunct-bound consciousness, which is the root of all wrong knowledge, being itself a wrong knowledge that arises only when we mistake ourself to be a physical body. A theoretical understanding of this philosophy and science is therefore useful only to the extent that it both motivates us to seek direct experience of true non-dual self-knowledge, and enables us to understand clearly the means by which we can attain such direct experience.

CHAPTER 6

True Knowledge and False Knowledge

As we saw in the previous chapter, true knowledge is not a state that we can newly attain, because it always exists as our own essential and fundamental consciousness, 'I am', which we never even for a moment cease to know. What prevents us from experiencing it as it really is, is only the false knowledge that we have superimposed upon it. What do we mean when we speak of 'false knowledge' or 'wrong knowledge'?

Except our basic knowledge 'I am', everything that we know is only a thought that arises in our mind, a form of knowledge that is inherently dualistic, involving as it does three seemingly distinct components, ourself as the knowing subject, something other than ourself as the object known, and linking these two a separate act of knowing. That is, when we feel 'I know such-and-such', this knowledge involves a knowing consciousness or subject called 'I', a known thing or object called 'such-and-such', and an action or process of doing called 'knowing'. These three components constitute the basic triad of which every form of objective knowledge is composed.

In this basic triad of objective knowledge, the verb 'know' may be replaced by some other verb, such as 'perceive', 'see', 'hear', 'taste', 'experience', 'think', 'feel', 'believe' or 'understand', but still this triad remains as the basic structure of every form of knowledge or experience other than our essential and fundamental knowledge, which is our knowledge of our own being, 'I am'. Since our fundamental knowledge 'I am' is non-dual, it does not involve any distinction between the consciousness that knows and itself that it knows, nor does it involve any separate act of knowing, because consciousness naturally knows itself simply by being itself, and not by doing anything.

Why do we say that all knowledge involving this triad is a false or wrong knowledge? Firstly, we say so because each component of this triad is a thought that we form in our mind by our power of imagination. Without our power of imagination, our power to form thoughts, we could not experience any knowledge other than 'I am'. Thus every knowledge other than 'I am' is essentially imaginary.

Even the idea that our knowledge of the external world is formed in our mind not only by our power of imagination, but also in response to actual external stimuli, is a thought that we form in our mind by our power of imagination. No reason or proof exists that can justify our belief that any of our knowledge actually corresponds to something outside our mind. All we know, and all we ever can know, is known only within our mind. Even the seemingly external world that we know through our five senses exists for us only within our mind, just as the world we know in a dream exists only within our mind.

Secondly, we say so because each component of this triad is a transitory appearance. Though the knowing subject, 'I', is relatively constant, in contrast to the objects known by it and its actions of knowing them, which are thoughts that are constantly changing, rising and then subsiding in our mind, each one being replaced the next moment by another, even this 'I', the subject who knows this constantly changing flow of thoughts, is transitory, rising only in waking and dream, and subsiding in deep sleep.

This subject who thinks and knows all other thoughts is our mind, our limited adjunct-bound consciousness that knows itself not merely as 'I am' but as 'I am this body'. Since this subject, all the objects known by it, and all its successively repeated actions of knowing those objects, are thus merely transitory appearances, they cannot be real, because though they appear to be real at one time, they cease to appear real at another time. Their seeming reality is therefore just a false appearance, an illusory apparition formed in our mind by our power of imagination.

Though all our knowledge other than 'I am' is thus an imaginary and false appearance, how does it appear to us to be real? Whatever we know appears to us to be real while we are knowing it. Even the world that we experience in dream, and the body which we then take to be 'I', appear to us to be real so long as we are experiencing that dream. There is therefore something that makes all our current knowledge appear to be real. What is that something?

Every knowledge, we have seen, consists of three components, the first and basic one being the knowing subject, 'I'. This subject is a compound consciousness formed by the superimposition of an imaginary adjunct, 'this body', upon the real consciousness 'I am'. Thus underlying every knowledge is the true knowledge 'I am', and it is this true knowledge or consciousness that gives a seeming reality to every knowledge that we experience.

How exactly is the reality of our basic knowledge 'I am' thus seemingly transferred to all the other knowledge that we currently superimpose upon it, even though that other knowledge is false? All our other knowledge is known only by our mind, which is the knowing subject, and which comes into existence only by imagining itself to be a body. Before imagining and knowing any other thing, our mind first imagines a body to be itself. That is, it confuses a body, which is a product of its imagination, with 'I am', which is its real and basic knowledge. Since 'I am' is real, and since our mind mistakes that imaginary body to be 'I am', it cannot but feel that body to be real.

Whether the body that it now imagines to be itself happens to be this body of the waking state or some other body in dream, our mind always feels that its current body is real. Since that current body is one among the many objects of the world that it is currently experiencing, our mind cannot but feel that all the other objects that it is currently experiencing are as real as the body that it now mistakes to be itself. In other words, since we mistake certain current products of our imagination to be ourself and therefore real, we cannot avoid mistaking all the other current products of our imagination to be equally real.

However, though our basic knowledge or consciousness 'I am' alone is real, and though all the other things that appear to be real borrow their seeming reality only from this consciousness, which is their underlying base and support, we are so accustomed to overlooking this consciousness and attending only to the objects or thoughts that we form in our mind by our power of imagination, that those objects and our act of knowing them appear in the distorted perspective of our mind to be more real than the fundamental consciousness that underlies them.

The only reason why we suffer from this distorted perspective is that we are so enthralled by our experience of duality or otherness, believing that we can obtain real happiness only from things other than ourself, that throughout our states of mental activity, which we call waking and dream, we spend all our time attending only to such other things, and we consequently ignore or overlook our underlying consciousness 'I am'.

This distorted perspective of our mind is what makes it so difficult for us to accept that our consciousness 'I am' alone is real, and that everything else is just an imagination or apparition. Whereas in our distorted perspective all our knowledge of this world appears to be solid, substantial, obvious and irrefutable, our underlying consciousness 'I am' appears in comparison to be something insubstantial and ethereal, something that we cannot quite know with the same degree of precision and certainty.

A clear example of the effect that this distorted perspective has upon our human intellect is the famous observation made by Descartes, '*Cogito ergo sum*', which means, 'I think, therefore I am'. What he implied by this conclusion is that because we think, we know that we are. But this is putting the cart before the horse. We do not need to think in order to know that we are. First we know 'I am', and then only is it possible for us to think, or to know 'I am thinking'.

More appropriately, therefore, his saying could be inverted as, 'I am, therefore I think', or better still as, 'I am, therefore I seem to think'. Even when we do not think, as in deep sleep, we know 'I am'. Our thinking depends upon our knowledge of our being – our fundamental consciousness 'I am' – but our knowledge of our being does not depend upon our thinking.

However, what Descartes observed is not altogether untrue. Whatever we know and whatever we think does indeed prove that we do exist. All our knowledge and all our thoughts are irrefutably clear proof of our existence or being.

However, to know that we exist, we do not need any such external proof, because our existence or being, 'I am', is self-evident. Even in the absence of any other knowledge or thought, we know that we are. In sleep, for example, we do not think or know any other thing, but we do experience that state, and we remember our experience of it now in this waking state, saying 'I slept'. We experience the thought-free state of sleep because in that state we do indeed exist and know that we are existing. Therefore our existence and our knowledge that we do exist do not need any proof, least of all the proof provided by our thinking and knowing other things.

Our existence or being is self-evident because it is self-conscious. That is, our being is conscious of itself, and hence it does not need the aid of anything else to know itself. In other words, we are self-conscious being, and hence without the aid of anything else we know ourself as 'I am' simply by being ourself.

Therefore our basic self-consciousness 'I am' does not depend upon any other knowledge, but all our other knowledge does depend upon our basic self-consciousness 'I am'. Hence our basic self-consciousness 'I am' is our one fundamental and essential knowledge.

In order to think, we must be, but in order to be, we do not need to think. And since our being is not separate from or other than our knowledge of our being, we can equally well say that in order to think, we must know that we are, but in order to know that we are, we do not need to think.

Since we always know 'I am', even when we know it mixed with other knowledge or thoughts, why should we say that such other knowledge obscures our knowledge of 'I am', preventing us from knowing it as it really is?

The true and essential nature of our consciousness 'I am' is mere being, because it is able to be without knowing any other thing, as we experience each day in deep sleep. Merely by being itself, it knows itself, because its being is itself the consciousness of its being. Thus it is a perfectly non-dual knowledge – a knowledge in which that which is known is that which knows it, a knowledge that involves no action, a knowledge that involves nothing but mere being.

On the other hand, all other knowledge involves not only being, but also an act of knowing, in addition to a distinction between the knower and the known. This imaginary act of knowing is superimposed upon the reality of our mere being, making it appear to us that the nature of our consciousness 'I am' is not merely to be, but is to know things other than itself.

Thus by the transitory rising of any other knowledge, the real and permanent nature of our true knowledge or consciousness 'I am', which is mere being, is obscured. Instead of knowing merely 'I am', we know 'I am knowing this' or 'I am knowing that'. Since all knowledge other than 'I am' is imaginary and therefore unreal, the knowledge 'I am knowing this' is merely a false or wrong knowledge – a knowledge in which an imaginary adjunct has been superimposed upon our basic and only true knowledge, 'I am', thus obscuring it by making it appear otherwise than it really is.

In order for us to know our true self as it really is, is it therefore sufficient for us merely to cease knowing anything else? If we merely cease attending to any other thing, do we thereby automatically attain true knowledge of our real self, 'I am'?

No, we do not, because in deep sleep we cease attending to or knowing anything other than ourself, but even then we do not have a clear knowledge of what we really are. If in deep sleep we knew ourself truly and clearly as we really are, we could not again mistake ourself to be something else – a physical body – in waking and dream. Though all knowledge of other things is removed in deep sleep, our consciousness 'I am' is nevertheless still obscured by a seeming darkness or lack of clarity of self-knowledge.

What is this darkness or lack of clarity that we experience in deep sleep, and that prevents us from clearly knowing the true nature of ourself, our real adjunct-free consciousness 'I am'?

In *advaita vēdānta*, our power of delusion or self-deception by which we seemingly prevent ourself from knowing our true nature is called *māyā*. The word *māyā* etymologically means 'what (*ya*) is not (*mā*)', and is defined as the power that makes that which is unreal appear to be real, and that which is real appear to be unreal.

This power of *māyā* or self-deception functions in two forms, as the power of veiling or obscuring called *āvaraṇa śakti*, and the power of scattering, dispersion, diffusion or dissipation called *vikṣēpa śakti*. The former, *āvaraṇa śakti*, which is our power of 'self-forgetfulness', 'self-ignorance' or lack of clarity of self-knowledge, is the root and primal form of *māyā*, because it is the original cause that always underlies the latter, *vikṣēpa śakti*, which is our power of imagination that enables us to project from within ourself a seemingly external world of multiplicity. Whereas *vikṣēpa śakti* functions only in waking and in dream, the underlying *āvaraṇa śakti* functions not only in waking and dream but also in deep sleep.

Our power of 'self-forgetfulness', which is our power of veiling or *āvaraṇa śakti*, can be compared to the background darkness in a cinema, without which no picture could be projected on the screen. All the thoughts that we form in our mind, including the seemingly external world that we project and perceive through our five senses, are like the pictures projected and seen on the cinema screen. The power that projects this picture of thoughts and a seemingly external world is our power of imagination, which is our power of diffusion or *vikṣēpa śakti*.

Just as the cinema projector could not project any picture if its indispensable light were not shining brightly within it, so our mind could not project the imaginary picture of this or any other world if its indispensable light were not shining brightly within it. This indispensable light that shines brightly within our mind enabling it to project this imaginary picture of thoughts and objects is our essential consciousness 'I am'.

The states of waking and dream can be compared to the state in which a film reel is rolling in the projector, producing an ever changing picture on the screen, whereas sleep can be compared to the state in which one film reel is finished and another is about to be threaded into the projector. All the while, however, the bright light in the projector is shining, so in the gap between the removal of one reel and the fitting of the next all that is seen on the screen is a light.

However, though at that time we can see no pictures on the screen, but only a frame of light, the background darkness of the cinema still remains. Similarly in deep sleep, though we do not experience any of the effects of *vikṣēpa śakti*, but only the essential light of consciousness, 'I am', the veiling power of 'self-forgetfulness' or *āvaraṇa śakti* still remains, preventing us from knowing our consciousness 'I am' as it really is, free from any adjuncts such as a seeming lack of clarity.

Our power of self-delusion or *māyā* can never entirely conceal our real self, because our real self is the consciousness that enables us to know the effects of our self-delusion. All our self-delusion or *māyā* can do is to obscure our real self by making it appear to be something other than what it really is. We always know 'I am', whether our mind is functioning, as in waking and dream, or in temporary abeyance, as in sleep, but we do not know it as it really is. In all these three states we know *that we are*, but we do not know *what we are*.

In waking and in dream we know 'I am this body, a person named so-and-so, and I am conscious of this world around me'. In deep sleep, on the other hand, we know ourself as being seemingly 'unconscious'. Thus in waking and dream our identification with a physical body and our consequent perception of a world around us is superimposed upon our fundamental consciousness 'I am'. Similarly in sleep our identification with the seeming 'unconsciousness' of that state is superimposed upon our fundamental consciousness 'I am'. That is, in all three of these states the true nature of our real self, our fundamental and essential consciousness 'I am', is obscured by the superimposition of illusory adjuncts.

As we have seen earlier, our present so-called waking state is essentially no different to the many dream states that we experience while asleep. Out of our sleep of self-forgetfulness, we create both waking and dream. Since we create both of these states only by our power of imagination, they are both merely imaginary states that do not exist in reality.

Though from our point of view in this present waking state we may be able to point out certain differences between our experience in waking and our experience in dreams, these differences are only superficial differences in the quality of each of these states, and not differences in their essential substance. Because our attachment to our body in this waking state is normally stronger than our attachment to our body in a dream, this waking state appears to us (at least now while we are experiencing it) to be more solid, fixed, consistent and lasting than an ordinary dream. However, merely because from our present point of view in this waking state there appear to be such differences between the quality of our experience in this state and the quality of our experience in dream, we cannot conclude that this waking state is actually any more real than a dream.

Both waking and dream are states that we experience only within our own mind. All that we experience or know in either of these two states is only a series of thoughts that we have formed within our mind by our power of imagination. In both these states we imagine a body, which we mistake to be ourself, and further imagine that through the five senses of that body we perceive an external world, which we mistake to be real. However, these bodies that we mistake to be 'I' and these worlds that we mistake to be real are all merely images that we form and experience within our own mind.

So long as we mistake ourself to be this mind – this consciousness that has limited itself by mistaking an imaginary body to be itself – we cannot know anything outside the limits of this mind. In both our waking and our dream states, we live our whole life only within our mind.

Since all that we know – other than our fundamental consciousness 'I am' – is known by us only within our mind, we have no valid reason to believe that any world or anything else other than 'I am' actually exists outside the confines of our mind. We consequently have no valid reason to believe that our present waking state is anything but another dream created entirely by our own self-deceiving power of imagination.

Under what circumstances, or in what condition, can a dream be experienced? A dream can occur only when there is an underlying sleep. When we are wide awake to the world around us, and to ourself as a particular body in that world, we cannot mistake another body to be 'I' or another world to be real. Only after we have fallen asleep, forgetting our normal waking self (this imaginary body that we now mistake to be ourself) and the fact that we are supposedly lying in our bed, can we mistake ourself to be some other imaginary body that is undergoing various experiences in some other imaginary world.

Therefore if our present waking state is only another dream, as we have good reason to suppose it is, there must be some sleep underlying it. What is that sleep that underlies this waking state – the sleep without which this waking state could not occur?

The difference between waking and sleep is that in waking we imagine ourself to be a particular body, whereas in sleep we forget this imaginary body-bound self of the waking state. Sleep is thus essentially a state of self-forgetfulness.

In our ordinary everyday sleep we forget our normal waking self, and because we have forgotten this waking self – this particular body that we now imagine to be ourself – we are able to imagine ourself to be some other body in dream. Though our waking self is supposedly lying asleep on a bed unaware of the world around it, we forget about this waking self and instead create another imaginary self for ourself in the dream state, identifying another body as 'I' and seeing another world around us. Therefore, just as the sleep that underlies an ordinary dream is a state of forgetfulness of our waking self, so the sleep that underlies this dream that we call our present 'waking state' must be a state of forgetfulness of our real self.

However, what do we actually mean when we define sleep as a state of self-forgetfulness? In what way do we forget ourself in sleep? Even in sleep, we never actually forget *that we are*, but only forget *what we are*. Because in sleep we know that we are, but not what we are, in dream we are able to mistake ourself to be some other body. If we had not forgotten our waking self in sleep, we could not imagine that other body to be ourself in dream.

Similarly, if we had not forgotten the true nature of our real self, which always exists as our adjunct-free consciousness 'I am', we would not be able to imagine ourself to be anything other than that. That is, we would not be able to imagine ourself to be one body in the waking state, to be another body in dream, and to be 'unconscious' in sleep. Thus the fundamental sleep that underlies all our dreams, including the present dream that we now mistake to be our waking state, is our sleep of self-forgetfulness – the sleep in which we have forgotten our real self, the true nature of our essential consciousness 'I am'.

Though in our present waking state we mistake the seeming 'unconsciousness' that we experienced in sleep to be merely an unconsciousness of our body and the world, in sleep we did not actually know or think 'I am unconscious of my body and the world'. Only in waking and dream do we think 'In sleep I was unconscious of my body and the world'. That which thinks thus is our mind, but since our mind was not present in sleep, it cannot accurately tell us what our experience in sleep actually was.

All we can now say about sleep is that, though we knew 'I am' in that state, it nevertheless appears to us now to be a state of seeming darkness, ignorance or lack of clarity. That seeming lack of clarity is the 'unconsciousness' that we appear to have experienced in sleep. But what actually is that seeming lack of clarity? About what is it that we seem to have lacked clarity in sleep?

Since no body or world existed in sleep, to say that we were unconscious of them is misleading. Saying that in sleep we were unconscious of our body and this world is like saying that in our present waking state we are unconscious of the body and world that appeared to exist in a dream. Since any body or world that we experience, whether in waking or in dream, is only an imagination – a collection of thoughts or mental images that appears only in our own mind – saying that we were unconscious of them in sleep is in effect saying that we were unconscious of our thoughts in sleep.

We could say that we are unconscious of our thoughts in sleep only if we actually had any thoughts in that state. When we say that we are unconscious of something, it implies that that thing actually exists, or at least appears to exist. Since in sleep we only experienced our own essential self-conscious being, 'I am', we have no reason to believe that anything other than that actually existed in that state.

Therefore the clarity of knowledge that we seem to have lacked in sleep can only be a clarity concerning what actually existed in that state, namely our own real self-conscious being. In other words, the 'unconsciousness' that we now imagine that we experienced in sleep is only our seeming lack of clear self-knowledge – our seeming lack of clarity concerning the real nature of our essential consciousness 'I am'.

In sleep we know that we are, yet we seem to lack a clear knowledge of what we are. Therefore the seeming darkness of sleep, which in our present waking state we mistake to be merely an 'unconsciousness' of the body and world that we are now experiencing, is actually just our lack of clarity of true self-knowledge – our so-called 'forgetfulness' or 'ignorance' of our own real self. If our real self, which is our essential consciousness 'I am', were not seemingly obscured by the veil of our self-forgetfulness or self-ignorance, sleep would be a state of perfectly clear self-knowledge.

In deep sleep, therefore, the adjunct that we superimpose upon our real self, and that thereby prevents us from clearly knowing its true nature, is only this veil of self-forgetfulness called *āvaraṇa*. Though this veil of self-forgetfulness can never prevent us from knowing 'I am', it makes us experience 'I am' in a distorted form, thereby enabling us in waking and dream to imagine that we are a physical body, and that through the five senses of this body we are seeing a world of multiple objects and people.

Because this veil of self-forgetfulness is the original cause of the illusory appearance of our mind, the compound consciousness that imagines 'I am this body', in *advaita vēdānta* it is described as our 'causal body' or *kāraṇa śarīra*. Just as the self-forgetfulness that we experience in sleep is our 'causal body', so our mind which arises out of this 'causal body' is our 'subtle body' or *sūkṣma śarīra* (as explained by Sri Ramana in the fourth paragraph of *Nāṉ Yār?* and in verse 24 of *Uḷḷadu Nāṟpadu*, both of which we cited in chapter three), and the physical body that our mind creates for itself by its power of imagination in waking and in dream is our 'gross body' or *sthūla śarīra*. That is to say, our physical body is a gross form of our mind, which in turn is a more subtle but nevertheless gross form of our self-forgetfulness.

Whenever our mind rises, whether in waking or in dream, it does so by imagining itself to be a physical body. But when it subsides in sleep, all its imaginations cease, and hence it merges back into its causal form, which is our veil of seeming self-forgetfulness. Our forgetfulness of our real self is thus the primeval sleep that underlies the appearance of both our waking and our dream states.

Is this primeval sleep of self-forgetfulness, which thus causes the appearance of both waking and dream, a state distinct from the ordinary deep sleep that we experience every day, or are they both the same state?

Though we can experience a dream within a dream (as we sometimes do when we think we have woken up from a dream, but later wake up again and find that our first 'waking' was only from one dream into another dream), we cannot experience a sleep within a sleep. Since dream is a state of duality and diversity, we can experience any number of dreams. But since sleep is a state devoid of differences or duality, there can only be one state of sleep.

That one and only state of sleep is our fundamental sleep of self-forgetfulness – the sleep that has come about due to our seeming lack of clear self-knowledge. This sleep of self-forgetfulness is the underlying cause for the rising of all other states – the original cause for the appearance of all duality. All our countless states of dream – including our present dream which, while we experience it, we imagine to be a waking state – arise only from this underlying sleep of self-forgetfulness. Therefore, the state of deep sleep that we experience every day is nothing other than this original sleep of self-forgetfulness that underlies the rising of both waking and dream.

Though waking and dream are both temporary states that occur in our long sleep of self-forgetfulness, we wrongly perceive sleep as being a short gap that occurs each day in our waking life. In truth, however, our present waking life is merely one of the many dreams that occur in our long sleep of self-forgetfulness.

Even now we are experiencing that sleep of self-forgetfulness, but within this sleep we are also experiencing a dream that we call our present waking life. The state of deep sleep that we experience every day is merely the state in which all our dreams have subsided, leaving only their underlying and causal state, our sleep of self-forgetfulness.

How do we forget our real self? In truth we always know our real self, and have never forgotten it. We only appear to have forgotten it. We can never really forget it, because we are the essential consciousness 'I am', and the very nature of this consciousness 'I am' is to be conscious of itself.

However, though our real consciousness 'I am' can never forget itself, we nevertheless somehow appear to mistake ourself to be our mind, which is a spurious and unreal consciousness that does not know its own real nature, and that thereby imagines 'I am this body'. Therefore to account for the appearance of this mind, we have to posit a seeming forgetfulness of our real self. However, this self-forgetfulness of ours exists only in the view of our mind, and not in the view of our original consciousness 'I am'. Our self-forgetfulness, therefore, is not real, but is merely an imagination – an illusory appearance that exists only in the view of our unreal mind.

Our self-forgetfulness, as we have seen, is the primal form of *māyā* or self-delusion, and *māyā* is *ya mā*, 'that which is not'. Our self-forgetfulness or lack of clear self-knowledge, therefore, is something that does not really exist.

Whereas our self-forgetfulness, which is our power of self-obscuration called *āvaraṇa*, is the primary form of *māyā*, our mind, which is our power of imagination or self-diffusion called *vikṣēpa*, is the secondary form of *māyā*. All forms of *māyā*, including not only its two basic forms of self-forgetfulness and self-diffusion, but also all the duality or multiplicity that arises from these two basic forms, are known only by our mind, and not by our original consciousness 'I am', whose nature is to know only its own being. Being known only by our mind, therefore, our self-forgetfulness and all that arises from it is only an imagination.

That is, though our power of imagination arises only from our self-forgetfulness, our self-forgetfulness is nevertheless a mere imagination. Our self-forgetfulness is in fact the primal form or seed of our power of imagination or mind, and as such it is itself that which appears to us as our mind. Our mind or power of imagination is therefore merely a gross form of our extremely subtle self-forgetfulness.

Such is the inexplicable and illusory nature of *māyā* that though our self-forgetfulness is the original cause that created the spurious and unreal consciousness we call our mind, it nevertheless does not exist except in the view of this unreal consciousness that it has created.

How then does this illusory self-forgetfulness arise? How do we appear to have forgotten our real self? Since we are in reality only our fundamental self-consciousness 'I am', which can never forget its own true nature, how can we even seemingly forget ourself?

Since we are in truth the unlimited consciousness 'I am', which alone is real, we alone truly exist. Since nothing exists other than ourself, there is nothing that can limit our freedom or our power in any way. Being the one and only absolute reality, therefore, we are perfectly free, and hence all powerful. Or to be more precise, we ourself are perfect freedom and absolute power, because freedom and power cannot be other than the only existing non-dual reality, which is our real self.

Therefore, other than ourself, there is no power that could make us forget our real self, or even seemingly forget it. Hence it must be only by our own freedom of choice that we have seemingly forgotten our real self.

Because we ourself are perfect freedom, we are free to be whatever we choose to be, and to do whatever we choose to do. We are free either to be our real self – that is, to remain just as we ever really are, as mere being, which is our own infinite non-dual self-consciousness 'I am' – or to imagine ourself to be a finite body-bound consciousness that experiences an imaginary world of duality.

In order to imagine ourself to be a limited body-bound consciousness, we must first choose to overlook or ignore our real nature as the unlimited adjunct-free consciousness 'I am', or at least to imagine that we have overlooked it. This imaginary overlooking or ignoring of our real self is what we call 'self-forgetfulness', and it occurs only by our own choice – by our own misuse of our unlimited freedom and power.

Though it is only by our own unlimited freedom and power that we thus imagine that we have forgotten our real self, once we have imagined thus, we have thereby seemingly become a limited body-bound consciousness, and hence we no longer experience our unlimited freedom and power, but instead feel ourself to be a finite creature possessing only very limited freedom and power. Because of our imaginary and self-imposed limitations, it is no longer possible for us to be whatever we choose to be, and to do whatever we choose to do. Our freedom of choice, therefore, is now limited.

However, even now we have the freedom either to attend to the thoughts or objects that we have created by our power of imagination, or to attend to our own essential consciousness in order to discover our real nature – who or what we really are. Only by such self-scrutiny can we remove the veil of self-forgetfulness with which we have seemingly concealed our true nature.

When we, as the absolute reality, seemingly choose to misuse our unlimited freedom and power to forget our real self and thereby to imagine ourself to be a finite individual, our power assumes the unreal form of *māyā*. But when instead we choose to use our unlimited freedom and power correctly to be merely as we really are, our power remains in its natural and real form, which in the language of mysticism or religion is called the power of 'grace'. Grace and *māyā* are thus one and the same power – the only power that really exists.

When we misuse our power to delude ourself, we call it *māyā*, and when we use it correctly to remain as we are, we call it grace. *Māyā* is the power of delusion or self-deception, while grace is the power of 'enlightenment' or clear self-knowledge.

Therefore, if we want to free ourself from *māyā*, we must turn our attention away from all other things towards our own essential consciousness 'I am' in order to know what we really are. When we do so, our own natural power of grace – which is the clarity of our essential self-consciousness, which ever shines peacefully in the core of our being as our own real self, 'I am' – will draw our attention towards itself by its overwhelming power of attraction, and will thereby dissolve the delusion of our self-forgetfulness within itself, which is the perfect clarity of true self-knowledge.

As we have seen, our self-obscuring and self-deceiving veil of self-forgetfulness is the sleep that underlies all the dreams that we ever experience, including our present dream, which we mistake to be a state of waking. This sleep of self-forgetfulness is what enables us to imagine that we are a limited person, who feels a particular body to be 'I', and who perceives a world of multiple objects through the five senses of that body.

The primal form of *māyā* that first enables us to forget ourself is our power of self-obscuration called *āvaraṇa śakti*, while the secondary form of *māyā* that then enables us to imagine a multitude of thoughts and objects that are seemingly other than ourself is our power of self-dissipation called *vikṣēpa śakti*. In waking and dream we experience the effects of both of these two forms of *māyā*, but in sleep we only experience the effect of the primal form of *māyā*, the power of self-forgetfulness called *āvaraṇa śakti*.

Therefore in order to free ourself from the power of *māyā* and thereby know our real self, we must not only set aside the false knowledge of multiplicity created by its *vikṣēpa śakti*, but must also pierce through the veil of self-forgetfulness cast by its *āvaraṇa śakti*. That is why in verse 16 of *Upadēśa Undiyār*, which we have discussed earlier, Sri Ramana does not merely say, '[Our] mind giving up [knowing] external objects is true knowledge', but instead says, '[Our] mind knowing its own form of light, having given up [knowing] external objects, alone is true knowledge'.

Without giving up attending to external objects, we cannot turn our attention inwards to focus it wholly and exclusively upon our 'form of light', which is our true self-consciousness 'I am'. But by merely giving up attending to external objects, we do not automatically focus our attention on our true consciousness 'I am'. Therefore Sri Ramana places 'having given up [knowing] external objects' as a subordinate clause, and places our 'mind knowing its own form of light' as the subject of the sentence.

True knowledge is not merely a state in which we have given up knowing any external objects, but is the state in which we clearly know our own true self. In sleep we give up knowing external objects, but we do not thereby attain true knowledge. In order to attain true knowledge, it is not sufficient for us merely to remove all our other forms of false knowledge – that is, our knowledge of multiplicity, duality or otherness – because mere removal of such false knowledge will not destroy its root and foundation, which is our forgetfulness of our own real self.

Removing our other forms of false knowledge without putting an end to our self-forgetfulness, which is our primal form of false knowledge, will result only in a temporary subsidence or abeyance of our mind. From such a state of abeyance, our mind will rise again, and when it rises, all our false knowledge of duality will rise again with it.

Our mind can rise and be active only by experiencing the false knowledge of otherness – that is, only by knowing duality – because as a separate individual consciousness its very nature is to know things that appear to be other than itself. However, even without knowing any duality, it can still continue seemingly to exist in a dormant seed-form, as it does every day in deep sleep. The seed-form in which it seemingly remains in sleep and other such states of abeyance is its 'causal body', which is its basic self-forgetfulness or lack of clarity of self-knowledge.

Therefore, to attain true knowledge, it is necessary for us not merely to make our mind subside temporarily in a state of abeyance, but instead to destroy it forever by putting an end to its original cause and supporting base, which is our forgetfulness or ignorance of our real self.

When we finally put an end to our self-forgetfulness by knowing our real self as it is, we will discover that our mind was merely an apparition or illusory superimposition that never really existed, just like the illusory snake that our imagination superimposed upon a rope. The state in which we thus discover that our mind is truly ever non-existent is described in *advaita vēdānta* as the state of 'mind-annihilation' or *manōnāśa*, and is the state that in both Buddhism and *advaita vēdānta* is called *nirvāṇa*, a word that means 'extinction', 'extinguished' or 'blown out'.

Being an illusory apparition, our mind can only be destroyed or annihilated by our recognising that it truly does not exist, which we can do only by knowing our real self. Just as we can 'kill' the illusory snake that we imagine we see lying on the ground only by recognising that it is merely a rope and not a snake, so we can 'kill' the illusory mind that we now imagine ourself to be only by recognising that it is merely our real self – our own unlimited adjunct-free consciousness 'I am'.

That is, when we know what we really are, we will discover that we were never the mind that we imagined ourself to be, and that that mind was merely a product of our power of imagination – an insubstantial shadow that appeared in the darkness of our ignorance or forgetfulness of our own real self.

Every day in deep sleep we remove all our false knowledge of duality, but because sleep is only a state of temporary abeyance of our mind, such false knowledge arises again as soon as our mind rises from sleep. However, instead of making our mind subside temporarily in a state of mere abeyance, such as sleep, if we destroy it by putting an end to our self-forgetfulness, it will never rise again, and hence all our false knowledge will be destroyed forever.

As Sri Ramana says in verse 13 of *Upadēśa Undiyār*:

> Subsidence [of our mind] is of two kinds, *laya* [abeyance] and *nāśa* [annihilation]. That [mind] which is in abeyance will rise. [But] if [its] form dies, it will not rise.

By certain forms of meditation or *yōgic* practices such as breath-control, it is possible for us to remove all our false knowledge of duality artificially and thereby to make our mind subside temporarily in a state of abeyance, sometimes even for a very prolonged period of time. But the only means by which we can destroy our mind is by knowing our real self, and we can know our real self only by scrutinising our essential consciousness 'I am'.

Therefore in verse 14 of *Upadēśa Undiyār* Sri Ramana says:

> When [we] send [our] mind, which subsides [only temporarily] when [we] restrain [our] breath, on the one path of knowing [our real self], its form will die.

The words that Sri Ramana uses in this verse to mean 'the one path of knowing' are *ōr vaṙi*, which can be taken to mean either *oru vaṙi*, the 'one path', the 'unique path' or the 'special path', or *ōrum vaṙi*, the 'path of knowing', the 'path of investigating', the 'path of examining' or the 'path of considering attentively'. Because examining and knowing our real self, our essential consciousness 'I am', is the unique and only means by which we can put an end to our self-forgetfulness, which is the cause and foundation for the illusory appearance of our mind and all its false knowledge, Sri Ramana deliberately chose to use these words *ōr vaṙi* here, knowing that they would thus give this double meaning.

When our mind subsides temporarily in sleep, or in any other similar state of abeyance brought about by some artificial means, why do we not thereby attain true knowledge? Since all our false knowledge of otherness is removed in sleep, what prevents us from knowing the real nature of ourself in that state? The only answer we can give is to say that our self-forgetfulness persists in sleep, and it does so because we have not put an end to it by knowing our real self as it is.

However, if we do not know anything other than 'I am' in sleep, why do we not know it as it is? What exactly do we know in deep sleep? Now in the waking state, when we mistake ourself to be our mind, we cannot say exactly what we experienced in deep sleep, because we as our mind did not exist at that time. That is, our waking mind cannot accurately tell what we experienced in deep sleep because it did not exist in that state.

We, however, did exist in sleep, and we knew that we existed at that time, because we now clearly know that we did sleep and that we did not know anything other than ourself at that time. We have a definite memory of having slept, even though we are unable to remember exactly what we experienced in deep sleep.

Since we wake up from sleep and again mistake ourself to be this body, we obviously did not experience a clear knowledge of our true self in that state. But though it is clear to us (at least from our present perspective as a waking mind) that sleep is not a state of perfect knowledge, we still do not know exactly what we experienced in sleep that prevented us from clearly knowing our true self. From the viewpoint of our present waking mind, we can vaguely recognise that we did experience our consciousness 'I am' in sleep, but we cannot say exactly in what form we experienced it.

To our present waking mind sleep appears to be a state in which we were enveloped by a confused cloud of seeming ignorance or lack of clarity of self-consciousness, just as in waking we are now enveloped by our confused identification of ourself with this particular body, and in dream we were enveloped by our confused identification of ourself with some other body. But though we do not know exactly what we experienced in deep sleep, other than the fact that we did experience 'I am', can we at least find a reason for our lack of clarity of self-consciousness in that state? That reason must be the same fundamental reason why we also lack clarity of self-consciousness in this present waking state, and in the state of dream.

Whatever may be the fundamental reason why we do not clearly know ourself in sleep, since that same fundamental reason is the underlying cause of our lack of clear self-knowledge not only in sleep but also in waking and in dream, all we need do is to find and do away with that cause now in our present waking state. If we can clearly know our real self now, that will destroy the inexplicable self-forgetfulness that underlies not only waking but also dream and deep sleep.

In our present waking state we do not know what we really are because we spend all our time attending only to things other than ourself, and never turn our attention to focus it wholly and exclusively upon our fundamental consciousness 'I am'. As a result of our thus not attending exclusively to our consciousness 'I am', we confuse ourself by imagining ourself to be something else.

Because we thus confuse ourself by mistaking ourself to be our body and mind in the waking state, and because our body and mind are absent in sleep, we continue to confuse ourself in that state by mistaking ourself to be in some way unaware of our real nature. However, since our mind is absent in sleep, we cannot in that state make any effort to focus our attention keenly upon our essential self-consciousness 'I am'. We can make such an effort only now in this waking state, or in dream.

In a dream, however, if we try to turn our attention towards our essential consciousness 'I am', we usually find that we awaken immediately from that dream into our present waking state. Because our attachment to the body that we mistake to be ourself in dream is not as strong as our attachment to this body that we now mistake to be ourself in this waking state, our attachment to that dream body is easily dissolved by our making even a little effort to attend to ourself.

However, if our self-attention in dream thus results only in our remembering our waking self, it is clearly not a very keen or deep self-attention. Since our illusory imagination that we are a body in dream is so easily dissolved by even a superficial self-attention, it is difficult for us to attend to ourself deeply and keenly in dream. Therefore it is only in the present waking state that we can seriously make an effort to attend to ourself deeply – that is, to attend wholly and exclusively to our essential self-consciousness 'I am'.

In a dream, if we cease to know any objects, but do so without actually knowing our waking self, we will slip either into deep sleep or into another dream. Similarly in this waking state, which is also a dream, if instead of trying to know our real self we merely try to give up knowing any of the objects or thoughts that we are experiencing, we will slip either into deep sleep or into another state of dream.

Therefore, in order to go beyond these three ordinary states of waking, dream and deep sleep, we must not only cease knowing other things, but must also remove our veil of self-forgetfulness by remembering our true self. That is, in order to awaken to our true self, we must turn our attention selfward to scrutinise and clearly know the true nature of ourself, our mere consciousness of being, 'I am'.

Though we know our essential consciousness 'I am' in all our three normal states of waking, dream and deep sleep, we know it in a different form in each of these states. In waking we know it in the form of this body, in dream we know it in the form of some other body, and in deep sleep we know it in the form of a seeming unconsciousness.

Since the form in which we know our consciousness 'I am' in each one of these states does not exist in the other two states, each of these forms is merely an illusory adjunct that we superimpose upon it. Therefore none of the forms in which we know it in any of these three states can be its true form.

If we clearly knew our consciousness 'I am' in its true form in any one of these three states, we could not mistake it to be anything other than that in the other two states. Therefore, since we experience ourself in a different form in each of these three states, and since we pass through each of these states repeatedly one after another, it is clear that we do not know the true form of our essential consciousness 'I am' in any of them.

However, since we are this consciousness 'I am', and since the very nature of this consciousness 'I am' is to be conscious of itself, it must be possible for us to know this 'I am' in its true form. In fact, at the very deepest level of our being, which is our absolutely pure and non-dual self-consciousness 'I am', we must even now know it clearly in its true form. Therefore, beyond our ordinary three states, which are all states of wrong knowledge, there must exist a state of true knowledge in which we always clearly know the real nature of our essential consciousness 'I am'.

Though this state of true knowledge – the state in which we are fully awake to the absolute reality of our own self – transcends all our ordinary three states, it nevertheless underlies them at all times, including this present moment. Therefore, in order to experience this fundamental state of true knowledge, all we need to do is to scrutinise and know our essential consciousness 'I am' at this precise moment.

Since this state of true knowledge transcends our ordinary three states, it must be devoid of all the false knowledge – all the imaginary knowledge of differences or duality – that we only experience in two of them. Therefore, since it is a state in which we experience no duality, it is a thought-free state like sleep, but since it is at the same time a state in which we experience absolute clarity of self-knowledge, it is also a state of perfect wakefulness. Hence in *advaita vēdānta* this fundamental state of true self-knowledge is sometimes described as the state of 'wakeful sleep' or 'waking sleep' – *jāgrat-suṣupti* in Sanskrit, or *naṉavu-tuyil* in Tamil.

Since this state of 'wakeful sleep' is beyond our three ordinary states of waking, dream and deep sleep, in *advaita vēdānta* it is also sometimes referred to as the 'fourth state', *turīya* or *turya avasthā*. Somewhat confusingly, however, in some texts another term is used to describe it, namely the 'fourth-transcending' or *turīyātīta*, which has given rise to the wrong notion that beyond this 'fourth state' there is some further 'fifth state'. In truth, however, the non-dual state of true self-knowledge is the ultimate and absolute state, beyond which no other state can exist.

Since it is the absolute state that underlies yet transcends all relative states, true self-knowledge is in fact the only state that really exists. Therefore in verse 32 of *Uḷḷadu Nāṟpadu Anubandham* Sri Ramana says:

> For those who experience waking, dream and sleep, [the real state of]

> 'wakeful sleep', [which is] beyond [these three ordinary states], is named *turiya* [the 'fourth']. [However] since that *turiya* alone exists, [and] since the three [states] that appear [and disappear] are [in reality] non-existent, [the one real state that is thus named *turiya* is in fact] *turiya-v-atīta* [that which transcends even the relative concept that it is the 'fourth']. Be clear [about this truth].

Our fundamental and natural state of 'wakeful sleep' or true non-dual self-knowledge is described as the 'fourth' only to impress upon us that it is a state that is beyond our three ordinary states of waking, dream and sleep. However, when we actually go beyond our three ordinary states by experiencing our fundamental state of true self-knowledge, we will discover that this fundamental state is the only real state, and that our three ordinary states are merely imaginary appearances, which are seemingly superimposed upon it, but which in reality do not exist at all. Therefore, though it is sometimes called the 'fourth state', the state of true self-knowledge or 'wakeful sleep' is in fact the only state that truly exists.

Hence, since the term *turīya* or the 'fourth' implies the existence of three other states, it is actually not an appropriate name for the only state that truly exists. Therefore, though the true state of 'wakeful sleep' is named *turīya*, it could more appropriately be named *atīta*, 'that which transcends'.

In other words, since it is the one absolute reality and is therefore completely devoid of all relativity, it transcends not only the three relative states of waking, dream and sleep but also the equally relative concept that it is the 'fourth' state. This is the reason why it is also described as *turīyātīta*, a term that literally means 'that which transcends the fourth'.

The above verse was composed by Sri Ramana as a summary of the following teachings that he had given orally and that Sri Muruganar had recorded in verses 937 to 939 of *Guru Vācaka Kōvai*:

> When all the states [waking, dream and sleep], which are seen as three, disappear in sages, who have destroyed ego [the self-conceited sense of being a separate individual], *turīya* [the 'fourth'], which is the exalted state, is that which predominates in them excessively as *atīta* [that which transcends all duality and diversity].

> Since the states [waking, dream and sleep] that huddle together [enveloping us] as the three components [of our life as an individual consciousness] are mere apparitions [that appear and disappear] in the non-dual *atīta* [the one all-transcending state], [which is] the state of [our real] self, [which is known as] *turīya* [the 'fourth'], [and] which is pure being-consciousness ['I am'], know that for those [three illusory states] [our real] self is the *adhiṣṭhāna* [the single base upon which they appear and disappear, and] in which they [must eventually merge and] become one.

> If the other three [states] were fit [to be described] as real, [only then would it be appropriate for us to say that] 'wakeful sleep', [which is the state of] pure *jñāna* [knowledge], is the 'fourth', would it not? Since in front of *turīya* [the so-called 'fourth'] those other [three states] huddle together [that is, they merge together and become one], being [revealed to be] unreal [as three separate states], know that that [so-called 'fourth' state] is [in fact] *atīta* [the transcendent state], which is [the only] one [real state].

Whereas the reality of our fundamental state of true self-knowledge is absolute, the seeming reality of our three ordinary states is merely relative – relative only to our mind, which alone knows them. However, when we experience the absolute state of true non-dual self-knowledge, we will discover that our mind was a mere apparition that never truly existed. Therefore when the phantom appearance of our mind is thus dissolved, all our three relative states of waking, dream and deep sleep, which are mere figments of our imagination, will dissolve along with it. After this dissolution of our mind, all that will remain is our natural state of 'wakeful sleep', the peaceful and non-dual state of absolute true knowledge.

All forms of duality or relativity are experienced by us only in the waking and dream states, and not in their underlying state, the state of deep sleep, from which they both arise. Since duality and relativity are known only by our mind, and since all things known by our mind are only thoughts that it forms within itself by its power of imagination, all forms of duality or relativity are mere imaginations, thoughts that we have ourself created.

Since our mind, which thus creates all duality and relativity, is itself a false form of knowledge – a spurious form of consciousness that arises only when we imagine ourself to be a body, which is itself just one of our imaginations – all forms of duality or relativity cannot be anything other than false or wrong knowledge.

Thus, since our mind is just a phantom that arises from the state of deep sleep, which is our sleep of self-forgetfulness, all the imaginary knowledge of duality or relativity that our mind experiences in waking and in dream arises likewise only from our sleep of self-forgetfulness. Therefore, since the non-dual state of true self-knowledge transcends not only the states of waking and dream but also their underlying state of deep sleep, it is the supreme and absolute state that transcends not only all forms of wrong knowledge, but also the fundamental self-forgetfulness which is the original cause of all wrong knowledge.

Since this absolute state of true knowledge is our natural state of being, it always exists within us as our own real self or essential consciousness, and hence we can experience it only by knowing ourself as we really are. Since we cannot know our real self unless we attend to it, the only means by which we can attain direct experience of true and absolute knowledge is to scrutinise keenly our innermost being or essence.

Though this true knowledge, which is our real self or essential being, is the reality underlying all the three states that we are now accustomed to experiencing, we cannot make the necessary effort to attend to it while we are in sleep. And though we are able to make this effort in dream, whenever we attempt to do so our dream is usually dissolved instantly, because as we discussed earlier most of our dreams are fragile states based upon a feeble sense of attachment to our dream body and to the world that we experience through that body.

Hence in practice it is generally possible for us to succeed in our effort to know our real self only now in this waking state. Therefore in verse 16 of *Upadēśa Taṉippākkaḷ* Sri Ramana says:

> In waking the state of sleep [the true state of 'wakeful sleep' or clear self-knowledge] will [naturally] result by [your] subtle investigation [or minute examination], which is [the practice of] constantly scrutinising yourself. Until [such] sleep shines suffusing [and absorbing your entire attention both] in waking [and] in dream, incessantly perform [or practise] that subtle investigation.

The reason why Sri Ramana says here that we should continue the practice of subtle self-investigation until the state of 'wakeful sleep' is experienced throughout both waking and dream is that he composed this verse as a summary of verses 957 and 958 of *Guru Vācaka Kōvai*, in which Sri Muruganar had recorded what he once said to a spiritual aspirant who complained that he was unable to experience the perfect clarity of self-consciousness or 'wakeful sleep' in dream:

> Do not be disheartened, losing [your] mental fortitude [by] thinking that [wakeful] sleep does not [yet] suffuse [and absorb your entire attention] in [your] dream [states]. If the firmness of [such] sleep is achieved in the present [state of] waking, the suffusion of [such] sleep [will also be experienced] in dream.
>
> Until the state of [such] sleep [is experienced] in waking, do not abandon [your] subtle investigation, which is [the practice of] scrutinising [your essential] self. Therefore, until [such wakeful] sleep shines suffusing [your entire attention] in dream, performing that subtle scrutinising investigation [is] imperative.

Waking and dream are both states in which we experience the appearance of otherness or multiplicity. The 'wakeful sleep' that we seek to attain is a state devoid of all such otherness, but is nevertheless a state of perfectly clear self-consciousness. Therefore so long as we experience either otherness or a lack of perfectly clear self-consciousness, we are still caught in the illusion of the three states, waking, dream and deep sleep. Hence we should persist in our practice of subtle self-investigation until we experience a perfect clarity of pure self-consciousness devoid of even the slightest trace of otherness, duality or multiplicity.

Whatever knowledge we may obtain about anything other than ourself is indirect and therefore open to doubt. The only knowledge that is direct is the knowledge or consciousness that we have of ourself as 'I am', and hence it alone can be certain and free of all doubt.

Before we know anything else, we first know our own existence as 'I am'. This knowledge or consciousness of ourself is our primary and essential form of knowledge. Without knowing 'I am', we could not know anything else. Our consciousness 'I am' can stand alone without any other knowledge, as we experience daily in deep sleep, but no other knowledge can stand without this consciousness 'I am'.

Whenever this single, undivided and non-dual consciousness 'I am' appears to know other things in addition to itself, it does so by seemingly limiting itself as a separate individual consciousness that identifies itself with a body, one among the many objects that it then seems to know. This individual consciousness which thus feels 'I am this body, a separate person living in this world of manifold objects' is not our primary and essential form of knowledge, but only a secondary form of knowledge, a distorted form of our original and primary knowledge 'I am'.

All objective knowledge is known only by this secondary form of knowledge, the separate individual consciousness that we call our 'mind'. Therefore objective knowledge is not the primary form of knowledge, nor even the secondary form of knowledge, but only a tertiary form of knowledge. This tertiary form of knowledge depends for its seeming existence upon the secondary form of knowledge that we call our 'mind', which in turn depends for its seeming existence upon the primary form of knowledge, our fundamental and essential consciousness 'I am'.

Unlike all other forms of knowledge, this primary form of knowledge, 'I am', does not depend upon any other thing, and hence it is the only knowledge that is absolute and unconditional. All other knowledge is merely relative. Since the secondary form of knowledge, our mind, can appear as a separate entity only by knowing the tertiary form of knowledge, the objective thoughts that it forms within itself, each of these two forms of knowledge exist relative only to the other.

Since it is known only by our mind, and thus depends for its seeming existence upon our mind, objective knowledge has no reality of its own but borrows its seeming reality from our mind. Objective knowledge can therefore be no more real than our mind that knows it. Is this mind, the individual consciousness that feels 'I am this body, a separate person who knows a world full of objects', real? No, it is not, because it is, as we have seen above, merely an imaginary and distorted form of our true and original consciousness 'I am'.

Though both our mind and all the objective knowledge known by it appear to be real, the reality of each is relative only to the other. Whatever is real only relatively is not really real at all, because in order to be truly real, a thing must be absolutely and unconditionally real. Only that which is absolutely and unconditionally real is real at all times, in all states and under all conditions, whereas that which is relatively real appears to be real only at certain times, in certain states and under certain conditions. Whatever thus appears to be real only at certain times, in certain states and under certain conditions, is merely an appearance, and hence it is only seemingly real.

Therefore, the only knowledge that can surely be considered as real or true knowledge is our direct, unconfused, clear and certain knowledge of our own essential consciousness 'I am'. Until and unless we attain such clear and certain knowledge, any other knowledge that we may attain will be uncertain and open to doubt.

Only when we attain true knowledge of our consciousness 'I am' will we be in a position to judge the truth and validity of all our other knowledge. Thus the belief that objective research can lead to true knowledge – a belief that is implicit in and central to the philosophy upon which all modern science is based – is philosophically unsound, and is based more upon wishful thinking than upon any deep or honest philosophical analysis.

All objective knowledge is known by us indirectly through the imperfect media of our mind and five senses, whereas consciousness is known by us directly as our own self. Therefore, if we seek true, clear and immediate knowledge, rather than attempting to elaborate our knowledge of objective phenomena by turning our attention outwards through our mind and five senses, we should attempt to refine our knowledge of consciousness by directing our attention selfwards, towards the essential consciousness that we always experience directly as 'I am'.

Though the philosophy and science of consciousness or true self-knowledge that we discuss in this book may seem to refute or deny the truth of all normal forms of human knowledge, it does not in fact deny the relative truth of any other philosophy, science or religion. It merely places them in a correct perspective. In the grand scheme of things, everything has its relative place, and this philosophy of self-knowledge enables us to understand the relative place of everything in a correct perspective.

The truth is that the 'grand scheme of things' and everything that has a place in it are all known only by our mind, and thus are ultimately only our thoughts. Since we cannot know anything except in our own mind, we have no adequate reason to suppose that anything exists outside of our mind.

Even the idea that things exist independent of our mind, and are therefore more than just our thoughts, is itself merely a thought or imagination. What the philosophy and science of consciousness refutes or calls into question, therefore, is not merely any particular thought, idea or belief that our mind may have about anything, but is ultimately the reality of our mind itself.

All dualistic systems of philosophy, science and religious belief are dealing with the truth – but not with the absolute truth. The truth or truths with which they are dealing are only some relative forms of truth, and because they are relative, the truths of one such system may appear to clash with those of another. However, the conflict between all the countless forms of relative truth can be reconciled when each is seen in its correct perspective, which is possible only from the standpoint of the absolute truth of non-dual self-knowledge – the fundamental consciousness 'I am', which is the impartial substratum and reality on which or in which all things appear and disappear.

Though the objective knowledge that we acquire by means of philosophy and science may appear to be true and valid knowledge from the relative standpoint of our mind, from the absolute standpoint of our real consciousness 'I am' it is not true knowledge. Whatever knowledge the human mind may acquire through philosophy, science, religion or any other means can only be relative knowledge, and not absolute or true knowledge.

Our mind is an instrument that can know only duality, relativity or limitations, and not that which is beyond all duality, relativity and limitations. However, the limit of our knowledge does not stop with our mind. Beyond our mind, or rather behind, beneath and underlying our mind, there is a deeper consciousness – our fundamental and essential self-consciousness, 'I am'. This essential self-consciousness or non-dual knowledge of our own mere being is itself the absolute knowledge – knowledge which is absolutely, unconditionally, independently and infinitely true, pure, clear and certain.

In this book we have been examining in detail the philosophy of self-knowledge, and showing how it calls upon us to question all our most basic assumptions about ourself and the world, and how it offers us a rational view of reality that is fresh and entirely different to the one that most of us are familiar with. However, this philosophy will be of little use to us if we do not understand that it is not only a philosophy but also a science – a science that requires of us a steadfast commitment to practical research.

As a philosophy it is insufficient in itself, and will remain merely a body of thoughts, ideas or beliefs like any other philosophy, unless and until we make it a direct experience by practising its empirical method of self-investigation. Any benefit that we may gain by studying and reflecting upon this philosophy will be of little real value to us unless we also attempt to put it into practice by repeatedly turning our attention back to our mere consciousness of being whenever we notice that it has slipped away to think of other things.

The true knowledge that we all seek to attain is not a body of thoughts, ideas or theories, or anything else that could be grasped by our mind, but is the state of conscious non-dual experience of being, in which the absolute reality, our own essential consciousness 'I am', knows only itself. Therefore, unless and until we actually turn our attention away from all thoughts and objects towards our own fundamental consciousness 'I am', we can never attain direct, certain and true knowledge of the absolute reality that underlies and contains – but nevertheless transcends – all relativity.

CHAPTER 7

The Illusion of Time and Space

Though in chapter three, while discussing the formation and dissolution of each of our consecutive thoughts, we said that each individual thought rises and subsides in an infinitely small period of time, this is not the entire truth, because time is itself an illusion created by the rising and subsiding of our thoughts.

Just as we imagine the physical dimension of space in order to create in our mind a conceptual image of a universe consisting of separate objects of diverse forms, so we imagine the physical and psychological dimension of time in order not only to create in our mind a conceptual image of events and changes constantly occurring within that universe, but also more importantly to create the illusion that the thoughts we think and the consequent experiences we undergo are formed and dissolved in a consecutive manner. Without first imagining the basic dimensions of time and space, we cannot form any image or thought in our mind, and hence these dimensions are inherent in each and every thought that we think.

We think that we perceive time and space outside ourself, and that we are just limited creatures who exist for a very short period within the vast duration of time and who occupy a very small part of the vast expanse of space. This perception, however, is just an illusion, because like every other perception, we experience the perception of time and space only within ourself, in our own mind or consciousness.

Though time and space appear to exist outside us, we have no way of knowing that they actually do exist outside of or independent of ourself, because all that we know or can ever know of time and space is only the images of them that we have formed within our own mind by our power of imagination. Therefore, like everything that we perceive within time and space, time and space themselves are merely mental images, conceptions or thoughts.

The conceptual dimensions of time and space are centred respectively around the notions of the present moment, 'now', and the present place, 'here'.

The concepts of past and future exist only with reference to the concept of the present moment, which is the central point in time. What was once present is now past, and what will once be present is now future. Both the past and the future are the present when they occur. But more importantly, the past and the future are both concepts that exist only in the present moment. Therefore, relatively speaking, the present is the only point in time that is real. Though all that passes by it is constantly changing, the present moment itself always remains without undergoing any change, and hence it is the static gateway through which we may pass from the illusion of ever-changing time to the reality of our ever-unchanging being.

As Sri Ramana says in verse 15 of *Uḷḷadu Nāṟpadu*:

> The past and future stand [only by] clinging to the present. While occurring, they too are only the present. The present [is] the only one [point in time that truly exists]. [Therefore] trying to know the past and future without knowing the truth of the present [is like] trying to count without [knowing the fundamental number, the unit] one [of which all other numbers are merely multiples or fractions].

The third sentence of this verse, '*nihaṙvu oṉḏṟē*', which literally means 'present [is] one', with a stress (the terminating letter *ē*) added to the word *oṉḏṟu* or 'one' implying 'only one', can be interpreted in various ways. It can be taken to mean, 'The present is the only one time', 'Only the present truly exists', or 'All these three times are only the one present'. However, in effect all these three interpretations mean the same thing.

Since while occurring each moment in time is the present, all moments in time, whether past, present or future, are only the present moment. The present is therefore the only moment in time that truly exists. Hence the three divisions of time, past, present and future, are truly not three, but only one – the one ever-present present moment.

In the *kaliveṇbā* version of *Uḷḷadu Nāṟpadu* Sri Ramana added two extra words before the initial word of this verse, *nihaṙviṉai* or 'the present', namely *nitamum maṉṉum*, which mean 'which always endures'. Thus he further emphasised the fact that the present moment is ever present, that all times are the present while they occur, and that the present is therefore the only time that actually exists – the only time that we ever experience directly and actually. All other times, both past and future, are just thoughts that occur in this present moment.

If we wish to estimate the value of something in a particular currency, we must first know the value of a single unit of that currency. Without knowing the value of the unit 'one', we cannot know the value of any other number. Similarly, we cannot know the truth of the past or the future if we do not know the truth of the present, because the present moment is the one basic unit of time – the sole substance of which all time is formed.

Just as the present moment, 'now', is the central point in the conceptual dimension of time, so the present place, 'here', is the central point in the conceptual dimension of space. Every point in space that we perceive or think of exists only with reference to this present place, the point in space at which we now feel ourself to be.

What determines which point in space and which point in time are experienced as being present? What we experience as the present place, 'here', and the present moment, 'now', is that point in space and time in which we feel ourself to be present. The presence of our consciousness of being, 'I am', is therefore what makes us feel that this place in space is present 'here', and that this point in time is present 'now'.

All definitions of time and place are relative to this fundamental time 'now' and this fundamental place 'here'. The past is the past because it is prior to this present moment, which we call 'now', and the future is the future because it is subsequent to this present moment. Similarly, all definitions of place such as 'near' or 'far', 'there' or 'elsewhere', are relative only to this present place, which we call 'here'. Therefore, since the definition of 'now' and 'here' is that these are the points in time and space in which we always experience ourself to be, all time and space ultimately exists only with reference to our essential, fundamental and ever-present consciousness of our own being, 'I am'.

Because we feel this particular body to be ourself, we feel that the point in space where this body now exists is 'here'. Thus our mind, the limited consciousness that feels 'I am this body', always feels itself to be here and now, in the present place and present moment. Since this limited consciousness 'I am this body', which is the knowing subject or first person, is always experienced as the central point in space, it is not only the 'first person' but also the 'first place'. That is, the first or fundamental place, the central point in space, which we call 'here', is only our own mind, the consciousness that we always feel to be the first person, 'I'. Every other place or point in space exists only with reference to this fundamental place, the ever-present first person.

Because we identify ourself with a particular body, we feel that we move about in space, whereas in fact space moves about in us. That is, because we are not this material body but only consciousness, all space exists only within us, and hence all movement in space occurs only within us. Wherever we appear to go, the present place 'here' goes with us. When we seem to move from one place to another, that other place becomes 'here', that is, it moves into and becomes the central place in our consciousness.

Thus, just as the present moment, 'now', is the static and unchanging moment through which all moments in time pass, so the present place, 'here', is the static and unchanging place through which, near which or far from which all places in space move. Therefore, just as the present moment is the static gateway through which we may pass from the illusion of experiencing ever-changing time to the reality of our ever-unchanging being, so the present place is the static gateway through which we may pass from the illusion of being a body that moves about in space to the reality of our ever-unmoving being.

Just as the first person, our consciousness 'I', is the primary or fundamental place, the central point in the space of our mind, so the second person, 'you', and the third person, the aggregate of 'he', 'she', 'it', 'this', 'that' and everything else that is other than 'I' or 'you', may be considered to be respectively the secondary and tertiary places or areas within our mental space. Therefore, what we call the 'three persons' in English grammar are known as the 'three places' in Tamil grammar. That is, in most languages the subject and all the objects known by it are grouped into three categories, but whereas in English and many other languages these three categories are called the 'three persons', in Tamil they are called the 'three places'.

This spatial conception of these three categories is based upon the fact that we experience each of them as occupying a different 'place' or point either in physical space or in our conceptual space. The first person, which in grammatical terms is the person who speaks or writes as 'I', is always experienced as being *here*, in the present place. The second person, which in grammatical terms is any person or thing that is spoken or written to as 'you', is experienced as being physically or conceptually *nearby*, in a place that is close to the first person. And the third person, which in grammatical terms is any person or thing that is spoken or written about as 'he', 'she', 'it', 'this', 'that', 'these', 'those', 'they' or 'them', is experienced as being physically or conceptually *elsewhere*, in a place that is other than that occupied by the first and second persons.

This spatial conception of these 'three persons', particularly that of the 'first person', is philosophically very significant, and is potentially very helpful to us in our understanding of the practice of self-investigation. In his teachings, therefore, Sri Ramana frequently used the Tamil equivalents of the English terms 'first person', 'second person' and 'third person'.

Since he used these terms in place of the usual philosophical terms 'subject' and 'object', he in effect divided all the objects known by us into two distinct groups. That is, he used the Tamil equivalent of the term 'second person' to denote all those mental objects or images that we recognise as being thoughts that exist only within our own mind, and the Tamil equivalent of the term 'third person' to denote all those mental objects or images that we imagine we are perceiving outside ourself through one or more of our five senses.

Whereas the 'second person' objects are those objects or thoughts that we recognise as existing only within the space of our own mind, the 'third person' objects are those objects or thoughts that we imagine we are perceiving in physical space, outside our mind. Thus the second person objects are those objects that we recognise as existing only within the field of our mental conception, while the third person objects are those objects that we imagine to exist outside the field of our mental conception, in the seemingly separate field of our sense perception.

This definition of the terms 'second person' and 'third person' differs from the normal definition of them, because Sri Ramana did not use them in their usual grammatical sense, but in a more abstract philosophical sense. The philosophical meaning that he gave to these terms does not correspond exactly to their usual grammatical meaning because, whereas the former is concerned with knowledge or experience, the latter is concerned only with language, either spoken or written.

That is, though we usually understand the term 'second person' to mean only 'you', the person, people, thing or things spoken or written to, and the term 'third person' to mean the person, people, thing or things spoken or written about, this definition of these terms is applicable only to the act of communicating through speech or writing. If we extend the use of these terms to apply to the act of knowing, we must form a new definition of them. In reference to the act of knowing, the term 'second person' means whatever we know most directly or immediately, while the term 'third person' means whatever we know more indirectly or mediately.

Compared to the objects that we perceive through the media of our five senses, the thoughts that we recognise as existing only within our own mind are known by us more directly or immediately, and hence they are our 'second person' thoughts or objects. Since the objects that we think we perceive outside ourself are known by us not only through the primary medium of our mind but also through the secondary media of our five senses, they are a comparatively indirect or more mediate form of knowledge, and hence they are our 'third person' thoughts or objects.

Though in Tamil these 'three persons' are collectively called the 'three places' or *mū-v-iḍam*, individually they are not called the 'first place', 'second place' and 'third place', but are called respectively the 'self-ness place', the 'place standing in front' and the 'place that has spread out'. The actual term used in Tamil to denote the first person is *taṉmai-y-iḍam*, or more commonly just *taṉmai*, which etymologically means 'self-ness' or 'selfhood', and which therefore denotes our sense of 'self', the subject or first thought 'I'. The Tamil term for the second person is *muṉṉilai*, which etymologically means 'what stands in front', and which therefore from a philosophical viewpoint denotes our most intimate thoughts, those mental objects or images that figuratively speaking stand immediately in front of our mind's eye, and that we therefore recognise as being thoughts that exist only within our own mind. And the Tamil term for the third person is *paḍarkkai*, which etymologically means 'what spreads out, ramifies, becomes diffused, expands or pervades', and which therefore from a philosophical viewpoint denotes those thoughts that have spread out or expanded through the channel of our five senses, and that have thereby been projected as the objects of this material world, which we seem to perceive through those five senses, and which we therefore imagine to be objects existing outside ourself.

The space of our mind is thus divided into three distinct parts, areas or fields, which we can picture as three concentric circles. The most intimate part of our mind, the innermost of these three circles, which is also their central point, is our first person thought 'I', our limited individual consciousness that feels 'I am this body', 'I am such-and-such a person'. The next most interior or intimate part of our mind, the field or circle that most closely surrounds our first person thought 'I', is all our second person thoughts, the objects that we recognise as existing only within our own mind, and that we therefore consider to be the field of our mental conception. The most exterior part of our mind, the outermost field or circle surrounding our first person thought 'I', is all our third person thoughts, the objects that we imagine we perceive in an external physical space, and that we therefore mistake as existing outside our mind. Thus the entire external universe and the physical space in which we imagine it to be contained is just the outermost part of the space that is our own mind, the part of that space which we consider to be the field of our sense perception.

Though in our imagination we make a distinction between the thoughts that we recognise as existing within ourself and the material objects that we imagine we perceive outside ourself, this distinction is actually false, because both are in fact only thoughts that we form within our own mind by our power of imagination. Whereas we recognise some of our thoughts to be only images that we form in our mind, we wrongly imagine certain of our thoughts to be objects that actually exist outside us, and that are therefore distinct from our thoughts and our thinking mind. In fact, however, even the objects that we think we perceive outside ourself are only our own thoughts – images that we have formed within our own mind.

Nevertheless, though this distinction between our second person thoughts and our third person thoughts is illusory, in our mind it appears to be quite real. So long as we imagine that we are perceiving objects outside ourself, we will continue to imagine that there is a real distinction between those objects and the thoughts that we recognise as existing only within our own mind. Therefore this seeming distinction between our second person objects, the thoughts that we recognise as existing only within our own mind, and our third person objects, the objects that we think we perceive outside ourself, will continue to appear to be real so long as our thinking mind appears to be real.

Because it appears to us to be real, Sri Ramana allows for this seeming distinction between the second person and third person objects, but he does so only to make clear to us that the term 'objects' includes not only all the material objects we think we perceive outside ourself, but also all the thoughts that we recognise as existing only within our own mind. Even our most intimate thoughts or feelings are only objects known by us, and are accordingly distinct from us.

Therefore, when Sri Ramana advises us to withdraw our attention from all the 'second persons' and 'third persons' and to focus it instead on the 'first person', what he wants us to understand is that we should withdraw our attention from all objects – both those that we recognise as being merely our own thoughts or feelings, and those that we mistake to be objects existing outside ourself – and fix it only upon our sense of self, 'I', which we always experience as being here and now, in this precise present point in space and time. In other words, in order to know our real self, we should withdraw our attention from all our thoughts – both our second person thoughts, which we recognise as being thoughts, and our third person thoughts, which we imagine to be material objects existing outside ourself – and should instead focus it wholly and exclusively upon our ever-present self-consciousness, our fundamental consciousness of our own essential being, 'I am'.

Since all objects are only thoughts that we form within our own mind, they depend for their seeming existence upon our mind, the subject or first person, which thinks and knows them. Therefore in verse 14 of *Uḷḷadu Nāṟpadu* Sri Ramana says:

> If the first person exists, the second and third persons will [also seem to] exist. If, by our investigating the truth of the first person, the first person ceases to exist, the second and third persons will [also] come to an end, [and the reality of] the first person, which [always] shines as one [the one non-dual absolute reality, which alone remains after the dissolution of these three false persons], will be [then discovered to be] our [true] state, [our real] self.

In the *kaliveṇbā* version of *Uḷḷadu Nāṟpadu* Sri Ramana added four extra words before the initial word of this verse, *taṉmai* or 'first person', namely *uḍal nāṉ eṉṉum a-t*, which together with *taṉmai* mean 'that first person, which is called "I am [this] body"'. Thus he defined the first person as being our *dēhātma buddhi*, our root thought or primal imagination 'I am this body', which is the distorted and spurious form of consciousness that rises as our mind from our real non-dual self-consciousness, 'I am'.

In the second sentence of this verse, the words that I have translated as 'the truth of the first person' are *taṉmaiyin uṇmaiyai*, in which the word *uṇmai* or 'truth' etymologically means 'be'-ness or 'am'-ness. Hence the 'truth of the first person' is the essential being or 'am'-ness of our mind or individual sense of self, which we experience as 'I am this body'. Whereas our mind is an objectified form of consciousness – a form of consciousness that imagines itself to be an object, this body – its truth or 'am'-ness is its true and essential non-objective self-consciousness, 'I am', which is the sole reality underlying its false appearance.

Our individual 'selfhood' or *tanmai*, which is the adjunct-mixed consciousness that feels 'I am this body', appears to exist only because we have failed to investigate or scrutinise the underlying truth or 'am'-ness of it closely. If we scrutinise this false first person consciousness closely in order to know its underlying truth or reality, we will discover it to be nothing other than our non-dual consciousness of our own being, 'I am', which is our real and essential self, our true state of mere being.

When we thus discover that our real 'selfhood' is merely our non-dual self-consciousness 'I am', we will thereby discover that our false individual 'selfhood', which is our distorted and dualistic consciousness 'I am this body', and which by thus identifying itself with a physical body has limited itself within the bounds of time and space, is a mere apparition that has never truly existed. Just as the illusory snake, which we imagined that we saw lying on the ground, disappears as soon as we see that it is nothing but a rope, so the illusory first person will disappear as soon as we discover that it is nothing but our real non-dual self-conscious being, 'I am'. When this illusory first person, our false individual 'selfhood', thus disappears, all the second and third person objects or thoughts, which were created and known only by this false first person, will disappear along with it.

Thus by scrutinising the present place, 'here', which is the precise point in space in which the false first person 'I' appears to exist, and which is the central point from which it conceives all thoughts and perceives physical space and all the objects contained within that space, we will discover that it is merely an unreal conception, a thought created by our own power of imagination. When we thus discover that this central point from which we seem to perceive the physical space around us is merely an imaginary apparition, an illusion of something that never truly existed, we will discover that what we mistake to be physical space is likewise just an imaginary apparition.

The sole truth or reality underlying not only the present place, 'here', but also all the other places in physical space that we perceive from this central point, is our fundamental and ever-present consciousness of being, 'I am'. In reality, therefore, the present place, 'here', is not a point in physical space, but is only our own self-conscious being. Our ever-present consciousness of being, which is the reality underlying our experience of being always in the present place, 'here', is what Sri Ramana means in the above verse by the words 'the truth of the first person'.

What exactly do we mean when we speak of scrutinising the present place, 'here'? The precise point in space that we feel to be 'here' is that point in which we feel ourself to be – that point at which we seem to experience our consciousness of being, 'I am'. Therefore, in order to scrutinise the precise present place, 'here', we must withdraw our attention from all other places – that is, from all other thoughts and objects – and focus it wholly and exclusively upon our fundamental and essential consciousness of being, 'I am', which alone is always present 'here' and 'now'.

Thus our experience of always being 'here', at this precise present point in space, serves as a valuable clue in our investigation of our consciousness of being, 'I am', just as the scent of his master serves as a valuable clue in a dog's search for him. Similarly, our experience of always being 'now', at this precise present point in time, serves as another equally valuable clue in our investigation of our consciousness of being.

Either of these two clues, if followed correctly and diligently, will unfailingly lead us to experience the absolute reality that underlies yet transcends all time and space, because the reality underlying what we now experience as the relative 'here' and 'now', the 'here' and 'now' that appear to exist in space and time, is the absolute 'here' and 'now', the eternally omnipresent fullness of being, which is our own real self, our fundamental and essential consciousness of our own being, 'I am'. Therefore, we should investigate and know the truth of either the present place, 'here', or the present time, 'now'.

Time is a constant flow from past to future. The present is that precise moment in time when the past ends and the future begins. With the passing of every moment, the present moment becomes part of the past, and a new moment, which was part of the future, becomes the present. If we break time down into its smallest fractions or moments, the duration of each such moment will be infinitesimal. Such infinitesimal moments pass so rapidly that the very instant each one appears it also disappears. A moment that is the immediate future moment at one instant, becomes the immediate past moment the next instant.

However, even to speak of a moment or instant of time is potentially misleading, because time is actually a continuous flow that does not consist of any entirely discrete or clearly definable units called moments. A moment is just a conceptual fraction of time, a fraction whose duration is arbitrary. The most infinitesimal moment is a point in time whose duration is zero, and the precise present moment is such a durationless point, because it is the immeasurably thin borderline or boundary that separates the past from the future. The very instant the past ends, the future begins. Therefore the borderline or interface between the past and the future is an infinitely fine point, a point that has no duration or extent.

All that exists between the past and the future is pure being. In the immeasurably brief instant between the past and the future, time stands still, and all happening ceases. Time requires some extent or duration in which to move, so in the infinitely small instant between the past and the future, time cannot move, and nothing else can happen. Therefore all we can experience in that infinitely small instant, in the precise present moment, is our own self-conscious being, 'I am'.

If we scrutinise the present moment minutely in order to discern exactly which instant in time is present, we will not be able to discover any discernible instant in time that can be called the precise present moment, 'now'. To discern the precise present instant in time, we must set aside both the past and the future. The moment immediately preceding the present moment is past, and the moment immediately following it is future. If we try to set aside even the most immediate, subtle and minute past and future moments, and to discern what exists between them, all we will find is our own unmoving and unchanging being – our ever-present self-consciousness, 'I am'.

Being unmoving and unchanging, our self-conscious being is timeless. Therefore, the precise present moment, the infinitesimal instant between the past and the future, is a timeless moment – a moment that exists beyond the dimension of time.

Thus our experience that the present moment is a point in time is an illusion, just as our experience that the present place is a point in space is an illusion. As we saw above, if we set aside all thoughts of any place other than this precise present place, 'here', and keenly scrutinise only this precise present place in order to discover what the truth or reality of it is, we will discover that it is truly not a point in physical space, but is just our own self-conscious being. Similarly, if we set aside all thoughts of any moment other than this precise present moment, 'now', and keenly scrutinise only this precise present moment in order to discover what the truth or reality of it is, we will discover that it is truly not a point in the passage of time, but is just our own self-conscious being. When we thus discover that there is no such thing as a precise present point in time, and that our experience of the present moment in time is therefore merely an illusion, an imaginary apparition, we will discover that the passage of time, which we always experience only in this illusory present moment, is likewise merely an imaginary apparition.

Since all points in time and all points in space are experienced only in this present point in time and this present point in space, they depend for their seeming existence upon these present points, the ever-present 'now' and 'here', which in reality are nothing but the presence of our ever-present consciousness of our own being, 'I am'. Therefore, our ever-present self-conscious being, 'I am', is the sole substance or reality not only of this present moment, 'now', and this present place, 'here', but also of the entire appearance of time and space.

Thus these two clues, the clue of the precise present place, 'here', and the clue of the precise present moment, 'now', both point to the same reality, our ever-present self-conscious being, 'I am', which is not limited either by time or by space. At certain times we may find it more helpful to follow the clue of 'here', at other times we may find it more helpful to follow the clue of 'now', and at other times we may find it more helpful to follow both of them simultaneously, but whichever of them we choose to follow, our attention should be focused wholly and exclusively upon our fundamental and ever-present consciousness of our own being, 'I am'.

When we investigate our non-dual consciousness of our own being, which we always experience as being 'here' and 'now', we will discover that time and space are both unreal imaginations, and that our non-dual self-conscious being is the only reality, the only thing that truly exists. Therefore in verse 16 of *Uḷḷadu Nāṟpadu* Sri Ramana says:

> When [we] investigate [that is, when we scrutinise ourself], except 'we' [our essential self or fundamental consciousness of being], where is time [and] where is place? If we are [a] body, we shall be ensnared in time and place. [But] are we [a] body? We are one [at each moment in time], now, then and always, one [at each] place [in space], here, there and everywhere. Therefore we, the timeless and placeless 'we', [alone] exist.

The superficial meaning implied by the rhetorical question 'Except "we", where is time and where is place?' is that time and space do not exist besides, apart from, or as other than us. However, its deeper meaning is that we alone exist, and time and space are completely non-existent, a fact that is reiterated in the last sentence of this verse.

In the *kaliveṇbā* version of *Uḷḷadu Nāṟpadu* Sri Ramana added three extra words before the initial word of this verse, *nām* or 'we', namely *uṇara niṉḏṟa poruḷ*, which literally mean 'the reality that stood to know', but which are a poetic way of saying 'the reality that exists knowingly', or more precisely 'the reality that exists and knows [its own existence]'. By placing these words before *nām* he defined exactly what he meant by it in this context. That is, when he asked, 'Except "we", where is time and where is place?', by the term 'we' he did not mean our object-knowing mind but only our real self – our essential and ever-existing self-conscious being, which we always experience as 'I am'.

Time and space are known only by our mind, and hence they depend upon it for their seeming existence. They are not known by our essential consciousness of being, which knows only itself, and hence they are not known by us in sleep, in which we experience only our own self-conscious being. However, though they are not known by our essential self-consciousness, they could not be known independent of it, because it is the sole reality that underlies and supports the appearance of the false object-knowing form of consciousness that we call our mind, in whose imagination alone they exist.

We are able to imagine ourself to be this mind, which experiences itself as a body that exists in time and space, only because we know ourself as 'I am'. However, whereas our mind and the time and space known by it are transitory appearances, we are the reality that always exists and knows its own existence. Since our self-conscious existence or being exists independent of time and space, it is the absolute reality – the only reality that truly exists. Hence Sri Ramana asks, 'Except "we", where is time and where is place?', implying thereby that we alone truly exist, and that time and space are mere appearances – mental images that have no real existence of their own.

Time and space appear to exist only because we imagine ourself to be a finite body. In truth, however, we are not any finite body, because though in our present waking state we imagine ourself to be this body, in dream we imagine ourself to be some other body, and in sleep we do not imagine ourself to be any body at all. When we imagine ourself to be a particular body, as in waking and dream, we experience both time and space, but when we do not imagine ourself to be any body, as in sleep, we do not experience either time or space.

However, whether or not we imagine ourself to be a body, we always remain the same one unchanging consciousness of being, 'I am'. In all times, in all places and in all states of consciousness, we are always in essence only this single, non-dual consciousness of our own being. Therefore Sri Ramana says in this verse, 'We are one [at each moment in time], now, then and always, one [at each] place [in space], here, there and everywhere'.

Since time and space, and everything else other than our essential consciousness of our own being, 'I am', appear and disappear, they are not real, but are merely illusory figments of our imagination. In reality, therefore, we not only transcend time and space, but are in essence absolutely devoid of time and space. We – this timeless and spaceless 'we', who are nothing other than absolute non-dual self-conscious being – alone exist.

In verse 13 of *Upadēśa Taṉippākkaḷ*, which is the original form in which he composed the above verse, Sri Ramana says:

> Except 'we', where is time? If, having not investigated [or scrutinised] ourself, we think that we are [a] body, time will devour us. [But] are we [a] body? We are always one, [in] present, past and future times. Therefore we, the 'we' who has devoured time, [alone] exist.

We imagine that we are a physical body only because we ignore or fail to pay due attention to our true and essential self-conscious being, and since the body that we imagine to be ourself is confined within the limits of time and space, we are thereby in effect swallowed by time. However, if we investigate ourself by keenly attending to our own essential self-conscious being, we will discover that we are not this finite body but are only the one infinite and therefore timeless reality, and thereby we will in effect swallow the illusion of time.

Since we are the one infinite reality, which exists in all times and all places, and since nothing can exist apart from or other than the infinite, we alone truly exist. Therefore the body that we imagine to be ourself, and the time and space in which this body is confined, are all mere apparitions, and in reality do not exist at all. This is the clear meaning of the last line of verse 16 of *Uḷḷadu Nāṟpadu*, which I have translated as, 'we, the timeless and placeless "we", [alone] exist', but which could also be translated as, 'we [alone] exist; time and place do not exist, [but only] we'.

The only way for us to experience this truth that we alone exist, devoid of all time and space, is for us to scrutinise our own consciousness of being, which always exists here and now, in this precise present point in space and time. So long as we continue to attend to or think of anything in time or space other than the precise present moment and the precise present place, we will continue to perpetuate the illusion of time and space – the illusion of ourself being a body, an object confined within the limits of time and space. But if we attend only to either the precise present moment or the precise present place, which are actually one and the same point, we will find in them no time or space, no duration or extent, and therefore no thought of any kind, but only our own absolutely non-dual consciousness of being, 'I am', which underlies yet transcends all time, all space and all forms of thought.

If we wish to locate either the precise present moment in time, the exact 'now', or the precise present place in space, the exact 'here', we have to look within ourself, to the very centre or core of our being, because only there can we find the infinitely minute and subtle interior point that always makes us feel that we are 'here' and 'now', no matter at which exterior point in time and space we happen to experience ourself as being.

When we look within ourself, focusing our entire attention on the innermost core of our being, our thinking mind will come to a standstill, and thus all our thoughts will cease. Our thoughts all occur within the flow of time, and within the multidimensional space of our mind. If we did not experience the one-dimensional flow of time, the constant flow of our mind from past to future, we could not form any thought. Similarly, if we did not experience our mind as a multidimensional space in which thoughts of diverse kinds rise and subside, there would be no space in which we could form any thought.

However, in the precise present moment there is no movement or flow, and in the precise present place there is no space. The precise present moment is a point in time that has no dimensions, no duration, and the precise present place is a point in space that has no dimensions, no extent. Therefore, in neither the precise present moment nor the precise present place can any thought be formed.

A dimension is a particular way of measuring or defining the extent of something, so anything that can be measured in any way, anything that has any definable extent, has dimension. Time is one-dimensional, because it is a unidirectional flow from past to future. Physical space is three-dimensional, because it has height, breadth and depth. The space of our mind is multidimensional, because not only does it contain the one-dimensional flow of time and the three-dimensional physical space, but it also has many other dimensions of its own, such as its five forms of sense knowledge, its various forms of conceptual knowledge, and its various forms of emotion.

Moreover, the space of our mind contains dimensions within dimensions. For example, the dimension of taste has six basic sub-dimensions, namely sweetness, sourness, saltiness, pungency, bitterness and astringency, the dimension of sight has various sub-dimensions such as colour, shape and distance, and each dimension of conceptual knowledge, such as abstract mathematical thought, has many sub-dimensions. All the many ways in which our mind can measure or define the extent of whatever it knows or experiences – the objects of its sense perception, its concepts, its emotions, and so on – are dimensions of its space.

All things that have dimension extend within that dimension. The extent to which any particular thing extends within any particular dimension is the measurement of that thing within that dimension. Except our fundamental consciousness of our own being, 'I am', everything that is known by our mind extends in one or more of the many dimensions that are experienced by it. All forms of objective knowledge extend in one or more dimensions.

Whereas everything else that we experience in time and space extends either in time or in space, or in both, the only things in time and space that do not extend in either of them are the precise present moment, 'now', and the precise present place, 'here'. The precise present moment has no definable or measurable duration, and the precise present place has no definable or measurable extent. If a thing extends in some dimension, it is confined within that extent, but if it does not extend in any dimension, it is not confined or limited in any way. Therefore, since they do not extend in any dimension, the precise present place and the precise present moment are free of all limitations, and hence they are the absolute 'here' and 'now'.

Since they are each an infinitely small point, we may imagine that the precise present moment and the precise present place are therefore limited. However, since they do not exist at only one particular point in time or space, they are not actually limited in any way. Though the precise present moment appears to be an infinitesimal point in time, it is nevertheless not limited or restricted to any one particular point in time, because every point in time is experienced as the present moment while it is occurring. Similarly, though the precise present place appears to be an infinitesimal point in space, it is nevertheless not limited or restricted to any one particular point in space, because many points in space are experienced as the present place at one time or another. Since the precise present moment exists at every point in time, and the precise present place exists at different points in space at different points in time, neither of them can be defined or delimited as existing at only one point. As soon as we attempt to define their location in time or space, time will have moved on and our definition will have become invalid.

Though the precise present moment and the precise present place appear to exist within the dimensions of time and space, at no time can their exact location within those dimensions be defined or cognised, because in truth they exist beyond the limitations of time and space. If we wish to discover their exact location, we cannot do so by looking outwards, towards the objective dimensions of time and space, but only by looking within ourself, towards the innermost depth of our being, towards the core of our consciousness, towards the precise point within us where we feel 'I am', 'I am here and now'.

The precise present moment and the precise present place cannot be located at any exact point in the objective dimensions of time and space because they are not objective points, but are subjective experiences. Therefore, though they appear to touch the objective dimensions of time and space, their existence is not limited or restricted to any fixed or clearly discernible point within those dimensions. Because they are the point at which we experience our timeless and placeless consciousness of being, 'I am', appearing to exist within the imaginary dimensions of time and space, they are the point at which the eternal meets the temporal, the infinite meets the finite, and the absolute meets the relative.

Though time is always moving on, and with each passing moment a new point in time becomes the present moment, and a new point in space becomes the present place, the precise present moment and the precise present place do not themselves move or undergo any actual change. Except these two precise points, everything in time and space is constantly moving and undergoing change. The precise present moment remains unmoving and unchanged through all time, and the precise present place remains unmoving and unchanged, no matter at which point in space it may be experienced.

Though all moments in time seem to flow through the present moment, in the precise present moment no flowing or movement of any kind actually takes place, because movement requires a dimension in which to move. Similarly, though many places in space seem to move into and thereby to become the present place, in the precise present place no movement, becoming or change of any kind actually takes place, because change requires a dimension in which to occur.

A thing can be said to change only if it can first be defined in some way, because only a definable or definite thing can undergo a definable or definite change. Consequently, since a definition is a form of measurement or appraisal that can be made only with reference to some dimension, a point with no dimension cannot be defined or delimited in any way, and hence it cannot undergo any definable change.

Therefore, being completely devoid of dimension, extension, limitation, definition, change and movement, the precise present point in time and the precise present point in space are absolute. Though everything else exists relative only to them, the precise present moment and the precise present place are not relative to anything else, because they exist independently, and remain unaffected by the flow of time or any movement that takes place in space.

The 'here' and 'now' that appear to extend in space or time – that appear to be measurable and definable – are only the relative 'here' and 'now'. Our conception of what constitutes the present moment, 'now', and the present place, 'here', is not fixed, but varies according to the context. For example, when we say 'now', we may mean this very second, this minute, or a larger period of present time such as today, or we may extend its meaning even further to mean nowadays, during this period in our lives or in history. Similarly, when we say 'here', we may mean this exact part of space that is now occupied by our body, or any particular point within our body, or any point that is close to our body, or we may extend its meaning further to mean the room, the house, the town or even the country in which we are now living. All such uses of these words 'here' and 'now' are relative. Any relative form of 'now' extends in time, and any relative form of 'here' extends in space, and hence they can be measured.

However, the precise present moment and the precise present place are points in time and space that have no extent, and that therefore cannot be measured. As we saw above, the precise present moment is the immeasurably fine boundary or interface between the past and the future. Where the past ends, the future begins, so the interface between them is an infinitely fine point that has no measurement or extent. Similarly, the precise present place is the immeasurably fine point that exists in the very centre of our perception of space.

Since they are both infinitely fine and subtle, and therefore not limited within any dimension, the precise present moment and the precise present place are not relative, but are the absolute 'here' and 'now'. Since movement and change cannot occur within an infinitely fine and therefore dimensionless point, and since the formation of thought involves movement and change, no thought can be formed within either the precise present moment or the precise present place, and hence the precise present point in time and space is the exclusive abode of our own self-conscious being, 'I am'.

Though we talk of the precise present moment and the precise present place as if they were two different things, they appear to be different only from the limited viewpoint of our finite mind. The difference between them is therefore merely conceptual. In reality they are one and the same.

The precise present moment and the precise present place are the single point at which time and space meet and become one. This single point, at which all dimensions meet, is itself devoid of any dimension. Though the dimensions that meet and become one in it are all relative, this single, non-dual and dimensionless point is itself devoid of all forms of relativity. All that is contained within it is our mere consciousness of our own being, 'I am'. But even to say this is not entirely correct. It does not merely contain our essential consciousness of our own being, it is synonymous with it. Our essential non-dual consciousness of our own being, 'I am', is itself the absolute 'here' and 'now', the precise present place and the precise present moment.

Because this absolute point has no dimensions, it cannot be measured in any way. It is therefore not only infinitely minute, but also infinitely vast. That is, because it is absolute, it is free of all limitations, and hence it is not limited as being merely the minutest, but is also the largest, the infinite whole that contains everything. It is both that which is contained within everything, and that within which everything is contained.

Everything, all time and all space, and all that is contained within time and space, is only a form of knowledge, a conception or a perception, and hence it is all contained within consciousness. And since no form of knowledge can exist without consciousness underlying it, consciousness not only contains everything, but is also contained within everything.

In fact, consciousness is the one fundamental substance of which all things are made. Therefore, since all forms of knowledge are in essence only our own consciousness, since our own consciousness is essentially self-conscious – that is, it is in essence just our consciousness of our own being – and since our consciousness of our own being is the absolute point that we experience as being the precise present place, 'here', and the precise present moment, 'now', this absolute point contains everything and is contained within everything.

In order to be contained within everything, this absolute point must be infinitely small, and in order to contain everything, it must be infinitely large. As that which is infinitely small, it contains nothing but our own essential self-conscious being, 'I am', but as that which is infinitely large, it contains everything, the totality of all our knowledge, both our true knowledge and our false knowledge. All that is known is ultimately known only in the precise present moment, 'now', and the precise present place, 'here' – in the absolute present, which is our own ever-present self-conscious being, 'I am', and which is the only point in time and space that truly exists.

CHAPTER 8

The Science of Consciousness

A science is a means of acquiring valid knowledge, knowledge that can be independently verified. But what is the correct definition of valid knowledge? Is knowledge valid merely because it can be independently verified, or is there some other more strict standard by which we can measure the validity of any given knowledge?

As we saw in chapters five and six, there are two forms of valid knowledge, knowledge that is relatively valid and knowledge that is absolutely valid. Accordingly, there are also two forms of science, relative science and absolute science. Except the spiritual science, which is the science of true self-knowledge or consciousness, all forms of science are relative sciences, because the knowledge they seek to acquire is only relatively valid.

From the relative standpoint of our life as an individual in this material world, the knowledge sought and acquired by the various branches of objective science may be valid and useful, but such knowledge is not absolutely true. It is not valid and true under all circumstances and in all conditions or states. The laws of science that we experience as true in this waking state may be experienced as untrue in dream. In dream, for example, we are sometimes able to defy the law of gravity by flying. The law of gravity, which is undeniably valid according to our experience in this waking state, is not always equally valid in dream.

All our so-called scientific knowledge, though valid according to our experience in this waking state, is not valid according to our experience in sleep. In fact, our experience in sleep calls into question the validity of all our knowledge and experience in this waking state. Though we may each be able to verify independently the validity of our scientific knowledge in this waking state, in sleep none of us can verify even the existence of this world.

In this waking state we assume that this world existed while we were asleep, but we have no means by which we can independently verify the validity of this assumption. To verify it, we must depend upon the testimony of other people who claim to have been awake while we were asleep, but those other people are part of the world whose existence we wish to verify, so they cannot be independent witnesses.

Some philosophers believe that though much of our knowledge concerning this world is relative, our knowledge of the laws of mathematics is absolute. They believe that since two plus two equals four under all circumstances and in all conditions, it must be an absolute truth. However, their assumption that it is true under all circumstances and in all conditions is incorrect, because it depends upon the obvious condition of the existence of two. In sleep we do not experience the existence of two, so none of the laws of mathematics are valid in that state. Mathematics is a science of duality and multiplicity, and as such it is inherently relative. It is relative primarily to our mind and its power of imagination, because only when our mind imagines the existence of more than one do the laws of mathematics come into existence.

All our knowledge of duality is relative, and therefore though it may be relatively valid, it is not absolutely valid. The only knowledge that we can consider to be absolutely valid and true is a knowledge that is perfectly non-dual – that is, a knowledge that knows only itself and that is known only by itself.

Any knowledge that is known by a consciousness other than itself necessarily involves duality, distinction and relativity. Therefore the only science that could be absolutely true and valid is the science of consciousness, or more precisely, the science of self-consciousness.

What is consciousness? It is our power of knowing, or our power to know. Or to be more precise, it is the power within us that knows. However, since that which knows is only we ourself, our consciousness is not something other than ourself, but is our very being or essence.

Of all the things that we know, the first is our own being, which we always know as 'I am'. All our other knowledge comes and goes, but this first and most basic knowledge 'I am' neither comes nor goes, but is experienced by us constantly, in all times and in all states. Thus our very nature as consciousness is to know ourself. Consciousness is always self-conscious, and it cannot but be conscious of itself – that is, of its own essential being or 'am'-ness.

The original and primary form of our consciousness is therefore our self-consciousness 'I am'. Whether or not our consciousness knows any other thing, it always knows itself. In every knowledge that it experiences, its basic knowledge 'I am' is mixed.

That is, our consciousness experiences all its knowledge of anything other than itself as 'I am knowing this'. Whereas it knows itself only as 'I am', it knows other things as 'I am knowing this'. However, though it always knows itself as 'I am', when it knows other things in addition to itself, it seems to ignore or overlook its own basic knowledge 'I am', and to give prominence instead to whatever else it is knowing.

Though our consciousness sometimes appears to be knowing things other than itself, its knowledge of those other things is only temporary, and hence that knowledge of otherness is not an essential part of its being. In sleep we know that we are, but we do not know anything else, so our knowledge of otherness is extraneous to our essential consciousness of our own being.

Since our consciousness of our own being is permanent, whereas our consciousness of otherness is temporary, there is a clear distinction between these two forms of our consciousness. The former is our essential consciousness, while the latter is a mere adjunct that is temporarily superimposed upon it. This temporary adjunct – which rises from our essential non-dual consciousness of our own being as a dualistic consciousness of otherness, and which thereby appears to be superimposed upon and intimately mixed with our essential consciousness – is the limited and relative form of consciousness that we call our 'mind'.

In order to know things other than itself, our mind must limit itself. But how can consciousness limit itself? Only that which has a definable or measurable extent is limited. Since consciousness has no boundaries, it has no such definable extent, so it is unlimited.

A limitation of any sort requires one or more dimensions within which it can set defined boundaries. But consciousness is not confined within any dimension, and therefore it does not have any boundaries that could limit it in any way. Since all dimensions, boundaries, limits and extents are concepts or thoughts that are known only by our mind after it has risen to know otherness, they are contained only within our mind and have no existence independent of it. How then does our mind confine itself within any limit?

Our mind limits itself by imagining itself to be one of the objects that it knows. That is, it first imagines itself to be a form, and then only does it know the forms of other things. A form is anything that is contained within boundaries, and that therefore has a definable extent in one or more dimensions. Every finite thing has a form of one type or another, because without a form a thing would have no limits and would therefore be infinite. Everything that we know as other than ourself is a form. Our thoughts, our feelings, our emotions, our perceptions and all other things that are known by our mind are forms, except of course our essential consciousness of our own being, which is formless and therefore infinite.

The form that our mind imagines to be itself is our physical body, through the five senses of which it perceives a world of objects and other bodies. Our mind cannot function or know anything other than its own being without first imagining itself to be the form of a physical body. Our identification with our physical body is so strong that we imagine that even our own thoughts occur only within our body. That is, we experience the grosser forms of our thoughts, such as our perceptions, our conceptions, our visualised imaginations and our verbalised thoughts, as if they were all occurring somewhere within our head, and we experience the more subtle forms of our thoughts, such as our feelings and emotions, as if they were occurring somewhere within our chest.

Whatever body we currently imagine to be ourself, whether our present body in this waking state or some other body in one of our dreams, we always imagine that all our mental activity is occurring within it, and that the world we perceive through its five senses exists outside it. In dream we mistake ourself to be some other body, but we still feel that all our mental activity is occurring within that body, and that the world we perceive through its five senses exists outside it.

However, though we experience our thoughts as if they were occurring within the body that we currently mistake to be ourself, we still feel them to be other than ourself. Having limited our consciousness by mistaking ourself to be this finite body, we experience everything else that we know as if it were other than ourself. By our very act of limiting ourself within the confines of a particular form, we are able to know all other forms as other than ourself.

In fact, however, our body, our thoughts and all the other objects that we know are only images that appear and disappear within our consciousness, and hence they have no substantial reality other than our consciousness. That is, all the forms that we know are just modifications that occur in our consciousness, like the waves on the surface of the ocean. Just as the water of the ocean is the sole substance of which all the waves are formed, so our consciousness is the sole substance of which all things known by us are formed.

Because we mistake ourself to be this body, we imagine that both the thoughts that seem to occur inside it and the objects that seem to exist outside it are all other than ourself. However, though it is absurd for us to imagine that any of these things, all of which we know only within our own mind, are actually other than ourself, this is less absurd than the confused imagination we have regarding this body, which we mistake to be ourself. Though we experience this body as if it were ourself, and as if we were limited within the boundaries of its form, we nevertheless experience it as an object. We talk of my arms, my hands, my legs, my head and even my body, as if these were our possessions, but at the same time we mistake them to be ourself.

Our knowledge about our exact identity is confused and unclear because, though we mistake the form of this body to be ourself, we still know ourself to be consciousness. Since this body and our mind, which mistakes it to be 'I', are actually experienced by us as two different things, we are unsure which is really ourself. When we say 'my body', we are identifying ourself with our mind, which cognises this body as an object. But we also sometimes say 'my mind', as if our mind were something distinct from ourself.

Because we know ourself to be consciousness, which is in fact infinite, but at the same time imagine ourself to be a body, which is finite, we are perpetually confused about our true identity. However, as a result of this confusion we feel ourself to be something limited, and hence we are able to know things as other than ourself.

Our mind is in reality nothing other than our essential consciousness 'I am', which is formless and therefore infinite, undivided and non-dual. Hence, since it is infinite, there is truly nothing other than it for it to know. However by imagining itself to be a finite form, it is able to know other forms as if they were truly other than itself.

Therefore our mind is able to know things other than itself only by deluding itself into experiencing itself as something that it is not – something that is actually just a product of its own powerful and self-deceptive imagination. Nothing that we experience in a dream is actually other than ourself, but by imagining ourself to be one of the imaginary forms that we experience in that dream, we experience all the other forms in that dream as if they were other than ourself.

All the duality or multiplicity that our mind seems to experience is therefore just a product of its self-deluding power of imagination, and it experiences all the manifold products of its imagination only by imagining that it is one among them. Therefore, though our mind is real as our essential and non-dual consciousness of being, as a consciousness that knows otherness it is merely a figment of its own imagination, and is therefore unreal.

We use the term 'mind' to refer to our consciousness only when it seems to know otherness. When it ceases to know any otherness, it ceases to be a separate finite entity, and therefore it remains as our infinite consciousness 'I am', which in reality it always is. As our true infinite consciousness, it knows only itself, but as our 'mind' it imagines that it knows other things and is thereby deluded.

As our mind we can never attain true self-knowledge, because as our mind we can only know our consciousness 'I am' mixed with the imaginary knowledge of otherness. That is, as our mind our power of attention, which is another name for our power of knowing or consciousness, is constantly directed towards other things, and is thereby diverted away from ourself – from our own essential being, 'I am'.

Therefore, if we are to attain true knowledge, we cannot do so through the medium of our mind. We must turn our power of attention, which we have till now been constantly directing outwards through the media of our mind and its five senses, away from our mind and all its thoughts, back on itself, towards our real consciousness 'I am'.

However, when we do so we are likely to find that initially we are unable to focus our attention wholly and exclusively upon our extremely subtle consciousness of being, 'I am', because our power of attention has become gross and unrefined due to our constant habit of attending only to our thoughts. Only by repeatedly attempting to focus our attention wholly and exclusively upon our essential consciousness 'I am' will we gradually gain the skill required to do so.

Only practice can make perfect. By repeated and persistent practice of turning our attention back on itself to discover what this consciousness 'I am' really is, we will gradually refine our power of attention, making it more subtle, clear and penetrating, and thus we will gain a steadily increasing clarity of knowledge of the real infinite and non-dual nature of our consciousness 'I am'. Finally, when our power of attention has been perfectly refined or purified – that is, when it has become freed from its present strong attachment to attend only to thoughts and objects – we will be able to know with perfect clarity our essential consciousness 'I am' as it really is, devoid of even the least superimposition of any limitation or identification with any other thing.

This empirical practice of self-attention, self-scrutiny, self-examination or self-investigation is the experimental method of the science of consciousness. The only practical means by which we can discover the true nature of consciousness is by turning our attention towards it. Since consciousness cannot be known as an object but only as our own knowing self, scientific research upon consciousness must therefore consist in our scrutinising our own consciousness with a keen, focused and one-pointed power of attention. Except by such self-attention or self-scrutiny, we can never attain direct knowledge or experience of our real consciousness 'I am' as it really is, devoid of any imaginary superimposition or limitation.

The consciousness 'I am' is not some unknown thing that we are yet to discover, because even now we all clearly know 'I am'. However, though we know 'I am', we do not know it as it really is. We know it in a limited and distorted form due to the false adjuncts that we superimpose upon it by our power of imagination. We know it wrongly as 'I am this body, I am a person named so-and-so, I am sitting here, I am reading this book, I am thinking about the ideas discussed in it' and so on and so forth.

All these adjuncts that we are constantly superimposing upon our consciousness 'I am' prevent us from knowing it as it really is. Therefore to know it as it is, we must look beyond all these adjuncts to the one basic consciousness that underlies them all. When we scrutinise our basic consciousness 'I am' with a keen and penetrating power of attention, all these false adjuncts will dissolve or drop off it, and thus we will know it as it really is.

Though we speak of our real consciousness 'I am' and our unreal consciousness 'I am this body', these are in fact not two different consciousnesses, but are merely two forms of the same consciousness, the one and only consciousness that exists. The true form of consciousness is only our pure non-dual consciousness of our own being, 'I am'. Our mind, the mixed or impure consciousness 'I am this body', by which all duality is known, is merely a false, distorted and illusory form of our one real consciousness 'I am'.

When it knows only itself, our one real consciousness shines as it is, devoid of all false adjuncts, but when by its power of imagination it seemingly knows things other than itself, this same one real consciousness appears as our mind. This one real consciousness 'I am' is our true self. Therefore, when we remain as we really are, knowing only ourself, we are the real non-dual consciousness 'I am', but when we direct our consciousness or power of attention away from ourself towards the imaginary world of thoughts, we seemingly become this mind.

Thus in reality our mind is nothing other than our non-dual real consciousness 'I am', just as the snake that is superimposed by our imagination upon a rope is in reality nothing other than that rope. Its seemingly separate and limited existence as 'mind' is merely an illusion caused by our lack of clear self-knowledge, just as the snake is merely an illusion caused by the lack of clear daylight. When we once shine a clear light upon the rope and thereby distinctly see it for what it is, we will never thereafter mistake it to be a snake. Similarly, when we once shine the clear light of our keenly focused attention upon our consciousness 'I am' and thereby know it distinctly as it is, we will never thereafter mistake it to be what it is not – any of the alien adjuncts by which we formerly defined it.

Since our mind is thus nothing other than our non-dual real consciousness 'I am', all it need do to know that consciousness is to turn its attention back on itself, away from all other things. However, when it does so, it ceases to be the limited individual consciousness that we call 'mind', and becomes instead the unlimited real consciousness 'I am', which in reality it always has been and always will be. Therefore that which knows our real consciousness 'I am' is not our mind but only that consciousness itself.

In recent years a renewed interest in consciousness has arisen among a still quite small group of scientists and academic philosophers. The 'science of consciousness', as it is sometimes known, is now a recognised even if still quite minor branch of modern science. However it is more commonly referred to as 'consciousness studies', because it is considered to be an interdisciplinary field of study involving contributions made by philosophy, psychology, neuroscience and other related disciplines.

Though these modern 'consciousness studies' sometimes describe themselves as the 'science of consciousness', or at least say that they are an attempt to move towards a 'science of consciousness', they should not be confused with the true science of consciousness that we are discussing here, because their understanding about consciousness and their methods of research are fundamentally different to the clear understanding and simple method of research taught by Sri Ramana and other sages. The radical difference between these two approaches lies in the fact that these 'consciousness studies' attempt to study consciousness objectively, as if it were an objective phenomenon, whereas sages teach us that consciousness can never become an object of knowledge, but can only be known truly as the essential reality underlying our mind, which is the subject that knows all objects.

In conformity with the fundamental demand made by all modern objective sciences, namely that scientists should seek to acquire 'objective knowledge' (knowledge that can be demonstrated and verified objectively) about any field of study in which they undertake research, modern 'consciousness studies' attempt to take an objective approach to the study of consciousness. Therefore, since in the limited view of our body-bound mind our consciousness appears to be centred in our brain, 'consciousness studies' place great weight upon the efforts of modern science to understand the relationship between the electrochemical activity in our brain and consciousness, which they imagine results from such activity. Moreover, since we generally take consciousness to mean consciousness of something, 'consciousness studies' are also very much concerned with understanding cognition and our subjective experience of the sensory stimuli that we seem to receive from the outside world.

In other words, the basic assumption made by philosophers and scientists who are involved in these modern 'consciousness studies' is that we can understand consciousness by attempting to study it as an objective phenomenon. However, anything that is known as an objective phenomenon is merely an object of consciousness, and is not consciousness itself. Since consciousness is the subject that knows all objective phenomenon, it can never itself become an object of knowledge.

Consciousness can be known or experienced directly only by itself, and not by any other thing. Therefore if we try to study consciousness as an objective phenomenon, we will only succeed in studying something that is not consciousness itself, but is merely an apparent effect of consciousness. If we truly wish to study consciousness and to understand what it really is, we must study it within ourself, as ourself, because we ourself are consciousness, and anything other than ourself is not consciousness but is only an object known by us.

So long as we experience any form of dualistic knowledge, that is, any knowledge involving a distinction between subject and object, consciousness will always be the knowing subject and never a known object. Therefore since time immemorial one of the fundamental principles of *advaita vēdānta* has always been that in order to know consciousness as it really is we must distinguish that which knows from that which is known.

This process, which in Sanskrit is often known as *dṛg dṛśya vivēka* or 'discrimination between the seer and the seen', is a fundamental prerequisite for us to be able to practise effective self-investigation. Until we understand this basic distinction between consciousness and even the subtlest object known by it, we will not be able to focus our attention wholly and exclusively upon our essential consciousness, and thus we will not be able to experience it as it really is – that is, as our pure and unadulterated consciousness of our own being, which is devoid of even the slightest trace of duality or otherness.

Unless modern scientists are willing to accept this fundamental but very simple principle, all their efforts to understand consciousness will be misdirected. Any scientist who imagines that they can understand consciousness by studying our physical brain, its electrochemical activity or its cognitive function, has failed to understand that all these things are merely objects that are known by consciousness as other than itself.

Our body, its brain, the many biochemical and electrochemical processes that occur within it, and the functioning of its cognitive processes, are all thoughts or mental images that arise in our mind due to our power of imagination, as also is the illusion that our consciousness is centred in our brain. In the actual experience of each one of us, our consciousness is always present and is clearly known by us as 'I am' even when we are not conscious of our present body or any other body, and though the rising and functioning of our mind is only a temporary phenomenon, no other phenomenon such as a body or brain can ever appear unless our mind rises to know it. Therefore, since we experience our mind whenever we experience our physical body or any other thing in this material world, we have no valid reason to believe or even to suppose that the existence of this world preceded the existence of our mind, or that our mind is a phenomenon that arises due to the functioning of our brain.

Since we experience our mind even when we do not experience our present body, as in dream, and even when we have no idea about the brain in this body, our mind is something that is clearly distinct from both our body and our brain. Moreover, since we experience our consciousness even when we do not experience our mind, our present body or any other body, as in sleep, our consciousness is something that is clearly distinct from both our mind and our body, and consequently from the brain in this body.

Since all that we know about our brain is just a collection of thoughts that arise in our mind, we can never discover the true nature either of our mind or of the basic consciousness that underlies it by studying the functioning of our brain. In fact by thinking in any way about our brain or any other such objective phenomenon, we are only diverting our attention away from ourself – that is, away from the consciousness that we seek to know.

Even if we knew nothing about our brain, we would still know 'I am', so if we truly wish to know the true nature of this basic consciousness that we experience as 'I am', we need not attempt to know anything about our brain. All we need do is to turn our attention away from everything that is known by us as other than our essential consciousness, and to focus it instead only upon our consciousness that knows all those other things.

However, when we actually turn our attention back towards ourself, whom we now feel to be a consciousness that knows things other than ourself, we will discover that our real self or essential consciousness is not actually a consciousness that knows any other thing, but is only the pure consciousness of being, which knows nothing other than itself. This pure non-dual consciousness of our own being is the real and fundamental consciousness that underlies and supports the illusory appearance of our mind, which is the consciousness that knows otherness, just as a rope is the reality that underlies and supports the illusory appearance of a snake.

Though the object-knowing form in which we now experience our consciousness is not its true form, we must nevertheless investigate it very minutely in order to discover the true consciousness that underlies it. Just as in order to see the rope as it really is we must look very carefully at the snake that it appears to be, so in order to know our true consciousness as it really is we must very carefully inspect the object-knowing consciousness that it now appears to be.

If instead of looking carefully at the seeming snake we were to look however carefully at any other thing, we would not be able to see the rope as it really is. Similarly, if instead of carefully inspecting our present consciousness, which now appears to know things other than itself, we make research however carefully on any of those other things that it appears to know, we will not be able to experience and know our true consciousness as it really is.

As we saw at the beginning of this chapter, all science is an attempt made by our human mind to acquire knowledge that is true and valid. Therefore the most important research that any scientist can undertake is to test the truth and validity of his or her own mind, since that is the consciousness by which he or she knows all other things.

If we are not able to verify the reality of our own knowing consciousness, which is what we call our 'mind', we will never be able to verify the reality of any other thing, because all those other things are known only by our mind. Therefore before considering undertaking any other research, every true scientist should first undertake research upon his or her own consciousness.

If we do not know the colour of the glasses we are wearing, we will be unable to judge correctly the colour of any of the objects we see. Similarly, if we do not know the reality of our own mind, which is the medium through which we know all other things, we will be unable to judge correctly the reality of any of those other things that we now appear to know.

As we have been observing throughout this book, our mind or knowing consciousness is a confused and unreliable form of consciousness. As a finite object-knowing consciousness, our mind functions basically as a power of imagination. Except our fundamental consciousness of our own being, 'I am', everything that we know through the medium of our mind is a product of our power of imagination. Even if we choose to believe that the world that we seem to perceive through our five senses is truly something that exists outside us and that it is therefore separate from ourself, a belief which is in fact entirely ungrounded, we cannot deny the fact that this world as we experience it in our own mind is nothing but a series of thoughts or mental images that we have formed by our power of imagination.

Moreover, on careful analysis, not only do we find that all the things that we know through the medium of our mind are mere products of our imagination, but we also find that our mind itself is merely a product of our imagination. Our mind does not exist in our sleep, but it rises as an image in our consciousness as soon as we start to experience a state of waking or dream. When it rises thus, we experience our mind as if it were ourself. That is, through our power of imagination we seem to become our mind, which is a knowing consciousness, that is, a consciousness that appears to know things other than itself.

Since our mind is not only a transitory phenomenon but also a mere figment of our imagination, whatever we may know through it is also both a transitory phenomenon and a figment of our imagination. Therefore any knowledge that we may acquire by making research on anything known by our mind is imaginary, and is no more real than any knowledge that we could acquire by making research on anything that we experience in a dream. Hence, though the knowledge that we acquire by making objective research in our present waking state may appear to be quite valid and true so long as we experience this waking state, it is in fact nothing but a figment of our imagination, and it therefore cannot help us to know and experience the absolute reality that underlies and transcends all imagination.

In order to experience that absolute reality, we must penetrate beneath our mind and all its imaginary creations by seeking to know the true consciousness that underlies it. Since we are the consciousness in which our mind and all its imaginations appear and disappear, we are that which underlies and therefore transcends it. Hence to penetrate beneath our mind we must know ourself – our real self or essential consciousness, which we always experience as 'I am' – and we can do so only by focusing our attention wholly and exclusively upon ourself, thereby withdrawing it from all the products of our imagination.

Only when we thus know our essential consciousness 'I am', which is the absolute reality underlying the transient appearance of our mind, will we be able to judge correctly the reality of all the other things that we know. Until then, we should not waste our time making research upon any other thing, but should concentrate all our efforts in making research upon our essential consciousness by persistently trying to centre our entire attention upon it.

One objection that philosophers and scientists often raise about this true science of consciousness is that its findings cannot be demonstrated objectively, and therefore cannot be independently verified. However, while it is true that we can never demonstrate the absolute reality of consciousness objectively, it is not true to say that it cannot be independently verified. Since consciousness is the basic and essential experience of each one of us, we can each independently verify its reality for ourself.

The real reason why most people, including many philosophers and scientists, and even people with exceptionally brilliant minds, tend to shy away from this science of consciousness or true self-knowledge, and also in most cases from the entire simple and rational philosophy that underlies it, is that they are too strongly attached to their own individuality, and to all the things that they enjoy experiencing through the medium of their minds. Unlike other philosophies and sciences, which allow us to retain our individual self and all our personal interests, desires, attachments, likes and dislikes, this philosophy and science require us to relinquish everything, including our own mind or individual self.

Until and unless we are ready to surrender our individual self and everything that comes with it, we will be unable to know and remain as the infinite and non-dual consciousness, which is our own real self. We cannot eat our cake and still have it. We have to choose either to keep it intact or to eat it. Likewise, we have to choose either to retain our mind or individual consciousness and all that it experiences, or to annihilate it by surrendering it in the all-consuming fire of true self-knowledge.

In the case of a cake, we do at least have a third option, which is to eat a part of it and to keep the rest of it intact, but in the case of self-knowledge we have no such intermediate option. We must choose either to imagine ourself to be this finite consciousness that we call 'mind', or to experience ourself as the infinite consciousness that we really are.

Some philosophers are fascinated by the profundity and power of this simple philosophy of absolute non-duality, but are nevertheless not willing to make the personal sacrifice that is required to experience the non-dual reality that it expounds, and therefore they enjoy giving lectures and writing books about it, but avoid actually practising true self-investigation, which is the empirical means by which true non-dual self-knowledge is attained.

Such philosophers are like a person who enjoys looking at a cake and reading about how tasty and enjoyable it is, but who never ventures to taste it himself.

Their failure to put into practice what they think they have understood clearly indicates that they have not truly understood the philosophy that they seek to explain to others. If we have really understood this philosophy, we will certainly try our utmost to put it into practice, because we will understand that such practice is the only means by which we can attain true and lasting happiness.

Each one of us can independently verify the absolute reality of our essential consciousness 'I am', but to do so we must pay the necessary price, which unfortunately most of us are not yet willing to do. The reason why we are not willing to do so is that we are too strongly attached to our individuality, and are therefore not ready to surrender it even in exchange for the perfect happiness of true self-knowledge.

However, our clinging thus to our individuality is the height of foolishness, because this individuality to which we cling with so much attachment is in fact the cause of all our unhappiness, and the only obstacle preventing us from enjoying the perfect happiness that is our own true nature. As Sri Ramana used to say, our unwillingness to surrender our finite individual consciousness together with all the petty pleasures and pains that it is constantly experiencing, when in exchange for it we can become the true infinite consciousness, which is the fullness of perfect happiness, is like being unwilling to give a copper coin in exchange for a gold one.

However, even if we are not yet entirely willing to surrender our individuality here and now, if we have at least understood that this is something that we must do in order to be able to experience true self-knowledge, which is the state of supreme and absolute happiness, we should not be disheartened but should persist in our attempts to focus our attention upon our basic consciousness of being.

Since our consciousness of being is the ultimate 'light', the light by which all other lights are illumined or known, it is the source of perfect clarity. Therefore the more we focus our attention upon it, the more it will enkindle a deep inner clarity in our mind, and this clarity of self-consciousness will enable us to discriminate and truly understand that real happiness can be experienced only in the state of 'just being', that is, the state in which we remain merely as the simple non-dual essence or 'am'-ness that we always really are.

When we discriminate and understand this truth with profound clarity of self-consciousness, we will be consumed by absolute love to know and to be the reality that we always are, and thereby we will effortlessly surrender our false individual self and merge forever in the infinite consciousness that is our own real self.

CHAPTER 9

Self-Investigation and Self-Surrender

Sri Ramana often said that there are only two means by which we can attain the experience of true self-knowledge, namely self-investigation and self-surrender. However, he also said that these two means or 'spiritual paths' are truly one in essence. That is, though they are described in different words, in their actual practice they are identical. What exactly are these two means or paths, how are they one in essence, what is their one essence, and why did he describe that one essence in these two different ways?

According to the ancient philosophy of *vēdānta*, there are four paths that lead to spiritual emancipation, namely the 'path of [desireless] action' or *karma mārga*, the 'path of devotion' or *bhakti mārga*, the 'path of union' or *yōga mārga*, and the 'path of knowing' or *jñāna mārga*. Of these four paths, the second and the fourth are the principal means, while the first and the third are merely subsidiary aspects of these two principal means. In other words, all the various types of spiritual practice or 'paths' can in essence be reduced to these two principal paths, the 'path of knowing' and the 'path of devotion'. If any practice does not contain an element of either or both of these two paths, it cannot lead us to the state of spiritual emancipation, the state in which we are freed from the bondage of finite existence.

To express the same truth in a more simple fashion, we can attain spiritual emancipation or 'salvation' only by experiencing true self-knowledge – that is, by knowing ourself to be only the real and infinite spirit or consciousness 'I am', and not this unreal and finite individual whom we now imagine ourself to be. In order to know ourself thus as the absolute reality, we must be consumed by intense love for our essential being, because if we are not consumed by such love, we will not be willing to relinquish our false individual self, which we now hold more dear than any other thing.

In other words, in order to attain spiritual emancipation we must know our essential being, and in order to know our essential being we must love it. Thus 'knowing' and 'love' or devotion are the two essential means by which we can attain emancipation from our present illusion of being a finite individual.

The more we love our essential being, the more we will attend to it, and the more we attend to it, the more clearly we will know it. Conversely, the more clearly we know our essential being, the more we will love it, because it is the true source of all happiness. Thus love and knowing go hand in hand, each feeding the other. We cannot know without loving, and we cannot love without knowing. Therefore the 'path of knowing' and the 'path of loving' or devotion are not two alternative means, but are just two aspects of the one and only means by which we can regain our natural state of absolute being.

The two means to attain true self-knowledge taught by Sri Ramana correspond to these twin paths of 'knowing' and 'devotion'. The practice of self-investigation is the true 'path of knowing', and the practice of self-surrender is the true 'path of devotion'. Therefore self-investigation and self-surrender are not two separate paths, but are just two aspects of the same one path – the only means by which we can experience the absolute reality, which is our own true and essential being.

Though Sri Ramana taught the practice that leads to true self-knowledge in these two different ways, describing it either in terms of self-investigation or in terms of self-surrender, he taught it most frequently in terms of the former. Let us therefore first consider this path of self-investigation. What exactly is this practice that Sri Ramana described as self-investigation, self-examination, self-scrutiny, self-enquiry or self-attention?

Though he used various words in Tamil to describe this practice, one of the principal terms that he used was the Sanskrit term *ātma-vicāra*, or more simply just *vicāra*. The word *ātmā* means self, spirit or essence, and is often used as a singular reflexive pronoun applicable to any of the three persons and any of the three genders, though in this context it would be applicable only to the first person, meaning myself, ourself or oneself. The word *vicāra*, as we saw in the introduction, means investigation or examination, and can also mean pondering or consideration, in the sense of thinking of or looking at something carefully and attentively. Thus *ātma-vicāra* is the simple practice of investigating, examining, exploring, inspecting, scrutinising or keenly attending to ourself – our own essential self-conscious being, which we always experience as our basic consciousness 'I am'.

In English the term *ātma-vicāra* is often translated as 'self-enquiry', which has led many people to misunderstand it to mean a process of questioning ourself 'who am I?'. However such questioning would only be a mental activity, so it is clearly not the meaning intended by Sri Ramana. When he said that we should investigate 'who am I?' he did not mean that we should mentally ask ourself this question, but that we should keenly scrutinise our basic consciousness 'I am' in order to know exactly what it is. Therefore if we choose to use this term 'self-enquiry' in English, we should understand that it does not literally mean 'self-questioning' but only 'self-investigation' or 'self-scrutiny'.

Because some people had misunderstood his teaching that we should investigate 'who am I?' or 'from where do I rise?', taking it to mean that we should ask ourself such questions, and were accordingly spending their time in meditation repeatedly asking themself these questions, towards the end of his bodily lifetime, when he composed the brief poem *Ēkātma Pañcakam*, Sri Ramana wrote in verse 2:

> Declare a drunkard who says, 'Who am I? What place am I?', as equal to a person who himself asks himself 'who am I?' [or] 'what is the place in which I am?' even though oneself is [always] as oneself [that is, though we are in fact always nothing other than our own real self or essential being, which clearly knows itself as 'I am'].

Though Sri Ramana sometimes described the practice of self-investigation in terms of questions such as 'who am I?' or 'from what source do I rise?', he did so only to illustrate how we should divert our attention away from all thoughts towards our own essential self-conscious being, which is what we always truly are, and which is the source from which we seemingly rise as our mind or individual sense of 'I'. That is, when he said that we should investigate 'who am I?', he meant that we should turn our attention towards our basic consciousness 'I' in order to scrutinise it and know what it really is. He did not mean that we should allow our mind to dwell upon the actual question 'who am I?', because such a question is only a thought that is other than ourself and therefore extraneous to our essential being.

We can know our own real self with perfect clarity only by focusing our entire attention on our own essential self-conscious being to the exclusion of all thoughts. By focusing our attention thus, we will withdraw our mind from all activity, and thus it will sink deep into our clear, thought-free and ever-motionless consciousness of our own mere being.

Instead of penetrating deep within our own essential being in this manner, if we keep our attention dwelling upon thoughts such as 'who am I?' or 'what is the source from which I have risen?', we will continue to float on the surface of our mind, being perpetually agitated by thoughts that rise and subside there like waves on the surface of the ocean, and will thereby prevent ourself from gaining the true clarity of thought-free self-consciousness, which ever exists in the innermost core or depth of our being.

By comparing a person who meditates upon thoughts such as 'who am I?' or 'what is the place in which I am?', expecting thereby to gain true self-knowledge, to a drunkard who prattles such questions due to the confusion and consequent lack of clarity that result from intoxication, Sri Ramana very emphatically asserts that if we meditate thus, we are as confused about ourself as a drunkard is, and that we have entirely misunderstood the practice of self-attentive and therefore thought-free being that he intended to teach us. Asking ourself repeatedly questions such as 'who am I?' is the very antithesis of the practice of *ātma-vicāra* or self-investigation that he taught, because as he often used to say, self-investigation is not 'doing' but only 'being'.

That is, self-investigation is not any action or activity of our mind, but is only the practice of keeping our mind perpetually subsided in our real self, that is, in our own essential and ever clearly self-conscious being. This is made clear by Sri Ramana in the sixteenth paragraph of *Nāṉ Yār?*, in which he defines the true meaning of the term *ātma-vicāra* or 'self-investigation' by saying:

> […] The name '*ātma-vicāra*' [is truly applicable] only to [the practice of] always being [abiding or remaining] having put [placed, kept, seated, deposited, detained, fixed or established our] mind in *ātmā* [our own real self] […]

In both Sanskrit and Tamil the word *ātmā*, which literally means 'self', is a philosophical term that denotes our own true, essential and perfectly non-dual self-conscious being, 'I am'. Hence the state that Sri Ramana describes in this sentence as *sadākālamum maṉattai ātmāvil vaittiruppadu* is the state of just 'being', in which we keep our mind firmly fixed or established in and as *ātmā*, our own essential non-dual self-conscious being.

The compound word *sadā-kālamum* means 'always' or 'at all times', *maṉattai* is the accusative form of *maṉam*, which means 'mind', *ātmāvil* is the locative form of *ātmā* and therefore means 'in self', and *vaittiruppadu* is a compound of two words, *vaittu*, which is a verbal participle that means 'putting', 'placing', 'keeping', 'seating', 'fixing' or 'establishing', and *iruppadu*, which is a gerund formed from the verbal root *iru*, which means 'be'. When it is used alone, this gerund *iruppadu* means 'being', but when it is appended to a verbal participle to form a compound gerund, it serves as an auxiliary verbal noun denoting a continuity of whatever action or state is indicated by the verbal participle. Therefore the compound word *vaittiruppadu* can be interpreted either literally as meaning 'being having placed', or idiomatically as denoting a continuous state of 'placing', 'seating', 'fixing' or 'keeping'. However there is actually no essential difference between these two interpretations, because the state in which we keep our mind continuously placed, seated, fixed or established in *ātmā* or 'self' is not a state of activity or 'doing', but is only the state of just 'being' as we really are.

Thus in this sentence Sri Ramana clearly defines the exact meaning of the term *ātma-vicāra*, saying that it denotes only the state of just 'being' – the spiritual practice of keeping our mind firmly established in and as *ātmā*, our own real 'self' or essential self-conscious being, 'I am'. In other words, *ātma-vicāra* or the investigation 'who am I?' is only the practice of just being as we really are – that is, just being in our true and natural state, in which our mind has subsided peacefully in and as our own essential self, our thought-free and therefore absolutely actionless self-conscious being.

Thus from this extremely clear, simple and unambiguous definition of *ātma-vicāra* that Sri Ramana has given in *Nāṉ Yār?*, and also from many other compatible truths that he has expressed elsewhere in his own writings, we are left with absolutely no scope to doubt the fact that the essential practice of self-investigation does not involve even the least activity of mind, speech or body, but is simply the non-dual state of mind-free and therefore perfectly inactive self-conscious being.

Since our real self is absolutely non-dual self-conscious being, we cannot know it by doing anything but only by being as it is – that is, by just being ourself, our own perfectly thought-free self-conscious being. Therefore true self-knowledge is an absolutely thought-free, non-dual and therefore non-objective experience of clear, uncontaminated self-conscious being. Hence in verse 26 of *Upadēśa Undiyār* Sri Ramana defines the non-dual state of true self-knowledge by saying:

> Being [our real] self is indeed knowing [our real] self, because [our real] self is that which is devoid of two. This is *tanmaya-niṣṭha* [the state of being firmly established in and as *tat* or 'it', the absolute reality called *brahman*].

Since our goal is only the non-dual state of self-conscious being, the path by which we can attain that goal must likewise be nothing other than self-conscious being. If the nature of our path were essentially any different from the nature of our goal, our path could never enable us to reach our goal. That is, since our goal is a state that is infinite and therefore devoid of all otherness, division, separation or duality, the only means by which we can 'reach' or 'attain' such a goal is just to be one with it by merging in it – that is, by losing ourself, our seemingly separate finite mind, entirely in it.

In other words, we cannot be firmly established as our own real non-dual self-conscious being by doing anything or by knowing anything other than ourself. No amount of 'doing' can enable us to merge completely in the real state of just 'being'. Hence in order to know and to be our own real self, we must attend to nothing other than ourself, our own essential self-conscious being.

Attending to anything other than ourself is an action, a movement of our mind or attention away from ourself. Attending to ourself, on the other hand, is not an action or movement, but is just an actionless state of being self-conscious, as we always really are. Therefore *ātma-vicāra* or 'self-investigation' is only the practice of being self-conscious – that is, the practice of being conscious of nothing other than our own self, 'I am'. Only by this simple practice of thought-free self-consciousness or self-attentiveness can we know who or what we really are.

However, though *ātma-vicāra* or 'self-investigation' is truly not any form of mental activity, such as asking ourself 'who am I?' or any other such question, but is only the practice of abiding motionlessly in our perfectly thought-free self-conscious being, in some English books we occasionally find statements attributed to Sri Ramana that are so worded that they could make it appear as if he sometimes advised people to practise self-investigation by asking themself questions such as 'who am I?'. In order to understand why such potentially confusing wordings appear in some of the books in which the oral teachings of Sri Ramana have been recorded in English, we have to consider several facts.

Firstly, whenever Sri Ramana was asked any question regarding spiritual philosophy or practice, he usually replied in Tamil, or occasionally in Telugu or Malayalam. Though he understood and could speak English quite fluently, when discussing spiritual philosophy or practice he seldom spoke in English, except occasionally when making a simple statement. Even when he was asked questions in English, he usually replied in Tamil, and each of his replies would immediately be translated into English by any person present who knew both languages. If what he said in Tamil was seriously mistranslated, he would occasionally correct the translation, but in most cases he would not interfere with the interpreter's task.

However, though he seldom expressed his teachings in English, many of the books in which his oral teachings were recorded during his bodily lifetime were written originally in English. Unfortunately, therefore, from such records we cannot know for certain exactly what words he used in Tamil on each particular occasion. However, from his own original Tamil writings, and from the record of many of his oral teachings that Sri Muruganar preserved for us in *Guru Vācaka Kōvai*, we do know what Tamil words he used frequently to express his teachings.

Therefore, when we read the books in which his teachings are recorded in English, we have to try to infer what words he may actually have used in Tamil. For example, when we read such books and find in them statements attributed to him such as 'ask yourself "who am I?"' or 'question yourself "who am I?"', in order to understand the correct sense in which he used whatever Tamil verb has been translated as 'ask' or 'question', we have to try to infer what that verb might have been.

The Tamil verb that is used most commonly in situations in which we would use the verbs 'ask' or 'question' in English is *kēḷ*. Besides meaning to ask, question or enquire, *kēḷ* also means to hear, listen to, investigate, learn or come to know, so if this were the verb that Sri Ramana used on any of the occasions in which the English books have recorded him saying 'ask yourself "who am I?"' or 'question yourself "who am I?"', the inner meaning that he implied by these words would have been 'enquire "who am I?"', 'investigate "who am I?"' or 'find out "who am I?"'.

Another Tamil verb that is often used in the sense of 'question' or 'enquire', and that Sri Ramana sometimes used when describing the practice of *ātma-vicāra* or self-investigation, is *vinavu*. Besides meaning to question or enquire, *vinavu* also means to investigate, examine, listen to, pay attention to, bear in mind or think of.

One example of the use that Sri Ramana made of this verb *vinavutal* is in verse 16 of *Upadēśa Tanippākkaḷ*, which we discussed in chapter six. The words in this verse that I translated as '[…] by subtle investigation [or minute examination], which is [the practice of] constantly scrutinising yourself […]' are *endrum tannai vinavum usāvāl*. The word *endrum* is an adverb meaning always, constantly or at all times, *tannai* is the accusative form of the pronoun *tān*, which means self, oneself, ourself, yourself and so on, and *usāvāl* is the instrumental form of the noun *usā*, which means subtle, close or minute investigation or examination. Together with its adverb *endrum* and its object *tannai*, the verb *vinavum* acts as a relative clause, which describes the nature of the *usā* or 'subtle investigation' and which means 'which is [the practice of] constantly scrutinising self'.

Being a relative participle form of *vinavu*, in this context *vinavum* means 'which is investigating', 'which is scrutinising' or 'which is paying attention to'. If taken at face value, *vinavum* could also be translated here as 'which is questioning', thereby implying that the *usā* or 'subtle investigation' that Sri Ramana refers to here is merely the practice of constantly questioning ourself. However, since the central idea in the first half of this verse is that 'in waking the state of sleep will result by subtle investigation', this 'subtle investigation' must be a practice that is much deeper than the mere mental act of questioning oneself, and hence we cannot do justice to the truth that Sri Ramana expresses in this verse unless we interpret *tannai vinavum* to mean 'which is investigating ourself' rather than 'which is questioning ourself'.

Like *kēḷ* and *vinavu*, most other Tamil verbs that could be translated as 'ask', 'question' or 'enquire' could also be translated as 'investigate', 'examine', 'scrutinise' or 'attend to'. Therefore just because in some English books we occasionally find statements attributed to Sri Ramana such as 'ask yourself "who am I?"' or 'question yourself "who am I?"', we should not conclude from these words that he meant that we should literally ask ourself 'who am I?', or that questioning ourself thus is the actual practice of *ātma-vicāra* or self-investigation.

In certain places where it has been recorded that Sri Ramana said 'ask yourself "who am I?"' or 'question yourself "who am I?"', the Tamil verb that he used may have been *vicāri*, which is the verbal form of the noun *vicāra*, because in such places he appears to be referring more or less directly to the following passage from the sixth paragraph of *Nāṉ Yār?*:

> […] If other thoughts rise, without trying to complete them [we] must

> investigate to whom they have occurred. However many thoughts rise, what [does it matter]? As soon as each thought appears, if [we] vigilantly investigate to whom it has occurred, 'to me' will be clear [that is, we will be clearly reminded of ourself, to whom each thought occurs]. If [we thus] investigate 'who am I?' [that is, if we turn our attention back towards ourself and keep it fixed firmly, keenly and vigilantly upon our own essential self-conscious being in order to discover what this 'me' really is], [our] mind will return to its birthplace [the innermost core of our being, which is the source from which it arose]; [and since we thereby refrain from attending to it] the thought which had risen will also subside. When [we] practise and practise in this manner, to [our] mind the power to stand firmly established in its birthplace will increase. […]

In this passage the Tamil verb that I have translated as 'investigate' is *vicāri*, which occurs once in the form *vicārikka vēṇḍum*, which means 'it is necessary to investigate' or '[we] must investigate', and twice in the conditional form *vicārittāl*, which means 'if [we] investigate'.

As the Tamil form of the Sanskrit verb *vicar*, the principle meaning of *vicāri* is to investigate, examine, scrutinise, ascertain, consider or ponder, but in Tamil it is also used in the secondary sense of 'enquire' in contexts such as enquiring about a person's welfare. This secondary sense in Tamil does give some slight scope for us to interpret the meaning of *vicāri* in this context as 'enquire', 'ask' or 'question', but even if we choose to interpret it in this rather far-fetched manner, we should understand that Sri Ramana does not mean that we should literally ask or question ourself 'who am I?', but only that we should figuratively ask or question ourself thus.

That is, if any words used by Sri Ramana can be interpreted to mean that we should ask ourself any question such as 'who am I?', we should understand that the true inner meaning of those words is that we should figuratively ask ourself 'who am I?' in the sense that we should keenly scrutinise ourself in order to know clearly through our own immediate non-dual experience what the real nature of our essential self-consciousness 'I am' actually is. Since the only real answer to this question 'who am I?' is the absolutely non-dual and therefore perfectly clear experience of our own true thought-free self-conscious being, the only means by which we can effectively 'ask' or 'question' ourself 'who am I?' – that is, the only means by which we can 'enquire' in such a manner that we will thereby actually ascertain who or what we really are – is to withdraw our attention entirely from all thoughts or objects and to focus it keenly and exclusively upon our own essential non-dual self-consciousness, 'I am'.

In his teachings Sri Ramana frequently employed ordinary words in a figurative sense, because the absolute reality about which he was speaking or writing is non-objective and non-dual, and hence it is beyond the range of thoughts and words. Since the one undivided and infinite reality can never be known objectively by our mind, but can only be experienced subjectively by and as our own essential non-dual self-consciousness, no words can describe it adequately, and hence its true nature can often be expressed more clearly by a metaphorical or figurative use of simple words rather than by a literal use of the more abstract technical terms of scholastic philosophy.

Since the true nature of the one absolute reality cannot be known by our mind or described by any words (which are merely tools created by our mind to express its knowledge or experience of objective phenomena), the only means by which we can merge in and as that non-dual and otherless absolute reality is likewise beyond the range of thoughts and words. Hence Sri Ramana often used simple words figuratively not only when he was expressing the nature of the one absolute reality, but also when he was expressing the means by which we can attain our true and natural state of indivisible oneness with that infinite reality.

Therefore when we read the spiritual teachings of Sri Ramana, we should not always take at face value the meaning of each word or combination of words that he uses, but should understand the inner meaning that he intends to convey by such words. This is not to say that his teachings are difficult to understand, or that they contain any hidden meanings. He did in fact express his teachings in an extremely open, clear and simple manner, and hence they are very easy to understand. However in order to understand them correctly we must attune our mind and heart to the truth that he was expressing and to the manner in which he expressed it.

Though one of the great strengths of his teachings – one of the reasons why they are so powerful and compelling – is the simplicity and clarity with which he expressed even the most subtle and profound truths, the very simplicity of his teachings can at times be deceptive. Just because he used very simple words, we should not overlook the fact that what he was expressing through those simple words was an extremely subtle truth – a truth that can be understood perfectly only by an equally subtle clarity of mind and heart.

The extremely subtle inner clarity that we require in order to be able to comprehend perfectly the truth of all that Sri Ramana expressed in his teachings will arise in us only when our mind has been purified or cleansed of all the desires and attachments that are now clouding it. However, though we may not now possess such perfectly unclouded inner clarity, to whatever extent our mind is purified we will be able to comprehend his teachings, and if we sincerely try to put into practice whatever we have been able to understand, our mind will gradually but surely be further purified and clarified.

Though we cannot expect to be able to understand his teachings perfectly from the outset, if we sincerely wish to understand them we should not only try to put our present imperfect understanding into practice, but should also continue to study his teachings carefully and repeatedly, because as our practice of self-investigation and self-surrender progresses and develops, we will be able to understand what we study with increasing clarity. This is why it is said that *śravaṇa*, *manana* and *nididhyāsana* – study, reflection and practice – should continue in the life of a spiritual aspirant until the final goal of true non-dual self-knowledge is attained.

In order to understand Sri Ramana's teachings as clearly and as perfectly as we can, we should not attempt narrowly to understand any of his words, writings or sayings in isolation, but should attempt to understand each of them comprehensively in the light of all his other teachings. Unless we understand all his teachings comprehensively, we will not be able to understand each individual teaching in its correct perspective. Only if we cultivate a truly comprehensive understanding of his teachings, will we be able to recognise and grasp the real inner meaning of the simple words that he uses figuratively, and will we thereby avoid the error of interpreting too literally any of his figurative expressions of the truth.

Therefore if we read in any book that Sri Ramana said, 'Ask yourself the question "who am I?"', or any similar statement, in order to understand what meaning he really intended to convey by such words, we should consider them carefully in the light of all his other teachings, particularly the teachings that he expressed in his own writings. When doing so, we should first consider whether or not the literal meaning of such a statement is entirely consistent with the fundamental principles of his teachings, because we should accept that literal meaning at face value only if it is clearly consistent with those principles. If it is not consistent, then we should consider whether the real meaning of that statement might perhaps be not merely its apparent literal meaning but only some other deeper and more figurative meaning.

If any statement attributed to Sri Ramana appears to be in any way inconsistent with the central principles of his teachings, there may be several plausible explanations for this. Firstly, it could be either an inaccurate recording or an inaccurate translation of what he actually said. Secondly, it could be one of the many instances in which he expressed his teachings in a modified or diluted manner in order to suit the limited understanding or maturity of mind of a particular questioner. Or thirdly, if it is an accurate recording of his actual words, and if it is not clearly an instance in which he deliberately diluted his expression of the truth to suit the individual needs of the concerned questioner, it could be a case in which the real meaning of his words is figurative rather than literal.

Though Sri Ramana did often express the truth in a diluted manner to suit the actual needs of whoever he was talking to, he usually did so only with regard to more general aspects of spiritual philosophy or practice, but not with regard to the actual practice of self-investigation, which is the very core of his teachings. Whenever he advised or prompted anyone to practise self-investigation, he expressed very clearly what that practice actually is. Therefore if he ever said any words that literally mean 'ask yourself "who am I?"' or 'question yourself "who am I?"', he was certainly not expressing the practice of self-investigation in a diluted manner but only in a figurative manner.

Just as he often figuratively described our real and essential self, which is formless, infinite, undivided and non-dual spirit or consciousness – consciousness that knows nothing other than itself, because there is nothing that is truly other than itself – as an *iḍam*, *sthana* or 'place', or sometimes more specifically as the 'birthplace' or 'rising-place' of our mind, our false finite object-knowing consciousness, and just as he also often figuratively described it as a 'light', so he might also have figuratively described the thought-free, actionless and non-dual practice of self-investigation as being a state of 'questioning ourself', 'enquiring [into or about] ourself' or simply 'asking who am I?'. However, just because he used words that literally mean 'place' or 'light' to denote our real self, we should not misinterpret his figurative use of such words as implying that our essential self is actually a place confined within the objective dimensions of space and time, or that it is actually a light that we can see objectively by either our physical eyes or our mind. Likewise, just because he occasionally used words that could be taken literally to mean 'question yourself', 'enquire [into or about] yourself' or 'ask yourself who am I?', we should not misinterpret his figurative use of such words as implying that the ultimate spiritual practice known as self-investigation is merely a mental act of asking ourself questions such as 'who am I?'.

In spiritual philosophy, an important distinction often has to be made between *vācyārtha*, the literal meaning of a word or group of words, and *lakṣyārtha*, its intended meaning. Whereas *vācyārtha*, the 'spoken meaning' or 'stated meaning', is merely the meaning that is superficially expressed by a particular word or group of words, *lakṣyārtha*, the 'indicated meaning' or 'target meaning', is the implied meaning that is really denoted by it – the true inner meaning that it is actually intended to convey.

In many contexts in which Sri Ramana talks of the question 'who am I?', the *vācyārtha* or meaning superficially suggested by these words is the verbalised thought 'who am I?', whereas the *lakṣyārtha* or true inner meaning that he actually intended these words to convey is the state in which we look keenly within ourself to see who or what this 'I' really is. Therefore if he says any words that superficially appear to mean that we should ask ourself the question 'who am I?', we should understand that the *lakṣyārtha* of such words is that we should focus our entire attention upon our consciousness 'I am' in order to know what exactly it is.

When we see his words translated as 'who am I?', in most cases the actual words that he used in Tamil were '*nāṉ yār?*' or '*nāṉ ār?*', which literally mean 'I [am] who?'. By placing *nāṉ* before *yār* or *ār*, that is, 'I' before 'who', he gave prime importance to it, thereby emphasising the fact that it alone is our *lakṣya* – our real target or aim.

In these words, '*nāṉ yār?*' or 'I [am] who?', the *vācyārtha* or superficial meaning of 'I' is our mind or ego, but its *lakṣyārtha* is our real self, our true adjunct-free self-conscious being, 'I am', which is the sole reality underlying this illusory apparition that we call our mind or ego. Likewise, the *vācyārtha* of 'who' is merely a question that we frame in our mind as a thought, but its *lakṣyārtha* is the keenly scrutinising attention that seeks to experience this 'I' as it really is – that is, to experience thought-free, unadulterated and therefore absolute clarity of true self-consciousness.

We cannot ascertain who or what we really are by merely asking ourself the verbalised question 'who am I?', but only by keenly attending to ourself. If Sri Ramana were to say to us, 'Investigate what is written in this book', we would not imagine that we could discover what is written in it by merely asking ourself the question 'what is written in this book?'. In order to know what is written in it, we must open it and actually read what is written inside. Similarly, when he says to us, 'Investigate "who am I?"', we should not imagine that he means that we can truly know who we are by merely asking ourself the question 'who am I?'. In order to know who or what we really are, we must actually look within ourself to see what this 'I' – our essential self-consciousness – really is.

In order to experience ourself as we really are, we must withdraw our attention from everything other than our own real self – our essential self-conscious being, 'I am'. Since the verbalised question 'who am I?' is a thought that can rise only after our mind has risen and is active, it is experienced by us as something other than ourself, and hence we cannot know who we really are so long as we allow our mind to continue dwelling upon it.

Therefore though we can use this verbalised question 'who am I?' to divert our attention away from all other thoughts towards our own essential self-consciousness 'I am', we should not continuously attend to it. As soon as we have used it effectively to divert our attention away from all other thoughts towards this consciousness that we experience as 'I', we should forget this question and attend keenly and exclusively to its target or *lakṣya*, which is 'I' – our own essential thought-free self-conscious being.

This letting go of the verbalised question 'who am I?' is a secondary but nevertheless valid meaning of the second half of the first sentence of the sixth paragraph of *Nāṉ Yār?*, in which Sri Ramana says:

> Only by [means of] the investigation 'who am I?' will [our] mind subside [or cease to be]; the thought 'who am I?', having destroyed all other thoughts, will itself in the end be destroyed like a corpse-burning stick [that is, like a stick that is used to stir a funeral pyre to ensure that the corpse is burnt entirely] […]

The primary meaning of the statement '[…] the thought "who am I?", having destroyed all other thoughts, will itself in the end be destroyed […]' is that which is implied when we understand the term 'the thought "who am I?"' to be a figurative description of the effort that our mind makes to investigate 'who am I?' – that is, the effort that it makes to turn its attention away from all other thoughts towards itself. This effort to investigate 'who am I?' is the *lakṣyārtha* or intended inner meaning of this term 'the thought "who am I?"'.

Since our mind has a strong and deeply engrained liking to attend to thoughts, which appear to be other than ourself, if we wish to turn our attention towards ourself in order to know 'who am I?', we have to make an effort to draw our attention back from all the thoughts that are now distracting it away from ourself. Since this effort to investigate 'who am I?' is made by our mind, Sri Ramana describes it figuratively as 'the thought "who am I?"'.

Since other thoughts can survive only when we attend to them, and since this effort to investigate 'who am I?' draws our attention away from all other thoughts, Sri Ramana says that this effort will destroy them all. Though our mind commences the practice of self-investigation by making this effort to attend to itself, as a result of this effort it will subside, because it can rise and remain active only by attending to thoughts. Therefore, since our mind will begin to subside as soon as it makes this effort to attend to itself, and since by persisting in this effort it will eventually subside entirely in the perfect clarity of thought-free self-consciousness, the effort that it makes to attend to itself will subside along with it. This is the real meaning that Sri Ramana intended to convey when he said, '[…] the thought "who am I?", having destroyed all other thoughts, will itself in the end be destroyed like a corpse-burning stick'.

Though this is the primary meaning of this statement, a secondary meaning of it is that which is implied when we understand the term 'the thought "who am I?"' to mean literally the verbalised thought 'who am I?'. This verbalised thought 'who am I?' is the *vācyārtha* or superficial meaning of this term 'the thought "who am I?"'. If we interpret this statement according to this more superficial meaning, we should understand that the verbalised thought 'who am I?' is only an aid that helps to remind us to direct our attention towards ourself, thereby drawing it back from all the thoughts that are now distracting it away from ourself.

The verbalised thought 'who am I?' will destroy all other thoughts only when we allow it to divert our attention away from those thoughts towards ourself, and it will itself be destroyed only when we allow it to divert our attention away from itself towards its actual aim or target, which is our essential self-conscious being, 'I am'. Just as a 'corpse-burning stick' is itself destroyed by the same fire that it stirs in order to destroy the corpse completely, so the verbalised thought 'who am I?', if used correctly, will itself be destroyed by the same fire of clear non-dual self-consciousness that it arouses and that destroys each and every other thought.

That is, if we use the verbalised thought 'who am I?' to divert our attention away from other thoughts towards ourself, it will thereby enkindle within us a fresh clarity of self-consciousness. This clarity of non-dual self-consciousness is the fire of true knowledge that alone can destroy not only each individual thought that arises, but also our mind, which is our first thought and the root of all our other thoughts. Though this clarity of thought-free self-consciousness will be aroused whenever we use the verbalised thought 'who am I?' to draw our attention back towards ourself, if we then keep our attention fixed firmly upon ourself, the verbalised thought 'who am I?' will thereby subside automatically along with all other thoughts.

Hence as a verbalised thought the question 'who am I?' can be of use to us only when other thoughts have arisen. As soon as it has helped us to divert our attention away from other thoughts towards ourself, this verbalised thought 'who am I?' has served its purpose. That is, by asking ourself questions such as 'who is thinking this thought?', 'who knows this thought?' or 'who am I?', we can remind ourself of the 'I' that is thinking, and thus we can turn our attention away from any other thought towards ourself. This turning of our attention towards ourself is the only benefit to be gained by asking such questions.

If we choose to use any thought such as the question 'who am I?' as a means to turn our attention away from other thoughts towards ourself, that selfward-directing thought will act like a portal or doorway through which we can enter the state of self-attentiveness or clear self-consciousness, which is our natural state of mind-free being that Sri Ramana calls *ātma-vicāra* or self-investigation. No thought, word, sentence or question can be the actual state of true non-dual self-consciousness, because all thoughts and words are just objective forms of knowledge, and hence they can exist only in the state of duality. As Sri Ramana says in verse 25 of *Upadēśa Taṉippākkaḷ*:

> Questions and answers [can occur] only in the language of this *dvaita* [duality]; in [the true state of] *advaita* [non-duality] they do not exist.

Just as a doorway is a means by which we can enter our house, but is not our house itself, so a thought such as 'who am I?' may be a means by which we can enter our own natural state of clear non-dual self-consciousness, but it is not our self-consciousness itself. If we wish to enter our house, we should not just stand at the doorway but should pass through it and leave it behind us. Similarly, if we wish to enter our real state of non-dual self-consciousness, we should not cling to any thought such as 'who am I?' but should pass through such thoughts and leave them behind us.

If we continuously dwell upon the thought 'who am I?', instead of passing through and beyond it, it will not enable us to enter into our natural state of thought-free self-conscious being. Therefore having turned our attention towards ourself by asking ourself 'who am I?', we should calmly subside without even the slightest thought into the innermost depth of ourself – that is, into the absolute isolation of our own true non-dual self-conscious being.

Though we may use a thought such as 'who am I?' as a means to turn our attention towards ourself and thereby to subside deep into our real thought-free self-conscious being, we should not imagine that the thought 'who am I?' is the actual practice of *ātma-vicāra* or self-investigation. The real practice of *ātma-vicāra* is only the state in which we have left behind all thoughts, including the thought 'who am I?', and have thereby sunk deep into our own essential and perfectly clear self-conscious being.

Therefore, having once asked ourself 'who am I?', we need not ask this same question again. In fact we should not ask it again, because once we have turned our attention successfully towards ourself, the verbalised thought 'who am I?' would only distract us away from our vigilantly attentive state of clear thought-free self-consciousness, just as any other thought would.

This is the reason why, whenever anyone asked Sri Ramana whether we should repeat the question 'who am I?' like a *mantra*, he replied emphatically that it is not a *mantra* and should not be repeated as such, and he explained that our sole aim while practising *ātma-vicāra* should be to focus our entire mind or power of attention in its source, which is our own self-conscious being. In the same context, he also sometimes stated explicitly that if the *vicāra* or investigation 'who am I?' were merely a mental act of questioning, it would be of no real benefit to us.

However, though he stated explicitly that we should not repeat the question 'who am I?' as if it were a *mantra*, and that the practice of *ātma-vicāra* is not merely a mental act of asking ourself this question, Sri Ramana did not actually say that we should never ask ourself this question, or that asking it is not of some value as an aid to our actual practice of *ātma-vicāra*. What he warned us to avoid was firstly the futile practice of misusing this question by repeating it in a parrot-like manner, and secondly the mistaken notion that *ātma-vicāra* is merely a mental practice of asking ourself this question either repeatedly or even occasionally.

If we carefully read all the teachings of Sri Ramana, which are expressed extremely clearly both in his original Tamil writings and in *Guru Vācaka Kōvai*, and somewhat less clearly in the various books in which they were recorded in English, we should be able to understand very clearly what the actual practice of *ātma-vicāra* or self-investigation is and what it is not. Though many passages in the various English books may appear to be unclear or confusing, if we study such books with discrimination in the light of his original Tamil writings and *Guru Vācaka Kōvai*, we should be able to sift and pick out all the grains of genuine wisdom from the chaff of imperfectly or inadequately recorded ideas.

Regarding the practice of *ātma-vicāra* or self-investigation, two of the fundamental truths that we should be able to understand by reading the various available books are as follows: Firstly, *ātma-vicāra* is not a mental practice of repeatedly asking ourself any question such as 'who am I?'. And secondly, asking ourself any such question even once is not actually an essential part of the practice of *ātma-vicāra*.

When we first try to practise self-attentiveness, we may find that asking ourself such questions occasionally is helpful as a means to divert our attention away from other thoughts towards ourself, but after we have gained even a little experience in this simple practice of self-attentiveness, we will find that it is easy for us to turn our attention towards our natural and clearly self-evident consciousness 'I am' without having to think 'who am I?' or any other such thought.

Whether or not we choose to use any question such as 'who am I?' as an aid in our effort to turn our attention towards ourself is ultimately irrelevant, because all that is actually necessary is that we focus our attention keenly and exclusively upon ourself – that is, upon our essential self-conscious being, 'I am'. The actual practice of *ātma-vicāra* or self-investigation is only this intense focusing of our entire attention upon ourself. This practice of intense and clear self-attentiveness or self-consciousness is not a thought or an action of any kind whatsoever, but is only the absolutely silent and peaceful state of just being as we really are.

Besides using the Sanskrit word *vicāra*, Sri Ramana used many other Tamil and Sanskrit words to describe the practice of self-investigation. One word that he frequently used both in his original writings such as *Uḷḷadu Nāṟpadu* and in his oral teachings was the Tamil verb *nāḍu*, which can mean seeking, pursuing, examining, investigating, knowing, thinking or desiring, but which with reference to ourself clearly does not mean literally either seeking or pursuing, but only examining, investigating or knowing.

He also often used the word *nattam*, which is a noun derived from this verb *nāḍu*, and which has various closely related meanings such as 'investigation', 'examination', 'scrutiny', 'sight', 'look', 'aim', 'intention', 'pursuit' or 'quest'. In the sense of 'scrutiny', 'look' or 'sight', *nāṭṭam* means the state of 'looking', 'seeing' or 'watching', and hence it can also be translated as 'inspection', 'observation' or 'attention'. Thus it is a word that Sri Ramana used in Tamil to convey the same sense as the English word 'attention'.

Since the term *ātma-vicāra* is a technical term of Sanskrit origin, in conversation Sri Ramana often used instead the more colloquial Tamil term *taṉṉāṭṭam*, which is a compound of two words, *taṉ*, which means 'self', and *nāṭṭam*, which in this context means 'scrutiny', 'investigation', 'examination', 'inspection', 'observation' or 'attention'. In English books that record or discuss his teachings, this term *taṉṉāṭṭam* is usually translated as self-attention, self-investigation or self-enquiry, but is also sometimes translated as 'seeking the self' or 'quest for the self'.

Though the verb *nāḍu* can mean to seek, search for or pursue, and though the noun *nāṭṭam* can correspondingly mean a quest or pursuit, when Sri Ramana uses these words in the context of self-investigation he does not mean that we should literally seek, search for, go in quest of or pursue our own self as if it were something distant or unknown to us, but that we should simply investigate, inspect, examine or scrutinise ourself – that is, that we should attend keenly to our own essential self-conscious being, 'I am', which we always experience clearly, but which we now mistake to be our body-bound mind or ego, our false finite object-knowing consciousness that feels 'I am this body'.

Another verb that Sri Ramana used in the same sense as *nāḍu* is *tēḍu*, which literally means to seek, search for, trace, pursue or enquire into. However, just because he used words that literally mean to 'seek' or 'search for', we should not imagine that the 'self' he asks us to 'seek' is anything other than ourself – anything other than that which we already and always experience as 'I'.

The practice of *ātma-vicāra*, *taṉṉāṭṭam* or self-investigation is not a practice of one 'I' seeking some other 'I', but is simply the practice of our one and only 'I' knowing and being itself. In other words, it is simply the absolutely non-dual practice of we ourself knowing and being ourself.

Since we are in truth ever self-conscious, in order to know ourself as we really are we do not need literally to 'seek' ourself but just to be ourself – that is, just to be as we really are, which is thought-free non-dual self-conscious being. Therefore the practice that Sri Ramana sometimes described figuratively as 'seeking' ourself is simply the practice of just consciously being ourself.

As we discussed earlier, Sri Ramana often used simple words in a figurative sense, and his use of the verb *tēḍu* is a clear example of this.

Therefore whenever he uses this verb *tēḍu* in the context of self-investigation we should understand that he is not using it literally to mean that we should seek some object that we do not already know, but is only using it figuratively to mean that we should 'seek' the perfect clarity of true non-dual self-knowledge by keenly scrutinising our own ever self-conscious essence, 'I am'.

Other words that he used to describe this extremely simple practice of self-investigation include the Tamil nouns *ārāycci* and *usā*, which both mean a close and subtle investigation or scrutiny, their verbal forms *ārāy* and *usāvu*, which mean investigating, examining or scrutinising keenly, the Tamil term *summā iruppadu*, which means 'just being', the Sanskrit term *ātma-niṣṭha*, which means self-abidance or being firmly established as our own real self, *ātma-cintana*, which means self-contemplation or 'thinking of self', *svarūpa-dhyāna*, which means self-meditation or self-attentiveness, *svarūpa-smaraṇa*, which means self-remembrance, *ahamukham*, which means facing 'I', looking towards 'I' or attending to 'I', and *ātmānusandhāna*, which in Sanskrit means self-investigation or close inspection of ourself, and which in Tamil is also used in the sense of self-contemplation. These and other words that he used all denote the same simple practice of focusing our entire attention upon ourself, that is, upon our essential self-conscious being, our fundamental consciousness 'I am', in order to know who or what we really are.

The practice of *ātma-vicāra* or self-investigation is therefore just a calm and peaceful focusing of our entire attention upon the innermost core of our being, and hence it is the same practice that in other mystical traditions is known as contemplation or recollection – recollection, that is, not so much in the sense of remembering, as in the sense of re-collecting or gathering back our scattered attention from all other things by withdrawing it into its natural centre and source, which is our own innermost being – our true and essential self-conscious being, 'I am'.

Whereas attending to anything other than ourself is an activity, a movement or directing of our attention away from ourself towards something else, attending to ourself is not an activity or movement, but is a motionless retention of our attention within ourself. Since we ourself are consciousness or attention, keeping our attention centred upon ourself is allowing it to rest in its natural abode. Self-attention is thus a state of just being, and not doing anything. It is consequently a state of perfect repose, serenity, stillness, calm and peace, and as such one of supreme and unqualified happiness.

Because the practice of self-investigation is thus a state of just being, a state in which our attention does not do anything but simply remains as it really is – as the perfect clarity of our natural non-dual self-consciousness – rather than describing self-investigation as 'self-attention' we could more accurately describe it as 'self-attentiveness'. That is, it is truly not a state of actively attending or 'paying' attention to ourself, but is instead a state of just being passively attentive or conscious of our own essential being.

Since we are in reality nothing other than absolutely and eternally clear self-conscious being, when we practise this art of just being self-attentive or self-conscious, we are merely practising being ourself – being our real self, being what we really are, or as Sri Ramana often used to describe it, simply being as we are.

Now let us consider the path of self-surrender. In this context what exactly does the word 'surrender' mean, what is the self that we are to surrender, and how can we surrender it?

In a spiritual context, the word 'surrender' means yielding, letting go, relinquishing everything, giving up all forms of attachment, renouncing all our personal desires, abandoning our own individual will, resigning ourself to the will of God, and submitting ourself entirely to him. Since the root of all our desires and attachments is our finite self – our sense of being a separate individual person – we can surrender all our desires and attachments completely and effectively only by surrendering this finite self. We cannot truly let go of everything that we consider to be 'mine' until we let go of everything that we consider to be 'I'.

The self that we are to surrender is therefore our false finite self, our mind or ego. Since this individual self is a mere illusion, which arises due to our imagining ourself to be something that we are not, we can surrender it only by knowing our true self as it really is. If we clearly know what we really are, we will be unable to imagine ourself to be anything else. Therefore, as soon as we know our true self, we will automatically give up or surrender all the false notions that we now have about ourself. We can therefore truly surrender our false imaginary self only by knowing our real self.

The state of surrender is the state in which we do not attach ourself to anything or identify ourself with anything. Of all our attachments, the most fundamental is our attachment to our body, because we mistake it to be ourself. Our mind or separate individual consciousness can rise only by identifying a particular body as 'I', so all our experience of duality or multiplicity is rooted in our identification of ourself with a body. Without first attaching ourself to a body, we cannot attach ourself to anything else. Therefore, in order to give up all attachment, we must give up our attachment to our body.

We are attached to our body because we mistake it to be ourself, and we mistake it to be ourself only because we do not have a clear knowledge of what we really are. If we knew what we really are, we could not mistake ourself to be what we are not. Conversely, until we know what we really are, we will be unable to free ourself from all the mistaken notions that we now have about ourself. Hence, so long as we continue to lack a clear and correct knowledge of ourself, we will continue to mistake ourself to be what we are not.

Therefore we cannot surrender ourself entirely without first knowing our real self, that is, without actually experiencing our real nature or essential being. In other words, in order to surrender our false individual self, we must focus our entire attention upon our essential being in order to know what we really are. Thus self-investigation is the only effective means by which we can surrender ourself entirely.

Therefore in the thirteenth paragraph of *Nāṉ Yār?* Sri Ramana defines true self-surrender by saying:

> Being completely absorbed in *ātma-niṣṭha* [self-abidance, the state of just being as we really are], giving not even the slightest room to the rising of any thought other than *ātma-cintana* [the thought of our own real self], is giving ourself to God. […]

The term *ātma-cintana* literally means 'self-thought' or 'thought of ourself', but could perhaps be better translated as 'self-contemplation', because in this context the word *cintana* or 'thought' does not actually mean 'thought' in the sense of a mental activity. Our mind is active only when we attend to anything other than ourself, and all its activity will therefore cease when we try to 'think' only of ourself. Thus 'self-thought' or 'self-contemplation' is not actually an act of thinking, but is only a perfectly inactive state of thought-free self-attentiveness or self-consciousness.

That is, when we try to 'think' of ourself, our attention will be withdrawn from all other thoughts and will remain motionlessly focused on ourself. Thus by 'thinking' of ourself exclusively we will avoid giving room to the rising of any other thought, and thereby we will remain calmly absorbed in self-abidance, the thought-free state of just being our own real self. Since in this state of clear self-attentiveness or firm self-abidance we do not rise as the separate thinking consciousness that we call our 'mind' or 'individual self', this is the state of complete self-surrender.

All action or 'doing', including our basic action of thinking or knowing thoughts, is a result of our failure to surrender our false individual self. We feel that we are thinking and doing other things only because we imagine ourself to be this thinking mind and this doing body.

That is, so long as we identify ourself with our body, speech or mind, we will feel that the actions of these instruments are being done by us. Everything that we experience ourself doing, 'I am walking', 'I am talking', 'I am seeing', 'I am hearing', 'I am thinking', 'I am feeling', 'I am knowing' and so on, is an effect of our identification of ourself with our body, speech, senses, emotions and mind.

All our actions and all our dualistic knowledge arise only because we identify ourself with these instruments of action and knowledge – this entire body-mind complex. Therefore, so long as we feel that we are doing anything or knowing anything other than our own essential self-conscious being, 'I am', we have not surrendered our attachment to this body-mind complex, or to our individual self, which identifies this complex as 'I'.

Since complete and perfect surrender is the state in which we have entirely renounced our individual self, and thus all connection with its body and mind, it is a state devoid of any action and any knowledge of duality. That which feels 'I am doing' or 'I am knowing' is not our real self, but only our false individual self. The nature of our real self is just to be, and not to do or know anything other than itself. Therefore, if we have truly surrendered our finite individual self, we will remain as mere being, and will not feel that we are doing anything or knowing anything other than our own self-conscious being. The state of true surrender is therefore a state of just being, and not a state of doing anything.

Since perfect surrender is only the state of just being, the means to attain that state must also be just being. The practice of self-surrender is therefore the cultivation of the skill just to be, and not to be this or that. How can we cultivate this skill? According to the principles upon which the path of self-surrender is based, we can cultivate it by surrendering our individual will to the will of God, that is, by giving up all our own personal desires, because our desires are the power that impels us to do actions, and that thereby prevents us from just being.

By cultivating the attitude 'Thy will be done; not my will, but only thine', we will be able gradually to reduce the strength of our own individual will – our likes and dislikes, our desires, attachments and aversions – and thus we will begin to deprive our mind of the force or power that impels it to be active. The more we are able to reduce the power of our individual will, the more our mind will subside, and the closer we will come to the state of just being.

In order for us to surrender ourself completely, we must give up all our desires. But is it possible for us to remain completely free of desire? Is it not natural for us to be always driven by some form of desire? Can we not surrender ourself to God simply by giving up all our selfish desires, and replacing them with unselfish desires?

We can answer this last question only by understanding what we mean by an unselfish desire. Some people believe that if they are concerned only for the welfare of others, and that if they sacrifice all their own personal comforts and conveniences and dedicate all their time and money to helping other people, they are thereby acting unselfishly and without any personal desire. However, even if we are able to act in such an 'unselfish' manner, which few if any of us are actually able to do, what actually impels us to do so?

If we are perfectly honest with ourself, we will have to admit that we act 'unselfishly' for our own satisfaction. We feel good in ourself when we act 'unselfishly', and therefore acting in this way makes us feel happy. Hence our desire to be happy is what ultimately and truly motivates us to act 'unselfishly'. There is therefore truly no such thing as an absolutely 'unselfish' desire, because underlying even the most unselfish desire is our fundamental desire to be happy.

We all desire to be happy. However, because we each have our own personal understanding of what makes us happy, we each seek happiness in our own individual way. All our actions, whether good or bad, moral or immoral, virtuous or sinful, saintly or evil, are motivated only by our desire for happiness. Whatever we may do, and whatever effort we may make, we cannot avoid having the desire to be happy, because that desire is inherent in our very being.

Is it then impossible for us to be completely free of all desire? Yes, it is, or at least in a certain sense it is. If by the word 'desire' we mean our basic liking to be happy, then yes, it is impossible for us ever to be free from it. However, our liking to be happy exists in two forms, one of which is correctly called 'love' and the other of which is correctly called 'desire'. What then is the difference between our love to be happy and our desire to be happy?

'Love' is the only suitable word that we can use to describe the liking to be happy that is inherent in our very being. Happiness is truly not anything extraneous to us, but is our very being, our own real self. Our liking for happiness is therefore in essence just our love for our own real self.

We all love ourself, but we cannot say that we desire ourself. Desire is always for something other than ourself. We desire things that are other than ourself because we wrongly imagine that we can derive happiness from them. We can therefore use the word 'love' to describe our liking to be happy when we do not seek happiness in anything outside ourself, but when we seek happiness outside ourself, our natural love to be happy takes the form of desire.

Therefore we can be completely free of desire only when our natural love of happiness is directed towards nothing other than our own essential being. We will never be able to free ourself from the bondage of desire until we replace all our desire to acquire happiness from other things with an all-consuming love to experience happiness only in ourself. In other words, we can transform all our finite desires into pure and infinite love only by diverting our liking for happiness away from all other things towards our own essential being.

The obstacle that prevents us from surrendering ourself entirely is our desire to obtain happiness from anything other than ourself. But how does such desire arise in the first place? If our love just to be is our real nature, how have we forgotten such love and fallen a prey to the vultures of our desires?

So long as we remain as our infinite consciousness of being, which is what we truly always are, we can experience nothing other than ourself. In such a state nothing exists for us to desire, and therefore we are perfectly peaceful and happy in ourself. But as soon as we rise as the finite body-bound consciousness that we call our 'mind' or 'individual self', we separate ourself seemingly from the happiness that we truly are, and we experience things that seem to be other than ourself. Having separated ourself from our own real self, which is infinite happiness and for which we therefore naturally have infinite love, we are overwhelmed by desire to regain that happiness.

However, because we have forgotten what we really are, and because we see our own self as the many objects of this world, we are confused and imagine that we can obtain the happiness we desire from those objects. Due to the illusory appearance of duality or otherness, we experience both our natural happiness and our natural love for that happiness as two pairs of opposites, pleasure and pain, and desire and aversion. That is, we imagine that certain things give us pleasure or happiness, and that other things cause us pain or suffering, and therefore we feel desire for those things that seem to give us happiness, and aversion for those things that seem to make us unhappy.

Thus the root cause of all our desire is our forgetfulness or ignorance of our own real self. When we ignore our true and infinite being, we imagine ourself to be a false and finite individual, and therefore we experience things that seem to be other than ourself, and feel desire for them, thinking that they can give us the happiness that we seem to have lost. Since our imaginary self-ignorance is the sole cause of all our desires, we can free ourself from them only by regaining our natural state of true self-knowledge.

Until we regain our true self-knowledge, we cannot remain free of desire. We may be able to replace our 'bad' desires by 'good' desires, but by doing so we will only be replacing our iron chains with golden ones. Whether the chains that bind us are made of iron or of gold, we will still be bound by them. Therefore, in order to experience true and perfect freedom, we must give up all our desires, both our base desires and our noble desires, which we can do only by knowing ourself as we really are.

Since we can achieve true and complete self-surrender only by experiencing non-dual self-knowledge, why is the path of self-surrender generally associated with dualistic devotion to God? Though Sri Ramana taught that we can surrender ourself completely only by knowing our real self, even he often described self-surrender in terms of dualistic devotion, and he did so for a very good reason.

In the thirteenth paragraph of *Nāṉ Yār?*, for example, when defining true self-surrender as the state of thought-free self-abidance, he describes it as 'giving ourself to God', and he goes on to explain the practice of self-surrender in terms of dualistic devotion to God:

> Being completely absorbed in self-abidance, giving not even the slightest room to the rising of any thought other than self-contemplation, is giving ourself to God. Even though we place whatever amount of burden upon God, that entire amount he will bear. Since one *paramēśvara śakti* [supreme power of God] is driving all activities [that is, since it is causing and controlling everything that happens in this world], why should we always think, 'it is necessary [for me] to act in this way; it is necessary [for me] to act in that way', instead of being [calm, peaceful and happy] having yielded [ourself together with our entire burden] to that [supreme controlling power]? Though we know that the train is carrying all the burdens, why should we who travel in it suffer by carrying our small luggage on our head instead of leaving it placed on that [train]?

Why does Sri Ramana explain self-surrender in such dualistic terms? The necessity to surrender ourself arises only when we mistake ourself to be a finite individual, and in this state we experience all duality as if it were real. As we saw in chapter four, so long as we feel ourself to be a finite person or individual consciousness, the world and God both exist as entities that are separate from us. God as a separate being is as real as our own separate individuality. Because we have limited ourself as a finite individual, the infinite love and power which is our own real self appears to us to be separate from us, and therefore we give it the name 'God'. It is this power of our own real self that Sri Ramana describes here as the 'one *paramēśvara śakti*', the one 'supreme-God-power' or 'supreme ruling power'.

Everything that happens in this world happens only by the 'will of God', that is, by the love of this one supreme ruling power. Since God is all-knowing, nothing can happen without him knowing it. Since he is all-powerful, nothing can happen without his consent. And since he is all-loving, nothing can happen that is not for the true benefit of all concerned (even though our limited human intellect may be unable to understand how each happening is truly good and beneficial). In fact, since he is the source and totality of all the power that we see manifest in this universe, every single activity or happening here is impelled, driven and controlled by him. As an ancient Tamil proverb says, '*avaṉ aruḷ aṉḏri ōr aṇuvum asaiyādu*', which means 'except by his grace, not even an atom moves'.

Since God is therefore bearing the entire burden of this universe, he can perfectly well bear any burden that we may place upon him. But what exactly do we mean when we speak of placing our burden upon him, and how can we do so? We all feel that we have some cares and responsibilities, but since God is responsible for everything, and since he is taking perfectly good care of everything, the truth is that we need not take any care or responsibility upon ourself.

Our only responsibility is to surrender ourself to him – that is, to yield our individual will to his divine will, which simply means to give up all our personal desires, fears, likes and dislikes, and thereby to leave all our cares and worries in his perfectly capable hands. If we surrender our individual will in this manner, he will take perfect care of us and will bear all our responsibilities.

However, our surrender does have to be sincere. We should not delude ourself by thinking we have surrendered to him, and then indulging in irresponsible behaviour. If we have truly surrendered our individual will to him, he will prompt our mind, speech and body to act in an appropriate fashion in every situation. But so long as we have any lurking desires, any likes or dislikes, we have to accept responsibility for any of our actions that result from such desires. However, even if we have not yet been able to relinquish all our desires, so long as we sincerely want to surrender to his will and make every effort to do so, we can be sure that he will guide our actions and safeguard us from falling a prey to the delusion 'I have surrendered myself to God'.

If we do think 'I have surrendered myself to God', we have still retained our individual 'I', so our so-called 'surrender' is merely a self-deception. When we have truly surrendered ourself to him, we will not exist as an individual to think anything. We will have lost ourself in the all-consuming fire of true self-knowledge, and therefore we will only remain as mere being.

Until such time, we should conduct ourself with perfect humility, both inwardly and outwardly, and we should never imagine that we have gained any sort of spiritual achievement. So long as we are aware of any otherness or duality – anything other than our mere consciousness of our own being – we are still mistaking ourself to be a finite individual, and hence we should understand that we have not truly surrendered ourself or gained any worthwhile spiritual achievement.

Avoiding any form of pride or self-delusion is an integral part of self-surrender. True self-surrender is total self-denial. As individuals we are nothing, and should understand ourself to be nothing. Without the aid of God we are absolutely powerless to do anything, even to surrender ourself to him. Therefore if we truly wish to surrender to him, we should pray for his aid, and should depend upon him entirely to safeguard us from the self-deceptive rising of ego and pride.

However, knowing our powerlessness and worthlessness, we should not feel dejected. As a finite, confused and self-deluded mind, we truly cannot do anything to attain true self-knowledge, but why should we even imagine that we need to do anything? Our responsibility is not to do anything, but just to be. In order to be, we must reject our mind along with its sense of doership, and simply surrender ourself to the supreme power of love that we call 'God'. If we have even the slightest wish to surrender ourself thus, he will give us all the aid that is necessary to make our surrender complete.

In truth, even the iota of liking to surrender ourself that we now have has been given to us by him, and having given us this small taste of true love for the infinite being that is himself, he will not cheat us by failing to nurture this seed of love that he has planted in our heart. Having planted this seed, he will surely nurture it and ensure that it grows to fruition – the state in which we are wholly consumed by our love for absolute being.

Therefore whenever we feel dejected, knowing how feeble is our love for just being, and how half-hearted are our attempts to surrender ourself, we should console ourself by praying to God in the manner shown to us by Sri Ramana in verse 60 of *Śrī Aruṇācala Akṣaramaṇamālai*:

> Having shown to me, who am devoid of [true] love [for you], [a taste of] desire [for you], bestow your grace without cheating [me], O Arunachala.

Sri Ramana has composed many prayers like this showing us how we should beseech God to help us in our efforts to attain the state of just being, because prayer is an important part of the process of self-surrender. God of course does not need to be told by us that we require his help, but that is not the true purpose of prayer. The purpose of prayer is to enkindle in our heart a sense of total dependence upon God. Since we cannot surrender ourself and attain the state of being merely by our own effort, we must learn to depend entirely upon God, because he alone can enable us to surrender ourself completely to him.

Moreover, since God exists in the core of our being as the core of our being, that is, as our own true self, whenever we pray to him, we need not think of him as some far-off being up in heaven, but can address our prayers to him directly within ourself, and thus we can make prayer one more opportunity to turn our attention towards our own innermost being.

All the help that we need to enable us to attain the state of just being is available to us in our own heart, that is, in the core of our being, which is the true abode of God, the supreme power of love. To obtain all the divine aid or grace that we need, we need not look anywhere other than in our own heart, our real self or essential being. All our efforts, prayers and attention should therefore be directed inwards, towards our own being.

This truth is clearly implied by Sri Ramana in verse 8 of *Upadēśa*

Undiyār:

> Rather than *anya-bhāva*, *ananya-bhāva* [with the conviction] 'he is I' is indeed best among all [forms of meditation].

In this context *bhāva* means 'meditation', but also has the added connotation of 'opinion', 'attitude' or 'outlook', and *anya* means 'other', whereas *ananya* means 'non-other'. Thus the meaning implied by *anya-bhāva* is meditation upon God considering him to be other than oneself, whereas that implied by *ananya-bhāva* is meditation upon God considering him to be not other than oneself. This meaning of *ananya-bhāva* is further emphasised by the words 'he is I', which are placed in apposition to it.

Therefore in whatever manner we may practise devotion to God, it is always better to consider him to be our own real self, rather than considering him to be other than ourself. The benefit of developing the attitude that God is our own real self or innermost being, and meditating upon him, worshipping him or praying to him accordingly is explained by Sri Ramana in verse 9 of *Upadēśa Undiyār*:

> By the strength of [such] meditation [or attitude], being [abiding or remaining] in the state of being, which transcends [all] meditation, is alone the true state of supreme devotion.

So long as we consider God to be other than ourself, whenever we think of him our attention will be directed outwards, away from ourself, but when we consider him to be our own real self or essential being, 'I am', whenever we think of him our attention will be directed inwards, towards the innermost core of our being. When our attention is directed away from ourself, our mind is active, but when our attention turns back to the core of our being, our mind becomes motionless and thereby subsides in the state of being, which transcends all thought or meditation. The state in which we thus remain subsided in the state of being is the true state of supreme devotion, because it is the state in which we have surrendered ourself entirely to God, who is our own essential being.

This state of just being, in which our mind or individual self has completely subsided, is not only the pinnacle of true devotion or love, but is also the ultimate goal and fulfilment of the other three spiritual paths, the paths of desireless action, union and knowing, as affirmed by Sri Ramana in verse 10 of *Upadēśa Undiyār*:

> Being [firmly established as our real self] having subsided in [our] rising-place [the core of our being, which is the source from which we had risen as our mind], that is *karma* and *bhakti*, that is *yōga* and *jñāna*.

Though it is our mind that sets out to practise any of the four 'paths' or types of spiritual endeavour, namely the path of *karma* or action performed without desire for any reward, the path of *bhakti* or devotion, the path of *yōga* or union, and the path of *jñāna* or knowing, our mind is in fact the only obstacle that stands in the way of our achieving the goal of these four paths. Therefore the final end of each of these paths can only be reached when our mind, which struggles to practise them, finally subsides in the state of being, which is the source from which it had originally risen. Thus complete self-surrender is the true goal of all forms of spiritual practice.

Even self-investigation, which is the true path of knowing or *jñāna*, is necessary only because we have not yet surrendered ourself completely. Since the correct practice of self-investigation is not doing anything, but is just being, we cannot practise it correctly without surrendering ourself – our 'doing' self or thinking mind. Conversely, since we cannot effectively surrender our false finite self without knowing what we really are, the correct practice of self-surrender is to keenly scrutinise ourself and thereby to subside in the state of just being. Thus in practice self-investigation and self-surrender are inseparable from each other, like the two sides of a single sheet of paper.

When we try to surrender ourself, we have to be extremely vigilant to ensure that our mind or individual self does not surreptitiously rise to think of anything. Since our mind rises only when we think of or attend to anything other than ourself, we can prevent it from rising only by vigilantly attending to the source from which it rises, which is our own real self.

When we thus attend vigilantly to our own innermost being, we will be able to detect our mind at the very moment it rises, and thus we will be able to crush its rising instantaneously. In fact, if we are vigilantly self-attentive, our mind will not be able to rise at all, because it actually rises only on account of our slackness in self-attention.

To return once again to our discussion of the thirteenth paragraph of *Nāṉ Yār?*, in the third sentence Sri Ramana asks, 'Since one *paramēśvara śakti* is driving all activities, why should we always think, "it is necessary [for me] to act in this way; it is necessary [for me] to act in that way", instead of being having yielded to that?'. Besides what we have discussed already, there are two more important points to note in this sentence.

Firstly, when he asks us why we should think that we need to do this or that, the meaning he implies is not only that it is unnecessary for us to do anything, but also that it is unnecessary for us to think anything. If we truly believe that God is doing everything, and is always taking care of every living being, including ourself, we will have the confidence to place upon him the burden of thinking for us, and thus we will be freed of the burden of thinking anything for ourself.

If we really surrender ourself entirely to God, he will take full control of our mind, speech and body, and will make them act in whatever way is appropriate in all situations. Only when we thus cease to think anything will our surrender to God be complete.

Secondly, the words that I have translated as 'instead of being having yielded to that' are very significant, because they are an apt description of what real self-surrender is. In the original Tamil, the words used by Sri Ramana are *adaṟku aḍaṅgi-y-irāmal*. The word *adaṟku* means 'to that' or 'to it', that is, to the one *paramēśvara śakti* or 'supreme ruling power'. The word *aḍaṅgi* is a verbal participle that means not only 'having yielded', but also having subsided, settled, shrunk, laid down, submitted, been subdued, become still, ceased or disappeared. The word *irāmal* means 'without being' or 'instead of being'. Thus the meaning implied by these words is that true self-surrender is a state of just being, that is, a state in which we remain as mere being, having yielded or submitted ourself to God, and having thereby subsided, settled down and become still, and having in fact ceased altogether to exist as a separate individual.

As we saw earlier, God is our own real self, and he appears to be separate from us only because we have limited ourself as a finite individual consciousness. In other words, as soon as we delude ourself into imagining that we are a finite individual, our own real self manifests as God, the power that guides and controls our entire life as an individual, and that thereby gradually leads us back towards our natural state of true self-knowledge.

However, God is not the only form in which our real self manifests to guide us back to itself. At a certain stage in our spiritual development, our real self also manifests as *guru*, and in this form it reveals to us through spoken or written words the truth that we ourself are infinite being, consciousness and happiness, and that to experience ourself as such we should scrutinise ourself and thereby surrender our false individual self. When we have once heard or read this truth revealed by our real self in the form of *guru*, and if we have been genuinely attracted by this truth, we have truly come under the influence of *guru*, and we are therefore well on our way to reaching our final goal of true self-knowledge.

This state in which we have come under the influence of *guru* is described by Sri Ramana in the twelfth paragraph of *Nāṉ Yār?* as being caught or ensnared in the 'glance of *guru*'s grace':

> God and *guru* are in truth not different. Just as that [prey] which has been caught in the jaws of a tiger will not return, so those who have been caught in the glance of *guru*'s grace will surely be saved by him and will never instead be forsaken; nevertheless, it is necessary [for them] to proceed [behave or act] unfailingly according to the path that *guru* has shown.

Though the real *guru* outwardly appears to be a human being, he is in fact God in human form, manifested as such in order to give us the spiritual teachings that are necessary to prompt us to turn our mind towards the source from which it had risen, and thereby to subside and merge in that source for ever. Or to explain the same truth in another manner, since the person who had previously occupied the body in which *guru* is manifested had surrendered himself entirely to God and had thereby been consumed in the fire of true self-knowledge, that which remains and functions through that body is only God himself. Therefore that which speaks, sees, hears and acts through the human form in which *guru* is manifested is not a finite individual, but is the infinite power of love and true knowledge that we otherwise call God.

This absolute oneness of God, *guru* and our own real self is the true significance of the Christian Trinity, as explained by Sri Ramana. God the Father is God as the power that governs this whole universe and the life of each individual in it, God the Son is *guru*, and God the Holy Spirit is our own real self. Though in the limited and distorted outlook of our mind they appear to be three distinct entities or 'persons', God, *guru* and self are in reality the one infinite and indivisible being.

Though thc word *guru* is used in many different contexts and may therefore mean a teacher of any ordinary art, science or skill, in a spiritual context it correctly denotes only the *sadguru*, the 'real *guru*' or 'being-*guru*', that is, the *guru* who is *sat*, the reality or true being of each one of us. Though there are many people who claim to be spiritual *gurus*, the true spiritual *guru* is very rare, and hence in a spiritual context the term *guru* should only be applied to those rare beings like Buddha, Sri Krishna, Christ, Adi Sankara, Sri Ramakrishna and Sri Ramana, who have a clear divine mission to reveal to us the path to attain true self-knowledge. No such real *guru* will ever claim to be the *guru*, either explicitly or implicitly, because the real *guru* is totally devoid of ego, and therefore knows himself only as 'I am' and not as 'I am God' or 'I am *guru*'.

Once we are caught in the influence of the real *guru*, we are like the prey that has been caught in the jaws of a tiger. Just as a tiger will unfailingly devour the prey it has caught, so *guru* will unfailingly devour us, destroying our mind or individual consciousness, and thereby absorbing us into himself, that is, making us one with our own true and essential being, which is what he really is.

However, Sri Ramana adds a cautionary note, saying that though *guru* will surely save us in this manner, and will never forsake us, we should nevertheless unfailingly follow the path that he has shown us. In the clause 'it is necessary to proceed unfailingly according to the path that *guru* has shown', the original Tamil word that I have translated as 'to proceed' is *naḍakka*, which means to walk, go, proceed or behave, and therefore it implies that we should conduct ourself or act in accordance with his teachings, or in other words, we should unfailingly practise the twin path of self-investigation and self-surrender that he has taught us.

The purpose of the manifestation of our real self in the human form of *guru* is to teach us the means by which we can attain salvation, which is the state of true self-knowledge. It did not manifest itself as *guru* merely for us to worship him as God, expecting him to bestow upon us any finite benefit or happiness either in this world or some other world.

The function of *guru* is the ultimate function of God, which is to destroy for ever our illusion of individuality – our delusion that we are the body and mind that we now imagine ourself to be – and he performs this function by teaching us that we should turn our attention inwards, towards our innermost being, in order to know our real self and thereby surrender our false individual self. Therefore, if we truly wish to be saved from our own self-imposed delusion, we must unfailingly do as *guru* has taught us, making every possible effort to attend to our essential being, 'I am', and thereby to surrender our finite self in the infinity of that being or 'am'-ness.

The grace of God or *guru* is always providing us all the help we need to follow this spiritual path, but we must take full advantage of that help by turning our mind inwards and thereby remaining in our natural state of just being, which is the true state of self-investigation and self-surrender. God or *guru* is always bestowing grace upon us by shining within us as 'I am', but we must reciprocate that grace or love by attending to 'I am'.

The reason why we have not yet attained salvation is that we continue to ignore the true form of grace, which ever shines within us as 'I am'. As Sri Ramana says in verse 966 of *Guru Vācaka Kōvai*:

> Since *uḷḷadu* [the absolute reality, 'being' or 'that which is'] alone is [the true form of] *tiruvaruḷ* [divine grace], which rises [clearly and prominently within each one of us] as *uḷḷam* [our 'heart', 'core' or essential consciousness 'am'], the fault of ignoring [or disregarding] 'that which is' is suited [to be considered as a defect that belongs] only to individuals, who do not unceasingly think [remember or attend to this grace, which shines lovingly as 'am'], inwardly melting [with love for it]. Instead, how can the fault of not bestowing sweet grace be [considered as a defect that belongs] to [God or *guru*, who is] 'that which is'?

Being ungracious, unloving, unkind or unhelpful is a fault that can be blamed only upon us individuals, who ignore and disregard the infinite and absolute reality – *uḷḷadu*, 'being' or 'that which is' – which shines within us effulgently as 'am' or 'I am', and not upon God or *guru*, who is that reality. God or *guru* never ignores us, but constantly shines within us as our own being or 'am'-ness, beckoning us lovingly to turn within and merge in him. However, though he is always making himself so easily available to us, we choose to ignore him constantly and to attend instead to our thoughts about our petty life as an individual in this imaginary world.

For us to attain salvation, only two things are necessary, the grace of God or *guru* and our own willingness to submit to that grace. Of these two indispensable ingredients, the former is always abundantly available, and only the latter is lacking. Until we are perfectly willing to surrender and lose our individuality, God or *guru* will never force us, but he will be constantly nurturing the seed of such willingness or love in our heart, helping it to grow until one day it consumes us.

Therefore, though *guru* will certainly save us and will never forsake us, it is essential that we should do our part, which is to submit ourself willingly to his grace, which is the perfect clarity of our own fundamental self-consciousness – our absolutely non-dual consciousness of our own being, 'I am'. The only way we can thus submit or surrender ourself to his grace is to 'think of' or constantly attend to our own essential self-conscious being, 'I am', melting inwardly with overwhelming love for it. Sincerely attempting to surrender ourself in this manner is what Sri Ramana meant when he said, 'Nevertheless, it is necessary to proceed unfailingly according to the path that *guru* has shown'.

In order to know our own real self, which is absolute, infinite, eternal and undivided being-consciousness-bliss or *sat-cit-ānanda*, we must be willing to surrender or renounce our false finite self. And in order to surrender our false self, we must be wholly consumed by an overwhelming love to know and to be our own real self or essential being.

So long as we feel complacent about our present condition, in which we have imaginarily limited ourself as this finite mind and body, we will lack the intense motivation that we must have in order to be sufficiently willing to surrender our false self. Since we now imagine our mind and body to be ourself, our attachment to them is very strong, and hence we will not be willing to surrender this attachment unless we are very strongly motivated to do so.

Our attachment to our mind and body is so strong that it induces us to delude ourself into a deceptive state of complacency, making us feel that our present condition is not as intolerable as it really is. Rather than recognising the fact that the deep dissatisfaction that we feel with our present condition as a finite body-bound individual consciousness is an inevitable consequence of our imaginary separation of ourself from the infinite happiness that is our own real nature, and that we can therefore never overcome this dissatisfaction by any means other than true self-knowledge – that is, other than experiencing ourself as the adjunct-free, infinite, undivided and therefore absolutely non-dual real self-consciousness 'I am' – we complacently continue our life as a body-bound individual imagining that we can achieve the happiness that we seek by enjoying the petty transient pleasures that we experience by satisfying any of our countless temporal desires.

This self-deceptive complacency is a serious problem that all true spiritual aspirants experience, and we must overcome it if we truly wish to surrender our false finite self and thereby to know our real infinite self. Since this deep-rooted complacency is an inevitable consequence of our having succumbed to our power of *māyā* or self-delusion, which is the power that causes us to imagine ourself to be this finite body and mind, we normally cannot overcome it unless we experience an intense internal crisis, such as being suddenly confronted by a profound inward fear of death.

Therefore when we reach a certain stage of spiritual maturity, the power of grace will generally induce us to experience some such internal crisis, and when we experience it we will be shocked out of our present sense of complacency and will therefore turn our attention selfwards with intense love to know what we really are.

In the life of Sri Ramana such an internal crisis occurred in the form of the sudden intense fear of death that he experienced when he was a sixteen-year-old boy. As we saw in the introduction to this book, this intense fear prompted him to turn his attention inwards to discover whether he was really the body, which is subject to death. So intensely did he focus his attention upon his innermost being – his essential self-consciousness 'I' – that he experienced it with perfect clarity, and thus he came to know from his own direct experience that he was not the mortal body but was only the immortal, eternal and infinite spirit, which is absolutely non-dual being, consciousness and bliss.

Sri Ramana describes this experience of his in the second of the two verses of the *maṅgalam* or 'auspicious introduction' to *Uḷḷadu Nāṟpadu*:

> Those mature people who have intense fear of death will take refuge at the feet of God, who is devoid of death and birth, [depending upon him] as [their protective] fortress. By their surrender, they experience death [the death or dissolution of their finite self]. Will those who are deathless [having died to their mortal self, and having thereby become one with the immortal spirit] approach the death-thought [or thought of death] [ever again]?

Though the Tamil word *am* literally means either 'those' or 'beauty', I have translated it here as 'those mature', because in this context the beauty that it denotes is the true beauty of spiritual maturity, which is the truly desirable condition in which our mind has been cleansed of most of its impurities – namely its cruder forms of desire – and is therefore ready to surrender itself entirely to God.

The fear of death is naturally inherent in all living beings, but it usually remains in a dormant form because we spend most of our time thinking about our life in this world and hence we seldom think about death. Even when some external event or some internal thought reminds us that we will sooner or later die, our fear of death seldom becomes intense, because the thought of death prompts us to think of the things in our life to which we are most strongly attached.

However, though it usually remains in a dormant form, our fear of death is in fact the greatest, most fundamental and most deep-rooted of all our fears. We fear death because it appears to us to be a state of non-existence – a state in which we ourself will cease to exist, or at least cease to exist as we now know ourself. Since we love our own being or existence more than we love any other thing, we fear to lose our own being or existence more than we fear any other thing. In other words, our fear of death is rooted in our self-love – our basic love for our own essential self or being.

The reason why we love our own self or being is that we ourself are happiness. Because by our very nature we love happiness, and because happiness is in fact our own being, we cannot avoid loving our own being or existence, and hence we cannot avoid fearing the loss or destruction of our being or existence. Therefore so long as we experience ourself as a physical body – that is, so long as we confuse our existence with the existence of a mortal body – we cannot avoid having a deep-rooted fear of death.

Hence the fear of death will always exist in us until we truly decide to free ourself from our self-created illusion that we are a mortal body. Because we imagine ourself to be this body, we are unavoidably attached to it, and therefore we fear to lose it. However, though we all know that one day our body will die, and that death can come at any time, our power of *māyā* or self-delusion lulls us into a state of complacency, making us imagine that death is far away, or that we do not really fear death.

Though we may imagine that we do not fear death, if our life is put in sudden danger, we will certainly respond with intense fear. However, as soon as the immediate danger is past, our fear will subside and we will continue our life in our usual state of self-deceptive complacency.

Though we experience intense fear of death whenever the life of our body is in extreme danger, the intensity of that fear is short-lived. It is not sustained because when we are confronted with death we react by thinking of our loved ones, our friends, our material possessions, our status in life and other such external things to which we are attached, and which we consequently fear to lose.

Even our religious beliefs can be a means by which we sustain the comfort of our complacency. If we believe, for example, that after the death of our body we will go to some other world called heaven, where we will be reunited with all our loved ones and friends, and where we will live with them an eternal life free from all suffering, that belief will help us to ward off our fear of death. Even if we have some less optimistic belief about life after death, so long as our belief is sufficiently comforting, as most such beliefs are, it will help us to feel complacent about the certainty of death.

So long as we lack true spiritual maturity or freedom from desire for anything external, the fear of death will impel our mind to rush outwards to think of our life in this world or the next, and due to such thoughts our attention will be diverted away from the thought of death, and thus our fear will lose its intensity. However, when we eventually gain true spiritual maturity, our reaction to the thought of death will be different.

If we are spiritually mature, the intensity of our desire for and attachment to external things, either in this world or the next, will be greatly reduced. Therefore, when we think of death, we will not fear to lose any external thing, but will only fear to lose our own existence or being. Since the last vestiges of our desire and attachment will be centred on our own very existence as an individual, and since we confuse our existence with the existence of whatever body we currently imagine ourself to be, when the thought of the death of our body arises within us, our mind will turn inwards to cling to its own existence or essential being.

This is what happened in the case of Sri Ramana. When the thought of death suddenly arose within him, his reaction was to turn his attention within, towards his own very being, in order to discover whether he himself would die along with the death of his body. Because his attention was focused so keenly on his own essential being or 'am'-ness, he clearly experienced himself without any superimposed adjunct such as his mind or body, and thus he discovered that his real self was not a mortal body or a transient mind, but was only the infinite, eternal, birthless and deathless spirit – the one true non-dual consciousness of being, which always knows 'I am' and nothing other than 'I am'.

In the first sentence of this second *maṅgalam* verse of *Uḷḷadu Nāṟpadu* Sri Ramana says:

> Those mature people who have intense fear of death will take refuge at the feet of *mahēśaṉ* [the 'great Lord'], who is devoid of death and birth, [depending upon him] as [their protective] fortress. [...]

This is a poetic way of describing his own experience of self-investigation and self-surrender. Though the word *mahēśaṉ*, which literally means the 'great Lord', is a name that usually denotes Lord Siva, the form in which many Hindus worship God, Sri Ramana did not use it in this context to denote any particular form of God, but only as an allegorical description of the birthless and deathless spirit, which always exists in each one of us as our own essential self-conscious being, 'I am'.

No name or form of God is truly devoid of birth or death – appearance or disappearance – because like all other names and forms the various names and forms in which devotees worship God are transitory appearances. They can appear only when our mind has risen to know them, and they disappear when our mind subsides. Therefore in this context the words 'the great Lord, who is devoid of death and birth' do not denote merely the *saguṇa* or qualified aspect of God – that is, God as he is conceived by our finite mind – but only his essential *nirguṇa* or unqualified aspect – that is, God as he is really, which is the nameless and formless absolute reality, our own true self-conscious being, which always knows its own existence without ever appearing or disappearing.

However, though in this context Sri Ramana is not actually describing any form of *saguṇa upāsana* or worship of God in name and form, by using the word *mahēśaṉ*, which is a personal name of God, he does allude to such worship. This allusion is intentional, because if we worship God in name and form with true heart-melting devotion, our mind will gradually be purified or cleansed of its cruder forms of desire, and thus it will eventually gain the maturity that is required for it to be able to surrender itself entirely to him.

However, no matter how much we may worship God in name and form, we cannot achieve the final goal of the path of devotion, which is the complete surrender of ourself to him, until we turn our attention inwards to worship him in the profound depth of our own heart – in the innermost core of our being – as our own true and essential being. In other words, in order for us to attain the true goal of *saguṇa upāsana* or worship of God in name and form, such worship must eventually flower into *nirguṇa upāsana*, which is the true worship of God as the one nameless and formless absolute reality, which always exists within us as our own essential self-conscious being.

We can experience God as he really is only when we turn our mind inwards – away from all names and forms, which are merely thoughts that we have formed in our mind by our power of imagination – and thereby allow it to dissolve in the absolute clarity of our own true and essential self-conscious being, which is the true 'form' or nature of God. However, in order to turn our mind inwards and thereby surrender it completely in the all-consuming light of God's own true being, we must have overwhelming love for him, and such love is cultivated by the practice of *saguṇa upāsana* or dualistic worship.

However, though the true love that we require in order to be willing to surrender ourself entirely in the absolute clarity of pure self-conscious being, which is the reality of both God and ourself, can be cultivated gradually by the practice of dualistic devotion, the quickest and most effective way to cultivate it is by the practice of non-dualistic devotion – that is, by the practice of self-attentiveness, which is the true adoration of God as our own real self or essential being.

Whether we cultivate the true love or willingness to surrender ourself entirely to the absolute reality, which is the infinite fullness of being that we call 'God', by dualistic devotion or by non-dualistic devotion, once we have cultivated it sufficiently any internal crisis such as an intense fear of death will impel our mind to turn inwards and to sink into the innermost depth of our own being in order to surrender itself entirely to him. Only when our mind thus merges in the source from which it had risen, which is our own true and essential self-conscious being, will its surrender to God become complete.

This complete surrender of our mind or individual self in the innermost depth of our own being is what Sri Ramana describes in this verse by the words 'will take refuge at the feet of God, who is devoid of death and birth, [depending upon him] as [their protective] fortress'.

In Hindu devotional poetry and literature the adoration of God is often described as bowing to his feet, falling at his feet, clinging to his feet, taking refuge in or at his feet, and so on, because such actions imply humility, devotion and submission. Therefore in Indian languages the term 'feet' has come to be synonymous with God as the ultimate object of worship or adoration.

Moreover, as Sri Ramana often explained, the term 'the feet of God' is an allegorical description of his true state – the egoless and perfectly non-dual state of unalloyed self-conscious being, which always shines within each one of us as 'I am'. In order to remind us that we can experience God as he really is only in the core of our own being, he always emphasised the truth that the 'feet of God' cannot be found outside but only within ourself. On one occasion, when a lady devotee bowed before him and caught hold of his feet saying, 'I am clinging to the feet of my *guru*', he looked at her kindly and said, 'Are these the feet of *guru*? The feet of *guru* are that which is always shining within you as "I I". Grasp that'.

Therefore the words 'those mature people will take refuge at the feet of God' mean that they will lovingly subside in the innermost depth of their own being, where they will experience God as their own real self. The only true refuge or fortress which will protect us from the fear of death and every other form of misery is the innermost core of our own being, which is the real abode of God and which, being the foundation that underlies and supports our mind and everything known by it, is figuratively described as his 'feet'.

In the second sentence of this verse Sri Ramana says, 'By their surrender, they experience death'. The death that they previously feared was the death of their body, but when the fear of that death impels them to take refuge at the 'feet of God', they experience death of an entirely different kind. That is, when they take refuge at the 'feet of God' by subsiding into the innermost depth of their own being, they will experience the absolute clarity of unadulterated self-consciousness, which will swallow their mind just as light swallows darkness.

Our mind or finite individual self is an imagination – a false form of consciousness that experiences itself as a body, which is one of its own imaginary creations. We imagine ourself to be this mind only because we ignore or fail to attend to our own true and essential being. If we knew what we really are, we could not mistake ourself to be any other thing. Hence, since our mind has come into existence because of our imaginary self-ignorance, it will be destroyed by the experience of true self-knowledge.

Therefore when we subside into our 'heart', the innermost core of our own being, where our true self-consciousness shines free from all adjuncts, all thoughts, all imaginations, all duality and all forms of limitation, our mind will disappear in the absolute clarity of that pure self-consciousness, just as an imaginary snake will disappear when we see clearly that what we mistook to be that snake is in fact only a rope. Because our mind is a false knowledge about ourself – an imagination that we are a material body – the experience of true self-knowledge will reveal that it is unreal.

Therefore the death that we will experience when we surrender our false individual self in the absolute clarity of true self-knowledge, which always shines in the innermost core of our being, is the death of our own mind. The death of our body is not a true death, because when our body dies our mind will create for itself another body by its power of imagination. As long as our mind survives, it will continue thus creating for itself one body after another. Hence the only true death is the death of our own mind.

However, though the experience of true self-knowledge is figuratively described as the death or destruction of our mind, we should not imagine that this implies that our mind has ever really existed. The death of our mind is like the 'death' of a snake that we imagine we see in the dim light of night. In the morning when the sun rises, that imaginary snake will disappear, because we will clearly see that it is in fact only a rope. Similarly, in the clear light of true self-knowledge our mind will disappear, because we will clearly recognise that it is in fact only our infinite and non-dual consciousness of our own essential being.

Just as the snake does not really die, because it never actually existed, so our mind will not really die, because it has never actually existed. Its death is real only relative to its present seeming existence. Therefore though in figurative terms the experience of true self-knowledge may be described as the death of our unreal self and as the birth of our real self, in reality it is the state in which we know that our real self alone exists, that it has always existed, and that our mind or unreal self has never truly existed.

In the third and final sentence of this verse Sri Ramana says, 'Will those who are deathless approach the death-thought?'. Here the word *sāvādavar*, which means 'those who do not die' or 'those who are deathless', denotes those who have surrendered themself entirely to God, thereby dying as their mind or mortal self, and thus becoming one with the immortal spirit, the infinite and eternal self-consciousness 'I am', which is the true and essential being of both God and ourself.

The rhetorical question 'will they approach the death-thought?' is an idiomatic way of saying that they will never again experience any thought of death. Death is just a thought, as also is the fear of death. We can think of death and experience fear of it only when we imagine ourself to be a mortal body.

Our body, its birth and its death are all mere thoughts or imaginations. When we imagine that we are this body, we accordingly imagine that we were born at some time in the past and that we will die at some time in the future. Who or what imagines all this? Only our mind imagines these and all other thoughts. If our mind is real, these thoughts are also real, but if we keenly scrutinise our mind to see whether it is real, it will disappear, and only our own essential self-conscious being will remain as the eternal and deathless reality.

Our mind, which imagines the existence of our body, its birth and its death, is itself a mere thought or imagination. It is a phantom that comes into existence only by imagining itself to be a mortal body, and though it will disappear when this body dies, just as it disappears every day in sleep, it will reappear by imagining itself to be some other body, just as it reappears in a dream or on waking from sleep. It will itself die or disappear permanently only when we surrender it in the absolute clarity of true self-knowledge.

Since death is a thought, and even the thinker of death is a thought, the true state of deathlessness or immortality is only the thought-free state of absolutely clear self-conscious being – the state in which our thinking mind has died. When by our complete self-surrender we abide permanently in this egoless and mind-free state of true immortality, we will never again be able to imagine the thought of death or any other thought.

Thus in this verse Sri Ramana describes both the goal and the means to attain that goal. The goal is the state of immortality, in which our thinking, fearing and desiring mind has died, and the means by which we can attain that goal is complete self-surrender, which we can achieve only by subsiding within ourself and taking refuge there in the birthless and deathless absolute reality, which is our own essential self-conscious being, 'I am'.

As we have been seeing throughout this chapter, the essence of both self-investigation and self-surrender is just being. So long as we feel ourself to be thinking or doing anything, our attention is not focused entirely upon our own being, and therefore we have not yet surrendered ourself entirely to God.

The essence of all spiritual practice can be summarised in two words, 'just be'. However, though these two words are the most accurate possible description of the only means by which we can attain the infinitely happy experience of true self-knowledge, most of us are unable to understand their full significance, and therefore we wonder how we can just be.

We are so accustomed to doing, and to considering that we cannot achieve anything without doing something, that we tend to think, 'what must I do in order to just be?'. Even if we have understood that being is not doing anything, and that we therefore cannot do anything in order to be, we still wonder how we can refrain from thinking or doing anything.

To save us from all such confusion, Sri Ramana gave us a simple clue to enable us to be without doing anything. That is, he taught us that in order to be without doing anything, all we need 'do' is to focus our entire attention upon ourself, that is, upon our own essential being 'I am'. Though this practice of focusing our attention upon our being may appear to be a 'doing', the only 'doing' that it actually involves is the withdrawing of our attention from all other things, because once our attention is thus withdrawn and allowed to settle on itself, all 'doing' will have ceased and only 'being' will remain.

Moreover, though this withdrawing of our attention from all other things towards our own innermost being may appear to be a 'doing' or action, it is actually not so, because in practice it is just a subsiding and cessation of all activity. That is, since our mind rises and becomes active only by attending to things other than itself, when it withdraws its attention back towards itself, it subsides and all its activity or 'doing' ceases. Thus this clue of self-attention which Sri Ramana has given us is an infallible means by which we can make our mind subside in our natural state of just being.

This subsiding of our mind in our natural state of being is what is otherwise known as complete self-surrender. True self-surrender is a conscious and voluntary cessation of all mental activity, and what remains when all our distracting thoughts have thus subsided is the clear and undisturbed consciousness of our own true being. Therefore just as self-attentiveness automatically results in self-surrender, so self-surrender automatically results in self-attentiveness, which is the true practice of self-investigation.

In fact, though we speak of self-investigation and self-surrender as if they were two different practices, they are not actually so, but are merely two seemingly different approaches to the same practice, which is the practice of just being – just being, that is, with full consciousness of our being. What exactly do we mean when we describe them thus as different approaches? Though in actual practice they are one and the same, they differ only in their being two different ways of conceptualising and describing the one practice of just being.

Whereas self-investigation is the practice of just being conceived in more strictly philosophical terms, self-surrender is the same practice conceived in more devotional terms. However, this distinction is not a rigid one, because when understood correctly from a deeper and broader perspective, self-investigation and self-surrender are in fact both based upon the same broad philosophy and are both motivated by the same deep love and devotion.

It is only in the view of people who have a superficial and narrow understanding of philosophy and devotion, and who therefore see them as being fundamentally different viewpoints, that this seeming distinction exists. If however we are able to recognise that philosophy and whole-hearted devotion to the absolute truth are essentially the same thing, we will understand that there is really no difference between self-investigation and self-surrender.

Therefore, since self-investigation and self-surrender are two names given to the same practice of self-attentive being, let us now consider this practice or art of being in greater depth.

CHAPTER 10

The Practice of the Art of Being

The art of being is the skill to remain firmly established in the actionless and therefore thought-free state of perfectly clear self-conscious being, which is the state of absolute self-surrender and true self-knowledge.

Like any other skill, the art of being is cultivated and perfected by practice. The more we practise it, the more we will develop the strength that we require to remain steadily poised in our natural thought-free consciousness of our own essential being.

How much practice each one of us will actually require in order to perfect our skill in this art of being will depend upon the relative degree of our present maturity or ripeness of mind. In the case of Sri Ramana, only a moment of practice was required, because at that time his mind was already perfectly ripe and therefore willing to surrender itself and be consumed in the effulgent light of infinitely clear self-consciousness. However, most of us do not possess even a fraction of such ripeness, so we require long and persistent practice of this art of being in order to develop it.

What do we mean when we speak of ripeness or maturity of mind? Our mind will be spiritually ripe when it has been purified or cleansed of all its desires – all its likes and dislikes, its attachments, its aversions, its fears and so on – and when it has thereby developed the willingness and true love to surrender itself entirely and thus subside peacefully in its own essential self-conscious being or 'am'-ness. Our desires are the obstacles that make us unwilling to surrender ourself to our infinite being, and therefore they are the cause and the form of our unripeness for self-knowledge.

How can we develop the spiritual ripeness that we require in order to be able to surrender ourself entirely in the state of absolute being? Though there are many means by which we can indirectly and gradually begin to cultivate such ripeness, ultimately we can perfect it only by practising the art of being. All the other countless forms of spiritual practice – such as selfless service, dualistic devotion, ritualistic worship, repetition of a name of God, prayer, meditation, various forms of internal and external self-restraint (including the important virtue of *ahiṁsā* or 'non-harming', that is, the compassionate avoidance of causing any form of harm or suffering to any living being), the 'eightfold limbs' of *yōga* and so on – are indirect means which can enable us gradually to purify our mind, cleansing it of the grosser forms of its desires and thereby ripening it, but only to a certain extent.

That is, since all spiritual practices other than the art of being involve an extroversion of our mind, a turning of our attention away from ourself towards something else, they can enable us to free ourself effectively only from the grosser forms of our desires and attachments, but not from the more subtle forms. Until and unless we begin to practise the art of being, keeping our attention fixed firmly and exclusively upon our own essential being, as our own essential being, we cannot gain the inward clarity and focus that is required to detect and prevent the rising of our mind and its desires at their very starting point.

How are we thus able to detect and prevent the rising of our mind by practising the art of being? When we practise this art, our attention is fixed upon our essential self-conscious being, which is the source from which our mind arises along with all its most subtle desires, and so long as our attention thus remains vigilantly and firmly fixed on, in and as its source, our mind will be unable to rise.

However, whenever due to even the slightest slackening of our vigilant self-attentiveness we allow our attention to waver and be diverted by any thought, we will thereby rise in the form of our thinking mind. But by repeatedly practising this art of self-attentive being, we will gain the skill to detect any such slackening in our vigilant self-attentiveness at the very moment that it occurs, and thus we will be able to regain our self-attentiveness instantly and thereby prevent the rising of our mind at the very moment that it occurs.

The more we practise this art of being, the more keen, sharp and clear our self-attentiveness will become, and thereby our skill in the art of crushing the rising of our mind in its very source will steadily increase. Every moment that we succeed in thus vigilantly preventing even the least rising of our mind, the desires that impel it to rise will be steadily weakened, and our love to remain peacefully in our natural state of just being will be proportionately strengthened, until finally it will totally overpower all our remaining and much weakened desires, thereby enabling us to surrender ourself entirely in the infinite clarity of true self-knowledge.

Other than this practice of keenly vigilant self-attentive being, there is no adequate means by which we can weaken and destroy all of our desires, including even our most subtle and therefore most powerful ones. All other spiritual practices involve some sort of activity of our mind, and so long as our mind is active, it will effectively be guarding and protecting all its innermost desires, including its fundamental desire to exist as a separate individual consciousness. By engaging our mind in any activity, we cannot destroy its basic desire for self-preservation, and so long as it retains this basic desire, it will continue to support and nourish it by cultivating other desires.

That is, our mind's desire for self-preservation, which is satisfied and supported by all forms of spiritual practice other than the totally self-denying art of vigilantly self-attentive being, cannot stand on its own, but must be accompanied by some desire or other for something other than itself. This need is satisfied by every other form of spiritual practice, because all such practices provide our mind with something other than itself to attend to – in fact, they force our mind to attend to something other than itself. Therefore no such practice can train our mind to relinquish all of its desires, particularly its desire to preserve its own separate existence.

Some other spiritual practices do force our mind to subside, but such subsidence is only temporary, because it is not accompanied by clear self-attentiveness. Therefore in the eighth paragraph of *Nāṉ Yār?* Sri Ramana says:

> To make the mind subside [permanently], there are no adequate means other than *vicāra* [investigation, that is, the art of self-attentive being]. If restrained by other means, the mind will remain as if subsided, [but] will emerge again. Even by *prāṇāyāma* [breath-restraint], the mind will subside; however, [though] the mind remains subsided so long as the breath remains subsided, when the breath emerges [or becomes manifest] it will also emerge and wander under the sway of [its] *vāsanās* [inclinations, impulses or desires]. The birthplace both of the mind and of the *prāṇa* [the breath or life-force] is one. Thought alone is the *svarūpa* [the 'own form'] of the mind. The thought 'I' alone is the first [or basic] thought of the mind; it alone is the ego. From where the ego arises, from there alone the breath also arises. Therefore when the mind subsides the *prāṇa* also [subsides], [and] when the *prāṇa* subsides the mind also subsides. However in sleep, even though the mind has subsided, the breath does not subside. It is arranged thus by the ordinance of God for the purpose of protecting the body, and so that other people do not wonder whether that body has died. When the mind subsides in waking and in *samādhi* [any of the various types of mental absorption that result from *yōgic* or other forms of spiritual practice], the *prāṇa* subsides. The *prāṇa* is said to be the gross form of the mind. Until the time of death the mind keeps the *prāṇa* in the body, and at the moment the body dies it [the mind] grabs and takes it [the *prāṇa*] away. Therefore *prāṇāyāma* is just an aid to restrain the mind, but will not bring about *manōnāśa* [the annihilation of the mind].

Before going on to discuss the efficacy of other forms of spiritual practice, Sri Ramana begins this paragraph by stating the important truth that 'To make the mind subside [permanently], there are no adequate means other than *vicāra* [investigation]'. Why is this so?

Since the state of true self-knowledge, which is the only state in which the mind will remain permanently subsided, is a state of just being, it cannot be brought about by any action or 'doing', but only by the practice of just being. Since *vicāra* or investigation, which is simply the practice of self-attentiveness, does not involve any action but is just a state of self-conscious being, and since every other form of spiritual practice is an action of one kind or another, *vicāra* is the only practice that will enable us to abide in the state of eternal, infinite and absolute being, which is the state of true self-knowledge.

This same truth is also clearly stated by Sri Adi Sankara in verse 11 of *Vivēkacūḍāmaṇi*:

> Action [*karma*, which generally means action of any kind whatsoever, but which in this context means specifically any action that is performed for spiritual benefit] is [prescribed only] for [achieving] *citta-śuddhi* [purification of mind] and not for [attaining] *vastu-upalabdhi* [direct knowledge or experience of the reality, the true substance or essence, which is absolute being]. The attainment of [this experience of] the reality [can be achieved only] by *vicāra* and not at all by [even] ten million actions.

That is, except *vastu-vicāra*, investigation or scrutiny of our essential being or reality, all spiritual practices are actions, and as such they can only serve to purify our mind and thereby make it fit to subside and remain permanently in our own essential being or *vastu*. However, though they can purify our mind to a certain extent, they cannot by themselves enable us to experience our own true being as it really is. In order to experience an absolutely clear knowledge of our being, we must give up all actions or 'doings' and must cultivate perfectly pure love for just being, which we can do only by *vicāra*, the practice of self-attentive being.

Therefore, when discussing the efficacy of other forms of spiritual practice in the eighth and ninth paragraphs of *Nāṉ Yār?*, Sri Ramana repeatedly emphasises that they are all only aids that can prepare us for the practice of *vicāra* or self-attentive being, but that by themselves they cannot bring about *manōnāśa*, the complete annihilation of our mind, which is the state of true self-knowledge or absolute self-conscious being.

Because the aim of Sri Ramana in the eighth paragraph is to explain the limited value of *prāṇāyāma* or breath-restraint, which is one of the central practices of *yōga*, he explains the principle that underlies *prāṇāyāma* in terms of the *yōga* philosophy. It is therefore only from the standpoint of the *yōga* philosophy that he says that the breath does not subside in sleep, that God has arranged it thus in order to protect the body, and that the mind takes away the *prāṇa* at the time of death.

However, from the viewpoint of his principal teachings, we should understand that all this is only relatively true, and is based upon the false belief cherished by most of us that the body and world exist independent of our mind. According to the truth revealed and explained by him on countless occasions, our body and the world exist only in the imagination of our own mind, like the body and world that we experience in a dream, and hence when our mind subsides in sleep or in death, not only does our breath or life-force subside and vanish along with it, but even our body ceases to exist.

The central import of this paragraph is the truth that is stated in the first two sentences. Our mind will subside permanently only by remaining firmly fixed in the state of self-attentive being, because only in that state will the truth be revealed that our mind is truly ever non-existent. If instead of practising the art of thus remaining fixed in the state of self-attentive being we try to make our mind subside by *prāṇāyāma* or any other means, it will remain as if subsided for a short while, as it does in sleep, but will again rise and wander under the sway of its deeply engrained impulsions or desires, which are not weakened in the least by such inattentive subsidence, any more than they are weakened in sleep.

Like *prāṇāyāma*, all other forms of spiritual practice except the art of self-attentive being are merely aids which enable us to restrain our mind temporarily, but which cannot by themselves enable us to destroy it. We can effectively destroy our mind only by remaining in our natural state of perfectly clear self-attentive being, and by no other means whatsoever.

This truth, which was explicitly stated by Sri Ramana in the first two sentences of the eighth paragraph of *Nāṉ Yār?*, is further emphasised by him with some more examples in the ninth paragraph:

> Just like *prāṇāyāma*, *mūrti-dhyāna* [meditation upon a form of God], *mantra-japa* [repetition of sacred words such as a name of God] and *āhāra-niyama* [restriction of diet, particularly the restriction of consuming only vegetarian food] are [just] aids that restrain the mind [but will not bring about its annihilation]. By both *mūrti-dhyāna* and *mantra-japa* the mind gains one-pointedness [or concentration]. Just as, if [someone] gives a chain in the trunk of an elephant, which is always moving [swinging about trying to catch hold of something or other], that elephant will proceed holding it fast without [grabbing and] holding fast anything else, so indeed the mind, which is always moving [wandering about thinking of something or other], will, if trained in [the practice of thinking of] any one [particular] name or form [of God], remain holding it fast [without thinking unnecessary thoughts about anything else]. Because the mind spreads out [scattering its energy] as innumerable thoughts, each thought becomes extremely weak. For the mind which has gained one-pointedness when thoughts shrink and shrink [that is, which has gained one-pointedness due to the progressive reduction of its thoughts] and

> which has thereby gained strength, *ātma-vicāra* [self-investigation, which is the art of self-attentive being] will be easily accomplished. By *mita sattvika āhāra-niyama* [the restraint of consuming only a moderate quantity of pure or *sattvika* food], which is the best among all restrictions, the *sattva-guṇa* [the quality of calmness, clarity or 'being-ness'] of the mind will increase and [thereby] help will arise for self-investigation.

Both *mūrti-dhyāna* and *mantra-japa* are practices in the path of dualistic devotion, and hence they are efficacious to the extent to which they are practised with genuine love for God. If we try to practise either of them without true love, our mind will constantly wander towards other thoughts because of the strength of its desire for whatever it happens to think about, and hence we will be unable to concentrate it entirely upon any single name or form of God. Therefore when Sri Ramana says that by practising either *mūrti-dhyāna* or *mantra-japa* our mind will gain one-pointedness, the meaning he implies is that our love for God will become focused and one-pointed. By thus concentrating our love and attention upon any one particular name or form of God, our desire to think other thoughts will be weakened, and our love to think of God will thereby gain strength. Once our mind has gained this strength of one-pointed love for God, it will be able to practise the art of self-attentive being easily.

Since our love for God cannot be complete until we surrender ourself entirely to him, any devotee who sincerely tries to think of God constantly will naturally develop a yearning to surrender himself or herself entirely to him. In order to surrender ourself thus, we must remain without doing or thinking anything, but simply being calmly and peacefully aware of the all-embracing presence of God.

Since God is the infinite totality or fullness of being, and since he is therefore present within each one of us as our own essential being, 'I am', surrendering ourself to him is nothing other than surrendering ourself entirely to being. In other words, it is just being submissively and firmly established in the state of deeply self-attentive and therefore thought-free being, which is the true state of *ātma-vicāra* or 'self-investigation'. Practising this art of self-attentive being is also therefore the true state of 'practising the presence of God', and for any mind that has developed the love to think of God constantly and one-pointedly, achieving this state of *ātma-vicāra* or self-attentive being will be easy and natural.

Therefore, though meditation upon a name or form of God is a mental activity and is therefore not in itself the state in which the mind has subsided in being, if practised with true and heart-melting love such meditation can be a great aid in leading our mind to the state of spiritual ripeness in which it will be genuinely willing to surrender itself entirely in the peaceful and all-consuming state of self-attentive being.

Whereas the practice of *prāṇāyāma* or breath-restraint will enable us to achieve merely a temporary state of mental subsidence, the practice of meditating with love upon a name or form of God will enable us to achieve the state of overwhelming love for God and consequent freedom from other desires, which is the state of mind that we require in order to be able to remain firmly established in our natural state of self-attentive being. However, just as the mental activity of meditating upon a name or form of God, if practised with true love, becomes an aid that prepares our mind for the practice of self-investigation or self-attentive being, so *prāṇāyāma*, if practised with the right attitude, can also become an aid that prepares our mind for the practice of self-investigation.

What is that right attitude with which a person should practise *prāṇāyāma*? It is the understanding that achieving a sleep-like state of temporary subsidence of mind is not a worthwhile aim, because it cannot enable us to weaken our desires, and that a true spiritual benefit can therefore be achieved by practising *prāṇāyāma* only if, before allowing our mind to subside in such a sleep-like state of abeyance, we use the calmness of mind brought about by *prāṇāyāma* to withdraw our attention from our breath and to fix it instead on our simple self-conscious being.

That is, as a means to calm our mind, which is usually agitated by many other thoughts, *prāṇāyāma* can give us a relatively thought-free space in which we can practise the art of self-attentive being with a minimum of distraction. However, this aid that can potentially be provided by *prāṇāyāma* is truly unnecessary, because we can remain in the state of self-attentive being only if we have genuine love for it, and if we have genuine love for it we will remain in it effortlessly without the need for any external aid such as *prāṇāyāma* to calm our mind. Moreover, because the relatively thought-free space provided by *prāṇāyāma* is produced by an artificial means and not by a reduction in the strength of our desires, if we try to make use of that space by withdrawing our attention from our breath and fixing it instead upon our own self-conscious being, we are likely to experience a powerful urge to think of anything else as soon as we try to attend to our being.

Therefore, if we really want to do something other than self-investigation in the hope that it will eventually help us to practise self-investigation, trying to meditate with love upon a name or form of God is a much safer and more beneficial course to follow than *prāṇāyāma*. However, if we truly understand that God is always present within us as our own essential self-conscious being, why should we make effort to attend to anything else instead of simply trying our best to be constantly attentive to our own being?

The other aid to self-investigation that Sri Ramana mentions in the ninth paragraph of *Nāṉ Yār?* is *mita sattvika āhāra-niyama*. The term *āhāra-niyama* means 'food-restraint', but since the Sanskrit word *āhāra* etymologically means procuring, fetching or taking, it can apply not only to the physical food that we take into our mouth, but also to the sensory food that we take into our mind through our five senses. Therefore, in order to keep our mind in a condition that is most favourable for us in our efforts to cultivate skill in the art of self-attentive being, we should by every reasonable means endeavour to ensure that both the physical food that we take into our body and the sensory food that we take into our mind are of a suitable quantity and quality.

The quantity and quality of the food we should consume is described by Sri Ramana as *mita* and *sattvika*. The word *mita* refers to the quantity of food we should consume, and means measured, limited, frugal or moderate. The word *sattvika* refers to the quality of food we should consume, and basically means pure and wholesome, or more precisely, endowed with the quality known as *sattva*, which literally means being-ness, 'is'-ness, essence or reality, and which by extension means calmness, clarity, purity, wisdom, goodness and virtue. The restriction or *niyama* of eating only *sattvika* food means abstaining from all types of non-*sattvika* food, which includes all meat, fish and eggs, all intoxicants such as alcohol and tobacco, and all other substances that excite passions or dull the clarity of our mind in any way.

Though Hindus usually consider milk products to be *sattvika*, in most cases nowadays this is no longer the case, because the modern dairy industry is based upon the cruel and exploitative practices of factory farming. Even milk that is produced by less cruel means such as organic farming is not entirely untainted by cruelty, because it is obtained from cows that have been bred to produce unnatural and therefore basically unhealthy quantities of milk, and because the usual fate of dairy cows and their calves is to end their life by being slaughtered either for their meat, their leather or both.

Since one of the important principles underlying the observance of consuming only *sattvika* food is *ahiṁsā*, the compassionate principle of 'non-harming' or avoidance of causing suffering to any living being, any food whose production involves or is associated with the suffering of any human being or other creature must be considered as being not *sattvika*. In our present-day circumstances, therefore, the only food that can truly be considered as being *sattvika* is that which is organically produced, fairly traded and above all vegan.

Besides the important and morally imperative principle of *ahiṁsā*, another important reason for taking care about the food we eat is that the effect that food has upon our mind is extremely subtle. If our food has been produced through the suffering of any creature, the subtle influence of that suffering will be contained in that food, and will affect our mind. Similarly if our food has been handled, processed or cooked by a person with unhappy or negative thoughts in their mind, the subtle influence of such thoughts will be contained in that food. Therefore it is generally recommended that a spiritual aspirant should as far as possible eat only food that is raw or that has been freshly cooked from raw or minimally processed ingredients by a person in a happy mood and with kind, caring and loving thoughts in their mind, because kindness and love are the most important *sattvika* ingredients that can be added to food.

With regard to the 'food' that we take into our mind through our five senses, we should as far as possible avoid attending to any sense objects that excite passion, greed, lust, anger, envy or any other such undesirable thoughts and emotions. Though we cannot always avoid being exposed to undesirable sights and sounds, we should try to keep such exposure to a minimum. Moreover, not only should we try to see and hear only *sattvika* sights and sounds, but we should also restrict the quantity of our sense perceptions to a *mita* or moderate level. In other words, we should avoid the habit of constantly bombarding our senses with unnecessary stimulation, which with all our modern technology is so abundantly available to us.

What exactly does all this have to do with practising the art of self-attentive being? In order for us to be able to remain steadily poised in the extremely subtle state of self-attentive being, it is essential that we restrain our desires and passions, reduce the quantity and vigour of our thoughts, and cultivate a contented, calm and peaceful attitude of mind. Such desirelessness, contentment, calmness and peace are qualities that in Sanskrit are described as *sattva-guṇa* or the quality of 'being-ness', which is the original and natural quality of our essential consciousness 'I am'.

Though this quality of *sattva* or 'being-ness' is the basic quality that always underlies the finite consciousness that we call our 'mind', our mental activity tends to cloud over and obscure it. Therefore besides this basic quality of *sattva* there are always two other qualities that function and compete in our mind, namely *rajōguṇa*, the dissipating quality of *rajas*, passion, emotion, restlessness, agitation and activity, and *tamōguṇa*, the obscuring quality of *tamas*, darkness, dullness, delusion, ignorance, insensitivity, heartlessness, cruelty, meanness, selfishness, pride and baser emotions such as anger, greed and lust. Whereas *sattva* is the natural quality of our essential being or *sat*, *rajas* and *tamas* are the respective qualities of the two basic aspects of our power of self-deception or *māyā*, the former being the quality of our power of dissipation or *vikṣēpa śakti*, and the latter being the quality of our power of obscuration or *āvaraṇa śakti*.

Our mind is composed of a mixture of these three qualities, but in ever-varying proportions. So long as it exists, each of them will always be present in it to a greater or lesser degree, and throughout our waking and dream states they will be competing to dominate it. At any given time one or more of them will predominate, and their relative predominance will influence our ability to be vigilantly attentive to our essential being, our consciousness 'I am'.

In order for us to be able to remain calmly and keenly attentive to our true but extremely subtle self-conscious being, the quality of *sattva* or 'beingness' must predominate in our mind, overpowering and suppressing the other two qualities. So long as either or both of the other two qualities predominate, our mind will lack the clarity and calmness that is required for us to be able to remain keenly self-attentive.

Sri Ramana used to illustrate this by means of two similes. Just as we would be unable to separate the extremely fine fibres of a silk cloth using a thick and heavy iron bar, so we will be unable to distinguish our extremely subtle being so long as our mind is under the sway of *tamas*, the dense and heavy quality of darkness, insensitivity and pride. Likewise, just as we would be unable to find an extremely small object in the dark using a lamp that is flickering in a strong wind, so we will be unable to discern our extremely subtle and unmoving being so long as our mind is under the sway of *rajas*, the dissipating and distracting quality of passion and restless activity. Therefore in order to be established firmly and steadily in our natural state of clear and unwavering self-attentive being, we should make every possible effort to cultivate and maintain a predominance of *sattva* in our mind.

Since the quality of our mind is strongly influenced by the quality of the physical food we eat, Sri Ramana says that by consuming only moderate quantities of *sattvika* food the *sattva* quality of our mind will increase, and this will help us in our practice of self-investigation. In order to cultivate this *sattva* quality, we should not just consume only *sattvika* food, but should also consume such food only in moderate quantities, because if we eat an excess quantity of even the most *sattvika* food, it will have a dulling effect upon our mind.

Whereas we can dispense with most other aids, such as *prāṇāyāma*, *mūrti-dhyāna* and *mantra-japa*, observing this restriction on the quantity and quality of food that we consume is one aid with which we should as far as possible never dispense, because whereas other aids distract our mind from our central aim of practising the art of self-attentive being, this restriction on the nature and quantity of our food is no distraction and can only help us in our practice.

If the art of self-attentive being were really difficult, we might require aids such as *prāṇāyāma*, *mūrti-dhyāna* and *mantra-japa* to help us to practise it, but it is in reality not at all difficult. In fact, it is the easiest thing of all, because whereas all other efforts that we make are unnatural to us, self-attentive being is our natural state and truly requires no effort at all. Effort appears to be necessary only because we have a greater liking to attend to other things than to abide attentively in our own being.

Our desire for and attachment to things other than ourself makes us unwilling to let go of everything and remain calm, unattached and unwavering in our thought-free natural state of self-attentive being, and our unwillingness to remain thus makes it appear difficult. However, in itself abiding in this true state of self-attentive being is not at all difficult. Therefore in the refrain and sub-refrain that he composed for his song *Āṉma-Viddai* Sri Ramana sings:

> What a wonder, *ātma-vidyā* [the science and art of self-knowledge] is [so] extremely easy! What a wonder, [so] extremely easy!
>
> [Our true] self is [so] very real even to ordinary [unlearned] people, that [in comparison even] an *āmalaka* fruit in [our] palm ends [paling into insignificance] as unreal.

The Sanskrit word *vidyā* basically means 'knowledge', but in actual usage it has a broad range of meanings including philosophy, science, art, learning or any practical skill. Thus the compound word *ātma-vidyā*, which in Tamil is generally modified as *Āṉma-Viddai*, means the practical science and art of knowing our own real self or essential being.

Our consciousness of our own being, 'I am', which is our true self, is our first and most basic knowledge, and hence it is clearly real to us at all times, even before we learn or understand anything else. 'As real as an *āmalaka* fruit in the hand' is an idiomatic way of saying that something is perfectly clear and obvious, but in comparison to our absolutely clear and real consciousness 'I am' even the clarity and reality of such a fruit in our hand pales into complete insignificance. When our true self or essential being 'I am' is so very real to each one of us, the science and art of knowing and being ourself is extremely easy – far easier than any other thing imaginable.

In order to know our own real self, we need not do anything. Because we ourself are the reality that we call our 'self' or *ātman*, we cannot know ourself as an object. We know objects by an act of knowing, that is, by paying attention to them. This act of paying attention to an object is a movement of our attention away from ourself towards that object, which we imagine to be other than ourself. Because the process of knowing anything other than ourself involves this stirring of our attention, arousing it from its natural state of reposing as our simple non-dual consciousness of being, and directing it outwards to something that seems to be other than ourself, it is an action or 'doing'.

However, we cannot know ourself in this same manner, because any movement or action of our attention takes it away from ourself. Therefore we cannot know ourself by any act of knowing, or by any other kind of 'doing'.

Because our real self is perfectly clear self-conscious being, we can know it only by being it, and not by 'doing' anything. By merely being self-attentive, we remain naturally as our own self-conscious being, without doing anything. Therefore, since this art of self-attentive being does not involve even the least action of our mind, speech or body, it is the easiest means – and in fact the only truly adequate means – for us to experience the infinite happiness of true self-knowledge.

Hence in verse 4 of *Āṉma-Viddai* Sri Ramana sings:

> To untie the bonds beginning with *karma* [that is, the bonds of action, and of all that results from action], [and] to rise above [or revive from] the ruin beginning with birth [that is, to transcend and become free from the miseries of embodied existence, which begins with birth and ends with death, only to begin once again with birth in another mind-created body], [rather] than any [other] path, this path [of simple self-attentive being] is exceedingly easy. When [we] just are, having settled [calmly and peacefully in perfect repose as our simple self-conscious being] without even the least *karma* [action] of mind, speech or body, ah, in [our] heart [the innermost core of our being] the light of self [will shine forth clearly as our non-dual consciousness of being, 'I am I']. [Having thereby drowned and lost our individual self in this perfectly peaceful and infinitely clear state of true self-knowledge, we will discover it to be our] eternal experience. Fear will not exist. The ocean of [infinite] bliss alone [will remain].

To attain this eternal experience of infinite happiness, we need not do anything by mind, speech or body, but must merely subside and settle calmly in our natural state of perfectly clear self-conscious being.

The words that Sri Ramana uses here to describe this state of just being are *summā amarndu irukka*. The word *irukka* is the infinitive form of the verbal root *iru*, meaning 'be', and is used idiomatically in the sense 'when [we] are'. The word *amarndu* is the present or past participle of the verb *amar*, which means to abide, remain, be seated, become still, become calm, become tranquil, rest, settle down or be extinguished. And the adverb *summā* means just, merely, leisurely, silently, quietly, calmly, motionlessly, inactively, without doing anything, or in perfect peace and repose. Since *summā* can be taken as qualifying both *amarndu* and *irukka*, the clause *summā amarndu irukka* means 'when [we] just are, having settled silently, calmly and peacefully in perfect repose'.

The sense of these three words, especially the word *summā*, is further emphasised by the preceding words, which mean 'without even the least action of mind, speech or body'. Therefore the practice of *ātma-vidyā*, the science and art of knowing our own real self, is just being, without even the least action of mind, speech or body – our mind having subsided and settled peacefully in and as our simple self-conscious being.

This practice of 'just being' or *summā iruppadu* is also clearly explained by Sri Ramana in the sixth paragraph of *Nāṉ Yār?*, where he defines it as 'making [our] mind to subside [settle down, melt, dissolve, disappear, be absorbed or perish] in *ātma-svarūpa* [our own essential self]'. Therefore, since this practice of *ātma-vidyā* is just being our own ever self-conscious being, and since it does not involve any action of our mind, speech or body, it is indeed 'exceedingly easy', far easier than any other 'path' or form of spiritual practice.

Nevertheless, due to the density of our self-imposed delusion or *māyā*, and due to the strength of our resulting desires, knowing and being our real self appears in the view of our mind to be difficult. That is, though the state of absolutely clear self-conscious being is truly our natural state, and though it is always experienced by us as 'I am', its natural clarity appears to our mind to be clouded and obscured by thoughts, which are impelled by our deeply rooted desires, and hence discerning it clearly in the midst of all these thoughts seems to our mind to be difficult.

This seeming difficulty will persist so long as our mind is under the sway of *māyā* and its *guṇas* or 'qualities', *tamas* and *rajas*. As we saw earlier, trying to focus our attention on our essential consciousness of being when our mind is under the sway of *tamōguṇa*, the obscuring quality of darkness and insensitivity, is like attempting to separate the fine threads of a silk cloth with the blunt end of a heavy iron bar, and trying to do so when our mind is under the sway of *rajōguṇa*, the dissipating quality of restlessness and agitation, is like attempting to find a tiny object in the dark with the aid of the flickering light of a lantern buffeted by a strong wind. Hence for those of us whose self-delusion and desires are strong, and in whose mind these two *guṇas* therefore predominate, calmly attending to and abiding as our own essential consciousness of being will appear to be not easy.

However, just as the only way to learn to talk is to talk, the only way to learn to walk is to walk, and the only way to learn to read is to read, the only way to learn the art of attending to and abiding as our own pure self-conscious being is to practise this art. However many times our attempts fail, we should persevere in trying again and again. As we do so, we will gradually but steadily gain the skill required to abide firmly as our own real self, our true and essential consciousness of being, 'I am'.

Self-abidance, which is the art of self-attentive being, is not impossible for anyone. All that is needed is persistent effort. Every moment that we are attentive to our natural consciousness of our own being, 'I am', however clumsily and imperfectly, the clear light of such relatively unadulterated self-consciousness will be cleansing and purifying our mind, dispersing the darkness of *tamōguṇa* and calming the agitation of *rajōguṇa*, and thereby allowing the natural clarity of *sattva-guṇa* or 'being-ness' to manifest itself.

To express the same truth in another way, when we practise the art of self-attentive being, the clarity of our self-attentiveness acts like the scorching rays of the sun, drying up all the seeds of desire in our heart and thereby rendering them infertile. Though the destruction of these seeds of our desires is the ultimate aim and purpose of all forms of spiritual practice, they can in fact be effectively destroyed – scorched and rendered infertile – only by the clarity of our self-attentive being-ness and by no other means.

These seeds of our desires – which in *vēdānta* philosophy are named as *vāsanās*, a word that is usually translated as latent mental 'tendencies' or 'inclinations', but whose actual sense can be better translated as latent mental 'impulsions' or 'driving forces' – are what rise and manifest in our mind as thoughts. Since their very existence is threatened by the clarity of our self-abidance or self-attentive being-ness, when we try to practise abiding in this state of self-attentive being they rise in rebellion, manifesting in our mind as innumerable thoughts of various kinds.

When they rebel against our self-attentive being-ness in this manner, the only way to vanquish them is to ignore them by keeping our attention firmly fixed upon our own essential being, as explained by Sri Ramana in the following passage from the sixth paragraph of *Nāṉ Yār?*:

> [...] If other thoughts rise, without trying to complete them [we] must investigate to whom they have occurred. However many thoughts rise, what [does it matter]? As soon as each thought appears, if [we] vigilantly investigate to whom it has occurred, 'to me' will be clear [that is, we will be clearly reminded of ourself, to whom each thought occurs]. If [we thus] investigate 'who am I?' [that is, if we turn our attention back towards ourself and keep it fixed firmly and vigilantly upon our own essential self-conscious being in order to discover what this 'me' really is], [our] mind will return to its birthplace [the innermost core of our being, which is the source from which it arose]; [and since we thereby refrain from attending to it] the thought which had risen will also subside. When [we] practise and practise in this manner, to [our] mind the power to stand firmly established in its birthplace will increase. [...]

No thought can rise without us to think it. Therefore the easy way for us to divert our attention away from each thought as and when it rises is to remember that it has occurred only to ourself. Instead of allowing ourself to be distracted by any thought that arises, if we vigilantly continue to remember only ourself, each of our thoughts will perish as soon as it attempts to rise, because without our attention it cannot survive.

If however we do become momentarily distracted by any thought, we should immediately divert our attention away from it towards ourself by remembering that it has occurred only 'to me'. As soon as we remember this 'me' to whom that thought had occurred, our attention will return to its source, which is our own consciousness of being, 'I am'.

This process of drawing our attention back towards our own self-conscious being by keenly scrutinising ourself in an attempt to discover 'who am I to whom these thoughts have occurred?' is what Sri Ramana describes when he says, 'If [we] investigate "who am I?", [our] mind will return to its birthplace'. Our mind is our power of attention, which becomes extroverted by thinking of things other than ourself, and its birthplace or source is our own being – our basic and essential self-consciousness 'I am'. Therefore when we divert our mind away from all thoughts and focus it exclusively in our being, we are simply returning it to its own birthplace, the source from which it had arisen.

Our mind rises only by imagining things other than itself, and those imagined things are its thoughts. Therefore, when we turn our mind or attention towards our own essential being, it is diverted away from all its imaginary thoughts, and hence it subsides in its source and remains as our mere self-conscious being. When we thus remain as being instead of rising as our thinking mind, our thoughts are all deprived of our attention, and since no thought can exist unless we pay attention to it, Sri Ramana adds that when our mind thus subsides in its birthplace or source, 'the thought which had risen will also subside'.

He then concludes by saying, 'When [we] practise and practise in this manner, to [our] mind the power to stand firmly established in its birthplace will increase'. That is, when we repeatedly practise this art of immediately turning our attention back towards its source whenever it is distracted even to the slightest extent by the rising of any thought, the ability of our mind to remain firmly and self-attentively established as mere being will increase.

Therefore repeated and persistent practice of this art of self-attentive being is the only means by which we can cultivate the ability and strength to remain unshaken by thoughts, and thereby to weaken and eventually destroy all our *vāsanās*, the seeds of our desires, which give rise to them.

This process of gradually fixing our mind or attention more and more firmly in our own essential self-conscious being by repeatedly and persistently withdrawing it from all thoughts of anything other than ourself is clearly described by Sri Krishna in two extremely important verses of the *Bhagavad Gītā*, verses 25 and 26 of chapter 6, which Sri Ramana has translated into Tamil as verses 27 and 28 of *Bhagavad Gītā Sāram*, a selection that he made of forty-two verses from the *Bhagavad Gītā* that express its *sāra* or essence:

> By [an] intellect [a power of discrimination or discernment] imbued with firmness [steadfastness, resolution, persistence or courage] one should gently and gradually withdraw [one's mind] from [all] activity. Having made [one's] mind stand firm in *ātman* [one's own real self or essential being], one should not think [even a little] of anything else.

> Wherever the [ever] wavering and unsteady mind goes, restraining [or withdrawing] it from there one should subdue it [by always keeping it firmly fixed] only in *ātman* [one's own real self].

The key words used here are *ātma-saṁsthaṁ manaḥ kṛtvā*, which literally mean 'having made the mind stand firm [or still] in self', and by clear implication they should be applied to each of the three sentences in these two verses. That is, we should gently and gradually withdraw our mind from all activity or thinking by making it stand firm and motionless in our essential self, having thus made it stand firm and motionless in our essential self we should refrain from thinking of anything whatsoever, and if due to our lack of vigilance it again wanders towards anything else, by making it stand firm once again in our essential self we should restrain its wanderings, withdrawing it from whatever it is thinking of, and thereby subduing it and making it subside in our essential self.

What exactly does Sri Krishna mean when he says that we should make our mind stand firm in self or *ātman*? The word *saṁstha* is the word *stha*, which literally means 'standing', qualified by the prefix *sam*, which literally means 'with' or 'together with', but which is used to express not only conjunction or union, but also intensity, completeness or thoroughness. Thus *saṁstha* means standing with, standing united with, standing firm, standing still, standing fixed, or simply firmly abiding, remaining or being. Hence the words *ātma-saṁsthaṁ manaḥ* denote the state in which our mind is firmly and motionlessly established in our essential being, as our essential being, having consciously subsided and thereby merged, united and become one with it. Therefore what Sri Krishna clearly implies by these words is that we should keep our entire mind or attention firmly fixed or keenly focused upon our real self or essential being, and should thereby remain firmly in the state of clear self-attentive being.

However, until our *vāsanās* or latent desires are greatly weakened, our mind will continue to be wavering and unsteady, and will therefore repeatedly rush out towards things other than ourself. When our mind is in such a condition, we cannot force it against its will to remain quietly and peacefully in our natural state of self-attentive being, and therefore by repeatedly practising this art of being steadfastly self-attentive we must gently and gradually train it and cultivate in it the willingness to withdraw from its habitual activity of thinking of things other than ourself.

The words in verse 25 that I have translated as 'gently and gradually' are *śanaiḥ śanair*. This repetition of the word *śanais*, which is an adverb meaning 'quietly', 'calmly', 'softly', 'gently' or 'gradually', conveys the sense that this practice of withdrawing from all activity by establishing our mind firmly in our own being should be done not only gently and without any force or compulsion, but also repeatedly and persistently.

This same sense is also conveyed in the next verse. That is, whenever and wherever our mind may wander, we should persistently practise restraining it, withdrawing it each time from the objects it is thinking about, and subduing it by establishing it firmly in our own essential being.

Whenever we succeed in our efforts to establish our mind thus in our real self or *ātman*, we should remain firmly established in that state of self-attentive being without thinking even the least about any other thing. By practising this art of repeatedly drawing our mind or attention back from thoughts towards ourself, we will gradually weaken and eventually destroy all our deeply rooted *vāsanās* or desires.

This process of destroying our *vāsanās* as soon as they rise in the form of thoughts is described by Sri Ramana in more detail in the tenth and eleventh paragraphs of *Nāṉ Yār?*. In the tenth paragraph he says:

> Even though *viṣaya-vāsanās* [our latent impulsions or desires to attend to things other than ourself], which come from time immemorial, rise [as thoughts] in countless numbers like ocean-waves, they will all be destroyed when *svarūpa-dhyāna* [self-attentiveness] increases and increases. Without giving room to the doubting thought, 'Is it possible to dissolve so many *vāsanās* and be [or remain] only as self?', [we] should cling tenaciously to self-attentiveness. However great a sinner a person may be, if instead of lamenting and weeping, 'I am a sinner! How am I going to be saved?', [he] completely rejects the thought that he is a sinner and is zealous [or steadfast] in self-attentiveness, he will certainly be reformed [or transformed into the true 'form' of thought-free self-conscious being].

Our *vāsanās* or latent desires, which are the driving forces that impel us to think, and our thoughts, which are their manifest forms, do not have any power of their own. They derive their power only from us. So long as we attend to them, we are feeding them with the power that is inherent in our attention.

As Sri Sadhu Om used to say, our attention is the divine power of grace, because it is in essence the supreme *cit-śakti* or power of consciousness, which is our essential being and the absolute reality. Our attention or consciousness is the power that underlies, supports and gives life to our imagination, and as such it is the power that creates this entire world of duality and multiplicity.

Therefore whatever we attend to is nourished and made seemingly real. Our desires and thoughts appear to be real only because we attend to them, and hence the power they seem to have is derived only from our attention. Just as our experience of a dream appears to be real and to have power over us only so long as we attend to it, so all our desires and thoughts appear to be real and to have power over us only so long as we attend to them.

Therefore if we fix our attention entirely and exclusively in our own essential being and thereby ignore all the thoughts that our *vāsanās* or latent desires impel to rise, we will deprive those latent desires of the power which they need to survive, and which they can obtain only from our attention. The more we thus deprive them of the attention they seek, the weaker they will become, and thus we will gain increasing power to resist the power of attraction with which they have till now been dominating us.

This is the reason why Sri Ramana said in the sixth paragraph of *Nāṉ Yār?*, 'When [we] practise and practise in this manner, to [our] mind the power to stand firmly established in its birthplace will increase'. That is, the more we practise this art of being vigilantly self-attentive, steadfastly ignoring all our impulses or desires to think of anything else, the more we will gain the strength to remain firmly established in our own naturally and ever clearly self-conscious being.

When our strength or power to remain firmly established in our self-conscious being thus increases, all our latent desires or *vāsanās* will be progressively weakened and will eventually lose the power that they now have to distract us away from our natural state of just being. This is the reason why Sri Ramana says that 'they will all be destroyed when *svarūpa-dhyāna* [self-attentiveness] increases and increases', and why he says that we should therefore give no room to the rising of any type of thought, but should instead 'cling tenaciously to self-attentiveness'.

Whatever thought we may feel impelled to think, by clinging tenaciously to self-attentiveness we can then and there weaken not only that particular impulsion or *vāsanā* but also simultaneously all our latent impulsions to think any thoughts, and with continued tenacity we can eventually destroy completely all our latent impulsions or desires. Therefore if we truly wish to destroy all our latent desires and thereby attain our natural state of true self-knowledge, we must be extremely tenacious and persistent in our practice of self-attentiveness, which is the true art of being.

What in practice does Sri Ramana mean by the words 'without giving room to thought' when he says here, 'Without giving room to the doubting thought whether it is possible to dissolve so many *vāsanās* and be only as self, we should cling tenaciously to *svarūpa-dhyāna* [self-attentiveness]', and when he says in the thirteenth paragraph, 'Without giving even the slightest room to the rising of any thought except *ātma-cintana* [the thought of self], being completely absorbed in *ātma-niṣṭha* [self-abidance] is giving ourself to God'? Not giving room to the rising of any other thoughts means ignoring them completely, not allowing them even the slightest space within the field of our attention or consciousness. But how in practice is it possible for us to exclude all thoughts from our consciousness? It is possible for us to do so only by filling our attention or consciousness wholly and exclusively with the 'thought of self', *svarūpa-dhyāna* or *ātma-cintana*, that is, with clear, keen and vigilant self-attentiveness.

Though Sri Ramana sometimes referred to self-attentiveness as the 'thought of self', using words that imply thinking such as *dhyāna* or *cintana*, he often clarified that it is actually a state of just being, and not a state of 'thinking' or mental activity. Therefore, since paying attention to anything other than ourself is 'thinking', and since being attentive only to ourself is a state not of 'thinking' but of just 'being', self-attentiveness is the only practical and effective means by which we can exclude all thoughts from our consciousness.

In the last sentence of this paragraph Sri Ramana assures us that if we are zealous or steadfast in self-attentiveness, we will certainly be 'reformed' or 'transformed'. The word that I have translated as zealous or steadfast is *ūkkam-uḷḷavaṉ*, which means a person who has *ūkkam*, impulse, ardour, zeal, strength, firm conviction and sincerity. Thus in this context the word *ūkkam* implies the same ardent tenacity and steadfastness that is emphasised by the words *viḍāppiḍiyāy piḍikka vēṇḍum*, which occur earlier in this paragraph and which I translated as 'should cling tenaciously to'. Clinging fast to self-attentiveness with such ardent tenacity, zeal, steadfastness and perseverance is essential if we truly wish to succeed in our efforts to attain absolute happiness, which can be experienced only in the calm and thought-free state of true self-knowledge.

The final word of this paragraph is *uruppaḍuvāṉ*, which etymologically means 'will become form', but which is commonly used in an idiomatic sense to mean 'will be elevated' or improved in body, mind or morals, and hence I have translated it as 'will be reformed' or 'will be transformed'. However, since the word *uru* or 'form' can also denote *svarūpa*, our 'own form' or essential self, in this context the meaning implied by *uruppaḍuvāṉ* is not merely that we 'will become morally reformed' or 'will be transformed into a better person', but is that we will be transformed into our own true and eternal 'form', which is thought-free, infinite, all-transcending, absolute and perfectly clear self-conscious being.

In the eleventh paragraph of *Nāṉ Yār?* Sri Ramana goes on to explain more about how the practice of self-attentive being enables us to destroy all our *vāsanās* or latent desires to experience things other than ourself:

> As long as *viṣaya-vāsanās* [latent impulsions or desires to attend to anything other than ourself] exist in [our] mind, so long the investigation 'who am I?' is necessary. As and when thoughts arise, then and there it is necessary [for us] to annihilate them all by investigation [keen and vigilant self-attentiveness] in the very place from which they arise. Being [abiding or remaining] without attending to [anything] other [than ourself] is *vairāgya* [dispassion] or *nirāśā* [desirelessness]; being [abiding or remaining] without leaving

> [separating from or letting go of our real] self is *jñāna* [knowledge]. In truth [these] two [desirelessness and true knowledge] are only one. Just as a pearl-diver, tying a stone to his waist and submerging, picks up a pearl which lies in the ocean, so each person, submerging [beneath the surface activity of their mind] and sinking [deep] within themself with *vairāgya* [freedom from desire or passion for anything other than being], can attain the pearl of self. If one clings fast to uninterrupted *svarūpa-smaraṇa* [self-remembrance] until one attains *svarūpa* [one's own essential self], that alone [will be] sufficient. So long as enemies are within the fort, they will continue coming out from it. If [we] continue destroying [or cutting down] all of them as and when they come, the fort will [eventually] come into [our] possession.

The investigation or *vicāra* 'who am I?' that Sri Ramana refers to here is the same practice of self-attentiveness that he referred to in the previous paragraph as *svarūpa-dhyāna* or 'meditation upon one's own essential form'. Since this practice of self-attentive being is the only means by which we can effectively weaken and eventually destroy all our *vāsanās* or latent desires, it is necessary for us to continue practising it tenaciously until all of them have been thoroughly eradicated. Since these latent desires are the driving forces that impel us to think, as long as any thought – any trace of a knowledge of anything other than our mere self-conscious being, 'I am' – appears in our consciousness, so long we should tenaciously persevere in clinging to keen and vigilant self-attentiveness.

So long as we continue to be vigilantly self-attentive, we will be effectively annihilating each thought that attempts to rise. Because our keen self-attentiveness will give no room for any thoughts to rise, as and when any latent desire attempts to rise in the form of a thought it will be immediately annihilated at the very moment and place in which it thus attempts to rise.

The 'place' or source in which and from which all our thoughts arise is our own essential being or consciousness, 'I am'. By self-attentiveness we remain in and as our self-conscious being, and thus we cut down each thought then and there as soon as it begins to rise.

If however our self-vigilance slackens even an iota, we will thereby give room to the rising of thoughts, and hence they will rush forth in great numbers in an attempt to distract our attention further away from our being. If we are attracted by these thoughts and therefore fail to regain our self-attentiveness immediately, they will continue to rise with great vigour and will thereby overpower us, subjecting us once again to the delusion of duality.

This self-negligence, self-forgetfulness or slackness in our natural self-attentiveness is named in *vēdānta* philosophy as *pramāda*. Since it enables our power of *māyā* or self-delusion to overpower us with the manifold products of our imagination, beginning with our illusory individuality and including all our desires, our thoughts and the objects of this world, since ancient times sages have repeatedly affirmed the truth that such self-negligence or *pramāda* is death. That is, when due to our self-negligence we slip down from our firm self-attentive abidance as being, we seemingly transform ourself into the finite and unreal individual consciousness that we call our 'mind', and we thereby in effect die to our infinite real self.

When we succeed in our attempts to cling tenaciously to self-attentiveness, we will thereby avoid attending to any other thing, or in other words, we will avoid imagining or thinking of anything other than ourself. Since the forces that impel us to imagine and know things other than ourself are our latent desires, we will be able to refrain from attending to any other thing only when we are able to avoid the fatal error of succumbing to the delusive attraction of the imaginary objects of our desires. Therefore whenever we remain without attending to anything other than ourself, we are at that moment remaining free from all our desires, and hence Sri Ramana says, 'Being without attending to [anything] other [than ourself] is *vairāgya* [dispassion] or *nirāśā* [desirelessness]'.

In this state of self-attentive being, in which all our imaginary knowledge of other things is entirely excluded, all that we know is our own non-dual consciousness of being, 'I am'. Since (as we have seen in earlier chapters) this non-dual self-consciousness 'I am' is the only true knowledge, because it is the only knowledge that is not finite or relative, Sri Ramana says, 'Being without leaving [our real] self [our own essential self-conscious being, 'I am'] is *jñāna* [knowledge]'. That is, whenever we are able to be without leaving our firm and attentive hold on our clear, natural and eternal self-conscious being, 'I am', we are at that moment experiencing only the one true, infinite and absolute knowledge.

Since not attending to anything other than ourself and not leaving ourself are just two alternative ways of describing our natural state of thought-free self-attentive being, after defining desirelessness as 'being without attending to [anything] other [than ourself]' and true knowledge as 'being without leaving ourself', Sri Ramana concludes by saying, 'In truth [these] two are only one'. That is, the only state of true desirelessness is the state of true self-knowledge. Since this state is not something alien to us but is our own natural and eternal state of being, we can begin to experience it even now by simply remaining vigilantly and firmly as our mere self-attentive being.

Because we always know 'I am', our consciousness of our own being is always present. However, because of our desire to pay attention to the thoughts and objects that we have created by our self-deceptive power of imagination, we tend to ignore or overlook this fundamental self-consciousness.

The more strongly our desires impel our mind or attention to flow out towards the objects of our imagination, the more we will tend to overlook our own essential self-conscious being. In other words, the stronger our desires become, the more dense our self-ignorance will grow. Conversely, the weaker our desires become, the more brightly and clearly our natural self-consciousness or self-knowledge will shine. In other words, the degree of our clarity of self-consciousness is inversely proportional to the strength of our desires and the consequent density of our thoughts or mental activities.

Therefore self-consciousness – or self-attentiveness, as we call it when we practise it as a spiritual exercise – is not something that is either white or black. That is, it is not a quality that is either present or absent, but is one that is always present but in widely varying degrees of clarity or intensity.

This is true, of course, only from the standpoint of our mind, which being an extroverted form of attention or consciousness never experiences its own essential consciousness of being with perfect and absolute clarity. From the standpoint of our real self, which is itself the absolute clarity of our consciousness of being, there are no relative degrees of self-consciousness, because its natural and infinite consciousness of its own being alone truly exists.

However, though the absolute truth is that our self-consciousness alone really exists, and that there is therefore no other thing that could ever obscure or diminish its intense and perfect clarity, in the relative and dualistic outlook of our mind self-consciousness appears to be something that we experience with varying degrees of clarity and intensity. From the standpoint of our spiritual practice, therefore, our aim should always be to experience our self-consciousness or self-attentiveness with the greatest possible degree of clarity.

Hence we should try to focus our attention so keenly on our own self-conscious being that all our awareness or knowledge of any other thing is entirely excluded. The more we are able by such keen self-attentiveness to exclude all other knowledge or thoughts, the more clearly and intensely we will become conscious of ourself as we really are.

In order to illustrate this process by which we can make our self-consciousness become increasingly clear and intense, Sri Ramana gives us the analogy of a pearl-diver who sinks deep into the ocean to collect a pearl. Our thoughts, which are the imaginary knowledge that we have of things other than ourself, are like the ever-restless waves on the surface of the ocean. The closer we are to the surface of our mind, the more we will be buffeted about by the movement of our thoughts. However, instead of floating about near the surface, if we sink, dive or penetrate deep into our being, we will increasingly approach the absolute core and essence of our being, which is entirely free of all such movement. The deeper we sink into our being, the less we will be affected by the movement of any thought.

Sinking or diving deep into ourself therefore means penetrating deep beneath the surface activity of our mind by focusing our attention ever more keenly, pointedly, exclusively and firmly upon our 'am'-ness – our fundamental consciousness of our own essential being, which we always experience as 'I am'. When our attention penetrates thus into the very essence of our being, our mind will subside or sink into the state of just being, and thus all its activity or thinking will automatically and effortlessly cease.

Only by repeatedly and persistently penetrating thus into the depth of our own 'am'-ness – our essential self-conscious being – will we eventually be able to reach its innermost depth or absolute core, which is itself the 'pearl of self', the perfect state of true and infinitely clear self-knowledge, which we are seeking to attain.

Sri Ramana often used this analogy of diving or sinking into water to illustrate how deeply and intensely our attention should penetrate into the innermost core or essence of our being. For example, in verse 28 of *Uḷḷadu Nāṟpadu* he says:

> Like sinking [immersing or diving] in order to find an object that has fallen into water, diving [sinking, immersing, piercing or penetrating] within [ourself] restraining [our] speech and breath by [means of a] sharp intellect [a keen, intense, acute and penetrating power of discernment or attention] we should know the place [or source] where [our] rising ego rises. Know [this].

The key words in this verse are *kūrnda matiyāl*, which mean by a sharp, pointed, keen, intense, acute and penetrating mind, intellect or power of discernment, cognition or attention, and they are placed in this verse in such a position that they apply by implication to all the verbs that follow them. That is, we should restrain our speech and breath by a keenly focused and penetrating intellect, we should dive or sink within ourself by a keenly focused and penetrating intellect, and we should know the source from which our ego rises by a keenly focused and penetrating intellect.

But what exactly does Sri Ramana mean in this context by these words *kūrnda mati* – a sharp, pointed, keenly focused and penetrating mind or intellect? The clue he gives us to answer this question lies in the last two verbs that they qualify. That is, since this keen and penetrating intellect is the means or instrument by which we can dive, sink, immerse or pierce deep within ourself, and by which we can thus know the source from which our ego rises, it must be an intellect – a power of discernment or attention – that is turned inwards and focused keenly, pointedly and penetratingly upon our real self or essential being, which is the source or 'place' from which our ego or individual sense of 'I' arises. Therefore a *kūrnda mati* is a keenly, sharply, intensely and penetratingly self-attentive intellect.

In this context it is important to note that though the Sanskrit words *buddhi* and *mati* are usually translated in English by the word 'intellect', they do not merely mean 'intellect' in the superficial sense in which this word is normally used in English. That is, in English the word 'intellect' is normally understood to mean just our superficial power of reasoning or rational thought, whereas in Sanskrit, Tamil and other Indian languages the words *buddhi* and *mati* convey a much deeper meaning than this.

The real meaning of these two words, particularly in the sense in which Sri Ramana uses the word *mati* in this verse, is 'intellect' in its original sense, which is derived from the Latin words *inter legere*, meaning 'to choose between', and which therefore denotes our power or faculty of discernment or discrimination. Therefore in this verse the word *mati* denotes our deep inner power of discernment or ability to distinguish and clearly recognise that which is real – a power that is derived not just from intellectual reasoning or rational thought, but rather from the profound natural clarity of pure self-consciousness which always exists within us, but which is usually clouded over by the density and intensity of our desires and attachments and our resulting thoughts.

Though in the philosophy of *advaita vēdānta* the two words *manas* or 'mind' and *buddhi* or 'intellect' are often used in such a way that they appear to denote two different entities, Sri Ramana clarified the fact that they are not actually two different entities but are just two different aspects or functions of one single entity – namely our finite individual consciousness, which we usually refer to as our 'mind'. Therefore whenever a distinction is implied in the meaning of these two words, the word *manas* or 'mind' denotes our mind in its more superficial and dynamic function as a power of thinking, feeling and perceiving, whereas the word *buddhi* or 'intellect' denotes our mind in its deeper and more static function as a calm power of inner clarity, discernment, discrimination or true understanding.

Hence the word *mati*, which is used in this verse as an equivalent of the word *buddhi*, means our mind, but rather than just our mind in a vague or general sense, it more specifically means our mind as a power of inner clarity and discernment – a power of attention that is capable of turning itself away from all appearances and focusing itself keenly and clearly upon the one reality that underlies them, namely our own essential self-consciousness 'I am'.

Since our mind is a separate individual consciousness that deserves this name 'mind' only so long as it attends to anything other than our own essential being, and since it subsides and becomes one with our being when it attends to it truly, wholly and exclusively, the keenly self-attentive 'mind' that is denoted by these words *kūrnda mati* actually ceases to be an individual mind or ego as soon as it becomes truly self-attentive and thereby submerges and sinks into the depth of our being, and thus it is transformed by its self-attentiveness into our real self, of which it is now wholly conscious. In other words, a truly *kūrnda* or keenly self-attentive mind is actually nothing other than our naturally and eternally self-conscious being.

Though Sri Ramana mentions 'restraining [our] speech and breath' in association with 'diving [sinking, immersing or piercing] within', it is not actually necessary for us to make any special effort to restrain either our speech or our breath, because just as our thoughts or mental activities will all subside automatically and effortlessly when we become intensely self-attentive, so too will our speech and breath. Therefore, if we undertake this simple and direct practice of self-attentive being from the very outset, there will never be any need for us to practise any of the artificial exercises of *prāṇāyāma* or breath-restraint, because by our mere self-attentiveness we will naturally restrain and bring to a complete standstill all the activity of our mind, speech, breath and body.

Since all these activities are merely imaginations that arise only when we allow our attention to leak out towards anything other than ourself, they will all disappear and become non-existent as soon as we effectively draw our entire attention back into the innermost depth or core of our being, which is the source from which it arises and flows outwards as our mind, intellect or ego.

Though the word *mati* is used in Tamil in the sense of mind, intellect, understanding, discrimination or discernment, it is actually a word of Sanskrit origin, and in Sanskrit besides these meanings it can also mean intention, resolution, will, desire or devotion. If we understand the words *kūrnda matiyāl* in this latter sense, they would mean 'by intense devotion or love'. Though this is not the principal meaning of these words in this context, it is nevertheless appropriate as a secondary meaning, because we will be able to sink or penetrate deep within ourself only if we have great love for the state of just being, which is the true form of God.

Unless we truly have intense love for being, we will be unwilling to surrender ourself to it, and hence our mind together with all its *vāsanās* or latent desires will continue to rise in rebellion whenever we try to cling firmly to self-attentiveness and thereby to sink deep into our innermost being. Devotion and desirelessness – that is, true love for being and freedom from desire for anything other than being – are like the two inseparable sides of a single piece of paper, and they each increase in direct proportion to the increase of the other. Therefore when Sri Ramana compares *vairāgya* or freedom from desire to the stone that a pearl-diver ties to his waist, saying that by submerging beneath the surface activity of our mind and sinking deep within ourself with *vairāgya* we can attain the 'pearl of self', he implies that in order to be able to sink to the innermost depth of our being we require not only *vairāgya* but also great love or *bhakti*.

Devotion and desirelessness, or *bhakti* and *vairāgya* as they are respectively called in Sanskrit and other Indian languages, are not only inseparable but are actually just two different ways of describing the same state of mind. However they are usually spoken of as two separate qualities because they are each a particular aspect of that one state of mind. Because they are both indispensable qualities that we require in order to be able to attain true self-knowledge, they are sometimes said to be the two wings by which we must learn to fly to the transcendent state of absolute being.

Both devotion and desirelessness arise due to another essential quality, which is called *vivēka*, a Sanskrit word that means discrimination, discernment or the ability to distinguish the real from the unreal, the eternal from the ephemeral, the substance from the form, or the actual truth from what merely appears to be true. True *vivēka* is not merely an intellectual understanding of the truth, but is a deep inner clarity that exists naturally in the core of our being and that arises in our mind when it becomes purified or cleansed of the grosser forms of its desires. An intellectual understanding of the truth is a useful starting point from which we can commence our inward search for the actual experience of true knowledge, but it will blossom into true discrimination or *vivēka* only if we apply it in practice by actually turning our mind inwards to discover the true nature of our essential being.

To the extent that our mind is purified of its desires, to that extent will the clarity of true discrimination or *vivēka* arise within it. Conversely, the more clearly we are able to discriminate, understand and be truly convinced that happiness exists only within ourself and not in any other thing, the stronger will both our devotion and desirelessness become. Thus true discrimination or *vivēka* enkindles in our mind true devotion or *bhakti* and true desirelessness or *vairāgya*, and true devotion and desirelessness clarify our mind, thereby increasing our power of discrimination.

The most potent and effective means by which we can enkindle the clarity of true discrimination in our mind is to be constantly and deeply self-attentive, because when we are self-attentive we are focusing our attention on our consciousness of being, which is not only the light that illumines our mind, but is also the infinite fullness and source of all clarity, knowledge or understanding. Or to explain the same thing in another way, when we are self-attentive we are warding off all the thoughts that cloud and obscure the infinite clarity of being that always shines in our heart or innermost core. Thus by self-attentiveness we are opening our heart to the true grace of God, which is our natural clarity of perfect self-consciousness, and which by its pure light will enable us to discriminate, understand and be truly and deeply convinced of the truth.

If our understanding and discrimination does not give us sufficient strength of conviction to enable us to withdraw our mind easily from everything other than ourself and to focus it intensely upon our own essential being, it must only be a superficial and unclear form of discrimination or *vivēka*. When our discrimination becomes truly deep, clear and intense – that is, when it becomes a truly *kūrnda mati* or keenly penetrating power of discernment – it will shine within us as an unshakeable strength of conviction, which we will experience as intense *bhakti* or love for our natural state of just being and as firm *vairāgya* or freedom from desire for anything other than being, and thus it will enable us to surrender our finite individual self, our mind or ego, and thereby sink effortlessly into the innermost depth of our essential being.

Just as the weight of a stone enables a pearl-diver to sink deep into the ocean, so the intensity of our *bhakti* and *vairāgya* will enable us to sink deep into the innermost core of our being. However, until we actually cultivate sufficiently intense *bhakti* and *vairāgya*, whenever we attempt to be vigilantly self-attentive, we will not be able to sink very deep but will continue to float just below the surface of our mind, where our thoughts will continue to disturb us. That is, our self-attentiveness will not be very deep and clear, but will continue to be shallow and clouded by the thoughts that we constantly like to think due to our lack of true *vairāgya* or desirelessness.

Our liking to think of anything other than ourself is the sole obstacle that prevents us from sinking deep into our real self-conscious being, and such liking is caused by our lack of true discrimination or *vivēka*. If we were truly convinced that happiness exists only within ourself and not in any other thing, we would certainly gain the love to subside into the peaceful thought-free depth of our own self-conscious being, and would therefore lose our desire to think of anything else. However, though we need this firm conviction, which arises as a result of clear discrimination, in order to be able to remain firmly and deeply self-attentive, the only way to gain it is by practising self-attentiveness.

By repeatedly and persistently practising the art of being self-attentive to whatever extent we can, we will gradually enkindle within our mind the necessary clarity of true discrimination or *vivēka*, and thus we will cultivate a steadily increasing strength of true love or *bhakti* and true desirelessness or *vairāgya*, which will in turn enable us to sink deeper into our naturally ever self-conscious being.

Thus the three inseparable qualities of *vivēka*, *bhakti* and *vairāgya* – which Sri Ramana describes collectively as *kūrnda mati* or a keenly penetrating power of discernment and love – will drive our mind deeper into our natural state of self-conscious or self-attentive being, and by sinking deep into this state we will cultivate and increase these three qualities. Therefore however weak or strong our present *vivēka*, *bhakti* and *vairāgya* may be, the only way for us to progress from where we now stand towards our goal of attaining the infinitely happy experience of true self-knowledge is to attempt repeatedly and persistently to be ever self-attentive.

After saying that in order to attain the pearl of self-knowledge we should sink deep within ourself with steadfast desirelessness, Sri Ramana goes on to say, 'If one clings fast to uninterrupted *svarūpa-smaraṇa* [self-remembrance] until one attains *svarūpa* [one's own essential being or real self], that alone [will be] sufficient'. Why exactly does he use the term *svarūpa-smaraṇa* or 'self-remembrance' here?

We never actually forget ourself, because we always know 'I am'. However, though we are always conscious of our own being as 'I am', we tend to ignore or overlook it because we are so interested in attending to things other than ourself, which are all mere products of our imagination. When our mind is thus constantly absorbed in thinking of things other than itself, it in effect forgets its own real self, its essential being, which does not think anything, but just is. Since all our thoughts or imaginations are thus constantly distracting our attention away from our natural consciousness of just being, we can put an end to their distracting influence only by trying to remember our being uninterruptedly.

Self-remembrance is therefore the antidote to our fascination with thinking of things other than ourself. However, because our desire to think of other things is so strong, when we try to cling fast to self-remembrance our mind will rebel and rise in the form of innumerable thoughts, thereby interrupting our effort to remember only ourself.

Whenever our self-remembrance is thus interrupted by the rising of other thoughts, we should again remember our being and thereby withdraw our attention from them. The more we practise remembering ourself in this manner, the more we will gain the strength and ability to cling exclusively and uninterruptedly to our remembrance of our own simple self-conscious being.

This practice or exercise of self-remembrance is not an attempt to regain the memory of something that we have forgotten, as for example we would try to remember where we had placed something that we have lost and are now trying to find, because our own self or essential being is always present and known by us, and is therefore something we have never really lost or forgotten. Rather this practice is an attempt to retain the memory of something that we wish to avoid forgetting, as for example we would try to remember constantly a person or thing whose memory gives us great joy. Self-remembrance is therefore simply another name for self-attentiveness, that is, being constantly attentive, conscious, mindful or aware of our own mere being or 'am'-ness.

Therefore this term *svarūpa-smaraṇa* or 'self-remembrance' that Sri Ramana uses here in this eleventh paragraph, the term *svarūpa-dhyāna* or 'self-meditation' that he used in the previous paragraph, the term *ātma-cintana*, 'self-thinking', 'self-thought', 'self-consideration' or 'self-contemplation' that he uses in the thirteenth paragraph, and the term *ātma-vicāra*, 'self-investigation', 'self-examination' or 'self-scrutiny' that he uses in many other places all denote the same simple practice of self-attentive being. As Sri Ramana says in the sixteenth paragraph of *Nāṉ Yār?*:

> […] The name '*ātma-vicāra*' [is truly applicable] only to [the practice of] always being [abiding or remaining] having put [placed, kept, seated, deposited, detained, fixed or established our] mind in *ātmā* [our own real self] […]

What exactly does Sri Ramana mean when he talks of putting, placing, keeping or detaining our mind in *ātmā* or our own real self? Our real self or essential being is the sole reality that underlies the appearance of our mind, and as such it is its source and natural abode. So long as we know nothing other than our own being, our mind remains naturally in and as our own infinite, undivided and non-dual real self. When however we begin to imagine and know anything other than our own being, our mind seemingly comes out from our real self as a separate and finite individual consciousness, whose nature appears to be thinking – that is, constantly attending to those other things, which it has created by its imagination. Hence putting, placing, keeping or detaining our mind in our real self means preventing it from rising and coming out as a separate thinking or object-knowing consciousness.

Therefore, since our mind comes out from our real self only by attending to things other than itself, and since it remains in our real self whenever it attends to and knows only our own being, putting, placing, keeping or detaining our mind in our real self means fixing or retaining our attention wholly and exclusively in our own essential self-conscious being, without allowing it to come out to know or experience any other thing.

Thus this simple definition given by Sri Ramana, which expresses perfectly the very essence of the practice called *ātma-vicāra* or self-investigation, can be paraphrased by saying that *ātma-vicāra* is a name that is applicable only to the practice of always being steadfastly self-attentive or conscious only of our own essential being, 'I am'.

Self-remembrance or self-attentiveness is a practice that we can train ourself to maintain even while we are engaged in other activities. Whatever we may be doing by mind, speech or body, we always know that we are, so by persistent practice it is possible for us to gain the skill to maintain a tenuous current of self-attentiveness in the midst of all our other activities. When we cultivate this skill to be always tenuously aware of our underlying self-consciousness throughout our waking and dream states, we will also become more clearly aware of our continuing self-consciousness in sleep.

That is, by persistently practising self-attentiveness or self-remembrance whenever our mind is free from any other work, we will gradually become so familiar with our natural and essential self-consciousness that we will continue to be tenuously aware of it even when our mind is engaged in activity, and even when it has subsided in sleep. Though we cannot be wholly or deeply attentive to our being when our mind is engaged in activity, we can nevertheless be tenuously attentive to it at all times. This is the state that Sri Ramana describes as 'clinging fast to uninterrupted *svarūpa-smaraṇa* or self-remembrance', and as 'always being or remaining keeping our mind fixed in *ātmā* or our own real self', and he says that practising thus 'alone is sufficient'.

Why does he say that 'clinging fast to uninterrupted *svarūpa-smaraṇa* or self-remembrance until we attain our own real self will alone be sufficient'? Though in the initial stages of this practice our self-remembrance will be frequently interrupted by the rising of thoughts and the consequent activity of our mind, and though in the more advanced stages of practice it may not be entirely interrupted but is nevertheless greatly diminished by whatever activity our mind may be engaged in, due to our persistence in this practice our *vāsanās* or latent desires to think of things other than ourself will be steadily weakened, and thus we will gain the *vairāgya* or freedom from desire that is required for us to be able to sink into the innermost depth of our being, where we can obtain the pearl of true self-knowledge.

So long as we mistake ourself to be this physical body, we will feel impelled to engage in physical, vocal and mental activities, if not at all times at least at certain times, because such activity is necessary for the maintenance of our life in this body. Therefore until we transcend this illusion that we are this body, we will not be able to remain completely untouched by the rising of thoughts. Hence sinking or diving deep within ourself is a practice that we cannot be engaged in uninterruptedly at all times.

However, though we cannot uninterruptedly and at all times be deeply, keenly, intensely and clearly self-attentive until we actually attain the perfect experience of true and absolute self-knowledge, even during the stage of practice we can strive to be uninterruptedly self-attentive at least tenuously. By trying to maintain at least a tenuous degree of self-attentiveness at all times, we can steadily weaken our latent desires and thereby make it easier for ourself to sink deep into our being at certain times, and by sometimes sinking deep into our being, we can gain an increased degree of clarity of self-consciousness, which will make it easier for us to maintain a tenuous but uninterrupted current of self-attentiveness even in the midst of various activities.

However, though attempting to maintain uninterruptedly a tenuous current of self-attentiveness in this manner is an important element of our spiritual practice, we cannot actually attain the true experience of absolute self-knowledge until we thereby gain sufficient *vivēka*, *bhakti* and *vairāgya* to be able to sink into the innermost depth of our being, where the bright and infinite light of perfectly clear and absolutely non-dual self-consciousness is eternally shining as 'I am'.

In the final two sentences of this eleventh paragraph Sri Ramana gives another analogy in order to illustrate what he had said in the first two sentences, namely:

> As long as *viṣaya-vāsanās* [latent desires for things other than ourself] exist in [our] mind, so long the investigation 'who am I?' is necessary. As and when thoughts arise, then and there it is necessary [for us] to annihilate them all by *vicāra* [self-investigation or self-attentiveness] in the very place from which they arise […]

The analogy he gives to illustrate this process of annihilating all thoughts as soon as they arise is as follows:

> […] So long as enemies are within the fort, they will continue coming out from it. If [we] continue destroying [or cutting down] all of them as and when they come, the fort will [eventually] come into [our] possession.

In this simile, the fort is our own real self, the core of our being, which is the source of our mind, and the enemies that reside within it are our *vāsanās* or latent desires for things other than our own being. In order to take possession of a fort, we must besiege it, and when we do so the enemies inside will not just remain there peacefully and submissively. For their own survival it is necessary for them to come out in an attempt to break our siege and replenish their food supply.

The food that our latent desires require for their gratification and survival is the knowledge of things other than our being. So long as we feed our mind with the knowledge of otherness or duality, it will survive and flourish, but if we deprive it of such knowledge, it will grow weak, because in the absence of such knowledge its separate identity or individuality will be dissolved. For its own survival, therefore, our mind will rise in rebellion as soon as we try to retain it in our mere being. That is, it will rebel by constantly trying to think of anything other than our own essential self-conscious being.

Since thoughts can rise only when we attend to them, they can be destroyed at the very place and moment that they arise only by our clinging tenaciously to self-attentiveness. If we are steadfast in our self-attentiveness or self-remembrance, every thought that our mind tries to think will perish due to its being ignored by us.

This ignoring of all thoughts by our clinging tenaciously to self-attentiveness is what Sri Ramana describes as cutting down all the enemies as and when they come out of the fort. Therefore if we persist long enough in our practice of self-attentive being, all our *vāsanās* or latent desires to think will eventually be destroyed, and our mind will thereby sink back into the source from which it arose.

This eventual sinking of our mind or attention back into our source or essential being is what Sri Ramana describes by saying that 'the fort will [eventually] come into [our] possession'. It is not necessary for us to continue struggling eternally to resist the attraction of things other than ourself and thereby to remain in our mere being, because by struggling to do so for a while we will be able to completely annihilate our desires, which make those other things appear to be so attractive.

Other things attract us because we wrongly believe that we can obtain happiness from them, and we believe this due to our lack of *vivēka* or true discrimination. However, by being constantly self-attentive, we will be feeding our mind with the natural clarity of *vivēka* that exists within us as the clear light of our ever self-luminous consciousness of our own being, and thereby we will steadily gain an increasingly strong conviction that happiness lies only within ourself and not in any other thing. The stronger this conviction becomes, the more our *bhakti* or love for our own being and our *vairāgya* or freedom from desire for anything other than our being will grow, and the easier it will therefore become for us to resist the false and delusive attraction of knowing anything other than being.

Therefore as a practice self-attentiveness is necessary for us only until such time as all our *vāsanās* or latent desires are destroyed by the dawning of true self-knowledge, whereupon we will discover that self-attentiveness or self-consciousness is the very nature of our being, and is therefore something that truly does not require any effort or practice. When our mind and all its *vāsanās* are thus destroyed by our experience of true self-knowledge, our false and imaginary individuality will be dissolved and we will remain effortlessly and eternally as the infinite and absolute consciousness of just being, 'I am'.

In this state of *manōnāśa* or complete annihilation of our mind, which is the state that is also known as *nirvāṇa* or total extinction of the illusion of our individual self, there is nothing further for us to do, and nothing other than our being for us to know. This is the true experience of Sri Ramana and all other sages, and it is clearly expressed by him in verse 15 of *Upadēśa Undiyār* and verse 31 of *Uḷḷadu Nāṟpadu*:

> When [his] mind-form is annihilated, for the great *yōgi* who is [thereby] established as the reality there is not a single action [or 'doing'], [because] he has attained his [own true] nature [which is actionless being].

> For one who is [completely immersed in and therefore one with] *tanmayānanda* [bliss composed only of *tat*, 'it' or the infinite and absolute reality], which rose [as true self-knowledge, 'I am I'] having destroyed [his finite individual] self, what single thing is there to do [or for 'doing']? He does not know any other thing but only [his own real] self. [Therefore] how to think [or who can think] that his state is such-and-such?

The state of true self-knowledge, which is the state of infinite and absolute happiness, is the state of just being – the state in which we have discovered that the finite thinking consciousness that we called our 'mind' was a mere illusion that existed only in its own limited and distorted view, and is therefore in reality entirely non-existent. Since our mind is the original cause, source and base of all activity, this mind-free state of just being is entirely devoid of even the least activity, action, *karma* or 'doing'.

Since this state of true self-knowledge is thus utterly devoid of our 'thinking', 'doing' and 'knowing' mind, it is also devoid of all knowledge of otherness or duality. Because it is therefore a state that completely transcends all thoughts and words, Sri Ramana asks how anyone could possibly conceive it or think of it as it really is.

Any conception that we may form in our mind about this state of true self-knowledge is therefore inaccurate, because it is merely an attempt to conceive the inconceivable. Likewise any words that we may use to describe it are inadequate, because they are merely an attempt to define the indefinable.

The state of true self-knowledge can never be known by our finite mind, but can be experienced by us only when our thinking mind is destroyed. In order to experience it, therefore, we must turn our mind inwards and drown it in its own source, which is our true and essential being. Hence we can never gain true knowledge from mere words, or by turning our attention outwards to read word-filled books, but only by turning our attention inwards to read the silent book of our own heart.

Words and books can serve a useful purpose only insofar as they point our mind in the right direction in which it must focus its attention in order to be able to experience true knowledge. However, even those few books that direct us to turn our mind selfwards will be truly beneficial to us only if we follow their directions and attempt to make our mind sink with true love and steadfast desirelessness into the deepest core of our own being.

Therefore instead of concentrating our efforts in repeatedly studying a few books that truly convince us and remind us of the need for us to turn our mind inwards, and in sincerely and persistently trying to practise the art of self-attentive being that those books teach us, if we continue reading innumerable books to gather more and more extraneous knowledge, we will be wasting our valuable time and distracting our mind from our true purpose, which is to give up all other knowledge and thereby to sink in the only true knowledge – the simple non-dual knowledge or consciousness of our own being, 'I am'.

Therefore in the sixteenth paragraph of *Nāṉ Yār?* Sri Ramana says:

> Since in every [true spiritual] treatise it is said that for attaining *mukti* [spiritual emancipation, liberation or salvation] it is necessary [for us] to restrain [our] mind, after knowing that *manōnigraha* [holding down, holding within, restraining, subduing, suppressing or destroying our mind] is the ultimate intention [or purpose] of [such] treatises, there is no benefit [to be gained] by studying without limit [a countless number of] treatises. For restraining [our] mind it is necessary [for us] to investigate ourself [in order to know] who [we really are], [but] instead [of doing so] how [can we know ourself by] investigating in treatises? It is necessary [for us] to know ourself only by our own eye of *jñāna* [true knowledge, that is, by our own selfward-turned consciousness]. Does [a person called] Raman need a mirror to know himself as Raman? [Our] 'self' is within the *pañca-kōśas* [the 'five sheaths' with which we seem to have covered and obscured our true being, namely our physical body, our *prāṇa* or life force, our mind, our intellect and the seeming darkness or ignorance of sleep], whereas treatises are outside them. Therefore investigating in treatises [hoping to be able thereby to know] ourself, whom we should investigate [with an inward-turned attention] having removed [set aside, abandoned or separated] all the *pañca-kōśas*, is useless [or unprofitable]. Knowing our *yathārtha svarūpa* [our own real self or essential being] having investigated who is [our false individual] self, who is in bondage [being bound within the imaginary confines of our mind], is *mukti* [emancipation]. The name '*ātma-vicāra*' [is truly applicable] only to [the practice of] always being [abiding or remaining] having put [placed, kept, seated, deposited, detained, fixed or established our] mind in *ātmā* [our own real self], whereas *dhyāna* [meditation] is imagining ourself to be *sat-cit-ānanda brahman* [the absolute reality, which is being-consciousness-bliss]. At one time it will become necessary [for us] to forget all that [we] have learnt.

To attain emancipation or salvation from the bondage of imagining ourself to be a finite individual we must know ourself as we really are, that is, as the non-dual, infinite and absolute consciousness of our own essential being. But where must we look in order to know ourself thus? Can we know ourself merely by looking in books or sacred texts? No, we obviously cannot, because to know ourself truly and accurately, we must look within ourself in order to discern the true essence of our own being.

That is, since we ourself are the 'self' that we wish to know, we can know ourself only by investigating or examining our innermost being with a keenly focused and inwardly piercing attention. Our power of attention, which is our power to direct and focus our consciousness upon something, is the basic and essential instrument by which we are able to know anything. Without attending to something, we cannot know it. Therefore, unless we actually attend to ourself very keenly and carefully, we cannot truly and accurately know ourself as we really are.

True self-knowledge is not just some theoretical knowledge that we may understand by our intellect, but is only a clear and direct non-dual knowledge that we can acquire only through actual self-experience. By attending to books that provide conceptual information about our real self, we can know only that conceptual information, but we cannot actually know ourself. Whatever conceptual information or theoretical knowledge we may acquire about ourself is extraneous to us, and hence it is something other than ourself. Learning some theoretical information about the taste of chocolate is entirely different to actually experiencing the taste of chocolate. Likewise, learning some theoretical knowledge about our own real self is entirely different to actually experiencing ourself as we really are.

We can never know ourself by looking outside ourself, but only by looking within. In fact, it is our habit of looking outside ourself, and our intense liking to do so, that actually prevents us from knowing ourself as we really are. We do not need any other knowledge to know ourself, because we always know 'I am'. All we need 'do' to know ourself is to remove all the extraneous knowledge that we have superimposed upon our basic knowledge of ourself as 'I am'.

The extraneous knowledge that we have superimposed upon ourself comes in many different forms, but what is common to all these manifold forms of knowledge is that we experience them all as 'I am knowing this'. What is real in this experience is only the 'I am' and not the 'knowing this', which is merely a transient appearance. Therefore, in order to know the real 'I am' as it is, all we have to 'do' is to experience it without the superimposition of this ephemeral apparition or adjunct 'knowing this'.

Of all the ephemeral and imaginary adjuncts that we superimpose upon our basic knowledge 'I am', the most fundamental are our body and the other objects that we mistake to be ourself. Because we imagine certain objects such as our body to be ourself, we imagine other objects outside this body to be other than ourself, and hence we create the illusion of a distinction between ourself and other things, and the parallel illusion of 'inside' and 'outside'.

In the philosophy of *vēdānta*, the objects that we imagine to be ourself are described as the *pañca-kōśas*, the 'five sheaths' or 'five coverings', because in effect they enclose or cover our real self, obscuring in our view its true and infinite nature. These 'five sheaths' that are classified in *vēdānta* are our physical body, our *prāṇa* or the life-force within this body, our thinking mind, our discerning intellect, and the happiness that we experience in sleep as a seeming darkness or ignorance.

Because the distinction between some of these 'sheaths' is rather arbitrary, this classification is often simplified by saying that our real self is seemingly enclosed within three bodies, our 'gross body', which means our physical body, our 'subtle body', which is our mind, and which is usually said to include both our *prāṇa* and our intellect, and our 'causal body', which is the seeming darkness-yet-happiness that we experience in sleep. However, how we choose to classify these phenomena that we imagine to be ourself is unimportant, because none of them are the real 'self' that we seek to know.

Sri Ramana mentions this term *pañca-kōśas* or 'five sheaths' in this context only to emphasise the fact that we experience ourself as if we existed inside these 'sheaths' or extraneous adjuncts, whereas we experience books as if they existed outside of them. Though books appear to exist outside ourself, we can know them and understand them only through the medium of at least three of these sheaths, namely the senses of our physical body, our mind and our intellect. However, to know our real self, we must set aside or ignore all of these five sheaths, since they are not really ourself, and we must concentrate our entire attention upon our essential self-consciousness – our fundamental consciousness of our own being, 'I am'.

Therefore, since we cannot study any book without mistaking ourself to be this body and mind, and since we cannot know our real self without giving up this mistaken identification, we can never know ourself merely by studying books. Since the ultimate import of all sacred texts and other truly useful books is that we should know ourself in order to experience true and perfect happiness, we must eventually forget all that we have learnt in books by turning our attention inwards with overwhelming love to know only our own real self or essential being.

Everything that we learn from books or from any other source outside ourself is an extraneous knowledge, which, having come to us at one time, must leave us at some other time. The only knowledge that is eternally with us is our basic knowledge 'I am', which is our consciousness of our own essential being.

However, though it is ever present and known by us as our own self-conscious being, the true nature of this eternal knowledge now appears to be clouded and obscured by the transient superimposition of all our other knowledge. Since no knowledge that comes and goes can give us permanent happiness, the only knowledge we should seek is perfectly clear and accurate knowledge of our own being – that is, knowledge of ourself free from the superimposition of any other form of knowledge.

The only truly useful and beneficial knowledge that we can acquire from books or other external sources, including even the most sacred and holy books, is the knowledge that impresses upon us and convinces us of the need for us to turn our attention selfwards in order to experience and directly know our own essential being. So long as our mind feels impelled by its desires to be active, studying a select few books that constantly, repeatedly and convincingly emphasise the truth that in order to experience eternal and infinite happiness we must know our own real self, and musing frequently upon the truth revealed in such books, will be a great aid in giving impetus to our love and efforts to practise self-attentiveness.

This three-fold process of repeatedly reading such books, musing upon their import, and trying to put what we learn from them into practice is known in *vēdānta* as *śravaṇa*, *manana* and *nididhyāsana*, and is recommended by Sri Ramana and other sages as the means by which we can gradually acquire the skill to remain steadfastly in the state of self-attentive being. However, though *śravaṇa* or reading the right type of books is recommended by Sri Ramana, this does not mean that we should read an endless number of books. Just a few really pertinent books are quite sufficient to support us in our efforts to practise self-attentiveness.

Whereas studying deeply a few truly pertinent books can be a great aid to our practice of self-attentive being, reading a vast number of books can be a serious impediment. Therefore in verse 34 of *Uḷḷadu Nāṟpadu Anubandham* Sri Ramana says:

> For people of little intelligence, wife, children and others [other relatives] form [just] one family. [However] know that in the mind of people who have vast learning, there are not [just] one [but] many families [in the form] of books [that stand] as obstacles to *yōga* [spiritual practice].

Though a strong attachment to our family can be an obstacle to our spiritual practice, because it can draw our mind outwards and make it difficult for us to remain free of thoughts in the state of self-attentive being, a strong attachment to all the knowledge that we have acquired from studying many books is a still greater obstacle, because it will fill our mind with many thoughts.

If we are really intent upon experiencing the true goal of *yōga*, which is perfectly clear self-knowledge, we will not feel inclined to read vast quantities of sacred texts or other philosophical books, because we will be eager to put into practice what we have learnt from a few really pertinent books which explain that simple self-attentive being is the only means by which we can experience that goal. If instead we feel enthusiasm only to study an endless number of books, we will merely succeed in filling our mind with countless thoughts, which will draw our attention away from our essential consciousness of our own being. Thus filling our mind with knowledge gathered from many books will be a great obstacle to our practice of self-attentive being.

Excessive study will not only fill our mind with innumerable thoughts, which will cloud our natural inner clarity of self-consciousness, but will also fill it with the pride of learning, which will prompt us to display our vast knowledge to other people, and to expect them to appreciate and praise it. Therefore in verse 36 of *Uḷḷadu Nāṟpadu Anubandham* Sri Ramana says:

> Rather than people who though learned have not subsided [surrendered or become subdued, humble or still], the unlearned are saved. They are saved from the ghost of pride that possesses [the learned]. They are saved from the disease of many whirling thoughts. They are saved from running in search of fame [repute, respect, esteem or glory]. Know that what they are saved from is not [just] one [evil].

Of all the obstacles that can arise in our path when we are seeking true self-knowledge, the desire for praise, appreciation, respect, high regard, renown or fame is one of the most delusive and therefore dangerous, and it is one to which the learned are particularly susceptible. Therefore in verse 37 of *Uḷḷadu Nāṟpadu Anubandham* Sri Ramana says:

> Though all the worlds are [regarded by them as] straw, and though all the sacred texts are within [their] hand, [for] people who come under the sway of the wicked whore who is *puhaṙcci* [praise, applause, appreciation, respect, high regard, renown or fame], escaping [their] slavery [to her], ah, is rare [or very difficult].

The first clause of this verse, 'though all the worlds are straw', implies that those of us who have studied vast amounts of philosophy may look down upon the normal mundane pleasures of this world, heaven and all other worlds as being a mere trifle, and may therefore imagine that we have renounced all desire for them. The second clause, 'though all the sacred texts are within hand', implies that we may have mastered a vast range of scholastic knowledge about various systems of philosophy, religious belief and other such subjects. However, in spite of all our vast learning and our seeming renunciation, if we fall prey to desire for the extremely delusive pleasure of being an object of praise, appreciation, admiration, respect, high regard, acclaim or fame, to free ourself of such desire is very difficult indeed.

The desire for appreciation and respect is very subtle and therefore powerful in its ability to delude us, and it is a desire to which even otherwise perfectly good people can easily fall a prey, particularly if they engage themselves in any activity that seems to benefit other people, such as teaching the principles of religion, philosophy or moral conduct through either speech or writing. This desire is particularly dangerous for a spiritual aspirant, because the pleasure we feel in being appreciated and respected derives from our attachment to our ego or individual personality – our delusive sense that we are the person who is appreciated and respected. Therefore, if we are sincere in our desire to attain true self-knowledge, we should be extremely vigilant to avoid giving any room in our mind to the rising of this desire.

Until we attain the non-dual experience of true self-knowledge, we will not be able to remain completely unaffected either by any recognition, respect, appreciation or praise that we may receive, or by any of their opposites such as disregard, disrespect, depreciation or criticism. Only when we attain true self-knowledge and thereby discover that we are not this individual person who is being recognised, appreciated or praised, or disregarded, disrespected, depreciated or criticised, can we be truly unaffected by them. Therefore in verse 38 of *Uḷḷadu Nāṟpadu Anubandham* Sri Ramana says:

> When we always abide unswervingly in our own [true] state [of non-dual self-knowledge], without knowing [the illusory distinction between] 'myself' [and] 'others', who is there besides ourself? What [does it matter] if whoever says whatever about us? [Since in that state we know that there is no one other than our own essential being, it would be as if we were extolling or disparaging ourself only to ourself.] What indeed [does it matter] if [to ourself] we extol or disparage ourself?

So long as we experience the existence of any person besides ourself, or the existence of anything other than our single, undivided and non-dual consciousness of our own being, 'I am', we should not imagine that we have attained true self-knowledge, or that we are impervious to all forms of appreciation and depreciation. Most importantly, we should never delude ourself by imagining that we can be a true spiritual *guru* to other people, or pose as such, because the true spiritual *guru* is only the 'person' who has ceased to exist as a separate individual person, having merged and dissolved in the absolute reality, thereby becoming one with it, and who therefore knows that the absolute reality, which is our own essential being, alone exists, and that there is truly no person other than it.

So long as we feel ourself to be a separate individual, we should always be wary of the delusion of pride, which can so easily rise within us. Even if, for example, we happen to write a book like this one that I am now writing, exploring and discussing the teachings of a true spiritual *guru* such as Sri Ramana, we should never allow ourself to fall prey to the subtle and powerful delusion of pride or egoism, imagining that we can claim credit for any clarity or wisdom that might appear in what we write.

If we are able to express any clarity of understanding about the nature of the absolute reality, or about the means by which we can attain it, we should understand that that clarity is not our own, but belongs only to the source from which it arises, which is the one absolute reality that exists within each one of us as our own essential self-conscious being, and which manifests outwardly in the form of the true *guru* in order to indicate the truth that we are that reality, and that to know it we must turn our attention back on ourself in order to experience and thereby drown in our own essential being. If we have truly understood the teachings of any manifestation of the one true *guru*, such as Sri Ramana, we will understand that as an individual person we are truly nothing, and that our mind or individual personality is a mere delusion, and is therefore not worthy of any praise or other form of appreciation.

Self-delusive pride is the greatest danger that can arise as a result of excessive study of sacred texts and other philosophical books. The real purpose of studying such books, and the only true benefit we can derive from doing so, is twofold. Firstly it is to understand clearly the means by which we can annihilate our ego, our sense of separate individuality, and thereby experience the one true and absolute knowledge, which is our non-dual consciousness of our own essential being. Secondly and still more importantly, it is to cultivate an overwhelming love to practise that means and thereby drown in the infinite happiness and peace of that true non-dual self-consciousness. Therefore in verse 35 of *Uḷḷadu Nāṟpadu Anubandham* Sri Ramana says:

> What [is the use of] people who do not intend to erase the letter [of fate], scrutinising where they who know the letter [the words written in books] were born, knowing [that] letter? O Sonagiri the Wise, say, who else [are they] but people who have acquired the erudition [or nature] of a sound recording machine?

The 'letter' is an idiomatic way of referring to destiny, the 'writing of fate', and also to the words written in books, the 'letter of the scriptures', as opposed to their spirit or true significance. The purpose or spirit of the words written in sacred texts is to teach us how we can 'erase the letters of fate' only by annihilating our ego or mind, which imagines that it is doing actions or *karmas* and experiencing the destiny or fate that results from such actions.

If we study the words written in sacred texts and other philosophical books, but still make no effort to put what we learn from those books into practice by turning our mind inwards to experience our own essential being, which is the source from which we as our ego were 'born' or originated, and thereby annihilating this ego, who experiences the letters of fate, all our study and erudition are of no use whatsoever.

Therefore, addressing God poetically as 'Sonagiri the Wise', Sri Ramana concludes that if we gain vast erudition by studying books which teach that we can attain true and lasting happiness only by annihilating our ego or mind, yet still have no intention to practise self-scrutiny, which is the only means by which we can annihilate it, we are merely gaining the erudition of a sound recording machine – that is, the ability to regurgitate repeatedly whatever words or concepts we have recorded in our mind as a result of our study.

What initially motivates us to read books on philosophy or religion is our desire to know the truth, but the true knowledge that we seek to acquire cannot be contained in any book or any words. True knowledge is only the absolute knowledge that lies beyond the reach of all thoughts and words.

The words and concepts that are expressed in philosophical writings can only show us the means by which we can attain the true knowledge we seek, which always exists within us as our fundamental non-dual consciousness of our own essential being, 'I am'. Therefore, in order to attain true knowledge, we must turn our attention away from books and concentrate it instead upon our own essential self-conscious being.

True *jñāna-vicāra*, investigation or examination of knowledge, is not the study of any philosophical concepts, but is only the keen and vigilant scrutiny of our own fundamental self-consciousness. Therefore in verse 19 of *Upadēśa Undiyār* Sri Ramana says:

> When [we] scrutinise within [ourself] 'what is the place in which it [our mind] rises as I?' [this false] 'I' will die. This [alone] is *jñāna-vicāra*.

The word which I have translated here as 'will die' is the compound verb *talai-sāyndiḍum*, which literally means 'becomes head-bent', that is, bows its head in shame, modesty or reverence, but which is commonly used in an idiomatic sense to mean 'dies'. So long as our mind or ego – our false individual sense of 'I', which is our basic consciousness 'I am' mixed with various adjuncts or *upādhis* that we imagine to be ourself – appears to exist, we cannot experience the true adjunct-free nature of our real self-consciousness 'I am' – that is, our unqualified, undivided, non-dual and absolute consciousness of our own essential being.

Since this mind, our false 'I' or ego, rises only by knowing things that appear to be other than itself, and since it seems to exist only so long as we allow it to continue dwelling upon those other things, in order to annihilate it we must turn it away from all its thoughts and concepts – that is, from all forms of knowledge that are extraneous to our fundamental self-consciousness – by concentrating it wholly and exclusively upon our own essential self-conscious being, which is the source from which it had arisen to know all those other forms of knowledge. No matter how many books we may read, we cannot attain true knowledge until and unless we forget all that we have learnt from them by thus concentrating our entire attention only upon our own true non-dual self-conscious being.

If we have great enthusiasm to study a vast number of books, and to remember all the concepts that we have learnt from them, we are likely to forget the true purpose of the books we study. Therefore, rather than reading many books, we would be wise to select a few books which clearly and repeatedly emphasise the need for us to turn our mind inwards and drown it in the source from which it has risen, and that thereby enkindle and sustain our enthusiasm to practise the art of vigilantly self-attentive and therefore thought-free being.

The most important books for us to study are those that contain the teachings of our own *guru*. Though all sages have taught the same truth, they each have expressed it in different terms and with differing degrees of explicitness, in order to suit the circumstances and the understanding of those they were addressing. Though our own real self has at various times manifested itself in the form of various sages, it has now manifested for us in the form of our own particular *guru* in order to teach us the truth in a manner that is best suited to our own particular needs.

It does not matter if we have never seen our *guru* in physical form, as most of us have never seen Sri Ramana, because he is always manifest and available to us in the form of his teachings. Therefore, though we should have respect for the teachings of all sages, the teachings of our own *guru* are sufficient for us and will provide us with all the help and guidance that we need in order to be able to turn our mind inwards and practise steadfastly the art of self-attentive being.

Whatever books we may read, we should always remember that the only true benefit we can derive from reading is an added impetus or urge to turn our mind inwards and remain firmly self-attentive. If a book does not enkindle in our mind a clear understanding and strong conviction that the only means by which we can attain true happiness is to practise persistently the art of self-attentive being, or if it does not reinforce our existing understanding and conviction concerning this truth, there is truly no benefit in our reading such a book.

In order for us to develop the skill that we require to hold fast to self-attentiveness – that is, in order for us to cultivate the necessary *bhakti* or love for our own being and *vairāgya* or freedom from desire for anything other than our being – we must be single-mindedly interested in and focused upon this one aim, and hence we should avoid as far as possible anything that distracts us from it or that scatters our single-pointedness. Therefore, though there may be many books that emphasise more or less directly that we should restrain our mind from running outwards and should instead turn it inwards to attend to our mere being, we would nevertheless be wise to avoid reading more than a select few such books, because the same truth is expressed in many such books in many different ways and with varying degrees of clarity and intensity, and hence by reading too many books our mind will tend to become scattered and thereby to lose its concentrated and keenly focused impetus to cling tenaciously to simple self-attentiveness.

Moreover, though repeatedly reading a select few books may help to clarify our understanding and strengthen our conviction, we should always remember that the truth we seek is not actually contained in those books but only within ourself. The truth or reality transcends all thoughts and words, so it can never be adequately expressed in any book, no matter how sacred we may hold that book to be.

The words in sacred books can never express the truth as it really is, but can only point our mind towards that truth, which exists in the innermost depth of our being. Therefore the benefit we can obtain from reading any book is very limited. As Sri Adi Sankara wrote in verse 364 of *Vivēkacūḍāmaṇi*, a hundred times greater than the benefit of *śravaṇa* or reading is the benefit of *manana*, musing or reflecting upon the truth that we have read, and a hundred thousand times greater than the benefit of *manana* is the benefit of *nididhyāsana* or keen self-attentiveness, which is the correct application of the truth we have learnt by *śravaṇa* and understood by *manana*.

In the first sentence of this sixteenth paragraph, Sri Ramana says that every sacred text or treatise teaches that to attain emancipation or salvation we should restrain our mind, and that teaching mind-restraint is therefore the ultimate aim or intention of all such texts.

However, though all sacred texts agree on the fact that we should restrain our mind, different texts explain what is meant by 'mind-restraint' in different terms. Some sacred texts emphasise only the less subtle aspects of mind-restraint such as curbing the grosser forms of our desires, but though we may curb many or even most of our desires, we cannot restrain our mind completely and perfectly unless we manage to prevent it from rising at all to know even the least thing other than ourself.

Therefore, since we can prevent or restrain the rising of our mind only by being vigilantly self-attentive, in the second sentence Sri Ramana clarifies the true meaning of the term mind-restraint or *manōnigraha* by saying, 'For restraining [our] mind it is necessary [for us] to investigate ourself [to know] who [we really are]'. What happens when we truly investigate ourself is revealed by him in verse 25 of *Uḷḷadu Nāṟpadu* and verse 17 of *Upadēśa Undiyār*:

> Grasping form [a body] it [our mind or ego] comes into existence. Grasping form [that body] it persists. Grasping and feeding on form [thoughts or objects] it flourishes abundantly. Leaving form [one

> body or one thought] it grasps form [another body or another thought]. [However] if [we] examine [it], [this] formless phantom ego takes flight. Know [that is, know this truth, or experience this disappearance of the ego by examining it].
>
> When [we] scrutinise the form of [our] mind without forgetfulness, [we will discover that] there is no such thing as 'mind' [separate from or other than our real and essential self]. For everyone, this is the direct path [to true self-knowledge].

That is, the more keenly we investigate, examine or scrutinise ourself, whom we now feel to be this finite individual consciousness that we call our 'ego' or 'mind', the more this 'mind' will subside and dissolve in our being, because, having no substantial existence or form of its own, it cannot stand in front of the clear and intense gaze of our self-attentiveness. When by repeated practice we gain the ability to maintain our self-scrutinising attentiveness without forgetfulness, our mind will eventually sink into the innermost depth or core of our being, where we will experience the infinite clarity of true self-knowledge, which will dissolve our mind entirely by revealing the truth that no such thing has ever really existed.

That is, in the clear light of true self-knowledge we will discover that we were never the mind that we imagined ourself to be, but were always the real, infinite and absolute consciousness of mere being, just as in the clear light of day we would discover that a rope that in the darkness of night we imagined to be a snake was never a snake, but was always only a rope. Like the snake, our mind is a mere figment of our imagination, and like the rope, our infinite consciousness of being is the sole reality underlying the illusory appearance of this mind. Just as we were actually seeing only a rope even when we imagined it to be a snake, so we are actually experiencing only our own infinite and absolutely non-dual self-consciousness even when we imagine it to be this duality-knowing consciousness that we call our 'mind'.

Therefore, since our mind is merely an illusion, an insubstantial, elusive and ever-fleeting phantom created by our own imagination, we can effectively restrain it only by knowing the truth that we are really not it, as we now imagine ourself to be, but are only the infinite fullness of being, consciousness and happiness. Until we know this truth as our actual experience of ourself, we will continue to be deluded by this imaginary mind, and we will never really be able to restrain it entirely. Hence, since we can know ourself as we really are only by keenly and attentively scrutinising our being, this practice of self-scrutiny, self-attentiveness or self-investigation is the only means by which we can thoroughly and effectively restrain our mind.

After saying that to attain *mukti* or emancipation we must restrain our mind, and that to restrain our mind we must investigate or examine ourself in order to know who or what we really are, Sri Ramana goes on to define true emancipation later in the same paragraph by saying:

> […] Knowing our *yathārtha svarūpa* [our own real self or being] having investigated who is [our false individual] self, who is in bondage, is *mukti* [emancipation or liberation]. […]

What exactly does he mean by saying that we are in bondage? The 'bondage' we are now in is not only our imaginary confinement within the limitations of this physical body, but is more fundamentally our imaginary confinement within the limitations of this finite consciousness we call our 'mind'. We are in reality the infinite non-dual consciousness that knows nothing other than its own being, which is absolute peace and perfect happiness. Therefore, by imagining ourself to be this finite mind, which rises by knowing duality or otherness, we are seemingly confining our perfectly happy and infinite being within the finite realm of dualistic knowledge, in which we experience a mixture of relative happiness and unhappiness.

If we want to be eternally free from all unhappiness, we must free ourself from the illusion that we are this finite mind, and to free ourself from this illusion we must know ourself as we really are, that is, as infinite being, consciousness and happiness. Since true self-knowledge is our real state of absolute non-duality, it is the state of infinite freedom, because when we experience it we will know that we alone exist, and that there is therefore nothing other than ourself to limit our freedom.

The bondage that we now experience is an illusion, a figment of our imagination, because in reality our infinite being is never limited or bound in any way. Therefore when we experience true self-knowledge, we will know the truth that we have always been perfectly free. Bondage is a state that is experienced only by our unreal mind, and not by our real self. Therefore, since bondage exists only in the limited and distorted view of our mind, and not in the unlimited and clear view of our real self, the concept of liberation or emancipation is true only in relation to our bondage-ensnared mind. Hence in verse 39 of *Uḷḷadu Nāṟpadu* Sri Ramana says:

> Only so long as [we imagine] 'I am a person in bondage', [will] thoughts of bondage and liberation [arise]. When [we] see [our real] self [by investigating] 'who is [this] person in bondage?', [our real] self, [which is] eternally liberated, will remain [alone experiencing itself] as that which is [always] attained. When [our real self remains experiencing itself thus], since the thought of bondage cannot remain, can the thought of liberation [alone] remain in front [of such clear self-knowledge]?

Liberation or true self-knowledge is not actually a state that we can newly attain, because in truth we are always the non-dual consciousness of being, which never ceases to know itself and which is therefore eternally liberated. However, since we now imagine ourself to be this bondage-ensnared mind, from the standpoint of this imaginary experience it is necessary for us to free ourself from this illusion of self-ignorance and bondage. Therefore so long as we experience ourself to be this mind, our notions of bondage and liberation are in effect quite true and perfectly valid. That is, so long as we experience ourself as being bound by limitations, our desire to attain true self-knowledge and thereby to be liberated from such bondage is both valid and necessary.

However, though it is necessary for us now to make every possible effort to attain true self-knowledge by investigating the reality of our mind, which is in bondage, when we actually experience the self-knowledge that we now seek, we will discover that we are not this bondage-ensnared mind but only our eternally liberated real self. When we thus discover that our bondage is entirely unreal, being a mere figment of our imagination, our liberation or emancipation from that bondage will also be unreal. That is, we will discover that we are eternally and infinitely free, and hence we will not feel that we have ever been freed or liberated from anything.

After defining *mukti* or liberation, and indicating that we can attain it only by investigating or scrutinising ourself, Sri Ramana goes on to define *ātma-vicāra* or 'self-investigation', and while doing so he contrasts it with the practice of *dhyāna* or 'meditation', saying:

> […] The name '*ātma-vicāra*' [is truly applicable] only to [the practice of] always being [or remaining] having put [placed, kept, seated, deposited, detained, fixed or established our] mind in *ātmā* [our own real self], whereas *dhyāna* [meditation] is imagining ourself to be *sat-cit-ānanda brahman* [the absolute reality, which is being-consciousness-bliss]. […]

Since self-investigation or *ātma-vicāra* is the practice of remaining with our mind fixed in our real self, which is infinite and absolute being, it is a practice of just being without any mental activity. In contrast, the term meditation or *dhyāna* is commonly understood to denote the practice of thinking or imagining ourself to be God or *brahman*, the infinite and absolute reality, whose nature is *sat-cit-ānanda* or being-consciousness-bliss, and as such meditation is merely a mental activity.

This radical distinction between the practice of true self-investigation or *ātma-vicāra* and the practice of meditating 'I am *brahman*' was often emphasised by Sri Ramana, as for example in verse 29 of *Uḷḷadu Nāṟpadu*, in which he says:

> Without saying 'I' by mouth, scrutinising by [our] inward sinking [diving or piercing] mind 'where does it [this mind] rise as I?' alone is

> the path of *jñāna* [the practice that leads to true knowledge]. Instead [of practising such deep thought-free self-scrutiny], thinking '[I am] not this [body or mind], I am that [*brahman* or the absolute reality]' is [merely] an aid, [but] can it be *vicāra* [self-investigation or self-scrutiny]?

True *vicāra* or self-investigation is only the practice of our sinking or penetrating inwards with our entire mind or attention focused on our source or true being, our fundamental consciousness 'I am'. Meditating or dwelling upon the thought that we are not this body or mind but are only the infinite and absolute reality may be an aid in helping us to convince ourself of our need to turn inwards to know ourself, but it cannot itself be the actual process of self-investigation, because it is an extroverted activity of our mind.

When sages and sacred books tell us that we are not this finite body or mind but are only the infinite and absolute reality, their aim is to prompt us to turn our attention inwards to scrutinise ourself in order to discover what we really are. Instead of turning and sinking inwards thus, if we merely think 'I am not this, I am that', we have clearly misunderstood the purpose of their teaching. Therefore in verse 32 of *Uḷḷadu Nāṟpadu* Sri Ramana says:

> When the Vēdas [or other sacred texts] proclaim 'that [absolute reality] is you', our thinking 'I am that [absolute reality], [and] not this [body or mind]' [and] not [just] being [that absolute reality by] examining ourself [to ascertain] 'what [am I]?' is due to lack of mental strength [or discrimination], because that [absolute reality] always abides as ourself.

When we are told 'that is you', we should investigate and know 'what am I?'. If instead we simply meditate 'I am that', Sri Ramana says that this is due to absence or lack of *uraṉ* or mental strength. The word *uraṉ* literally means strength of will, self-control or knowledge, but in this context it means specifically strength of conviction. If we are truly convinced that we are that, we will not feel any need or desire to meditate 'I am that', but will instead feel only a strong urge and love to scrutinise ourself in order to discover 'I am what?'.

Since that absolute and infinite reality always exists as our own real self or essential being, we cannot know it until we know ourself. Therefore if we truly have love for the infinite fullness of being that we call 'God', we should meditate only upon ourself, and not upon any thought of God, or even upon the thought 'I am God'.

Any thought that we form in our mind is an imagination, and is experienced by us as something other than ourself, so no thought can be God. Whatever may be our conception of God, that conception is not God, and does not come even close to defining him, because he is the infinite reality, which transcends all thoughts and mental conceptions.

The thought of God is useful to us only so long as we imagine ourself to be this finite individual who feels 'I am this body', but if we get rid of this imagination by knowing ourself as we really are, no thought of God will be necessary, because we will experience him directly as our own real self. Until we experience him thus, thinking of him is beneficial, but rather than thinking of him as other than ourself, thinking of him as our real self is more beneficial. Therefore in verse 8 of *Upadēśa Undiyār* Sri Ramana says:

> Rather than *anya-bhāva* [considering God to be *anya* or other than ourself], *ananya-bhāva* [considering him to be *ananya* or not other than ourself], 'he is I', is indeed best among all [ways of thinking of God].

However, since God is our own real self, rather than meditating 'he is I' or thinking of him as not other than ourself, putting aside all thoughts of God and meditating only upon our own self or essential being is the most perfect way of meditating upon him. If we are truly convinced that 'he is I', why should we continue thinking repeatedly 'he is I', instead of just being keenly self-attentive in order to experience ourself as the pure and infinite being that we really are? Therefore in verse 36 of *Uḷḷadu Nāṟpadu* Sri Ramana asks:

> If we think that we are [this] body, that [meditation] which is thinking [instead] that 'no [we are not this body], we are that' is a good aid [to convince and remind us of the need] for abiding [in the state of true non-dual self-consciousness, in which we experience ourself] as 'we are that [absolute reality]'. [However] since we [in truth always] abide as that, why [should we be] always thinking that we are that? [In order to know that we are human] do we [need to] think 'I am a man'?

Thinking that we are God or the absolute reality is beneficial only insofar as it can help us to convince and remind ourself that we should not rise as this thinking mind but should instead abide as our own real self, which is that absolute reality, whose nature is just being and not doing or thinking anything. But just as we do not feel any need to think 'I am a human being', because we always experience ourself as such, so there is no need for us to think repeatedly 'I am that', because we are always that, whether or not we think so.

Therefore, since we are in truth always only that absolute reality, our aim should be to experience ourself as such, and in order to experience ourself thus, we must subside in our being, remaining without rising to think anything. Therefore in verse 27 of *Uḷḷadu Nāṟpadu* Sri Ramana says:

> The state of [just] being, in which 'I' [this mind] does not rise [as a seemingly separate entity], is the state in which we are that. Without

> scrutinising the place [abode or source] where 'I' rises, how [is it possible for us] to reach the loss of [our individual] self, [which is the egoless state] in which 'I' does not rise? Without reaching [this state of egolessness or annihilation of our individuality], say, how [can we remain] abiding in the state of [our own real] self, in which [we experience ourself as] 'myself is that'?

We can experience ourself as God, the infinite and absolute reality, only in our natural state of complete egolessness, in which we do not rise as a separate individual 'I' or mind. In order to remain without rising as this mind, we must keenly scrutinise our innermost being, which is the source from which we have risen. When we keenly, vigilantly and unwaveringly scrutinise our innermost being, we will sink and merge into it, becoming one with it, and in the resulting state of egoless non-dual self-consciousness we will experience the truth that we are the absolute reality that we now call 'God' or *brahman*.

This practice of keen, vigilant and unwavering self-scrutiny or self-attentiveness is the practice of 'being having placed [our] mind in [our real] self', which Sri Ramana described when he said, 'The name "*ātma-vicāra*" [is truly applicable] only to [the practice of] always being [abiding or remaining] having put [placed or fixed our] mind in *ātmā* [our own real self]', and it is the only means by which we can effectively restrain or prevent the rising of our mind. In contrast to this simple practice of self-attentive being, which is entirely devoid of mental activity, the practice of meditating 'I am the absolute reality' is a mental activity, and hence it actually sustains the rising of our mind and prevents its subsidence.

In practice, the meditation or *dhyāna* that Sri Ramana described when he said, '[...] whereas *dhyāna* is imagining ourself to be *sat-cit-ānanda brahman* [the absolute reality, which is being-consciousness-bliss]', is just a process of remembering some information that we have learnt from sacred books or sages, namely that we are in truth the absolute reality, which is infinite being, consciousness and happiness, and trying to imagine ourself as such. So long as we practise such *bhāvana* or imaginative meditation, we clearly do not know our real self, because if we did, we would not feel any need for such practice. Therefore, since we do not know our real self, we clearly do not know *brahman* or the absolute reality, nor do we know the true experience of being infinite being-consciousness-bliss. For our self-ignorant mind, terms such as God, *brahman*, the absolute reality and *sat-cit-ānanda* or being-consciousness-bliss all denote only mental concepts, and not any actual experience.

Sri Ramana concludes this sixteenth paragraph by saying, 'At one time it will become necessary [for us] to forget all that [we] have learnt', because all the information that we have learnt, including all that we have learnt from sacred books about God or the absolute reality, is only a collection of thoughts or mental conceptions, whereas the reality transcends not only all thoughts and concepts, but even the mind which thinks and knows such thoughts and concepts. Therefore, to know ourself as the absolute reality or *brahman*, we must forget all such thoughts and even our mind that thinks them, and must instead remain self-attentively as our own mere being, which is devoid of all thoughts and mental activity.

When Sri Ramana defines *dhyāna* or 'meditation' as the practice of 'imagining ourself to be *sat-cit-ānanda brahman*', we should not confuse his use of the word *dhyāna* in this context with his earlier use of the term *svarūpa-dhyāna* or 'self-meditation' in the tenth paragraph. The Sanskrit word *dhyāna* derives from the verbal root *dhyai*, which means to think of, imagine, meditate upon, ponder over, reflect upon, consider or recollect, and hence it literally means meditation, thought or reflection. As such, *dhyāna* is definitely a mental activity, a process of imagining or thinking of something.

However, when the word *dhyāna* is applied to ourself as in *svarūpa-dhyāna*, it does not literally mean meditation or thinking, because our real self or being is not an object that we think of. If we try to think of or meditate upon ourself, our thinking mind will begin to subside, because it can rise and be active only by thinking of or attending to things other than itself. Therefore the practice of *svarūpa-dhyāna* or 'self-meditation' is unlike all other forms of meditation, because it is not a mental activity or any form of 'doing' or 'thinking', but is just the state of self-attentive being.

The true meaning of 'meditating' upon being, the reality or 'that which is', is beautifully explained by Sri Ramana in the first of the two verses of the *maṅgalam* or 'auspicious introduction' to *Uḷḷadu Nāṟpadu*, which he initially composed as a two-line verse in *kuṟaḷ veṇbā* metre, in which he said:

> How to [or who can] meditate upon [our] being-essence? Being in [our] heart as [we truly] are alone is meditating [upon our being]. Know [this].

However, in order to match the metre of all the other verses in *Uḷḷadu Nāṟpadu* and to explain in more detail the subtle truth that he expressed so succinctly in this *kuṟaḷ* verse, he later added to it two opening lines, thereby transforming it into its present form, which is a four-line verse in *veṇbā* metre, in which he says:

> Other than *uḷḷadu* ['that which is' or being], is there consciousness of being? Since [this] being-essence [this existing substance or reality which is] is in [our] heart devoid of [all] thought, how to [or who can] think of [or meditate upon this] being-essence, which is called 'heart'? Being in [our] heart as [we truly] are [that is, as our thought-free non-dual consciousness of being, 'I am'] alone is meditating

[upon our being]. Know [this truth by experiencing it].

The Tamil original of this verse is a beautiful composition rich in alliteration and profound in meaning. Of its fifteen metrical feet, the first fourteen begin with the syllable *uḷ*, which is a root word that has two distinct but closely related meanings. That is, *uḷ* is the base of a tenseless verb meaning 'to be' or 'to have', and is also a separate but related word meaning 'within', 'inside' or 'interior'.

Of the fourteen words in this verse that begin with this syllable *uḷ*, eight are various words derived from the former sense of *uḷ* as the base of a tenseless verb meaning in this context 'to be', while the other six are words derived from the latter sense of *uḷ* as a word meaning 'within', 'inside' or interior'. Of these six words, three are forms of *uḷḷam*, which means 'heart', 'core', 'mind', 'consciousness' or 'self', and the other three are *uḷḷal*, which means 'thought', 'thinking' or 'meditating'.

The first sentence of this verse is a simple question, but one with a very deep and broad meaning, '*uḷḷadu aladu uḷḷa-v-uṇarvu uḷḷadō?*' As a noun *uḷḷadu*, which is a term used in Tamil philosophical literature to denote the reality, truth or spirit, is both a compound noun meaning 'that (*adu*) which is (*uḷḷa*)' and a gerund meaning 'being'. However these two meanings are essentially identical, because 'that which is' is not other than or any way distinct from its own natural state of being, and hence they are both appropriate in this context. The word *aladu* can be an adversative conjunction meaning 'or', 'if not' or 'else', or it can mean 'except as', 'other than' or 'besides'. The compound word *uḷḷa-v-uṇarvu* means 'consciousness which is', 'existing consciousness', 'being consciousness' or 'consciousness of being', and *uḷḷadō* is an interrogative form of the third person singular verb *uḷḷadu* and therefore means 'is there?' or 'does [it] exist?'.

Thus this first sentence gives various shades of meaning such as 'If being were not, could there be consciousness of being?', 'Except as [other than or besides] that which is, is there [any] consciousness of being?' or 'Can [our] consciousness of being ['I am'] be other than [our] being?'. Though all these shades of meaning are closely related, parallel and compatible with each other, they are each an alternative and helpful way of understanding the same basic truth.

Among the various shades of meaning implied in this first sentence, an important one derives from the fact that *uḷḷadu* means 'that which is', and therefore in its literal sense it denotes only that which really is, and not anything which merely seems to be. That is, it does not denote merely a relative, finite, partial or qualified form of being, but only the absolute, infinite, indivisible and unqualified form of being – the being which really is. Hence an important meaning implied in this sentence is that if there were not an absolute being, could we be conscious of being?

That is, we are conscious of being only because there is something that really is – something that is absolutely, unconditionally, infinitely, eternally and immutably real. Thus this sentence is a powerful argument that establishes the truth that our mere consciousness of being clearly indicates the existence of an absolute reality – an unqualified form of being, an essential 'is'-ness or 'am'-ness which underlies all forms of knowledge.

This essential and absolute being is our own being, 'I am', because 'I am' is the fundamental being which we always experience and which is the base for our knowledge of all other forms of being. Since our essential being or 'am'-ness underlies and supports all our knowledge, including our knowledge of time, space and all other such limiting dimensions, it itself must transcend all limitations and must therefore be eternally, immutably, infinitely and absolutely real.

Though the word *uḷḷadu* or 'that which is' may superficially appear to denote some being that exists as 'that', an object other than ourself, this is not the sense in which Sri Ramana intends us to understand it. That which really exists, and which we always know as existing, is only our own being, which we experience as 'I am'.

Our knowledge or consciousness of the being or existence of any other thing appears and disappears, and is therefore just an ephemeral apparition. Moreover, the 'consciousness' that knows the being or existence of other things is only our mind, and those 'other' things that it knows are all merely thoughts or mental images that it forms within itself by its own power of imagination. Since both our mind and all the 'other' things that it knows appear and disappear, their seeming reality is finite, relative and conditional, and hence they cannot be the absolute reality that is denoted by the word *uḷḷadu* or 'that which [really] is'.

Therefore, in the context in which Sri Ramana uses it, the word *uḷḷadu* does not denote any seeming reality that our mind knows as other than itself, but denotes only the absolute reality that underlies and supports the appearance of our mind. That is, it denotes only our own being, the first person being 'I am', and not any other form of being, any second or third person being such as 'it is'. This fact is made even more clear by Sri Ramana in the second sentence of this verse, in which he says that the *uḷḷa-poruḷ*, the 'substance that is' or 'reality that is', exists in our heart and is devoid of thought, and that it is in fact that which we call our 'heart' or the core of our being. Therefore the words *uḷḷadu* and *uḷḷa-poruḷ* denote only the thought-free reality that exists within us as our own essential being.

Whereas most sacred texts and other philosophical writings that attempt to establish the existence of God or the absolute reality do so by arguing that there must be an absolute cause, source or basis for the appearance of this world, in this first sentence of *Uḷḷadu Nāṟpadu* Sri Ramana establishes the existence of the absolute reality by simply pointing out that we could not be conscious of our own being or existence if we were not that which really is. That is, if we did not really exist, we could not know 'I am'. Therefore our own essential self-conscious being, which we always experience as 'I am', is absolutely real.

Since all other things depend for their seeming existence or being upon our knowledge of them, they are all merely relatively real, and not absolutely real. The only thing that we know as the absolute reality is our own essential being or 'am'-ness, whereas the being or 'is'-ness of all other things, including both this entire world and any God whom we conceive as being separate from our own being, are only relative forms of reality.

Therefore in this simple sentence, 'If that which is were not, would there be consciousness of being?', Sri Ramana indicates that the only evidence we require to prove the existence of the absolute reality, 'that which really is', is our simple consciousness of our own being. Thus he implies that, since our knowledge of all other things depends upon our knowledge of our own being, 'I am', any argument that we may give to establish the existence of the absolute reality based merely upon the seeming existence of otherness instead of upon our fundamental knowledge of our own being is inherently flawed.

This is why all the usual arguments about the existence or non-existence of God can never be resolved unless we first consider the reality of our own existence. We can never establish the existence of the absolute reality or 'God' on the basis of the seeming existence of this world, but only upon the indubitable existence of ourself.

Because we know the world, we know that we certainly exist to know it. The existence of the world may be a mere apparition or imagination, like the seeming existence of the world that we know in a dream, but our own existence is undoubtedly real, because if we did not really exist, we could not know either our own existence or the seeming existence of any other thing. Therefore Sri Ramana begins the main text of *Uḷḷadu Nāṟpadu* by saying in verse 1:

> Because we see [or perceive] the world, accepting [the existence of] one *mudal* [first principle, origin, source, base, fundamental reality or primal substance] which has a power which is manifold [or diverse, that is, a power to appear as if it were many diverse things] is indeed unavoidable. The picture of names and forms [this entire world-appearance], the seer [our mind which perceives it], the underlying [or existing] screen [on which it appears] and the shining light [of consciousness by which we perceive it] – all these are he [this one primal substance], who is [our own real] self.

The one *mudal* – the sole fundamental reality, basic essence or primal substance – which Sri Ramana refers to in this verse, and which he says is our own real self, is the same absolute reality that he describes as *uḷḷadu* or 'that which is' in the first *maṅgalam* verse. Because we know 'I am', we know that this one original, fundamental and absolute reality, which is our own real self or essential being, does indeed exist. And because when we rise as our mind we seemingly experience within it many other things besides our own being, we know that our single self-conscious being has the power to appear as if it were many diverse things.

All these diverse things – namely this entire world-appearance, which rises in our mind as series of mental images and which is like a motion picture projected upon a screen, our mind, which experiences this picture, the underlying 'screen' or substratum of being from which, in which and upon which both our mind and this whole picture of ever-changing mental images appear, and the clear light of consciousness that enables us to experience this entire dream-show – are in essence only the one primal substance or fundamental non-dual reality, which is our own real self or essential being. That is, because all this multiplicity arises in us like a dream, and disappears when our mind subsides in sleep, the substance from which it is formed is only our own non-dual self-conscious being, which is the one fundamental and absolute reality.

Though in this verse Sri Ramana seems to affirm the existence of this one non-dual absolute reality on the basis of our experience of this world-appearance, he actually begins this verse with the word *nām*, which means 'we', thereby placing emphasis not upon the world as such, but only upon ourself, who seem to perceive this world. This emphasis is reiterated by him still more strongly in the final words of this verse, *tāṉ ām avaṉ*, which mean 'he who is self', and which therefore clearly indicate what he actually means by the term 'one *mudal*', namely that 'he', the 'one *mudal*' or God, who is the one fundamental reality or primal substance that underlies and appears as all this multiplicity, is only our own real self or essential being. Thus in this verse Sri Ramana actually establishes the existence of the absolute reality based not upon the seeming existence of the world, but only upon the indubitable existence of ourself, who seem to cognise it.

However, whereas in this first verse of the main text of *Uḷḷadu Nāṟpadu* he establishes the existence of the absolute reality in an indirect manner based upon our transient consciousness of this world, in the first sentence of the first verse of the *maṅgalam* or 'auspicious introduction' to *Uḷḷadu Nāṟpadu* he establishes it in a direct manner based upon our permanent consciousness of our own simple being. That is, whether or not we perceive this world, we always experience the absolute reality, 'that which is', because we are always conscious of our own essential being, 'I am'.

Since we always clearly know our own being or 'am'-ness, it is indeed 'that which really is', and hence we need no other evidence to convince ourself of the indubitable existence of 'that which is'. We, who are in essence the self-conscious being that we always experience as 'I am', are ourself that which truly is, that which definitely is, that which exists unconditionally and independently, and which is therefore absolutely real.

Another shade of meaning conveyed in this first sentence is based upon the meaning implied by the compound word *uḷḷa-v-uṇarvu*. That is, since *uḷḷa-v-uṇarvu* means 'being-consciousness' or 'consciousness of being', and since the first and fundamental form in which we are conscious of being is the consciousness or knowledge that we have of our own being, which we experience as 'am', the meaning implied by *uḷḷa-v-uṇarvu* is this basic consciousness 'am', which is our first person consciousness of our own being. Since 'am' is a predicate, it must have a subject, and that subject can only be 'I', which is the real being denoted here by the word *uḷḷadu*. Therefore, one meaning implied in this first sentence is: 'If the fundamental being "I" did not really exist, could we experience this consciousness "am"?'.

Moreover, since *aladu* means not only 'unless' or 'if not' but also 'other than' or 'besides', another parallel but slightly different shade of meaning conveyed in this sentence is: 'Can our consciousness 'am' be other than our essential being "I"?'. That is, our consciousness of our being, which is denoted by the word 'am', is not other than our being, which is denoted by the word 'I'.

When we interpret *aladu* as meaning 'other than', this same basic meaning stands even without our involving the inferred words 'I' and 'am'. That is, one meaning that is clearly conveyed in this first sentence is: 'Other than that which is, is there [any] consciousness which is [to know that which is]?', or more simply, 'Other than being, is there [any] consciousness of being?'.

In other words, consciousness is itself being, because if it were other than being, consciousness would not be and therefore could not know being. This is the same crucially important truth that Sri Ramana expresses in very similar words in verse 23 of *Upadēśa Undiyār*:

> Because of the non-existence of [any] *uṇarvu* [consciousness] other [than *uḷḷadu*] to know *uḷḷadu* ['that which is' or being], *uḷḷadu* is *uṇarvu*. [That] *uṇarvu* itself exists as 'we' [our essential being or true self].

The crucial truth which is stated explicitly in this verse of *Upadēśa Undiyār*, and which is also implied clearly in this first sentence of *Uḷḷadu Nāṟpadu*, is in perfect accord with the experience of each one of us, because the basic form in which we each experience our consciousness is as our consciousness of ourself or our own being. Our consciousness is conscious of its own being because, since it is consciousness, its being is essentially self-conscious. Or to express the same truth more directly, we are conscious of our own being because, since we ourself are consciousness, our being is essentially self-conscious, and hence our consciousness and our being are inseparable. That is, we are not only being or *uḷḷadu*, 'that which is', but are also consciousness of being or *uḷḷa-v-uṇarvu*, 'that which is conscious of that which is'.

Yet another shade of meaning, one that is important in the context of the rest of this verse, derives from the fact that *uḷḷa* is not only the infinitive, relative participle and adjective form of the verb *uḷ*, and thus means 'to be', 'which is', 'existing', 'being', 'true' or 'real', but is also the infinitive of the verb *uḷḷu*, and thus means 'to think'. Viewed in this latter sense, the meaning of this first sentence would be, 'Other than that which is, is there a consciousness to think [of it]?'. That is, since we are not separate from the absolute reality upon which we wish to meditate, we can only meditate upon it truly by experiencing it as ourself, and since it is devoid of all thoughts, we can experience it as ourself only by experiencing ourself without any thought as our own simple self-conscious being.

The second sentence of this verse is a longer but still quite simple question, '*uḷḷa-poruḷ uḷḷal aṟa uḷḷattē uḷḷadāl, uḷḷam eṉum uḷḷa-poruḷ uḷḷal evaṉ?*' The compound word *uḷḷa-poruḷ*, which denotes the same real and absolute being that is denoted by the word *uḷḷadu* in the first sentence, literally means the thing, entity, reality, substance or essence which is, or in other words, the existing reality or being essence. The word *uḷḷal* means 'thought' or 'thinking', and *aṟa* means 'devoid of'. The word *uḷḷattē* is a locative form of *uḷḷam* and therefore means 'in [our] heart', that is, in the core or innermost depth of our being, and *uḷḷadāl* means 'since [it] is'. The words *uḷḷam eṉum uḷḷa-poruḷ* mean 'the being-essence, which is called heart', *uḷḷal* here means 'thinking' or 'meditating', and *evaṉ* means 'how' or 'who'.

Thus this sentence means, 'Since [this] being-essence is in [our] heart devoid of [all] thought [or all thinking], how to [or who can] meditate [upon this] being-essence, which is called [our] heart?'. That is, since our true and essential being transcends and is therefore devoid of all thoughts, how can any person think of it, conceive it or meditate upon it?

In this sentence the use of the word *uḷḷam* or 'heart' is very significant, because Sri Ramana not only says that our essential being exists in our heart or innermost core, but also says that it is called our heart. In other words, *uḷḷam* or 'heart' is just another name for our essential being, which is the infinite and absolute reality. Since our 'heart' or innermost core is our own real self, we ourself are the absolute reality or being that exists in our heart as our heart.

Moreover, in literary Tamil *uḷḷam* can be used as an alternative form of *uḷḷōm*, the first person plural form of the verb *uḷ*, and as such it means 'are' as in 'we are'. In this context, however, *uḷḷam* is not intended to mean 'are' as a first person plural verb, but rather 'are' as an inclusive form of the first person singular verb 'am', and hence we can translate it simply as 'am'. Interpreted in this sense, therefore, the words *uḷḷam eṉum uḷḷa-poruḷ* would mean the 'being-essence, which is called "am"'.

Thus by using this word *uḷḷam* in this context, Sri Ramana indicated that the real meaning of the word 'heart' or 'core' when used in a spiritual context is only our essential self-conscious being, 'am', and also that an appropriate name for the absolute reality, the essence or substance that just is, is not only 'heart' or 'core' but also 'am'. In fact, since the word 'am' necessarily implies the word 'I', and vice versa, either jointly or separately 'I' and 'am' are the most appropriate of all the names we can use to denote the absolute reality or 'God', because the absolute reality is always experienced directly by each one of us as 'I am'.

In the third sentence Sri Ramana concludes by defining what true 'meditation' upon the reality is, saying '*uḷḷattē uḷḷapaḍi uḷḷadē uḷḷal*'. As we have seen, *uḷḷattē* means 'in [our] heart', or by implication 'in am', and *uḷḷal* here means 'meditation' or 'meditating'. The word *uḷḷadē* is the gerund *uḷḷadu* meaning 'being' with the intensifying suffix *ē*, which means 'alone', 'itself', 'certainly' or 'indeed'. Thus these three words *uḷḷattē uḷḷadē uḷḷal* mean 'being in [our] heart [or 'am'-ness] alone is meditating', or in other words, being in our real self or essential self-conscious being, 'I am', is truly 'meditating' upon it.

However, the most important word in this sentence is *uḷḷapaḍi*, because it explains precisely what is meant by the words *uḷḷattē uḷḷadē* or 'only being in [our] heart'. How exactly we are to be in our heart or true being is *uḷḷapaḍi*, which means 'as [it] is' or 'as [we] are'. But what does Sri Ramana actually imply in this context by using this term 'as [it] is' or 'as [we] are'? The meaning he implies is 'devoid of thought' or 'without thinking', because in the previous sentence he revealed the true nature of our being-essence saying that it exists within us 'devoid of [all] thought' or 'devoid of [all] thinking'.

Moreover, since he indicated in the first sentence that our true being is itself our consciousness of being – in other words, that our true being is self-conscious – and that we are therefore the perfectly non-dual consciousness of our own being, 'I am', he uses this term *uḷḷapaḍi* here not only to imply 'devoid of thinking' but also to imply 'as our non-dual consciousness of being' or 'as our non-dual self-consciousness'. Therefore the meaning of this entire sentence, '*uḷḷattē uḷḷapaḍi uḷḷadē uḷḷal*', is: 'Being in [our] heart as [we truly] are [that is, as our thought-free non-dual self-conscious being, 'I am'] alone is meditating [upon our being, which is the absolute reality]'.

The final word with which Sri Ramana then concludes this verse is *uṇar*, which is an imperative meaning 'know' or 'be conscious', and which implies in this context either 'understand this truth' or 'experience your real being by thus being as you really are'.

Thus in this verse the conclusion to which Sri Ramana leads us is that we can never conceive or think of the absolute reality, which is both our being and our consciousness of our being, because it transcends all thinking and can therefore never be reached or grasped by any thought, and that the only way to 'meditate' upon it or to know it is therefore just to be it as it is, that is, as our simple thought-free and non-dual consciousness of our own being, 'I am'.

In the first of the two verses of his *pāyiram* or preface to *Uḷḷadu Nāṟpadu*, Sri Muruganar writes that Sri Ramana joyfully composed this clear and authoritative text in response to his request, 'So that we may be saved, [graciously] reveal to us the nature of reality and the means to attain [join, reach, experience or be united with] it'. Accordingly, in this first *maṅgalam* verse Sri Ramana reveals to us both the essential nature of reality and the means by which we can experience it, which is possible only by our being one with it.

In the first two sentences of this verse Sri Ramana reveals several crucial truths about the nature of the one absolute reality, which is *uḷḷadu* or 'that which is'. Firstly he explains that it is not only being but also consciousness, because other than 'that which is' there cannot be any consciousness to know 'that which is'. Therefore 'that which [really] is' is self-conscious – that is, it is absolutely non-dual self-conscious being.

Secondly he says that that truly existing reality or 'being-essence' exists devoid of thoughts, or devoid of thinking. That is, it is not a mere thought or mental conception, but is the fundamental reality that underlies and supports the seeming existence of our thinking mind and all its thoughts. However, though it supports the imaginary appearance of thoughts, in reality it is devoid of thoughts, and hence devoid of the thinking consciousness that we call our 'mind', because both this thinking mind and its thoughts are unreal. In the clear view of the one self-conscious reality, thoughts do not exist, because they appear to exist only in the distorted view of our mind, which is itself one among the thoughts that it imagines and knows.

Thirdly he says that it exists 'in heart', that is, in the innermost core of our being. In other words, it is not merely something that exists outside us or separate from us, but is that which exists within us as our own essential reality. He also adds that it is called 'heart', thereby indicating that the word 'heart' does not merely denote the abode in which the reality exists, but more truly denotes the reality itself. Moreover, since the word *uḷḷam* means not only 'heart' but also 'am', by saying that the truly existing reality or 'being-essence' is called *uḷḷam* Sri Ramana reveals that it is not something that exists as an object but is our own self – our essential being or 'am'-ness.

In other words, the absolute reality exists not only in us but also as us. It is the real 'heart' or core of our being. That is, it is our own very essence, substance or reality. It is that which we really are. Other than as the one absolute reality, we truly do not exist.

Because we mistake ourself to be this thinking mind or object-knowing consciousness, the one fundamental reality is said to exist within us, but this is only a relative truth – a truth that is only true relative to the distorted perspective of our mind, which experiences dualities such as subject and object, 'self' and 'other', 'inside' and outside', and so on. Since the one fundamental reality transcends all such dualities, the absolute truth about its nature is not merely that it exists within us, but that it exists as us.

Finally, by asking, '*uḷḷa-poruḷ uḷḷal evaṉ?*', which means 'how to [or who can] meditate [upon this] being-essence?', Sri Ramana emphasises the truth that since the absolute reality is that which transcends thought, it cannot be conceived by mind or reached by thought. Therefore, since its nature is such, what is the means by which we can 'reach' it, 'attain' it or experience it as it really is?

Since it is not only that which is completely devoid of thought, but is also that which is essentially self-conscious, and since it is our own 'heart' or essential being, the only way we can experience it is by just being it. In other words, the only means by which we can 'attain' this one non-dual absolute reality is by simply remaining as we always truly are – that is, as our own true, essential, thought-free, self-conscious being. Therefore in the third sentence of this verse Sri Ramana says, 'Being in [our] heart as it is alone is meditating [upon this truly existing reality, which is called 'heart']', thereby declaring emphatically that this practice of 'being as we are' is the only means by which we can experience the absolute reality as it is.

Thus in this first *maṅgalam* verse Sri Ramana succinctly reveals both the essential nature of reality and the means by which we can 'reach' it, 'attain' it or experience it as it really is. Hence in a nutshell this verse expresses the very essence of *Uḷḷadu Nāṟpadu*, and all the other forty-one verses of this profound text are a richly elaborated explanation of the fundamental truths that he expressed so briefly yet so clearly and powerfully in this first verse.

Indeed, since it reveals so clearly not only the nature of the one absolute reality but also the only means by which we can actually experience it, this verse summarises the essence not only of *Uḷḷadu Nāṟpadu* but of the entire teachings of Sri Ramana. Therefore it is truly the *cūḍāmaṇi* or crest-jewel of his teachings, and if we are able to understand its full import correctly, comprehensively and clearly, we have truly understood the very essence of his teachings.

As in all his other teachings, in this verse Sri Ramana explains to us the nature of reality for a single purpose, namely to direct our mind towards the one practice that will actually enable us to experience reality as it truly is. Unless we understand the real nature of our goal, we will not be able to understand why the only one path by which we can 'reach' that goal is to practise just being as we always really are.

If our goal were something other than ourself, there would be some distance for us to travel in order to reach it. But since we ourself are the goal that we seek, there is absolutely no distance between us and it, and hence the path by which we can reach it cannot be essentially any different from it. That is, between us and our goal, which is our own real self, there is truly no space to accommodate any path that is other than our goal. Hence our path and our goal must be one in their essential nature. Since our goal is just thought-free self-conscious being, our path must likewise be just thought-free self-conscious being. This is the essential truth that Sri Ramana reveals so clearly in this verse, and that he reiterates in so many different words throughout his other teachings.

In our natural state of absolutely non-dual self-knowledge, which is our goal, our experience of our thought-free self-conscious being is effortless, because it is what we always really are. However in our present state, in which we imagine ourself to be this thinking mind, we appear to be not devoid of thought, as in truth we are, and hence we feel that we have to make effort to experience our thought-free self-conscious being. Thus the only difference between our path and our goal is the effort that now seems to be necessary in order for us to abide in our natural state of thought-free self-conscious being.

In this path, the effort that we have to make is not actually an effort to be, because we always effortlessly are, but is an effort to avoid mistaking ourself to be this thinking mind. So long as we imagine ourself to be this mind, we do not experience ourself as the true thought-free self-consciousness that is our real nature. Therefore in order to avoid mistaking ourself to be this thinking mind, we have to make effort to focus our entire attention upon our essential self-conscious being, 'I am', thereby withdrawing it from all thoughts.

This state in which we focus our entire attention upon our own self-conscious being, thereby excluding all thoughts, is the true state of 'meditation', which Sri Ramana describes in this verse as *uḷḷattē uḷḷapaḍi uḷḷadē* or 'only being in heart as it is [or as we are]'. That is, since the true nature of our essential self or 'heart' is just thought-free self-conscious being, 'being in heart as it is' is just the state of abiding calmly and peacefully in our own essential self as our own essential self – that is, free of all thoughts as our own true non-dual self-conscious being, 'I am'.

Thus the only path by which we can 'reach' or 'attain' our own essential self, which is the one and only absolute reality, is this simple practice of keenly attentive self-consciousness – self-consciousness that is so keenly attentive that it gives absolutely no room for the rising of any thought. Since no thought can rise unless we attend to it, when we focus our entire attention upon our own essential self-consciousness, 'I am', we automatically exclude the possibility of any thought arising.

That is, thoughts arise only because we think them, and this act of thinking involves an imaginary diverting of our attention away from our essential self-consciousness, 'I am'. Therefore the only effective means by which we can remain completely free of all thoughts – and hence completely free of our mind, which can rise and appear to exist only by thinking – is by just being attentively, keenly and vigilantly self-conscious.

This state of thought-free and therefore mind-free self-conscious being alone is the state that Sri Ramana describes as 'being as we are', and it is not only our path but also our goal. When we practise this vigilantly attentive and therefore thought-excluding self-consciousness with effort, it is the path, and when we experience it effortlessly as our unavoidable natural state, it is our goal, which is the absolutely non-dual state of true self-knowledge.

The experience of true self-knowledge that we will attain by practising this art of being as we really are, without thinking of any other thing, is clearly described by Sri Ramana in the fifth and final verse of *Āṉma-Viddai*:

> In the *uḷḷam* [heart, mind or consciousness] which investigates [itself] within [itself], [by just being] as it is [as clear self-conscious being] without thinking of [anything] other [than itself], *ātmā* [our real self], which is called Annamalai [and which is] the one *poruḷ* [absolute reality or essential being] that shines as the eye to [our] mind-eye, which is the eye to [our five physical] senses beginning with [our] eyes, which illumine [or enable us to know the material world, which is composed of the five elements] beginning with space, [and] as the space to [our] mind-space, will indeed be seen. [For us to be able to remain thus as we really are] grace is also necessary. [In order to be a suitable receptacle to imbibe grace, we should] be possessed of love [for just being as we are]. [Infinite] happiness will [then] appear [or be experienced].

The word Annamalai is a name that Sri Ramana often used when referring to God, the absolute reality, which is the *paramātman*, the transcendent spirit 'I am', the one real self of all living beings. Using the word *kaṇ* or 'eye' as a metaphor for consciousness, he describes this absolute reality as the 'eye to [our] mind-eye, which is the eye to [our five physical] senses beginning with [our] eyes, which illumine [or enable us to know the material world, which is composed of the five elements] beginning with space'.

That is, the absolute reality is our essential self-consciousness – our fundamental consciousness of our own being, 'I am' – which is the true light of consciousness that illumines our mind, enabling it to know both itself and all other things, which are merely thoughts that it forms within itself by its power of imagination, which is a distorted function of consciousness. There is truly no 'eye', 'light' or consciousness other than our fundamental non-dual consciousness of our own being, but when we imagine that consciousness to be our mind, it is seemingly reflected in the adjuncts or *upādhis* that we imagine to be ourself, and thereby it seems to know things other than itself.

That is, the limited consciousness that we call our 'mind', and which Sri Ramana here refers to as our 'mind-eye', is a reflected and thereby distorted form of consciousness, an apparition whose sole underlying reality is our real non-dual consciousness of being. Hence he describes our real consciousness as the 'eye to [our] mind-eye' not because it actually knows anything through our mind, but because it is the one reality that we mistakenly experience as our mind. Since our mind could not know anything if the light of our real consciousness were not shining within it as 'I am', that 'light' is the 'eye' that illumines our mind.

Our mind is in turn the 'eye' to our five senses, because it is the consciousness that sees through our eyes, hears through our ears, and so on. Our five senses function like lenses through which we direct our mind in the form of our attention to perceive the seemingly external world, which is considered to be composed of five 'elements' or basic qualities known as space, air, fire, water and earth (which in approximate terms may be described respectively as the qualities of accommodation, motility or non-cohesive fluidity, transformation, cohesive fluidity and solidity). Since this directing of our attention through our senses thus enables us to know this imaginary world, Sri Ramana says figuratively that our senses 'illumine [the material world, which is composed of the five elements] beginning with space'.

Besides describing the absolute reality, which is our own real self, our fundamental and essential consciousness of being, as the 'eye to [our] mind-eye', he also describes it as the 'space to [our] mind-space'. The physical space or *bhūtākāśa* in which all the objects of this universe are contained is itself contained within our mind-space or *cittākāśa*, which is in turn contained within our consciousness-space or *cidākāśa*.

That is, just like the world that we experience in our dream, this entire universe and the physical space in which it is contained are mere thoughts or mental images that we form in our mind by our power of imagination, and hence the 'space' in which this physical space is contained is our own mind. Likewise, since our mind rises and subsides within ourself, the 'space' in which this 'mind-space' is contained is our own fundamental consciousness of our being.

In order for us to 'see' or experience within ourself this absolute reality, which is *ātman*, our own true self or spirit, the 'eye to [our] mind-eye' and the 'space to [our] mind-space', Sri Ramana says we only have to 'investigate within as it is without thinking of [anything] other'. That is, we have to investigate or scrutinise ourself within ourself, by just being as we really are, that is, as our clear self-conscious being, without thinking of anything other than ourself. Only by practising this art of simple self-attentive being can we experience the absolute reality as our own self or essential being.

However, after saying this, Sri Ramana adds an important proviso, '*aruḷum vēṇumē*', which means 'grace also is certainly necessary'. What exactly is the 'grace' that he refers to here, and why does he emphasise the need for it in this context?

Grace is a power – the supreme and only truly existing power. It is the power that is inherent in our real self, and that is indeed not different from our real self, because our real self is absolute, infinite and therefore perfectly non-dual being, consciousness, happiness and love. Grace is the power of love, the love that our real self has for itself, the love that it has just to be as it is, as perfectly self-conscious and infinitely blissful being.

Grace is therefore not a power that is extraneous or alien to us. It is our own power, our power of love for ourself – for our own essential self-conscious and blissful being.

Our power of grace is the true and original nature of all other forms of power. The first other form of power that seemingly arises from grace, which is the only real power, is our power of *māyā* or self-delusion. Our power of *māyā* arises because we seemingly choose to forget or ignore our true, infinite, undivided and non-dual self-conscious being, and to imagine ourself to be a finite consciousness that experiences the existence of duality or otherness. This self-imposed self-forgetfulness or self-ignorance is not real, but is a mere imagination, and it is experienced not by our real self, but only by our mind, which is itself part of the imagination that it experiences.

Other than our mind or power of imagination, which is just a distorted and illusory function of our simple non-dual consciousness of being, there is no such thing as *māyā* or self-delusion. Our power of *māyā* arises in the form of our own mind, and it and its effects appear to exist only so long as we imagine ourself to be this mind – that is, only so long as we ignore our true non-dual self-conscious being, and therefore fail to investigate or scrutinise the real, fundamental and essential nature of our mind. If we keenly scrutinise our mind, which we experience as our seemingly finite individual consciousness 'I', in order to discover what it really is, it will dissolve and merge in our true non-dual self-conscious being, because it has no reality other than that.

However, in order for us to investigate or scrutinise our mind effectively,

Sri Ramana says that grace is necessary. Why is this so? When we undertake the practice of self-investigation or self-attentive being, we feel ourself to be this mind, which is the power of *māyā* or self-delusion. If we believe that we can attain our natural state of true self-knowledge by our own efforts, that is, by the power of our own mind, we will surely fail, because our mind is the power of self-delusion, and hence it will delude us in an infinite variety of ways in order to ensure its own survival. In order for us to attain true self-knowledge, therefore, we must surrender our mind, that is, we must entirely dissociate ourself from it. So long as we continue to cling to the illusion that this mind is ourself, it will continue to delude us.

Therefore, since we cannot rely upon the power of our mind to enable us to experience ourself as we really are, upon what power must we instead depend? Only upon the power of grace, which is the source from which our mind derives its limited power. We can attain absolute true knowledge only by the infinite power of grace, and not by the finite power of our mind, because no finite power can produce an infinite or absolute result.

Therefore, so long as we continue to experience ourself as this finite consciousness that we call our 'mind', which we will continue to do until it is dissolved entirely in the clarity of true self-knowledge, we must depend entirely upon the power of grace to motivate us and impel us in our efforts to practise the thought-free and therefore mind-free art of self-attentive being.

How in practice can we depend entirely upon the power of grace? Or in other words, how can we avoid depending even in the least upon the self-delusive power of our mind?

The answer is given by Sri Ramana in the next clause, '*aṉbu pūṇumē*', in which *aṉbu* means 'love' and *pūṇumē* literally means 'put on', 'wear', 'undertake', 'assume', 'be possessed of', 'be yoked with', 'be caught by', 'be ensnared by', 'be entangled with' or 'be fettered with'. Thus *aṉbu pūṇumē*' basically means 'be possessed of love', or simply 'have love'.

Only by true, whole-hearted and all-consuming love for our natural state of just being can we truly become a receptacle fit to receive, imbibe and assimilate grace. As explained by Sri Ramana in verse 966 of *Guru Vācaka Kōvai*, which we discussed in the previous chapter, grace is always available to us, existing in the core of our being as the clear light of our own absolute self-consciousness, 'I am'. To receive, imbibe and assimilate it, therefore, all we need do is to turn our entire attention towards it. But in order to be able to turn and keep our attention firmly fixed in the clear light of grace, which is our own essential consciousness of being, devoid of even the least contamination in the form of thinking or knowing otherness, we must have overwhelming love for being.

What obstructs and obscures the clear light of grace is only the rising of our mind with all its restless activity of thinking and its resulting knowledge of duality or otherness. Therefore we can experience and assimilate grace only to the extent to which our mind subsides, or in other words, only to the extent to which we surrender ourself to being.

Normally, however, our mind is not willing to surrender itself entirely by subsiding self-attentively in our own essential being, and hence when we try to turn our attention towards ourself it rises in rebellion, trying to think of anything other than our simple being. Only when we succeed in cultivating overwhelming *bhakti* or love for just being, and consequently steadfast *vairāgya* or freedom from even the least desire to think of anything other than being, will our mind willingly submit to its own annihilation.

The overwhelming and all-consuming love for absolute being that we require in order to be able to surrender ourself entirely to the infinite fullness of being that we call 'God' is cultivated within us both by the magnetically attractive power of grace, which is always shining in the innermost core of our being as infinite peace, happiness and love, and by our responding to it by willingly turning our attention towards it and thereby trying to abide as our own naturally self-conscious being.

All we can 'do' to cultivate the required love in our heart is to yield to the attracting power of grace by tenaciously persevering in our practice of the art of self-attentive being. If we sincerely and repeatedly attempt to keep our entire attention fixed in our mere being, grace will bestow upon us every form of help that we need, both inwardly and outwardly, and will thereby steadily nurture within us the true love that we require.

The power that motivates us and enables us to turn our mind inwards and to abide firmly as our simple self-conscious being is not the power of our mind, but only the power of true love or grace, which is the power of our own real self. The power of our mind is a power of extroversion, self-delusion and egocentric desire, and hence it can never enable us either to turn within or to remain firmly in the egoless and thought-free state of just being. It is in fact the power that by its very nature drives our attention outwards and therefore prevents us from abiding as being.

Therefore we should never imagine that by our own egotistical power we can attain the non-dual experience of true self-knowledge. Without the power of grace we can never cultivate the perfectly submissive and heart-melting love that we require to abide eternally as the infinite and mind-free reality.

If we imagine that we can attain the supreme and egoless state of absolute oneness with the infinite reality by the finite power of our own mind and our mind-driven efforts, we are merely allowing our mind to delude us into believing its power to be real. The seeming power of our mind is not only trivial in comparison with the infinite power of grace, but is actually entirely unreal. It is in truth merely a self-deceptive illusion, and if we scrutinise it keenly to discover the reality that underlies it, it will dissolve and disappear in the clear light of pure self-conscious being.

So long as our mind tries to assert its own power in an attempt to turn its attention away from all thoughts towards itself, it is merely struggling with itself, thereby giving reality to its own seeming existence, and hence it will not be able to subside truly and completely. It can subside completely only by lovingly yielding itself and all its self-assertive power to the true power of grace, which is the naturally attractive power of the perfect peace and happiness that we can experience only in the state of thought-free self-conscious being. Hence we will be able to surrender our mind completely only when, by the all-loving power of grace and by our reciprocal love and effort just to be, we steadily gain the inner clarity that is necessary for us to be able to experience fully the overwhelming attraction of the infinitely blissful state of just being.

When we sincerely, lovingly and submissively persevere in practising the art of being to the best of our ability, the power of grace, which is the infinite happiness of absolute self-conscious being, will steadily attract our mind more and more strongly, and thus it will naturally draw it gently within, into the innermost depth of our being, where it will consume it in the perfect clarity of true non-dual self-knowledge.

What we will then experience is expressed by Sri Ramana in the final clause of this verse, '*iṉbu tōṇumē*', which means simply 'happiness will certainly appear' or 'happiness will certainly shine forth'. That is, when, by the power of grace and by our responding to it appropriately by willingly subsiding into our natural state of self-conscious being, we are finally overwhelmed entirely by our love for just being, the apparition of our unreal mind or ego will vanish, and in its place we will experience ourself as infinite and eternal happiness.

In order to yield ourself entirely to the power of grace and thereby just to be as we really are, we must be extremely vigilant to avoid giving even the least room to the rising of our thinking mind. Since we allow our mind to rise only by imagining anything other than our own being, in order to avoid allowing it to rise we must keep our attention firmly fixed in our mere being. In other words, to be as we really are, we must be vigilantly self-attentive.

Sri Ramana has therefore taught us that vigilantly, steadfastly and tenaciously practising this art of self-attentive being is the only means by which we can surrender our mind or false individual self entirely and thereby experience our real self or infinite being. To practise this art successfully we must have a true and deep love for being. That is, we must have a sincere and wholehearted love just to be, and not to be 'this' or 'that' or anything else.

So long as we have even the least liking or desire for anything other than being, we will be impelled by that desire to rise as our mind to experience that thing. Therefore we must free ourself from all our desire for anything other than our essential being, and as we saw earlier, the only way we can do so effectively and entirely is by clinging tenaciously to our practice of self-attentiveness or *svarūpa-dhyāna*.

Self-attentive being is both our means and our end – our path and our goal. Since the nature of our true self or absolute reality is eternally self-conscious being, being that is ever clearly conscious only of itself and of nothing else, we can experience it only by being as it is – that is, as thought-free self-conscious being. The only difference between our path, which is our practice of self-conscious being, and our goal, which is our natural and effortless state of self-conscious being, lies in the effort that we now seem to require in order to remain as our self-conscious being.

The effort that we now require to remain as our naturally and eternally self-conscious or self-attentive being is only the effort we need to make in order to resist the impelling force of our own desires. Our desires impel us to rise as this finite object-knowing consciousness we call our 'mind', to imagine things other than ourself, and to attend to or think of those 'other' things. Therefore so long as even the least desire remains in our heart, we have to make a tenacious effort to remain attentively as our self-conscious being.

Effort is the application of force. To resist the driving force of our desires and to remain steadily and motionlessly poised as being, we have to apply an equal and opposite force. That opposite force is the force of our love to be. If the force of our love to be is not equal to or greater than the force of our desires to think, our desires will overpower us and we will begin to think of the objects of our desire. Therefore the practice of the art of being is the practice of cultivating the force of our love to be and applying it to resist the delusive force of our desires for other things.

By repeated and persistent practice of this art of self-attentive being, we will steadily gain the love we require to remain effortlessly as being. Only when our love grows by means of our sincere and tenacious efforts to be ever self-attentive, and when it thereby finally overwhelms us entirely, will we achieve the skill to remain effortlessly in our natural state of just being, which is our thought-free and therefore perfectly clear self-consciousness, 'I am'.

The love we have just to be is the purest and most perfect form of love. Since our natural state of just being is the true form of God, attending to and thereby abiding as our essential being is the only way we can truly express our love for God. As Sri Ramana says in verse 9 of *Upadēśa Undiyār* and verse 15 of *Upadēśa Taṉippākkaḷ*:

> By the strength of [such *ananya*] *bhāva* [the attitude or conviction that God is not other than ourself], being [abiding or remaining] in *sat-*

> *bhāva* [our natural state of being], which transcends [all] *bhāvana* [imagination, thinking or meditation], is alone *para-bhakti tattva* [the true state of supreme devotion].
>
> Since God exists as *ātmā* [our own real self or essential being], *ātmānusandhāna* [self-contemplation or self-attentiveness] is *paramēśa-bhakti* [supreme devotion to God].

When we rise as our mind or finite individual self, we seemingly separate ourself from God, who is our own true being, and thereby we commit the 'original sin' of imagining divisions in the infinite and indivisible being that is God. By imagining ourself to be separate from God, we are defiling his infinity, reducing him in our view to something less than the infinite fullness of being that he really is. Therefore if we wish to restore to God what we have unrightfully usurped from him, we must surrender our finite self back into his infinite being, and we can do this only by remaining in the egoless state of absolutely non-dual self-consciousness, which is our natural state of infinite, undivided and therefore thought-free being.

In order to be able to give ourself entirely to God in this manner, we must be overwhelmed by an unreserved and all-consuming love for him. So long as we retain even the least love for our existence as a separate individual, we will resist yielding ourself entirely to him. However, the more we practise abiding as our perfectly thought-free and clearly self-conscious being, the more we will experience the taste of the infinite peace and happiness which are the real nature of our being, and thereby our love for being will steadily increase, until eventually it will consume our mind and drown it for ever in the ocean of infinite being, consciousness, happiness, peace and love.

Abiding in this state of absolute bliss is the true way of serving God in the manner in which he wants us to serve him. This important truth about the only manner in which we can render real service to God is stated by Sri Ramana in verse 29 of *Upadēśa Undiyār*:

> Abiding permanently in this state of *para-sukha* [supreme or transcendent happiness], which is devoid of [both] bondage and liberation, is abiding in the service of God.

When we imagine ourself to be a finite individual, we are doing a great disservice to God, because we are thereby making it necessary for him to draw us back into himself. Therefore so long as we imagine ourself to be separate from him, nothing that we may do is truly a service to him. The only service he requires of us is for us to surrender ourself entirely to his will, which is that we should remain happily as one with himself. Therefore surrendering our finite self by abiding as our essential non-dual self-conscious being, which is both the thought-free state of supreme happiness and the absolute reality that we call 'God', is truly abiding in his service.

Since our natural state of supreme happiness is the state of just being, it is completely free of any doing or thinking, and hence it is devoid of all thoughts, including the thoughts of bondage and liberation. Bondage and liberation are a pair of opposites, and therefore they exist only in the unreal state of duality. In the non-dual state of true self-knowledge or absolute oneness with God, all thoughts of bondage and liberation disappear along with our thinking mind and all its imaginary duality.

When we first learn about this art of self-attentive being, and understand the importance of practising it to our utmost ability, many of us wonder how we can practise it in the midst of all our day-to-day activities. Our mundane life in this world and the absolute truth taught by Sri Ramana and other sages appear to be two completely different states of reality, divided by such a vast chasm that it is difficult for us to imagine how we can in practice even begin to reconcile the two of them. How can we actually practise this art of being when our mind is being constantly pulled hither and thither by the outward demands of our life in this world and by the inward pressure of our desires and attachments?

Whatever may be the circumstances of our life, and however great may be the external and internal pressures upon us, we always know 'I am'. Therefore the chasm that we imagine existing between ourself and the absolute reality is unreal. The absolute reality is our simple self-conscious being, which we always experience as 'I am', and therefore it is our nearest and dearest. There is nothing so close or so dear to us as the absolute reality, because it is our own real self.

Since we always experience it as 'I am', it is always possible for us to attend to it. Nothing can truly prevent us from being self-attentive whenever we want to be. The imaginary chasm or divide that seems to separate us from the infinite fullness of being, consciousness and happiness is in fact nothing but our own desires.

However, our desires have no reality or power of their own. They appear to be real and powerful only because we give them reality and power by attending to them. If we steadfastly ignore them by clinging tenaciously to self-attentive being, they will be powerless to distract us from our natural state of being.

In practice, however, most of us experience difficulty in holding firmly and uninterruptedly to self-attentiveness, because our desire to think of other things is greater than our love to remain as our naturally thought-free and self-conscious being. But no matter how much difficulty we experience, if we persist in our efforts to draw our attention back to our own being whenever we notice that it has slipped away to think of other things, we will gradually gain the skill – the love and desirelessness – that we require to remain simply as our self-conscious being.

As Sri Sadhu Om used to say, 'Where there's a will there's a way, but where there's no will there's a hill'. That is, if we sincerely want to practise self-attentiveness, we will find that it is possible for us to do so, even if only falteringly and intermittently, but if we lack a sincere wish to practise it, we will feel that it is too difficult for us. Ultimately all difficulty is in our own mind, because it can never really be difficult for us to be self-attentive, even if only momentarily. If we feel that being self-attentive is too difficult for us, we feel so only because we really do not have sufficient will even to try, or after trying a little to persist in our attempts.

Even if we are able to be self-attentive only momentarily, that will be sufficient as a start. However, to gain a real benefit from such momentary self-attentiveness, we must persist in our attempts to catch such moments as frequently as possible, and to hold on to each such moment as long as possible. The more frequently we remember to withdraw our attention towards ourself, and the longer we manage to maintain our self-attentiveness each time that we thus catch it, the more quickly we will cultivate the love that we require to be firmly self-attentive.

One question that is often raised is whether or not it is necessary for us to sit with closed eyes in order to practise self-attentiveness. The simple answer to this is that it is certainly not necessary, because we can be self-attentive whatever our body may be doing or not doing, and whether our eyes are open or closed.

Self-attentiveness has nothing to do with either the posture of our body or the closing of our eyes, but is only a matter of our attention. Our eyes may be open but our attention may still be focused on our being, and conversely our eyes may be closed but our attention may nevertheless be dwelling upon thoughts of things other than ourself.

However, though it is not essential for us to sit in 'meditation' with closed eyes in order to practise self-attentiveness, it may sometimes be helpful for us to do so. In order to sink into a state of deep and intense self-attentiveness, we may find it helpful to refrain not only from mental activity but also from physical activity.

However refraining from physical activity does not necessarily mean sitting with our eyes closed. Our body may be sitting or lying or in any other posture, so long as our attention is not on it but only on our essential self-conscious being. Likewise, our eyes may be open or closed so long as our attention is not going outwards either to see or to think of any object in the outside world.

The attitude we should have to our body whenever we attempt to experience clear and intense self-attentiveness is expressed by Sri Ramana in the words *piṇam pōl tīrndu uḍalam*, which mean 'leaving the body like a corpse', and which were the words that he added between verses 28 and 29 when he expanded the two plus forty verses of *Uḷḷadu Nāṟpadu* into a single verse in *kaliveṇbā* metre. Though he added these words to the last line of verse 28, in their meaning they form part of the first sentence of verse 29, which with their addition means:

> Leaving [our] body like a corpse, and without saying 'I' by mouth, scrutinising by [our] mind sinking [diving or piercing] inwards 'where does [this mind] rise as I?' alone is the path of *jñāna* [the practice that leads to true knowledge]. [...]

In this context, 'leaving [our] body like a corpse' may either refer to the attitude with which we should withdraw our attention from it, or to the posture in which we should leave it. When as a sixteen-year-old boy Sri Ramana was overwhelmed by a sudden and intense fear of death, he lay down like a corpse and turned his entire attention towards his essential being in order to discover whether his being or 'I' would survive the death of his physical body. Because he withdrew his attention entirely from his body, his mind and all other things, and instead focused it wholly and exclusively upon his consciousness of his own being, he instantly experienced true self-knowledge, and thus his mind was dissolved for ever in the infinite and absolute reality.

Thus in his own case Sri Ramana not only withdrew his attention from his body as if it were a lifeless corpse, but also laid his body down as if it were a corpse that had been laid out in preparation for its cremation. This does not mean, however, that we should necessarily lie down when we practise self-attentiveness. We certainly can practise self-attentiveness while lying down, but in practice we may often find it preferable to sit instead of lying, because while sitting upright it is usually easier for us to remain alert and thereby to avoid drowsing off into sleep or a dream.

However the posture of our body really does not matter, because the only thing that is important during our intense practice of just being is that our attention is withdrawn entirely from our body and from every other object or thought, and instead focused keenly and vigilantly upon our mere consciousness of being.

Therefore when Sri Ramana said, 'leaving [our] body like a corpse', he did not merely mean that we should physically lay it down like a corpse, but that we should mentally withdraw our attention from it as if it had become a lifeless corpse – something with which we no longer have any connection. Since our sole aim during moments of intense practice is to penetrate deep within our being, we must entirely disregard our body, and hence we should not concern ourself in the least with its posture or any other such trivial matter.

So long as our attention is fixed only on ourself and on nothing else, it does not matter what posture our body may be in, or whether it happens to be active or inactive. As Sri Ramana used to say, the only *āsana* (posture) that is required is *nididhyāsana* (deep contemplation or attentiveness, which in the context of his teachings means keen self-attentiveness). In fact we may often find it easier to be self-attentive while our body is engaged in some mechanical activity such as walking, which does not require any significant attention, than when we are sitting or lying down with our eyes closed, because as soon as we close our eyes to meditate upon our being, our mind tends to struggle to resist such meditation or self-attentiveness, and hence we may quickly forget why we have closed our eyes and instead begin thinking of anything except our own being.

If we sincerely attempt to practise self-attentiveness whenever our mind is not pressingly engaged in any other work, we will soon find what suits us best in terms of bodily posture or activity. Whether we are sitting, lying, walking or engaged in any other physical activity, we should attempt as frequently and as intensely as circumstances permit to focus our attention keenly on our being, or at least to maintain a certain degree of self-attentiveness. Therefore all questions about bodily posture are missing the whole point of the art of self-attentive being, which is that we should concentrate our entire attention upon our being and should thereby ignore our body and all other things.

Another question that is often raised is whether or not we should set aside certain periods of time each day to practise self-attentiveness. Again the answer to this question is that it is not necessary for us to do so, but that we may find it to be helpful.

It is all a matter of personal preference and lifestyle. So long as we find it helpful, we should set aside certain periods of time each day to practise self-attentiveness, but if we find that our set periods of 'meditation' are just becoming a mechanical routine, and that we are not really spending those periods usefully engaged in clear and steady self-attentiveness, we should find some better way of ensuring that we spend some time each day engaged in self-attentiveness.

To experience our true and essential being with perfect clarity does not in truth require any time. If we have an overwhelming and all-consuming love to know ourself, we can attain true and eternal self-knowledge by just a moment of total self-attentiveness, as Sri Ramana himself did.

Just as death is something that happens in an instant, and is not something that we can ever experience partially, so the experience of true self-knowledge 'happens' in an instant, and can never be experienced partially. Either we imagine ourself to be a finite individual, as we do so long as we still feel that our self-attentiveness or self-conscious being is a practice and not something entirely natural and unavoidable, or we are wholly consumed by the absolute clarity of true self-knowledge, in which case we will know that we have always been nothing other than infinite and perfectly clear self-conscious being.

Our aim during practice, therefore, is to experience that one moment of absolute unqualified self-attentiveness. Hence long periods of 'meditation' are not necessary. It may be helpful for us at times to sit quietly for a while attempting to focus our attention wholly and exclusively upon our being, but if our mind rebels too strongly we should relax for a while and try again later with a fresh and calm mind. If we struggle for too long a period to oppose the force of our desires to think, our mind will become agitated, and will therefore cease to be a suitable instrument for practising self-attentiveness. But if we relax our efforts for a while and allow our mind to become relatively calm once again, then we will be able to practise self-attentiveness with a renewed vigour.

In practice what we need is not long hours seated in a desperate struggle to maintain continuous self-attentiveness, but rather many brief periods of time here and there throughout each day when we try with fresh vigour and intense enthusiasm to experience our naturally ever self-conscious being. During the midst of our normal daily activities, there are many times when our mind is not pressingly engaged in any particular work, and normally during such times we allow our mind to wander and think of many trivial and unnecessary matters. Each such time is a precious opportunity for us to be self-attentive.

Most of the thoughts we think each day are not pressingly urgent, but are merely the way in which our mind usually chooses to occupy itself. Therefore if we have a true love for self-attentiveness, instead of wasting most of our day in idle thoughts, we can very easily spend many moments here and there attempting to be self-attentive. This frequent drawing of our mind back towards ourself is what Sri Ramana sometimes referred to as the practice of 'self-remembrance'.

Therefore, as Sri Sadhu Om used to say, what we need is not long periods of 'meditation', which usually turn out to be merely a futile struggle attempting to resist the force of our desire to think, but is rather just many intermittent attempts to be self-attentive. If we remember to make such intermittent attempts frequently throughout the day, each individual attempt may only last a brief while, but all such brief attempts will together add up to a considerable amount of time spent in the state of self-attentive being.

By thus practising self-attentiveness intermittently, we will make each attempt with a fresh vigour and therefore a more intense clarity. Rather than longer periods of unsteady and therefore unclear self-attentiveness, shorter periods of more intense and therefore clearer and more precise self-attentiveness will be more beneficial.

Yet another question that is sometimes raised is whether it would not be beneficial for us to renounce all our worldly activities and responsibilities and to dedicate ourself solely to a life of contemplation. For some people a lifestyle of external renunciation may be beneficial, but for most of us such a lifestyle is not only unnecessary but also inappropriate. What is really important is not external renunciation but only internal renunciation.

Whatever may be our external lifestyle, we are always free inwardly to renounce our desires and attachments. If we succeed at least partially in such inward renunciation, no external lifestyle will be an obstacle to our practising the art of self-attentive being. Conversely, however, if we fail inwardly to renounce our desires, no amount of external renunciation will be of any use to us. The only obstacle to our practice of self-attentiveness is our own desires, and is not anything in the external world.

Our ability to be clearly and steadily self-attentive is proportionate only to our love for being and our corresponding freedom from desire for anything else, and has nothing to do with our external lifestyle. No matter what our external lifestyle may be, if we have even a little love to know ourself and to be free of our desires, we will to that extent be able to practise the art of self-attentive being.

However, though our external lifestyle cannot directly influence our ability to be self-attentive, our practice of self-attentiveness may to some extent influence our lifestyle. That is, since our practice will gradually weaken and erode our desires, we will naturally begin to lose interest in many of the seeming pleasures of life that we formerly desired, and hence we will feel contented with a simpler, less extroverted and less busy style of life.

However, there is really no need for us to concern ourself about the outward mode of our life, because our external life is moulded by our destiny, and our destiny is ordained by God in such a way that will be most beneficial to our spiritual progress. Whatever we experience in our outward life is according to the will of God, and is therefore what is most conducive to our practice of self-attentive being.

Even the seeming difficulties and obstacles that arise in our life are intended by God to create in our mind the state of *vairāgya* or desirelessness, which is otherwise called equanimity or 'holy indifference'. Only if we learn to be inwardly detached from our life in this world, will we gain the strength that we require to turn our mind inwards to drown in the perfect clarity of true self-knowledge.

For most of us, this spiritual path of persistently trying to practise the art of self-attentive being may appear at times to be anything but a smooth, peaceful and trouble-free course, because our self-deluded and desire-driven mind will certainly try to create many obstacles in our way. However, whatever obstacles our mind may create, we can overcome all of them by undaunted perseverance. Except by tenaciously persevering in our practice of self-attentiveness, there is no way that we can effectively overcome all the seeming obstacles that we as our mind create for ourself.

One of the many self-deceptive tricks that we as our mind tend to play on ourself is to expect and look for some cognisable results from our practice, and to feel dejected when we do not experience the results that we hope for. However, any cognisable results that we may experience on this path are deceptive, because they are experienced only by our mind, whose nature is to delude itself with appearances, and to distort and thereby see out of proportion whatever it happens to experience. Therefore nothing that is experienced by our mind can be a true indicator of our spiritual progress.

As Sri Ramana used to say, our perseverance is the only true sign of our progress. That is, if we persevere in our practice, that is clear evidence of our love for being, and so long as we have that love, we are surely making progress. If, on the other hand, we fail to persevere, that indicates that we lack the love that we require to make rapid progress. However, if we make even a little effort to be self-attentive, or at least have a liking to try, to that extent we do have love for being, so we should not feel dejected because of our inadequate perseverance, but should continue to persist in our attempts to whatever extent we find possible. Even a little sincere effort will go a long way towards cultivating in our heart the true love that we require to reach our ultimate goal of absolute self-knowledge.

Whenever we find that our enthusiasm and perseverance are faltering, we should read once again the teachings of Sri Ramana, or books that explore and discuss their import and significance, and we should ponder deeply over their meaning, because such repeated *śravaṇa* (reading) and *manana* (musing) will rekindle our enthusiasm to persevere in *nididhyāsana*, the practice of keen self-attentiveness. We cannot force our mind to remain calmly and peacefully self-attentive, but by repeated *śravaṇa*, *manana* and *nididhyāsana* we can gently tempt it to return again and again to our natural state of peaceful self-attentive being.

Our mind is like a runaway horse, and our natural state of calm self-conscious being is like its stable. Just as we would not use physical force to catch and pull a runaway horse back into its stable, but would simply tempt it to return willingly by gently and patiently holding a handful of grass in front of it, so we should not try in vain to overcome our desires and the resulting self-deceptive workings of our mind by confronting and fighting with them, but should gently and stealthily tempt our mind by whatever means possible to return willingly to our natural state of serene self-conscious being, which is its source and natural abode.

Until our mind is completely dissolved in the infinite luminescence and clarity of true self-knowledge, we will continue to experience ourself as a finite individual, and as such we will feel ourself to be one among the many living beings in this world, and hence we will have to interact constantly with other people. When we interact with other people, our deeply rooted *vāsanās* or mental impulsions will tend to rise vigorously to the surface of our mind in the form of subtle and therefore strong likes and dislikes, attachments and aversions, possessiveness, selfishness, greed, lust, anger, jealousy, pride, egoism and other such undesirable feelings and emotions.

Thus our interactions with other people are a good opportunity for us to recognise such bad qualities in ourself, and to resist the sway that they hold over us by applying the *vairāgya* or 'holy indifference' that we are gradually cultivating through our practice of self-attentive being. Therefore in the last two paragraphs of *Nāṉ Yār?* Sri Ramana gives us some valuable tips regarding the inward attitude with which we should interact with other people and conduct ourself in this world. In the nineteenth paragraph he says:

> There are not two [classes of] minds, namely a good [class of] mind and a bad [class of] mind. The mind is only one. Only *vāsanās* [impulsions or latent desires] are of two kinds, namely *śubha* [good or agreeable] and *aśubha* [bad or disagreeable]. When [a person's] mind is under the sway of *śubha vāsanās* [agreeable impulsions] it is said to be a good mind, and when it is under the sway of *aśubha vāsanās* [disagreeable impulsions] a bad mind. However bad other people may appear to be, disliking them is not proper [or appropriate]. Likes and dislikes are both fit [for us] to dislike [or to renounce]. It is not proper [for us] to let [our] mind [dwell] much on worldly matters. It is not proper [for us] to enter in the affairs of other people [an idiomatic way of saying that we should mind our own business and not interfere in other people's affairs]. All that one gives to others one is giving only to oneself. If [everyone] knew this truth, who indeed would refrain from giving?

The only thing that we should truly dislike is our own likes and dislikes, because they agitate our mind and disturb our natural peace and equanimity. We dislike certain people because we feel they are the cause of the irritation and annoyance that we feel when we interact with them or think of them, but in fact the real cause of our irritation and annoyance is only our own likes and dislikes. If we were completely free of likes and dislikes, no other person could make us feel any aversion or other negative emotion.

What truly disturbs us when we interact with a person we dislike is not actually that person's *aśubha vāsanās* or disagreeable impulsions, but is only our own *aśubha vāsanās*, because our *aśubha vāsanās* are what manifest as our likes and dislikes. Our likes and dislikes are both forms of desire, and like all forms of desire they drive our mind outwards, away from the infinite peace and happiness that exists in the core of our being.

Therefore if we truly wish to turn our mind inwards and thereby dissolve it in our perfectly clear consciousness of being, we must reject all our likes and dislikes, and develop instead a love only for being.

All our selfish attitudes, feelings, emotions, reactions and behaviours, such as our possessiveness, greed, lust, anger, jealousy, pride and egoism, are rooted in our likes and dislikes. Therefore to the extent to which we are able to free ourself from our likes and dislikes, we will accordingly free ourself from all forms of selfishness and from all the disagreeable feelings and emotions that they arouse in us. Since our interactions with other people tend to bring to the surface of our mind all our deep-rooted likes and dislikes, they are God-given opportunities for us not only to identify our likes and dislikes but also to curb them.

By practising the art of self-attentive being, we cultivate the skill to restrain not only our likes and dislikes but also their root, which is our mind. Hence our practice of self-attentiveness will make it easier for us to recognise and curb the likes and dislikes that arise in our mind when we interact with other people. Conversely, by curbing our likes and dislikes when we interact with other people, we are cultivating our *vairāgya* or freedom from desires, and this will in turn help us in our practice of self-attentive being.

When Sri Ramana says that it is not proper for us to allow our mind to dwell much upon worldly matters, or for us to interfere in the affairs of others, he does not mean that we should be indifferent to the sufferings of other people or creatures. It is right for us to feel compassion whenever we see or come to know of the suffering of any other person or creature, because compassion is an essential quality that naturally arises in our mind when it is under the sway of *sattva-guṇa* or the quality of 'being-ness', goodness and purity, and it is also right for us to do whatever we reasonably can to alleviate such suffering.

However, suffering is an unavoidable fact of embodied existence, and there is little that we with our limited powers can do to alleviate the many forms of suffering that exist and will always exist in this world. Therefore if we allow our mind to dwell upon the sufferings and injustices in this world, we will only lose our own peace of mind, and to little or no avail.

Rather than imagining that we can really do anything significant to alleviate the suffering in this world, it would be more beneficial if we simply take care to avoid contributing in any way to that suffering. For example, hundreds of millions of animals are subjected to unnecessary and unjustifiable suffering due to the cruel practices of factory farming, and every day millions of them are cruelly slaughtered just to satisfy the unnatural and inhumane craving that people have to eat their flesh. This is a sad fact of life, and a very sorry reflection on the so-called civilisation and humanity of the modern human race, but there is little we can actually do to prevent all such cruelty from happening. However, though we cannot prevent it, we can easily avoid contributing to it simply by refraining from eating meat, fish, eggs or any other animal-derived products.

Similarly, so many unjustified wars are fought in this world, all as a result of human greed, and every year more than a hundred million children and adults die of starvation and other poverty-related causes, in spite of all the abundant food and other material resources that a large section of the human race are enjoying. Many factors contribute to such sufferings, but at the root of all those factors lies human selfishness and greed. Though in the complex economy of the modern world, in which we are all to some extent unavoidably involved, it is difficult for us to know exactly what effects our means of earning and each of our spending habits and other forms of behaviour are having on the lives of those less fortunate than ourself, to whatever extent possible we should try to avoid contributing by our own actions to the sufferings that are caused by this unjust economy, and we can avoid this by simplifying our lifestyle and minimising our dependence upon material possessions and other objects of sense enjoyment.

Most importantly, however, though we cannot know all the repercussions that each of our actions may be having on other people and creatures, we do know that the root cause of much of the suffering that exists in this world is the selfishness and greed that exists in the minds of people like ourself. Therefore, to avoid contributing to the sufferings of others, the most essential thing that we must do is to root all selfishness and greed out of our own mind, and we can do this effectively only by turning our mind inwards to drown it in our own self-conscious being, which is the source from which it rises together with all its selfishness and greed.

So long as our mind is turned outwards, dwelling upon worldly matters or trying to interfere in the affairs of other people, we will be overlooking the defects that exist in our own mind. Therefore, before trying to rectify the defects of this world or of other people, we should first succeed in rectifying our own defects, which we can effectively do only by withdrawing our attention entirely from this world and from matters that concern other people, and vigilantly focusing it upon our own self-conscious being in order to curb and prevent the rising of our mind, which is the root of all our defects. This is the reason why Sri Ramana says that it is not proper for us to allow our mind to dwell much upon worldly matters, or for us to interfere in the affairs of others.

Moreover, in the final analysis, this world and all the sufferings that we see in it are created by our own power of imagination and exist only in our own mind, just as the world and the sufferings that we see in a dream are. If we feel compassion on seeing the sufferings of other people and animals in our dream, and if we wish to alleviate all such suffering, all we need do is to wake up from that dream. Likewise, if we truly wish to put an end to all the sufferings that we see in this world, we must strive to wake up from this dream that we mistake to be our waking life, into the true waking state of perfectly non-dual self-knowledge, by tenaciously practising the art of self-attentive being.

However, though our life in this world is in fact just a dream, so long as we experience this dream we should not dismiss the sufferings of others as being simply unreal and therefore of no consequence. We who experience this imaginary dream are ourself a part of it, and hence everything that we experience or witness in this dream is just as real as we are.

So long as we feel ourself to be a person – a body-bound mind – who is experiencing this dream, we cannot but feel that the joys and sufferings that we are undergoing are perfectly real, and so long as we thus feel that our own joys and sufferings are real, we cannot deny that the joys and sufferings of other people and creatures are equally real and just as consequential. Hence, since we each naturally wish to avoid any form of suffering being caused to ourself, we should wish equally strongly to avoid any form of suffering being caused to any other sentient being.

Therefore, when Sri Ramana advises us to avoid interfering in the affairs of others or allowing our mind to dwell much upon worldly matters, he does not suggest that we should avoid such actions of body, speech or mind due to heartless indifference, but only that we should do so due to holy indifference – compassionate indifference, truly loving and caring indifference.

Sri Ramana never advised anyone to be heartlessly indifferent – uncaringly and unkindly indifferent – to the sufferings of others. On the contrary, through his own actions he clearly exemplified how compassionate, tender-hearted and caring we should all be, and how strictly we should avoid causing even the least *hiṁsā* or harm to any other living being.

Though Sri Ramana seldom taught the importance of compassion explicitly in words, he did teach it very clearly through his own life – through his every action and attitude. In every situation, his attitude and his response through speech or action clearly demonstrated his unbounded love, compassion, tender-heartedness, kindness, consideration and *ahiṁsā* – sensitive and careful avoidance of causing any harm, injury or hurt to any living being.

Compassion, kindness and love shone through every action of Sri Ramana because that is what he was. His very being was itself the fullness of love – infinite and all-inclusive love. Because his seeming individuality had merged and been consumed in the infinite light of true self-knowledge, he was truly one with the absolute reality, whose nature is perfectly non-dual and indivisible being, consciousness, happiness and love.

He therefore loved all of us – each and every sentient being – as his own self, because he experienced himself as the one infinite reality, other than which none of us can be. He truly was and is the real and essential self of each and every one of us, and hence none of us can be excluded from his infinite love – his all-inclusive self-love – which is his own essential being.

Therefore the seeming 'person' that was Sri Ramana was a perfect embodiment of *parama karuṇā* – supreme compassion, grace, kindness and love. His kindness and love were equal to all. To him sinner and saint were all alike. He showed the same simple care, kindness, tenderness, love and compassion to people whom we may consider to be bad as he did to people whom we may consider to be good.

His love and kindness were absolutely impartial. He showed no greater love, kindness or concern for his most sincere devotees – those who most truly understood and put his teachings into practice – than he did either for those people who disregarded him, disparaged him or even ill-treated him, or for those devotees who were unconcerned about his teachings, or who misunderstood them, or who even tried to distort, misinterpret or misrepresent them.

In fact, if he ever seemed to show any partiality, it was not for those who loved him most sincerely, but only for those who had least love or no love at all for him. Devotees who loved him most sincerely, and who earnestly tried to follow his teachings by turning their mind inwards and surrendering it to him in the core of their being, sometimes felt that outwardly he seemed to ignore them, and to give his attention only to other less sincere devotees. However, if they understood him correctly, they knew that he outwardly gave his attention to those who were most in need of it, and that if he outwardly ignored us it was only to encourage us to turn inwards to seek the true form of his love, which is always shining blissfully in our heart as our own non-dual self-conscious being, 'I am', waiting to draw us within by its magnetic power of attraction.

The reason why he showed equal love and kindness to each and every person, irrespective of the fact that a particular person may have been the worst of sinners or the greatest of saints, was that in his view there is no essential difference between a sinner and a saint, between an atheist and a devotee, or between a cruel person and a kind person. He knew that in essence every person is the same single non-dual self, which he experienced as himself. If at all there seems to be any such thing as a separate person, he or she appears to be such only due to his or her imaginary ignorance of the true nature of the one real non-dual self, which we all always experience as our own essential self-consciousness, 'I am'.

Not only are we all in essence the same one non-dual self, but as people we are all also equally ignorant of our own true nature. Even our theoretical knowledge of our own true nature does not make us any less ignorant than another person who has no such theoretical knowledge, because this theoretical knowledge exists only in our own mind, which arises only because of our basic underlying self-ignorance or self-forgetfulness.

In our self-ignorant view, Sri Ramana appears to us to be a person like us, and even our honest belief and conviction that he is in reality not a person but only our own infinite real self is a faith that exists only in our own mind. So long as we experience ourself as a person, and not as the one infinite and undivided real self, we cannot experience Sri Ramana as our own essential self, but can only know him as a person, albeit a person immeasurably superior to ourself.

Therefore in our self-ignorant view, Sri Ramana seemed to be a person, and as such he seemed to see each one of us as a separate person. However, even insofar as he seemed to see each of us as a person, he did not see any essential difference between us. He saw us all as being equal in our ignorance of our real self. In his view there was no person who was any more or any less ignorant than any other person. We either know ourself as we really are, or we ignore our real nature and experience ourself as a person – a finite body-bound mind.

Since in his view we are all equally ignorant, we are all equally in need of his *kāraṇam illāda karuṇai* – his causeless grace, mercy, compassion, kindness and love. Nothing that we can do can make us worthy of his grace, and equally nothing that we can do can make us unworthy of his grace. Just as the rain falls on the good and evil alike, his divine grace and love is equally available to all creatures, including the greatest saints and the most evil sinners, the most brilliant intellectuals and the dullest of fools, the richest and the poorest, kings and beggars, human beings and all the so-called lesser animals.

His grace or love is uncaused because it is his essential nature. As the one infinite real self, he cannot but love us all as himself, because he experiences us all as himself. Since his grace is infinite, and not dependent upon any cause other than itself, it can never either increase or decrease. In truth it is the only reality – the one absolute reality, which is eternal, immutable and self-shining.

Though Sri Ramana is truly the one infinite reality that we call 'God', who is always making his grace available to each and every one of us by shining eternally in the innermost depth of our heart as our nearest and dearest – our own true self-conscious being, 'I am' – he manifested himself in human form in order to teach us that we can experience the perfect and ever-undiminishing happiness that we all seek only by turning our mind selfwards and thereby surrendering it in the absolute clarity of our own non-dual self-conscious being, which is the true form of his grace or love.

His human form was thus an embodiment of *parama karuṇā* or supreme compassion, grace, mercy, tender-heartedness, kindness, care and love, and as such no creature could ever be excluded from his infinite kindness and love. And though his human form passed away in 1950, before most of us were even born, his grace, love and inner guidance are ever available to us, because they are the one eternal reality that ever shines within us as 'I am', our own most beloved self. Moreover, not only does he always remain as our own essential self, but he also continues to be manifest outwardly in the form of his precious teachings, which are still available to remind us constantly of our need to turn selfwards in order to experience the infinite happiness of true self-knowledge.

In order to avail of his love or grace in all its infinite fullness, all we have to do is to turn selfwards and to drink thus at the source from which it springs. Though his grace is always helping us, so long as we attend to anything other than our own essential self we are ignoring it, and by doing so we are in effect closing the doors of our heart on it, obstructing it from flowing forth and consuming us in its infinite clarity.

His grace is the light of consciousness that shines within us, enabling us to know both ourself and all the imaginary objects that we have created in our mind. Both subject and object are illumined only by his grace, and without his grace as their essential substance and reality they could not even seem to exist.

However, so long as we attend to any form of object – whether the objects that we recognise as being only thoughts in our own mind, or the objects that we imagine exist in a world outside our mind – we are misusing the light of his grace, and we are distorting his infinite non-dual self-love and experiencing it as our desire for some objects and our aversion for other objects. Rather than misusing his grace in this manner to know objects, or expecting it to fulfil any of our petty desires, we should derive true benefit from it by using it to know ourself.

That is, our mind, which is the distorted light of consciousness that we now use to know objects, is a reflected form of our original light of self-consciousness, which is his grace. Therefore if we turn our mind away from all objects towards the source of its light, it will merge in that source like a ray of sunlight that is reflected from a mirror back towards the sun. By thus turning the reflected light of our mind back on ourself, we are surrendering ourself to our original light of grace – our fundamental self-consciousness, 'I am', which is the true form of love that we call 'Sri Ramana'.

When Sri Ramana manifested himself in human form, the compassion, tender-heartedness, kindness and love that he showed towards every person he encountered was an outward expression of the infinite, eternal, undivided and non-dual love that he experienced as his own self, and that always shines within each one of us as our own essential self-conscious being, 'I am'. Therefore the impartiality of his outward kindness and love demonstrated clearly the absolute impartiality of his true inward grace, which is always surging in the heart of every sentient being.

The same love that he showed to all people he showed to every other creature. He did not consider any animal to be any less worthy of his kindness, love and compassion than any human being, and animals naturally responded to the love they felt in him, and therefore approached him without any fear. Numerous stories and incidents in his life have been recorded that beautifully illustrate his extraordinary relationship with both wild and domesticated animals – the tender-heartedness, kindness, care and love that he showed to them, and their reciprocal fondness for and trust in him.

Moreover, not only was he equally kind to and caring about individual animals of every species, but he also showed his strong disapproval whenever any person treated unkindly or caused any harm to any animal. He would not tolerate or allow people to kill even poisonous animals such as snakes and scorpions, and he pointed out that our fear of such animals is caused only by our attachment to our own bodies. He said that just as we cherish our life in our present body, so every other creature equally cherishes their life in their present body, and hence we have no right to deprive any creature of its cherished life, or to cause it harm or suffering of any kind whatsoever.

One very clear illustration of his unbounded and absolutely impartial compassion and love was an incident that occurred when he was a young man. One day while he was walking through a thicket his thigh accidentally brushed against a hornets' nest, disturbing its numerous occupants, who immediately flew out in a rage and began to sting his offending thigh. Understanding their natural response, and feeling sorry for the disturbance that he had accidentally caused them, he stood quite still and, in spite of the intense pain that they were inflicting upon him, patiently allowed them to sting his thigh until they were all fully satisfied and returned to their nest. In later years, when Sri Muruganar wrote a verse (which is now included in *Guru Vācaka Kōvai* as verse 815) asking him why he felt repentant and allowed the hornets to sting his thigh even though the disturbance he caused them was not intentional, he replied by composing verse 7 of *Upadēśa Taṉippākkaḷ*, in which he said:

> Though the swarming hornets stung the leg so that it became inflamed and swollen when it touched and damaged their nest, which was spread [and concealed] in the midst of green leaves, and though it [the act of disrupting their nest] was a mistake that happened accidentally, if one did not at least feel sorry [pity for the hornets and repentant for the trouble caused to them], what indeed would be the nature of his mind [that is, how thoroughly hard-hearted and insensitive it would be]?

By his own life and example Sri Ramana taught us the great importance not only of kindness, love, tender-heartedness, consideration, compassion and *ahiṁsā*, but also of humility, selflessness, desirelessness, non-acquisitiveness, non-possessiveness, non-wastefulness, generosity, contentment, self-restraint, self-denial and utter simplicity of lifestyle. None of these qualities were cultivated or practised by him with any effort, but were all quite effortless, because they were natural effects of his absolute egolessness.

Because he did not experience himself as an ego, a finite and separate individual consciousness, he did not experience any person, animal, plant or inanimate object as being other than himself, and hence in the infinite fullness of his love – his absolutely non-dual self-love – there was no room for even the least trace of selfishness, greed, desire, attachment, possessiveness, unkindness, insensitivity or any other defect that tends to arise when we mistake ourself to be a finite body-bound ego or mind. He therefore lived what he taught, and taught only what he himself lived.

His actions, his attitude and his response to each person, to each animal and to each outward situation and event were therefore teachings that were no less powerful or significant than his spoken and written words. He exemplified in his life the same state of absolute egolessness that he taught us as being the only goal worth seeking. Therefore, though we cannot emulate his perfectly egoless life so long as we mistake ourself to be a person, a body-bound mind or ego-consciousness, we can learn much from it, and if we truly wish to lose our false individual self in our own natural state of absolutely egoless self-conscious being, we should humbly and sincerely try to apply what we are able to learn from his outward life in our own outward life.

That is, if we truly wish to be absolutely egoless, we must begin even now to practise the selfless qualities and virtues that are natural to egolessness. If we do not love and cherish such qualities, we do not truly love the state of perfect egolessness.

The consistently selfless simplicity of Sri Ramana's lifestyle was legendary and witnessed by thousands of people. Though his devotees built an *āśrama*, a community dwelling-place and religious institution, around him, he never claimed anything as his own. And though there were rich people who offered him and honestly desired to give him anything that he might want, he availed himself of nothing other than the minimum food, clothing and shelter that were necessary for the survival of his body.

From the time he left home at the age of sixteen till the end of his bodily lifetime, he lived the simple life of a *sādhu*, a religious mendicant. His only clothing was a *kaupīna*, a simple loincloth. Until his devotees built a simple dwelling-place for him, he lived only in caves or in *maṇḍapams*, open temple hallways. Even in the later years of his life, when he lived in a small hall that his devotees had built for him, its doors were open to visitors day and night, and he shared it freely with other permanent or temporary residents, who lived and slept there with him. He had no private life or time for himself, but was available always for anyone who needed him.

He preferred to eat only the simplest of food, and even when he was offered any type of special food, whether a delicacy such as a sweet or a savoury titbit, an elaborately prepared feast, or even a medicinal tonic for bodily health, he would eat it only if it were first shared equally with all people who were present. Just as he shared his shelter, his time and his entire life with everyone in his presence, so he shared with them freely and equally whatever food or other material thing he was given.

The only type of food that he strictly avoided, and that he advised others to avoid equally strictly, was any form of non-vegetarian food such as meat, fish or eggs. In this and many other ways he taught us emphatically that we should always avoid any action that would cause even the least harm, injury or suffering to any creature.

By both his words and his example he taught us the virtue of perfect *ahiṁsā* or compassionate avoidance of causing any harm, injury or hurt to any sentient being. Through his life and his teachings he clearly indicated that he considered *ahiṁsā* or 'non-harming' to be a greater virtue than actively trying to 'do good'. Whereas *ahiṁsā* is a passive state of refraining from doing any action that could directly or indirectly cause any harm or suffering to any person or creature, 'doing good' is an active interference in the outward course of events and in the affairs of other people, and even when we interfere thus with good intent, our actions often have harmful repercussions.

When we try to do actions that we believe will result in 'good', we often end up causing harm either to ourself or to others, or to both. The danger to ourself in our trying to do 'good' to others lies principally in the effect that such actions can have on our ego. If we engage ourself busily and ambitiously in trying outwardly to do 'good', it is easy for us to overlook the defects in our own mind, and to fail to notice the subtle pride, egotism and self-righteousness that tend to arise in our mind when we concentrate on rectifying the defects of the outside world rather than rectifying our own internal defects.

Moreover, what we consider to be 'good' is often quite different to what other people consider to be 'good', so unless we are very careful the 'good' that we try to do to others may in fact be unwanted. Even if we feel strongly that our idea of 'good' is right and some other people's idea of it is wrong, we should be careful not to try to impose our idea of 'good' upon them, because when we do so our efforts will only create resentment and conflict, which will usually result in causing more harm than any actual good.

Most actions have multiple effects, so the repercussions of our actions are often not what we intend them to be. The greater the 'good' that we try to do, the greater the harm that may result. Since the beginning of human history, many social, political and religious reformers have come and gone, but none of their attempted reforms have ever resulted in unmixed good. Any action or series of actions that has a significant impact upon this world inevitably results in a mixture of good and bad – benefit and harm.

Many of the greatest evils and injustices in this world have resulted from supposedly well-intentioned social, political, economic or religious reforms. Even in the name of God countless conflicts have occurred, which have sometimes even resulted in cruel persecutions, wars and terrorism. From all this we should understand that attempts to do good can result in great harm, and that our primary moral duty is therefore to avoid causing any harm rather than to try to do any good.

In many situations, far greater good can result by our refraining from doing any action than could possibly result by our doing any action, because whatever good might result from any action that we could do would not compensate for the harm that would result from it. In other words, our inaction – our just being without doing anything – can often be truly more beneficial than any amount of action or 'doing' could be.

As a general rule, if any action is likely to cause harm to any sentient being, we should refrain from doing it, even though it may also result in some good. Moreover, whatever action we may decide either to do or to refrain from doing in any particular situation, we always should remember that the ultimate good, which is the infinite happiness of true self-knowledge, can never be achieved by any amount of action or 'doing', but only by just 'being' – that is, by our abiding peacefully in our own natural state, which is the egoless, thought-free and therefore absolutely actionless state of perfectly clear self-conscious being.

This is not to say, however, that we should not do anything to help other people or creatures when an immediate need arises, but only that we should not be too ambitious in our desire to do good. We should respond appropriately to any situation we find ourself in, but we need not actively seek situations in which we imagine that our help may be required. Moreover, even when a situation does arise in which our help appears to be required, we should take care to do only whatever help or 'good' is truly appropriate, and we should at the same time be very vigilant not to cause any form of harm in our attempt to do good.

From the example set by Sri Ramana, we should understand that it is good for us to be always humble, unselfish, kind, caring, considerate, gentle, compassionate, generous and sharing, and that all our outward actions and reactions – which in many cases may appropriately include our refraining from doing certain actions or any action whatsoever – should always be guided by these inward qualities of mind and heart. The great importance of such true generosity, kindness and care was clearly emphasised by Sri Ramana when he concluded this nineteenth paragraph of *Nāṉ Yār?* by saying:

> […] All that one gives to others one is giving only to oneself. If [everyone] knew this truth, who indeed would refrain from giving?

All that we give to others (especially the tender-hearted love, kindness, compassion, sympathy, affection, care and consideration that we give to them) we are giving only to ourself because no one – no person, animal, plant or any other thing – is truly other than ourself, our essential self-conscious being or 'am'-ness.

This is the real meaning of the teaching of Christ, 'Thou shalt love the Lord thy God with all thy heart, and with all thy soul, and with all thy mind […] Thou shalt love thy neighbour as thyself' (*Matthew* 22.37, 39, and *Mark* 12.30-31). We cannot truly love either God or our neighbour – any of our fellow sentient beings – as ourself unless we actually experience them as ourself, and if we do not love them as ourself, we cannot really love them with all our heart, soul and mind.

Love for anything other than ourself can never be a whole love, but can only be a divided and therefore partial love, because we always love ourself more than we can ever love any other person or thing. Therefore if we truly wish to love either God or our neighbour wholly – with all our heart, soul and mind – we must experience them as ourself, and in order to experience them thus, we must experience ourself as we really are – that is, as the one infinite and indivisible absolute reality, which is the real essence or true substance of all that is. Hence, since we cannot experience ourself thus as the one infinite, undivided, non-dual and all-inclusive whole so long as we attend to anything that appears to be other than ourself, in order to experience and love both God and our neighbour as ourself, we must withdraw our mind entirely from their imaginary outward forms and focus it keenly and exclusively upon our own essential self-conscious being, 'I am', which alone is their real and essential form.

Therefore until we merge and lose ourself entirely in our natural state of absolutely non-dual self-conscious being, which alone is the state of true self-knowledge, our love for God and for our neighbour will only be partial and imperfect. However, even though we may not yet actually experience and love all our fellow sentient beings as ourself, if we have really understood at least theoretically that they are truly not other than ourself, we will naturally feel compassion for them and will therefore empathise with all their sufferings. When we feel such compassion and empathy for all sentient beings, we will naturally refrain as far as possible from causing even the least harm or suffering to any of them.

However, our love, compassion and concern for other people and animals should not lead us to believe that we can do any great good in this world, or that this world needs us to reform it. Whenever any person told Sri Ramana that he had an ambition to reform the world in some way or to do any other such 'good', he would say, 'He who has created this world knows how to take care of it. If you believe in God, trust him to do whatever is necessary for this world'. On many occasions and in many ways, Sri Ramana made it clear that our duty is not to reform the world but only to reform ourself.

To people who lacked subtle understanding, he would say that since this world is created by God, he knows how to take care of it, thereby indicating that this world is exactly as God intends it to be, and that he intends it to be thus for the true benefit of all concerned. However, to people of more subtle understanding, he would say that this world is a creation of our own mind, and exists only in our mind in the same manner that a dream exists only in our mind, and that whatever defects we see in this world are therefore reflections of our mind's own defects. Hence, rather than trying to reform the reflection, we should try to reform the source of it, which is our own mind. If we reform our mind by restoring it to our natural state of just being, its reflection will also merge and become one with our true being, which is the infinite fullness of unalloyed happiness and love.

Though all the manifold problems of this world can be effectively solved only by our turning our mind inwards and drowning it in its source, which is our own absolutely non-dual self-conscious being, so long as our mind is turned outwards, we will continue to mistake ourself to be just a body-bound person – one among the many such body-bound creatures living in this material world. When we thus mistake ourself to be a finite person, we inevitably become involved in the activities of our body, speech and mind, and our actions unavoidably have an effect upon other people and creatures.

Therefore in this dualistic state of activity we are responsible for the effects of our actions, and hence we must take care not to cause any harm to any of our fellow embodied beings. The benefit of our thus carefully practising the virtue of *ahiṁsā* or 'non-harming' is twofold. Not only do we thereby avoid as far as possible causing any harm or suffering to any other sentient beings, but we also thereby cultivate the tenderness of mind that is required for us to be able to turn within and merge in our natural state of just being.

If we are heartlessly indifferent to the sufferings of others, we will not be able to succeed in any effort that we may make to turn within, because such heartlessness is caused only by the density of our ego – by our strong attachment to and identification with our own individual self. Only when our attachment to our own ego is greatly attenuated will we have the *vairāgya*, desirelessness or detachment that is necessary for us to be able to relinquish all thoughts or attention to anything other than our own essential self-conscious being, and as an inevitable consequence of this attenuation of our ego, true heart-melting kindness, love and compassion will also naturally arise within us.

Only to the extent to which our ego and all its desires and attachments are truly attenuated will the real love for just being arise in our heart. When this true love for just being arises within us, it will impel us to try repeatedly to withdraw our mind from all objects and to rest in our own essential self-conscious being. However, until our love for just being consumes us entirely, our mind will often slip down from our natural state of self-conscious repose, and whenever we thus experience this seemingly external world our heart-melting love for just being will manifest as tender-hearted compassion, kindness, love and consideration for all other sentient beings, who are each in essence nothing other than our own self-conscious being.

Sri Ramana used to say that *bhakti* is *jñāna-mātā* – that is, that devotion or love is the mother of true self-knowledge. In this context *bhakti* means true heart-melting love for just being – love, that is, for our own infinite self-conscious being. Since our true self-conscious being is infinite, it knows no other, and hence if we truly love our own being we will not feel anything – particularly any sentient being – to be excluded from it or from our love for it.

Therefore so long as we experience even the least duality or otherness, our true love for just being will be experienced by us as a tender-hearted and all-inclusive love and compassion for our fellow sentient beings. Hence if we cultivate true love for just being, as we will naturally do by our persistent practice of self-attentiveness, we need make no separate effort to cultivate any other qualities such as compassion, tenderness or kindness for other sentient beings, because such qualities will result automatically from our love for true being.

However, though we need not make any special effort to cultivate qualities such as compassion or sensitivity for the feelings of others, by cherishing such qualities we can indirectly nourish our love for just being, which alone can enable us to experience the egoless state of true self-knowledge. Only an extremely tender-hearted mind will be overwhelmed by such great love for just being that it will be willing to surrender itself entirely, turning its attention wholly towards its own self-conscious core or essence and thereby subsiding and merging within, losing itself in the absolute clarity of true non-dual self-knowledge.

Just as compassion is a natural effect of true love for just being, so *ahiṁsā* or 'non-harming' is a natural effect of compassion. If we feel true compassion and tenderness for the feelings of others, we will automatically take care not to do any action that might cause any harm or suffering.

Therefore the most important quality that we should strive to cultivate is the true love to subside and rest in our natural state of self-conscious being. If we cultivate this one essential quality, all other qualities will flourish effortlessly and naturally in our heart.

Absolute *ahiṁsā* is possible only in the non-dual state of true self-knowledge. The first *hiṁsā* or 'harm' – that is, the first action that causes harm, injury and suffering both to ourself and to all 'others' – is the rising of our own mind. When our mind does not rise, everything remains peacefully merged in the true state of non-dual self-conscious being, which is the state of infinite happiness. The imaginary rising of our mind is not only the primal form of *hiṁsā*, but is also the cause and origin of all other forms of *hiṁsā*.

Therefore, so long as we imagine ourself to be this body-bound mind or ego, we cannot experience absolute *ahiṁsā*, and we cannot entirely avoid doing any form of *hiṁsā*. Hence if we truly wish to avoid causing any harm whatsoever, we should not only try carefully to regulate all our actions of mind, speech or body in accordance with the morally imperative principle of *ahiṁsā*, but should also try to destroy the root cause of every form of *hiṁsā*, which is our own mind or ego. In order to destroy this root cause of all suffering, the only means is to turn our mind away from all otherness or duality and thereby to drown it in the infinite clarity of our own self-conscious being. This is the reason why Sri Ramana says in the nineteenth paragraph of *Nāṉ Yār?*:

> […] It is not proper [for us] to let [our] mind [dwell] much on worldly matters. To the extent possible, it is not proper [for us] to enter [or interfere] in the affairs of other people […].

The fact that we can truly do good to the world only by withdrawing our mind from it and searching within ourself for the real cause of all suffering is aptly and beautifully illustrated by the compassionate life of Lord Buddha. Like Bhagavan Ramana, Bhagavan Buddha was an embodiment of *parama karuṇā* or supreme compassion, kindness and love. As a young man, when he came to know of the inevitable sufferings of embodied existence such as disease, old age and death, he was overwhelmed by an intense desire to discover the root cause of all suffering and the means to destroy that cause. Therefore, though he had great love for his wife, son, father, aunt and other relatives and friends, he left them all and lived the life of a wandering mendicant, earnestly searching for the true knowledge that would put an end to all suffering.

Though at an early stage of his search he hoped to attain such knowledge by practising severe bodily austerities, he eventually understood that no such external means could enable him to attain the truth that he was seeking, and that he could attain it only by searching calmly within himself. Thus by turning his mind away from his body and this world, he was able to experience the true state of *nirvāṇa* – the absolute extinction of his mind or false finite self.

The reason why Lord Buddha left his beloved wife, child and other relatives was not because he did not care for them. He left them only because his love for them was so great that he could not bear the thought that he was powerless to save them from the inevitable sufferings of embodied existence, and he was therefore determined to find the means to do so.

Only because his love and compassion were so great that he was impelled to withdraw his mind from those he loved most in order to find the real solution to the sufferings of all embodied beings, was he able to attain the true knowledge that enabled him to teach us all the means by which we can attain *nirvāṇa*, the true state of just being, in which all suffering is extinguished along with its cause, our mind or illusory sense of finite selfhood.

In order to attain true self-knowledge – the state of absolutely non-dual self-conscious being – and thereby to extinguish the root of all suffering, we need not outwardly renounce either our family or the entire world, as Lord Buddha did, but we must inwardly renounce all thought of our false finite self and everything else other than our own essential self-conscious being. Still more importantly, in order to be sufficiently motivated to be able to surrender or let go of our false finite self, we must be impelled by the same intensity of tender-hearted love that impelled Lord Buddha and every other true sage to melt inwardly and surrender themself in the all-consuming fire of true self-knowledge.

All the suffering that we see in this world is only a dream that arises due to the rising of our own mind, so if we are truly concerned about the sufferings of others, we should earnestly try to wake up from this dream by surrendering our self-deceptive mind in the clarity of our own essential self-conscious being. However, though true heart-melting love for our own essential being, which is also the essential being of every other person and creature, is the only means by which we can wake up from this dream of duality or otherness, our present finite love will blossom as the absolute fullness of infinite love only when we have actually destroyed this illusory dream of duality in the perfect clarity of true non-dual self-knowledge.

This world and everything that we experience in it, including our body and our own individual personality with all its likes and dislikes, appear to exist only because we have risen as this finite object-knowing consciousness that we call our mind. Therefore if our mind subsides and ceases to exist as a separate individual consciousness, everything else will also subside and cease to exist. Hence in the final paragraph of *Nāṉ Yār?* Sri Ramana concludes by saying:

> If [our individual] self rises, everything rises; if [our individual] self subsides [or ceases], everything subsides [or ceases]. To whatever extent we behave humbly, to that extent there is goodness [or virtue]. If [we] are restraining [curbing, subduing, condensing, contracting or reducing our] mind, wherever [we] may be [we] can be [or wherever we may be let us be].

The key word in the second sentence of this paragraph is *taṙndu*, which I have translated as 'humbly', but which is actually the past or perfect participle of *taṙ*, a verb that has many meanings such as to bow, worship, fall low, be low, be bowed down, become subdued, be suspended, be deep, be engrossed in anything, descend, decline, sink, diminish, decrease, stay, rest, stop, bend, droop or hang down. In this context, therefore, proceeding or behaving *taṙndu* means conducting ourself humbly in this world, submitting to the will of God, with our mind subsided, subdued, submerged or resting calmly in our own essential self-conscious being.

To the extent that we live our life thus, says Sri Ramana, there is *naṉmai* – goodness, righteousness, benefit, benefaction, virtue or morality. That is, the relative goodness of any of our actions or of our behaviour in general is determined solely by the extent to which, while acting or behaving, we are truly humble, subdued, desireless, calm, equanimous and resigned to the will of God.

In the final sentence Sri Ramana says that if we are able to be thus, always restraining, curbing, subduing or reducing our mind, 'wherever [we] may be [we] can be' or 'wherever [we] may be let [us] be'. These concluding words, *eṅgē-y-irundālum irukkalām*, imply that in whatever place or circumstances we may be placed in our life, it is always possible for us just to be. If we always keep our mind subsided in our true and natural state of self-conscious being, no external circumstances can prevent us from remaining thus.

Therefore, since we have no duty or responsibility other than just to be in our own self-conscious and blissful being, and since there is no higher happiness than simply to be thus, *summā irukkalām* – let us just be.

Bibliography

When citing the Tamil writings and other recorded teachings of Sri Ramana in this book, I have given my own translations, many of which are based largely upon the explanations and Tamil prose renderings of Sri Sadhu Om.

The following are some details about the works that I have cited:

Philosophical poems of Sri Ramana

Upadēśa Undiyār (உபதேச வுந்தியார்) – a Tamil poem of thirty verses that Sri Ramana composed in 1927 in answer to the request of Sri Muruganar, and that he later composed in Sanskrit, Telugu and Malayalam under the title *Upadēśa Sāram*, the 'Essence of Instruction'.

Uḷḷadu Nāṟpadu (உள்ளது நாற்பது) – the 'Forty [Verses] on That Which Is', another Tamil poem that Sri Ramana composed in 1928 when Sri Muruganar asked him to teach the nature of the reality and the means to attain it.

Uḷḷadu Nāṟpadu Anubandham (உள்ளது நாற்பது அனுபந்தம்) – the 'Supplement to Forty [Verses] on That Which Is', a collection of forty-one Tamil verses that Sri Ramana composed at various times during the 1920's and 1930's.

Ēkāṉma Pañcakam (ஏகான்ம பஞ்சகம், also known as *Ēkātma Pañcakam*) – the 'Five [Verses] on the Oneness of Self', a poem that Sri Ramana composed in 1947, first in Telugu, then in Tamil, and later in Malayalam.

Āṉma-Viddai (ஆன்ம வித்தை, also known as *Ātma-Vidyā Kīrtanam*) – the 'Song on the Science of Self', a Tamil song that Sri Ramana composed in 1927 in answer to the request of Sri Muruganar.

Upadēśa Taṉippākkaḷ (உபதேசத் தனிப்பாக்கள்) – the 'Solitary Verses of Instruction', a collection of twenty-seven Tamil verses that Sri Ramana composed at various times.

Devotional poems of Sri Ramana

Śrī Aruṇācala Akṣaramaṇamālai (ஸ்ரீ அருணாசல அக்ஷர மணமாலை) – the 'Marriage Garland of Letters' or 'Garland of Imperishable Union', a Tamil hymn of 108 verses addressed to God in the form of the holy hill Arunachala, which Sri Ramana composed spontaneously one day in 1914 or 1915.

Śrī Aruṇācala Aṣṭakam (ஸ்ரீ அருணாசல அஷ்டகம்) – the 'Eight [Verses] to Sri Arunachala', another Tamil hymn that Sri Ramana composed at about the same time.

Prose writings of Sri Ramana

Nāṉ Yār? (நான் யார்?, also known as *Nāṉ-Ār?*, நானார்?) – 'Who am I?', a treatise of twenty paragraphs that Sri Ramana wrote in the late 1920's, of which all but the first paragraph are an edited version of a collection of answers that he had given to a series of questions asked by Sri Sivaprakasam Pillai in the years 1901 to 1902.

Vivēkacūḍāmaṇi Avatārikai (விவேகசூடாமணி அவதாரிகை) – the introduction that Sri Ramana wrote, probably in 1903 or 1904, to his Tamil prose translation of Sri Adi Sankara's great philosophical poem, *Vivēkacūḍāmaṇi*.

Ancient text translated by Sri Ramana

Bhagavad Gītā Sāram (பகவத் கீதா சாரம்) – the 'Essence of the *Bhagavad Gītā*', a selection of forty-two verses from the *Bhagavad Gītā* that Sri Ramana translated as a Tamil poem.

Oral teachings of Sri Ramana recorded by Sri Muruganar

Guru Vācaka Kōvai (குருவாசகக் கோவை) – the 'Series of *Guru*'s Sayings', the most comprehensive and reliable collection of the sayings of Sri Ramana, recorded in 1255 Tamil verses composed by Sri Muruganar, with an additional 42 verses composed by Sri Ramana (of which 27 are included in *Upadēśa Taṉippākkaḷ*, 12 in *Uḷḷadu Nāṟpadu Anubandham*, 2 in *Ēkātma Pañcakam* and 1 in *Uḷḷadu Nāṟpadu*).

The Tamil originals of most of these works are available in several books, often with basic explanations or detailed commentaries, and many translations of them are available in various languages. However, the principal source of all of them, except *Upadēśa Taṉippākkaḷ* and *Guru Vācaka Kōvai*, is *Śrī Ramaṇa Nūṯriraṭṭu* (ஸ்ரீ ரமண நூற்றிரட்டு), the 'Collected Works of Sri Ramana', published by Sri Ramanasramam, Tiruvannamalai, Tamil Nadu, India (www.sriramanamaharshi.org).

The principal source of *Upadēśa Taṉippākkaḷ* is *Śrī Ramaṇōpadēśa Nūṉmālai – Viḷakkavurai* (ஸ்ரீ ரமணோபதேச நூன்மாலை – விளக்கவுரை), a Tamil commentary by Sri Sadhu Om on all the philosophical poems of Sri Ramana, published by Sri Arunachalaramana Nilayam, Tiruvannamalai, India (www.sriarunachalaramananilayam.org).

The original Tamil text of *Guru Vācaka Kōvai*, and a Tamil prose rendering by Sri Sadhu Om, are published as two separate volumes by Sri Ramanasramam. A complete English translation by Sri Sadhu Om and myself, together with comments by both Sri Muruganar and Sri Sadhu Om, is published separately by Sri Arunachalaramana Nilayam.

Transliteration and Pronunciation

The transliteration scheme that I use here is based upon several closely related schemes, namely the International Alphabet of Sanskrit Transliteration (IAST), the scheme used in the *Tamil Lexicon*, the National Library at Kolkata romanization scheme, the American Library Association and the Library of Congress (ALA-LC) transliteration schemes and the more recent international standard known as 'ISO 15919 Transliteration of Devanagari and related Indic scripts into Latin characters'.

The table below summarises this transliteration scheme. In the first column I list all the diacritic and non-diacritic Latin characters that I use to transliterate the Tamil and Sanskrit alphabets; in the second column I give the Tamil letter that each such character represents (followed in square brackets where applicable by the Grantha letter that is optionally used in Tamil to denote the represented sound more precisely); in the third column I give the Devanagari letter that it represents; and in the last column I give an indication of its pronunciation or articulation.

In the Tamil and Devanagari columns, a dash (–) indicates that there is no exact equivalent in that script for the concerned letter in the other script. In the Tamil column, round brackets enclosing a letter indicates that it is pronounced and transliterated as such only in words borrowed from Sanskrit or some other language. Likewise, in the Devanagari column, round brackets enclosing a letter indicates that it is not part of the alphabet of classical Sanskrit, though it does occur either in Vedic Sanskrit or in some other Indian languages written in Devanagari.

Vowels:

a	அ	अ	Short 'a', pronounced like 'u' in cut
ā	ஆ	आ	Long 'a', pronounced like 'a' in father
i	இ	इ	Short 'i', pronounced like 'e' in English
ī	ஈ	ई	Long 'i', pronounced like 'ee' in see
u	உ	उ	Short 'u', pronounced like 'u' in put
ū	ஊ	ऊ	Long 'u', pronounced like 'oo' in food
ṛ	–	ऋ	Short vocalic 'r', pronounced like 'ri' in merrily
ṝ	–	ॠ	Long vocalic 'r'
ḷ	–	ऌ	Short vocalic 'l', pronounced like 'lry' in revelry (not

			to be confused with the Tamil consonant ள், which is also transliterated as *ḷ*)
ḹ	–	ॡ	Long vocalic 'l'
e	எ	(ऎ)	Short 'e', pronounced like 'e' in else
ē	ஏ	ए	Long 'e', pronounced like 'ai' in aid
ai	ஐ	ऐ	Diphthong 'ai', pronounced like 'ai' in aisle
o	ஒ	(ऒ)	Short 'o', pronounced like 'o' in cot
ō	ஓ	ओ	Long 'o', pronounced like 'o' in dote
au	ஔ	औ	Diphthong 'au', pronounced like 'ou' in sound

Consonantal diacritics:

ḵ	ஃ	–	Tamil *āytam*, indicating gutturalization of the preceding vowel, pronounced like 'ch' in loch
ṁ	–	◌ं	Sanskrit *anusvāra*, indicating nasalization of the preceding vowel, pronounced like 'm' or (when followed by certain consonants) 'ṅ', 'ñ', 'ṇ' or 'n'
ḥ	–	◌ः	Sanskrit *visarga*, indicating frication (or lengthened aspiration) of the preceding vowel, pronounced like 'h' followed by a slight echo of the preceding vowel

Consonants:

k	க்	क्	Velar plosive, unvoiced and unaspirated
kh	(க்)	ख्	Velar plosive, unvoiced but aspirated
g	க்	ग्	Velar plosive, voiced but unaspirated
gh	(க்)	घ्	Velar plosive, voiced and aspirated
ṅ	ங்	ङ्	Velar nasal
c	ச்	च्	Palatal plosive, unvoiced and unaspirated (pronounced like 'c' in cello or 'ch' in chutney)
ch	(ச்)	छ्	Palatal plosive, unvoiced but aspirated
j	ச் [ஜ்]	ज्	Palatal plosive, voiced but unaspirated
jh	(ச்)	झ्	Palatal plosive, voiced and aspirated
ñ	ஞ்	ञ्	Palatal nasal
ṭ	ட்	ट्	Retroflex plosive, unvoiced and unaspirated
ṭh	(ட்)	ठ्	Retroflex plosive, unvoiced but aspirated
ḍ	ட்	ड्	Retroflex plosive, voiced but unaspirated
ḍh	(ட்)	ढ्	Retroflex plosive, voiced and aspirated
ṇ	ண்	ण्	Retroflex nasal
t	த்	त्	Dental plosive, unvoiced and unaspirated

th	(த்)	थ्	Dental plosive, unvoiced but aspirated
d	த்	द्	Dental plosive, voiced but unaspirated
dh	(த்)	ध्	Dental plosive, voiced and aspirated
n	ந்	न्	Dental nasal
p	ப்	प्	Labial plosive, unvoiced and unaspirated
ph	(ப்)	फ्	Labial plosive, unvoiced but aspirated
b	ப்	ब्	Labial plosive, voiced but unaspirated
bh	(ப்)	भ्	Labial plosive, voiced and aspirated
m	ம்	म्	Labial nasal
y	ய்	य्	Palatal semivowel
r	ர்	र्	Dental tap (in Tamil phonology) or retroflex trill (in Sanskrit phonology)
l	ல்	ल्	Dental lateral approximant
v	வ்	व्	Labial semivowel
ṙ	ழ்	–	Retroflex central approximant (transliterated as *ḻ* in the *Tamil Lexicon*, and commonly transcribed as *zh*)
ḷ	ள்	(ळ्)	Retroflex lateral approximant
ṯ	ற்	–	Alveolar plosive, unvoiced (pronunciation of ற only when it is muted, that is, not followed by a vowel)
ḏṟ	ற்	–	Alveolar plosive, voiced (pronunciation of ற only when it follows ன்)
ṟ	ற்	–	Alveolar trill (pronunciation of ற when it follows and precedes a vowel)
ṉ	ன்	–	Alveolar nasal
ś	(ச்) [ஶ்]	श्	Palatal aspirated sibilant, pronounced somewhat like 's' in sure (or 'sh' in she)
ṣ	(ச்) [ஷ்]	ष्	Retroflex aspirated sibilant, pronounced somewhat like 's' in sure (or 'sh' in she), but with the tongue curled further back
s	ச் [ஸ்]	स्	Dental aspirated sibilant, pronounced like 's' in see
h	க் [ஹ்]	ह्	Voiced glottal fricative

For a more detailed explanation of this transliteration scheme and a fuller explanation about the pronunciation of each letter, please refer to the document 'Transliteration, Transcription and Pronunciation' on my website (www.happinessofbeing.com/Transliteration.pdf).

Glossary

In this glossary, {T} after a word indicates that it is Tamil, {TS} indicates that it is a Tamil form of a Sanskrit word, {Ts} indicates that it is a Tamil word or phrase derived partly from Sanskrit, and {S} indicates that it is Sanskrit (though most of the Sanskrit words listed here are also used frequently in Tamil spiritual literature, either in the same or a euphonically modified form).

A

a {T} that, those (a demonstrative prefix)
ā {T} come into being, become, be, happen, occur, be done, be completed, be fit, be appropriate, be proper – see *ādal*, *ām*, *āy*, etc.
abhēda {S} not different, undivided, identical
ādal {T} being, becoming (verbal noun formed from *ā*)
aḍaṅgi {T} yielding, submitting, subsiding (tenseless verbal participle of *aḍaṅgu*)
aḍaṅgu {T} yield, submit, subside, shrink, be subdued, be still, settle, cease, disappear – see *aḍaṅgi*
adaṟku {T} to that
adaṟku aḍaṅgi-y-irāmal {T} 'instead of being having yielded to that'
ādhāra {S} support, substratum, ground, container
adhiṣṭhāna {S} standing place, base, substratum, ground, abode
ādi {S} beginning
ādi-guru {S} original *guru*
a-dvi-tā {S} no-two-ness
advaita {S} non-duality
advaita vēdānta {S} non-dualistic *vēdānta*
aham {S} 'I'
aham {T} inside, heart, home, abode, space
ahaṁ brahmāsmi {S} 'I am *brahman*'
ahamukham {Ts} inward facing, introspection, introversion, 'I'-ward facing, self-attentiveness
ahandai {TS} (*ahantā* {S}) ego
ahantā (*ahaṁtā*) {S} 'I'-ness, ego – see *ahandai*
āhāra {S} food
āhāra-niyama {S} food-restraint
ahiṁsā {S} non-harming
ajñāna {S} ignorance, lack of self-knowledge – see *ajñāni*
ajñāni {S} a person who lacks self-knowledge
ākāśa {S} space – see *bhūtākāśa*; *cidākāśa*; *cittākāśa*
akhaṇḍa {S} unbroken, unfragmented, undivided, indivisible, whole, entire
akṣara {S} imperishable, letter [of the alphabet], syllable – see *Śrī Aruṇācala*

Akṣaramaṇamālai
akṣaramaṇamālai (*akṣara-maṇa-mālai*) {Ts} marriage garland of letters, fragrant garland of letters, garland of imperishable union – see *Śrī Aruṇācala Akṣaramaṇamālai*
allāh {Arabic} God
am {T} beauty (or before a word beginning with '*m*', *am* can also be the demonstrative prefix *a* [meaning 'that' or 'those'] with an extra '*m*' added for euphonic conjunction)
ām {T} [it] is, [they] are (singular or plural future or habitual third person form of *ā*); which is, which are, who is, who are (future or habitual relative participle of *ā*)
āmalaka {S} a grape-sized fruit
amar {T} abide, remain, be seated, become still, rest, repose, settle
amarndu {T} settling, having settled (tenseless verbal participle of *amar*)
anādi {S} beginningless
ānanda {S} happiness, joy, bliss (see also *sat-cit-ānanda*)
ānandamaya kōśa {S} 'sheath' composed of happiness (the self-ignorance that remains in sleep, even though the mind has subsided)
ananta {S} endless
ananya {S} non-other, not other, otherless, without otherness
ananya bhāva {S} meditation on [God as] not other [than ourself]
anātmā {S} non-self, not self
anattā {Pāḷi} (*anātmā* {S}) non-self, not self, devoid of self, no self
aṉbu {T} love
aṉbu pūṇumē {T} be possessed with love
aṉḏṟi {T} except, besides, without
āṉmā {TS} (*ātmā* {S}) self
āṉma-viddai {TS} (*ātma-vidyā* {S}) science of self (see also *Āṉma-Viddai*; *ātma-vidyā*)
Āṉma-Viddai {TS} '[Song on] the Science of Self'
annamaya kōśa {S} 'sheath' composed of food (the physical body)
anta {S} end
antar {S} within, inside
antarmukham {TS} inward facing, introspection, introversion, self-attentiveness
anubandham {TS} appendage, appendix, supplement – see *Uḷḷadu Nāṟpadu Anubandham*
anugraha {S} grace, kindness
anusandhāna (*anusaṁdhāna*) {S} investigation, close inspection, contemplation
aṇu {S} atom
aṇuvum (*aṇu-v-um*) {Ts} even an atom
anya {S} other, another
anya bhāva {S} meditation on [God as] other [than ourself]
ār {T} who (interrogative personal pronoun) – see *Nāṉ-Ār?*, *yār*
ār {T} become full, spread over, abide, be, combine with, eat, experience, obtain, put on, wear, gird, bind (also used in poetry as a relative participle meaning 'which is', 'which is combined with', 'which is bound by')
ārāy {T} investigate, scrutinise, examine, inspect, explore

ārāycci {T} investigation, scrutiny, inspection, exploration, research
a̱ri {T} know, cognise, experience, be conscious of – see *a̱rivu*, *a̱riyādu*, etc.
a̱rivē (*a̱rivu-ē*) {T} consciousness alone, consciousness certainly
a̱rivē nā̱n {T} consciousness alone [or certainly] is 'I'
a̱rivu {T} knowledge, consciousness (noun formed from *a̱ri*)
a̱riyādē (*a̱riyādu-ē*) {T} only not knowing
a̱riyādē muyalum {T} 'which [we] practise only [due to] not knowing'
a̱riyādu {T} not knowing (negative tenseless verbal participle of *a̱ri*)
artha {S} aim, purpose, meaning, substance, wealth, property, object, thing
aruḷ {T} grace, benevolence
aruḷum vēṇumē {T} grace also is certainly necessary
aruṇācala {TS} Arunachala (the name of the sacred hill at the foot of which Sri Ramana lived, and which he worshipped as a physical manifestation of God and *guru*, our own real self)
Aruṇācala Akṣaramaṇamālai {Ts} – see *Śrī Aruṇācala Akṣaramaṇamālai*
Aruṇācala Aṣṭakam {TS} – see *Śrī Aruṇācala Aṣṭakam*
āśā {S} desire – see *nirāśā*
asaiyādu {T} [it] does not move
āsana {S} sitting, abiding, posture
asat {S} unreal, non-existent
asher {Hebrew} that, which, what, who (a 'relativizer', a word that indicates a relative clause, like a relative pronoun in English)
asi {S} [you] are – see *tat tvam asi*
asmi {S} [I] am
aṣṭakam {TS} collection of eight parts (especially a poem of eight verses) – see *Śrī Aruṇācala Aṣṭakam*
āśrama {S} 'ashram', hermitage, abode of an ascetic, religious institution formed around such an abode, dwelling-place of a religious community
aṣṭan (*aṣṭa* in compound) {S} eight
asti {S} [it] is, [it] exists, there is, existence, presence, being
asti-bhāti-priya {S} being-illumination-love
aśubha {S} ugly, unpleasant, disagreeable, inauspicious, bad, evil
aśubha vāsanā {S} disagreeable propensity
atiśaya śakti {S} extraordinary power, wonderful power
atītam {TS} that which has gone beyond, that which transcends
ātmā {S} self, spirit (nominative singular form of *ātman*, serving in Tamil as both its nominative and its inflectional base)
ātmānusandhāna (*ātma-anusaṁdhāna*) {S} self-investigation, self-contemplation
ātma-cintana {S} self-contemplation
ātma-jñāna {S} self-knowledge
ātma-jñāni {S} sage, one who knows self
ātman (*ātma* in compound, *ātmā* in nominative) {S} self, spirit, soul, life, essence (also serves as the reflexive pronoun for all persons and genders: oneself, myself, yourself, itself, ourselves, etc.)
ātma-niṣṭha {S} self-abidance, being established in self
ātma-saṁsthaṁ manaḥ kṛtvā {S} 'having made the mind stand firm in self'

ātma-siddhi {S} self-attainment
ātma-sukha {S} self-happiness
ātma-svarūpa {S} our essential self, the 'own form' of ourself
ātma-vicāra {S} self-investigation, self-scrutiny, self-attentiveness, self-enquiry
ātma-vidyā {S} science of self
Ātma-Vidyā Kīrtanam {TS} 'Song on the Science of Self'
ātmāvil (*ātmā-v-il*) {TS} in self (locative singular form of *ātmā*)
a-t-taṉmai {T} that first person
āttumā {TS} (*ātmā* {S}) self
avaṉ {T} he
avaṉ aruḷ aṉḏri ōr aṇuvum asaiyādu {T} 'except by his grace, not even an atom moves'
āvaraṇa {S} covering, veiling, hiding, concealing, obscuring
āvaraṇa śakti {S} power of veiling, concealing, obscuration
avasthā {S} state, condition
avatārikai {TS} (*avatārikā* {S}) introduction
āy {T} having become, being, as (tenseless verbal participle of *ā*; often used as an adverbial suffix, like '-ly' in English)
ayaṁ {S} this
ayaṁ ātmā brahma {S} 'this self is *brahman*'

B

bahirmukham {TS} outward facing, extroversion
Bhagavad Gītā {S} 'Divine Song', 'Song of God'
Bhagavad Gītā Sāram {TS} 'The Essence of the Song of God'
Bhagavān {S} Lord, God
Bhāgavatam {S} '[Book] about God' – see *Śrīmad Bhāgavatam*
bhakti {S} devotion, love
bhakti-mārga {S} path of devotion
bhāti {S} shining, light, illumination, knowledge, consciousness
bhāva {S} being, state, state of being, way of thinking, attitude, idea, concept, opinion, conviction, contemplation, meditation
bhāvanā {S} forming in mind, imagination, thought, meditation
bhramaṇa {S} wavering, bewilderment, confusion
bhūtākāśa (*bhūta-ākāśa*) {S} physical space
brahman (*brahma* in compound and in nominative neuter [not to be confused with the nominative masculine, *brahmā*, which is a name of God as the creator]) {S} God (as pure impersonal being), the absolute reality, the infinite spirit, the one non-dual being-consciousness, 'I am', our essential being or real self, the source, ground and substance of all things
brahma-ṛṣi {S} sage who experiences himself as *brahman*
Brahma Sūtra {S} 'Aphorisms about *Brahman*'
buddhi {S} intellect, mind, faculty of discernment, discrimination, reason, understanding (see also *dēhātma buddhi*)

C

cakra {S} wheel, circle, mystic centre in the body
cāvādavar {T} – see *sāvādavar*

cāyndiḍum {T} – see *sāyndiḍum*
cidākāśa (*cit-ākāśa*) {S} space of consciousness
cintana {S} thinking, thought, meditation – see *ātma-cintana*
cit {S} faculty of knowing or experiencing, that which knows, experiences or is conscious, consciousness (particularly pure non-objective consciousness), awareness (also a verb meaning to know, experience, cognise, perceive, observe, attend to, be attentive, be conscious); (like other Tamil and Sanskrit words that are translated as 'consciousness' or 'awareness', such as *aṟivu*, *uṇarvu*, *jñāna* and *prajñāna*, in the teachings of Sri Ramana *cit* means not merely the state of being conscious but more specifically *that which is conscious*, namely ourself)
cit-jaḍa-granthi {S} the knot that binds consciousness to the non-conscious [body]
cit-śakti {S} power of consciousness
citta {S} mind, will, faculty of volition
cittākāśa (*citta-ākāśa*) {S} mind-space
citta-bhramaṇa {S} mental wavering, bewilderment, confusion
citta-śuddhi {S} purification of mind
cittattiṉ {TS} of mind (an oblique case form of *cittam*, often serving as a genitive form of it)
cittattiṉ śānti {TS} peace of mind
cogito ergo sum {Latin} '[I] think therefore [I] am'
col {T} – see *sol*
coṯporuḷ {T} – see *soṯporuḷ*
cūḍāmaṇi (*cūḍā-maṇi*) {S} crest-jewel
cummā {T} – see *summā*
cummā-v-iru {T} – see *summā iru*

D

darśana {S} seeing, looking, perception, discernment, vision, experience
daśamaṉ {TS} tenth man (a personal noun formed from *daśama*, tenth)
dēha {S} body
dēhātma buddhi {S} 'body [is] myself' notion, 'I am the body' sense
dēva {S} god, deity, divine being
dharma {S} that which upholds, supports, sustains, preserves, maintains, restrains, keeps in place or regulates; nature, function, duty, obligation, righteousness, fundamental correctness, order, how anything should be or act, moral law, justice, religion [as an ordered and correct way of life, rather than as a particular set of beliefs or doctrines], law [of human nature and spiritual development] ('*dharma*' is an extremely important and deeply meaningful concept in all philosophies and religions of Indian origin, which are collectively described as the 'dharmic religions'; the word derives from the verbal root *dhṛ*, which means hold, uphold, carry, support, sustain, preserve, maintain, hold together, hold back, restrain, keep in place, control or regulate; everything – even an insentient object, an element such as fire or water, or any abstract quality – has its own *dharma*, that which holds it together, making it what it is, preventing it from being anything else, its essential nature, its particular property or quality, its function, its 'duty', its order, how it should be or act, the law of its being and action; since we are sentient, rational and social beings, with a sense of right and wrong, and aspiring to rise

above the limitations of our present finitude, our *dharma* includes our moral *dharma*, our social *dharma*, our religious *dharma*, our spiritual *dharma*, our natural duties and obligations in every area of our lives, all of which collectively constitute our *svadharma* or 'own *dharma*'; likewise, every society or section of society, every profession or trade, every social role, every familial relationship, every mode of life or stage of life, has its own particular *dharma*)

dhātu {S} layer, element, constituent, ingredient

dhyai {S} contemplate, meditate on, think of, imagine, recollect, bear in mind

dhyāna {S} contemplation, meditation, mindfulness, attentiveness

dīrgha {S} long-lasting

dṛg {S} – see *dṛś*

dṛg-dṛśya-vivēka {S} discrimination between the seer and the seen

dṛś (*dṛk* or *dṛg* in compound) {S} seeing, looking at, knowing, discerning, sight, eye, that which sees, that which knows (consciousness, the subject, seer or knower)

dṛśya {S} visible object, that which is seen, that which is known (the object, seen or known)

dṛṣṭi {S} seeing, sight

dvaita {S} duality

dvandva (*dvaṁdva*) {S} pair [of opposites] – see *iraṭṭai*

E

-ē {T} an intensifier, a suffix used for emphasis (meaning 'only', 'alone', 'itself', 'certainly', 'indeed')

edu {T} what

edu nāṉ? {T} 'what [am] I?'

ego {Greek} I

ego eimi {Greek} I am

ehyeh {Hebrew} [I] am

ehyeh asher ehyeh {Hebrew} '[I] am that [I] am'

eimi {Greek} [I] am

ēka {S} one, the one

ēkāṉmā (*ēkāṉma* in compound) {TS} – see *ēkātman*

Ēkāṉma Pañcakam {TS} – see *Ēkātma Pañcakam*

ēkātman (*ēka-ātman*; *ēkātma* in compound) {S} one self, 'self, the one [reality]' (see also *Ēkātma Pañcakam*)

Ēkātma Pañcakam (*Ēkāṉma Pañcakam*) {TS} 'Five [Verses] on Self, the One', 'Five [Verses] on the Oneness of Self'

ēkātma vastu {S} the one self-substance

eṇ {T} think, consider, meditate upon, scrutinise

eṉḏrum {T} always, for ever, constantly

eṉḏrum taṉṉai viṉavum usāvāl {T} 'by subtle investigation, which is constantly scrutinising self'

eṅgē {T} where indeed, wherever (interrogative pronoun *eṅgu*, meaning 'where', with intensifying suffix *ē*)

eṅgē-y-irundālum irukkalām {T} 'wherever [one] may be [one] can be', 'wherever [one] may be let [one] be'

eṇṇa {T} when [we] think, consider, meditate upon, scrutinise
eṇṇa naṙuvum {T} 'when [we] scrutinise, it will vanish'
eṉṉum {T} who says, which says, which is called (a quotative relative participle [like *iti* in Sanskrit], which often functions like inverted commas enclosing the preceding word or clause)
eṉum {T} who says, which says, which is called (a poetic abbreviation of *eṉṉum*)
eppōdum {T} always, at all times
ergo {Latin} therefore
ēttiṉum {T} even if one worships
evaiyum {T} everything
evaiyum kāṇum {T} which sees everything

G

garbha {S} womb, embryo
gati {S} way, path, means, refuge, liberation
gītā {S} song – see *Bhagavad Gītā*
granthi {S} knot
guṇa {S} [finite] quality, property, attribute
guru {S} [spiritual] teacher, guide
Guru Vācaka Kōvai {Ts} 'Series of *Guru*'s Sayings'

H

hiṁsā {S} harm, injury, hurt
hṛdaya {S} heart, core, essence

I

icchā {S} wish, desire, liking, inclination
iḍam {T} place, location, position, station, site, situation, state, room, space, abode, home, ground (see also *muviḍam*)
iladāl {T} since [it] is not, since [it] is devoid of
iṉbu {T} happiness
iṉbu tōṇumē {T} 'happiness will certainly appear'
iṉṉāṉ {T} so-and-so, such a person
irāmal {T} not being, without being, instead of being (tenseless verbal negative participle of *iru*)
iraṭṭai {T} pair [of opposites], *dvandva*
iraṭṭaigaḷ {T} pairs [of opposites] (plural form of *iraṭṭai*)
iru {T} be, exist, remain
iṟudi {T} end, limit, cessation, death
iṟudi taṉṉai-y-uṇarndu tāṉ-ādal {T} 'finally knowing ourself [and] being ourself'
irukka {T} to be, when [one] is, when [we] are
irukkalām {T} let [us] be, let [one] be, [one] can be
irukkiṟēṉ {T} [I] am
irundālum {T} even if [one] is, though [one] is
iruppadu {T} being, existing, remaining (verbal noun formed from *iru*, be, exist, remain)
iruḷ {T} darkness (of self-ignorance), spiritual ignorance
īśaṉ {TS} God
īśaṉ sannidhāna {TS} (*īśa-saṁnidhāna* {S}) presence of God

J

jaḍa {S} non-conscious, insentient, material, lifeless matter
jāgrat {S} [state of] waking, wakefulness
jāgrat-suṣupti {S} waking sleep
jāla {S} net, snare, web, deception, collection, multitude
japa {S} whispering, repetition [of a name of God, prayer or *mantra*], invocation
jīva {S} life, living being, soul
jīvātmā {S} personal self, soul
jñā {S} know, be conscious of, cognise, ascertain, experience
jñāna {S} knowledge, consciousness (often used to mean *ātma-jñāna*, self-knowledge)
jñāna-dṛṣṭi {S} knowledge-sight
jñāna-mārga {S} path of knowledge
jñāna-mātā {S} mother of knowledge
jñāna-vicāra {S} knowledge-investigation
jñānēndriya {S} sense organ
jñāni {S} a knower, sage, one who knows [self]

K

kaḍa {T} pass through, go across, exceed, excel, transcend, escape from) – see *kaḍandu*
kaḍandu {T} transcending (tenseless verbal participle of *kaḍa*)
kaḍandu-uḷḷavaṉ {T} he who exists transcending
kaḍavuḷ {T} God
kālam {TS} time
kalaṅgārē (*kalaṅgār-ē*) {T} they will certainly not deluded
kaliveṇbā {T} an extended version of the *veṇbā* metre
kalpanā {S} mental creation, imagination, fabrication, mental image – see *kaṯpaṉai*
kaṇ {T} eye
kāṇ {T} see, perceive, discover, know, experience (also used in poetry as a verbal noun meaning 'seeing', etc.)
kaṇḍavarē (*kaṇḍavar-ē*) {T} only those who have seen
kāṇum {T} which sees, perceives, knows (relative participle of *kāṇ*)
kāraṇa {S} cause
kāraṇa śarīra {S} causal body
kāraṇam illāda karuṇai {Ts} causeless grace
karma {S} action, activity
karma-mārga {S} path of action
karma-vāsanā {S} propensity or desire that impels one to do action
karmēndriya {S} organ of action
kartṛtva {S} doership
karu {T} (*garbha* {S}) embryo, egg, efficient cause
karuṇā {S} compassion, grace
karuṇai {T} – see *karuṇā*
karuvām ahandai (*karu-v-ām ahandai*) {Ts} 'ego, which is the embryo'
kāṭci {T} that which is seen, sight, vision, appearance
kaṯpaṉai {Ts} (*kalpanā* {S}) mental creation, imagination, fabrication, invention,

mental image, illusion, illusory superimposition

kaṯpaṉaigaḷ {Ts} imaginations, illusions, mental images (plural form of *kaṯpaṉai*)

kaupīna {T} loincloth

kēḷ {T} hear, listen, learn, ask, question, investigate

khaṇḍa {S} broken, fragmented, divided, division, break, part, fragment

kīrtanam {TS} song, praise

kōśa {S} 'sheath', covering

kōvai {T} stringing, series, succession, arrangement – see *Guru Vācaka Kōvai*

kṛ {S} do, make, cause, effect – see *kṛtvā*, *kṛtya*

kṛtvā {S} having done, made (past participle of *kṛ*)

kṛtya {S} action, function – see *pañcakṛtya*

kṣaṇika {S} momentary

kuṟaḷ veṇbā {T} a two-line version of the *veṇbā* metre

kūr {T} be abundant, intense, sharp, keen, acute, penetrating – see *kūrnda*

kūrnda {T} sharpened, pointed, sharp, keen, acute (past relative participle of *kūr*)

kūrnda mati {Ts} sharp, piercing, acute, keen, concentrated, subtle, discerning mind

L

lakṣya {S} aim, target, goal

lakṣyārtha (*lakṣya-artha*) {S} target meaning, intended meaning

laya {S} lying down, temporary subsidence, abeyance

M

mā {S} not

mahākartā (*mahā-kartā*) {S} the 'great doer' (God)

mahāraṇya (*mahā-araṇya*) {S} great forest, desert, wilderness

maharṣi (*maha-ṛṣi*) {S} great 'seer', sage

mahāvākya (*mahā-vākya*) {S} great saying

mahēśaṉ (*mahā-īśaṉ*) {TS} great Lord, God

mai {T} darkness, ignorance

-mai {T} suffix denoting an abstract state or quality (similar to the suffix '-ness' in English) (see also *naṉmai*; *taṉmai*; *uṇmai*; *viṇmai*)

mālai {TS} (*mālā* {S}) garland – see *akṣaramaṇamālai* and *nūṉmālai*

manaḥ {S} mind (nominative, accusative or vocative singular form of *manas*)

maṉam {TS} (*manas* {S}) mind

maṇam (*maṇa* in compound) {T} marriage, union, fragrance – see *Śrī Aruṇācala Akṣaramaṇamālai*

manana {T} thinking, considering, pondering, musing, reflection

manas {S} mind (see also *maṉam*)

maṉattai {TS} mind (accusative singular form of *maṉam*)

maṇḍapam {TS} temple hall

maṅgalam {TS} auspiciousness, verse composed as an auspicious introduction

maṉidaṉ {TS} (*manu-ja* {S}) man, male person

māṉiḍaṉ {TS} (*mānuṣa* {S}) man, human being

māṉiḍaṉāy (*māṉiḍaṉ-āy*) {Ts} having become human, being human, as human, as [a] man

māṉiḍaṉāy irukkiṟēṉ {Ts} '[I] exist as [a] man', '[I] am [a] man'

maṉṉu {T} be permanent, endure, remain long, stay, persevere, be steady, abound –

see *maṉṉum*
maṉṉum {T} which endures (relative participle of *maṉṉu*)
manō- (for *manas* in compound) {S} mind, of mind
manōlaya {S} abeyance of mind
manōmaya kōśa {S} 'sheath' composed of mind
manōmayam {TS} (*manōmaya* {S}) composed [only] of mind
manōmayam-ām kāṭci {Ts} 'vision which is composed of mind', mind-made appearance
manōnāśa {S} annihilation of mind
manōnigraha {S} mind-restraint
mantra {S} sacred syllable, word, phrase (such as a name of God or a prayer)
mantra-japa {S} repetition of a *mantra*
mārga {S} path, way, means (see also *bhakti mārga*; *jñāna mārga*; *karma mārga*; *yōga mārga*; *vaṟi*)
mātā {S} mother
mati {S} mind, intellect, power of discernment (see also *buddhi*; *kūrnda mati*; *nuṇ mati*)
matiyāl (*mati-y-āl*) {TS} by mind (instrumental form of *mati*)
mati-y-iladāl {Ts} 'since it is devoid of consciousness'
mātra {S} mere, only, nothing but
mauna {S} silence
-maya {S} suffix meaning 'made of', 'composed of', 'consisting only of' – see *ānandamaya*, *annamaya*, *manōmaya*, *prāṇamaya*, *tanmaya*, *vijñanamaya*
māyā {S} that which is not (see *yā mā*), illusion, delusion, self-deception
mey {T} reality, truth
meypporuḷ (*mey-p-poruḷ*) {T} real substance, true essence, reality, God
meypporuḷ-viḷakkam {T} light of the real substance (consciousness of being, 'I am')
mita {S} measured, moderate
mudal {T} origin, cause, root, base
muḍiyum {T} [it] will end, cease, be possible
mukti {S} liberation, emancipation
muṉṉilai (*muṉ-nilai*) {T} 'that which stands in front', the second person
muppuḍi {Ts} (*tripuṭi* {S}) triad, three factors [of objective knowledge] (knower, knowing and known)
muppuḍigaḷ {Ts} triads (plural form of *muppuḍi*)
mūrti-dhyāna {S} meditation on a form [of God]
muttoṟil (*mu-t-toṟil*) {T} threefold function [of God]
mūviḍam (*mū-v-iḍam*) {T} 'three places', three persons (in grammar) (see also *muṉṉilai*; *paḍarkkai*; *taṉmai*)
muyal {T} begin, undertake, attempt, practise, make effort, exert, persevere – see *muyalum*
muyalum {T} which [we] undertake, practise (relative participle of *muyal*)

N

na-iti {S} 'not [this]' (see also *nēti nēti*)
naḍakka {T} to walk, proceed, behave
nāḍu {T} seek, pursue, inspect, examine, investigate, explore, know

nām {T} we (inclusive of whoever is addressed)
nāma-rūpa {S} name-form
nāṉ {T} 'I'
Nāṉ-Ār? {T} 'I [am] Who?', 'Who am I?'
nāṉ ār iḍam edu {T} 'who am I? what is the place [from which I arose]?', 'what is the place where I abide?'
nāṉ eṉum sol-poruḷ {T} 'the import of the word I'
nāṉ iṉṉāṉ {T} 'I [am] so-and-so'
nāṉ maṉidaṉ {Ts} 'I [am a] man', 'I [am a] male person'
nāṉ māṉiḍaṉ {Ts} 'I [am a] man', 'I [am] human'
nāṉ māṉiḍaṉāy irukkiṟēṉ {Ts} 'I exist as [a] man', 'I am [a] man'
nāṉ nāṉ {T} 'I [am] I'
nāṉ yār? {T} 'I [am] who?', 'who am I?'
Nāṉ Yār? {T} 'I [am] Who?', 'Who am I?'
naṉavu {T} [state of] waking, wakefulness
naṉavu-tuyil {T} waking sleep
naṉmai (*nal-mai*) {T} goodness, righteousness, benefit, virtue, morality
nāṟpadu {T} forty – see *Uḷḷadu Nāṟpadu*
naṙuvum {T} '[it] will vanish'
nāśa {S} annihilation, destruction – see *manōnāśa*
nāṭṭam {T} investigation, examination, scrutiny, inspection, observation, attention, attentiveness
nēti nēti (*na-iti, na-iti*) {S} 'not [this], not [this]' (implying '[I am] not [this adjunct], nor [this adjunct]', the word *iti* being a quotative indicator that is equivalent to the use of inverted commas in English)
nididhyāsana {S} deep contemplation, meditation, attentiveness, observation, scrutiny (derived from the verb *nidhyai*, in which the prefix *ni* means down, deep, back, in or within, and *dhyai* means to contemplate or meditate on, from which *dhyāna* is derived)
nihaṙviṉai {T} present time
nihaṙvu (often transliterated as *nihaḻvu* and transcribed loosely as *nihazhvu*) {T} present time
niṉaivu {T} thought, mind
niṉḏṟa {T} which stands, exists, abides, remains, endures, continues, is permanent (though it is actually the past relative participle of the verb *nil*, it indicates permanence and hence implies continuity from past to future)
nirāśā (*nir-āśā*) {S} without desire, desirelessness
nirguṇa (*nir-guṇa*) {S} without qualities, without [finite] properties, unqualified
nirguṇa brahman {S} '*brahman* without [finite] qualities', the unqualified reality, God (as pure being, 'I am', the impersonal ground, essential substance or infinite whole)
nirguṇa upāsana {S} worship without attributes, worship of the unqualified reality (God as pure being)
nirvāṇa {S} blown out, extinguished, extinction, annihilation
niṣṭha (or *niṣṭhā*) {S} standing in, fixed in, grounded in, being in, abiding in, intent on, devoted to, attached to, steadiness, firmness, abidance, attachment, devotion,

application, skill, familiarity with, certain knowledge of, position, condition, state

nitamum maṉṉum {T} 'which always endures'

nitya {S} innate, fixed, perpetual, eternal

niyama {S} restraining, restraint, restriction

nūl {T} thread, treatise, scientific text, spiritual text, scripture – see *nūṉmālai* and *nūṯriraṭṭu*

nuṇ {T} subtle, refined, precise, acute, sharp, discerning

nūṉmālai (*nūl-mālai*) {Ts} garland of texts – see *Śrī Ramaṇōpadēśa Nūṉmālai*

nuṇ mati {Ts} discerning mind

nūṯriraṭṭu (*nūl-tiraṭṭu*) {T} collection of texts, compilation of texts – see *Śrī Ramaṇa Nūṯriraṭṭu*

O

oḍukkiḍavē {T} when it is subdued, reduced, condensed, dissolved, merged, destroyed

oḷi {T} light

oḷirum {T} [it] shines

oḷiyāl (*oḷi-y-āl*) {T} by light (instrumental form of *oḷi*)

oṉḏru {T} one

ōr {T} one, an

ōr {T} consider attentively, investigate, examine, know (also used as a poetic form of the relative participle *ōrum*)

ōr vaṙi {T} 'one path', 'investigating path', 'knowing path', 'path of investigation [or knowing]'

oru {T} one, a

ōrum {T} which investigates, which knows, investigating, knowing (relative participle of *ōr*)

P

paḍarkkai {T} that which has spread out [and become remote], the third person

pākkaḷ {T} verses (plural form of *pā*) – see *taṉippākkaḷ*

pañcakam {TS} collection of five parts (especially a poem of five verses) – see *Ēkātma Pañcakam*

pañca-kōśa {S} five 'sheaths' or coverings

pañcakṛtya (*pañca-kṛtya*) {S} five functions (of God)

pañcan (*pañca* in compound) {S} five

pañca vāyu {S} five 'vital airs'

para-bhakti {S} supreme devotion

parama-īśa-bhakti {S} – see *paramēśa-bhakti*

parama karuṇā {S} supreme compassion

paramārtha (*parama-artha*) {S} most excellent aim, principle meaning, ultimate substance, true essence, highest truth, entire truth, ultimate reality

pāramārthika {S} related to the ultimate reality, truest, most essential (adjectival form of *paramārtha*)

pāramārthika satya {S} essential truth, ultimate reality, absolute reality

paramātman {S} supreme self

paramēśa-bhakti (*parama-īśa-bhakti*) {S} supreme devotion to God

paramēśvara śakti (*parama-īśvara-śakti*) {S} supreme power of God

para-sukha {S} supreme happiness
parā-vāk {S} supreme word
pati {S} lord, master, God
pāyiram {T} preface, introduction (especially a verse or group of verses explaining the genesis of a work or giving a synopsis of its subject matter)
pēr {T} name
pēr-uruvil {T} 'in name and form', 'nameless and formless'
piḍikka {T} to cling to (infinitive of *piḍi*, catch, grasp, hold, cling to)
piṇam {T} corpse
piṇam pōl tīrndu uḍalam {T} 'leaving the body like a corpse'
pōl {T} like
poṉ {T} gold
pōṉḏra {T} which resembles
poṟi {T} sense organ, mind
poruḷ {T} substance, essence, reality
poy {T} falsity, unreality, illusion, deceptive appearance (also used adjectivally to mean 'false', 'unreal', 'illusory')
poy mai-y-ār niṉaivu aṇuvum uyyādu oḍukkiḍavē {T} 'when thought, which is unreal darkness, is destroyed without reviving even an iota'
pōy {T} going, having gone
prajñāna {S} pure consciousness (adjunct-free self-consciousness, 'I am')
prajñānaṁ brahma {S} 'pure consciousness is *brahman*'
pramāda {S} intoxication, negligence, carelessness, inattentiveness (in a spiritual context, specifically self-negligence or lack of self-attentiveness)
prāṇa {S} breath, life, life-force, vitality
prāṇamaya kōśa {S} 'sheath' composed of breath
prāṇāyāma {S} breath-restraint
prārabdha {S} action (*karma*) that has begun to give fruit, destiny, fate
prasthāna {S} source, origin, starting point
prasthāna-traya {S} triple source
pratibhāsa {S} appearance, semblance, illusion
prātibhāsika {S} seeming, existing only as an appearance
prātibhāsika satya {S} seeming reality
pravṛtti {S} outgoing effort, extroverted activity
priya {S} love, kindness, loving, beloved, liked, pleasing
puhaṟcci {T} praise, applause, appreciation, adulation, eulogy, fame, renown, glory, celebrity
pūṇumē {T} put on, wear, be adorned with, be possessed of, be yoked to, be ensnared in
pūjā {S} worship (particularly ritual worship), adoration, reverence
pūrṇa {S} filled, full, complete, entire, whole, fullness, completeness, entirety
puruṣa {S} man, human being, person, primal 'person', supreme being, spirit (as the original source and substance of everything)

R

rajas {S} passion, emotion, restless activity
rajō- (for *rajas* in compound) {S} passion, emotion, restless activity

rajōguṇa {S} quality of passion (*rajas*)
ram {S} settle, become calm, rest, experience joy, give joy, delight, please
ramaṇa {S} joy, pleasure, that which gives joy, beloved, lover, husband
Ramaṇa Nūṟiraṭṭu {Ts} – see *Śrī Ramaṇa Nūṟiraṭṭu*
ramaṇōpadēśa (*ramaṇa-upadēśa*) {Ts} teachings of Sri Ramana – see *Śrī Ramaṇōpadēśa Nūṉmālai*
Ramaṉōpadēśa Nūṉmālai {Ts} – see *Śrī Ramaṉōpadēśa Nūṉmālai*
ṛṣi {S} (commonly transcribed as *rishi*) 'seer', sage
rūpa {S} form, outward appearance, nature (see also *nāma-rūpa*; *svarūpa*)

S

śabda {S} sound, noise, word
śabda jālaṁ mahāraṇyaṁ {S} 'great forest of snares of words'
saccidananda (*sat-cit-ānanda*) {S} being-consciousness-bliss (see also *sat-cit-ānanda*)
sadā {S} always, ever, continually, perpetually
sadākālam (*sadā-kālam*) {TS} always, at all times
sadākālamum maṉattai ātmāvil vaittiruppadu {Ts} 'always being keeping mind fixed in self'
sadguru (*sat-guru*) {S} real *guru*, being-*guru*, true spiritual teacher
sādhakattil {TS} in spiritual practice (locative singular form of *sādhakam*)
sādhu {S} good person, gentle person, saintly person, religious mendicant
saguṇa (*sa-guṇa*) {S} with qualities, with [finite] properties, qualified
saguṇa brahman {S} '*brahman* with [finite] qualities', the qualified reality, God (as a 'person' or separate being)
saguṇa upāsana {S} worship with attributes, worship of the qualified reality (God as a person)
sahitar {TS} person who is joined to, connected with, associated with, possessed of
śakti {S} power
samādhi {S} state of mental stillness, subsidence, absorption, composure, intense meditation, unwavering contemplation
saṁhāra {S} drawing together, closing, contraction, dissolution, destruction [of the universe]
saṁsāra {S} flowing together, going about, wandering, spreading among, being diffused, moving thoroughly, restless activity [of mind]
saṁstha {S} standing together, standing firmly, abiding, resting in, being as
śanaiḥ śanair (*śanais śanais*) {S} gently gently, calmly and gradually
śanais {S} calmly, quietly, softly, gently, gradually
sanātana {S} ancient, primeval, eternal, everlasting, constant, perpetual
sanātana dharma {S} that which eternally upholds, supports, sustains, maintains, holds together, keeps in place or regulates; eternal law [of human nature and spiritual development], eternal 'religion' (that is, religion as an ordered and correct way of life, rather than as any particular set of beliefs or doctrines)
sankalpa (*saṁkalpa*) {S} volition, intention, wish, will, desire
sankalpa sahitar {TS} person possessed of volition
sannidhāna (*saṁnidhāna*) {S} nearness, presence
śānti {S} peace, tranquillity, calmness

sapta {S} seven

sapta dhātu {S} seven constituents [of the physical body] (namely chyle, blood, flesh, fat, bone, marrow and semen)

sāra {S} essence, substance, core, pith (see also *sāram*)

sāram {TS} essence

śarīra {S} body

sarva {S} all, entire, whole, every

sarvakartā (*sarva-kartā*) {S} all doer, one who does everything (God)

śāstra {S} rule, precept, teaching, instruction, book, scientific treatise, religious treatise, scripture, sacred book

sat {S} being, existing, existence, that which is, reality, truth, essence, real, true, right, good, honest, wise

sat-bhāva {S} real being, state of being

sat-cit {S} being-consciousness

sat-cit-ānanda {S} being-consciousness-bliss

sattva {S} being-ness, reality, calmness, clarity, purity (the true nature or essence of the mind and all its creations)

sattva-guṇa {S} quality of being-ness, calmness, clarity, purity

sāttvika {S} pure, pristine, endowed with *sattva*

satya {S} true, real, truth, reality

sāvādavar {T} those who do not die, immortals

sāyndiḍum {T} [it] hangs down, bends down, lies down, breaks (like branch under pressure)

siddha {S} accomplished, fulfilled, effected, achieved, attained, acquired, person who has accomplished [either a spiritual or non-spiritual goal]

siddhi {S} accomplishment, [spiritual or supernatural] attainment, miraculous power

śiva-svarūpa {S} God as our 'own form' or real self, the absolute reality

smaraṇa {S} remembering, bearing in mind, remembrance, mindfulness, attentiveness, meditation

sol {T} word, term, saying (also a verb meaning to say, speak)

sol-poruḷ {T} – see *soṯporuḷ*

soṯporuḷ (*sol-poruḷ*) {T} word-substance (the substance, import or meaning of a word)

sorūpam {TS} (*svarūpa* {S}) 'own form', essential self

śravaṇa {S} 'hearing', learning, studying, reading

śrī {S} light, lustre, radiance, splendour (often used as an honorific prefix [meaning 'sacred'] before the names of deities, holy people, places or objects)

Śrī Aruṇācala Akṣaramaṇamālai {Ts} 'Marriage Garland of Letters to Sri Arunachala', 'Fragrant Garland of Letters to Sri Arunachala', 'Garland of Imperishable Union with Sri Arunachala'

Śrī Aruṇācala Aṣṭakam {TS} 'Eight [Verses] to Sri Arunachala'

Śrīmad Bhāgavatam {S} 'Sacred [Book] about God'

Śrī Ramaṇa Nūṯrirattu {Ts} 'Compilation of Sri Ramana's Texts', 'Collected Works of Sri Ramana'

Śrī Ramaṇōpadēśa Nūṉmālai – Viḷakkavurai {Ts} 'Commentary on Sri Ramana's

Upadēśa Nūṉmālai (Garland of Teaching Texts)'

sṛṣṭi {S} letting go, bringing forth, discharging, emission, projection, creation [of the universe]

sthāna {S} standing, state, situation, place, locality, abode

sthiti {S} standing, staying, continuing, enduring, maintenance, sustenance [of the universe], state, situation, condition

sthūla {S} massive, gross, material, physical

sthūla dēha {S} physical body

sthūla śarīra {S} physical body

śubha {S} bright, beautiful, pleasant, agreeable, auspicious, good, righteous, virtuous, pure

śubha vāsanā {S} good inclination, agreeable propensity

śuddhi {S} cleansing, purification, purity, clearness

sukha {S} easy, pleasant, agreeable, ease, comfort, happiness

sūkṣma {S} subtle, fine, minute, keen, acute, sharp

sūkṣma śarīra {S} subtle body (the mind, ego or soul)

sum {Latin} '[I] am'

summā {T} easily, leisurely, inactively, at rest, at ease, peacefully, happily, quietly, silently, barely, merely, just (perhaps derived from *sukhamā*, a Tamil adverbial form of the Sanskrit word *sukha*)

summā amarndu irukka (*summā-v-amarndirukka*) {T} 'when [one] just is, having settled'

summā iru (*summā-v-iru*) {T} just be, quietly be, be without activity [of mind, speech or body]

summā irukkalām (*summā-v-irukkalām*) {T} 'let us just be'

summā iruppadu (*summā-v-iruppadu*) {T} just being

śūnya {S} empty, void

suṣupti {S} sleep (dreamless deep sleep)

sūtra {S} thread, cord, string, short string of words, aphorism, concise instruction, text consisting of a string of aphorisms (especially aphoristic instructions)

sva {S} own (referring to any of the three persons or three number [singular, dual or plural]), one's own, oneself (also serves [like *ātman*] as a reflexive pronoun)

svarūpa {S} own form, own nature, essential self

svarūpa-darśana {S} seeing self, self-discernment, self-experience

svarūpa-dhyāna {S} self-attentiveness, self-contemplation, self-meditation

svarūpa-smaraṇa {S} self-remembrance, self-attentiveness

sva-svarūpa-anusandhāna {S} self-investigation, self-inspection, self-contemplation, self-attentiveness

T

talai {T} head (literally or figuratively)

talai-sāyndiḍum {T} [it] head-bends, becomes head-bent, hangs [its] head [in shame or modesty], dies

tamas {S} darkness, delusion

tamō- (for *tamas* in compound) {S} darkness, delusion

tamōguṇa {S} quality of darkness (*tamas*)

taṉ {T} self (inflexional base of *tāṉ*, and its oblique case form, often used as a genitive [of self, his, her, its, one's own])

tāṉ {T} self (also serves as a third person pronoun [he, she or it], an indefinite pronoun [one or anyone], the reflexive pronoun for all persons and genders [oneself, myself, yourself, itself, ourselves, etc.], and an intensifying suffix [certainly, only or alone])

tāṉ-ādal {T} becoming self, being self

tāṉ ām avaṉ {T} 'he who is self'

taṉadu {T} of self, his, her, its, one's own (a genitive form of *tāṉ*)

taṉadu oḷiyāl eppōdum uḷḷadu {T} 'that which always exists by its own light'

tāṉē (*tāṉ-ē*) {T} self itself, self alone, self certainly

tāṉē tāṉē tattuvam {T} 'self itself alone certainly is the reality'

taṉi {T} singleness, solitude, independence, uniqueness, purity (also used adjectivally) – see *taṉippākkaḷ*

taṉippākkaḷ (*taṉi-p-pākkaḷ*) {T} solitary verses – see *Upadēśa Taṉippākkaḷ*

taṉmai (*taṉ-mai*) {T} 'self-ness', the first person

taṉmaiyiṉ (*taṉmai-y-iṉ*) {T} of the first person (an oblique case form of *taṉmai*, used as a genitive)

taṉmaiyiṉ uṇmai {T} the truth of the first person

tanmātra (*tat-mātra*) {S} 'it-only', merely that, basic element, essence

tanmayānanda (*tat-maya-ānanda*) {S} bliss composed only of *tat* ('it', the absolute reality)

tanmaya-niṣṭha (*tat-maya-niṣṭha*) {S} abidance as *tat* ('it', the absolute reality)

taṉṉai {T} self (accusative singular form of *tāṉ*)

taṉṉai-y-uṇarndu {T} knowing self

taṉṉāṭṭam (*taṉ-nāṭṭam*) {T} self-investigation, self-observation, self-scrutiny, self-attentiveness

taṉṉuḷ (*taṉ-ṉ-uḷ*) {T} within self, in oneself

tāṙ {T} fall low, descend, decline, sink, subside, stay, stop, rest, bend down, bow down, be subdued

tāṙndu {T} falling low, subsiding, bowing down, being subdued, being humble (tenseless verbal participle of *tāṙ*)

tat {S} it, this, that (the third person neuter pronoun, which is used in philosophy to denote *brahman*, the one non-dual absolute reality)

tat tvam asi {S} 'it you are', 'that thou art'

tattuvam {TS} reality – see *tattva*

tattva (*tat-tva*) {S} it-ness, that-ness, reality, truth, principle (used to denote both the one absolute reality, and any of the variously enumerated ontological principles)

tēḍu {T} seek, search for, enquire into, examine, investigate

Tipiṭaka {Pāḷi} (*Tripiṭaka* {S}) 'Three Baskets' (the oldest written collection of the teachings of Lord Buddha, popularly known as the 'Pāḷi Canon')

tiraṭṭu {T} gathering, collection, compilation – see *nūṯriraṭṭu*

tirōbhāva {S} – see *tirōdhāna*

tirōdhāna {S} concealment, obscuration, veiling

tīr {T} end, expire, vanish, separate, leave, cease, die, perish – see *tīrndu*

tīrndu {T} ending, separating, leaving (tenseless verbal participle of *tīr*)

tiru {T} brightness, brilliance, lustre, splendour, eminence, distinction, fortune, blessing, holiness, sacredness, divinity (used like *śrī* as an honorific prefix [meaning 'sacred'] before the names of deities, holy people, places or objects) – see *tiruvaruḷ*

tiruvaruḷ (*tiru-v-aruḷ*) {T} divine grace

tōṉḏṟum {T} [it] will appear, arise, become visible, come to mind, be known, become clear

tōṇumē {T} [it] will certainly appear, become known

traya {S} triple, threefold, consisting of three

tripuṭi {S} triad, three factors [of objective knowledge] (knower, knowing and known)

turiya {TS} (*turya* {S}) fourth (the 'fourth' state, the state of clear thought-free self-consciousness, also known as 'waking sleep')

turīya {S} fourth (the 'fourth' state)

turīya (or *turya*) *avasthā* {S} the fourth state

turīyātīta (*turīya-atīta*) {S} fourth-transcending, that which transcends the fourth (an alternative name of *turīya*, so called because it transcends the three false states of consciousness, waking, dream and sleep, and hence is not actually the 'fourth' but the only real state)

turiya-v-atīta {TS} (*turīyātīta* {S}) fourth-transcending

turya {S} fourth (the 'fourth' state)

tuyil {T} sleep

U

uḍal {T} body

uḍal nāṉ {T} '[this] body [is] I', 'I [am this] body'

uḍal nāṉ eṉṉum a-t-taṉmai {T} that first person, which is called 'I [am this] body'

uḍalam {T} body

Udāna {S/Pāḷi} 'Joyous Exaltation'

ūkkam {T} impulse, ardour, zeal, exertion, effort, firm conviction

ūkkam-uḷḷavaṉ {T} he who has zeal, he who makes [earnest] effort

uḷ {T} be, exist, have (a tenseless verb, from which most of the following words beginning with *uḷ* are derived)

uḷ {T} within, inside, interior, heart, mind

uḷ-mai {T} 'be'-ness, 'am'-ness

uḷḷa {T} to be, which is, who is, being (as an adjective), existing, real, true, actual (infinitive, relative participle and adjective form of *uḷ*)

uḷḷa {T} to think (infinitive of *uḷḷu*, think, cogitate, meditate)

uḷḷa-poruḷ {T} substance which is, real substance, being-essence, existing reality

uḷḷa-v-uṇarvu {T} consciousness which is, existing consciousness, being consciousness, real consciousness

uḷḷadē (*uḷḷadu-ē*) {T} only being

uḷḷadu {T} being (verbal noun formed from *uḷ*, be), that which is (*uḷḷa-adu*), that which [really] exists

Uḷḷadu Nāṟpadu {T} 'Forty [Verses] on Being', 'Forty [Verses] on That Which Is'

Uḷḷadu Nāṟpadu Anubandham {Ts} 'Appendix to *Uḷḷadu Nāṟpadu*'

uḷḷal {T} thinking, thought, meditation (verbal noun formed from *uḷḷu*)

uḷḷam {T} mind, heart, spiritual core (also a poetic form of *uḷḷōm*, which means '[we] are', and which is thus an inclusive way of expressing our singular consciousness of being, '[I] am')

uḷḷattē (*uḷḷattu-ē*) {T} in heart, only in heart, in heart itself

uḷḷavaṉ (*uḷḷa-avaṉ*) {T} he who is, he who exists, he who has

uḷḷu {T} think, remember, cogitate, meditate, investigate

ūṇ {T} that which is eaten, food

ūṉ {T} flesh, meat, body

ūṇ ādal kāṇ {T} 'becoming food [is] seeing'

ūṉ ār karu ahandai {Ts} ego, [which is] the body-bound embryo

uṇar {T} be conscious of, know, experience, feel, understand, examine, scrutinise, think

uṇara {T} to know (infinitive of *uṇar*, know, be conscious of)

uṇara niṉḏṟa poruḷ {T} 'the reality that stands [exists, endures or continues] to know', 'the reality that exists and knows'

uṇarndu {T} knowing, having known (tenseless verbal participle of *uṇar*)

uṇarvu {T} consciousness, knowledge, clear discernment, perception, feeling, sense, awakening (noun formed from *uṇar*, know, be conscious of)

undiyār {T} a particular poetic style – see *Upadēśa Undiyār*

uṇmai (*uḷ-mai*) {T} 'being-ness', existence, being nature, essence, reality, truth

upadēśa {S} pointing towards, indicating, instructing, specifying, instruction, teaching

Upadēśa Nūṉmālai {Ts} 'Garland of Teaching Texts' – see *Śrī Ramaṇōpadēśa Nūṉmālai*

Upadēśa Sāram {S} 'Essence of Instructions', 'Essence of Teachings'

Upadēśa Taṉippākkaḷ {Ts} 'Solitary Verses of Instruction'

Upadēśa Undiyār {Ts} 'Teachings in [the poetic style called] *Undiyār*'

upādhā (or *upadhā*) {S} place upon, superimpose, take up, seize

upādhi {S} adjunct, superimposition, disguise, substitute, that which is put in place of something else, that which is mistaken to be something else

upādhi-uṇarvu {Ts} adjunct-consciousness, adjunct-knowledge, adjunct-sense

upalabdhi {S} acquisition, attainment, perception, knowledge

upaniṣad {S} any one of a group of philosophical texts in the Vēdas (see also Index of Texts)

upāsana {S} waiting upon, serving, attendance, reverence, adoration, worship, meditation, contemplation, being intent upon

upāya {S} coming near, approach, way, means, that by which an aim is reached or achieved

upēya {S} aim, goal, that which is to be approached, reached or achieved

upēyamum tāṉē upāyamum tāṉē {Ts} 'the aim is only self, and the means is only self'

urai {T} speaking, saying, telling, explanation, interpretation, exposition, commentary – see *viḷakkavurai*

uraṉ {T} mental strength

uru {T} form

uruvil (*uru-v-il*) {T} in form (locative form of *uru*), formless (privative form of *uru*)

uruppaḍuvāṉ (*uru-p-paḍuvāṉ*) {T} [he] will be formed, reformed

usā {T} subtle investigation, close examination, keen scrutiny
usāvāl (*usā-v-āl*) {T} by subtle investigation (instrumental form of *usā*)
usāvu (or *usavu*) {T} ponder, consider, investigate keenly
uy {T} live, subsist, revive, escape, be saved – see *uyyādu*
uyarvu {T} height, elevation, loftiness, eminence, greatness (also used adjectivally to mean 'lofty', 'eminent', 'superior')
uyir {T} life, soul, living being
uyyādu {T} not living, not escaping, not reviving, without reviving (tenseless verbal negative participle of *uy*)

V

vācaka {S} speaking, telling, saying, word – see *Guru Vācaka Kōvai*
vācya {S} spoken, told, said, expressed – see *vācyārtha*
vācyārtha (*vācya-artha*) {S} spoken meaning, expressed meaning, literal meaning
vai {T} put, place, seat, keep, hold, maintain, fix – see *vaittu*
vairāgya {S} dispassion, freedom from desire, desirelessness, indifference (from *vi-rāga*, without passion, desire, liking, interest)
vaittu {T} placing, keeping, holding, fixing (tenseless verbal participle of *vai*)
vaittiruppadu (*vaittu-iruppadu*) {T} keeping fixed, being keeping, being having kept (verbal noun formed from *vaittiru*, a compound verb in which *iru* [be] serves as an auxiliary to *vaittu* [keeping])
vāk {S} word
vaṙi (often transliterated as *vaḻi* and transcribed loosely as *vazhi*) {T} path, way, means
vāsanā {S} disposition, propensity, tendency, inclination, impulsion, desire (derived from *vāsa*, meaning abiding or remaining, because a *vāsanā* is a disposition that remains in the mind as a result of previous actions or experiences)
vastu {S} substance, essence, reality
vastu-upalabdhi {S} direct knowledge of the reality or true essence
vastu-vicāra {S} scrutiny of our essential reality
vattu {TS} (*vastu* {S}) substance
vattuvām (*vattu-v-ām*) {T} which is the substance
vēda {S} knowledge (derived from *vid*, to know), the 'Vēdas' (all or any one of the four groups of ancient scriptural texts, the *Ṛg-Vēda*, *Yajur-Vēda*, *Sāma-Vēda* and *Atharva-Vēda*)
vēdānta (*vēda-anta*) {S} the 'end' or final conclusion of the Vēdas (the spiritual philosophy and science expounded in the *Upaniṣads*, *Brahma-Sūtra* and *Bhagavad Gītā*, and elucidated by many sages including SrI Ramana)
vēdāntic {English adjective formed from *vēdānta*}
veṇbā {T} a four-line Tamil poetic metre (see also *kaliveṇbā*; *kuṟaḷ veṇbā*)
vēṇḍum {T} [it] is wanted, desired, needed, necessary, indispensable (often used with an infinitive as an optative auxiliary to mean that one should or must do a certain action or be in a certain state)
vēṇum {T} [it] is needed, necessary, indispensable (as *vēṇḍum*)
vēṇumē {T} [it] is certainly needed
vicar {S} investigate, examine, scrutinise, ascertain
vicāra {S} investigation, examination, scrutiny

vicāri {TS} (*vicar* {S}) investigate, examine, scrutinise, inspect, explore
vicārikka {TS} to investigate
vicārikka vēṇḍum {TS} [it] is necessary to investigate, [one] should investigate
viḍāppiḍiyāy (*viḍā-p-piḍi-y-āy*) {T} firmly, tenaciously, incessantly (literally, unleaving-graspingly)
viḍāppiḍiyāy-p piḍikka vēṇḍum {T} [it] is necessary to cling tenaciously, [one] should cling tenaciously
viddai {TS} (*vidyā* {S}) knowledge, science
vidyā {S} knowledge, philosophy, science, practical art, learning
vijñānamaya kōśa {S} 'sheath' composed of discriminative knowledge
vikṣēpa {S} throwing out, projection [of thoughts that form the world appearance], throwing about, scattering, dispersion, dissipation, distraction, confusion, agitation
vikṣēpa śakti {S} power of projection, dispersion, dissipation
viḷakkam {T} light, lamp, clearness, elucidation, explanation
viḷakkavurai (*viḷakka-v-urai*) {T} explanation, interpretation, exposition, commentary – see *Śrī Ramaṇōpadēśa Nūṉmālai – Viḷakkavurai*
viṉavu {T} question, enquire, investigate, examine, scrutinise, listen, pay attention to, bear in mind, hear
viṉavum {T} which scrutinises, which is scrutinising (relative participle of *viṉavu*)
viṇmai (*viṇ-mai*) {T} sky-ness (illusory like the blueness of the sky)
viṉai {T} action (*karma*),
viṉai-mudal {T} doer (literally, origin or cause) of action, subject (as the originator of any action)
viśēṣa {S} distinction, difference, peculiarity, speciality, special quality, excellence
viṣaya {S} extent, range, region, domain, sphere, sphere of activity, [worldly] affair, sense 'region', sense perception, sense object, sense pleasure, object of desire
viṣaya-vāsanā {S} desire that impels one to attend to sense perceptions and worldly affairs, and to seek enjoyment in such things
viśiṣṭādvaita (*viśiṣṭa-advaita*) {S} differential non-duality, qualified non-duality (an ancient philosophy that is distinct from the absolute non-duality of *advaita*, because it maintains that differences are real and not just false appearances)
vittu {T} seed
vittu-p-pōṉḏra {T} 'which resembles a seed', seed-like
vivēka {S} discrimination, discernment, power to distinguish the real from the unreal
Vivēkacūḍāmaṇi (*vivēka-cūḍā-maṇi*) {S} 'Crest-Jewel of Discrimination'
vyavahāra {S} doing, activity, conduct, affair, occupation, transaction, business, commerce, disputation, litigation, mundane matter
vyāvahārika {S} transactional, related to worldly affairs, mundane, commonplace, relative (adjectival form of *vyavahāra*)
vyāvahārika satya {S} transactional reality, mundane reality, relative reality

Y

yā {S} she who (feminine form of *ya* or *yad*, who, which or what)
yā mā {S} she who is not, that which is not, what is not (see *māyā*)
yār {T} who (interrogative personal pronoun)
artha {S} aim, purpose, meaning, substance, wealth, property, object, thing

yathārtha (*yathā-artha*) {S} according to the meaning, genuine, actual, real, true
yathārtha svarūpa {S} real self
yatna {S} effort, exertion, energy, zeal, endeavour, striving
yōga {S} yoking, joining, uniting, union, means [to attain union]
yōga-mārga {S} path of union
yōgi {S} one who is seeking union, one who has attained union
yōgic {English adjective formed from *yōga*} pertaining to *yōga*

Made in United States
North Haven, CT
14 June 2024

53605124R00274